Canadian Federalism:
Myth or Reality

Canadian Federalism: Myth or Reality

edited by

J. Peter Meekison

Methuen

Toronto   London   Sydney   Wellington

Canadian Federalism: Myth or Reality

Published in Toronto by Methuen Publications
(A Division of the Carswell Co. Ltd.)
and in London by Methuen & Co Ltd

Library of Congress Catalog Card Number 68-8671

SBN 416 99540 3/42

Printed and bound in Canada

Contents

Part Four
Federal-Provincial Financial Relations

Part Five
Cooperative Federalism

Part Six
Quebec and Canadian Federalism

Contributors

A. H. BIRCH   *Professor of Political Studies, The University, Hull.*

EDWIN R. BLACK   *Associate Professor of Political Studies, Queen's University.*

ALEXANDER BRADY   *Professor Emeritus, Department of Political Economy, University of Toronto.*

R. M. BURNS   *Director, Institute of Intergovernmental Relations, Queen's University.*

M. CADIEUX   *Under Secretary of State for External Affairs.*

ALAN C. CAIRNS   *Associate Professor of Political Science, University of British Columbia.*

J. A. CORRY   *Vice-Chancellor and Principal, Queen's University.*

MARTHA SUE FLETCHER   *Doctoral Candidate in Political Science, Duke University.*

EUGENE FORSEY   *Research Director, Canadian Labour Congress.*

EDGAR GALLANT   *Director, Federal-Provincial Relations Division, Department of Finance, Canada.*

A. W. JOHNSON   *Assistant Deputy Minister, Department of Finance, Canada.*

ALLEN R. KEAR   *Doctoral Candidate in Political Science, Université Laval.*

BORA LASKIN   *Supreme Court of Ontario.*

JEAN-MARC LEGER   *Le Devoir.*

JEAN LESAGE   *Leader of the Opposition, Province of Quebec, Prime Minister of the Province of Quebec, 1960-1966.*

W. S. LIVINGSTON   *Professor of Government, University of Texas.*

JAMES H. LYNN   *Federal-Provincial Relations Division, Department of Finance, Canada.*

JACQUES-YVAN MORIN   *Associate Professor of Law, Université de Montréal.*

STEVEN MULLER   *Vice-President for Public Affairs, Cornell University.*

LESTER B. PEARSON   *Professor of International Affairs, Carleton University, Prime Minister of Canada, 1963-1968.*

JEAN-LUC PEPIN   *Minister of Trade and Commerce, former Parliamentary Secretary to the Minister of Trade and Commerce.*

LOUIS-PHILIPPE PIGEON   *Supreme Court of Canada, former Professor of Law, Université Laval.*

JOHN P. ROBARTS   *Prime Minister of the Province of Ontario.*

MITCHELL SHARP   *Secretary of State for External Affairs, Minister of Finance, 1965-1968.*

DONALD V. SMILEY   *Professor of Political Science, University of British Columbia.*

ROBERT STANFIELD   *Leader of the Opposition, House of Commons, Canada, Premier of the Province of Nova Scotia, 1956-1967.*

MICHAEL STEIN   *Associate Professor of Political Science, McGill University.*

CHARLES D. TARLTON   *Assistant Professor of Political Science, Muir College, University of California.*

PIERRE ELLIOTT TRUDEAU   *Prime Minister of Canada, Minister of Justice, 1967-1968.*

Preface

Events in recent years have caused a number of people to study the federal system; to examine its theoretical bases, its development and its problems. This aspect of Canadian politics has received so much attention that it seems worthwhile to pull together a number of writings and speeches on the subject. The basic purpose of the collection is to give students of Canadian government and politics some idea of the complexity of the federal system and some conception of the issues which currently confront Canada.

To accomplish this objective, the material has been arranged by content into six parts. It is hoped that the first part will provide students with some understanding of federalism as a form of government. The material in the other five sections has been selected to illustrate the intricacies, development, operation and dilemmas of Canadian federalism. An effort has been made to include as much up-to-date material as possible. Some of the essays in each section could logically have been included in more than one section but the final organization appears the most useful.

This collection, like any other book of essays, does not exhaust the literature on this subject. Indeed, a number of excellent works and documents had to be excluded prior to publication. Ideally, the essays will suggest sources and areas for additional research, and will stimulate discussion by exposing readers to a variety of viewpoints. In short, it is hoped that the volume will be useful as a teaching device.

I would like to thank the authors and publishers who gave me permission to reprint the material contained within this volume. The responses received were extremely gratifying. I would also like to thank Joyce and Roger Burke, Linda Anderson and Jean-Claude St. Onge, University of Alberta graduate students who helped me in preparing the manuscript.

University of Alberta   J. P. M.
Edmonton
August 20, 1968

Introduction

Should a collection of essays have an introduction? Of what use is a brief essay at the beginning of such a collection which "introduces" the reader to the subject? Many essays of this kind merely sketch out in abbreviated form the contents of the volume. The danger of this approach is that the student will pick and choose his reading based on the editor's comments. Should an introduction not arouse the reader's curiosity and give him guidelines for study? A number of questions follow naturally from such a thesis. What should the reader expect from a collection of essays on a topic as controversial and complex as Canadian federalism? What terminology will the student encounter throughout the text? Finally, what approaches to the topic might prove useful? Once these questions are answered, the text becomes more meaningful. It gives the reader a feeling for and an awareness of the subject which perhaps he did not have before.

Central to any federal system is its constitution, the document which sets down the powers of the two levels of government. The constitution is a reference point or a bench mark. But constitutions change over time; amendments are enacted, interpretations are made by governments and the judiciary, and conventions and usages are developed. Specific clauses take on different meanings and significance while other sections may be ignored or quietly forgotten. The essential point to be remembered is that the constitution provides the legal framework within which the federal system evolves. One recent event concerning Canada's constitution seems an appropriate mechanism for preparing the student for the following collection of essays.

At the close of the Constitutional Conference of February 1968, the participants agreed to establish a "Continuing Constitutional Conference" and a "Continuing Committee of Officials". Although the terms of reference of these two groups were not restricted, seven areas were singled out for specific scrutiny and discussion. These were: official languages, fundamental rights, distribution of powers, reform of institutions linked with federalism (e.g. the Senate and Supreme Court), regional disparities, amending procedure and mechanisms of federal-provincial relations. The study of (and hopefully some agreement on the resolution of) these matters is to be conducted during the next few years. Presently, efforts to predict the outcome of these discussions would be futile. At best, one can offer suggestions as to the future structure of the Canadian federal system based on the historical development of it and other federal systems.

Confronted with the prospect of either a new constitution or a revised British North America Act, some knowledge of the interpretation and operation of the present constitution is essential. In addition, an understanding is required of how the federal system has been adjusted and shaped since its inception to reflect the changes within Canadian society. What problems have existed with respect to interpretation of the division of powers? What mechanisms for consultation between the provinces and federal government have evolved? To what degree have the fiscal needs of the provinces been balanced with their fiscal means? What influences have the cultures and subcultures of the regions of Canada had on the development of the federal system? Comprehension of what exists and what went before is required before one can tackle the problem of what ought to be the federal system of the future.

It should be realized that any changes in the Constitution, as far as they affect the federal system, will be determined to a great extent by the current interpretation of the words and clauses of the British North America Act, the conventions which are at the moment operative in Canadian federalism and the realities of political bargaining. We are not starting with a clean slate nor one which can be wiped clean.

Before providing solutions, one must identify the problem or problems. What is federalism? What are the necessary conditions for establishing and maintaining a federal state? Why do some federations succeed while others do not? What are the factors which produce change within a federal system? These general questions are only a beginning. From here one must proceed to a study of the Canadian system and pose more specific questions: What are the historical factors which have influenced the development of Canadian federalism? What institutions are essential to the establishment of a federal state in a bicultural country? What political, economic, social, cultural and geographic factors must one consider in contemplating revisions of the present system? These questions and others arise because federalism, as a political system, is far more complex than it initially appears. Like the hidden dangers of an iceberg, nine-tenths of its problems may be submerged below the surface.

Once questions like the above have been presented, students must come to grips with the terminology of federalism. In writing about federal governments, authors have usually given certain areas a prominent position in their analyses. One finds discussions on the constitution, the division of powers, the division of revenues, the governmental structure, the position and protection of minorities and the relationship between the levels of government. From these studies a number of theories or explanations of federalism have emerged. One encounters terms such as "classical federalism", "quasi-federalism", "devolutionary federalism", "dual federalism", "cooperative federalism", "creative federalism" and "joint federalism". While these terms are used to designate certain phases or aspects of the federal phenomenon or a particular federal system at a certain point in time, their universal applicability is open to some doubt.

Into this maze of questions and terms one must fit the Canadian federal system. The purpose of the following collection is to uncover as many areas of controversy as possible in order to familiarize the reader with existing and future problems, and to give him some ability to evaluate critically solutions proposed by the authors. For this purpose, the material has been divided into six major sections. Each part represents a different facet of the subject, and, while each section can be considered separately, they are interdependent. For example, while one can study the significance of federal-provincial conferences as they relate to cooperative federalism, the subject matter of many of these meetings has been fiscal problems.

Before a detailed discussion of Canadian federalism is presented, the reader is introduced to the subject of federalism in a theoretical way. While the first four essays do not exhaust the literature on the theories of federalism, they do indicate the number of approaches which may be used in studying this subject. They provide the conceptual framework for the material on Canada which follows. The five sections of the collection which deal specifically with Canada represent the major areas in which studies have been conducted.

Finally, a word on the essays themselves. They have been selected, not to give a particular point of view, but to show the diversity of thinking on this topic, and to give the reader some idea of the extent of material available. Some of the selections come from public documents, while others are works analyzing specific features of the federal system. The authors, who come from widely divergent backgrounds, are representative of the people who have given perhaps the most attention to analyses of the Canadian federal system.

While many have concentrated their studies on these areas in particular, there is a paucity of research in other areas of the subject. For example, very little has been written about federalism and the party system. Only scant attention has been paid to the federal features of national political institutions such as the Supreme Court, the Senate, the bureaucracy or even Parliament itself. It is all very well, for example, to state that representation in the Cabinet is determined in part by geographical considerations. But of what significance is such a statement? How does the geographical distribution of Cabinet positions influence decision making in this body? How effectively do Cabinet ministers represent the interests of their provinces?

Further questions may be posed: How do pressure groups in Canada operate? How is their influence and operation modified by the federal system? To what extent is parliamentary government compatible with federalism? These and other questions remain to be answered by students of Canadian government. Other areas of research in which some of the devices used in comparative government might prove useful for analysis are comparisons of decision-making at the provincial level and of policy outputs of the provincial governments. To what degree are these decisions and policies influenced by the federal system? Understanding of these differences may yield additional information on federalism. In brief, new approaches to the problem must be devised if our understanding of the subject is to be expanded. It is an exciting topic, one that is constantly changing, and one that offers challenges to the inquiring mind.

Part One

What is Federalism?

Part One

What is Liberalism?

1 Approaches to the Study of Federalism *

A. H. Birch

One of the features of the post-war world has been the proliferation of
constitutions which describe themselves as federal. Not surprisingly, this development has been accompanied by a considerable increase in interest in the academic study of federalism. But federalism is, of course, a concept which has no
fixed meaning: its meaning in any particular study is defined by the student in
a manner which is determined by the approach which he wishes to make to his
material. The aim of this article is to examine four approaches that have been
made to the subject since 1945 and to consider their value in the light of three
examples. These are the establishment of the federations of Nigeria and Malaysia and the attempt, so far unsuccessful, to create a federation of East Africa.

The Institutional Approach

The writer who has exerted the greatest influence on the study of federalism
in Britain is undoubtedly K. C. Wheare, and a whole generation of students
have been brought up to regard federalism in Wheare's terms. His book written
during the war and published in 1946,[1] is a comparative analysis of some of the
characteristics of the four governmental systems that were then generally
regarded as federal. His method was to construct a kind of model by isolating
the common features of these systems which led observers to describe them as
federations. These features were defined first in terms of constitutional law and
then in terms of the political relationships which had developed on the basis
of the constitutional provisions. The greater part of the book consists of a series
of comparisons and contrasts of developments in the history and government
of the four countries, carefully analysed to illuminate the relationship of these
developments to the federal model, as defined.

In recent years Wheare's approach has fallen out of favour, particularly
among American writers.[2] The most common complaint made is that it is legalistic, though it is not immediately apparent why this should be regarded as a criticism. The essence of his analysis is that somewhat similar circumstances in the
four countries have produced somewhat similar constitutional provisions
which in turn have led to the development of institutions and political relationships which can usefully be compared. Comparative government is such a tricky
and elusive subject that it may well be thought a virtue rather than a defect
that the approach should be disciplined by a framework of constitutional law.

The real basis for the tendency to turn away from Wheare's approach, I

---

*From *Political Studies*, Vol. XIV, No. 1, 1966, pp. 15-33. Reprinted by permission of
the author and Oxford University Press.
[1]*Federal Government*, Oxford University Press, London, 1946.
[2]M. J. C. Vile has suggested an interesting and helpful modification of Wheare's
model, but in what follows I am concerned with approaches which are radically different
from Wheare's, not those which are simply modifications. See M. J. C. Vile, *The
Structure of American Federalism*, Oxford Universtiy Press, London, 1961, Ch. 10.

think, is not any shortcoming in his analysis but the fact that the approach cannot usefully be applied to many of the federations that have been established, successfully or otherwise, since the war. The roll includes India, Pakistan, Indonesia, Malaya, and Malaysia in Asia; Nigeria, Libya, Ethiopia, the Mali Federation, Uganda, the Central African Federation, and the Republic of Cameroon in Africa; the German Federal Republic and perhaps Yugoslavia in Europe. They have all described themselves as federal but hardly any of them conform to Wheare's model. If the student keeps to this approach all that he can say about most of these new systems of government is that they are not really federal, in the sense defined. This is entirely logical but not, perhaps, entirely satisfying.

Of course a model of federation which would enable one to deal with all these countries would have to be a very sketchy model, and it is likely that the comparisons that could be made on the basis of such a model would be equally sketchy. The student has a choice here (as in other branches of comparative government) between using a fairly elaborate and well-defined model which enables him to say a good deal about a few countries or using a more exiguous model which enables him to say a little about a large number of countries. The choice is for each student to make. But in this case those who choose the second alternative are forced to define federalism in terms other than legal, for the constitutions of these numerous post-war federations are extremely varied.

A Sociological Approach

It is not surprising that some writers have attempted to define federalism in sociological terms. The undisputed leader in this enterprise is W. S. Livingston, who published an article on the topic in 1952 which was incorporated with minor amendments into the opening chapter of his subsequent book.[3] Livingston's point is that federalism is essentially a phenomenon of social diversity rather than one of constitutional mechanics. "The essence of federalism", he says, "lies not in the constitutional or institutional structure but in the society itself".[4] And since all countries are characterized by some social diversity, all countries have some tendency to be federal. "There is no point at which it can be said that all societies on one side are unitary and all those on the other are federal."[5] These diversities which exist, in differing degrees, in all societies, are said to be reflected and expressed in political phenomena which Livingston calls "federal instrumentalities". A fair number of these instrumentalities must emerge before it would be reasonable to describe the political systems as a whole as federal, but no definition or classification can be attempted, for federalism is

---

[3]See W. S. Livingston, "A Note on the Nature of Federalism", in *Political Science Quarterly*, Vol. LXII, No. 1, March 1952, and *Federalism and Constitutional Change*, Clarendon Press, Oxford, 1956.

[4]*Federalism and Constitutional Change, op. cit.*, p. 2.

[5]*Ibid.*, p. 5.

"not an absolute but a relative term".[6] It follows that what Livingston offers us is not so much a model as a dimension or, to use his own term, a spectrum.

It is not at all easy to see what help we can derive from this approach to the subject. It is, of course, true that federal institutions are frequently, though not always, a reflection of social diversity, and virtually all writers on the subject (including Wheare) have said as much. The point is not whether this is true but whether it is useful as a tool of analysis, and a study of Livingston's book yields at least three reasons for doubting the utility of the approach.

First, it is clearly very difficult to make any firm generalizations about the members of a category of which the membership is undefined, and since the main object of this kind of comparative study is to produce generalizations it would seem that the approach is somewhat self-defeating. Second, we may note that Livingston is forced to include a wide variety of phenomena under his heading of "federal instrumentalities", including laws, regulations, theories, concepts and attitudes. Propositions based upon this use of language are bound to be somewhat cloudy: they may not be invalid but they are unlikely to be specific enough to be helpful. An example is the proposition that "ultimately the instrumentalities enter into and become part of the (psycho-sociological) complex which determines the nature of the instrumentalities".[7] This is undoubtedly true but it cannot be said to advance our understanding of the subject significantly. Third, it is fair to observe that in the main body of his book Livingston is unable to use the conceptual framework which is outlined in the first chapter. The remaining 300 pages contain a straightforward and somewhat legalistic account of the process of constitutional amendment in federal states, and the book as a whole would have gained in coherence if the opening chapter had comprised a brief recapitulation of Wheare's model of federal government in place of the attempt to develop a sociological approach.

It would seem, therefore, that Livingston has failed to develop an approach to the study of federalism that is genuinely novel. His introductory chapter is novel, but when he gets down to specific examples his analysis has the same kind of institutional basis as Wheare's. The other two approaches I shall consider are very different in method and object. Wheare and Livingston deal with political systems which have a set of institutions in common and their analyses show the limited range of ways in which the similar problems resulting from these institutions have been met. The writers I shall now discuss deal with political systems whose institutions vary quite widely and their aim is to search for uniformities, much as other scholars have tried to establish uniformities about dictatorships or democracies or developing societies. It is sometimes asked whether this kind of enterprise can ever produce worthwhile results. Possibly the following discussion will contribute to this continuing debate.

Federalism as a Process

An attempt to develop a flexible model of federalism has been made by a

---

[6]*Ibid.*, p. 4.
[7]*Ibid.*, p. 7.

number of writers who refer to federalism as a process rather than as a static
pattern of government. C. J. Friedrich attempted to summarize this approach in
a paper presented to the Sixth World Congress of the International Political
Science Association and it will be convenient to quote from his summary.[8]
Friedrich describes a federation as "a union of groups, united by one or more
common objectives, but retaining their distinctive group character for other
purposes".[9] This description can be applied not only to a federal state but also
to an alliance, a functional association of states, or a union of groups within a
state (such as the Trades Union Congress). Federalism is said to be the process
of federalizing; that is, the process of achieving a union of groups which retain
their identity. It follows that "federalism may be operating in both the direction
of integration and differentiation. For both the transformation of the British
Empire into the Commonwealth of Nations and that of European states into a
United States of Europe (as envisaged and initiated) are federalizing processes".[10]

This approach thus directs our attention to one of the features of post-war
politics: the development of a wide variety of political systems and organizations in which decision-making is divided between a central authority and a
number of regional authorities. This, broadly speaking, is what federations
which conform to Wheare's model have in common with those that do not
conform to that model, and what both have in common with several other forms
of political association. Scholars who follow this approach seek to identify the
factors making for integration and those impeding integration in a variety of
situations, and have shown that the social and economic forces at work are
often the same, even though in one context they contribute to nation-building
while in another they contribute to international integration. To view federalism
in this way is to view it in a broad perspective which helps us to understand
some of its features and draws our attention to what may appropriately (if
inelegantly) be called its dynamics.

There is, of course, a certain price to pay. If federalism is defined in such
general terms there may be difficulty in deciding whether certain political
systems are to be regarded as federal at any particular time. For Friedrich the
difficult case is the Soviet Union. On page 5 we are told that "the hitherto
common invasion of the sphere of power of the republics of the Soviet Union
argues against the presumption that the Soviet Union constitutes a genuine
federalism"; on page 10 we learn that "the evolution of Soviet federalism
suggests that within limits the absence of constitutional democracy is no bar to
the federalizing process"; and on page 16 it appears that "in the Soviet Union

---

[8]The quotations which immediately follow are from C. J. Friedrich, "New Tendencies
in Federal Theory and Practice", mimeographed, 1964. See also Friedrich's chapter in
Elmer Plischke (ed.), *Systems of Integrating the International Community*, Van Nostrand,
Princeton, N.J., 1964; and the work of K. W. Deutsch and his associates.

[9]*Ibid.*, p. 2.

[10]*Ibid.*, p. 2. See also Ernst B. Haas, *The Uniting of Europe*, Stanford University Press,
Stanford, Calif., 1958 and "International Integration: European and Universal Processes", in *International Organization*, Vol. XV, 1961.

the formal federalism of the government structure is rendered largely nugatory by the integrating force of the C.P.S.U.". But every classification has its borderline cases and this particular difficulty may not be very important, since the test of this approach to the study of federalism must be the success of those who follow it in identifying the factors which influence the speed and direction of progress in the federalizing process.

It is hazardous to generalize about such a considerable body of literature but it seems safe to say that the factors generally suggested as important are economic, social and cultural. The factors most commonly identified as creating the conditions for federal integration are the expectation of economic advantage and the existence of social and cultural bonds which generate a feeling of community. K. W. Deutsch and his collaborators have listed nine conditions as "essential conditions" for what they call an "amalgamated security-community" (which would include all the forms of union with any reasonable claim to be regarded as federations).

These conditions include "a distinctive way of life", expectation of economic gains, and "unbroken links of social communication".[11] But what is conspicuously absent from the list is any mention of the political circumstances in which the politicians who alone can create an amalgamated security-community are likely to do so. Without this the list is potentially misleading, to put it no higher. W. H. Riker has pointed out that the evidence of history shows that these nine conditions are neither necessary nor sufficient for the amalgamation of political units, which prompts him to ask the pertinent question of how they can be considered "essential".[12] Riker's own approach focusses directly on the political aspects of federalism.

Federalism as a Bargain

Riker defines federalism in a very simple and formal way saying that a constitution is federal if it provides for two levels of government, each of which has "some guarantee (even though merely a statement in the constitution)" of its contained autonomy within its sphere.[13] He notes that this kind of constitution is always the result of a political bargain which takes place in a historically unique situation, but he proceeds to an examination of these situations which yields the discovery that two conditions have always been present. He concludes that these conditions should be regarded as necessary conditions for the striking of a

---

[11]K. W. Deutsch et al., Political Community and the North Atlantic Area, Princeton University Press, Princeton, 1957, p. 58.

[12]W. H. Riker, Federalism: Origin, Operation, Significance, Little Brown and Co., Boston, 1964, pp. 15-16.

[13]Ibid., p. 11. He does not worry about the hypothetical problem posed by Mackenzie and Chapman of a system in which the regional governments enjoy only the power to determine the shape of postmen's helmets, though he comes near it when he suggests at one point that the question of whether the Soviet Union is a federation depends upon whether the republics have genuine autonomy in the sphere of cultural affairs. See W. J. M. Mackenzie and B. Chapman, "Federalism and Regionalism", Modern Law Review, Vol. XIV, No. 2, April 1951, pp. 182-194.

federal bargain. The first condition is the existence of politicians who wish to expand the area of territorial control, either "to meet an external military or diplomatic threat or to prepare for military or diplomatic aggression",[14] but prefer to expand without the use of force. The second condition is the willingness of the assenting politicians to surrender part of their independence, either because "they desire protection from an external threat" or because "they desire to participate in the potential aggression of the federation".[15]

The other question with which Riker deals is that of the conditions for the maintenance of a federal system. Here again his examination of historical evidence leads him to a single, but more tentative, conclusion: that whether or not a federal system survives depends on the nature of the party system that develops. It does not, that is, depend on the division of governmental powers, on the extent of governmental activities, or on the survival of provincial loyalties and a belief in states' rights: these factors influence the nature and working of the federal system, but it is the structure of the parties which determines how long the system itself is maintained.

Though these conclusions can be outlined in a few lines, they are not insubstantial. Given that the model of federalism is sketchy enough to permit the inclusion of twenty or more somewhat diverse systems, it would be absurd to expect a comparative analysis to produce many generalizations. Riker's conclusions are a significant achievement, provided the evidence supports them. It is also interesting to see that Riker's approach to the subject enables him to deal in a specific and useful way with some of the social factors with which Livingston was concerned but which he did not make explicit, such as the nature and effects of regional cultural differences and the changing pattern of citizens' loyalties to different levels of government.[16]

The Value of These Approaches

It is a little difficult to compare the value of these approaches to the study of federalism because although the aims of the authors overlap they are nevertheless not the same. Wheare's aim is to make possible a detailed comparative study of the small numbers of federal systems which conform to his model. The aim of writers like Friedrich and Deutsch is to elaborate the forces and conditions, thought to be mainly social and economic, which facilitate and stimulate the federalizing process.[17] Riker's aim is to establish the conditions, claimed to be entirely political, which are necessary for the making and maintenance of the federal bargain as he has defined it. These approaches can be compared only

---

[14]Riker, *op. cit.*, p. 12.

[15]*Ibid.*

[16]*Ibid.*, pp. 103-116. The analysis is brief and the evidence is somewhat uneven as between one country and another, but this does not affect the value of the conceptual framework.

[17]I do not intend to suggest that Friedrich and Deutsch agree on everything, only that their approaches to the study of federalism are similar enough for it to be appropriate to include them in the same category in this paper.

in respect of the fact that each points to a set of conditions in which a new federation is likely to be created. They cannot usefully be compared in respect of their other virtues, such as Wheare's discussion of constitutional and administrative problems in federations, Deutsch's discussion of other forms of economic and political integration, and Riker's discussion of the conditions for the maintenance of federal systems.

The conditions which are proposed by these authors as necessary for the creation of a federation can be summarized as follows. K. C. Wheare considers that most, if not all, of six conditions must be satisfied:

1. a sense of military insecurity and of the consequent need for common defence;
2. a desire to be independent of foreign powers, for which union is a necessity;
3. a hope of economic advantage from union;
4. some previous political association;
5. geographical neighbourhood;
6. similarity of political institutions.[18]

K. W. Deutsch and his collaborators postulate nine conditions:

1. Mutual compatibility of main values;
2. a distinctive way of life;
3. expectations of stronger economic ties or gains;
4. a marked increase in political and administrative capabilities of at least some participating units;
5. superior economic growth on the part of at least some participating units;
6. unbroken links of social communications, both geographically between territories and sociologically between different social strata;
7. a broadening of the political elite;
8. mobility of persons at least among the politically relevant strata;
9. a multiplicity of ranges of communications and transactions [19]

W. H. Riker regards two conditions as pre-eminent:

1. A desire on the part of the politicians who offer the bargain to expand their area of influence by peaceful means, usually either to meet an external military or diplomatic threat or to prepare for military or diplomatic aggression and aggrandizement;
2. a willingness in the part of the politicians who accept the bargain to give up some independence for the sake of union, either because they desire protection from a military or diplomatic threat or because they desire to participate in the potential aggression of the federation.[20]

---

[18]See Wheare, *op. cit.*, pp. 37-38.
[19]See Deutsch *et al.*, *op. cit.*, p. 58.
[20]See Riker, *op. cit.*, p. 12.

The following sections of the paper will be devoted to a brief discussion of developments in Nigeria, in East Africa, and in Malaysia, with the hope that these examples will cast some light on the value of the three approaches to the student who wishes to analyse the factors involved in the establishment of a new federation.

The Nigerian Federation

The main outlines of this story are well known and need not be repeated.[21] It is clear that in Nigeria the last four of Wheare's conditions were present and it is arguable that the second condition was also present: certainly the British Government wanted Nigeria to remain united and would have delayed independence if one or more regions had insisted on separation, though it is not likely that independence would have been long delayed. Wheare's first condition was not present, as the former French colonies which surround Nigeria did not present any kind of military threat. But as Wheare stipulates only that most of the six conditions must be present the case of Nigeria supports his generalization.

Of Deutsch's conditions, numbers 3, 4, 5, 9, and (with some reservations) 6 were present. But the Muslim and aristocratic north had a different way of life and was dominated by a different set of values from those which obtained in the two southern regions; it is doubtful whether federation was accompanied by a broadening of the political elite; and there was little mobility of top persons between regions.[22] The Nigerian example therefore confirms Riker's view that Deutsch's nine conditions cannot be regarded as essential.

Riker's own account of the Nigerian situation is somewhat misleading. He cites the expansionist ambitions of Ghana as the external threat, saying that "during the time just before and during the Nigerian achievement of independence, Nkrumah's emphasis on Pan-Africanism was at its height and no Nigerian leader could fail to be aware of the proximity of the western (and depressed and minority) region of Nigeria to Ghana".[23] In fact the western region was the most prosperous of the three and at the time of the bargain its leaders showed no disposition whatever to sympathize with Nkrumah's ambitions.[24] However, it is certainly true that diplomatic considerations were a

---

[21]See James S. Coleman, *Nigeria: Background to Nationalism*, University of California Press, Berkeley, 1958; Kalu Ezera, *Constitutional Developments in Nigeria*, University Press, Cambridge, 1960; and Richard L. Sklar, *Nigerian Political Parties*, Princeton University Press, Princeton, 1963.

[22]There had been some mobility of junior government officials from the East to the North, but the programme of "Northernization" was launched to counteract this.

[23]Riker, *op. cit.*, p. 31.

[24]The writer acted as consultant to the western region government from 1956 to 1958 and feels able to report this with some certainty. It is also the case that the western leader's attitude to Ghana was well known in West Africa: it was expressed in speeches and in frequent editorials in the Action Group newspaper, the *Daily Service*. Further, in the federal elections of December 1959 the Action Group announced its "opposition to any form of political union among the West African states". See R. O. Tilman

factor in the establishment of this federation. The two groups whom it is rea-sonable to regard as the proponents of continued political union were the British and the leaders of the N.C.N.C. The British were clearly motivated by diplo-matic considerations and the N.C.N.C. leaders, having played a dominant role in the nationalist movement, hoped to have a large influence on the politics of an independent Nigeria and saw great diplomatic advantages in the fact that, if it remained united, it would be the most populous country in Africa.[25]

The western and northern leaders can appropriately be regarded, in Riker's terms, as the acceptors of federation. Both wished to preserve their own lead-ership in their own area and had some fears of the ambitions of the N.C.N.C., a party which was to some extent the vehicle of an ideology, as opposed to the western and northern parties which were based on tribal and cultural organiza-tions. But the western leaders knew that an independent state of western Nigeria would be in a very precarious position because of the minority tribes in the west and the strength of the N.C.N.C. in organizing both these tribes and certain dissident elements among the Yoruba peoples (for instance, in Ibadan). More-over, they knew that a claim for independence would immediately precipitate a conflict over the status of Lagos. Feeling that a two-state federation of southern Nigeria would also be dominated by the politically ambitious easterners, the western leaders therefore accepted the idea of a federation of three states, hoping to ensure that the powers of the central government would be fairly restricted.

The northern leaders accepted federation with more reluctance, partly be-cause they were fairly content with the status quo and thought that it would be a poor exchange if British rulers were replaced by southern Nigerians. However, once it became clear that the colonial regime was reaching its last days the northern leaders had to face the prospect that regional independence would leave the north extremely poor (the poorest of the three regions), with a grave shortage of middle-grade officials (the north being far more dependent on British officials than the other two regions), and in a precarious position because their traditional enemies in the south could cut off their communications with the coast at a moment's notice. They therefore agreed to accept the proposal for a federation, strengthened by the knowledge that the population of the

---

and Taylor Cole (eds.), *The Nigerian Political Scene*, Duke University Press, Durham, N.C., 1962, p. 128. It was not until June 1961 that Chief Awolowo, by then disappointed in his personal political ambitions, changed his mind on this score: an extraordinary reversal of view which was one of a succession of steps which led eventually to his imprisonment for treason. His policies up to 1960 are explained and illustrated in *Awo: the Autobiography of Chief Obafemi Awolowo*, University Press, Cambridge, 1960.

[25]Of course economic and social considerations also motivated the N.C.N.C. leaders: Riker's point is not that diplomatic considerations must be dominant, only that they must always be present. It is also true that the N.C.N.C. leaders were over-optimistic about the political influence they could exert in a federation, believing as they did that they would be able to offset the numerical preponderance of northerners by winning a fair number of seats in the north region in association with their allies in the Northern Elements Progressive Union.

north would entitle it to at least half the seats in the federal legislature.[26]

The situation in Nigeria was therefore more complex than Riker suggests, and is unusual in the sense that the potential threats which acted as inducements to those who accepted the proposal came from other parts of the federation, not from other countries. But it is of course true that considerations of political power and diplomacy were a factor in the establishment of this federation. It follows that the Nigerian case can probably be regarded as an example of Riker's rule, provided that the rule is so interpreted or amended as to allow the threat to come from prospective partners in the federation as well as from outside. An amendment to cover this will be suggested below.

The Proposed Federation of East Africa

The idea of a federation of the East African territories that were until recently administered by Britain has been intermittently under discussion for over forty years. It was advocated by Winston Churchill when he was Colonial Secretary in 1922 and by L. S. Amery when he was appointed to that office in 1924. It was investigated by a series of commissions and committees during the following years, all of which reported with varying degrees of emphasis that the idea had economic advantages but political and administrative drawbacks. After 1931, when a Joint Select Committee of Parliament canvassed opinion in Kenya, Tanganyika, and Uganda, one of the main obstacles was the feeling among Africans that such a development would extend the area of influence of the European settlers who already had a good deal of influence in the government of Kenya.[27] From then until the independence of these countries became imminent constructive discussion focussed on the development of common services and economic integration, not on federation as such.

At the end of the World War II the three territories had a common market (instituted in 1927), a common currency, a single court of appeal, and a single system of posts and telegraphs. There was an annual governors' conference which was replaced in 1948 by the East Africa High Commission, with a Central Legislative Assembly and power to administer a number of common services. These included rail transport (as from 1949), civil aviation, docks and harbours, the collection of income tax, locust control, and research organizations in medicine, agriculture, and veterinary science. In December 1961, when Tanganyika became independent, the High Commission was replaced by the East African Common Services Organization. The functions of EACSO were substantially the same as those of the High Commission, but its executive was responsible to

---

[26]The differences of attitude between the regions were reflected in many of the negotiations. Thus one of the main subjects of controversy at the 1957 Constitutional Conference was the control of the police, the British and the eastern leaders wanting federal control while the western and northern leaders wanted regional control. Again, in their submissions to the Fiscal Commission of 1957-8 the government of the eastern region proposed a more centralized tax system than that advocated by the governments of the western and northern regions.

[27]See *Reports of the Joint Select Committee in Closer Union in East Africa*, Cmnd. 3254 and 3378 of 1931.

the three territorial governments instead of to the British Government and its constitution provided for amendment by agreement of the three governments.[28] There was, therefore, a considerable measure of functional integration in East Africa when the idea of federation was given new life by Julius Nyerere in June 1960.

Speaking at Addis Ababa, Nyerere proposed that the four East African territories (including Zanzibar) should federate as soon as they achieved independence, and he went so far as to suggest that Tanganyika would be willing to see its own independence day postponed by a few months if the four territories could then be given independence simultaneously. He repeated this suggestion at the P.A.F.M.E.C.A. meeting at Nairobi in January 1961, saying: "The feeling of unity which now exists would be whittled away if each country gets its independence separately and becomes open to the temptations of nationhood and the intrigues of those who find their strength in the weakness of small nations".[29] In Kenya this proposal got a mixed reception. The Legislative Council passed a resolution declaring that federation was both economically and politically desirable, but the government rejected as impracticable the suggestion that independence should be synchronized. In Uganda the leaders of all three parties took the view that it would be premature to discuss federation before the country's own constitutional problems were resolved.[30]

However, the leaders of Kenya and Uganda became more ready to talk about federation after they had achieved what seemed to be solutions to their internal constitutional problems, and in June 1963 a joint statement pledging their governments to the goal of federation was issued by the President of Tanganyika and the Prime Ministers of Kenya and Uganda. In this statement federation was commended both as a step towards Pan-African unity and as a move which would bring economic benefits to the area. It was announced that to achieve these aims: "a working party is being established which will prepare a framework of a draft constitution for the Federation of East Africa. It will report back to a full conference of East African governments", to meet in "the third week of August".[31]

In the event this confident prediction was not fulfilled. The working party failed to reach agreement and the conference was not held. During 1964 the army revolt in Tanganyika, the revolution in Zanzibar, and the subsequent "amalgamation" of Tanganyika and Zanzibar effectively occupied President Nyerere's attention, and there are signs that his future international involvements may be to the west and the south rather than to the north. Meanwhile economic co-operation between the East African countries has been under

---

[28]For an analysis of the structure and role of EACSO, see J. S. Nye, Jr., "East African Economic Integration", *Journal of Modern African Studies*, Vol. I, No. 4, 1963.

[29]Quoted in A. J. Hughes, *East Africa: the Search for Unity*, Penguin Books, Harmondsworth, 1963, p. 233. In saying this Nyerere may also, of course, have been motivated by the desire to press the British Government to bring forward the dates of independence for the other territories.

[30]*Ibid.*, pp. 231-234.

[31]The full statement is printed in an appendix to Hughes, *op. cit.*

strain and some restrictions have been imposed on the free trade of commodities between them. In June 1965 the government of Tanzania announced its intention to withdraw from the common market and to establish its own currency.

These are the bare bones of the story of the proposed East African Federation. The question with which we are concerned is how this story should be interpreted. Should the student adopt Wheare's approach, looking for a mixture of geographical, economic, and political factors; or Deutsch's with its heavy emphasis on economic and social factors; or Riker's, with its exclusive concern with the political, diplomatic and strategic aspects of the situation?

There can be little doubt that the first inclination of nearly all commentators is to concentrate on the economic and social factors. Four main arguments have led people both to commend federation in East Africa as desirable and to predict it as a probable development. First, the common market has stimulated economic development and a federal union with complete internal free trade would be even more beneficial.[32] Second, it should not be assumed that the common market and EACSO will survive for long after self-government unless a further step towards unity is taken: functional integration of this kind is to be regarded not as a point of equilibrium but as a stage in the federalizing process, with political union as the next stage. Third, overseas investors tend to be more willing to invest in a large country (providing it appears to have a fair chance of political stability) than in a number of small countries.[33] Fourth, territorial boundaries in East Africa are entirely arbitrary, often cutting tribal communities in two; while tribal rivalries might be more easily contained in a federal union in which no tribe would comprise more than four or five per cent of the population.[34]

All these arguments and others were canvassed at a conference on the problems of East African federation which was sponsored by the University of East Africa and held at Nairobi in November 1963. The general tendency of participants in the conference (most of whom were politicians from the three mainland territories) was to discuss federation in terms of economic and social advantages on the one hand, political and administrative difficulties on the other.[35] The advantages were agreed to be very considerable; the difficulties (e.g. the fact that the states had slightly different institutions and the problem of giving the states some influence over federal planning decisions) did not seem insurmountable. Yet at the time of writing the proposal for a federation

---

[32] In the common market there are a number of artificial impediments to trade between territories. See *Report of the East African Economic and Fiscal Commission*, Cmnd. 1279 of 1961, pp. 15 and 63.

[33] See, for instance, the report by the Federation of British Industries on the prospects of investment in Nigeria.

[34] On this last point see Burudi Nabwera, "Federation", mimeographed, Nairobi, 1963, p. 3.

[35] It will be appreciated that this is a personal impression. The main papers of the conference have been published in Colin Leys and Peter Robson (eds.), *Federation in East Africa*, Oxford University Press, Nairobi and London, 1965.

is in eclipse. This is the problem of this approach, spotlighted by the fact that in East Africa all of Deutsch's nine conditions appear to be satisfied. So, for that matter, are all but the first two of Wheare's conditions.

It is evident that although economic arguments loomed large in the discussions over federation, the situation cannot be understood simply in these terms. One indication of this is that the negotiations do not appear to have taken the shape they would have done if economic considerations had been primary. There is substantial agreement among economists that Kenya has derived most of the benefit from the common market, that Uganda's benefits have been very small, and that Tanganyika may not have benefited at all.[36] If there were more complete economic integration the territorial disparities in terms of benefit would necessarily be greater, except in so far as Tanganyika and Uganda were either compensated by fiscal means or given special advantages in the planning of industrial location.[37] Since all the straws in the wind pointed to increasing strains within the customs union after the participating governments gained full independence, with the possibility of Uganda and/or Tanganyika taking protective measures, the economic logic of the situation required that Kenya should propose federation as a way of safeguarding the customs union and that the other countries (particularly Tanganyika) should demand guarantees of fiscal compensation and a sizeable influence in planning decisions as a price of their agreement. Instead, Julius Nyerere proposed federation and has consistently taken the view that the three governments should commit themselves to political union before bothering about details of that kind. From the economic point of view, this makes no sense at all: it makes sense only if Nyerere's primary motives were political and diplomatic.

If the latter assumption is made, Nyerere's role as the proposer of federation can be interpreted as a move to expand the area of influence of himself and his party, and to create a large East African state which would be in a good position to assume the leadership of the Pan-African movement. The reluctance of the governments of the other countries, particularly Uganda, to accept the proposal can be interpreted as the natural reluctance of political leaders to surrender autonomy when they were under no external threat and either did not desire to participate in the diplomatic aggression that union would make possible or did not feel confident they would have anything but a subordinate role in the proposed federal government.

Nobody would suggest that this is the whole truth of the matter. The suggestion is the more limited one that this approach enables the student of politics to pick out the factor — namely a prospect of political, diplomatic or strategic gain for all parties — which must be present if the negotiations for federal union are to succeed. The so-far abortive attempts to form a federation of East Africa

---

[36]See, for instance, Dharam Ghai, "Territorial Distribution of the Benefits and Costs of the East African Common Market" in Leys and Robson, *op. cit.*, where it is argued that Tanganyika has suffered a slight net loss from the operation of the customs union.

[37]See Benton F. Massell, *East Africa Economic Union*, Rand Corporation Research Memorandum, Santa Monica, 1963, *passim*.

would seem to afford striking confirmation of the value of Riker's contribution to the theory of federalism.

The Establishment of the Federation of Malaysia

This example is clearer than that of East Africa because diplomatic and strategic considerations were openly paramount in Malaysia. The story in a nutshell is that federation was proposed first by the government of Singapore, anxious to transfer control of internal security and allied matters to Kuala Lumpur; was proposed secondly by the British Government, worried about Singapore and anxious to give the Borneo territories independence without leaving them in a hopelessly vulnerable position in relation to Indonesia; and was accepted by the government of Malaya, mainly because of its concern about the possibility that Singapore might otherwise become a threat to the security of the area.

The proposal for some form of merger between Singapore and Malaya was made by successive chief ministers in Singapore between 1955 and 1960 — first by David Marshall, then by Lim Kew Hock, and then by Lee Kuan Yew. The proposals were unacceptable to the Malayan Government mainly because the inclusion of the predominantly Chinese electorate of Singapore would upset the delicate balance of multi-racial politics by means of which the Malays, with fifty per cent of the population of Malaya, have contrived to control the political situation.

However, in the first five months of 1961 the Tunku Abdul Rahman (Prime Minister of Malaya) changed his mind on this issue. One factor in this was the imminence of the end of the five-year agreement made in 1958 whereby internal security in Singapore was controlled jointly by the governments of Singapore, Malaya, and the United Kingdom. Another was that Lee Kuan Yew succeeded in persuading the Tunku that the People's Action Party (the ruling party in Singapore), though left-wing, was firmly anti-communist and more reliable than any likely alternative. Allied to this was the growth of opposition from the extreme left in Singapore and the loss of a by-election which shook public confidence in the ability of the People's Action Party to win the next general election.[38] These developments increased the disposition of the Malayan leaders to see the advantage and indeed the necessity of a merger which would put defence and internal security in Singapore under the control of a federal government at Kuala Lumpur.

In this same period the British Secretary for Commonwealth Relations proposed to the Tunku that it would be advantageous to include the three British Borneo territories with Singapore and Malaya in a federation. The convenience of this to the British Government was clear; its great attraction to the Malayan Government was that it would enable the Chinese and left-wing electorate of Singapore to be offset by the inclusion of a considerable non-Chinese and not-left-wing electorate in the Borneo territories. In May 1961 the Tunku announced

---

[38]See Michael Leifer, "Politics in Singapore", *Journal of Commonwealth Political Studies*, Vol. II, 1963-1964, pp. 102-119.

that he saw advantages in the creation of a federation which would include both Singapore and the Borneo territories, and the matter was henceforth the subject of public discussion and private negotiation.

The public discussion emphasized the concern of government leaders with the possibility that Singapore might become the Cuba of Asia. Lee Kuan Yew delivered twelve broadcast talks in the autumn of 1961 which were intended to expose communist attitudes in Singapore and to justify his government's decision to join the proposed federation.[39] He insisted that the main fear of the communists and their allies was that internal security in Singapore would pass into the control of Kuala Lumpur; that the communist object was either to secure the abolition of the Internal Security Council and the subsequent independence of Singapore by itself or else to keep Singapore under British rule, so that their opposition to the government could "be camouflaged as an anti-colonial struggle";[40] and that it was his government's intention that security in Singapore would in fact be transferred to an elected federal government which could not be accused of colonialism. The Tunku took a similar line, saying in a speech to publicity officers of his party that:

> The most important point is that the constitution of Singapore will come to an end and with it two issues will be faced: firstly, whether Singapore becomes independent; and, secondly, whether Singapore should merge with the Federation of Malaya.
>
> It is impossible to grant independence to Singapore because of the danger of its going communist, and if it goes communist it would with the help of the communist powers try to overrun the whole of Malaya . . . . Therefore to prevent this most unhappy and disastrous state of affairs occurring, the only course open to us would be to accept Singapore as a member of the Federation of Malaysia.[41]

The private negotiations took place at first between Lee Kuan Yew and the Tunku, and subsequently involved the spokesmen for the Borneo territories. They first established the main terms for the merger between Singapore and the mainland, which related to citizenship, to representation in the federal legislature, and to Singapore's wish (which was granted) to retain control over education and labour. Bargaining continued from July 1961 until the very eve of the inauguration of the federation,[42] and resulted in an extremely complicated set of constitutional arrangements in which the different states of the federation

---

[39]See Lee Kuan Yew, *The Battle for Merger*, Government Printing Office, Singapore, 1962, which comprises the text of these talks together with twelve documentary appendixes.

[40]*Ibid.*, p. 45.

[41]Speech printed in *Malayan Times*, September 25, 1962, quoted in Gordon P. Means, "Malaysia: a new Federation in Southeast Asia", *Pacific Affairs*, Vol. XXXVI, No. 2, Summer 1963, pp. 138-159.

[42]Nine points were not agreed until 8 and 9 July 1963, when Lee Kuan Yew and the Tunku settled them in meetings in the Ritz Hotel, London, one or two of the agreements being jotted down on the back of an envelope, photographs of which were subsequently published by the Singapore Government. See *Malaysia Agreement: Exchange of Letters*, Misc. 5 of 1963, Singapore.

enjoy differing degrees of autonomy.[43] Despite this flexibility the terms offered proved unacceptable to the rulers of Brunei, which has remained outside the federation. The details of the constitution are not relevant to this article, but it is worth noting that Singapore, with a population of 1.6 millions, was given only 15 seats in the federal legislature, whereas Sabah and Sarawak, with a combined population of 1.2 millions, have 40 seats between them.[44] The governing Alliance Party of Malaya moved quickly into the Borneo territories and in the first elections for the federal legislature (the Dewan Ra'ayat) it won all 16 seats in Sabah and 20 of the 24 seats in Sarawak. Since it won 89 of the 104 seats in Malaya in 1964 it had 125 members in a house of 159 seats, in which all the Singapore representatives (12 People's Action Party and 3 Barisan Sosialis) were in opposition. The Borneo territories thus filled the role for which they were cast, but whether the Alliance Party will continue to be so successful there must be a matter for speculation. If racial tensions were to increase this would probably weaken its position, since it would be seen as a Malay-dominated party in states in which only a minority of the population are Malays.[45]

This outline of the formation of the Federation of Malaysia is substantially different from that given by Riker, who cites the possibility of Indonesian aggression as the only threat and regards the British and the Malayan Governments as the proposers of federation and the other territories as the acceptors.[46] I do not think that his account can be accepted in its present form. Malaysia is a federation which would almost certainly not have been created in the absence of threats to the security of one or more of the participating territories, but the threats were as much internal as external, and it was a desire for protection that motivated the proposers (Singapore and Britain, on behalf of the Borneo territories) as well as the acceptor. It follows that this example is not quite covered by Riker's generalizations as they are now formulated. Since the Nigerian example was also one in which the threats were internal, I suggest that the generalizations stand in need of amendment to cover situations of this kind. The following proposition is offered as a substitute for the two conditions proposed by Riker:

> A necessary condition for the establishment of a federation is that the political leaders of all the territories involved should believe that union would either (a) help to protect one or more of the territories from an external or internal threat, whether actual or potential, to the security of

---

[43]For details, see *Malaysia Agreement*, Cmnd. 2094 of 1963; H. E. Groves, *The Constitution of Malaysia*, Malaysia Publications, Singapore, 1964; Milton E. Osborne, *Singapore and Malaysia*, Data Paper 53 of Cornell University Southeast Asia Programme, Ithaca, N.Y., 1964; and Wang Gungwu (ed.), *Malaysia: a Survey*, Pall Mall Press, London, 1964.

[44]The official justification of this was that Singapore retained control of education and labour, which are federally controlled in the Borneo territories.

[45]See Robert O. Tilman, "Elections in Sarawak" and Frances L. Starner, "Malaysia and the North Borneo Territories", both in *Asian Survey*, Vol. III, No. 10 and No. 11, October and November 1963, pp. 507-518 and pp. 519-534.

[46]Riker, *op. cit.*, p. 31.

the established regime or (b) enable them to benefit from the improved diplomatic or military position that the larger unit could be expected to enjoy; though it is not necessary that the considerations influencing the leaders of the various territories should be identical.

It should also be noted that all of Wheare's six conditions were present in Malaysia (provided 800 miles of ocean are not regarded as a bar to "geographical neighbourhood"). Of Deutsch's nine conditions only numbers 3, 4, 5, and 9 were satisfied.[47]

Conclusion

It may be appropriate to conclude with a very brief comment about method. My own belief is that the kind of comparative study most likely to be fruitful is that which takes as its starting point the existence of somewhat similar arrangements which have evolved or have been devised in a limited number of countries, themselves not entirely dissimilar, to meet similar needs. The object of this kind of study is to show how these arrangements have been modified in the course of time by the pressure of circumstance and by differences in the political traditions of the countries involved, and how far interesting points of similarity remain. As one example, I followed this approach in my study *Federalism, Finance and Social Legislation in Canada, Australia, and the United States*.[48] The problems analysed were similar and the countries were similar enough for comparisons to be fruitful. One result of the study was a set of general comments about the financial predicament of the poorer states in a federal system. These comments were not presented as generalizations which could be applied without further study to any federal system, but they did indicate the kind of dilemma which the poorer states in other federations (or potential federations) would be likely to experience, and in this sense they were of general significance.

The approach followed by Riker and by Deutsch is unlike this in that, instead of beginning with similarities and showing differences, they begin with a large variety of different situations and try to establish uniformities. This method is inherently more difficult, not only because no scholar can be expected to have a detailed knowledge of more than a few countries but also because the method involves such a radical process of abstraction and generalization that the sense

---

[47]This analysis is not invalidated by the fact that Singapore has left the Federation since this article was written. The reason for the rift is that the dominant Malay elements in the Alliance Party are not willing to tolerate electoral competition from a non-Malay party led by Lee Kuan Yew. In the objective situation little has changed, but there has been a shift in the assessment by Malay leaders of the relative importance of the threats to their position from (a) the possible election of a pro-communist government in an independent Singapore and (b) the development of a challenge to their political power from a Chinese-led Malaysian party deriving leadership and finance from Singapore. However, this development may indicate the importance for the maintenance, as distinct from the establishment, of a federation of some of the social factors discussed by Deutsch *et al.*

[48]Clarendon Press, Oxford, 1955. The introductory chapter to the book contains a brief discussion of comparative method.

of concrete reality is apt to disappear. But in spite of these difficulties, Riker has succeeded in pointing to the importance of certain kinds of political consideration in the formation of federations, and this may be counted a real, if limited, gain in a period in which it seems fashionable to assume that economic and social factors are pre-eminent.

2   A Note on the Nature of Federalism*

W. S. Livingston

Federalism as a Juridical Concept

Almost every treatment of federal government and its problems has begun with the assumption that the problem here concerned is one of legal formalism and formal jurisprudence. Nearly all theorists have been at pains to point out that a federal constitution is a device for associating a number of distinct political and constitutional entities in such a manner that a new body is produced which is above and different from those that have come together. But the component states still retain their identity, sacrificing to the collectivity only such powers and functions as are necessary for the implementation of the purpose for which the association is formed. Or, as it is described in some instances, the powers of the central government are devolved upon the subordinate bodies in such a way that both central and regional units are thenceforth endowed with certain powers and functions of which neither can be deprived by the other. This is to say that the central government's functions cannot be assumed by the local governments, or the local governments' by the central. Each is placed in relation to the other in a position of autonomy; neither is subordinate and each may exercise within its sphere the full extent of its powers. There is also substantial agreement among writers on federalism that the extent of these powers is strictly limited by the simultaneous existence of comparable, though never identical, powers in the other unit. The problem thus becomes that of the proper delineation of these spheres. Where is the boundary between the central and the component governments to be drawn? How much power does the central government have and how much power do the local units have? This attempt to quantify power seems to be characteristic of the juridical approach to the problems of federal government.

In order that this line of demarcation between the two governments may be precise and understood by all it is ordinarily considered necessary that the constitution of a federal state be written. Most writers have held it impossible

---

*From *Political Science Quarterly*, Vol. LXVII, No. 1, March 1952, pp. 81-95. Reprinted by permission of the author and The Academy of Political Science.

for a distribution of this nature to be produced by the slow evolution of institutions such as is found in Great Britain. The experience of federal governments in the modern world is cited to show that in fact they all do have written constitutions. Only a written constitution, it is held, could precisely assign powers and functions in the necessary manner.

Once the distribution of powers is made, the accounts continue, it must be protected; and this requires that some kind of obstacle be put in the way of constitutional change. If the component units have entered the federation on the understanding that they are to possess certain rights and functions, then these must not be taken from them except in circumstances where some agreed-upon criterion demands such reassignment. Conversely the powers of the general government must not be alienated unless this is clearly necessary. In order to protect the allotment of powers to local and central units, the constitution must be *rigid*. By this is meant simply that to amend the constitution a procedure different from (that is, more difficult than) that of ordinary legislation is to be used. Indeed, since Lord Bryce published his *Studies in History and Jurisprudence* the definition of a rigid constitution has turned on this very point. A rigid constitution, as contrasted with a flexible one, has come to mean one that can be amended only by a procedure more difficult than that by which ordinary laws are made.

This procedure for constitutional amendment in a federal state, it is ordinarily said, must be designed to protect the federal allocation of governmental powers and functions. Since one of the purposes of employing a federal rather than a unitary constitution is to assure the different units of their proper and agreed-upon share in governmental activity, the power to amend the constitution cannot be lodged in either the general government exclusively or in the local governments exclusively, for this would permit the one to take from the other without its consent those functions that it desires to retain. Hence the federal system necessitates an amending procedure in which the consent of both the general and the local governments must be secured before any change can be made. But, the accounts continue, this does not mean that the consent of all the local governments is necessary, for this would effectively cripple the federation and prevent all important change; it would also, according to some, transform the federation into a confederation. But the procedure must consist of some form of consent on the local level as well as some form of consent on the national level. Usually the need for local concurrence takes the form of a requirement that a majority or more of the component units must consent to the amendment, though the means by which this consent is secured and measured vary greatly.

It requires little demonstration to show that the constant emphasis throughout this chain of thought is on the legal aspects of federal organization. The questions are always of a legal nature. How much power? What vote is required? Upon what right may this or that action be based? Does it violate the constitutional distribution of power? Does it violate the principles of federalism? The ordinary treatment of federalism is based upon a legalistic foundation and its problems are treated as problems of constitutional law.

The Operation of Federal Institutions

This is assuredly a convenient method of approaching the problem and in many instances it is the only possible one. But it is not the only one. If a question arises that requires a legal answer, it can be answered only in legal terms. But the validity of such an answer is limited to the frame of reference within which the question is posed. Legal answers are of value only in the solution of legal problems. And federalism is concerned with many other problems than those of a legal nature.

Above and beyond this legalism there is an aspect of federalism that has been largely ignored. The essential nature of federalism is to be sought for, not in the shadings of legal and constitutional terminology, but in the forces — economic, social, political, cultural — that have made the outward forms of federalism necessary. Federalism, like most institutional forms, is a solution of, or an attempt to solve a certain kind of problem of political organization. It is true, on the whole, that federal governments and federal constitutions never grow simply and purely by accident. They arise in response to a definite set of stimuli; a federal system is consciously adopted as a means of solving the problems represented by these stimuli.

Whether a constitutional structure may properly be called federal, however, depends not so much on the arrangement of the institutions within it as it does on the manner in which those institutions are employed. Institutions have a habit of serving purposes other than those for which they are designed. The passage of time produces changes in the purposes of any society and these new purposes are reflected in new modes of operating old institutions which frequently retain their original forms. Thus a society may possess institutions that are federal in appearance but it may operate them as though they were something else; and, what is more likely, it may possess a unitary set of institutions and employ them as though they were federal in nature. The institutions themselves do not provide an accurate index of the federal nature of the society that subtends them.

Federalism as a Sociological Phenomenon

This leads us another step forward in the analysis. We have said that institutions may not be suited to the actual needs of the society and this point will be explored in greater detail later. If one could know exactly how the institutions are operated, one would have a much more accurate picture of the nature of the society itself. But the picture would still be incomplete and unclear; for institutional devices, both in form and in function, are only the surface manifestations of the deeper federal quality of the society that lies beneath the surface. The essence of federalism lies not in the institutional or constitutional structure but in the society itself. Federal government is a device by which the federal qualities of the society are articulated and protected.

Every society, every nation if you will, is more or less closely integrated in accordance with its own peculiar historical, cultural, economic, political and other determinants. Each is composed of elements that feel themselves to be

different from the other elements in varying degrees and that demand in varying degrees a means of self-expression. These diversities may turn on all sorts of
questions — economic, religious, racial, historical; any of these can produce in
a certain group within the population a demand for such self-expression. Furthermore, these diversities may be distributed among the members of a society
in such a fashion that certain attitudes are found in particular territorial areas,
or they may be scattered widely throughout the whole of the society. If they
are grouped territorially, that is geographically, then the result may be a society
that is federal. If they are not grouped territorially, then the society cannot be
said to be federal. In either case coherence in the society may depend on the
devolution upon these groups of the exercise of functions appropriate to the
diversities that they represent. But in the first case only can this take the form of
federalism or federal government. In the latter case it becomes functionalism,
pluralism or some form of corporativism.

I realize that in using the term federal only in this restricted territorial sense
I am taking from it some of the meaning attributed to it by writers who profess
to see federal elements in the various forms of pluralism, such as feudalism or
corporativism. But I suggest that these writers have added a meaning that was
not there before and one that introduces an element of confusion into the term.
No government has ever been called federal that has been organized on any but
the territorial basis; when organized on any other it has gone by another name.

It is true that the geographical diversities may not always follow the boundary lines of the component units. In many countries, and particularly in the
United States, the operation of the federal system has displayed patterns of
diversity that are more nearly associated with regions or groups of states than
with the individual states themselves. This is easily understood. Federalism
embraces not merely a diversity of opinion on one issue but a whole pattern
of diversities on a number of issues. It can scarcely be expected that state
boundary lines will be adequate to mark off areas in which opinions differ on
all possible questions. Indeed on many, or even most, questions the state boundaries will be of little significance in thus eliminating the areas of diversity.
Federal organization is not perfect in every case.

No one supposes that it is, however. Component states exist because of some
great significant diversity of such importance that it is felt that only a federal
organization can offer it sufficient protection. Day-to-day issues may easily and
reasonably produce alignments that follow regional lines. Regionalism in this
sense is a valid manifestation of the federal principle. It conforms to the criterion suggested above, namely, that the diversities in the society be grouped
territorially. It should be noted, moreover, that regionalism in the politics of a
federal country is made possible only by the federal allocation of functions to
the states themselves. The fact that several states within a larger region are
dominated by similar opinions and hence unite in an effort to transform these
views into policy does not detract from the importance of the states as the basic
units of the federal system.

On the other hand, federalism becomes nothing if it is held to embrace diversities that are not territorially grouped, for there are then no territorial units

that can serve as components of the federal system. I readily agree that this is a question of the definition of federalism and that society can be organized in accordance with any principle upon which there is substantial agreement among the members of the society. But if the distribution of powers, which is the essential feature of the federal structure, is made between the nation as a whole and component units that are functional in character, such as industries, trade unions, churches, and so on, then the traditional and, I think, necessary quality of federalism is lost. We confuse two distinct principles when we apply the terminology of federalism to a society organized on a functional basis.

It may be objected that the federal division of powers among territorial areas is in reality functional, since these areas differ from one another on questions of a functional character. I agree. But the important point is that they are territorially organized. Such areas naturally differ in opinions, in composition, in interests, in function. This, however, only brings us back to the point that they differ. If there were no functional differences, there might be no need for federalism. But the point that must be emphasized is that these functional differences are territorially grouped; and thus they provide a reason for and a demand for a federal system of government.

Federal Institutions as a Reflection of Societal Diversities

The nature of a society is roughly reflected in the external forms of its political and constitutional arrangements; and it is true that the extent to which the society is federal can be more or less accurately measured by the extent to which these external forms are federal. The institutional patterns reflect the federal quality of the societies in varying degrees; they may be more or less "federal" in the way in which they manifest the degree to which the political society behind the institutional facade is integrated or diversified. But the institutional patterns and the constitutional structure are far from an adequate test of the federal qualities of the society; dependence upon them alone can lead to serious error in assessing the nature of the society itself.

If these did serve as an accurate measurement of the society, the problems of the constitution maker and of the political analyst would be much simpler and this essay would not have been written. But the weighing of the various forces that go into the making and maintaining of a political community is an extremely difficult task. Those who devise institutions can never be sure that the institutions they devise will accurately represent the nature of the society or will be adequate to the needs they are designed to fulfill. Moreover, social patterns are constantly changing. What may be good for today will very likely be outmoded and less adequate by tomorrow. Finally, institutions mean different things to different people; the same set of institutions may produce widely different results when adopted and operated in different communities. Hence there can be no assurance at any time that the institutional patterns fit the needs of the society below.

From this it follows that the real nature of the society cannot be divined merely by an analysis, however brilliant and profound, of the institutions only. No amount of reading of constitutions can properly inform the analyst about the societies served by those constitutions. The nature of the political society can be examined only by observing how the institutions work in the context of that society. It is the operation, not the form, that is important; and it is the forces that determine the manner of operation that are more important still.

The Spectrum of Federal Societies

This is no less true of federalism than it is of any other form of political organization. Federalism is a function not of constitutions but of societies. Viewed in this way, it will be seen that federalism is not an absolute but a relative term; there is no specific point at which a society ceases to be unified and becomes diversified. The differences are of degree rather than of kind. All countries fall somewhere in a spectrum which runs from what we may call a theoretically wholly integrated society at one extreme to a theoretically wholly diversified society at the other. Some are more unified than others; some are more diversified than others; and the differences between adjacent societies in this spectrum may be so slight or so incommensurable as to be incapable of assessment. But that there is a gradation is clear from observing societies that are widely separated in the spectrum.

As one moves from one end of this hypothetical spectrum to the other the societies encountered are more and more diversified. And the more diversified the society, the greater is the necessity of providing some means for articulating the diversities; for these diversities are nothing less than tensions and as tensions they demand and require means of self-expression. But there is no point at which it can be said that all societies on one side are unitary and all those on the other are federal or diversified. If a society contains territorial groups that are so different from the rest of the society that they require some instrumentality to protect and articulate their peculiar qualities, then the society is likely to provide some means for the creation of such an instrumentality. One such circumstance doubtless does not make a society or a constitution federal. But two or six or twenty may produce a result that may be properly so called.

It cannot be said that when a society is just so diversified, it requires a federal constitution. In the first place we are unable to quantify social and political forces to the degree necessary to warrant such a demarcation; and secondly the forces themselves are incommensurable. (Which is more diversified, a society rent by religious schisms or one in which the members are divided by differences of language?) Societies employ instrumentalities for the expression of diversities in accordance with what men in particular societies think is necessary; and this view of what is necessary and what is not will vary considerably from society to society. Thus some societies which would seem to be highly diversified are able to get along with a set of institutions that seem to be nearly unitary; and, conversely, some that seem quite unified adopt institutions that we call federal. It may be that one especially strong unifying tendency in a society, such as a long historical tradition of unity, will overcome diversities of economic interest, language and the like which, in another society, with a weaker historical tradition, would necessitate federal institutions.

Types of Diversities

The social diversities that produce federalism may be of many kinds. Differences of economic interest, religion, race, nationality, language, variations in size, separation by great distances, differences in historical background, previous existence as separate colonies or states, dissimilarity of social and political institutions — all these may produce a situation in which the particular interests and qualities of the segments of the larger community must be given recognition. At the same time these differences must not be too great, else the community must break up into independent groups. Federalism cannot make coherent a society in which the diversities are so great that there can be no basis for integration.

There is no way to estimate the relative weights of these factors except in results; we have observed already that they are largely incommensurable. But it seems clear that some are more significant than others, at least within a single society. For example a society that enjoys a uniformity of social and political background can still hold together despite cleavages in other matters. The point is that the diversities and similarities are of many different kinds and when taken together they produce a total picture of the extent to which the society is integrated or diversified.

The total pattern of these diversities produces a demand for some kind of federal recognition of the diversities. This demand must in most cases meet a counterdemand (or inertia, which is equally a force) for increased unity or integration. These two demands or forces — the one impelling toward autonomy and independence for the component units, the other impelling toward centralization and the suppression of diversity — meet each other head on; the result of their conflict is the federal system. The federal system is thus an institutionalization of the compromise between these two demands, and the federal constitution draws the lines of this compromise. The constitution will be more or less federal in accordance with the relative strength of the two demands. Thus societies in which the demand for integration is stronger than the demand for decentralization will produce a set of institutions that is more nearly unitary; and a contrary situation will produce a contrary result. It is in this sense that federalism is a matter of degree and not of kind. The varying degrees of federalism are produced by societies in which the patterns of diversity vary and in which the demands for the protection and articulation of diversities have been urged with more or less strength. But what determines the federal quality of the government is not only the constitution that draws the lines of the compromise but the whole pattern of instrumentalities that are employed as a result of these demands.

Types of Instrumentalities

The diversities within a society require certain instrumentalities for their expression and protection. Just as the diversities take many forms, so do the instrumentalities; the latter are designed to fit the needs of the former. But the relation and correspondence between the diversities and the instrumentalities that express them will vary from society to society. A diversity that requires one kind of instrumentality for its expression in one social complex will require another kind in another social complex. So also similar instrumentalities in different social complexes will serve different kinds of diversities. It is this fact that has been largely ignored by most analysts of federal institutions.

We are too prone to say that federal constitutions must contain a certain five or eight or ten characteristics and that all constitutions lacking any of these are not federal. Such a set of criteria ignores the fundamental fact that institutions are not the same things in different social and cultural contexts. Two societies equally diversified with respect to a particular matter may require very different instrumentalities for the implementation of that diversity. By the same token, similar institutions or instrumentalities in different social contexts may serve to implement dissimilar diversities.

The word "instrumentality" is a broad one and necessarily so; but we must be clear about what is meant. First of all, it does not mean merely a clause in the constitution, though such clauses may be examples of such instrumentalities and it may be said that the provisions of the constitution are a good rough guide to the pattern of instrumentalities, though they become less adequate with the passage of time. But the word includes not only the constitutional forms but also the manner in which the forms are employed; it includes the way in which the constitution and its institutions are operated. Beyond this, moreover, it includes many things that are far from constitutional in importance in the ordinary sense of the word. It includes such things as habits, attitudes, acceptances, concepts and even theories. It includes perhaps the rules of the American Senate, the make-up of the Canadian cabinet, the zeal of the Baptist Karens in Burma. All these may serve as instrumentalities for the expression of the diversities within a society, and whether a country is federal or not may best be determined by examining the pattern of these instrumentalities and not by checking its constitution against an *a priori* list of the characters of a federal constitution.

Federal Constitutions and Federal Instrumentalities

Indeed the documentary constitution may be a poor guide in attempting to discover whether or not the society itself is federal. Several South American countries have adopted federal constitutions and yet an examination of those countries reveals a rather high degree of integration. Are we to infer that Soviet Russia is more federal than, say, the United States because it provides in its constitution for a right of secession?

Other examples may better illustrate the point. It is meaningless to insist that the Union of South Africa is unitary and not federal because of certain characteristics of its constitution. I should be quite willing to agree that the component units may be overwhelmed by the central government, if the testimony of the constitution is to constitute the only evidence. But I should at the same time insist that what is significant is, not what the constitution says, but how the people of South Africa employ it. The fact is that in many instances South Africa operates its institutions as though its constitution were federal; it works federally despite the unitary character of its legal forms. If one examines the

South African polity from a strictly legal or constitutional point of view, it is clearly unitary. But if one probes deeper into the processes of politics one quickly perceives that federalism is still an operative principle in that society.

A similar argument may be advanced in regard to Great Britain, a country whose constitution is most often cited as being typically unitary. Many elements of British public life are witness to the vitality of the federal principle on British society. Indeed there would seem to be an operative right to secede from that community, exemplified by the withdrawals from it in recent years of such elements as Burma and Ireland. If Northern Ireland or Scotland, or perhaps even other elements, were to seek actively for secession, it seems most unlikely that the right would be challenged. A right of secession as an operative idea in a society suggests diversities of a rather acute nature and places that society, as far as the particular point is concerned, well over toward the diversity side of the spectrum of federalism. Federal elements in Great Britain take other forms as well. Northern Ireland has its own parliament; Scotland has its own courts and legal system as well as its own church. Scotland, furthermore, is especially protected in the House of Commons by a Scottish Committee which deals with questions pertaining to that area. If the central government were to attempt to abolish any of these institutions, the outraged complaints of injustice would bear adequate witness to the extent to which this society is diversified and to the necessity of providing these instrumentalities for the articulation and protection of the federal qualities.

Even France under the *ancien régime*, which is ordinarily considered to have been a very highly centralized executive state, manifested certain federal qualities. The laws and customs of the provinces were far from standardized. Each had its own legal code, its own body of customary law, its own historical tradition and a very considerable degree of local patriotism.

The Causal Relation Between Federalism and its Instrumentalities

The point has been made that the pattern of forces within the society changes with the passage of time. Society is never static but changes constantly in accordance with the interplay of the various dynamic forces within it. As a result, the diversities within the society wax and wane in intensity so that the need for their articulation increases or decreases. A complex of psychological and sociological factors may require one type of instrumentality at one time and another type at some other time. As the nature of society changes, demands for new kinds of instrumentalities are created and these demands are met by changing or abolishing old instrumentalities and substituting new ones in their place. But it can scarcely be hoped that the instrumentalities will keep pace with the changing pattern of social relationships, and as a result the pattern of instrumentalities tends to lag behind the changes in society itself (though it may be observed that the functioning of the instrumentalities will not be so rigid in this respect as the constitutional forms).

This is complicated further by the fact that the instrumentalities, once put into operation, become rigidified and acquire a status of their own. They become substantive instead of merely adjectival; they become ends in themselves instead of merely means toward other ends. Their procedures become standardized; they may take on an honorific quality; they become matters of pride to the diverse elements that they serve; and ultimately the instrumentalities enter into and become part of the psycho-sociological complex itself.

This is by no means an unusual occurrence; almost every society manifests this tendency in one form or another. The Scottish Committee of the British House of Commons, mentioned above, is an example. This Committee was at the outset a device, an instrumentality, to permit the organized expression of Scottish opinion on affairs that directly concerned Scotland; it is still that. But it is also much more, for it has become a thing of value in itself, a thing to be preserved because it is an essential part of the federal relation between England and Scotland.

Another example is the Supreme Court of the United States which began as a mere court of law. But as judicial supremacy developed in the United States the Supreme Court became more and more an institution that connoted the maintenance of justice in federal relations in this country. (It came to mean many other things as well, but it is the federal arrangement that concerns us here.) Few men now claim that the Court is a mere court of law; and few men would dare to disturb its position without serious consideration of the effects of such a change on the shifting balance of national power and state power. The Court has ceased to be a mere instrumentality and has entered into the psycho-sociological complex that determines the nature of the instrumentalities.

Another example is to be found in the United States themselves. America adopted a federal constitution at the outset because the elements that were to make up the new country were so diversified that they could be brought together in no other form. But since that time the Federal Constitution has continued in force and has collected around it all the aura of a highly revered institution. As other states have entered the union they have taken their places in the federal arrangement and have found that all the prerequisites and particularities of the established states have accrued to them. Although at the time of their entry these later states may not have been sufficiently diversified to justify such special treatment, they rapidly acquired such consciousness of individuality that they now would be unwilling to part with the instrumentalities that permit the expression of that individuality. It is doubtful that the two Dakotas warranted the dignity of separate statehood at the time of their entry into the union; but who can deny now that, having lived as states for a number of years, they would look with disfavor upon any proposal to deprive them of their individuality by merging them into one? The Constitution, which endows the states with the characteristics of diversity, treats them indiscriminately and thus tends to create diversity where none previously existed. The Constitution with its federal plan, though designed as an instrumentality, has become a part of the complex of sociological and psychological values that constitutes the pattern of diversities. It is no longer merely an instrumentality serving to protect and articulate the diversities; it has itself become a part of that complex of values which *is* the pattern of diversities and which determines the pattern of the instrumentalities.

Thus the problem of the student of federalism is made much more difficult, for he cannot clearly distinguish between society and the instrumentalities it employs. Similarly with the problems of the statesman; he cannot devise means to accomplish new ends without disturbing the old relationship, for the old means have themselves become ends and the old techniques have become values.

The effort to draw the distinction must be made, however; for otherwise we end by confusing cause with effect and by attributing to the instrumentalities values that belong properly to the anterior diversities. The student of federalism must probe deeper than the institutional patterns, for these are but the products of the diversities in the society; it is to the pattern of these diversities that we must go if we would assess the federal qualities of the society.

3   Symmetry and Asymmetry as Elements of Federalism: A Theoretical Speculation*

Charles D. Tarlton

This short essay is mainly speculative. It attempts to highlight a principal weakness in theoretical treatments of the concept of federalism, and to offer modifications of the federal concept. It is not in any sense a complete theoretical statement of federalism. Nor is it meant to survey writings on federalism, although it is generally based on a wide sampling from those writings.

Specifically what I want to suggest is that in studies of federalism the prevailing emphases avoid sufficient consideration of the diverse ways in which each member state in a federal system is able to relate to the system as a whole, the central authority, and each other member state. The federal relationship, in any realistic sense, means something very much different to nearly every participant unit in the system. Among the several states in a federal union, cultural, economic, social, and political factors combine to produce variations in the symbiotic connection between those states and the system.

Two concepts, both to be explored in greater detail in a later section, can be introduced and their general content suggested here. The first, the notion of *symmetry* refers to the extent to which component states share in the conditions and thereby the concerns more or less common to the federal system as a whole. By the same token, the second term, the concept of *asymmetry* expresses the extent to which component states do not share in these common features. Whether the relationship of a state is symmetrical or asymmetrical is a question

*From *The Journal of Politics*, Vol. XXVII, No. 4, November 1965, pp. 861-874. Reprinted by permission of the author and publisher.

of its participation in the pattern of social, cultural, economic, and political characteristics of the federal system of which it is part. This relation, in turn, is a significant factor in shaping its relations with other component states and with the national authority . . . .

The most common form of analysis of federalism has been formal and legal. The working of a federal government has been viewed as a question of constitutional law. The balance between the general government and the local authorities is cast in terms of rights, powers, and judicial determinations. The basic assumptions of most writers on federalism have involved the requirement that a federal government needs a constitution so that the sharing of authority essential to the federal principle can be laid down and maintained. Analysis of federalism, then, has entailed investigation of the ways in which those formalized relations contained in the constitution are interpreted and applied. . . .

Federalism is almost universally defined implicitly in terms of component political and legal units sharing equally the federal relationship among themselves and with the general government. The federal relationship is usually visualized as that between the Federal Government and the State (or all of the States collectively). Regardless of the criteria by means of which federalism is delineated, a federal system is or is not deemed *federal as a whole*. This results in an important distortion because of the obvious fact that a federal system may be more or less federal throughout its parts. That is, the quality and levels of federalism present in the relationship between the central government and each component government considered separately may vary in significant ways throughout the system. The "federalism" of the system is likely to be variegated and disparate among all the essential units.

A principal element in federal relationships, both essential to understanding federalism and too often not carefully distinguished and recognized, is the symmetry of the federal system. What I mean by symmetry is the level of conformity and commonality in the relations of each separate political unit of the system to both the system as a whole and to the other component units. The overall extent to which the federal system is characterized by a harmonious pattern of states partaking of the general features of the federal nation is at the core of the symmetry of federalism. The specific elements and the degree of symmetry in the relations of a single member state to the system and to other states and in the total pattern of federalism throughout the system are equally important in assessing the quality of federalism.

The Symmetrical Model

An ideal symmetrical federal system would be one composed of political units comprised of equal territory and population, similar economic features, climatic conditions, cultural patterns, social groupings, and political institutions. In the model symmetrical system each of the separate political units would in effect be miniature reflections of the important aspects of the whole federal system.

Each state would, because of this basic similarity, be concerned with the solution of the same sorts of problems and with the development of the same sorts of potential. There would be no significant differences from one state to another in terms of the major issues about which the political organization of a state might be concerned. Nor would there be significant differences in terms of the political machinery and resources with which the state would approach those major issues.

In the model symmetrical federal system each state would maintain essentially the same relationship to the central authority. The division of power between central and state governments would be nearly the same in every case. Representation in the central government would be equal for each component polity, and support of the activities of that central government would also be equally distributed.

In the symmetrical model no significant social, economic, or political peculiarities would exist which might demand special forms of representation or protection. The basic justification for having a federal constitutional arrangement rather than a unitary one would be found in the completeness and integral character of the various political sub-systems. Separate political existence rapidly becomes a self-justifying arrangement as political loyalties granted to local governments become permanent features of the prevailing political ideology. Each member state, while similar in most important features to every other member state and to the overall character of the federal society, would be a separate unit possessing general problems of its own in the solution of which local authority would be thought to be best suited. The federal authority would, in the main, be limited to concerning itself with those problems either common to the federal system *qua* system (e.g., problems of international relations), or requiring system-wide attention and resources for solution.

The Asymmetrical Model

The ideal asymmetrical federal system would be one composed of political units corresponding to differences of interest, character, and makeup that exist within the whole society. The asymmetrical federal system would be one in which, as Livingston says of federal systems generally, the diversities in the larger society find political expression through local governments possessed of varying degrees of autonomy and power. Again, following Livingston, an asymmetrical federal government is one in which political institutions correspond to the real social "federalism" beneath them.

In the model asymmetrical federal system each component unit would have about it a unique feature or set of features which would separate in important ways, its interests from those of any other state or the system considered as a whole. Clear lines of division would be necessary and jealously guarded insofar as these unique interests were concerned. In the asymmetrical system it would be difficult (if not impossible) to discern interests that could be clearly considered mutual or national in scope (short of those pertaining to national existence *per se*).

The Character of Federal Governments

Livingston, after developing his theory of socio-cultural federalism, argued that with it he was able to arrange societies in order according to the degree to which they were really federal or unitary. He came a step further than the formal-legal treatments of federalism which allowed really only for determining whether a state was constitutionally federal or unitary and whether that form was being purely applied or not. But both Livingston's categories and criteria and those of the formal-legal approach are only capable of leading to such judgments with respect to an entire political system. That is, they can classify whole nations as being federal or unitary or (in Livingston's case) some degree of either. They are unable, however, to provide a theoretical framework suitable for discerning areas of "federalism" or "non-federalism" within a single system. The upshot of this is that they cannot say to what extent parts of the system might be more or less "federal" than others. In assessing and evaluating whole federal governments the ability to discern the pattern of federalization throughout the whole system is crucial.

Thus ordinarily discussions of federalism in the United States have been more or less limited to (1) attention to the particular areas in which state-federal relationships are concentrated, e.g., education, highway construction, the grant-in-aid programs, criminal and civil law, and interstate commerce problems, (2) concern over the growing "octopus" of federal authority and the erosion of "states' rights," and (3) the origins and meanings of federalism in American political history. The general concern seems to have been with the condition of federalism in the United States at large. Now, certainly there is good reason to be concerned with the ways in which federalism has developed, just as there is good reason, in the broader theoretical sense, to pursue the kind of social/functional analyses that Livingston has suggested. But, while these are useful concerns, they go only part of the way.

No federal arrangement is likely to be made up of states each of which stands in exactly the same relationship to the whole system. In actual cases each component unit will tend to reflect (or not to reflect) the overall national character to a greater or lesser extent. A federal system which resembled the symmetrical model would be a very different one and would involve very different legal, political, and economic problems than one which resembled the asymmetrical model. In this connection many important characteristics of the federal relationship can best be explained by a system of analytical categories which take account of the level, nature, and distribution of the system's symmetry. One basic characteristic that can adequately be explained only in this way is federal-state conflict, what might be termed the "secession-potential" of the federal system.

The question of federal-state conflict must be approached in terms of the shared goals, aspirations, and expectations of the elements constituting the federal union. When, through a particular asymmetry in the relationship between a state and the federal authority in consideration of basic processes and needs, the policies pursued and the conditions demanded by a single component state are importantly foreign to those of the overall system, then federal-state conflict is likely to be the result. It should be stressed at this point that where state-federal conflict occurs it is most likely to stem from complaints limited to one or just a few of the member states. It is rare for conflict to occur between the central government and all the states simultaneously.

Therefore federal-state conflict is a likelihood where the relationship between local and central authorities corresponds to the image of the asymmetrical situation, and where that asymmetry is characteristic only of a few of the states in their relation to the whole. To a real extent, then, the degree of harmony or conflict within a federal system can be thought of as a function of the symmetrical or asymmetrical pattern prevailing within the system. Most real federal states, however, would be somewhere between the complete harmony of the symmetrical model and the complete conflict potential of the asymmetrical model.

For example, the levels of conflict or harmony between California and Washington, D.C., or Mississippi and Washington, D.C., can be viewed in relation to the symmetry of each state's relation to the whole of the United States. The character of society in California is much closer to the pattern of society in the nation at large. Mississippi (or the hard core Southern states generally) differs in a variety of important ways from the social, economic, cultural, and ideological configurations of the nation. Conflict between California and the Federal Government is likely to be less frequent and less intense than in the case of Mississippi. The prevailing attitude of public officials toward the legal and political details of the federal-state relationship is also likely to vary greatly between California and Mississippi. The most basic factor involved and leading in the direction of explaining this difference is the symmetry of the underlying social-political relationship each state has to the nation at large.

I am compelled, at this point, to engage in some unorthodox speculations regarding the relation between the symmetry of a political society and its suitability for federal or unitary political organization. Concern for logical neatness has led, in writings on federalism, to the conclusion that the more diverse the elements within a political system, the better it is suited for federalism, and that the more homogeneous the political society the clearer the need for unitary forms. There is a limit, however, in that the diversity can in some cases be so great that not even "federalism" can provide adequate bases for unification under a single political authority. These propositions appear to be pure common sense, but I am suggesting that this is deceiving, that they are not as true in all cases as they are assumed to be, and that they are often downright false and misleading.

A viable federal system can be examined from at least two points of view. One can concentrate on the question of the desirability of adopting a federal system in a particular set of social and political circumstances, or one can inquire into the workings of a particular extant federal system with a view to unearthing the factors contributory to its success. Depending upon the emphasis, the questions asked and the answers accepted must be very different.

Whether a particular country or collection of countries should adopt a federal structure is intimately bound up with the question of the symmetry of the whole. If, in the underlying structure, diversity is overwhelmingly predominant (approximating the asymmetrical model), then (according to the logic of the orthodox view of federalism's requisites) there exists a presumption of the applicability of some utilization of the federal principle, assuming, of course, that the diversity is not such as to preclude even federal forms. The argument would entail something to the effect that the various significant diversities ought to find political expression and protection within the system as a whole. Federalism, it is maintained, provides the necessary expression and protection.

The question, of course, really involves setting a hierarchy of values by means of which to judge the overall desirability of federalism. It can not turn simply on the logical formula "diversity, then federalism." The question of the workability of the system comes energetically to mind. Whether a state can function harmoniously with a federal constitution will, I argue, be a result of the level of symmetry within it. The higher the level of symmetry, that is the more each particular section, state, or region partakes of a character general and common to the whole, the greater the likelihood that federalism would be a suitable form of governmental organization. On the other hand, if the system is highly asymmetrical in its components, then a harmonious federal system is unlikely to develop. If a formula were to be extracted from this, it would read: *The elements of similarity among component units of a federal system must, if that system is to function at an optimum level of harmony, predominate over existing elements of diversity.* Where diversity of elements is the rule, then it follows (presuming that sufficient political power and motivation exist to achieve unity *at all*) that a unitary and centralized system would be better. When diversity predominates, the "secession-potential" of the system is high and unity would require controls to overcome disruptive, centrifugal tendencies and forces.

Following this reasoning and applying it to a brief discussion of the quality of federalism in the United States, certain interesting conclusions are reached. *First*, the functioning of federalism in the United States has fluctuated with changes occurring in the underlying makeup of its basic components. Periods of greatest harmony in the relations between states and the federal authorities and among states themselves have paralleled periods in which the differences among the states have been overshadowed by the factors compelling to symmetry. *Second*, the periods of conflict and tension within the American federal system have been at times when particular interests and problems in some of the component states have developed independently to such proportions that their protection and expression overrode considerations of the common interest. In order for the political parcelling-out of authority basic to any definition of federalism to be part of a working system it is essential that the component units have shared characteristics to such an extent that the common pursuits are never lost sight of. *Third*, regions of the country where federalism is most hotly questioned, its constitutional features most frequently argued, and the propensity for subverting national interest the highest are just those areas in which certain problems have taken such deep hold of political life that they destroy the symmetry of the federal relationship. If the entire United States reflected relationships like those typical of the states of the Deep South, then federalism in the United States would long since have perished. Areas within the nation whose relationship to the whole is generally asymmetrical are just those areas in which federal presence is most keenly felt and in which meaningful participation in national affairs most often necessitates compulsion.

The concept of federalism has been a major panacea in Western political thought for an incredible range of problems — from the creation of new nation-states, the provision of government in metropolitan areas, to the creation of organizations designed to prevent international war. Federalism has been a kind of universal answer to the question of overcoming problems of diversity and disparity in the interests of harmony and unity. Whenever events have seemed to demand cooperation and coordination, while interests and anxieties have held out for the preservation of difference and diversity, the answer has almost unfailingly been some form of federalism. It is in this connection, then, that a clear understanding of the strengths and weaknesses, the benefits and liabilities, the predictability and the surprises of federalism is particularly important.

If there is anything of merit in the speculations which comprise the bulk of this essay, it seems clear that much of the ordinary optimism regarding the near magical qualities of federalism can profitably be reexamined. The most basic question that must be asked, then, is: To what extent can "federalism" be expected to sustain the stimulus to and the need for unity in the face of the pressures of separatism? The answer, plainly, is: To the extent that the forces of unity are dominant. Unless there is some factor or set of factors which clearly and inexorably push in the direction of commonality, then the pressures of asymmetry will increasingly present themselves, making continued federal existence nearly impossible.

This is a discomforting way of thinking about federal principles of governmental organization because among the implications that derive from it is the idea that diversity, a factor so often raised by proponents of increased local autonomy in federal systems, tends really to necessitate increased central authority if the system is to continue operating as a system. Relieving the tensions and discord often attendant upon asymmetrical systems requires not further recognition of the elements of diversity and their protection in the complicated processes of ever-increasing federalization, but rather increased coordination and coercion from the centralizing authorities in the system. The implications of this kind of thinking about the federal process may entail serious skepticism regarding the feasibility of using federalism as a means of politically organizing local, regional, national, and international communities.

4 Federal Political Systems and Federal Societies *

Michael Stein

In the past few years a number of studies have been published which offer different approaches and interpretations to the subject of federalism. Until these recent studies appeared, the theory of federalism was embodied largely in the work of K. C. Wheare. Wheare published the first truly path-breaking book in the comparative study of federalism shortly after World War II.[1] He defined federalism as that system of government in which the federal and regional governments are both coordinate and independent. In applying this definition, he stressed the sharp division in the powers and functions of two co-equal sovereignties as a basis for classifying systems of government as federal. Wheare's definition was derived primarily from his analysis of the American constitution and, in particular, its formally sharp division of powers between national and state governments.

Wheare also compared the constitutions of governments with their actual workings in order to classify such governments as federal or non-federal in practice. He found that only three then existing constitutions met his criteria of "federal" — the United States, Australia and Switzerland. Canada, the fourth system that he analyzed in depth, did not qualify as a "federal constitution" primarily because the powers of disallowance and reservation of provincial legislation accorded the federal government effectively nullified the co-equal status of the provincial governments. Wheare then turned to the actual workings of these governments, and found that the governments of the United States, Australia, Switzerland and Canada all more or less fulfilled his criteria of a working federal government. Wheare justified his inclusion of Canada as an operative federal system by noting that the powers of disallowance and reservation had been very infrequently applied, especially since the turn of the century.

Wheare recognized that his criteria of coordinate, but independent, status for the two levels of government, and his implicit notion that the functions of government should somehow be carried out independently by the two different levels of government were only components of an ideal-typical definition. His discussion of the evolution of a preponderant financial position of the federal government over provincial governments as a result of depression and post-war economic strains reveals this.[2] Nevertheless, Wheare was optimistic that the approximate coordinate and independent relationship between the two levels of

*From *World Politics*, Vol. XX, No. 4, July 1968. Reprinted by permission of the author and publisher. The author wishes to acknowledge his indebtedness to Professors Robert J. Jackson and Donald C. Rowat of Carleton University and Mr. Peter H. Solomon, Jr., of Columbia University, for their comments on this paper and to the students in his seminar on Federalism at Carleton.

[1] K. C. Wheare, *Federal Government*, 4th ed., Oxford University Press, London, 1963. The first edition was published in 1946.

[2] *Ibid.*, Chapters 6-8.

government would continue into the post-World War II period, with some modifications in the financial and administration sphere. He also was confident of the continuing utility of federal forms of government in post-World War II conditions. His ideal-typical definition of federalism became the most widely accepted basis for a classificatory scheme and for comparing federal systems of government in such problem areas as financial and administrative relations between the two levels of government, relationships between the court systems at both levels, and the composition of legislatures at the two levels of government.

Wheare, however, neglected several important problem areas which are vital to the working of any federal government. Among them are the party system, and the role of pressure groups and political movements, and the effect of political attitudes on the system. Probably the most important, as both W. H. Riker and Aaron Wildavsky have argued, is the political party system. The relationships between the two levels of government are dependent on the kinds of relationships which members of political parties at both levels establish with each other. Often in a federal system the members of the political parties operating governments at the regional level are co-partisans of those operating governments at the federal level. In such instances informal party relationships became important to federalism. At other times members of the governing parties at the regional level belong to opponent parties of the governing parties at the national level. The rivalry between the parties can be an important factor in determining legislative and administrative relations between the two governments. The federal structure of government also affects the pattern of organization of these different parties, the relationships between the extra-parliamentary party and the parliamentary caucuses at both levels of government, and the organization of election campaigns. The parties in turn not only affect the pattern of relationships between the two levels of government through the internal relationships of their members, but also the patterns of party finance from region to region. These are only a few of the similarities between the pattern of relationships of political parties operating within federal structures which can be illuminated by comparative analysis.

For almost two decades Wheare's definition of federalism stood unchallenged in the textbooks of political science, and in numerous government documents. However, not long after his book first appeared, several scholars began to cite some shortcomings in what seemed to be an overly narrow definition of federalism, based on legal and juridical writings. Several of these often neglected essays, written in the 1950's and early 1960's, are reprinted in the first three sections of Aaron Wildavsky's *American Federalism in Perspective*. One of them by W. H. Livingston is worthy of special attention.

Livingston's critique was directed at the limitations which a formal-legal definition of federalism imposes on the kinds of problems with which students of federalism concern themselves. In his perceptive view,

> . . . the essential nature of federalism is to be sought for, not in the shadings of legal and constitutional terminology, but in the forces — economic, social,

political, cultural — that have made the outward forms of federalism necessary. Federalism, like most institutional forms, is a solution of, or an attempt to solve a certain kind of problem of political organization . . . . [F]ederal governments and federal constitutions never grow simply and purely by accident. They arise in response to a definite set of stimuli; a federal system is consciously adopted as a means of solving the problems represented by these stimuli.[3]

According to Livingston, the stimuli for the outward forms of federalism were the forces which he described as "the federal quality of the society". A federal society is one in which diversities are grouped territorially.[4] Where societies exist in which diversities are grouped in some other way, then the society is not federal, and there is little likelihood that its political institutions will be federal in form. On the other hand, where diversities are grouped territorially, the likelihood is that these territories will be assigned functions appropriate to their diversities, and federal forms will be established.

Livingston was careful to point out that these diversities may not be precisely translated into political forms which follow the strict boundary lines of the principal geographic cleavages in the society. Administrative and historical considerations generally weigh most heavily in determining how such political boundaries defining the regional units in a federal system should be drawn. For example, in Canada the federal form of government established in 1867 was primarily the product of a compromise between French- and English-speaking groups in the then united Province of Canada. Two separate provinces, Ontario and Quebec, were established in which each of the two principal language groups comprised a majority. Nevertheless, there were large minorities of both groups concentrated along the borders of each province. The provincial boundaries were not redrawn to encompass them.

Livingston did not make clear precisely what kinds of diversities he thought were crucial in defining his concept of "federal society". He seemed to be speaking of differences in language, religion, ethnicity or historical tradition, which distinguish groups of people living in one concentrated area from those of neighbouring areas. These differences form the basis of federalism when such groups attain sufficient power to permit their political representatives to insist upon retaining important functions in those areas in which they constitute an overall majority.

Can Livingston's concept of "federal society" be made more precise? Can one distinguish between a society which is "federal" and one which is not? And what utility is there in identifying a "federal society", assuming some consensus can be reached on what is meant by the term?

It seems to me that some degree of consensus has already been reached on the meaning of "federal society". Several other students of federalism, including R. L. Watts and Aaron Wildavsky, have adopted Livingston's terminology and

---

[3]W. S. Livingston, "A Note on the Nature of Federalism", *Political Science Quarterly*, Vol. LXVII, No. 1, March 1952, pp. 83-84.
[4]*Ibid.*, p. 85.

applied it in their own writings. Watts limits Livingston's use to "that segment of the spectrum [of societies] in which the pressures for unity and diversity are fairly closely balanced".[5] Watts introduces here a notion of equilibrium, which is absent in Livingston's analysis. He defines federal society as that kind of inclusive social system in which social forces making for diversity among differentiated communities are in approximate balance with forces making for unity. He does not, however, suggest indices which might permit the student of federalism to identify the kind of society and the type of equilibrium which he envisages. Nor does he provide a list of criteria which distinguish "federal societies" from other kinds of societies. Are the United States and Australia, despite the comparative homogeneity of social groups in their respective societies, to be characterized as "federal societies"? If not, what kind of societies are they? And how does one account for the adoption and continued operation of federal political forms in these systems?

Aaron Wildavsky deals with this problem. He distinguishes between what he calls "structural federalism" and what he refers to as "social federalism".[6] For Wildavsky, "structural federalism" exists today in societies like Australia largely because a structural framework of federalism was originally adopted and has created vested interests which support its retention rather than because of the social makeup of territorially based groups. The political framework of federalism is no longer a minimum condition for the survival of Australia as a nation-state, as it apparently once was.

Surprisingly, Wildavsky considers the United States, despite the relative homogeneity of its territorially concentrated communities in terms of language, religion, and historical experience, to be a type of "social federalism" rather than "structural federalism". Wildavsky disagrees with writers such as Riker, who see the United States as sufficiently integrated at present to abandon federalism if its national political leaders choose to do so. The disagreement between Wildavsky and Riker demonstrates how important it is to define the concept of "federal society" with greater precision.

It seems to me that the concept of "federal society" can be most usefully applied if it is confined to a society which is conterminously both "polyethnic" and multilingual in makeup. The major cleavage defining societies of this type is a product of ethnic and linguistic differences. Where a society is constituted of territorially based communities which are clearly differentiated by language and ethnicity, then one can expect to find a federal society. The cleavage defining such a "federal society" may be reinforced by other factors such as religion, geography and economics, which also help to create a sense of belonging to distinctive communities. However, the ethnic and linguistic factors are determining factors in the decision concerning the nature of the larger political order which each community wishes to establish in union with other communities. If

---

[5] R. L. Watts, *New Federations, Experiments in the Commonwealth*, Oxford University Press, Oxford, 1966, p. 95.

[6] Aaron Wildavsky, "Party Discipline Under Federalism: Implications of the Australian Experience", Aaron Wildavsky (ed.), *American Federalism in Perspective*, Little Brown and Co., Boston, 1967, p. 178.

the aforementioned social conditions are present, then the political leaders of the distinctive communities will "bargain" for sufficient autonomy for themselves and their followers to prevent the establishment of a system more centralized than a federal union.

Once the "federal bargain is struck", to use William Riker's phrase, then forces in the society will again operate on and be shaped by the political structure.[7] Here the concept of "federal political system" becomes relevant. The first student of federalism to use the concept "federal political system" in conjunction with "federal society" was R. L. Watts. Watts borrowed the concept from the writings of David Easton and others. He extends K. C. Wheare's definition of federal government to subsume all political systems in which jurisdictions and functions are divided between central and regional governments, so that neither is totally subordinate to the other. He includes systems in which one level of government is stronger or more powerful than the other.[8]

Watts does not really apply the concept "political system" in a systematic manner. He focusses almost exclusively on the formal structures of government which manifest federal features. He does not include those political or power relationships outside the formal structures of authority which ultimately produce authoritative decisions for the members of a society. In particular, he does not deal systematically with those aspects of political parties, interest groups, elite groups and political attitudes which are shaped by, and in turn shape the operation of federal political systems.[9]

Watts also does not distinguish between the more inclusive aspects of a society's political behaviour encompassed by the concept "political system", and those aspects which are peculiarly influenced by and influence the federal structure. The concept "federal political system" is narrower in meaning and scope than is the general concept of "political system".

A "federal political system", then, in my view is that form of political system (of a nation-state) in which the institutions, values, attitudes, and patterns of political action operate to give autonomous expression to both the national political system and political culture and to regional political subsystems and subcultures (defined primarily by ethnic linguistic factors). The autonomy of each of these systems and subsystems is counterbalanced by a mutual interdependence. This balance maintains the overall union.

The concepts used by Livingston and Watts can be fruitfully combined with those of William Riker. Riker focusses on the specifically "political" variables in any federal arrangement. A mutual desire among negotiating communities for territorial expansion by means other than conquest, and a mutual interest in security against an outside neighbour are for Riker the two major factors producing a "federal bargain". Once the "bargain" is struck, a number of other variables come into play in maintaining the federal system. Riker explores the

---

[7]William H. Riker, *Federalism: Origin, Operation, Significance*, Little Brown and Co., Boston, 1964.

[8]Watts, *op. cit.*, p. 13.

[9]Watts was hamstrung by lack of information about informal political processes within the new federations. This point is made below, p. 44.

relationship between fiscal and administrative arrangements (which he refers to as the "administrative theory of federalism"), the influence of the federal institutions of government, and the pattern of political attitudes (which he describes as "patriotism") as they relate to the maintenance of federalism. He concludes that none of these factors is crucial to the maintenance of federalism. Rather, the pattern of relationships operating within the party system is the key factor preserving the federal bargain over time. In his words,

> Whatever the general social conditions, if any, that sustain the federal bargain, there is one institutional condition that controls the nature of the bargain in all the instances here examined and in all others with which I am familiar. This is the structure of the party system, which may be regarded as the main variable intervening between the background social conditions and the specific nature of the federal bargain.[10]

Riker considers his approach to be a more purely political one, in opposition to the sociological approaches adopted by such writers as Karl Deutsch.[11] However, there is nothing in my opinion which prevents a synthesis of the two approaches in comparing certain federal systems. The concept "federal political system" can incorporate both pure power political relationships and more inclusive socio-political patterns of action.[12] The patterns of political relationships in polyethnic federal systems which are comparable are those which operate within the limits set by the federal bargain. They also emanate from comparable territorially based cleavages in these societies. Thus, in the same way as one speaks of the interactions between societies and their political systems, one can speak of the interaction between the "federal" or polyethnic factors in a society and the "federal" patterns of power political relationships which operate in any federal political system.

By "federal" patterns of power political relationships I mean simply those bargains, compromises and balances in power relationships between the representatives of the major ethnic-linguistic communities which operate within the formal and informal structures (such as the executive, legislature, judiciary, political parties and political groups). Within the legislature a compromise might be arranged through special representation provisions, or through linguistic guarantees. Within the executive a bargain may exist in the representation of different regions in cabinet decision-making. Within the judiciary the scope of different legal systems and the representation of judges from the different communities and legal traditions strengthens the bargain. Within political parties, an agreement to give representation on party executives to the members of different communities, and an arrangement to separate national and regional party structures in parties which bear the same name and are part of the same

---

[10]Riker, *op. cit.*, p. 136.

[11]*Ibid.*, p. 16.

[12]The distinction between pure power political relationships and socio-political patterns of action is often blurred in the literature. By socio-political patterns of action I mean all those behaviour patterns which directly or indirectly contribute to authoritative decision-making in a society. Pure power political relationships are those which specifically involve power, authority and rule, defined in a coercive sense.

tradition, also involves implementation of the federal bargain. These delicate compromises are worked out in part through mutual adherence to the strict terms of the original constitution and in part through informal understandings between the representatives of the member communities in the federal society.

It seems to me that R. L. Watts, implicitly rather than explicitly, has confined his concepts and his analyses to just such types of federal systems and societies. Watts compares societies which manifest aspects of federalism both in their social structure and in their political structure. The patterns of political relationships are sufficiently similar to lend themselves to comparison. Thus Watts selected such widely divergent political systems as India, Pakistan, Malaysia, Nigeria, the Federation of Rhodesia and Nyasaland, and the West Indies Federation for comparison.

Watts has applied the concepts of "federal society" and "federal political system" in answering two major questions: 1) what causes new nations to adopt federal forms, and 2) how well have these forms worked once they have been adopted? The focal point of his analysis of the first question is the "federal society", or the forces of unity and diversity in these six societies which influenced them to strike a "federal bargain". These forces include a balance in desire and capacity for both unity and diversity between different ethnic-linguistic groups; a balance in economic goals and capabilities between the negotiating communities; a balance between shared historical traditions and those historical memories making for differentiation between these communities; a balance of the desire to achieve political independence from the colonial power and of the realization of the limited possibilities of achieving such independence except under a federal system, and so forth. After comparative analysis, Watts argues that the factors making for federation in the six societies he compares vary from federation to federation.[13] Despite the large number of factors which he lists, Watts' analysis of the forces in a federal society is, in my opinion, still incomplete. It is not sufficiently multi-dimensional to encompass other societal factors which might have been even more important in producing the federal bargain. For example, a balance in social and economic transactions and a balanced set of mutual perceptions between the negotiating communities may also have influenced them to negotiate the bargain. Karl Deutsch gives these factors special prominence in his discussion of the preconditions for security-communities, of which a federal system is one sub-type.[14]

Watts also neglects to weight his factors in terms of their relative importance. Riker gave two factors, the desire for security from external attack and the desire for territorial expansion through diplomatic negotiation, a major place in his analysis. This may be true for some communities but not for others.[15] Wheare, Watts and Deutsch all emphasized non-political factors, which may be more important than the political factors as preconditions for the bargain in some federal systems. What is needed, then, is a technique for measuring the

---

[13]Watts, *op. cit.*, pp. 65 ff., 90 ff.

[14]K. W. Deutsch *et al.*, *Political Community and the North Atlantic Area*, Princeton University Press, Princeton, 1957, p. 58.

[15]Birch makes this point in his excellent review of Riker. See pp. 7-9 in this volume.

relative weight of the variety of factors impinging on the federal bargain.

In his second question, namely how well the forms worked once applied in practice, Watts claims to focus on the interactions within what he calls the "federal system". In fact, however, because so little information is available about the federal institutions of these new federations other than those falling strictly within the formal governmental sphere, Watts was forced to confine his analysis to the formal distribution of legislative and executive authority in these new federations.

Political scientists have now come to include the informal political structures in their analyses of political systems. Concepts have been developed in comparative politics which give some precision to such institutions and patterns of action as political parties, pressure groups, political movements, cliques and factions; competing elites; and political cultures and subcultures. This is particularly the case in developed and westernized political systems, where the informal institutions, informal patterns of political action, and the patterns of political attitudes which comprise the infrastructure of any political system show striking similarities, particularly as they relate to the federal political structure.

What kinds of questions might one ask about the relationship between the aforementioned patterns of action and the federal structure? I have already listed several problem areas involving the relationship between political parties and the federal structure. In the case of pressure groups and other competitive structures, one might investigate the following: What kinds of pressure groups and political movements are formed with the specific purpose in mind of representing one of the ethnic-linguistic communities? How do they act on the central and regional decision-making centers? Are their activities in influence concentrated more on the central government or on the regional governments? How intense are these pressures on the two levels of government? What is the internal structural pattern of these groups, unitary, federal or confederal? How well represented are the different ethnic-linguistic communities in the internal decision-making processes of such groups? What overall role do such groups play in preserving or destroying the federal bargain?

With regard to competing elites, one might explore the following: Are the ethnic-linguistic communities equally represented within the society's "power elite"? When their representatives join the "power elite", do they continue to champion their community's interests? Or do they abandon their community ties and become part of a "national" political community? What role do they play in decisions made by the central government affecting the demands and interests of the ethnic-linguistic communities? Are they deliberately recruited from their ethnic-linguistic community in order to strengthen the federal bargain?

Finally, one can investigate some questions relating political cultures and subcultures to the federal structure. What are the major subcultures within the federal society? Do they correspond with the various ethnic-linguistic communities? What are the comparative loyalties felt towards the central and regional governments of the federal political system? How efficacious a role do the individual members of the major communities feel they perform in the national and regional political systems and subsystems? How do changing perceptions about the national and regional governments affect the behaviour of the various ethnic-linguistic communities towards these governments?

In which federal systems might these questions be investigated? There are several contemporary federal systems which fall easily into the category of "federal societies" (defined in terms of polyethnicity and multilingualism) which also have federal governmental structures. Most of them, however, have very little experience as operative political systems. Among the mature federations, Switzerland and Canada are the most outstanding examples. The former system has achieved a considerable success as a model of stable federalism. The latter is now experiencing serious strains after one hundred years of what seemed to most outside observers to be a highly stable and durable federalism as well. I shall use Canada then as a laboratory for applying some of the concepts which I have discussed above.

At present, after one hundred years of what seemed a firmly established and stable federal political system, Canada is undergoing what the Royal Commission on Bilingualism and Biculturalism aptly referred to as a "crisis in the Confederation partnership" in its Preliminary Report published just over two years ago.[16] There has been a growing realization among politically aware Canadians that the Commission's diagnosis was correct. The federal bargain between French- and English-speaking Canadians struck one hundred years ago is in serious danger of coming unhinged.

What tools can political scientists apply to explain why this bargain is now endangered? Why has it been maintained for one hundred years without seemingly a threat to its continued existence? What are the possibilities for its future maintenance, if reforms are introduced? Where are the changes most needed, at the constitutional level, within formal governmental institutions, or within informal political institutions such as the political party system, the pressure groups, and in the political attitudes which French- and English-speaking Canadians have towards each other?

As has been previously mentioned, Riker argues that the crucial factor maintaining the federal bargain in any political system is the party system. In the case of Canada, I think this is correct. However, writers on Canadian federalism had not given much attention to the relationship between the Canadian party system and federalism. We know very little about the power relationships and bargains struck between French- and English-speaking Canadians within the parliamentary caucuses and extra-parliamentary parties, between members of each language group belonging to the same political party at the provincial and national levels, etc. Such aspects are just beginning to be systematically studied by these political scientists. But their study can be facilitated by the application of some of the hypotheses suggested in the Wildavsky reader

---

[16]*A Preliminary Report of the Royal Commission on Bilingualism and Biculturalism,* Queen's Printer, Ottawa, 1965, p. 13. The Preamble reads: "Canada, without being fully conscious of the fact, is passing through the greatest crisis in its history. The source of the crisis lies in the Province of Quebec." It is also interesting that the Commissioners describe Canada as a nation-state containing "two societies".

by Truman and Grodzins in the case of the American party system, by Wildavsky and Davis in the case of the Australian party system (which, because Australia has a parliamentary cabinet type of government, is more similar to the Canadian case than is the United States), by Muller in the case of the Canadian system itself, and by Riker.[17]

It seems to me that one of the prime factors which will determine whether the "federal bargain" will endure in Canada is the accommodation that will be worked out between French- and English-speaking Canadians in the two major parties at the federal and provincial levels, and also that between French- and English-speaking Canadians in the minor parties, the New Democratic Party and the Social Credit Party. If, for example, accommodations can be made for French-speaking Canadians living outside the Province of Quebec so that they can be educated in and retain their own language (and these accommodations are negotiated both within the cabinet and upper levels of the administration and within the caucuses of the federal and provincial parliamentary parties), then the possibilities for maintaining the federal bargain are enhanced. This assumes that the major negotiating communities, the French- and English-speaking communities, are willing to maintain their electoral confidence in these long-standing parties, and the leading partisan representatives of both major communities are also willing to preserve the federal bargain.

In a similar manner, the internal composition, structure and bargaining within the leading pressure groups will affect the durability of the federal bargain. For example, the major union in Canada, the Canadian Labour Congress (CLC) is a confederation of provincial and locally organized unions. One of these provincial unions is the Quebec Federation of Labour (QFL), which represents a substantially larger proportion of the working class in Quebec than their major competitors, the Confederation of National Trade Unions (CNTU). The latter, however, has adopted a more radical stance with regard to the role of Quebec in Confederation. Consequently it has expanded its membership at the expense of the QFL. This has caused the members of the QFL to demand a more sympathetic attitude on the part of Canadian labour as a whole to such questions affecting the French-Canadian community as its representation in the decision-making processes of the union, use of the French language at work, and so forth.

Other subjects of crucial importance in this negotiating process are the entire array of federal and provincial powers and the linguistic and regional composition of the federal and provincial courts, the ethnic-linguistic composition of the federal administration, and the bicultural composition of a national capital district.

However, all this assumes that the two dominant ethnic-linguistic communities retain their confidence in the traditional parties and pressure groups. The existence of different types of structures of political competition such as political movements within French Canada opposed to the existing bargain threatens to undermine the prospects for a negotiated settlement. Here the analysis of the

---

[17]Wildavsky, *op. cit.*, pp. 23-24, 51-59, 81-181.

major right- and left-wing political movements dedicated to the independence of Quebec becomes relevant. Comparative analysis has something to contribute to the question of whether such movements of independence can make sufficient headway in the Province of Quebec to undermine the federal bargain.

It has been found by students of political movements that under severe conditions of deprivation (of an economic, status, or other sort) and psychological strain, individuals in any society will seek outlets in the form of some episodes of collective protest behaviour.[18] In the case of two party systems in which one party has been dominant for a long period of time, so that the major opposition party is no longer seen as a credible alternative to the dominant party, the individuals in that society will tend to vote for third party alternatives which appeal to their attitudes of discontent.[19] In the case of Quebec, the independence parties of the right- and the left-wing, the Ralliement Nationale and the Rassemblement de l'Indépendence Nationale, have competed in one provincial election, in 1966, and together gained only about 10% of the vote.

The Union Nationale, one of the major parties provincially, is at present still committed to maintaining the Confederation pact, although it seeks significant reforms in the federal structure. It succeeded in capturing power from the Liberals, which had also pledged to maintain the bargain. Federally all the major and minor parties have agreed to support the Confederation settlement. Much depends, then, on whether the two major parties provincially can hold their electorate to a program of reform within the existing federal structure. The condition of the electorate depends largely on the fluctuating economic and social conditions in the province. If conditions worsen, French-Canadians may feel themselves attracted to parties opposed to the existing system. For, given the fact that a predominance of force is held in federal hands, the most likely way that independence can be achieved for Quebec is by election to power of an independence party (or the achievement by such a party of sufficient bargaining power through a balance of power position to win the major parties away from their pledge to maintain the bargain).

Alternatively, one of the major provincial parties might unilaterally decide to opt out of the federal bargain. It seems to me that this is not at present a likely possibility. Premier Johnson of Quebec, leader of the Union Nationale, has expressed his desire to maintain the Confederation pact if certain reforms favourable both to the Province of Quebec and to French-Canadian interests are enacted. The provincial Liberal party, the other major party, has recently had a showdown within its ranks in which the *indépendentistes*, led by the colourful René Lévesque, were defeated in their bid to commit their party to separatism. The party now appears to be firmly under the control of those pledged to retain the federal bargain.

What would be the signs of changing French-Canadian attitudes towards the

[18]Neil J. Smelser, *Theory of Collective Behaviour*, Free Press of Glencoe, New York, 1962, p. 14 ff. Also Maurice Pinard, "One-Party Dominance and Third Parties", *Canadian Journal of Economics and Political Science*, Vol. XXXIII, No. 3, August 1967, pp. 358-373.

[19]Pinard, *op. cit.*, p. 361.

federal pact? Clearly, public opinion polls and studies of changing attitudes of Quebeckers towards the federal pact are an important indicator. A recent public opinion poll revealed that, whereas 70 per cent of Quebeckers favour some constitutional change, only 7 per cent are committed to outright separatism.[20] Of course the attitudes of English-speaking Canadians towards implementing the kind of reforms which French-speaking Canadians are now demanding must also be studied.

The use of these tools of analysis cannot give us more than a very rough approximation of what is likely to occur in Canada. We cannot know for sure whether the bargain will be maintained or not. Its preservation will depend on the willingness of French- and English-speaking Canadians to retain their trust in the federal pact. This trust rests ultimately on mutual understanding and confidence on the part of the leading representatives of both communities. They must agree that their welfare can best be enhanced through a willingness to let the members of the other community live in the enjoyment of their "full personality as a community" (to use a common French-Canadian phrase). It seems to me probable that such a confidence will be maintained over the long run in Canada.

The questions concerning the relationship between the informal political structures of a society and federalism are, as stated earlier, relevant to other systems besides that of Canada. In particular, where modern societies have ethnic-linguistic cleavages which reinforce each other, creating distinct communities along territorial lines, similar problems related to the structure of the political system arise. If such societies have adopted federal forms as a minimum condition for the formation of political communities, then it is likely that conflicts will arise which will translate themselves into federal political problems. Ethnic-linguistic differences between separate communities tend to polarize around the federal structure because political power, both potential and actual, exists for these communities within the spheres of jurisdiction and functions assigned them by the federal legal-political structure. Thus the problems that have been discussed in relation to the "federal society" and "federal political system" of Canada, exist in similar form in other clearly "federal societies" such as Switzerland, Yugoslavia, the Soviet Union among developed systems, and India, Pakistan, Nigeria, among some less developed systems.

It is also possible to apply these concepts comparatively to multicultural societies which do not have federal structures (for example, Belgium), in order to assess the possibilities for adoption and workability of federal forms. And comparatively homogenous societies with federal structures, such as Australia and the United States, can be analyzed to assess whether federalism can survive over the long run in a system which lacks the solid underpinnings of multicultural societies within federal structures.

---

[20]This poll was conducted for the Canadian Broadcasting Corporation in October 1967.

Part Two

Canadian Federalism: An Overview

5 Constitutional Trends and Federalism *

J. A. Corry

The design of . . . [the federal systems of Canada, the United States and Australia] was shaped under the influence of liberal ideas. They began, and continued for some time, under the impulse of individualism, legalism, and *laissez faire*. From an examination of these three constitutions comes the definition of federalism we have found meaningful: general and regional governments of co-ordinate authority, each independent of the other in its appropriate sphere, ruling over the same persons and the same territory under the benign surveillance of a court. This is classical federalism in the Anglo-American mode.

Classical federalism saw the national and state governments in the system as independent entities, each going its own way in the enjoyment of its own powers under the check of a watchful electorate with a minimum of either association or collision. Because the electorates would limit narrowly the actual use made by governments of their extensive legislative powers under the constitution, the governments would not run afoul of one another so long as each minded its own business. If some governments forgot themselves and encroached on the domains of others, the courts would remind them of their proper place. Indeed, the genius of place would have its way, in Virginia and Massachusetts, in Quebec and Nova Scotia. Both unity and genuine diversity would flourish.

With due allowances for the imperfect realization of ideals in action, for the general untidiness of political processes, and for one major breakdown in the War between the States, the classical federalism worked with considerable success until World War I. Thereafter it was subjected to increasing trials and was finally transformed into something quite different in the depression of the thirties, something which is called co-operative federalism, or the new federalism. Although the change has been effected without striking amendments in the formal constitutions of any of the three countries, the alteration in the working governmental structures of the United States, Canada and Australia has been profound. Whether the essential reality of these structures can now be called federal at all depends, of course, on one's definition of federalism. At any rate, the reality has moved far away from what I have called classical federalism.

There has been a persistent and rapid acceleration in the centralizing of the prime initiative in government, if not so much in the formal exercise of governmental power. The umpiring of each of these federal systems seems to be slipping out of the hands of the judges into the hands of the politicians, where decisions are taken on a view of policy rather than as a matter of law. The co-ordinate governments no longer work in splendid isolation from one another but are increasingly engaged in co-operative ventures in which each relies heavily on the other. Before considering the outlines of these develop-

*From A. R. M. Lower, F. R. Scott, *et al.*, *Evolving Canadian Federalism*, Duke University Press, Durham, N.C., 1958, pp. 95-125. Reprinted by permission of the author and publisher.

ments, we should remind ourselves of some of the forces thrusting in this direction.

Great improvements in transportation and communication within the free trade area that each federation provides have knit the economic life of each federation into an interdependent whole. The separate chambers of the states are insulated no longer. Instead, conduit pipes and high voltage wires link them together, transmitting economic pressures and economic shocks throughout the country. The exercise by one government of its undoubted powers often has serious repercussions on some or all of the others by the transmission of political pressures and political shocks.

Economic individualism has been displaced by a mixed economy of a strongly collectivist cast. In part, it is a private collectivism of giant corporations, national trade associations, and national trade unions, which we are always being driven to try to match by extending the authority of national governments. In part, it is a public collectivism in which *laissez faire* has given way to a dispensation in which governments are many things to all men.

Governments intervene in the social and economic spheres in at least three different and important ways. First, they respond to complaints of social and economic maladjustment with regulatory action in one sector of affairs in ways which impinge on other sectors and other governments. Second, to meet their housekeeping needs and to finance the services they provide, the several governments in the federation taken together impose a weight of taxation which seriously affects economic decisions, the level and distribution of economic activity. The dominant economic theories of the time gravely warn governments to give serious thought to finding the least burdensome and disruptive, or perhaps I should say the most beneficial, way to raise a given total of public revenues. Because it is so hard for seven or eleven, much less fifty, governments to take thought effectively together, the tendency is for the national governments to take strong leadership in taxation policy. Third, because economic concentration and the tinkering of governments have diminished greatly the self-adjusting capacity of the economy, the national governments have gone a considerable way towards assuming responsibility for over-all guidance of the economy.

The experience of national action gained in two World Wars, improvements in communications, additional bundles of social and economic data, improved in reliability by statistical techniques, to say nothing of electronics, have made it easier for the national governments to take the initiative on a wide front. The fact that in the last ten years of uneasy peace these federations have had to remain girded for war has strengthened the case for the dominance of national governments in the field of taxation. But the material factors, to which for the most part consideration has been restricted so far, will not alone account for the decisive leadership the national governments are taking. In countries where governments are as responsive to popular moods as they are in Australia, Canada, and the United States, there must be widespread acquiescence, if not active support, for the enlarged role of the national government. If the people of the several states and provinces remained stubbornly determined to find their principal collective expression as Tarheels or Bluenoses, we should not have arrived where we are. So it seems necessary to put as a major factor in the superseding of the classical federalism some nationalizing of sentiment.

The cautious phrasing of this statement may seem to some quite unnecessary. Of course, we have become Americans, Canadians, and Australians. What began as sheer expediency has come to have an independent and inspiring value of its own. We have become nations in Renan's sense that our people are conscious of having done great things together in the past and want to stick together to do great things in the future. We now see many things we did not always see in the past that we want to accomplish in unity together, and are willing to use our national governments as means to these ends even if pursuit of them entails sacrifices of interests, both individual and parochial. Certainly this is true as far as it goes, but it does not go the length of saying how many things, of what kinds, and at what sacrifices.

Some say the nationalizing of sentiment has gone so far that the vitality of federalism which depends on some balance of provincial and national feeling has been destroyed. There are some awkward facts in the way of such a conclusion. There has not been any strong swelling of sentiment in favor of drastic centralizing amendments or of reducing the states and provinces to administrative instruments of national governments. If we leave aside the income tax amendment of 1913 as perhaps equivocal, Americans have not put forward, let alone approved, any formal amendment to enlarge national power at the expense of state power. Perhaps an obliging Supreme Court has made any such action unnecessary, a point to be considered later. Since 1867, Canadians have put forward and pushed through two amendments, and two only, which enlarge the powers of Parliament at the expense of the provinces — the unemployment insurance and old age pensions amendments.

Two other important facts about Canada are to be noted. First, repeated efforts to get agreement on a method of amending the portions of the B.N.A. Act which define provincial powers and privileges have failed completely. Second, all attempts to get general agreement on a comprehensive and enduring settlement of federal-provincial public finances have also failed. We have, it is true, negotiated, since World War II, three successive sets of federal-provincial tax agreements, but only because the federal government, in the end, relied on its constitutional advantages in the field of taxation and negotiated separate agreements with each province that was prepared to deal.

It is clear that national unity is not strong enough to bring Canadians to agreement on these matters. While Quebec has been in the forefront of the resistance, she has not been there alone by any means. On the other hand, it must be said that all the discussions just referred to have been directed at getting the agreement of provincial premiers and cabinets who have a vested interest in provincial status and power which the several provincial electorates perhaps do not share fully. Having no provision for plebiscites, on such issues, we do not know what the electorates would say. Yet there is no evidence that the provincial electorates have been dismayed, or even disturbed, by the reluctance of their governments to make concessions for the sake of agreement.[1]

In Australia formal amendment requires approval by majorities of the electorates of four of the six states, as well as by a nationwide majority. The Australian Parliament has proposed some twenty centralizing amendments, and only two of these have secured the needed popular majorities. Most of the Australian writers I have read still insist, in the face of these verdicts, that "the States are no longer vital political entities in any basic sense",[2] and that these impressive refusals of enlarged authority to the Commonwealth Parliament do not spring from any loyalty to federalism as such. The electoral votes are explained rather as votes against paternalism in general or against the particular proposals in question on the ground that they should not be enacted by any legislature, state or national. This explanation does not carry full conviction to me, partly because until I know more, I would be disposed to regard a vote for *laissez faire*, hopeless and misguided though it may be, as an unequivocal vote for the classical federalism.

In Canada we have no plebiscites of this kind to explain one way or the other, unless the rejection of the Liberal party in the 1957 and 1958 national elections can be interpreted as a rejection of the centralizing policies of the Liberal Government. Of course, we do not need plebiscites at all to know that the Quebec electorate is generally opposed to centralization, whether it be by formal amendment or through the informal drift of prime initiative to Ottawa. In a negative way, as noted above, the other provincial electorates have shown that they see no urgency for nationwide agreement on at least some broad and vital issues. But we do not know what positive views, if any, these other electorates have on the question of the piecemeal centralizing of initiative in the national government.

We do know something of the attitudes of the provincial premiers and cabinets to this question. The positions they adopt and the courses they pursue over a period of time probably reflect the balance of opinion in their respective provinces. Therefore it seems highly significant that in the recurring tax negotiations and agreements of recent years, all provincial governments except Ontario and Quebec have given up, for three successive five-year periods, the right to levy personal and corporate income taxes and succession duties in return for guaranteed annual grants from the federal treasury. In fact, Ontario did give up personal and corporate income taxes for one five-year period, and for a second period has given up the right to levy the personal income tax. So it, too, has been a participant, if not so fully committed as the other eight English-speaking provinces, in transactions with a strongly centralizing effect, increasing the leverage of the national government on the policies of provincial governments as well as on the economy of the country.

In these negotiations and deals, Quebec alone has had a completely consistent position. Since 1945 Premier Duplessis has refused to enter into a tax

---

[1]Equally, of course, one has to say that on June 9, 1957, there was little evidence of the restiveness of the Canadian electorate over twenty-two years of Liberal rule.

[2]S. J. Butlin, "The Problem of Federal Finance", *Economic Record*, Vol. XXX, 1954, p. 11.

agreement with the national government. Since 1951 this has entailed a considerable sacrifice in the revenues he otherwise could have had for provincial purposes. He does not want grants from Ottawa. He does not want Ottawa to assume burdens for purposes that lie within the scope of provincial legislative power, such as grants to the universities. All he wants of the national government is that it should get out of his way, allow him effective freedom to tax heavily personal and corporate incomes and successions, and allow his government to carry the full cost of whatever services it decides Quebec is to have. He wants to go it alone, and so far has been prepared to take the risks and pay the price for provincial autonomy.

Generally speaking, the other provincial premiers do not appear to be willing to pay the price of being genuinely masters in their own houses. They either press for, or readily acquiesce in, federal assumption of burdens relating to costly services which traditionally, to say the least, have been regarded as provincial responsibilities: education, highways, welfare, electric-power development, and so on. We are now to have provincial health insurance schemes, in aid of which the federal government somewhat reluctantly promised large federal grants. As far as one can judge, the strongest pressure for the Dominion to take up this costly venture came from Premier Frost of Ontario.

All federal commitments for objects that are either constitutionally or traditionally the responsibilities of the provinces increase the dependence of the Dominion on personal and corporate income taxes and reduce the room for effective provincial exploitation of these tax sources. The provincial premiers do not stop at the point of encouraging new direct federal expenditures. Each goes on to urge, in addition, that the Dominion proposals for compensating the provinces for giving up these tax sources are quite inadequate, that Dominion grants to the provinces should be greatly increased. At each round of negotiations, these grants are sharply increased. In effect, the provincial governments, Quebec excepted, are doing all they can to ensure that the Dominion will continue its dominant role in public finance and fiscal manipulation, and that genuine provincial initiative will be correspondingly curtailed. The provincial electorates, Quebec again excepted, do not seem to mind.

Of course, a just appreciation of the lines pursued by provincial premiers in tax negotiations must take account of their dilemmas. The requirements of national defense have always to be taken into account. Given the level of provincial services and expenditures established in response to electoral demand, if not social need, most provincial governments could not make ends meet at all by scorning tax agreements and the large federal grants they produce, and levying their own personal and corporate income taxes. Partly because of the concentration of control of the economy, a very large proportion of the high personal and corporate incomes are concentrated in two or three provinces. The other seven or eight provinces must either acquiesce in a much lower level of government services or conspire with the Dominion in a scheme for taxing and redistributing this concentrated income. I think it is correct to say that the reflective members of the Canadian community in all provinces, except perhaps Quebec, have decided that the first alternative is unfair and unjust, and therefore approve the second.

Ontario is the province which would best be able to go it alone. Indeed, Ontario would profit immensely from complete dismantling of the tax agreements. She did, in fact, oppose the first postwar tax agreements, adhering to the bucolic wisdom of former Premier Mitchell Hepburn, who had said many years earlier that Ontario wouldn't be made a milch-cow for the rest of the Dominion. By 1951 Ontario had changed her mind, had acquiesced in the policy of centralized taxation, and had entered into a tax agreement. The change of mind was, in part at least, due to a recognition of some justice in the claims of the poorer provinces that much of the wealth pooled in the richer provinces is produced by the skill and effort of people in other provinces, and that some of it should be redistributed for their benefit. That is to say, Ontario has loyalties that go beyond her boundaries and distract her from any crusade for a self-centered provincial autonomy.

Indeed, a self-centered state's rights or provincial autonomy is no longer practicable. It is not practical at all for states and provinces in these three federations to think of themselves as did the American states before, and even after, the War between the States or as the older Canadian provinces tended to think of themselves until after World War I. They cannot think of themselves as independent principalities, bowing only to federal dictates on foreign policy and foreign trade and a few other matters. They threw all this away when they allowed themselves to be drawn into an interdependent economy which undermined whatever secure economic base they may previously have had within their own boundaries. Even the rich and powerful states in the federation compromised their positions when they brought within their walls the Trojan horse of big enterprise with nationwide interests and outlook, which, by its very nature, cannot be loyal to any self-centered provincialism. In so committing themselves, states and provinces gave up the power to develop or maintain widely differing economic relationships and sharply divergent social and cultural patterns. In fact, before interdependence had gone very far, the American states found they could not live together half slave and half free, if I may use a term which points to the fateful differences but does not express them fully. In this discovery they pointed up a lesson for all federal systems to learn in their maturity, if not before.

Alberta soon found it was not free to follow the genius of Social Credit in building the New Jerusalem in the foothills. If Saskatchewan under the C.C.F. had attempted full-scale socialism it would have run into much more trouble than the mere timidity of free enterprise about exploring for oil. Actually, the C.C.F. in Saskatchewan has chosen to work within the postulates of the mixed economy, which is the dominant economic pattern for the country as a whole. It has found there room for considerable experiment and variety in adapting the mixed economy to the distinctive genius of Saskatchewan for public and co-operative enterprise.

If it is said that Quebec has managed so far to maintain a culture markedly different from that of the other provinces, it must be recalled that for most of its people and over most of its area, Quebec culture has rested, until very recently, on a base of relatively self-sufficient agriculture. The very rapid industrialization in Quebec in the last fifteen or so years has caused much internal stress and strain. Much of the stress is due to the unremitting pressure exerted, for example, through trade unions and corporate enterprise to establish there the urban industrial pattern accepted by the rest of Canada. Quebec is being caught up in the logic of the interdependent economy and of large-scale industrial enterprise.

A province cannot now hope to run successfully against the tide of national development unless, of course, it associates with enough other provinces to turn the tide, in which event we have national, not provincial, action. The most it can hope to hold is freedom for minor adventure, for embroidering its own particular patterns in harmony with the national design, for playing variant melodies within the general theme.

It can hope to be free to decide to have rather more public ownership and rather less private enterprise, more or less social security and provincial regulation of economic life. It can hope to adjust policy on education and conservation of natural resources to distinctive provincial needs and aims, and so on. But it is everywhere limited in the distance it can go by having become part of a larger, although not necessarily a better, scheme of things. Its main role now is to lighten the curse of bigness.

In support of this conclusion I have so far produced only big nationwide enterprise, the interdependent economy, and some admittedly equivocal evidence on the nationalizing of sentiment. This testimony alone is not enough. Economic interdependence does not always draw communities together; big cartels do not always foster integration effectively — witness the World Wars of the twentieth century. There must be, in addition, a will to work together in solving the problems posed by interdependence. If that will emerge, it will find its main instrument in the initiatives of the national government and legislature. But it is not clear to me that there are firm popular majorities in the several states with this united will. It is little more than twenty years since an almost spontaneous mass revolt took place in Alberta and more such may well be possible, even if somewhat unlikely. The truth is that the bulk of the people are not really aware of what is at stake in federal-state issues. They probably want the best of both worlds, state governments that respond fully to regional aspirations and a national government with power to spawn an increasing range of services, deploring only the outrageously high taxation.

Whatever may be the truth about popular loyalties, it seems clear that sentiment is rapidly being nationalized among the elites, meaning by this term no more than the leaders of minority groups, the persons whose occupations or interests lead them either into close relationships with government or into sustained reflection about it.

The active persons in many occupations and interests have been drawn into national associations. Whether or not these organizations become pressure groups in the strict sense, association in them has marked effects on those who take part. Their horizons are widened and they breathe the large air of broader understanding and sympathies. The relations of French-speaking and English-speaking Canadians have improved immensely in recent years. Much of both the decline in recriminations and the rise in generosity comes from the meeting each year in national associations of one kind and another of relatively small numbers of persons of the two language groups who reach not only understanding but friendship. They recognize themselves and one another as Canadians.

Associations of this kind break down barriers and clear ground for common action. When the members of such associations find they have common problems, they are led easily to think of attacking them on the broadest possible front, which is the national front. The welfare elite increasingly pins its hopes on the national government, for initiative and the setting of standards at least. The agricultural elite still wants governmental action at both state and national levels but wants the essential frame of policy determined at the latter level. The trade union elite wants national standards in labor matters. In Canada the education elite, if that is a permissible description of the National Conference of Canadian Universities, has been pressing strongly for federal subventions to university education.

Most striking of all are the changing attitudes of the business elites. In the long retreat of *laissez faire* in the first third of the century, substantial business interests fought many determined rearguard actions from the bastions of state power and judicial review in an effort to stem the advance of federal legislative action. Over the last twenty years they have almost given up the struggle, not so much because *laissez faire* is a lost cause but rather because events have made them change their minds. Industrial concentration has proceeded at a rapid pace. One industry after another has come to be dominated by a few great corporations. These mammoths and a number of more nebulous but nevertheless very real industrial combinations have deployed themselves in a nationwide arena.

The men who control them are compelled to think in nation-wide, if not national, terms. They do not want *laissez faire*, or the free fluctuating market, or the unco-ordinated tinkering of many state or provincial governments. Instead, they want stability in prices, in labor relations, in monetary, fiscal, and other governmental policies, so that they can engage in long-range planning for their industry. They want the economy to be manageable, and, within the limits, to be managed with a foresight which takes their nationwide concerns into account. Because foresight on the scale that they want implicates the national government and its powers at many points, they want to be able to bring a persuasive influence to bear upon the national government. Instead of being closeted with their attorneys to find ways of frustrating national governments, they are now in conference on friendly terms with presidents, cabinet ministers, and senior officials at the national capitals. A wise precept says, "If you can't lick 'em, join 'em," and one may guess that the great managers would now consider a partnership with the national government if suitable terms could be arranged.

This is not quite the managerial revolution, but it is a profound change. Adolf Berle calls it "administered capitalism" in a brilliant paper[3] in which he

---

[3]"Evolving Capitalism and Political Federalism", in A. W. Macmahon (ed.), *Federalism, Mature and Emergent*, Doubleday, New York, 1955, pp. 68-82.

sketches the anatomy of the change and discusses its significance for federalism. He speaks only about the United States, but it is possible to discern the outlines of a similar change taking place in Canada on a smaller scale and at a somewhat slower pace. In the last twenty years Canadian business interests have not challenged seriously the constitutional validity of federal legislation in the courts. Significantly, the one case in this period which reproduced some of the atmosphere of battles long ago was brought by grain traders (who still believe in the free market) seeking to have declared unconstitutional a wartime regulation of the federal government which, in effect, denied them windfall profits arising from decontrol of the price of barley.

From 1912 to 1932 interests engaged in the insurance business urged the courts again and again to hold that the Parliament of Canada has no constitutional power to regulate the business of insurance. By 1941 Canadian financial interests, including the insurance companies, had become the strongest supporters of the main recommendations of the Royal Commission on Dominion-Provincial Relations, recommendations which proposed to stabilize public finance and restore confidence and credit mainly through greatly enlarged action by the federal government. Shaken by widespread defaults in the depression and terrified by the revolt against financial orthodoxy in Alberta, they were driven to take a nationwide view of their affairs and to pin their hopes on the national government.

The tax agreements, which were first undertaken as a wartime measure and which have continued to the present, give the sole power of levying personal and corporate income taxes and succession duties to the national Parliament. These far-reaching fiscal powers joined to federal monetary powers have been used courageously and with considerable effectiveness to stabilize the economy during the war and postwar periods. The fiscal initiative of the national government has not only kept the attention of business leaders focused on Ottawa but has also earned a grudging appreciation from the clear-headed ones. Despite incantations about free enterprise and imprecations about the scandalous tax burden, few of them want to return to a situation in which each of eleven governments dips into personal and corporate incomes as it sees fit. National government planning in fiscal matters is the least of the horrible evils that must be endured in a polity where high taxation seems inevitable.

To say that business leaders in Canada are coming to look more favorably on the federal government does not mean that they have all succumbed to this temptation or that those who have really favor all that the federal government does. Those whose interests are concentrated on the development and exploitation of the natural resources of a single province naturally want the federal government to leave them alone while they cultivate the good will of the provincial government. Big business with nationwide interests sees more readily how helpful the national government could be. At the same time, it finds the federal government's scrutiny of combines and monopolies somewhat hampering and can be expected to urge on the courts a narrow interpretation of the power of the federal government in this field. All that is asserted is that nationwide interests establish some kind of bond with the national government.

There is considerable ground for thinking that the business and other elites are coming to accept the preeminence of the national governments and to concentrate their efforts on ways and means of getting effective influence in the national arenas. In the main they are the active leaders of opinion, and they are likely, in the long run, to carry electoral opinion in most states and provinces. If this is so, the federal balance is being tipped decisively in favor of the national power, and it is hard to see how state governments and national governments can continue to be genuinely co-ordinate authorities. In constitutional law the states may long continue to be co-ordinate, but politically they are likely to sink to a subordinate position.

Much the greater part of this paper so far has been taken up with speculation about the focus of opinion and sentiment in electorates and influential groups. It has had to be speculation because, as far as I know, this aspect of federal trends has not been studied with detailed care. Nevertheless, in these democratic aggregates with which we are concerned, sentiment and opinion, molded and canalized no doubt by material factors, will decide where power lies. Because power alone can balance power, the provinces and states have to keep strong and vigorous bodies of opinion on their side if they are to stop the aggrandizement of national governments.

For a long time we believed, admittedly without being fully correct, that the boundaries of power were pretty clearly marked out by the Constitution. In practice, uncertainties about these boundaries were expounded, if not always completely clarified, by the courts. In the classical federalism, the courts were the arbiters of the system. Even if it would not be quite correct to say that they held the balance between state governments and national governments (since, allowing for some exceptions in the case of the Judicial Committee of the Privy Council, the courts did follow the election returns), they nevertheless tipped the balance one way or the other from time to time. Here we come on a constitutional trend of the greatest importance. The courts are retiring, or being retired, from their posts as the supervisors of the balance.

If the consistent course of decision in the last twenty years is a reliable index, the Supreme Court of the United States has retired. By very wide interpretations of the interstate commerce clause and of the general welfare clause as it relates to the federal spending power, the Court has come very close to holding that Congress can direct the economic life of the country — and influence its social and political structure through the spending power — as it sees fit. It has not excluded the states from intervention in the areas of economic life formerly thought to be their exclusive preserves but rather has enabled Congress to oust them by overriding legislation. At the same time, by restrictive reinterpretation of the due process clauses, it has freed both state legislatures and Congress from the restraints formerly imposed by these clauses on legislative regulation of economic affairs. Judicial review by the Court continues to be important in two main matters — in restraining the states from encroachment on fields that are either clearly exclusive federal domain under the Constitution or that have been occupied by federal law, and in the safeguarding of fundamental civil liberties against encroachments by governments. In so far as the federal balance is concerned, "recent judicial doctrine encourages the determination of both power and action by legislation, so that for most purposes, the national policy-makers are the arbiters of the federal system."[4]

Of course, this does not necessarily mean that Congress is rapidly denuding the states of all effective power. The states do not lack defenders in Congress, and so far state interests have been treated with circumspection, if not generosity. It does mean that contests about state power have to take place largely in the national political arena and that a flexible method of experimental shifting of powers back or forth between the nation and the states has been achieved. It also means that, in federal relations as in many other aspects of our affairs, leadership in social adjustment to rapid and complex change has shifted from courts to legislatures, and law has been replaced in part by policy.

It would be quite wrong, however, to say that the Supreme Court of Canada is retiring from its post as supervisor of the federal balance in Canada. Indeed, the Supreme Court has recently proclaimed its strict adherence to the classical federalism by holding that neither the federal Parliament nor a provincial legislature can constitutionally delegate any portion of the exercise of its legislative powers to the other.[5] Ironically enough, it seems clear that Parliament can delegate its legislative powers to a provincial cabinet or other provincial executive agency or even to a tramp in the street, and that provincial legislatures can equally delegate their powers to the Governor-General in Council or to some agency of the federal executive.[6] The reason that the Parliament and the legislatures cannot delegate to one another is that their capacity for lawmaking is limited by the B.N.A. Act to the classes of subject exclusively conferred on them therein. The Supreme Court sticks to the notion of exclusive and rigidly separated spheres of power. There is here no encouragement for experimental trading back and forth of legislative power between the nation and the provinces.

There is, however, some ground for thinking that the Supreme Court is being retired from this post, or perhaps rather being relieved of many of its duties at this post, by forces outside itself. It is well known that, on the whole, the Judicial Committee of the Privy Council gave a narrow, restrictive interpretation of the powers of Parliament under the B.N.A. Act and a correspondingly wide interpretation to the powers of the provincial legislatures. Faced with this condition and seeing no hope of drastic constitutional amendment, those who have been concerned over the past twenty years with finding means of national action which would meet what they thought were, or would be, national needs have tried to turn the flank of the constitutional obstacles.

One of the reasons for persuading provinces voluntarily to give up personal and corporate income taxes and succession duties to the Dominion was to give the Dominion massive fiscal powers. On the assumption that the power of the

---

[4]Harvey C. Mansfield, "The States in the American System", in *The Forty-Eight States*, The American Assembly, New York, 1955, p. 30.

[5]*Attorney General of Nova Scotia* v. *Attorney General of Canada*, [1951] Sup. Ct. Can., 31.

[6]*Prince Edward Island Potato Marketing Board* v. *H. B. Willis, Inc. and Attorney General of Canada*, [1952] 2. Sup. Ct. Can., 392.

Dominion over its "public property" conferred by s. 91.1 gave by implication a wide federal spending power, big spending programs were undertaken. Vigorous use of its constitutional powers over monetary and foreign trade policy, of its constitutional- and contractual-fiscal powers, and of its assumed spending power for objects within the exclusive legislative authority of the provinces, has given the federal government enormous leverage on the provinces as well as on the national economy. This has been achieved without undertaking much legislative action of dubious constitutionality on which the Judicial Committee of the Privy Council or the Supreme Court would have had a chance to rule.

At first glance it seems extraordinary that no one has challenged the constitutionality of the assumed spending power before the Supreme Court. It accounts for a very large portion of the heavy taxation about which everybody groans. Yet a little reflection will show that proof of the unconstitutionality of federal spending for objects outside federal legislative power would prove far too much for almost anybody's comfort. A great many of the substantial interests of the country now derive advantages from it, and the rest of them have not given up hope of doing so. The provincial governments which, as pointed out earlier, are always urging new projects on the federal government, do not want to challenge it. Federal spending now supports so much of the established political, social, and economic structure of the country that prudent men hesitate to take steps that might wipe it out.

More generally, it can be said that neither the provincial governments nor big business interests are testing federal legislative action in the courts as vigorously as they used to. No spectacular cases challenging federal legislative power have recently come to the Supreme Court. An arbiter who is rarely appealed to is still an arbiter, but his importance diminishes *pro tanto*. Perhaps this is happening to the Supreme Court of Canada. I say perhaps, because conclusions should not be based on trends of twenty years or less, which may turn out to have been merely temporary aberrations.

The negative side of the development is that the Court is not being asked to rule against Parliament so often. On the positive side, Dominion-Provincial conferences, notably those held to negotiate about tax agreements every five years, have become clearing houses for many disputed issues between the Dominion and the provinces. One can almost say that the various stresses and strains of the system are negotiated down to tolerable compromises in the course of hammering out the next tax agreements. In Australia, where fiscal power and policy have also been centralized and the states are dependent for a large part of their revenues on the central government, as in Canada, annual premiers' conferences perform somewhat more systematically functions similar to those of the Dominion-Provincial conferences. The Australian premiers' conference mediates between the states and the nation in much the same way as does the United States Senate. Because of the discipline imposed by cabinet government in Australia and Canada regional interests cannot express themselves as freely in the national parliaments as they do in the United States Senate. They do express themselves through the state and provincial premiers in negotiations with the national governments. The Australian and Canadian mechanisms differ from that used in the United States, but they also give the appearance of a political process replacing, or at any rate supplementing more extensively than in earlier years, the judicial process.

The political processes have a flexibility and an easy adaptability to the dominant moods of the country that constitutional amendment and judicial interpretation both lack. There will continue to be regional aspirations which, even if they cannot have free play in a mature federalism, still have to be recognized and reckoned with. There will still be regional resistance by the people in the poorer areas against the tribute levied on them by the metropolitan areas. All these stresses and conflicts need to be negotiated and compromised in *ad hoc* arrangements, particularly where the electorates do not seem disposed to say clearly whether they are federal or unitary in spirit.

At any rate, we are likely to have to live for a long time with the equivocal structure called co-operative federalism. It has arisen because several separate governments share a divided responsibility for regulating a single economic and social structure. It is most unlikely that any constitution could be devised which would enable each to perform its specific functions adequately without impinging seriously on the others. So their activities are inevitably mingled and co-operative arrangements must be worked out. In the result, formal powers are not co-terminous with operating responsibilities; the two levels of government as well as the several state and provincial governments interpenetrate one another in many places and ways. Under the heat and pressure generated by social and economic change in the twentieth century, the distinct strata of the older federalism have begun to melt and flow into one another.

Little can be said about co-operative federalism in the compass of a paper, and it is a subject on which saying a little is not very useful. An outsider can surely be excused for saying that he finds the ramifications of co-operative federalism in the United States bewildering, particularly if he adds that neither Canada nor Australia has been able to make nearly so many promising applications of it. The most effective instrument of its vertical, or federal-state, manifestations in the United States has been the federal grant-in-aid, which has been used with great flexibility, ingenuity, and imagination, if not always with fully satisfying results.

Its achievements are very largely due to two features of the American governmental structure, the strict separation of powers at both state and national levels and the loose structure of command within the state executives. The separation of powers shields the formulation and operation of co-operative schemes from the more niggling reservations of politicians. Because state administration is not fully integrated under the command of the governors, many governors cannot control effectively the arrangements that state officials make with officials of the federal government. In some measure, perhaps, the exigencies of government in Washington deny the President and his staff effective control of officials at their end.

The result is that federal and state officials, many of whom have a professional devotion to their tasks, are relatively free to develop administratively satisfactory arrangements for the federal aid programs. Nothing like these conditions prevail in Australia or Canada because of responsible, cabinet government. Federal and state cabinets will not — indeed cannot — keep political considerations out of co-operative federalism. More than that, there is an integrated command of administration under premiers, prime ministers, and cabinets. Officials know they have to be sure of the support of their ministers before taking significant positions in matters as political as Dominion-provincial relations.

These differences explain in large measure why the federal grant-in-aid is less used and less flexible in Canada and Australia. To help with the imbalance of state and provincial revenues and responsibilities as well as to meet effectively the special cases of the poorer states, efforts have gone into securing a federal monopoly of levying the progressive taxes in return for which large unconditional grants are made to the states and provinces. Having possessed themselves of these revenues without federal conditions or controls on their use, the states and provinces develop their own services and programs as they see fit. Federal-state co-operative arrangements are not undertaken except where there are special and compelling reasons, as for example in the administration of proposed health insurance schemes in Canada. The tendency is for the provinces to become dignified and haughty pensioners rather than partners of the national government.

Given the political conditions in which it would have to be worked, it is not clear whether Canada and Australia could really secure the important advantages that the technique of the federal grant-in-aid offers. On the other hand, it must be said that the broad fiscal powers that the Australian and Canadian national governments have secured are important, if not indispensable, instruments for maintaining stability and coherence in the public finance system and in the economy at large. The maxim that the power to tax is the power to destroy has a special poignancy for present-day polities with the prevailing high levels of taxation. Perhaps we exaggerate the practical usefulness of cyclical budgeting which broad fiscal powers make so attractive in theory. It would be difficult to exaggerate the menace to economic stability and rationality of a number of unco-ordinated taxing authorities each trying to dip deeply into the flow of income. Perhaps the American economy is sufficiently productive to stand it without serious distortion and disruption. The Australian and Canadian economies almost certainly are not.

Whatever the different configurations of co-operative federalism are and however well they may be working, the ingenuity and resource that have gone into the adaptation of the classical federalism to the complexities of the twentieth century in the last two decades is remarkable. In the mid-thirties the prospects that polities with significant federal elements in their constitutions could survive the tribulations from which they then suffered seemed dim. The prospects now appear to have improved greatly. We can at least hope to operate big government with a moderate amount of centralization and at the same time preserve many of the values of wide participation and decentralized decision. Those who want to get back the substance of the classical federalism will have to reduce greatly big business, big government, and economic interdependence.

6 The Rowell-Sirois Report, Provincial Autonomy, and Post-War Canadian Federalism *

Donald V. Smiley

On May 3, 1940, the Royal Commission on Dominion-Provincial Relations presented its report to the Prime Minister of Canada. This report, along with the specialized studies undertaken by direction of the commission, constitutes the most comprehensive investigation of a working federal system that has ever been made. In spite of the scope and quality of the commission's work, its analysis of federal-provincial relations has had surprisingly little influence on the directions that the theory and practice of Canadian federalism have taken since 1945. More specifically, the concept of provincial autonomy which is central to the commission's argument has been denied explicitly or implicitly by such influential writings on the Canadian federal system as the so-called Green Book proposals submitted by the federal government at the Dominion-Provincial Conference on Reconstruction in 1945,[1] the Report of the Royal Commission on National Development in the Arts, Letters and Sciences,[2] Mr. Maurice Lamontagne's book, *Le Fédéralisme canadien*,[3] and the Report of the Quebec Royal Commission on Constitutional Problems,[4] as well as by the actual developments in federal-provincial relations since the Second World War.

At the present time of uncertainty in the Canadian federal system it seems desirable to re-examine the perspectives of the Rowell-Sirois Report.[5] This paper attempts to analyse one of these perspectives—provincial autonomy in the fields of health, welfare and education.

Provincial Autonomy in the Rowell-Sirois Report

The emphasis on provincial autonomy in the performance of a very wide range of public functions which pervade the analysis of the Rowell-Sirois Commission has given rise to much less comment than the commission's relatively few but significant proposals for transferring particular provincial responsibilities to the federal authorities and for sharing functions previously the exclusive concern of the provinces between the two levels of government. Indeed, viewed against

*From *Canadian Journal of Economics and Political Science*, Vol. XXVIII, No. 1, February 1962, pp. 54-69. Reprinted by permission of the author and publisher. This paper was presented at the annual meeting of the Canadian Political Science Association in Montreal on June 9, 1961.

[1]*Submissions and Discussions*, King's Printer, Ottawa, 1946.

[2]King's Printer, Ottawa, 1951.

[3]Les Presses de l'Université Laval, Quebec, 1954.

[4]Queen's Printer, Quebec, 1956.

[5]*Report of the Royal Commission on Dominion-Provincial Relations*, King's Printer, Ottawa, 1940, reprinted 1954, Bk. II, p. 80. All page references in this paper are to the 1954 reprint, hereafter cited as *Report*.

the constitutional impasse of the 1930's the report is a somewhat cautious document.[6]

It is fundamental to the commission's analysis that the highly integrated nature of the Canadian economy makes it appropriate for the provinces to perform a very wide range of public functions without the direct involvement of the federal authorities.

> As striking as the economic interdependence of Canadian provinces is their political, social and cultural individuality. The Commission's recommendations are based, in accordance with its terms of reference, on the economic and financial analysis it has made. But the Commission appreciates the existence of many non-economic and non-fiscal factors, and its recommendations are not those which might have been made for a more homogeneous country. No allocation of jurisdiction, over education and social services, for example, would be satisfactory which did not take full account of the existing loyalties to provincial traditions and institutions. The Commission's plan seeks to ensure to every province a real and not an illusory autonomy by guaranteeing to it, free from conditions or control, the revenues necessary to perform those functions which relate closely to its social and cultural development.[7]

It appears implicit in the commission's analysis that the desirability of provincial autonomy to safeguard regional particularisms is more pressing in relation to health, education, and welfare services than to the regulatory activities of government. In regard to welfare the report states, "provincial responsibility for social welfare should be deemed basic and general; Dominion responsibility, on the other hand, should be deemed an exception to the general rule, and as such should be strictly defined". It was recommended that welfare responsibilities be transferred from the provinces to the federal level only in relation to unemployment and contributory old age pensions, and then only after the commission had taken some pains to demonstrate that there would be substantial disabilities to provincial action.[8] Of health services it asserted, ". . . there are pronounced regional differences in Canada in social philosophy which are bound to affect public health legislation. Centralization of jurisdiction might not, therefore, conduce to progressive action in public health, or to national unity in general".[9] As in welfare, federal activity should be limited to a relatively few residual functions whose limits should be carefully defined — research, statistical and other staff services, activities ancillary to other federal responsibilities, leadership in establishing uniform standards where such are desirable,

---

[6]It might be argued that the *Report* was conditioned by the commission's terms of reference which directed it in part to ". . . express what in their opinion, subject to the retention of the distribution of legislative powers essential to a proper carrying out of the federal system in harmony with national needs and the promotion of national unity, will best effect a balanced relationship between the financial powers and the obligations and functions of each governing body, and conduce to a more efficient, independent and economical discharge of governmental responsibilities in Canada". *Ibid.*, Bk. I, p. 10.

[7]*Ibid.*, Bk. II, p. 80.

[8]*Ibid.*, Bk. II, pp. 24-28 and 40-42.

[9]*Ibid.*, Bk. II, p. 34.

and leadership in co-ordinating provincial activities to avoid overlapping and deficiencies in health services.[10] The commission rejected the many proposals made to it in regard to federal aid for general education on the ground that "a free hand in something so important to the social and cultural life of the people seems to us to be vital to any provincial autonomy worthy of the name";[11] the commission did, however, give cautious approval to small annual Dominion grants to the Canadian universities.[12] Thus full provincial responsibility in the fields of health, welfare, and education, with the exception of a relatively few federal residual responsibilities, was seen by the commission to be essential to the maintenance of those provincial particularisms which were strategic in the establishment of the Canadian federal system and whose continuing existence made necessary the preservation of that system.

The Commission had a precise idea of what it meant by provincial autonomy. A province has genuine independence only if it has the revenues at its disposal to carry out those functions for which it is responsible, free from federal control in respect to those functions; the master-solution of the report was aimed at ensuring that each province was put in a financial position to provide, if it chose, a level of provincial services at average national standards without subjecting its citizens to provincial taxation above the national average.[13] The commission implicitly rejected the notion that has been propagated by latter-day defenders of provincial rights that provincial autonomy is genuine only if the provinces have exclusive access to the more lucrative fields of direct taxation. The commission also rejected the position that the federal government had a direct responsibility for the standards at which particular provincial services were rendered; this was to be in the last analysis the duty of the respective provincial electorates. In rejecting proposals for federal grants-in-aid to education the commission argued, ". . . the representations appear to us to go too far in denying the right of each province to decide the relative importance of expenditure on education and expenditure on other competing services. . . . Our financial proposals aim at placing every province in a position to discharge its responsibilities for education (on a scale that is within the means of the people of Canada) if it chooses to do so. Once this position is established it seems to us best that education, like every other form of welfare service in a democratic community, should have to fight for its life, and that a generous provision for the education of the children of the nation should depend, not on any arbitrary constitutional provision, but on the persistent conviction of the mass of the people that they must be ready to deny themselves some of the good things of life in order to deal fairly by their children. . . ."[14] Along the same lines the Report stated in relation to the proposed national adjustment grants to the provinces:

---

[10]*Ibid.*, Bk. II, pp. 34-35.
[11]*Ibid.*, Bk. II, p. 50.
[12]*Ibid.*, Bk. II, p. 52.
[13]See *Ibid.*, Bk. II, "Abstract of the Leading Recommendations", pp. 269-276.
[14]*Ibid.*, Bk. II, p. 51.

It should be made clear that while the adjustment grant proposed is designed to enable a province to provide adequate services (at the average Canadian standard) without excessive taxation (on the average Canadian basis) the freedom of action of a province is in no way impaired. If a province chooses to provide inferior services and impose lower taxation it is free to do so, or it may provide better services than the average if its people are willing to be taxed accordingly, or it may, for example, starve its roads and improve its education, starve its education and improve its roads. . . . But no provincial government will be free from the pressure of the opinion of its own people and if, when it applies for an increased adjustment grant on the basis of need, it has to produce figures which indicate that although it might, without specially heavy taxation, have provided better education but did not do so, it has, of course, to justify this to its own voters.[15]

The kind of solution the commission recommended thus relieved the federal authorities of the responsibility for guaranteeing the standards of particular provincial services or of influencing the priorities the provinces set in relation to the functions assigned to them.

The commission had little enthusiasm for "co-operative federalism" through the device of federal grants-in-aid of particular provincial activities. An astute and closely reasoned analysis of the conditional grant procedure was made following in the main the trend of Professor J. A. Corry's specialized study "Difficulties of Divided Jurisdiction", and the commission pointed out what appeared to them to be the inherent defects of this technique in the Canadian setting.[16] There are almost inevitable rivalries between federal and provincial authorities involved in administering joint programmes; under the cabinet system with its union of politics and administration these rivalries can be resolved only at the political level and thus irrelevant partisan considerations are introduced into the implementation of these programmes. Federal supervision of shared activities is seldom effective and is usually restricted to checking on the regularity of provincial expenditures; this leads to further differences between federal and provincial officials as the former are characteristically Treasury and auditing personnel preoccupied with protecting the federal purse while the lattter are involved with the provision of particular services. In practice too, it is rarely practical for the federal authorities to withdraw a grant from a province which fails to adhere to the conditions imposed by the federal authorities in respect to that grant. The general conclusion is that, "The experience with conditional grants leads us to doubt whether joint administration of activities by the Dominion and a province is ever a practical way of surmounting constitutional difficulties. Where legislative power over a particular subject is divided it is ordinarily desirable that these powers should be pooled under the control of a single government in order to secure unified efforts in administration".[17] The report does, it is true, give cautious and

---

[15]*Ibid.*, Bk. II, p. 84.
[16]*Ibid.*, Bk. I, pp. 257-259.
[17]*Ibid.*, Bk. I, p. 259.

qualified approval to the use of federal conditional grants where the amounts of money involved are relatively small and where the programmes can either be routine or subject to scientific standards of performance which eliminate differences between the federal and provincial officials involved.[18] However, in most situations the aim was a clear-cut delineation of the respective responsibilities of the federal and provincial governments and the unified control of particular programmes by one or the other. Furthermore, the commission's emphasis on the desirability of a mutual power of delegation between provinces and Dominion and between Dominion and provinces[19] suggests a procedure by which particular functions might be transferred completely from one to the other as an alternative to joint arrangements in the implementation of these programmes.

In summary, provincial autonomy is fundamental in the commission's concept for a viable Canadian federal system. Such autonomy was justified on three grounds — cultural, political, and administrative: (1) It is necessary for the preservation of provincial particularisms; (2) It makes possible the effective accountability of provincial public authorities to provincial electorates, particularly in relation to the respective priorities that are placed on provincial programes; (3) It makes possible the unified control over the administration of particular provincial functions necessary to the vigorous implementation of public policies relating to such functions.

To the commission, then, the major implications of the integration of the national economy lay in the desirability of giving the federal authorities exclusive access to the major field of direct taxation with the corresponding responsibility of effecting some redistribution of financial resources among the provinces rather than the alleged need for federal involvement in the range or standards of provincial functions. Further, in the commission's view the fact that particular problems have come to have more than provincial significance does not by itself justify federal action in respect to those problems; in perhaps its most striking sentence the report asserts in respect to health functions, "Mere importance of a service does not justify its assumption by the Dominion".[20] It is this last judgment which most sharply distinguishes the underlying philosophy of the commission from much of the more recent thinking about Canadian federalism and the directions that the Canadian federal system has taken.

Developments in Federal-Provincial Relations Since 1945

The final breakdown of the Dominion-Provincial Conference on Reconstruction in May, 1946, signalled the second failure in five years to evolve a comprehensive settlement of the relations between the two levels of government and no subsequent attempts have been made. The rejection of a solution on the general lines proposed by the Rowell-Sirois Commission can be attributed to the obstruction of the governments of Ontario, Alberta, and British Columbia. However, the character of the so-called Green Book proposals presented by the fed-

[18]*Ibid.*, Bk. I, p. 257.
[19]*Ibid.*, Bk. II, pp. 72-73.
[20]*Ibid.*, Bk. II, p. 34.

eral Government at the opening of the Conference on Reconstruction in the spring of 1945,[21] with their emphasis on shared programmes and their rejection of the principle of equalization, indicates that by that time the federal authorities had, for whatever reasons, turned their back on the broad solution of the Rowell-Sirois Report and accepted an alternative which would have reduced the provinces to a subordinate and dependent role in the Canadian federal structure.

Canadian federalism as it has developed since 1945 has not patterned itself according to either of the comprehensive solutions sponsored by the federal Government at the conferences of 1941 and 1945-46 respectively. Rather, the action of the federal authorities after the latter conference in attempting to negotiate tax-sharing arrangements with each of the provinces was the beginning of a process of continuous and piecemeal adjustment between the two levels of government, which is still going on. To an overwhelming degree, these adjustments have come about through interaction between federal and provincial executives — the tax-sharing arrangements, the various kinds of shared cost programmes, the activities of the Continuing Committee on Federal Provincial Fiscal and Economic Relations and other *ad hoc* and standing committees, and so on — rather than through formal constitutional amendment or through an evolving pattern of judicial interpretation of the British North America Act. Thus any discussion of contemporary Canadian federalism which revolves about the traditional concerns of students of federal systems — residual powers, judicial review, procedures of constitutional amendments, and other matters relating to the formal constitutional structure — is somewhat unprofitable. The federal aspects of the Canadian constitution, using the latter term in its broadest sense, have come to be less what the courts say they are than what the federal and provincial Cabinets and bureaucracies in a continuous series of formal and informal relations determine them to be.

The Canadian constitution has in fact become a more flexible instrument than those who faced the impasse of the 1930's could have visualized. There is a recognition of this actual or potential flexibility in much of the recent writing on the Canadian federal system, a recognition that significant developments in federal-provincial relations can come about without either a change in the pattern of judicial interpretation of the BNA Act or of amendment to that Act. The Green Book proposals contemplated sweeping and permanent changes in the Canadian federal system; although the Minister of Labour mentioned, almost in passing, the desirability of a constitutional amendment making possible mutual delegation between Parliament and the provincial legislatures which would apply to industrial relations and other matters,[22] the delegation amendment was not central to the Government's plan, as it was in the Rowell-Sirois Report; and the Minister of Health and Welfare, a constitutional lawyer in his own right, asserted of the Government's comprehensive programme for national health insurance, "It is believed that none of these proposals involves

---

[21]*Submissions and Discussions*, pp. 55-108, pp. 111-118.
[22]*Ibid.*, pp. 75-76.

any change in the constitutional jurisdiction or responsibility of federal and provincial governments under the British North America Act".[23] The Massey Report envisages almost a new dimension in the responsibilities of the federal authorities with its sweeping proposal for federal involvement in cultural development; there is no hint in the report that the implementation of any or all of these recommendations would necessitate any amendment of the BNA Act, and the laboured argument made to justify federal responsibility in cultural matters ends with the astounding, and from the constitutional point of view, question-begging assertion that "If the Federal Government is to renounce its right to associate itself with other social groups, public and private, in the general education of Canadian citizens, it denies its moral and intellectual purpose, the complete conception of the common good is lost and Canada, as such, becomes a materialistic society".[24] The continuing debate over a more appropriate procedure for constitutional amendment also reflects an underlying assumption of the possibilities of significant constitutional development by other means. The debate in the 1930's was an intensely serious one because those who supported reform were clearly bent on important amendments, particularly those which would increase the scope of federal jurisdiction in matters of economic regulation and social welfare; during the last decade or so, if I have understood the situation, the impulse for a new amending procedure has sprung very largely from the symbol of colonial status represented by the existing arrangements rather than from any sense of urgency relating to the need for substantive changes in the BNA Act. It has, of course, proved possible to effect amendments transferring significant fields of jurisdiction to Parliament after unanimous provincial consent, as the amendments of 1940 and 1951 relating to unemployment insurance and old age pensions respectively have demonstrated. More important in dispelling the previous sense of urgency, however, is the recognition that significant changes can and do come about in delineating the respective responsibilities of Ottawa and the provinces without formal amendment of the British North America Act.

There are three major procedures for adjustment on what one might call the executive side of federal-provincial relations — co-ordination through *ad hoc* and standing committees of the federal and provincial cabinets and bureaucracies, the delegation of federal powers to provincial executive agencies, and the exercise of the federal spending power on objects usually regarded as provincial and/or local responsibilities. Of these the third device, the use of the federal spending power, has the most direct implication for provincial autonomy.

Contemporary Canadian federalism has seen the growth of a very large number of *ad hoc* or standing committees of federal and provincial executive officials. In 1957 Dr. K. W. Taylor, the Deputy Minister of Finance, made a tabulation of sixty-four federal-provincial committees "more or less formally constituted, and that have either continuing terms of reference, or terms of

[23]*Ibid.*, p. 89.
[24]*Report of the Royal Commission on National Development in the Arts, Letters and Sciences*, King's Printer, Ottawa, 1951, p. 8.

reference that will keep them operating for a considerable period of time".[25] In generality of function these range from the Continuing Committee on Federal-Provincial Fiscal and Economic Matters to the Co-ordinating Agency on Diseases of the Beaver. Most of these committees meet in Ottawa and the chairman and secretary are provided by the federal government. A recent article by Professor Richard Leach reveals the extent of inter-provincial executive relationships, most of them of an informal and continuing nature.[26] The establishment of the Federal-Provincial Relations Division in the Federal Department of Finance, the Continuing Committee on Federal-Provincial Fiscal and Economic Matters, and the Quebec Department of Federal-Provincial Relations, along with the various *ad hoc* and standing committees on more specialized matters, appears to indicate a more profound emphasis than in the past on the executive aspects of federalism.

Legislation enacted by Parliament in 1949 and 1954 delegating federal authority to executive agencies operating under provincial legislation signals another device for delineating federal-provincial responsibilities apart from constitutional amendment or judicial review of the BNA Act. In a 1951 decision the Supreme Court affirmed a series of earlier cases that inter-delegation between Parliament and provincial legislatures was invalid.[27] However, it appears that there is no constitutional objection if delegation is made by Parliament to an executive agency operating under provincial legislation.[28] Thus the Agricultural Marketing Act of 1949[29] authorized the Governor-in-Council to delegate to any agency which under provincial law had the authority to regulate intra-provincial trade in agricultural products the power to exercise regulatory responsibilities over the extra-provincial and international aspects of agricultural marketing. Similarly, the Motor Vehicle Transport Act of 1954[30] authorized provincial regulatory boards to exercise powers over the interprovincial and international aspects of commercial road transport.

The third device lending flexibility to our constitutional arrangements is the exercise of the federal spending power on objects traditionally regarded as being within the exclusive concern of the provinces and/or local governments. In some circumstances payments have been made directly to individuals (family allowances) and to private groups (Canada Council grants). Unconditional grants to the provinces have been made under the tax-sharing agreements and supplementary subsidies to the Maritimes. In other cases payments have been made to local governments through grants in lieu of taxes on federal properties and grants for land assembly and winter works programmes. Particular capital

[25]"Coordination in Administration" in *Proceedings of the Ninth Annual Conference of the Institute of Public Administration of Canada*, pp. 253-259.

[26]"Interprovincial Cooperation", *Canadian Public Administration*, Vol. II, No. 2, June 1959, pp. 83-99.

[27]*A.G. Nova Scotia* v. *A.G. Canada*, [1951] S.C.R. 31. For a criticism of the decision see John R. Ballem, *Canadian Bar Review*, Vol. XXIX, 1951, pp. 79-86.

[28]*P.E.I. Potato Marketing Board* v. *H. B. Willis Inc. and A.G. Canada*, [1952] 4 D.L.R. 146.

[29]*Revised Statutes of Canada*, 1952, c. 6.

[30]*Statutes of Canada*, 1953-54, c. 59.

projects over which the provincial legislatures have exclusive responsibility like the St. Mary's and South Saskatchewan developments and the Canso Causeway have been aided by federal funds. Most importantly for provincial autonomy, a very large number of federal conditional grants to the provinces, and these increasingly involve local governments also, have been established, particularly in the fields of health, welfare, and vocational education.

The exercise of the spending power provides a means by which the federal government can by unilateral action involve itself in many matters which under traditional understandings of the constitution have been the exclusive concern of the provinces. Although it is not within my competence to judge the constitutionality of the various uses of this power, which have been justified as an exercise of an inherent prerogative power of the federal Crown to disburse its revenues as it chooses subject only to prior parliamentary authorization and as exercises of Parliament's jurisdiction over "The Public Debt and Property", it appears to a layman to be the most superficial sort of quibbling to assert that when Parliament appropriates funds in aid of say, vocational training or housing, and enacts in some detail the circumstances under which such moneys are to be available that Parliament is not in fact "legislating" in such fields.[31] There are four limitations faced by the federal authorities in augmenting their power through this mechanism. First, the provincial and local governments have the unchallenged right to participate or not in shared programmes, although federal financial inducements combined with popular and perhaps internal bureaucratic pressures may in many circumstances make this alternative illusory. Second, the federal government cannot in most cases oust the provinces from the primary administrative responsibilities in the fields assigned to them by the constitution; that is, federal and provincial objectives must be implemented through provincial or local agencies. Third, conditional grants have little relevance to the sharing of power in respect to regulatory functions. Fourth, in line with current understandings of the BNA Act,[32] the federal Parliament is precluded from contributing to a particular provincial activity from the proceeds of a federal levy made for that purpose. Within these limits, however, the exercise of the federal spending power provides an important device for overcoming the rigidities in the division of responsibilities between the federal and provincial authorities delineated by the BNA Act as judicially interpreted.

What criteria have been used to justify the expenditure of federal funds on

---

[31]It must of course be admitted that in the case of conditional grants federal legislation is inoperative in the absence of provincial and/or local action.

[32]There are some unresolved constitutional ambiguities in this area. The only case dealing directly with such a situation was *A.G. Canada* v. *A.G. Ontario*, [1937] A.C. 355, in which the Judicial Committee declared the federal *Unemployment and Social Insurance Act* of 1935 invalid as an invasion of provincial jurisdiction over property and civil rights. See also Leon Mercier Gouin and Brooke Claxton, *Legislative Expedients and Devices Adopted by the Dominion and the Provinces*, Ottawa, 1939, Ch. 3, "Grants in Aid for Objects not Under Dominion Jurisdiction"; and the evidence given by F. P. Varcoe, Deputy Minister of Justice, to the Joint Committee of the Senate and House of Commons on Old Age Security, *Minutes of Proceedings and Evidence*, King's Printer, Ottawa, 1950, 1161-1172.

behalf of particular provincial functions? Most of the argumentation proposing or upholding such actions in Parliament and elsewhere amounts to no more than assertions that the matter in question is of vital importance to someone or other and *ipso facto* Ottawa should do something about it; proponents of particular measures do not ordinarily feel obliged to demonstrate why provincial or local action has been inadequate — whether these governments lack the financial resources to support the function, or contrariwise whether they have the resources and choose not to give the activity a sufficiently high priority in their expenditure patterns. Thus the dominant consideration dictating federal involvement has been the assumed significance of a particular function in contradiction to the principle enunciated by the Rowell-Sirois Commission that "mere importance of a service does not justify its assumption by the Dominion"[33] and to any acceptable theory of federalism.

The following generalizations can be made about the existing conditional grant programmes:

First, several of the existing arrangements embody what appear to be permanent obligations for the federal government. When Dr. Luella Gettys investigated the seven existing programmes of federal conditional grants to the provinces in 1937-38 she discovered that only two, those related to old age pensions and employment offices, were regarded as of a continuing nature.[34] Several of the largest of the current schemes, more particularly those related to hospital services, welfare, and operating expenditures for vocational training, can reasonably be viewed as continuing commitments assumed by the federal government.

Second, the federal authorities have in most cases chosen to share in only part of the provincial and local costs incurred in particular aided functions. In most cases administrative costs are not shareable. Under the Hospital and Diagnostic Services Act federal grants are paid on behalf of patients undergoing treatment for mental illness and tuberculosis only if such treatment is given in a general hospital. In the Trans-Canada Highway programme costs of acquiring rights-of-way are not shareable. Other examples could be given. Also, grants are sometimes made for relatively narrow functions as is the case with the nine existing grants for specific provincial health programmes and grants for forest inventories, forest fire protection, and reforestation. Thus federal action can reasonably be viewed not only in terms of federal support for particular provincial activities but also in terms of Ottawa's desire to limit its contributions, for reasons which are often not easy to discover, to particular aspects of these programmes.

Third, the financial arrangements relating to particular programmes have been designed with little apparent concern for the relative fiscal capacities of the provinces or their respective financial needs in respect to particular functions. The general rule has been for the federal government to pay the same proportion to all provinces of the shareable costs incurred in grant-aided func-

---

[33]*Report*, Bk. II, p. 34.

[34]*The Administration of Canadian Conditional Grants,* Public Administration Service, Chicago, 1938.

tions. There have been refinements. Under the Hospital Insurance and Diagnostic Services Act the federal contribution to particular provinces is related both to national average *per capita* costs and to the average *per capita* costs in those provinces. Under a 1956 amendment to the Trans-Canada Highway Act the federal government will contribute ninety per cent of the shareable costs incurred by each province in building one-tenth of its approved mileage while maintaining its fifty per cent contributions to the costs of other mileage as provided for in previous legislation. Some of the federal grants for vocational education are related to the numbers of persons between fifteen and nineteen years of age in the respective provinces. A proportion of the health grants for tuberculosis control and child and maternal health are allocated on the basis of the relation between provincial population and deaths from tuberculosis and infant mortality respectively in the previous five-year period. However, there has been relatively little effort devoted to evolving sophisticated measures of either the needs of provinces in relation to particular services or of over-all provincial fiscal capacities which have characterized some of the central government grants to local authorities and many of the federal grants-in-aid to the American states.

Fourth, in most of the major shared cost programmes the conditions of federal and provincial participation, including the standards of acceptable provincial performance, are evolved through protracted negotiations between officials of the two levels of government. Federal standards are thus seldom determined by unilateral action and it must be remembered that in some of the grant-aided functions the provinces have at their disposal a much larger supply of specialized skills than does the federal government; and in these circumstances the justification for central control that is operative in many instances of provincial-local relations where the receiving jurisdictions are deficient in expertise, is absent.[35]

Fifth, the bias of the conditional grant system is towards health and welfare services. It is estimated that in 1961-62 the federal government will disburse $415,898,000 to the provinces for these functions, including hospitalization. This is 75.6 per cent of the total estimated for conditional grants for all purposes.[36]

The Nature and Relevance of Provincial Autonomy

The existing conditional grant programmes pose a direct challenge to provincial autonomy as that concept was defined in the Rowell-Sirois Report. Provincial discretion is limited in four directions by these programmes:

First, the present arrangements distort the priorities that the provinces would otherwise give to particular functions. Perhaps the most significant decisions a provincial government can make and can be held responsible for are budgetary ones — decisions relating to the respective priorities in the expenditures of

---

[35]For circumstances relating to provincial-local relations see my article "Local Autonomy and Central Administrative Control in Saskatchewan", *Canadian Journal of Economics and Political Science*, Vol. XXVI, No. 2, May 1960, particularly pp. 303-306.

[36]*House of Commons Debates* (unrevised), July 11, 1961, p. 7915.

available resources on schools, roads, welfare and health services, on vocational as against general education, curative as against preventive health services, the direct provision of services by the province as against subventions to the local authorities. We can deduce that under existing arrangements total provincial expenditures, including proceeds from conditional grants, are distributed among public functions rather differently than if the provinces had the same resources with no conditions attached to their use. We can also assume that the distribution of the resources available to the provinces from sources other than conditional grants is different from what it would be if no such grants were available; it is reasonable to conjecture that the existing policies influence the more prosperous provinces to spend less from non-grant sources on grant-aided services than they would otherwise do and the poorer provinces more. To put this in another way, if federal assistance is available on behalf of a service which a prosperous province would otherwise provide at the same or almost the same cost, the grant in effect is an unconditional subsidy which the province may use either to pay for other services or to hold taxes at a lower level than otherwise, while in a poorer province which conceivably might not provide the services at all if there were no federal help available, the provincial proportion of the cost might be met either by higher provincial taxation or by using provincial moneys which would otherwise be spent on non-grant-aided services. If this general argument is valid, one of the effects of the present grant arrangements is to increase the disparities between the abilities of the wealthier and poorer provinces to finance non-grant-aided services like secondary highways and elementary education. At any rate, the priority-determining function of provincial cabinets and legislatures is restricted by conditional grant programmes and there is no evidence that the federal authorities in inaugurating such programmes have had regard for their implications for the over-all pattern of provincial services or the impact of these programmes on the abilities of the provinces to perform other functions.

Second, existing policies place limits on the discretion of the provinces in formulating objectives related to particular shared functions and in implementing these objectives. For example, present arrangements in the field of welfare might make it difficult for a province to embark on policies either of eliminating categorical assistance programmes in favour of assistance based on need regardless of the circumstances occasioning such need or of implementing categorical programmes different from those supported by the federal government. In the field of senior citizens' housing the policies of Central Mortgage and Housing Corporation and provincial welfare officials in regard to the relative usefulness of hostel accommodation and self-contained dwellings for senior citizens' housing have sometimes been different. In these kinds of circumstances the formulation and implementation of programme objectives by the provinces is restricted by federal action and it is yet to be demonstrated that federal judgment has been, according to any reasonable criteria, "better" than that of the provincial authorities.

Third, provincial discretion is restricted by the uncertainties of future federal policies in relation to shared functions. Provinces are almost inevitably frustrated in long-term budgetary and programme planning when any such plans may be upset by federal action. Much of this uncertainty relates of course to the failure of the two levels of government to evolve stable divisions of tax sources and revenues. Provincial uncertainty as to federal actions in shared programmes has to some degree been mitigated, however, in those fields where there has grown up a tradition of prior consultation between Ottawa and the provinces in respect to new programmes or to changes in existing programmes and where long-term agreements relating to particular functions have been signed. It is probably true that provincial uncertainty is occasioned more by the continuing possibility of the federal government's sponsoring new programmes, to take advantage of which would impose new burdens on provincial revenues, than by the possibilities of changing federal policies in relation to existing programmes. Although consultative procedures have become more widespread and constructive in the past decade, Premier T. C. Douglas's complaint at the 1950 Federal-Provincial Constitutional Conference is not altogether inapplicable to the present and it is significant that Mr. Douglas spoke as the leader of an administration more committed than most to long-term budgetary and programme planning:

> Without consultation with the provinces it [the federal government] is vacating the field of rental control, after permitting substantial rent increases, and thus thrusting upon the provinces the responsibility of meeting a social crisis.
>
> Without consultation with the provinces, it has announced a comprehensive irrigation scheme, which we now learn must be supported by substantial provincial contributions.
>
> Without consultation with the provinces, it has announced the construction of a Trans-Canada highway, and it is later found that the provinces will not only have to stand fifty per cent of the cost of construction but also the entire cost of the right-of-way.
>
> Without consultation with the provinces, it has decided upon a housing program for which every province must contribute twenty-five per cent of the cost, without regard to its ability to pay.
>
> By these unilateral decisions, the federal government has embarrassed the provinces in respect to their capital programs and has virtually dictated policies to which their consent has not been obtained.[37]

Fourth, several of the existing programmes restrict the provinces in dealing as they choose with the local authorities within their boundaries. The traditions and practices of provincial-local relations differ profoundly among provinces and much is to be gained by preserving these differences in this complex and rapidly changing field. However, several of the federal grant programmes — those relating to hospital construction and hospital insurance, vocational education, low-rental housing and urban land assembly, municipal winter works, and others — involve local authorities directly or indirectly and must inevitably have some impact on provincial objectives in relation to particular

[37]*Proceedings*, p. 23.

local functions. Further, such federal involvement complicates the attempts of at least some of the provinces to base their subventions to local governments on some objective standards of local fiscal need and to evolve a more rational allocation of responsibilities and revenue sources between provincial and local governments.

Provincial autonomy finds its justification in three major sets of considerations: (1) the desire to preserve certain territorially-defined particularisms; (2) the desire to disperse political power and to make those who exercise such power effectively accountable to those over whom such power is wielded; (3) the desire to promote vigour and effectiveness in the implementation of public policies.

The relation of the division of powers between the federal and provincial governments and the maintenance of territorially located particularisms has not been systematically examined; perhaps here is a fertile field for collaboration between the political scientist and the cultural anthropologist. In regard to these particularisms in their most critical form, the existence of English-speaking and French-speaking cultures in Canada, I should rather summarily reject two extreme points of view. The first is that of the Tremblay Report whose essential argument is that governmental as well as all other human activities are culturally determined and that therefore most significant exercises of federal power are a challenge to the minority cultures.[38] This point of view forgets that there are values other than the protection of cultural particularisms to be sought through federalism and that there are some exercises of federal power, say for example in the regulation of weights and measures or agricultural research, which have few cultural connotations. At the other extreme it might be asserted that the minority culture has adequate protection if the guarantees in the BNA Act relating explicitly to minority rights are upheld; this position overlooks the existing scope of federal activity, particularly in the fields of health, welfare, and education, and the possible implications of such activity for French-speaking Canadian society. However, the kinds of restrictions on provincial autonomy that I have described above bear both upon Quebec and the other provinces, although it is understandable that Quebec's suspicion of shared programmes should be more profound than that of other provinces.

Provincial autonomy, indeed federalism itself, finds its major justification in liberal views about the desirability of dispersing political power and of making those who hold such power effectively accountable to those over whom power is exercised. Alan Barth forcefully states part of this aspect of the Western political tradition in the first sentences of his *Government by Investigation*: "Political liberty consists of limitations upon the authority of governments. It is in the nature of power to expand and seek its own aggrandizement. Through a variety of rationalizations — in the name of efficiency or economy, in the name of public welfare, in the name of national security — power presses always at the boundaries prescribed for it and can be held within these boundaries

---

[38]Quebec Royal Commission on Constitutional Problems, *Report*, Vol. II, part 3, Queen's Printer, Quebec, 1956, especially Ch. 1, "Culture, Nation, Society".

only by countervailing power."[39] Thus federalism, in Professor Arthur Macmahon's words, "lessens the risk of monopoly of political power by providing a number of independent points".[40] This dispersal of political power can, of course, take place along other than territorial lines,[41] although in Canada with its size and regionally based diversities there have been strong influences from the first for the allocation of significant public functions to regional units. There is the desirability not only of dispersing power but of making those who hold it effectively accountable. The parliamentary system operating under circumstances where there is both cabinet and party solidarity provides an effective mechanism by which those who wield executive and legislative power can be made accountable. Accountability, however, is attenuated when functions are shared between two or more levels of government.

Provincial autonomy is necessary for the vigorous and effective implementation of public policy. The Rowell-Sirois Commission made a perceptive analysis of the impact of joint federal-provincial control over the administration of particular public functions.[42] Essentially the argument is that effective administration requires unified direction, which is almost inherently impossible in shared programmes in the Canadian setting except in those few circumstances where objective and agreed-upon standards of performance can be evolved.

The kinds of considerations which I have described would, at least in my scale of preferences, have to give way if it could be demonstrated that the provinces would not in fact provide the functions allocated to them in an effective manner. Such an argument might have two bases. First, it might be asserted that the provincial elected and appointed executives have neither the competence nor the integrity to perform adequately. This proposition would I think be difficult to demonstrate, particularly in view of the substantial advances in establishing the merit system that have been made since the Second World War in most of the provincial bureaucracies. A second and more serious argument might be that some or all of the provinces are too small to make feasible the employment of the specialized personnel and equipment necessary for the adequate provision of particular provincial services. This objection could not be met without careful empirical investigation. However, on the surface it appears that all but one or two of the provinces are at least potentially viable units for the provision of most services allocated to them, particularly if the federal authorities are imaginative in providing a range of research and other specialized staff services which may be made available to the provinces without significantly limiting their autonomy.

Provincial autonomy is obviously incompatible with the claim that Canadian citizens as such have the right to *defined* standards of health, welfare, and edu-

---

[39]The Viking Press, New York, 1955, p. 3.

[40]Quoted in "On the Theory of the Federal State" in Sigmund Neumann, *The Democratic and the Authoritarian State*, Free Press, Glencoe, Ill., 1957, p. 220.

[41]See the analysis of Arthur Maass on the distinction between the "areal" division of power and the "capital" division of power in Arthur Maass (ed.), *Area and Power*, Free Press, Glencoe, Ill., 1959, pp. 9-25.

[42]*Report*, Bk. I, pp. 257-259.

cation services and the corollary of this proposition that the federal authorities have in the last analysis the responsibility of securing these rights. Apart from the provision of Section 93 of the BNA Act relating to denominational schools, the appropriateness of Ottawa's interposing its judgment between Canadians and their duly-elected provincial and local governments is by no means self-evident. However, the devising of explicit standards of provincial performance by the federal authorities, in consultation with the provinces or otherwise, and the enforcement of these by the federal government in connection with conditional grant programmes is only one of the possible procedures for attaining adequate performance by the provincial and local government in respect to particular functions. Assuming that a government has the financial resources permitting the provision of a particular service at adequate levels, the level at which the service will actually be provided will be determined in the long run by popular views about acceptable performance in respect to that activity. These views will in turn be determined by a complex and little-understood interaction between the public and the standards evolved by groups professionally involved in the provision of particular services — roads, education, welfare, hospitalization, and so on. Thus, where there are large numbers of people who change their residences from province to province, where there are relatively easy means of communication, and where there are close and constructive relations among persons professionally engaged in particular public functions, we can expect that popular expectations will tend to become more uniform as time goes on. From this point of view then, the federal government can, without inhibiting provincial autonomy, do much to equalize the standards at which provincial and local services are provided by ensuring that the provinces have the financial resources to provide, as they choose, adequate levels of service, by undertaking research and other staff activities relating to provincial and local functions, and by fostering fruitful contacts among officials throughout Canada engaged in the provision of particular services through such groups as the Dominion Council of Health and the various other advisory committees to the minister of health and welfare on specialized health matters.

Can the existing conditional grant arrangements with their restrictions on provincial autonomy be defended as egalitarian devices? As has been pointed out the bias of the conditional grants as a whole is towards health and welfare services and a very strong argument can be made that total provincial expenditures for these functions, including the proceeds from federal conditional grants, are greater than if the provinces had equivalent financial resources available with no strings attached as to their use. Further, federal participation in social assistance and hospitalization has aided enormously in resolving the residence problem to the egalitarian end that needy persons are not denied access to benefits because of their failure to establish legal residence in particular local or provincial jurisdictions. However, the present shared cost programmes have serious deficiencies as equalization devices among the provinces. In spite of the refinements previously mentioned, most of the programmes pay little regard to the relative fiscal capacities of the provinces or their particular needs in respect to particular functions. Further, it may be surmised that the increased expenditure in aided functions in the less prosperous provinces has been induced by the federal government partially at the expense of provincial and local services in which Ottawa does not share, and thus has increased the inequalities among provinces in respect to those latter activities.[43] The present arrangements give the federal authorities relatively little scope of channelling federal money into those expenditures where deficiencies in particular functions are most acute, and Ottawa moneys can be and are used to support facilities in some provinces at a level which others will not attain in the foreseeable future.

The case for provincial autonomy in health, welfare, and education is somewhat different than where the purely regulatory functions of government are concerned. Speaking broadly, in an integrated national economy the existence of different provincial practices is more disadvantageous in regulatory matters than where service activities are concerned. However, in line with the Rowell-Sirois analysis, there is much to be said for a clear-cut delineation of responsibilities between the two levels of government in both kinds of situation.

Unless international crisis makes federalism wholly irrelevant, provincial autonomy as that concept was defined in the Rowell-Sirois Report continues to be a worthy value to be sought through the Canadian federal structure. In the existing Canadian setting there seems no reason to think that we must make the hard choice between the broad social and political values which provincial autonomy can foster and the effective provision of particular provincial and local services.

7   A Different Perspective on Canadian Federalism *

Edwin R. Black
Alan C. Cairns

Traditional interpretations of Canadian federalism have stressed constitutionalism, legalism, the powerful influence of economic factors, and the impact of distinctive geographic and ethnic communities. These interpretations are clearly inadequate. The constitutional approach, with its structural emphasis, fails to

---

43See the surmise of Premier Shaw of Prince Edward Island at the Dominion-Provincial Conference of July, 1960, when he said in speaking of the conditional grants "There remains the doubt. . . whether the improvement in certain fields may not in some provinces have been purchased at the cost of some stagnation or retardation of improvement in other fields, such as education". *Proceedings of Dominion-Provincial Conference*, Queen's Printer, Ottawa, 1961, p. 75.

*From *Canadian Public Administration*, Vol. IX, No. 1, March 1966, pp. 27-45. Reprinted by permission of the authors and publisher. This paper was prepared initially for one of a series of radio lectures and for publication in Louis Sabourin (ed.), *Le Système politique du Canada: Institutions fédérales et québécoises*, University of Ottawa Press, 1968.

explain political behaviour. While closer to real life, the conventional economic wisdom has been too obsessed with the centralist assumptions implicit in attempts to enlarge Ottawa's historic role in managing the economy. Regional aspects of the traditional interpretations seem to be viewed either as self-evident facts whose continued existence requires no further explanation or as inconvenient impediments to national unity which really ought to go away. It seems essential, therefore, to investigate neglected elements of regionalism in order to explain contemporary developments. The deficiencies thus far suggested have been compounded by two divergent ethnic traditions of scholarship. While English-speaking scholars stressed the challenges of nation-building across vast distances, their French-speaking colleagues concentrated on problems associated with "la survivance".

The construction of more adequate explanations requires a fresh perspective which recognizes these salient characteristics of the Canadian polity:

1. Almost regardless of the impact of the "French fact" on the state as a whole, the maintenance of a federal form of government is required by the diversities of the English-speaking communities.

2. Since 1867 Canadians have been engaged in more than the construction of a new state; they have been building provinces and complex series of relationships between governments and societies as well.

3. Economic and social factors respond to political forces just as political forces respond to them.

4. The survival of a federal system depends upon the flexibility of its constitutional process in accommodating demands unforeseen at its birth.

A general preoccupation with discovering forces tending to create an impressive nation-state led many to ignore the creation and effects of social, political, and physical communication networks within the provinces, the growth of regional economies with international as well as national ties, and the burgeoning provincial bureaucratic and other elites which confidently manage state systems bigger in scope, competence, and importance than some foreign sovereignties. It is suggested that adding these perspectives to the more usual approaches will provide better explanations of Canadian politics than those to which we have been accustomed.

Federal systems are characterized by a division of lawmaking and administrative authority between a central government and several regional governments. Each type of government controls some significant aspects of public activity and is supreme within its own jurisdictional sphere. The difficulty of distinguishing boundary lines between governments has customarily required court arbitration the results of which were bound to displease at least one party and its supporters. For much of the past century the Judicial Committee of the British Privy Council had ultimate authority to determine the precise meaning of the powers distributed by the British North America Act. Thus arose the popular Canadian sport of lambasting British jurists who were usually accused of misinterpreting the clear meaning of sections 91 and 92, and particularly the relationship between the peace, order, and good government clause and the enumerated subjects following it. In essence, the British law lords were being asked to settle political questions arising from a changing, pluralist society whose governments were federally organized by a legal document. Much of the legal writing on Canadian federalism seems, however, to demand interpretation of the constitution according to technicalities encrusting the legal framework within and around which the actual system operates.

"Legal answers," Professor Livingston reminds us, "are of value only in the solution of legal problems. And federalism is concerned with many other problems than those of a legal nature."[1] Federalism is translated into governmental forms when a particular constellation of forces leads men to create institutions permitting diverse territorial groups to express themselves politically and to resist incorporation into the homogenizing framework of a unitary state. Logically, then, it is more important to analyse the federal nature of society than to analyse the legal framework it uses to achieve its diverse public goals.

The value of a socio-political approach is emphasized by the experience of Confederation's first three decades. John A. Macdonald and his colleagues had provided the federation with a highly centralized framework. That the new state was a most reluctant federation is shown by the division of functions and revenues and by the superior-inferior legal relationships contemplated between the central and the provincial governments. The concessions made to the pressures of geography, ethnic identities, and previous histories were restricted to as few as possible while the political institutions of the central government took on a strong majoritarian bias. In reflecting the principle of representation by population, the House of Commons was, and is, a highly majoritarian body. The Senate's organization displayed greater fidelity to regional considerations, but its general power and, in particular, its ability effectively to articulate the interests of the provinces was seriously inhibited from the outset. The chief executive officer of the provincial governments was a central government appointee, and the federation's Supreme Court owed its creation in 1875 to the central Parliament. The majoritarianism and centralization built into the legal structure of Canada can scarcely be denied.

It is highly significant that even though Macdonald, its chief architect, presided over this structure for a quarter of a century, it still proved incapable of resisting provincial assertions of local independence. One satisfactory explanation for this development may be found within the context of a new federal regime lacking even as much legitimacy as the former colonies had enjoyed. Confederation was the accomplishment of a small group of elites who neither sought nor obtained popular support for the new undertaking; this aspect of its origins effectively denied the new central government that widespread feeling of patriotic sentiment which it required to struggle successfully with recalcitrant provinces. The Fathers had gambled that the new polity would win legitimacy by its performance, particularly in terms of economic growth and rising standards of living throughout the country. That gamble failed. Within a few years of the union celebrations, economic depression set in and lasted almost

[1] W. S. Livingston, *Federalism and Constitutional Change*, Clarendon Press, Oxford, 1956, p. 1.

three decades; only with the opening up of the prairies and the resultant wheat boom did that prosperity arrive which had been hoped for thirty years earlier. An inevitable consequence of this initial absence of legitimacy was the central government's inability to withstand strong pressures for enlarged areas of provincial self-assertion. From the '80's on, constitutional decisions began to favour the provinces, thus confirming the underlying realities of Canadian society. By 1896, when Laurier assumed office, the political system was established as thoroughly federal in nature — whatever might have been the intentions of the Fathers and their legal draughtsmen.

The course of Canadian federalism has displayed cyclical swings from centralization to decentralization and back again. One should beware, however, of equating centralizing periods with times of social integration. Centralization has been primarily a product of emergencies such as the years of birth, of war, and of depression when the very survival of the country was thought to be at stake. During the two world wars, Canada was largely run as a unitary state with the provinces subordinating their separate claims for a temporary period. But even war did not prove a completely effective solvent of internal differences. While English-speaking Canadians generally answered Ottawa's demands for complete support in the face of external crises, French Canadians were more hesitant; with their much longer identification with North America and the consequent weakening of their ties with Europe, the French-speaking people saw little justification for the demands put upon them by the majority. Both wars were marked by conscription crises which deepened the cleavages between the two main racial groups. The First World War decimated Conservative support in Quebec, with damaging effects on the party system as a whole, while the Second World War was skilfully exploited by Duplessis, whose reactionary regime helped isolate Quebec from the rest of Canada. If the war periods brought the English communities closer together, they did so at the expense of seriously weakening French Canadians' identification with the federal government. The unifying effects of the depression of the 1930's have also been miscalculated. While intellectuals of English expression were fond of arguing that the fluctuations of modern industrialism made federalism obsolete, federal governments at Ottawa were characterized by timid leaderships in considerable contrast to the demagogues elected to power in Quebec, Ontario, and Alberta who were volubly hostile to any accretion of power by the central administration. Thus, even when the facts of social crises seemed to indicate an imperative need for centralized political direction, Canadians have shown little disposition to scrap their regional political systems.

On the whole, Canadian experience gives little credence to the belief that federalism is a transitional stage on the road to a unitary state. While federalism has changed significantly in response to new demands, its basic feature of two levels of government each wielding important powers seems to be durable. Indeed, at the present time, the question is not whether provincial governments can withstand centripetal pressures which would diminish their significance, but whether the federal system can successfully contain the powerful decentralizing pressure welling up from below without losing its essential character.

To survive and to thrive politically, a federation must be flexible enough to adapt to radical changes in circumstances over time. The presence of permissive political styles and of effective techniques for making short-run experimental adjustments in areas such as federal-provincial relations is especially helpful. But federations are dependent in their structures on legal distributions of authority, and constitutional adaptation is generally thought to require legal rather than political or customary procedures. Such legal procedures tend to be cumbersome, time-consuming, and rigid. During the '30's, structural changes were widely desired but neither of the major legal avenues of adaptation — formal amendment or judicial reinterpretation of the constitution — proved to be fruitful directions in which to seek desired reforms. The amending process was too difficult and too permanent, while the courts, dependent on the fortuitous arrival of appropriate cases, were much too unpredictable in their decisions. Lacking the expertise in assessing modern society with which political decision-makers are furnished, the courts exhibit great difficulty in giving shaded responses in complex problem areas, and in Canada they have been largely restricted to the black-and-white approach of ruling legislation either *intra vires* or *ultra vires*. In contrast with the American Supreme Court, which effectively kept the U.S. constitution abreast of societal shifts, the Canadian jurists were unwilling to consider political or sociological aspects of a case, and preferred to rule according to the technicalities of legal construction. The "constitutional impasse" referred to so frequently in the literature of the '30's reflects a despair of ever achieving structural changes in a federal system apparently tied to legal procedures. The courts specialized in delineating jurisdictional boundaries just at the time that public interest seemed to require blurring the boundaries. For these reasons, the courts and the formal amending process have been increasingly bypassed as mechanisms for resolving conflicts in the federal system.

All the more remarkable then, in the face of inadequate legal provisions for adaptation, is the occurrence of more important changes in Canadian federalism during the past quarter century than those of the preceding seventy years. The depression's revelations of the perils of an unregulated economy combined with the war years to foster an enhanced peacetime role for the state. Although the process is not completely clear, an increase in public economic control and much wider public provision of welfare services have been generally correlated in the western democracies with the type of dramatic speed-up in industrialization and urbanization that Canada experienced during the 1940's. The exigencies of fighting the war had led the federal government to assume many of the normal provincial powers, but when the war ended Ottawa proved most reluctant to return these powers to the provinces. Immediately after 1945 federal politicians were seeking votes with fresh fervour, the electorate was demanding more extensive government services, egalitarian sentiments were growing, and the public was largely indifferent to constitutional niceties of federal-provincial dividing lines. No wonder, then, that postwar federal governments exploited their overall dominance in the taxation field in an effort to orient the federation more or less permanently in a centralist direction. Previous concern for provincial autonomy was probably reduced, and an enhanced role for the

federal government was legitimized by the ineffectiveness of provincial governments during the depression which stood in stark contrast with the federal
government's much touted efficiency during the war years.

For the reconstruction period a series of highly centralist programs was
drafted by senior civil servants at Ottawa. Presented as a package at the Reconstruction Conference, these policy proposals were vigorously rejected by provincial politicians, and the federal cabinet had to settle for achieving its objectives
for postwar federalism on an *ad hoc* basis. Although the long-term direction of change was generally understood to be centralist, federal politicians
were content to operate in the short run. They had, so they thought, developed
a going concern. The anticipated postwar depression had not materialized. The
country was prosperous. The prairie revolt of the '30's had subsided into
agrarian reformism in Saskatchewan and conservative business administration
in Alberta. Duplessis had amassed large electoral majorities in Quebec, but his
antipathy to Ottawa was an irritant rather than a threat to the developing
centralization. The Liberals at Ottawa seemed possessed of almost permanent
tenure on the government side of the House of Commons, and to many observers the system seemed stable almost to the point of boredom. That these halcyon
days are separated from the political excitement and uncertainty of the present
by only ten years appears scarcely credible.

The federal structure had adjusted to the wartime crisis chiefly by monarchical
force majeure with the emergency-powers legislation finding retroactive approval
from the courts which evoked a defence-of-the-realm power said to be implicit
in the constitution. Alternatives to the formal amending and judicial instruments of flexibility were found after the war in the new networks of bureaucratic and political collaboration which blurred jurisdictional lines between
governments. A host of committees brought specialist civil servants together
to develop and administer intergovernmental agreements and to discuss exten-
sions of joint endeavours to solve problems outside any single jurisdiction.
Periodic tax rental conferences provided a forum wherein federal and provincial
ministers decided the allocation of the federation's total tax resources for the
next five-year period. By these mechanisms[2] views were exchanged, tensions
eased, and significant changes introduced into the federal system by short-term
agreements capable of ready alteration should circumstances require it. In
short, the practical workings of the federal system in the postwar decades came
to be decided more and more by politicians and administrators who shared a
common interest in making the system work rather than in determining its internal dividing lines. The result was an intertwining of the activities of ten (later
eleven) governments through cooperative arrangements which made the British
North America Act a less and less accurate guide for the determination of
which government provided which service.

The many changes in the working constitution which developed in the post-

---

[2]J. H. Aitchison, "Interprovincial Cooperation in Canada", in J. H. Aitchison (ed.),
The Political Process in Canada, University of Toronto Press, Toronto, 1963; a summary
of federal-provincial taxation arrangements may be found in the Canadian Tax
Foundation's *The National Finances, 1962-63*, Toronto, p. 117.

war period are all the more remarkable when contrasted to the relatively slight impact on the system made by formal and visible changes to the founding document. The levelling of jurisdictional barriers resulted in a "fused federalism" characterized by involvement of the federal administration in virtually all of the provincial areas of "exclusive" jurisdiction: natural resources, social welfare, highway building, higher education, local government, and so on. The Sirois Commission had proclaimed earlier that the "mere importance of a service does not justify its assumption by the Dominion", but this opinion in no wise inhibited the federal government's diligence in discerning some kind of national interest in a great many provincial services in order to justify its intervention. The intervention was primarily accomplished through the mechanism of conditional grants. Close analysis of the conditional grants programs provides little compelling evidence that any consistent definition of the national interest was involved in their development.[3] On the contrary, they seem to have resulted from a series of complex bureaucratic and popular pressures and the desire of federal politicians to gain political capital by aiding popular causes directly. Most striking, however, of all the postwar changes was the virtual solution of the constitutional impasse of the '30's. The most important instruments in its solution besides conditional grants were the tax-rental agreements. These pacts while informal and legally unenforceable,[4] effected a massive shifting of provincial taxation powers to the federal government in return for huge transfer payments without strings attached. Both conditional and unconditional grants programs were accomplished by political agreements supported by a liberal use of the central government's spending power and did not require either constitutional reallocation of functions or formal transfer of fiscal rights from one level of government to another.

Critics of cooperative federalism in this period have seen it as largely a one-way street. While consultations did take place in some areas, the federal government launched conditional grant sorties into provincial fields quite often without even informing those provincial administrations which were supposed to help finance the federal initiatives. The selective nature of federal financial inducements often distorted priorities which the provinces had set up for their own fields of constitutional authority, but there was no *quid pro quo*; the provinces whose policy-making autonomy was effectively diminished by Ottawa's manoeuvres were not compensated with any influence over the exclusive federal areas of policy-making. These tendencies led Professor J. A. Corry to observe in 1958 that the most a province could then hope for was "freedom for minor adventure, for embroidering its own particular patterns in harmony with the national design, for playing variant melodies within the general theme. . . . It is everywhere limited in the distance it can go by having become part of a larger, although not necessarily a better, scheme of things."[5] The determinants

---

[3]D. V. Smiley, *Conditional Grants and Canadian Federalism*, Canadian Tax Paper No. 32, Canadian Tax Foundation, Toronto, 1963.

[4]Bora Laskin, *Canadian Constitutional Law*, 2nd ed., Carswell, Toronto, 1960, p. 659.

[5]J. A. Corry, "Constitutional Trends and Federalism", in A. R. M. Lower, F. R. Scott, *et al.*, *Evolving Canadian Federalism*, Duke University Press, Durham, N.C., 1958, p. 108.

of this kind of federalism he located primarily in an interdependent economy requiring national regulation, the growth of large and powerful enterprises whose attention was focused on the federal government, and to a nationalizing of sentiment, especially among elites.

The pressures toward extension of federal government involvement came almost entirely from English Canada, a sign of potential trouble that was either unnoticed or ignored even when the federal prime minister was a French Canadian. "Pressures towards new federal initiatives are quite indiscriminate," Professor Smiley has observed, pointing out that English-speaking Canadians came to demand leadership and money from Ottawa for a great variety of matters they regarded as worthy national purposes. To this he adds:

> Anglo-Canadians have ordinarily not felt it necessary to demonstrate the administrative or other disabilities of exclusively provincial action or the constitutional appropriateness of their proposals; the case usually goes no further than a demonstration that the subject under discussion is of great importance and *ipso facto* Ottawa should do something about it.[6]

A number of English-speaking elite groups continued to behave as they had during the war — as if they lived in a unitary rather than a federal state. While their actions were influenced by lack of concern rather than any design to destroy federalism, the consequences were clear — a kind of centralization by indirection.

In 1955 Parliament was ramrodded by a cabinet that felt strong enough to seek the indefinite retention of over-riding powers almost the equal of those it had enjoyed during the war.[7] Today the pressures for decentralization have been so fired up by resurgent provincialism that many have questioned the very survival of the federal government as a decisive body. The factors lying behind this change are not easily deciphered because of its recency but some indication of the more important causes can be suggested. Popular commentators have been prone to attribute the change to the new Quebec, but such attribution is incomplete at best. French Canada has made a significant impact on the federalism of the '60's but, even if Quebec had remained quiescent, it is likely that pressures for change emanating elsewhere in the system would have had an almost similar impact.

Relevant factors in the swing from centralization back to decentralization include:

1. A return to peace-time normalcy.

2. An important diminution in the legitimacy of the governing party at Ottawa, especially with respect to any proposed federal initiatives outside its constitutional sphere of jurisdiction.

3. A mid-century decline in the importance of the powers constitutionally

---

[6]D. V. Smiley, "Two Themes of Canadian Federalism", *Canadian Journal of Economics and Political Science*, Vol. XXXI, No. 1, February 1965, p. 86.

[7]For a discussion see: John Meisel, *The Canadian General Election of 1957*, University of Toronto Press, Toronto, 1962, p. 7.

assigned to Ottawa and a corresponding magnification in social importance of the provincial powers.

4. A relatively great increase in the competence and confidence of provincial administrations and a consequent growth in elites who identified their prospects with the fortunes and favours of the provincial governments.

The period of centralization from which the country is rapidly receding was in large part the aftermath of war, depression, and a degree of collectivism inspired by them. As the influence of these crises waned, so did the justification for federal political dominance. The provinces, in continually asserting their needs and rights to more tax money, have had the obvious justification that they and not Ottawa are constitutionally entrusted with authority over most of the expanding areas of government activity. In 1939, federal, provincial, and municipal governments shared almost equally in total government expenditures in Canada. Under wartime pressure the federal share rose to 87 per cent in 1944. By 1963 the federal share had dropped to 46 per cent, the provincial share had risen to 26 per cent, and the municipal was 28 per cent.[8] One recent analysis indicates that if there are no major changes in defence spending and no major reallocation of functions between governments, each level of government will be spending about one-third of the total by 1980 — a return to the pre-war division.[9] Given provincial responsibility for municipalities, such a trend would put two-thirds of the total government expenditures in Canada under provincial jurisdiction.

Much of the federal government's current dominance in the taxation system has been justified by the size of defence expenditures and the need for Canada-wide economic stabilization and growth policies. But in recent years the use of fiscal policy to counter economic fluctuations appears to have declined in significance. The Conservative government's willingness to let the tax rental system expire in 1962 was a major indication of this change. Professor Hood has observed:

> Anti-recessionary fiscal policy is now less capable of providing support for monetary policy than at any time since the war. This feeling derives essentially from the fact that the provinces have so strategic a role in both tax and expenditure policy by virtue of the relative weights of their budgets and from the fact that much of the initiative for changes rests with them.[10]

Canadian defence expenditures are also declining dramatically from their peaks of ten and twenty years ago, and in this connection it might be suggested that defence expenditures today are unlikely to lead to the same degree of voter

---

[8]Canadian Tax Foundation, *The Provincial Finances, 1965*, Toronto, 1965, p. 3.

[9]David Ivor, "General Expenditure Analysis", in Canadian Tax Foundation, *Report of Proceedings of the Fourteenth Annual Tax Conference*, Toronto, 1960, p. 103. For a similar analysis see Eric J. Hanson's discussion on municipal tax problems in the Canadian Tax Foundation's *Report of Proceedings of the Seventeenth Annual Tax Conference*, Toronto, 1963.

[10]William C. Hood, "Economic Policy in our Federal State", *Canadian Tax Journal*, Vol. XII, No. 6, November-December 1964, p. 394.

support for the federal government as equivalent expenditures on education, roads, and even sewers elicit for provincial and local governments.

The federal government's ability to offer uncompromising resistance to provincial pressures for decentralization has been seriously reduced. The capacity of the party system to contain the country's major centrifugal forces and to reconcile them was impaired by the social crises of war and depression, and it has never really recovered. The Diefenbaker revolution of 1957-58 was a climactic revelation of the traditional party system's failure to bring together and give effective expression to the new postwar mixture of disparate social forces demanding recognition. While restructuring is obviously taking place, informed opinion is virtually unanimous that no federal party effectively incorporates the interest and allegiance of the new bureaucratic and political elite in power in Quebec. A by-product of these changes in the party system has been the failure of a legislative majority to emerge in the House of Commons to legitimate the work of the last two governments. The continued lack of majority support has clearly sapped the nerve of the once-confident Liberal Party leaders and diminished the authority which formerly supported federal cabinet ministers in their forays into provincial fields. The atmosphere of uncertainty engendered by this situation inevitably pervades the psychological context of federal-provincial relations. Since the beginning of the '60's, federal political leaders have been unable to radiate a meaningful sense of Canadian purposes with which their citizens could identify. In decided contrast to this central government weakness has been the decisive leadership of the provincial premiers. Most provincial ministries are faced with ineffectual oppositions, and many have enjoyed exceptionally long tenure. While some of it can be described only impressionistically, the combination of federal weakness and provincial strength has undoubtedly strengthened the hands of the provinces in their negotiations with Ottawa.

One's assessments of the Canadian state as a whole should not be too much influenced by the preceding judgments about the relative weakness of governments at Ottawa in the '60's. For nearly a century Canadians have undergone the common experience of living together within the same political community, and in the process something of a common identity and habit of cooperation has emerged. The populace is bound together by numerous country-wide institutional arrangements, both formal and informal, in government, politics, economics, and socio-cultural matters. The importance of the political system as a whole in determining the life opportunities of Canadians from coast to coast and in providing the framework of law and regulation within which men work, struggle, and live has helped to create an identity which, if it be not strongly based on emotion, finds its roots in a curious combination of rational interest and customary self-identification. Rising standards of living and improved communications have widened the range of contact for many Canadians far beyond that of a century ago. Less and less do people live out their lives within the confines of a single community or province; as their experience of other districts and other people expands, so do the standards change by which they assess the performance of particular political systems.

The process of state-building has given rise to a concept of Canadianism which seeks to minimize the disabilities which attend the accidental location of birthplace. This concept, which is a particular expression of egalitarianism, has facilitated satisfaction of some of the poorer provinces' claims, whether stimulated by a sense of historical injustice or by simple envy. Whatever the source of grievance, voters in the poor regions have been unwilling to accept the consequences of poverty in terms of public services. The interaction of inequalities in provincial revenue capacities with the widening frames of reference within which people judge their lot resulted in pressures for federal action to redress the perceived inequities. Funds were transferred from the wealthy to the less fortunate provinces with the federal administration performing the redistribution. Such recent attempts to reduce regional differences in public services, and consequently to minimize the price Canadians pay for their federal way of politics, are but modern manifestations of conventions and understandings which have been fashioned during the past century for promoting the welfare of the various provincial communities. That regional grievances are satisfied, at least partially, through the transfer of funds from the centre outwards rather than by the consolidation of functions at Ottawa reveals the persistent resistance to centralization. It is not for us to assess the degree to which that resistance is based on the hostility of provincial elites to any reduction in their roles, as distinguished from the tenacity of community identification.

The institutional protection of the provinces at the federal capital, originally a task of the politically enfeebled Senate, has been assumed by the cabinet whose members not only are responsible for their government departments but are spokesmen as well for the interests of their home provinces. Appointments to the Supreme Court, the Board of Broadcast Governors, the Board of Transport Commissioners, and numerous other central government institutions reflect to a greater or lesser extent the division of Canada into a number of regional societies and interests whose explicit recognition is essential to the legitimation of central government activities.

The distinctive regional interests and identifications underpinning the federal structure have long been thought to be temporary aberrations from the norm, and doomed to eventual disappearance. Many have agreed with Professor Alexander Brady who argued that the "socio-economic forces of modern industrialism tend to quicken the pace from federation to legislative union".[11] Professor Corry claimed that an interdependent economy with its nationally oriented big businesses would inexorably drive Canadian federalism in a centralist direction; American students like Karl Deutsch have argued similarly that regional emotional identifications become progressively weaker as transcending relationships are created by the forces of economic integration.[12] The thesis that federalism would disappear under the impact of modern economic development has been

---

[11]Alexander Brady, "Report of the Royal Commission on Dominion-Provincial Relations", *Canadian Historical Review*, Vol. XXI, No. 3, September 1940, p. 247.

[12]Karl Deutsch, *et al.*, *Political Community and the North Atlantic Area*, Princeton University Press, Princeton, 1957, Ch. 2 and 3.

a popular one, but its application to Canada's experience encounters serious difficulties and must be reappraised.

The continuing power and influence of the provincial governments in Canadian federalism is intimately related to the importance of their considerable economic functions. The budgets of Ontario and Quebec together come close to equalling one-third of the federal budget, and the expenditures of all provincial governments exert a weighty influence on the country's economy as a whole. All but three of the provinces cover vast land areas whose lavish natural resources are exploited at the sole discretion of the provincial cabinets. The boom in most of the northern hinterlands is subject to their exclusive jurisdiction. Large numbers of frontier towns and communities are spread across Canada from Quebec westward, and their citizens are well aware that their immediate future is tied much more closely to the provincial capitals than to the federal. Such settlements have ever had their eyes focused on provincial legislatures because of their primary responsibility for most elementary and essential services — particularly those of local political organizations, health and sanitation, and communications (at first railways and now highways). The provincial orientation of frontier communities is given extra significance by the distribution of legislative representation which favours the rural districts to a greater extent in the provincial assemblies than in the House of Commons.

Even though the decline in the agricultural portion of the labour force is ironing out some of the differences in the provincial economies, they remain dissimilar in several important aspects. Canada's generally heavy dependence on foreign trade is reflected in the substantial connections which the regional economies have with international markets as well as with each other. The importance of these international links helps to explain the growing international role of the provincial governments, especially with regard to the expansion of their economies. Provincial missions to foreign capitals seeking trade, investment, and technical knowhow are becoming commonplace. Many of these regional enterprises are virtually independent of the country's finance capitals and are able to attract sizeable investment funds from abroad. The large funds which the Canada Pension Plan will make available to the provincial treasuries will augment even the smaller provinces' autonomy from the centre.

That socio-political structures need not be dictated by the alleged integrating effects of an evolving economic system seems to be quite clear. It is worthwhile noting the frontal assault being made on this primitive version of economic determinism in Quebec. From the French-Canadian viewpoint, economic interdependence poses a serious challenge to a distinct culture and must therefore be countered by an even greater emphasis on the provincial government — the only one which French Canadians control. Political integration is not an inevitable consequence of urbanization, industrialization, and rising standards of living. The Canadian experience suggests that whatever integrating effect industrialism does exert is a function of the degree to which the internal economy is interlocking and approaches self-sufficiency. The Canadian economy falls far short of optimum conditions in this respect.

The disparate regional economies are complemented by the existence of distinguishable socio-political communities at the provincial level. The Canadian population is dispersed widely, and the provincial boundaries are still geographically meaningful except on the prairies. Despite improved communications, the country's great distances still require bureaucratic and political decentralization and seriously inhibit the ready dissolution of parochial identifications. While the psychological fibres may be weak in some of these provincial societies, they are sustained not only by their relative geographic isolation from each other but by networks of economic, cultural, and political self-interest. Their identities are reinforced by a large number of institutions organized along provincial lines. Many of these, such as political parties and associations of school teachers and school trustees, can be explained by the need of influencing the provincial political institutions. There are, however, many other organizations with few if any obviously public functions which organize within the same limits: churches, fraternal groups, ethnic associations, model railroaders, and other hobby and handicraft groups. There seems to be no obviously political need for organizing the Junior Red Cross League and the United Nations Associations along provincial lines, but that those associations are so structured is witness to the perceived naturalness of provincial boundaries for such purposes.

What this reveals is that since 1867 Canadians have been engaged not only in state-building but in province-building as well. The existence of separate provincial governments automatically elicits a more intense pattern of communications and associational activity within provincial boundaries than across them. Mechanisms set in motion by the creation of political institutions permit provinces such as Saskatchewan and Alberta which possessed little sociological legitimacy at their birth to acquire it with the passage of time and creation of a unique provincial history.

Probably the most important aspect of province-building concerns the growth of influential provincial elites in politics, administration, and resource based industries. Recent writings on federalism have often remarked on the nationalization of elites as a factor in attenuating provincialism. Such nationalization is based on the high degree of geographical mobility of elites and the tendency of professionals to identify with their counterparts across the country. They belong to national organizations, read the same journals, and attend frequent conferences tending to build up horizontal ties of loyalty. They belong to sub-cultures based on particular skill endowments and seem to have no geographical reference points. While these are important factors, they can be over-emphasized, for it is certain that not all elite groups possess an undiluted national orientation; in fact, elite groups exist which furnish potent incentives and supports for the expansion of provincial power against that of the federal government.

Members of the political elites, and particularly those involved in minor parties with only remote hopes of success in the federal field, may well see the province as the main arena for the pursuit of power. Capable people who are not at all interested in the preoccupations of federal policy-makers are often attracted by the type of activities in which provincial governments engage. The attractiveness of provincial politics for the public-spirited may be enhanced by statistical factors as well. Although the financial rewards are slighter and the duties less demanding the provincial legislatures make available more than twice the number of seats to be found in the House of Commons, and the chances of an able man winning a post in the provincial cabinet are infinitely better than they are at Ottawa.

For many of the new professional groups and some of the old engaged in public service the provincial administrations are almost the only source of employment. Professional educators, forest biologists, electrical power generation specialists, highway engineers, public safety inspectors and scientists, social workers, and large numbers of skilled program administrators find their lives intimately bound up with the size and prosperity of provincial governments. Professor Guindon's provocative interpretation of the new Quebec in terms of a bureaucratic revolution[13] seems especially to the point here. He indicates that the chief sources of dissatisfaction with confederation are found among intellectuals who, in French Canada, provide the legitimating ideas for political movements and among members of the postwar middle class located in the bureaucratic organizations that evolved to meet the problem of mass migration from country to city. In French Canada the bureaucrats are found overwhelmingly in the public and semi-public sectors, and their personal progress and prosperity have depended upon a rapid expansion in the scope and tempo of provincial government activity. Their demands for greatly expanded public support of their activities helped bring on a political crisis in federal-provincial relations that still exists.

The marked improvement in the competence and confidence of the public bureaucracies in almost every province has been a factor of peculiar influence in the course of federal-provincial relations during the past ten years. Civil service reforms, the elimination of patronage, entrance by competition, and security of tenure were introduced first at the federal level but began to spread at a slow pace to the provincial governments. Today the process is almost complete and it is no longer safe to assume that administrative competence resides only in federal hands. In many areas of public activity the real expertise is found only at the provincial level. In the fields of education, natural resource administration, municipal affairs, roads, law enforcement, and local economic promotion, the provincial civil servants will be found to be more numerous and generally more competent than the federal.

The improved quality of their civil services helps to invalidate the assumption, present at confederation and not yet dead, that the provinces should be entrusted with functions of only secondary importance. The traditional English-Canadian view of the federation as a pyramid or hierarchy becomes anachronistic with the location of superior administrative talent within the provincial rather than the federal functional departments. This redistribution of administrative competence has removed much of the paternalism from federal-provincial relations in specific areas, and we can expect provincial administrators and their political superiors to become even less likely to accept federal leadership as they grow more aware of their own capacities.

New political orientations within provincial cabinets are combining with this

---

[13]Hubert Guindon, "Social Unrest, Social Class, and Quebec's Bureaucratic Revolution", *Queen's Quarterly*, Vol. LXXI, No. 2, Summer 1964, pp. 150-162.

growing administrative competence to revolutionize the management of regional economic resources. During the 1950's it seems clear that provincial cabinets formulated their budgets with inadequate views of the future and were seldom prepared to make hard choices allocating different priorities to different services. That picture has changed. More and more cabinets plan their public policies within a broad context of long-range projections and expectations of economic development. Every example of *ad hoc* federal intervention in provincial fields becomes more difficult to tolerate because of the disruption in provincial planning; federal-provincial cooperation, requiring as it now does the fitting together of many governments' plans and expectations, grows more difficult to achieve. Saskatchewan's premier was the first to complain of such federal government disruptions, while the Quebec government, to take another case, has opposed conditional grants programs not only on principled grounds but because it wished to establish its own policy priorities within a coherent development program free of any environmental disturbances caused by federal activity.

The Quebec government's official demands for a general withdrawal of the federal programs in provincial areas and for radical increases in the province's effective fiscal capacity are clearly of major importance for the federal system. Within four or five years the Lesage government demanded and secured more changes in federal-provincial relations than Premier Duplessis had brought about in twenty years. Quebec's silent revolution of the '60's involved a major political breakthrough by a new and influential class which Duplessis had treated with indifference despite its special degree of concern for the consequences of government decisions. The Lesage electoral victory permitted a virtual seizure of power by these once-scorned bureaucrats of the middle class, and a dramatic change in public attitudes toward the role of the state was set in motion.

Under the old regime there had been a widespread distrust of the state. Both Taschereau and Duplessis were hostile to what they regarded as paternalism, while French-Canadian Catholic thought displayed a general preference for private rather than public action to ameliorate social conditions. In any case, the grossly inadequate provincial administration could not possibly have played any role other than the negative one. Bureaucracy, in Weber's sense, simply did not exist, for neither Taschereau nor Duplessis appears to have tried to separate governmental from private affairs. The corruption, nepotism, and incompetence of the provincial government suffered neither electoral disapproval nor moral stigma except in a few relatively ignored journals of opinion.

By contrast, the present government gives state power a positive emphasis as the main collective instrument of modernization and as the main instrument for controlling an economy whose ownership and managerial positions are largely in "foreign" hands. Governmental power is now being used in Quebec with a vigour and élan which makes most other provincial governments and the federal administration seem insipid by comparison. Since maximum exploitation of potential provincial powers requires expanded financial resources and the fullest possible arena for provincial legislative action, demands for more "tax room" and for federal withdrawal from provincial jurisdictions were both logical and inevitable.

Little general attention has been paid to province-building in Canada, or even to the related aspects of regional communication patterns, provincially oriented elites, and the development of overall planning approaches by a number of provincial cabinets. The natural desire of provincial elite groups to reduce planning uncertainties caused by outside interests such as the federal government contains implicit dangers of movements toward provincial autarchies. While speculation is hazardous, the possibility of accentuated economic regionalism must be scouted and guarded against if the federal system is to retain any significant control over its economic future.

While outside our immediate concerns, the recent emergence of the federal-provincial conference as an institution of unique influence in Canadian affairs must be noted. This institution must, in fact, be accounted the only effective instrument available today for the authoritative resolution of some of the federation's most insistent political questions. Some of the probable consequences of this development for the various elected bodies can already be discerned. At the very least, it seems, even further reductions may be expected in the effectiveness of Canadian parliaments as controllers of national and provincial policy-makers. What more may come in connection can only be guessed at.

The capacity of political systems to maintain their legitimacy over a long period of time is not easily addressed. As we have noted, the formal structure of Canadian federalism is reflected and reinforced in scores of other associational patterns both public and private. Political federalism is not the simple creature of existent, social, economic, and geographical forces, but is itself a creative influence. Governments within the system tend to create their own supports through a variety of methods; among them are the charisma surrounding all distant authority, the identification of particular groups with the fortunes of particular governments, the socializing of men to accept their political environment as the natural one, and the complex intertwining of modern government with society that endows any major proposal for change with widespread and often unforeseen consequences for all parts of the structure. This reciprocal relationship between federalism and the society it serves infuses both levels of government with durability and continuity by sustaining the divided system of loyalties that a working federalism requires. But the supports that governments build for themselves remain largely invisible. One level of government may appear to be much the more soundly underpinned by public loyalty until, perhaps, some dramatic event serves to thrust public sentiments for the "neglected" government to the fore. Certainly there lay beneath the apparently stable, centralized federalism of the postwar years a number of potent factors leading to a divergence between the system's form and the demands being put upon it. As we have seen, these demands have overwhelmingly favoured a relaxation of central authority and an increase in the provincial. So insistent has this pressure become that Canadian federalism is undergoing the greatest crisis since its inception.

Prediction of future developments is especially hazardous because for the first time since the depression Canadians are discussing the basic features of their federalism with passion and vigour. This renewed concern for fundamentals and its attempts to find guiding principles is one of the most important manifestations of the changing climate. The Laurendeau-Dunton Commission, the proposals for amending and delegation procedures, the swelling critique of conditional grants and the consequent opting out provisions, the ending of tax rentals, and the frequent demands for a new constitution are all indicative of a revived concern for the basic ground rules governing Canadian federalism. At the time of writing most of the basic issues appear to be open, but how long they will remain so is uncertain.

A new consensus on the purposes and structures of the Canadian state is clearly needed. The continued appropriateness of the federal form of government has been suggested by the analysis presented here. But if the state is to survive as a federation, it must embody a delicate balance between the forces of centralization and decentralization, a balance that obtains not only within the country as a whole but within each region as well. Tension arises not from changes in the relative significance of the push-pull pressures in the system as a whole but primarily from interregional disagreements about their relative importance. The centrifugal forces in Quebec and British Columbia cannot be offset by the centripetal forces in Ontario. That is a recipe for civil war.

To discuss Canada's federal system primarily in legal and economic terms is to misunderstand it from the beginning, and to discuss its problems in terms of ripping up the B.N.A. Act and beginning again from scratch is to hand over the decision to the separatists both east and west. The present structure has exhibited a marvellous degree of flexibility, but if the assumption gains currency that this structure must be scrapped and a new constitution written in both form and substance, then the prospects will not be hopeful. Rewriting constitutional documents is neither a mere exercise in legal logic nor a simple process of transforming a few accounts from this side of the ledger to that. In rewriting such documents one embarks on the reshaping of the entire set of interdependent relationships between government and peoples which has evolved during a full century. If necessary, Canadians will undoubtedly undertake this complex task, but for them to attempt it lightheartedly and without a full understanding of the present system would be an act of political immaturity for which succeeding generations would long curse their ancestors.

8 The Dynamics of Federalism in Canada*

A. W. Johnson

The Conflicting Elements in Federalism

The adjustments that must be made in a federal state in response to change take their form from the very nature of federalism, which — simply and without gloss — is a form of government designed to get the best of two worlds: the advantages of a unified state and the benefits of the diversity which is inherent in the peoples and the regions which make up the state. The compromise between these two conflicting elements in a federal country is institutionalized in a constitution, the centrepiece of which is a division of the power to govern between the central government and provincial authorities. If there is not much governing to be done, the compromise is not too complicated, and if the societies being governed are static, the compromise is likely to be lasting and stable. But remove these two conditions — static simplicity — and the federal state encounters difficulty. The equilibrium between the machinery which fosters unity and that which preserves diversity is upset: the values attaching to unity or to diversity themselves are changed; and even the meaning of unity and the meaning of diversity may be altered.

These two conflicting elements of federalism are found in an exaggerated degree in Canada, for the objectives of diversity are rather two-dimensional here. The first dimension arises out of the linguistic-cultural duality of our country. This has meant that the first and most obvious goal of diversity is the preservation and the promotion of the French culture on the one hand and the cultures of English-speaking Canada on the other, including now not only the culture of the other founding race, the British, but also the heritages of many other peoples.

The second and less obvious dimension of diversity embraces all the other objectives of classical federalism, most of them having to do with the goals of a pluralistic society. In such a state a diversity of values and interests and social units is to be found, with the institutions of government having been designed to preserve this diversity. Federalism is one such institution. The development of a monolithic state is less to be feared where federalism prevails; the citizen is able to turn to one government to counteract the actions of another. The ability of the individual to control or to influence government policy is enhanced by virtue of the existence of more than one level of government. Regional and sec-

*From *Canadian Journal of Political Science*, Vol. I, No. 1, March 1968, pp. 18-39. Reprinted by permission of the author and publisher. A paper presented to the annual meeting of the Canadian Political Science Association at Ottawa on June 8, 1967. The text has been revised in detail but not in substance and does not take account of major developments in federal-provincial or Ottawa-Quebec relations since June 1967. The author wishes to acknowledge the very direct and substantial contribution of his colleague, Edgar Gallant, director of the Federal-Provincial Relations Division of the Department of Finance, to the development and presentation of the ideas contained in this paper.

tional differences are more likely to be preserved as are the historical differences between groups and units of government within that society. Similarly differences in economic interests can more adequately be represented in the formulation of public policy where regional governments as well as representatives in national organs of government speak for these interests. All of these elements of pluralism in a federal state are to be found in the several provinces of Canada.

These two dimensions of diversity in Canada have been more or less constant, with the one, the preservation of two languages and two societies, having been the more obvious and the more persistent, and the other, the preservation of a pluralistic society, having been less tangible and rather more fluid.

The objectives of unity, on the other hand, are more or less obvious depending upon the times in which one lives. In times of international crisis, the importance of a common defence against external threats becomes more self-evident. In times of economic crisis, the importance of strong central management of the economy becomes more apparent to the average citizen. In times of political or cultural crisis, the requirements of unity, or at least the cost of disunity, become more evident.

During periods of calm, on the other hand, the objectives of unity are less apparent, more likely to be obvious primarily to those who are expert on or have occasion to concern themselves with the functioning of the country. In times of economic equilibrium it is more likely to be the specialist who understands the importance to all of Canada of the central measures for maintaining economic stability, for increasing the productivity of labour and capital across the country, for enlarging rather than compartmentalizing markets for Canadian products. In times of prosperity it is more the technocrat who understands the underlying mechanism of income redistribution measures, by which the citizen in one part of the country is persuaded to pay taxes to relieve the poverty of others in other parts. In times of comfort and ease, it is the artist or author who is more likely to perceive the importance to Canadian cultural achievements of measures which defend the country against external assaults of a cultural kind. Only if these mechanisms of unity were to cease functioning for an extended period is it likely that the full realization of their importance would be borne in on every citizen.

These conflicting elements of unity and diversity are to be found in any federal state — an obvious proposition, perhaps. The process by which they are reconciled is probably equally apparent — that of shifting power as between the central and the provincial governments or *vice versa*. But to understand fully the mechanisms of adjustment, it is helpful to consider the adjustments to which a country is exposed or may be called upon to undergo.

The Environment to which Canadian Federalism Must Adjust

The extent of the changes which Canada currently is undergoing may appear to be obvious, but I found that an inventory of them gave me a better sense of their magnitude and complexity, and of their effect upon federalism in our country. The dominant change, of course, has been the decision of French Canadians to participate fully in Canadian and North American society and to share in its economic benefits, while at the same time preserving and promoting their unique culture. The price of this change — from the earlier and easier course of preserving the French-Canadian culture through isolation — is profound adjustments, both for French- and English-speaking Canadians. Within English-speaking Canada there have been changes of another sort: the dilution, the adaptation, even the weakening, of the British culture brought about by the immigration since the Second World War of almost two million persons of European and other stock. Within both English- and French-speaking Canada the shifts of population from rural to urban areas, and the substitution in so many regions of industrialization for agriculture, have brought technological, social, and cultural changes which have further disrupted the earlier patterns of life.

Along with these changes there has been a growing obsolescence of the old bonds and the old symbols which united Canadians — both as between English- and French-speaking Canadians and as between the peoples within each of these two societies. The Union Jack, the Commonwealth, the church, the frontier, even connections with one's motherland have little appeal as symbols of unity for the younger people of today. And the institutions which have united us and have the potential for uniting us have come to be taken for granted or have lost their unifying force — the CBC, transcontinental railways, Air Canada, even the common denigration of Toronto and the shared suspicion of Ottawa.

Changes in the Canadian economy also have worked to force adjustments in the machinery of federalism. The balance between the various sectors of the economy has changed substantially: manufacturing and processing have developed to a point that they now outrank by two to one the contribution to Canadian production of agriculture, mining and logging. The regional balance has shifted, too, with much of the West having joined Ontario in the club of the wealthy, leaving the Maritimes and to a lesser extent Quebec striving to achieve their rate of growth. The infrastructure of the economy — transportation, energy, communications, social capital — has been elaborated, and has become a more important if more complicated element in Canada's economic development. Financial markets have grown and developed to the point that national and international capital flows, through a network of financial intermediaries, now provide substitutes for branch banking and direct foreign investment as sources of capital for growth and development.

Along with these social, cultural, and economic developments there has been a significant change in the social ethics of Canadians, and in their tendency to use government to achieve their ends. Governments now are expected to see to it that the economy is kept fully employed, to ensure that it grows at a satisfactory rate, and somehow to enable all regions to share in the growth. They are expected, too, to contribute to the well-being or even the efficiency of the several sectors of the economy and to the infra-structure and the financial markets which serve them. In the field of social policy, income redistribution, through taxes and transfers, has replaced relief cars as the vehicle by which higher-income people contribute to those in lower income brackets. And income redistribution now is supplemented by state welfare measures. In addition, Canadians have added medical and hospital care to education as services which should be removed from the market and purchased by the state for the citizen. And public services generally are thought to be important enough that the residents of richer regions are called upon to contribute to the governments of poorer ones.

These are the changes brought about by internal forces in the Canadian society. Increasingly international pressures too will force — are forcing — changes on Canadian society. The protected domestic market is giving way to larger market areas. The small company is giving way to the international corporation. International capital markets are replacing small and insulated local ones. External influences upon domestic monetary and fiscal policy are being brought to bear through international consultations, as well as through international markets. The concept of equalization is being broadened so that individual Canadians are contributing not only to other Canadians, and to other provincial governments in Canada, but also to the poorer nations of the world. Culturally, the development of satellite communication is bringing and increasingly will bring to Canada the cultures of many nations — not only American — and will subject our cultural development to international tests.

The Forces of Diversity and the Forces of Unity:
a State of Disequilibrium

Curiously, despite the nationalization and even the internationalization of the technological and economic environment in which Canada lives, the forces of diversity have gathered force relative to those of unity. This, of course, is not peculiar to Canada. Provincial functions have grown in importance relative to the functions of the central government: expenditures upon education and health, upon roads and urban development, have multiplied at the very time that economic management, income redistribution, and defence have been losing their glamour. Efforts on the part of the federal government to assume control or at least a measure of influence over provincially administered programs have been stoutly resisted by Quebec, the consistent champion of provincial rights. Other provinces have taken similar positions intermittently, as political personalities or government ideologies or simply concern over centralized decision-making have changed over time.

With these changes, the fiscal power of the provinces has increased relative to that of the federal government, this being the result not only of higher provincial and municipal taxes but also of very large fiscal transfers from the federal to provincial governments. The economic power of certain provinces has increased too, with the consequence that British Columbia, Alberta, and Saskatchewan, in addition to Ontario, now have the fiscal as well as the constitutional independence to pose as antagonists of the federal government as and when they wish.

The engines of unity, on the other hand, have tended to weaken. The threat of external aggression no longer unites Canada, and carping about the personal characteristics of Americans or Englishmen is no real substitute. The British Crown has long since ceased to be looked upon as a protector of the rights of French Canadians and now is regarded as a symbol of unity largely among those English-speaking Canadians who belong to an older generation. Other symbols of Canadian unity, and common institutions across the country, have, as I have said, tended to weaken or to be taken for granted. New engines of unity, in the form of common public services such as nation-wide social security programs and projects like the Trans-Canada Highway, have in no small measure been transformed into provincial enterprises in the eyes of the public, as provincial governments have learned how to turn conditional federal grants to their advantage.

Paralleling, and partly as a consequence of, this growth in the relative power of those engines of diversity, the provincial governments, has been a growing conflict between the two levels of government. The role of the state has so increased that it is scarcely possible for the federal government to exercise its powers without affecting provincial programs, or for provincial governments to occupy their jurisdiction without affecting federal policies. The federal government cannot use monetary and fiscal policies to stabilize the economy without employing taxes which the provinces want for their purposes or without affecting through monetary policy the rate at which the provinces and their municipalities must borrow. It cannot seek to influence the rate of economic growth through the use of tariff, tax, and expenditure measures without affecting the regional industrial development measures of the provinces. It cannot use the tax-transfer mechanism — a combination of income tax and income maintenance measures such as family allowances and old age security payments — to redistribute income without its having an effect on provincial welfare programs.

The provincial governments, in their turn, cannot, because of their very fiscal power, make tax and expenditure and borrowing decisions without affecting the stability of the Canadian economy. They cannot exercise their jurisdiction over education, over their resources, or over the various aspects of property and civil rights — be it health, welfare or the regulation of financial institutions — without affecting the rate of growth of the economy. Nor can they undertake regional economic development programs without having an effect upon the allocation of resources in Canada, and an indirect influence upon parallel federal measures.

The inevitable frictions which accompany the side-by-side existence of federal and provincial programs have been exacerbated by alleged invasions of provincial jurisdiction by the federal government and *vice versa*. The federal power has been used, knowingly and intentionally, to alter provincial priorities. It has sometimes been used, too, unknowingly and unintentionally, in such a way as to affect the very administration of provincial programs. Similarly the provinces, or certain of them, have sought by hard political pressure and negotiation to lay claim to jurisdiction long accepted as being federal — the mineral rights of Hudson Bay, for example, and certain aspects of international relations.

These are some of the general tensions in present-day Canadian federalism. To them must be added the paramount pressure upon our federation: the presence in Canada of a French-Canadian minority which is no longer prepared to accept a subordinate role in Canadian society. Here one finds the strongest desire for diversity. Here one finds the smallest attachment to the symbols of unity. Here one finds language and culture adding inflammation to the common suspicion of Bay Street and St. James Street, Westmount and Ottawa. Here one finds a determination to protect the integrity of the French-Canadian social entity from the erosion which would be the product of an unthinking drift toward centralization.

Somehow, in the face of and out of all these social and economic changes, all these federal-provincial and Quebec-Ottawa frictions, must come a new balance between the conflicting elements of unity and diversity in our Canadian federation. The question is which way to go.

Alternative Directions for Canadian Federalism

There is no shortage of prescriptions. But there are, it seems to me, only four main alternatives. One is to move toward more centralization of government, on the assumption that diversity must ultimately suffer anyway as we become more a part of the North American and ultimately of the international community. The second is to strengthen the regionalization of government, generally, on the assumption that the advantages of unity can be preserved even through a weakened federal government, with perhaps some buttressing from intergovernmental machinery or agreements. The third alternative is to provide for a greater regionalization of government in Quebec only, on the assumption that a higher degree of centralization would prevail in the rest of Canada, and the parallel assumption that the advantages flowing from this centralization would not seriously be diminished by the Quebec decentralization either for the country as a whole or for Quebec in particular. The fourth alternative is somehow to marry the stronger regional governments and a strong central government — the role of government as a whole having increased   on the assumption that strong federal and provincial governments can somehow reconcile and harmonize their priorities, policies, and administrative practices.

I shall consider each of these alternatives in turn, not with a view to determining which of them is to be preferred, but rather with a view to identifying the essential characteristics of each alternative and the questions or the problems which seem implicit in it. It should then be possible better to consider how these alternatives would function in balancing the forces of unity and diversity in Canada, not only now but in the future.

The Alternative of Centralization

The case for greater centralization, on the face of it, is very strong. There *is* greater interdependence as between the provinces of Canada, today, however much it may be obscured by the very complexity of the mechanics of interdependence: and the growing interdependence of the nations of the world will likely strengthen intra-national interdependence before the national state is eroded by the growth of the international community. The structure and the scale of Canadian industry is geared to Canadian markets and to Canada's trade and other policies. The infrastructure of our economy has been developed to serve the country as a whole, not just a group of more or less discrete regions. The social ethics of Canadians have developed on a national basis too: the citizen now is contributing to the welfare of other citizens 3,000 miles away, not just to his neighbour. The institutional structure serving Canadians — governmental, private and professional — is to a considerable extent country-wide in character. Above all, Canada is an open economy and an open society, vulnerable to external pressures of all kinds; to subdivide the Canadian community would be to make it even more open and more vulnerable.

Having said this, I think it is now generally accepted that progressive and general centralization simply will not work in Canada. The accumulation of steps in this direction, such as those which resulted from the programs of postwar reconstruction and from the social reform of the last two decades, has contributed to friction and disequilibrium in our federation. Quebec would rather separate than be submerged, and the peoples and the premiers of English-speaking Canada would have to become uncharacteristically submissive before a substantial centralization of government could be realized. Indeed, when carried to its logical conclusion, centralization defeats the very objective of federalism — pluralism; by its nature it cannot be expected to demonstrate those characteristics of flexibility which are so important in a diverse and divergent country.

The Alternative of General Decentralization

The second alternative, the progressive decentralization of government powers throughout Canada, has many attractions too. It would meet the demand of Quebec governments that more of the powers of government be concentrated in Quebec City, thus better enabling Quebeckers to be "maîtres chez nous". Equally, it would enable other provincial governments to pursue more vigorously the regional or provincial economic development programs to which all of them now are committed. It would lend itself to the preservation of cultural and historical differences, the strength of which is manifest to anyone who travels across Canada. It would make it easier for all provinces to develop their own priorities and to adapt their public services to the peculiar needs of their people. Conflicts with national economic and social policies would be minimized by virtue of the diminished role of the federal government.

But the cost of this alternative, too, is high. In economic terms, the vehicles of national economic policy would tend to remain static, or be diminished, as provincial economic powers grew. Federal fiscal policy would decline in importance as the fiscal resources of the central government were progressively transferred to the provinces; increasingly the voluntary participation of provincial governments would be essential to the development of a meaningful national fiscal policy. Monetary policy would come to have more effect upon provincial financial and developmental policies, as reliance upon this tool of policy grew and as the scale of provincial fiscal activity was enlarged; increasingly the provinces would expect to be consulted at least on the direction if not on the details of credit policy. Trade policy, too, would tend to become the subject of federal-provincial discussion, and perhaps negotiation, as the provinces sought to adapt this instrument to their several development goals. Provincial regulation of financial institutions would proliferate, and there would be a strong temptation to shape the investment policies of these institutions to serve provincial ends.

The potential economic cost of general and progressive regionalization is the most evident cost of this course for Canadian federalism. A coherent and an effective national economic policy would be possible only through intergovernmental agreement. Decisions on fiscal and monetary matters, difficult enough in a large central apparatus, would tend to become halting, uncertain, and muddied by compromise, as the several governments sought a consensus. Regional economic policies would tend to proliferate and the misallocation of resources would tend to increase, as each region pursued its own development. The Canadian government would be less and less able to speak with authority and assurance in international councils, with all this would imply for international confidence in Canada's ability to manage her own economic affairs.

Socially and culturally the same fragmentation would tend to emerge. As the provinces pursued independent social and education policies, there would be less and less sense of being a Canadian. As people moved between provinces they would be irritated by substantial differences in public services and their feeling for Canada would diminish as their irritation increased. Independent broadcasting and communications policies would weaken the sense of cultural unity in the country. The diminished sense of Canadianism would test the willlingness of British Columbians and Ontarians to contribute toward equalization payments to the poorer provinces, and ultimately, perhaps, even to income maintenance payments to individuals. This would be the consequence not only of a decline in the sense of mutual responsibility, but also of a suspicion that the transfer payments were not being used wisely or that they were being used to enhance the competitive position of the recipient provinces.

I think social scientists would agree that the equilibrium between the forces of unity and diversity must lie somewhere between these two extremes of centralization and decentralization. The consequences of these alternatives, however, should be borne in mind, for they illustrate vividly some of the problems and the pitfalls which must be avoided if other approaches are to be successful.

Special Status for Quebec

The third way to balance the forces of unity and diversity in Canada — the first of the two which lie between the extremes of centralization and decentralization — is to provide for a greater regionalization of government in Quebec only. This increase in regionalization could take the form of a special status for

Quebec within the present federal structure, or it could call for giving to that province associate state status. In either case a substantial measure of centralization would be expected to prevail in the rest of Canada.

The appeal of *statut particulier* is understandable. Quebec is *not* a province like the others, however much the other nine may differ from one another, and one should reasonably expect therefore a differentiation in particular government programs as between that province and the rest of Canada. Moreover, if progressive regionalization in the whole of Canada would seriously weaken the central government, it does not follow logically that the same price would be paid if that course were to be followed only in Quebec. The questions to be asked, therefore, are of a different order, having to do largely with the major shifts which would be involved under *statut particulier* in the burdens and benefits of confederation, and in the patterns of influence inherent in our machinery of government.

There are four elements to *statut particulier*, if I understand this approach to federalism correctly. First, under this proposal the government of Quebec would assume full responsibility for most if not all federal-provincial programs and would receive from the federal government a fiscal transfer which would fully compensate the province. The government of Quebec would similarly be compensated for new federal-provincial programs — such as medicare — whether or not the province undertook a program similar to that required in other provinces. Secondly, the government of Quebec would under this approach assume responsibility for certain purely federal programs, principally the family allowance and old age security income maintenance programs, and again would be compensated by means of a fiscal transfer from the federal government. Thirdly, the government of Quebec would be given the right to be consulted in respect of other federal policies, including fiscal, tariff and trade policies, and probably monetary policy. I am not entirely clear from what has been said by the proponents of this approach just how many areas of policy would be involved in these consultations or precisely what the process of consultation would entail. The importance of what *is* meant in terms of the constitutional arrangements called for will be self-evident. Fourthly, the government of Quebec might expect to assume certain aspects of federal jurisdiction, such as the right to conclude international arrangements, at least in fields of provincial jurisdiction and certainly to develop something of an international personality. These I think are the principal propositions which have been advanced at one time or another by the people advocating *statut particulier*.

This approach to the balancing of the forces of unity and diversity in Canada is one of the important alternatives being considered in Quebec; as such it deserves serious discussion in the rest of the country. I content myself here with an attempt to identify some of the questions which would arise, the problems which would be encountered, if an effort were made to adapt Canadian federalism to this model. I realize that in so doing I display one of the more wearisome traits of the civil servant, that of cocking a critical eye at a new idea. I can only plead that it is in the very nature of my training to search out the consequences of proposals in order adequately to examine their feasibility.

Moreover the capacity of this structure to adapt itself to the shifting forces, indeed the shifting requirements of unity and diversity, in Canada can only be judged by this kind of evaluation.

The first question I have identified has to do with the effect of *statut particulier* upon the efficiency of economic policy in Canada, and upon the distribution in different parts of the country of the benefits and the burdens of economic policy. As conceived by its authors, the effect of *statut particulier* on fiscal arrangements would be to transfer 100 per cent of the individual income tax and anywhere between 50 and 100 per cent of the corporation tax to the government of Quebec. This would mean that the effect of federal tax measures, whether used for stability or for growth, would be felt largely in the provinces other than Quebec, while the economic benefits of these measures would be felt across the whole country. Quebec's use of its extra share of the income taxes would also be felt across the country, albeit indirectly, but the Quebec legislature, not the Parliament of Canada, would be the organ of government responsible for these policies. To the extent, therefore, that federal policies continued to be relied upon as the balance wheel of the economy, the people and the governments of the other provinces would have to be prepared to accept the application of these policies in their part of Canada, though not in Quebec, and rely upon the voluntary co-operation of the government of Quebec for the application of similar policies in that province. The same reasoning would apply, of course, to the expenditure side of fiscal policy, given the additional expenditures that would be financed in Quebec from that province's extra share of the income taxes.

Federal monetary and trade policies, unlike fiscal policy, would continue to apply in the whole of Canada, one gathers. However, they would be formulated in the context of special consultations with Quebec, unless, of course, the other provinces were to insist upon similar rights. A good deal would turn upon the meaning of consultation. If it were to mean that Quebec, or in the alternative any provincial government, were to have the right to express its views on federal economic policy, the situation would not be too dissimilar from the present. If on the other hand, there were to be some moral or constitutional obligation upon the government of Canada to gain the consent of Quebec — as is sometimes suggested by the provinces with respect to the level of federal income taxes — then it is difficult to visualize any region in Canada being prepared to give Quebec a priority voice in these economic policies. If this analysis is sound, then *statut particulier*, in these areas of economic policy, would tend to lead to general regionalization, the consequences of which I have already considered.

The same analysis would apply to regional economic policies. *Statut particulier*, according to its authors, would call for Quebec's exercising full control over all federal regional development policies, including, presumably, ARDA, ADA, and similar federal measures. Some draw the further inference that to make economic sense Quebec should also have a voice in general economic policies — fiscal and credit, tariff and trade, and manpower training and mobility — since regional economic measures can function properly only if they operate in harmony with these general policies.

Special status in the field of regional economic policy, therefore, could come to mean the use by the government of Quebec of a whole range of special powers for the purpose of influencing its industrial and resource development: its larger share of the corporation tax, its control over special federal regional measures, its right to consult with the central government on federal economic policy, as well as the more familiar loan, guarantee and industrial estates programs to be found in all provinces. The question implicitly raised by such a regime will be obvious: given the different economic interests of the several provinces of Canada, and given the keenness of competition between them for industrial and resource development, would *statut particulier* be acceptable to the people and the governments of the other provinces or would it lead instead to general regionalization?

A second important question about *statut particulier* is its effect upon social policy and upon the distribution of the benefits and burdens of the several federal and federal-provincial programs involved. Shared-cost programs in the fields of health and welfare already have been the object of a good deal of discussion; indeed Quebec now enjoys special status in respect of the well-established programs in this field — at least until other provincial governments take advantage of a federal offer under which they too could assume full fiscal responsibility for the major health and social assistance programs. New federal-provincial programs, on the other hand, have not provided any special option for Quebec: that province like all others must start a universal and public medical care program, to use this example, in order to qualify for the new federal medical care grants. And Quebec like the other provinces has been told by the federal government that when its medical care program is well established, new fiscal arrangements will be considered under which it could assume full fiscal responsibility for its program. To give Quebec special status in respect of new programs such as this would mean offering to the government of that province full federal compensation, whether or not a qualifying program were started. For this system to work, however, the other provinces would have to refrain from asking for similar treatment, and Parliament would have to be prepared to legislate accordingly. For to offer the same option to all provinces would in effect be to offer them unconditional grants — some $360 million in the case of medical care, a temptation I can scarcely see the provinces resisting — or Parliament to withdraw the offer altogether. Put more generally, the logical conclusion of the system proposed is either for Parliament to refrain altogether from trying to stimulate new country-wide health and welfare programs or for Parliament to extend an unconditional fiscal benefit to Quebec only.

The extension of *statut particulier* to social policies which are purely federal — essentially the income redistribution measures — would raise a different aspect of the benefit-burden question. Here the proposal is that the government of Quebec would become the sole agency responsible for income redistribution measures in Quebec, with federal income maintenance programs such as family allowances and old age security pensions being replaced by Quebec government measures. The only official proposal which has been made calls for the transfer

to the government of Quebec of most federal income redistribution measures —
including both the family allowance and old age security payments to persons,
and federal equalization and other payments to the provincial government —
and provides that the government of Quebec would be compensated by the
transfer to it of 100 per cent of the federal income tax on persons and much
of the tax on corporations.

The advocates of this form of particular status recognize that tax revenues
from the rest of Canada would have to continue to flow into Quebec, in one
way or another, if taxes in that province were not to rise as a result of the
assumption by the provincial government of full responsibility for income
redistribution within its borders. It is well known that income in Quebec is
below the national average, with the result that federal income redistribution
measures, which apply automatically across Canada, now result in a net inflow
into Quebec of some $200 million a year (1967-68 figures). The suggestion is,
therefore, that the Parliament of Canada should continue to be responsible for
making payments to the government in Quebec (preferably by means of tax
transfers), but that it should forego any constitutional right to make payments
to persons in Quebec. Thus the disposition of the contributions of taxpayers
outside of Quebec toward income maintenance within Quebec would be
solely within the discretion of the government of the province. The question, it
will be evident, is whether Canadians outside of Quebec would willingly
accept the proposition that they ought to make contributions to maintain the
revenues of the *government* of Quebec, but that they ought not to make
contributions to maintain the incomes of the *people* of Quebec.

The second question raised by this aspect of *statut particulier* also concerns
Canadians outside of Quebec. Would the politicians in other provinces refrain
from asking for the same privilege Quebec politicians would be receiving,
namely the right to write and send all family allowance and old age security
cheques? If they did not — if they too wanted to assume responsibility for
these programs — the federal government's role in income redistribution
gradually would be dismantled. Such a prospect raises even more fundamental
questions than does *statut particulier*. For income redistribution, through a
combination of taxes and transfer payments, has come to be considered one of
the principal characteristics of nationhood and to the citizen one of the more
obvious evidences of citizenship; it is doubtful that this tax-transfer mechanism
could be dismantled without jeopardizing one of the unifying strands of the
Canadian community.

The third question that particular status for the government of Quebec
could raise would develop from the accretion in the fiscal power of the province,
resulting from the transfer to it of certain federal powers such as those just
discussed. Currently the federal government equalizes and stabilizes the revenues
of *all* provinces, under a kind of fiscal income test, universally applied. Such
an arrangement is consistent with a form of federalism under which all provinces
have similar constitutional powers. Under *statut particulier*, however, the government of Quebec would have superior constitutional powers in relation to those
enjoyed by other provinces — for example, its special ability to influence

Canada's economic policy and its competitive advantages in the field of industrial and economic development. One is driven to wonder whether these present intergovernmental arrangements would persist in the face of this new balance of power. Would there arise in the minds of other provincial governments, for example, the question as to whether Quebec was in a position to combine its special fiscal status with the equalization payments, toward which the citizens of the other provinces contributed, to finance competitive tax or expenditure incentives to industry? Put more generally, would intergovernmental arrangements, under which all provinces benefit and contribute equally, persist or would special fiscal status enjoyed by one provincial government force a readjustment designed to bring into balance the fiscal power and the fiscal responsibilities of all governments?

The particular status approach to federalism would raise questions concerning the machinery of government in Ottawa, as well as those concerning intergovernmental arrangements. Under the system proposed, as I understand it, Parliament would no longer have jurisdiction, so far as the people of Quebec were concerned, with respect to income redistribution measures, new federal-provincial programs, or regional economic development, to take three examples. Moreover, under some formulations the Quebec government would be recognized as the responsible spokesman for the views of Quebeckers on purely federal economic policies. In effect, therefore, cabinet ministers in the Quebec government would have replaced Quebec members of Parliament as the responsible spokesmen for the views of Quebeckers on a wide range of matters which had been federal, and which would remain under federal jurisdiction in respect of the other provinces. What adjustments would be required in the machinery of government to make it consistent with these new arrangements is a complicated question, which I leave to constitutional experts. But it seems evident to the layman that the Parliament of Canada would come to legislate on two classes of questions: those in which it had jurisdiction throughout Canada and in which Quebec MP's had a vote, and those in which the opposite was the case. The broader the range of responsibilities transferred to the government of Quebec, the more Parliament would be legislating in respect of the nine provinces only, with the Quebec legislature legislating in respect of Quebec. The effect of this transfer of powers, if carried to the conclusion advocated by some, would be a relatively independent Quebec, associated with the rest of Canada to the extent that it was advantageous to do so. Parliament would legislate for the two parts of Canada only in respect of such matters as tariffs and trade, currency and monetary matters, and presumably defence.

This leads to my final, and to me the most fundamental question about this direction for Canadian federalism. What would be the reaction of Canadians to the diminution in the degree of pluralism implied under *statut particulier*, by comparison with that provided for under the present constitutional division of powers? For Quebeckers the new regime would mean a shift to their provincial government of certain powers which now lie within the central government's domain or are shared with the federal government. Such a shift would imply both that Quebeckers would to a greater degree be "maîtres chez nous", and correspondingly that they would be the subjects of what would be more like a unitary provincial state. For Canadians in other provinces, too, *statut particulier* likely would lead more in the direction of a unitary state, as it became easier and more convenient to centralize powers in Ottawa. Quebec would no longer be in the vanguard of the forces of diversity, and of the remaining provincial governments so many are so small that it would be difficult for them to oppose any trend toward centralization.

So Canada might well be faced with a paradox: in an effort to strengthen the forces of diversity in Canada, through greater regionalization of government in Quebec, the nation might end up by diminishing the forces of pluralism.

The Associate State

This result is almost explicit, I would think, in the other variant of greater regionalization of government in Quebec — the associate state proposal. The essence of this alternative, if I understand it correctly, is to create two virtually sovereign states, one English and one French, and then to provide for the delegation by them to a new confederal body of certain defined and limited powers. Some of the advocates of this approach would assign to the confederal body roughly those powers given up by the members of the European Common Market; others would assign it broader powers, including trade and monetary policy and international relations. Whatever the case this approach seems to assume a centralization of powers in both states — a kind of "dual centralism".

Most of the questions which arise in respect of *statut particulier* would be resolved under the associate state approach. For there would no longer be a federal state or federal machinery, as we know it, within which a new balance would have to be found between the influence of Quebeckers and the people of other provinces. According to the authors of this proposal each state would influence equally the common economic policies; they would be developed through negotiations within the new confederal apparatus. Each state would have its own regional development policies, subject of course to the agreed economic policies. Each would have its own income redistribution system and its own social security measures. In short, under this approach the machinery of government would be adjusted in a quite fundamental way: by substituting for the federal Parliament and government of elected representatives a confederal apparatus operated by delegates appointed by the government of the two member states. Mutual self-interest would be relied upon to force a reconciliation of the conflicting interests of the two states.

The associate state approach poses, not the problems of adjustment within a federation if this understanding of the proposal is correct, but rather the question as to whether the needs of mutual interdependence would be sufficient to guarantee, in the face of the influence of our single powerful neighbour, the creation and then the survival of a new confederal country. A common economic market is assumed, for example. With such a major division in the country, however, the proponents of the associated states would have to consider whether British Columbia and the Prairie provinces would not prefer a common market with the United States to one which included Ontario and possibly the new state of Quebec. And they would have to consider too whether the old ties of the Atlantic provinces to the New England states would not impel these provinces in the same direction. In the field of social policy, it would be equally logical to consider whether the English-speaking state would continue to feel under an obligation to provide equalization payments or transfer payments to the state with which it now had to negotiate common economic policies. Or would English-speaking Canadians consider that Quebec under these circumstances was too independent a nation to qualify for equalization and too rich to qualify for foreign aid? It seems to me, in other words, that the preoccupations of the new states would not be those of today; they would be with their new status in relation to one another and in relation to an increasingly interdependent world.

Supposing, however, that the two states *were* to be established and were to function as their advocates suggest, the second question is whether the new state of Quebec would in fact gain the degree of independence its authors anticipate. The economy of Quebec would be more exposed to external influences than Canada's now is; economic logic would suggest that the governors of the new state would discover that control over monetary and fiscal policy would not be sufficient to enable them to follow a truly independent economic policy. Similarly they could be expected to find that control over the institutional repositories of Quebec savings would be subject to external contraints: rigid regulation of Quebec financial institutions might well reduce the inflow of capital from Canada and the United States, even to the extent that total investment in Quebec might decline. More important, the advocates of the associate state might find that the limitations of an open society could extend even to the promotion of the French language and culture — that the government of Quebec might be more inhibited than it has been, for example, about legislating with respect to the use of the French language in private business. For unless the rate of economic growth were to increase in Quebec — and it could indeed decline if it were subject to more protection or more direction — per capita income would decline relative to that elsewhere in North America, and increasing numbers of Quebeckers might choose to migrate to English-speaking areas. Only a return to a closed society, this line of reasoning suggests, would insulate Quebec from the constraints of an open economy and an open society. It is even possible that the presence as neighbours of 215 million English-speaking people might impose similar if less powerful constraints on the development of the French-Canadian culture within Quebec, bearing in mind that the new English-speaking Canada would no longer have any sense of obligation concerning the protection or preservation of that culture. Similar but more powerful constraints could be expected to operate in respect of Quebec's influence in international affairs.

Pursuing this logic, the new English-speaking Canada would be faced with similiar constraints upon its independence. But its will to survive would have been weakened, in part because of the greater similarity between the cultural traits of English-Canadians and those of their American neighbours, and in part because of the newly exaggerated or newly emphasized divergence between the economic interests of Ontario and those of eastern and western Canada. Even the advantages of regional diversity might not be preserved if the nine remained together: the preoccupation with survival would almost certainly require a greater centralization of power, and this would militate against even this advantage of survival.

The creation of associated states, then, if this analysis is sound, would not be the product of a shift in emphasis between the forces of unity and those of diversity *within* Canadian federalism. Rather it would involve the termination of confederation, and the creation of two new states, one of them a unitary state and the other either a unitary or a federal state, but with the two federated as closely as negotiations within the confederal apparatus would allow. Such an approach, it will be evident, really falls outside my framework of analysis, which was to examine how an equilibrium is established between the forces of unity and diversity within a single federal state.

Strong Regional Governments and a Strong Federal Government

Statut particulier, then, remains as one of the two alternatives which lie between progressive and general regionalization and progressive centralization of government in Canada. The other alternative which is being currently advocated is a marriage between a strong federal government and strong or stronger provincial governments. At first sight this proposition appears to be self-contradictory: if regional governments are to grow in strength, it must surely be at the expense of the central government. The advocates of this alternative point out, however, that this need not be the case: the role of government generally has grown so greatly that it is possible to have a federal government as strong as it has been, or as it is, while at the same time strengthening the role of the provincial governments.

It must be acknowledged that the marriage of governments, like the marriage of people, is the untidiest of all solutions. The respective powers of husband and wife, even if spelled out in some detail in a marriage contract, will vary over time as the family grows, as the husband's occupational responsibilities increase, as the wife's interests change and expand, and as both are thrown together again when the children leave the home. Nor will their responsibilities be mutually exclusive: the husband's decisions concerning his job will affect the family's finances and hence the manner in which the children are reared; the wife's decisions concerning the family will in turn affect the family's finances and hence the husband's occupational aspirations. Only if the family becomes monolithic — if either husband or wife somehow submerges the personalities of the other members of the family — does it become unequivocally clear how marriage works.

So it is with central and provincial governments in a changing federal state, argue the advocates of this fourth approach to Canadian federalism. No matter how carefully, or recently, the division of powers has been drawn, the exercise by the central government of its powers inevitably will affect the activities of provincial governments and *vice versa*. Constitutional lawyers perceived this long ago, it is pointed out, when they developed the "aspect theory": there will be aspects of provincial legislation which will touch upon federal powers and *vice versa*; only the "central tendency" of the legislation can be used as a guide to its constitutionality. The only escape from this untidiness is a unitary state — achieved in Canada either by centralization or by separation.

The advocates of the strong central-strong regional government approach hold that the present division of powers, with some modification, is capable of serving as a satisfactory framework within which the forces of unity and diversity could adjust over time. Some would modify the division of powers fairly substantially, through constitutional amendment; others less so. But whatever the case, most advocates seem to hold that the division of powers must be stated generally enough to make possible adjustments over time, as society and technology change, as the role of government grows, and as the forces of internationalization advance.

This approach to federalism calls, secondly, for a reversal of the cumulative influence the federal government has come to have, through shared-cost programs, over provincial government decisions. And it calls for a greater respect on the part of the federal government than it has often displayed in the past for those areas of provincial jurisdiction which are critical to the preservation and the promotion of cultural diversity, in particular education. The recent proposal of the federal government to transfer to the provinces fiscal resources to enable them to assume full responsibility for well-established health and social assistance programs, and the new program of fiscal assistance in respect of higher education, illustrate the mechanisms by which this shift in emphasis would be acccomplished.

It is not entirely clear what the strong central-strong regional government advocates would do about new federal-provincial programs. Some of them argue that the federal government should refrain altogether from using its spending power to induce the provinces to undertake new programs within their jurisdiction — that it should use this power only to make unconditional grants to the provinces. Others argue that it should initiate new federal-provincial programs only when a clear provincial consensus in favour of them has emerged. Still others argue that federal-provincial programs remain one of the important vehicles by which the forces of unity are renewed in Canada and that the federal government should employ this vehicle when Parliament has decided that it is in the national interest to do so. Whatever their views about the manner in which the spending powers should be used, the proponents of this approach would avoid a cumulative centralization of powers by transferring to the provinces full fiscal responsibility for continuing federal-provincial programs, once they had become well established.

Thirdly, the powers of the central government, to look at the other end of the balance, would also be strengthened under this approach to the adjustment of the forces of unity and diversity in Canada. Its authors point out that adherence by the federal government to the spirit of the constitution would give it a stronger base from which to resist provincial invasions of federal jurisdiction. The constitution would be used both ways, in other words: as a basis for resisting federal raiding of provincial jurisdiction, and *vice versa*. One important element in the strengthening of the federal power would be a return by the federal government to that primary principle of public finance and of government which holds that "the government which spends is the government which should tax"; under such a regime, the provinces would have to increase their income taxes whenever they needed the revenues rather than expect the federal government progressively to reduce its income taxes.

A fourth element in the strong central-strong regional government approach is the suggestion that the federal government would be expected to adapt more of its programs to regional needs and regional differences. The principle that all federal measures must be capable of equal and similar application in all regions is rejected by the spokesmen for this approach as being invalid in certain areas of public policy: they point out that in fact there have been regional programs for years, such as the Prairie Farm Rehabilitation Act and the Maritime Marshlands Reclamation program. Thus the federal government would and should as a matter of policy adapt its institutional structure to the important differences which exist in the country.

Finally, the advocates of strong central-strong regional government propose as part of their system that the federal government should adopt an even more vigorous bilingual-bicultural policy in governing Canada. The federal civil service should be bilingual, in Ottawa and in other areas where Canada's two languages are spoken; the nation's capital should be made a model of bilingualism and biculturalism; French should be the language of instruction in those schools in Canada where there are enough French-Canadians to warrant it; and French or English should be taught in schools throughout the country as second languages.

These, I think, are the principal elements in the strong central-strong regional government approach to federalism.

While the advocates of this approach seem neither to be disposed to generalize nor to advance their views in the form of a general theory, there are I think certain generalizations which emerge from what they say. They are arguing, with respect to the first dimension of diversity in Canadian federalism, the preservation of pluralism, that the provinces should continue to enjoy similar constitutional powers, and that the federal government should continue to exercise constitutional jurisdiction evenly across the country. They are suggesting, moreover, that the powers of the provinces should be such that each province is able to develop its own particular status, but that none should be able to do so at the expense of the others. As for the federal government's role in the preservation of diversity, it is argued that the central government should ensure, through the exercise of its economic and other powers, that personal incomes and provincial government revenues are maintained at reasonable levels across the country, thus enabling the people and the governments of the several provinces to preserve and develop their own regional and cultural characteristics. It is argued, further, that the federal government can also contribute to the goal of diversity by refraining from unnecessary interventions in the affairs of provincial governments, and, more positively, by adapting its own programs to the unique needs and characteristics of the several regions of Canada. As for the second dimension of diversity in Canada — the duality of language and culture — the advocates of the fourth approach are contending that the preservation of the language and cultural rights of French Canadians is as much a job for the Parliament of Canada as it is for the legislature of Quebec. They argue that these rights should be properly protected throughout the country; that Canada as a whole, not Quebec alone, should be the homeland for the French Canadians. The question, they seem to be suggesting, is not whether the government of Quebec should be given particular powers because five-sixths of all French Canadians live in that province but rather whether the French-Canadian society should enjoy the same rights in English-speaking Canada as the English-speaking society enjoys in Quebec. Turning to the forces of unity in Canadian federalism, the advocates of the strong central-strong regional government approach point out that under their regime the federal government would remain a strong national government, able to perform the responsibilities normally associated with a central government. Parliament's powers would remain unimpaired; provincial "raids" upon its jurisdiction would be resisted. It would continue to be responsible for external affairs, defence, the principal elements of economic policy, and those common social and cultural policies which are essential to nationhood.

As with the particular status alternative, a number of questions arise out of any attempt to evaluate this approach to Canadian federalism. First, can the existing division of powers between the federal and provincial governments withstand the strains to which it is currently being subjected? Differences of opinion as to what the constitution means, or ought to mean, are in constant evidence, particularly as between English- and French-Canadian constitutional authorities. Competing generalizations are common, for example, as to what economic powers would be the 1967 equivalent of those which were known or were assigned to the central government in 1867. Controversy persists as to what would be the 1967 equivalent of the education power which was assigned to the provinces a hundred years ago. To generalize, the question which arises is whether the constitution must be modernized if it is to contribute to a resolution of today's frictions, or whether, alternatively, today's frictions would be exacerbated if an effort were made to rewrite the constitution.

The second question raised by the strong central-strong regional government approach is whether federal and provincial programs can exist side-by-side and can be harmonized by intergovernmental consultation or whether a clearer compartmentalization of powers is required to solve current differences between the federal and provincial governments. If the latter is to be preferred, is a greater compartmentalization of powers possible in today's interdependent society? Or must one reconcile oneself to the expectation that the exercise of exclusive jurisdiction by the federal government will nearly always affect some provincial program or *vice versa*? If this is so, if the muddier course of attempting to harmonize federal and provincial programs must be accepted, coupled with some doctrine of paramountcy where a definite locus of responsibility must be fixed, what shape should the machinery for harmonization or consultation take? When will consultation imply simply the development by each government of an adequate understanding of the interests and the policies of the other governments? When will it centre upon the shape or even the details of particular programs, with each government accepting responsibility for consulting the others as to how a particular policy or program ought to be fashioned, in order to take account of parallel or related programs? And when should consultations be expected to influence the choice as between competing priorities *within* governments and legislatures in an effort to rationalize decisions on priorities as *between* governments and legislatures?

This leads to the obvious but often overlooked question as to whether consultation has to do with influence or control. Should federal-provincial conferences have as their objective the attempt on the part of provincial governments to influence federal ministers and *vice versa* or should these meetings be looked upon as forums in which *decisions* are made? If the latter were to be the case, what would be the machinery for determining when a sufficient consensus had been reached to be binding on all participating governments and what changes would be required in the relationship of governments to their legislatures if the decisions of federal-provincial conferences were to be binding? If influence is to be the goal of intergovernmental consultations, what would be the appropriate form for such consultations? What machinery would be required to ensure that an adequate and an adequately equal opportunity were open to each government to attempt to influence the others in their decisions?

The third question that emerges when one considers this approach to Canadian federalism is whether the use of the federal spending power needs to be reviewed; whether it confers upon the central government an unintended *de facto* power over the provinces; whether it is a necessary vehicle for the practical expression of national aspirations or for the practical resolution of national problems. The spending power has been used so widely and with such great effect by the federal government that it can scarcely be ignored: it is the primary basis for income maintenance payments to persons, for industrial incentive payments to industry, for unconditional equalization payments to the provinces, and for conditional or shared-cost grants to the provinces. Its use by federal governments for influencing provincial priorities through shared-cost programs has raised in the minds of certain authorities the question as to whether the spending power has not come to rival in importance the division of powers in determining the effective role of the federal government. This being so, the question must be considered, with respect to the spending power as with respect to the division of powers, whether or not an attempt to clarify the intent of the constitution would contribute to a reduction in the tensions in our federation.

A fourth and more fundamental question which must be faced in considering the strong central-strong regional government approach to federalism is whether its premises are sound. Is pluralism a realistic goal in modern society, or must one reconcile oneself to the gradual centralization of government — in the Canadian context to the development of two relatively centralized states? If gradual centralization is inevitable, is it reasonable to expect that pluralism could be expected to persist in the North American context — that an English-Canadian society and a French-Canadian society could be expected to flourish in a US-dominated North America — if this is an unreasonable expectation within the Canadian context?

If there remains a place for pluralism in modern society and if it is a reasonable premise that two societies can flourish within a single federation, is it a reasonable expectation that this country can be made a homeland for both French and English Canadians? Or must one expect the French-Canadian society to expire except in Quebec? This is probably the fundamental question which must be answered by Canadians. For the French Canadian the question is whether a return to isolation — and separation is essentially a modern version of isolation — is the price he is prepared to pay to protect his culture or whether indeed this is the way in which his culture will flourish. For the English Canadian, on the other hand, the question is whether French Canadians are to be forced into the isolation of Quebec and ultimately perhaps into separation by a refusal on the part of English Canadians to give to the French-Canadian society equal status wherever this is possible, by a refusal to embrace the advantages of a second society in Canada.

These are the questions which become apparent when one attempts to evaluate critically the strong central-strong regional approach to federalism in Canada. It will be only too evident that this approach, like that of particular status, carries with it its own questions and poses its own problems. This should scarcely be surprising given our starting proposition that the essence of federalism is a delicate balance between the engines of unity and the engines of diversity, and a vigilant concern that the balance is maintained as the environment changes and the role of government evolves.

Conclusion

This brings me to the most difficult part of this paper — the end. I say this because while one normally expects a speaker to come to a conclusion, a civil servant is not supposed to come to conclusions — at least not audibly or noticeably and certainly not in public. But there are a few things I would like to say.

The proposition with which I began was a simple one: that federalism is a compromise between the conflicting elements of unity and diversity within a single state. Except in a society which is both simple and static the equilibrium between these forces will be subject to constant change, with the mechanism of adjustment being the shift in power, or in the exercise of power, as between the central and provincial governments and *vice versa*. I went on to examine the several ways in which the forces of unity and diversity in Canada might be brought into a new balance, given the state of disequilibrium which presently prevails in our federation and the forces of change with which we are yet confronted.

It is not for me to make a choice between the alternative models of federalism. But I venture to suggest some of the conditions which I hope will apply in the making of the choice. We need a fuller and a more rigorous account of how these several approaches to federalism would function. We need a more critical analysis of their consequences and of their implications. We need to weigh carefully the quantum of change which Canadians may be expected to withstand before adjustments in the name of equilibrium might be transformed into forces of disequilibrium. We need to consider the relative contribution to the debate over Canada's future both of constitutional principle and of social and economic analysis. And we need to consider the importance to this debate of a clear understanding of the processes of government and how they function. In all of this the attention and the talents of Canada's social scientists are urgently required.

9 Federalism and the Party System in Canada*

Steven Muller

The purpose of this article is to suggest that there is a causal and necessary link between Canada's achievement of a relatively stable and coherent two-party system in the Dominion Parliament and the considerable variety of parties established in the Canadian provinces. Normally such parties as the Co-operative Commonwealth Federation (C.C.F.) and Social Credit are characterized as splinter parties in a national two-party system. This is in part quite justified. These parties do compete for seats in the Dominion Parliament and have never attained a very large representation there. But classification of these parties, and of the Union Nationale in Quebec, merely as national splinter parties obscures the true nature of Canada's party system. It may be useful to conceive that within the context of Canadian federalism, the national party system has two distinct layers, and that these are mutually inter-dependent but can be separated for purposes of analysis. One layer of the national party system services the parliamentary institutions at Ottawa. The other layer applies to the tension between the Dominion government and the governments of the provinces.

It is suggested here that as ruling parties in one or more provinces, the so-called splinter parties of the first layer constitute an essential part of the second layer of the Canadian party system. As elements of this second layer, parties such as the C.C.F. or Social Credit are not merely also-rans for power in the Dominion Parliament. Far greater is their importance as factors in the federal balance of powers between Ottawa and the provinces. The maintenance of this federal balance is perhaps the most acute problem of Canadian politics. It is,

*Prepared for delivery at the 1961 Annual Meeting of the American Political Science Association, St. Louis, Sheraton-Jefferson Hotel, September 6-9, 1961. Reprinted by permission of the author.

in fact, so acute that a special dimension of the national party system appears to have emerged to oblige it.

The argument that follows therefore assumes that a party that wins power in a Canadian province plays three major roles. Obviously, it functions within the party system of its particular provinces; it is a factor in the top layer of the national party system, which involves control of the Dominion Parliament; it also functions in the second layer of the national party system, which balances central and sectional interests within the federal structure. The roles of provincial ruling parties within provincial party systems and as contributors to the party politics of the Dominion Parliament have been variously studied, but too little recognition is evident of their special functions as a safety valve for sectional interests. The hypothesis is advanced that this special function is performed within the second layer of the national party system, and that the effectiveness of the stable two-party process in the Dominion Parliament depends upon its fulfillment. It also seems that the character and operation of the second layer of the Canadian party system is unique, and that it owes its existence to the complex, inexorable logic of Canadian federalism.

The Canadian Confederation is not inherently stable. It is a truism that divisive forces threaten Canada's national unity. Everyone is aware of the problem of the French Canadians, self-consciously nationalistic, rooted in their language, their church, their customs, and therefore different from other Canadians. In fact, the situation of the French Canadians is so dramatic, their destiny so colorful, that over-concentration on the social problem for national unity they represent may blur recognition of other centrifugal forces no less powerful. These are primarily economic in origin. It must never be forgotten that the natural economic drift of North America runs, like the course of its rivers and mountain ranges, on a north-south axis. Canada has created her national economy on an east-west axis in defiance of nature. Penned between the frontier of the United States and a vast arctic hinterland, the Canadian economy has no vertical, only horizontal mobility.

The problem thus posed for Canadian national economic development has never been solved, although its difficulties have failed to defeat Canadians, who have manfully fought and to an extent subdued them. There are in Canada at least four major and quite distinct economic regions: the Atlantic Maritimes, the industrial and commercial heartland of Quebec and Ontario, the Western prairies, and the Pacific Coast. The logic of economic geography would link each to a southward partner region in the United States; the logic of national politics yokes them together. The compulsion of political nationalism is characteristically negative. To be Canadian is above all to be North American without being American (i.e., pertaining to the United States — and the usage galls north of the border), or British, or French. A common defiance of external pressures remains the most important factor that unites Canadians with conflicting interest — the bluenose from the Atlantic Coast, the French Canadian, Irish Canadian, British Canadian, the farmer of East European descent in the prairies. There is a sharp difference here between Canada and the United States. In the States, clashing interests of sections and diverse peoples were and still are being overcome by an unrivalled homogenizing national prosperity, created essentially within the national frontiers and financed by domestic capital. Canada is poorer and lacks economic self-sufficiency. She has depended on London and New York for capital investment. At the sacrifice of a shared, homogeneous North American prosperity, she has austerely defied absorption into the economy of the United States. Her various regional interests — economic and social — retain their separate vigor virtually undiminished. The national politics of Canada involves a tense and struggling adjustment between national and sectional power quite different from the United States.

Canadian political institutions reinforce and cater to this tension. Confederating in 1867, in pursuit of greater autonomy from Britain and in fear of the ambitions of a United States still in arms after the Civil War, the statesmen of the first four Provinces adopted federalism. They sought to make a nation; some hoped that their projected system would one day evolve into a unitary regime; but at the time French and British Canada could live as one only within a federal pattern that guaranteed their differences. The national purpose of the Fathers of Confederation is clearly evident in the British North America Act. In contrast to the Constitution of the United States, which had just endured the war between the States, the B.N.A. Act assigns both the general and residual powers of government to the Dominion, not the provinces. By means of lieutenant-governors appointed by the Dominion government, the latter could disallow provincial legislation.[1] The design was created for the conquest of sectionalism from the center.

But it was not to be so. It is commonly known that the decisions of the Judicial Committee of the Privy Council abridged the general powers of the Dominion government and enhanced the legislative powers of the provinces.[2] After 1887, it is equally clear, the power of disallowance of provincial acts came to be less and less frequently used. What is often not emphasized sufficiently is that this frustration of the hopes of national supremacy over sectionalism was not merely the result of caprice on the part of alien judges. Professor Brady is right in maintaining that these decisions "gave judicial expression to the upsurge of provincialism, evident from the early eighties to the decade after the First World War".[3]

In 1867 Canada consisted of Ontario, Quebec, Nova Scotia and New Brunswick. By 1905 Ontario and Quebec had been vastly enlarged, and the Dominion had nine provinces: Manitoba was created in 1870, British Columbia joined in 1871, Prince Edward Island in 1873, and Alberta and Saskatchewan were established in 1905. Sectional development, fed by immigration, was proceeding rapidly. Macdonald's national policy, inherited and adapted by Laurier, had linked the nation east to west by rail, maintained a tariff barrier against economic aggression from the United States, and had hugely lessened dependence

---

[1]B.N.A. Act, 91; 58, 56, 90.

[2]See especially *Tennant* v. *Union Bank* (1894) and *Snider* v. *Hydro-Electric Commission of Toronto* (1925).

[3]Alexander Brady, *Democracy in the Dominions*, 3rd ed., University of Toronto Press, Toronto, 1958, p. 46.

on Britain. The nation existed, but sectional differences had grown apace with its progress. At the very heart of Canadian federal politics a classic pattern of tension between Dominion and Provincial governments was fully developed, around the focal point of financial relations. Dominion-Provincial financial arrangements symbolize Canadian diversity more validly than the problem of the French Canadians; and as a symbol and a fact they offer a rather neglected clue to the nature of the national party system.

I will not include here a detailed review of the manifold intricacies of Dominion-Provincial financial relations in Canada.[4] Suffice it to explain that, from Confederation onward, the Dominion government has necessarily subsidized the Provincial governments. Deprived by the federal constitution of revenues from external trade, but not released under that constitution from their diverse functions, the four original Provinces received subsidies in the form of per capita grants and debt allowances from the Dominion. The terms fixed for these subsidies were meant to be final, and they were embodied in detail within the constitution itself.[5] In fact, they have been subject to constant bargaining and revision ever since Nova Scotia obtained "better terms" almost at once, in 1869. The number of provinces and the divergent pressures grew; the alteration of subsidies has been virtually continuous.[6]

The problem has had an extra dimension ever since British Columbia and Prince Edward Island were first given additional subsidies in the early 1870's in lieu of land turned over to federal public domain. Time and again the provinces have besieged Ottawa for better terms; final settlement has succeeded final settlement. After the impact of the depression and the Second World War the present basis for an approach to the problem was developed. This involves the exchange of increased and adjustable subsidies to the provinces for exclusive "rental" by the Dominion government of the personal income tax, corporation taxes, and succession duties.[7]

For our present purposes the significance does not lie in the constitutional and technical labyrinth enclosing the problem, but in the basic fact that the governments of the provinces, meaning, of course, the parties that control them, inevitably must struggle and bargain for higher subsidies with the government at

---

[4]The best account of the matter up to the Second World War can be found in J. A. Maxwell, *Federal Subsidies to the Provincial Governments in Canada*, Harvard University Press, Cambridge, Mass., 1937.

[5]B.N.A. Act of 1867, 118.

[6]Professor Dawson counts "over twenty special revisions and three general revisions since Confederation". Robert MacGregor Dawson, *The Government of Canada*, 2nd ed., University of Toronto Press, Toronto, 1954, p. 120.

[7]The rental of the taxing power had to be devised because of the ambiguity of the British North America Act, which in section 91(3) gives to the Dominion Parliament the right of "The raising of Money by any Mode or System of Taxation," but in section 92(2) gives to Provincial legislatures the power of "Direct Taxation within the Province in order to the raising of a Revenue for Provincial Purposes"; thus exposing Canadians potentially to confiscatory levels of double direct taxation. Dawson hypothesizes the resident of Alberta who had an income of $1,000,000. In 1938, before the post-war rental schemes went into effect, he would have been liable for 105% of this amount in Dominion and provincial income taxes. Dawson, *ibid.*, p. 123.

Ottawa, meaning, of course, the majority party in parliament. This is true even when the party in power in a province is nominally the same as the party in power in Ottawa. And here we approach the nature of the second layer of the Canadian national party system.

In the first layer, two groups of adversaries are pitted against each other in the Dominion Parliament in what is essentially a two-party system. These are parliamentary parties in nature, with relatively weak national organization. They operate in the British parliamentary context, which decrees that elections come irregularly and with little advance warning. (The sharp contrast with the regularity of Congressional elections in the United States and with the galvanizing national impact of the Presidential election must be noted.) For effective organization these national parliamentary parties depend upon the services of provincial organizations. The textbooks advise that "the provincial association is the effective head of the party organizations in Canada".[8]

These provincial associations may bear the same name as the national parliamentary party, but they are in fact nearly autonomous. A national parliamentary party may in a Dominion election usefully be served by a provincial organization wholly autonomous and bearing a distinct and different name. The classic illustration of this is the role of the Union Nationale in Quebec. In its post-war heyday it helped the Liberals nationally to capture the bulk of Quebec's seats in the Dominion Parliament in four elections, and aided the Progressive-Conservatives in a fifth. Also, dominance of a province by a provincial party organization does not guarantee that the organization will deliver federal representation to its nominal partner in the Dominion Parliament. Social Credit governed in Alberta and British Columbia in 1958, but all of Alberta's and most of British Columbia's seats in the last federal election went to the Progressive-Conservatives, and none to Social Credit.

This is no doubt confusing, but it is nevertheless logical, and the logic is that of the second layer of the national party system. Centrifugal sectional forces are very strong in Canada. These forces are to a large extent institutionalized in the politics of the Canadian provinces. These politics, and the parties that control them, are inevitably pointed toward conflict with Ottawa. And it is therefore true, as Professor Dawson suggests, that "while it may be advantageous for a Dominion Government to have its own party in power in the provinces, it may well be that a Provincial Government is more secure if it is politically opposed to the party in power in Ottawa".[9]

The logic of the second layer lays down its own classic cyclical pattern. A Dominion government will be established with a majority in the federal parliament that rests on the support of a majority of the provincial party organizations. As that government stays in power in Ottawa, the governments of the provinces will gradually turn against it. Where the parties in power in the provinces bear the same name as the party in power in Ottawa, these parties in the provinces will tend to face defeat. To complete the cycle, a majority of party organizations in the provinces hostile to the government in power at Ottawa will

[8]Thus Dawson, *ibid.*, p. 529.
[9]*Ibid.*, p. 574.

in the end elect the opposition party to office in the Dominion Parliament. Thus, for example, when the Liberal party under Mackenzie King returned to power in Ottawa in 1935, Liberal parties were in power, alone or in coalition, in all of the then nine provinces except Alberta, where Social Credit had just come into office. When the Liberal party was defeated in the Dominion election of 1957, Liberal parties remained in power, alone or in coalition, in only three of the provinces; and in two of these, Manitoba in 1958 and Prince Edward Island in 1959, Progressive-Conservative governments came into office at the next provincial election.

In this fashion, the two layers of the national Canadian party system interact, and their inter-relationship is perhaps the most complex and unique phenomenon in Canadian politics. To win a Dominion election, a party must appeal for a national consensus, in face of all the divisive forces rampant on the political stage. From the birth of the Dominion it was apparent that a party appealing exclusively to either French Canadians or British Canadians could not hope to encompass a national consensus. In fact, such a party would, in its very nature, embody a threat to Canada's survival as a single nation. Total hostility from either of the two main racial groups also dooms a party's national chances. Flaws of leadership and historical circumstances deprived the Conservative party of the capacity to appeal to French Canadians for decades after the First World War. Until recently, therefore, it seemed that the Conservatives were doomed to be in opposition at Ottawa as a normal matter of course. To achieve national consensus and a national majority, parties must surmount not only social but economic divisions as well. This they can do mainly by advocating strong government to promote national economic development, which holds the promise of increased prosperity for a country still underpopulated, and still far from able to make full use of enormous natural resources. Strong national leadership, to keep the country together, to combat external pressures, and to develop the economy despite adverse geographical factors — this Canada needs and has usually received. It is what the parties successful in Dominion elections promise.

The themes are perennial: a national policy of energetic promotion, be it of a national railway or of natural gas; the vigorous assertion of separateness from the United States, running the gamut from protective tariffs to the attempt to force a distinctly Canadian culture into being. Only the theme of the British connection has altered, with the reality of completely achieved autonomy. The old negative separatist tone appears to be giving way to a more positive search for a forceful Canadian contribution to the Commonwealth. As all observers since Lord Bryce have noted, ideological questions play little role in Dominion politics. National circumstances do not encourage them.

Strong leadership at Ottawa appealing to Canadian nationalism, however, is never so strong as to be able to destroy the centrifugal forces at work. Sectional interests remain and must be somehow accommodated. In the absence of effective institutions to accommodate them within the Dominion government itself, they express themselves in the second layer of the party system. For practical purposes, sectional interests translate themselves into issues of provincial rights. What Canada requires is balance. Strong national leadership is required if the country as one is to survive at all. Yet national leadership which attempts to eliminate, or even override, sectional claims would be destructive. Therefore, provincial centers of power must exist to counter the power at Ottawa and keep it within bounds. However, a rigid, permanent conflict between Dominion and provinces would be intolerable. So the power in the provinces, as in Ottawa, must be flexible. At times the provinces must sustain leadership at Ottawa, at other times frustrate it.

This is the essence of living Canadian federalism, and it is largely accomplished in the interplay between the parties in the provinces and the parties in the Dominion parliament. What is distinctively Canadian in the process is the vigor of provincial rights and what they represent, as well as the fact that the struggle for balance between them and the wider national interest is institutionalized in the party system. It is more usual in federal systems to find this struggle, often less severe than it is in Canada, institutionalized within the federal apparatus itself. So it is in the United States, chiefly within the Congress. But not in Canada, where the federal parliamentary institutions are unsuited to this purpose.

The Canadian House of Commons does not represent the provinces. Seats are allocated among and within the provinces roughly on the basis of population. The two forces in conflict in the House are normally the party of government and the opposition, which in the British tradition acts as a potential alternative government. Never far from the prospect of the next election, both government and opposition party must, as we have seen, bear in mind the need to appeal to a national consensus. To protect their political future, both attempt to mute and smother manifestations of divisive sectional forces. More than the government party is able to, the opposition party may choose to pose as the champion of provincial rights, and thus of sectional interests. But its freedom of action is also restricted. It dare not press issues to the point where its own opportunity to rally a national majority is endangered. Nor dare it make such commitments to provincial rights as will prevent its capacity for strong national leadership should it come to power at Ottawa. Operating under the authority of the Cabinet much as in Britain, the Canadian House of Commons tends very much to be the place where the policies of the government are put forth and enacted and where the two major parties in contention strive respectively to maintain or to achieve their appeal to a national majority.

It is well known that the Canadian Senate is not an effective institution, either for the accommodation of thrusting provincial interests or for most other purposes. This body of aged appointees, the great majority of whom owe their tenure to political services rendered in their more active days to the government that named them, does not even represent the provinces equally.[10] Even

---

[10]The normal membership of the Canadian Senate is 102. In essence the body is designed to give representation to four major geographic areas. Thus Ontario and Quebec each have 24 Senators; the Western provinces have 24 Senators in all, six each for British Columbia, Manitoba, Saskatchewan and Alberta; and the Maritimes originally had 24 Senators, ten each for Nova Scotia and New Brunswick, four for Prince Edward Island. With the entrance of Newfoundland the balance was altered by the addition of six Senators for the island.

at the outset of Canadian Confederation the Senate was designed less as an organ of federal representation than as a bulwark of social conservatism. And, as Professor Brady points out, whatever federal role was intended for the nominees for life has now been largely diluted, since they are not compelled to possess a practical accountability to their provinces or their regions.[11] A weak second chamber, the Canadian Senate plays only a minor role in the parliamentary process, and virtually no significant role at all in Canadian federalism.

Within the Dominion Cabinet, to be sure, all or at least most of the provinces are represented. The process of Cabinet-making in Canada is made exceptionally difficult by the need of the ruling party to maintain its national strength by squeezing into the government as extensive a representation as possible from the ten provinces. However, such representation flows primarily only in one direction. It lacks a genuinely reciprocal character, and thus it does not serve to institutionalize the struggle for the federal balance completely in the Cabinet. The governing party does not pick a Cabinet in order to resolve federal conflicts. It seeks to have ministers from every province to demonstrate its truly national character and to sustain as widespread an allegiance as possible. There is a crucial overlap of purposes which falls short of identity.

In one sense a minister (or ministers) from a province does, of course, represent it. He can express a provincial or regional point of view, dispense some patronage and otherwise play an effective partisan role on behalf of his provincial party. But as a member of the Cabinet oriented toward the British model he is not consistently an effective bargainer for provincial interests. Only at the very formation of a government does he have an opportunity to make a really strong case for his province. An effective leader of the party in control of a province who is asked to join a Dominion Cabinet being formed can make his acceptance conditional upon *quid pro quos* that will benefit his province. Once in office, however, his ability to work for the provincial interest is limited by the practice of Cabinet solidarity. The collective decisions of the Cabinet are of necessity oriented toward preservation and promotion of the national consensus. And most men will temper their advocacy of a provincial case once it is clear that they will pay with a loss of office if they persist too far.

It is hard to be absolutely clear on this point. Obviously a Prime Minister and a Cabinet majority will go to great lengths to avoid a rupture that would see one of their number resign on the sensitive issue of provincial rights. Any Cabinet formed by the ruling party at Ottawa will seek to retain the strongest fealty possible from among affiliated or allied provincial parties, and to accede to the needs of the latter whenever practicable. But the momentum of divergent forces is never arrested; no balance of forces is permanent. Provincial demands, especially financial demands, are by their very nature insatiable. Better terms here, a boon there are inevitably followed by demands for still better terms, bigger boons. As a Dominion government stays in power it becomes impossible to gratify continually all that is sought by the provinces, even those governed by allied parties. In fact there is a danger that provincial demands feed on satisfaction. If too much is given by Ottawa too soon, the point may very early be

---

[11]Brady, *op. cit.*, p. 522.

reached within the Cabinet where the line is drawn against provincial pressures. It is here, then, that the logic of the second layer asserts itself most forcibly. Within a province the feeling is apt to grow that the provincial cause — most often symbolized by financial terms though it may in actuality have a far more complex composition — is no longer best served by having the ruling party in the province represented in the Cabinet of the ruling party at Ottawa. Such representation may have resulted in recognized initial benefits to the province. But soon there may be talk that the province's representative (or representatives) has been in Ottawa too long, that he no longer stands for the provincial interest. It may not be immediately practicable, or indeed desirable, to change parties both in the province and in Ottawa, and thus to await the next great stride in the provincial cause at the moment of formation of the new Dominion Cabinet. But it may very well seem of advantage to overturn the ruling party in the province. This puts at the head of the provincial government men who no longer belong to the ruling party at Ottawa, but who at least will therefore be free to put the provincial case forward without reservation.

There are conflicting considerations involved, of course. Is it indeed wiser to trade muted advocacy of the provincial cause within the Dominion Cabinet for strident efforts made outside the pale? Where the ruling party in the province and the ruling party in the Dominion are affiliated under the same name, prudent concessions from Ottawa may long persuade provincial voters to continue support of the affiliation and not to rupture it. Of greater interest to the argument at the moment is the alternative of keeping in power in a province a government not affiliated to either of the two major parties in contention at Ottawa. Is this perhaps the strategy that gives the most effective flexibility to the provincial case?

Such an autonomous party, in essential control over the province, is free to bargain with both of the contending parties at Ottawa each time there is a Dominion election. It will be rewarded each time that it supports a winner at Ottawa. True, it is not likely to be rewarded with direct partisan representation within the Dominion Cabinet. On the other hand, however, its leaders remain free to criticize and differ with the Dominion government as they choose. The leaders of the ruling party in the Dominion can never ignore the autonomous party in the province as long as it rules there and has the effectively dominant provincial electoral organization. A Dominion election is always in the offing, and for the Ottawa leaders each Dominion election means that the process of bargaining for support from provincial organizations must be resumed.

No doubt the leaders of the two major parties in contention at Ottawa find such thinking vexatious and deplorable. But its potential appeal for the voters of a province seems real and apparent. The most virulently divergent pressures away from national consensus exist among French Canadians and in the West. It is then perhaps no accident, that until 1960 Quebec voters for years chose to support the Union Nationale in the province while usually voting Liberal in Dominion elections. Also, the Western provinces, with the very recent exception of Manitoba, are each in the control of a party not affiliated with either of the main contenders for Dominion power. Social Credit appears to be thoroughly dominant within Alberta and British Columbia, and not since the war has the C.C.F. lost control of Saskatchewan.

These circumstances are scarcely understandable except in terms of Canadian federalism and a second layer of the national party system. The so-called ideology of Social Credit seems scarcely relevant to the conduct of provincial government by the party, and of almost equal irrelevance to its voters. The Union Nationale, given the leadership of the late M. Duplessis and French Canadian nationalism, was and is not encumbered with an ideology that could be so labelled. There is, of course, a socialist-progressive point of view that distinguishes the C.C.F. ideologically, but there is little evidence of its relevance to provincial voting in Saskatchewan. It seems most likely that voters in general support these provincial parties with a pragmatic perception of the federal circumstances under discussion, i.e., with recognition of the two layers comprising the national party system.[12]

Two obvious dangers attend this conception of an autonomous or nearly autonomous ruling party within a province as the most effective bargaining agent with Ottawa. Both have been evident in Canadian politics. The first is that dominance of provincial politics by one party will breed corruption and neglect or abuse of power. It is at this point that the third dimension of the party system relates to the two national layers. Sometimes the political situation within a province will prevent voters from continued support of the traditionally dominant party, even if the effectiveness of the latter in bargaining with the Dominion government is undiminished. This may be the result of evident flagrant abuses of office held too long and too securely. Or it may follow, as in the recent case of the Union Nationale in Quebec, the loss by the traditional ruling party of its dominant personality.

In the event, the replacing of a ruling provincial party which was not affiliated with either of the two major parties in the Dominion Parliament is hard to assess in terms of its impact on both layers of the national party system. Usually, such a provincial party could be replaced only by a provincial party affiliated with one or the other of the two Ottawa contenders. The first question must be whether the shift in the province is temporary and is soon to be undone again, after the repudiated party has undergone internal reform. The second question, if the shift seems semi-permanent, is whether the victory of a provincial party affiliated with one of the two parties in the Dominion Parliament signals an alternation in Ottawa. For example, with regard to Quebec today, it is not

---

[12]My thesis is supported by brief suggestive statements made by F. H. Underhill, "Canadian Liberal Democracy in 1955", in G. V. Ferguson and F. H. Underhill, *Press and Party in Canada*, University of Toronto Press, Toronto, 1955, pp. 27-46, and by Dennis Wrong, "The Pattern of Party Voting in Canada", *Public Opinion Quarterly*, Vol. XXI, No. 2, Summer 1957, pp. 252-264. It runs directly counter to the views of Howard A. Scarrow as expressed in his "Federal-Provincial Voting Patterns in Canada", *Canadian Journal of Economics and Political Science*, Vol. XXVI, No. 2, May 1960, pp. 289-298. Mr. Scarrow attempts a comparative manipulation of Canadian provincial and United States state election statistics and concludes from this effort, which proves sterile, "that no simple formula is likely to provide an adequate understanding of the motivation underlying split or alternating elections within a federation".

yet clear whether the Union Nationale will make a comeback soon within the province, or whether its fortunes have suffered a lasting reversal. And it is even less clear whether the success of the provincial Liberal party in Quebec signals the return of the Liberals to power in Ottawa or not. What is rather more clear is that lengthy dominance by one party is, despite disadvantages, habitual in Canadian politics, both at the Dominion level and in many of the provinces.

The second danger consists of the possibility of sterile deadlock or destructive hostility between the Dominion government and the governments of one or more of the provinces. This is in fact a constant potential threat within the structure of Canadian federalism. It is a threat not often realized because it is suicidal. The basic fact of the matter is that most Canadians are fully aware both of the need for strong national leadership that will hold the country together, and of the pressures of centrifugal forces pulling away from national unity. Awareness means more than recognition in this case. It means acceptance. The existence of centrifugal and centripetal forces is taken for granted, as is the tension between them. They serve as a basis for all Canadian political calculations.

Quite naturally both forces are embodied in the constitution, which demands their interaction. The Dominion must finance the provinces because it depends on governmental services only the provinces can render. The latter cannot function without the financial support of Ottawa, nor without the context of a nation consensus which the Dominion government represents. Both forces are also institutionalized in the national party system, requiring the parties at Ottawa to bargain with provincial parties, either as such, or more frequently as the governments of provinces. To bargain is the antithesis of deadlock or naked hostility. Prolonged bitterness between Dominion and provincial governments can work to the advantage of neither.

Nevertheless, there have been occasional lapses into excess. Two illustrations of unusual interest come to mind. One is the famous quarrel in 1940 between the Ontario Liberal administration led by Mitchell Hepburn and the Dominion Liberal government headed by Mackenzie King. This reached its peak when the Ontario legislature, dominated by the provincial Liberal party, passed a motion of censure on the conduct of the war effort by the Dominion government. Thus challenged, Mackenzie King went to the country and was returned to power with an increased majority. The number of Liberals returned to the Dominion Parliament from Ontario declined by only one, from fifty-six in 1935 to fifty-five. At the next provincial election in Ontario, in August 1943, the provincial Liberal party was crushingly defeated. (Mitchell Hepburn had earlier resigned as provincial Premier, on 21 October 1942.)

Of particular significance is the fact that this open breach occurred between a provincial and the Dominion party nominally affiliated under the Liberal name, which suggests that such nominal affiliation does not destroy the near-autonomy of a provincial party organization. Also of interest is the result of the conflict for the provincial party. Undoubtedly there was some feeling in Canada in the early years of World War II that the King government was not sufficiently vigorous in its war effort at Britain's side, and the voters of Ontario were as a group perhaps more loyal to the British connection than those of other provinces. However, the head-on challenge to the Dominion government flung down by the Ontario Liberal administration went too far in its expression of a divergent interest. Implicitly rebuked by King's success in the Dominion elections of 1940, and bitterly divided within itself, the provincial Liberal party lost its hold on Ontario.[13]

The other illustration is the notorious "five-cent speech" delivered by Mr. King in 1930. Speaking during the depression, Mr. King said:

> So far as giving money from this federal treasury to provincial governments is concerned. . . I might be prepared to go a certain length possibly in meeting one or two of the western provinces that have Progressive premiers at the head of their governments, but I would not give a single cent to any Tory government. . . . May I repeat what I have said? With respect to giving moneys out of the federal treasury to any Tory government in this country for these alleged unemployment purposes, with these governments situated as they are to-day, with policies diametrically opposed to those of this government, I would not give them a five-cent piece.[14]

Shortly after this speech the Liberal Administration of Mackenzie King fought a general election. The speech was extensively used against the government. In the election the Liberals were defeated. No one could claim that they were defeated solely or even primarily because of Mr. King's utterance. Still, there can be little doubt that his statement was excessive and disastrous. Were such a view to become policy for a Dominion government *vis-à-vis* provincial governments affiliated with the opposition party at Ottawa, the basis of Canadian federalism would be destroyed. In Canada the center can no more wipe out sectional divergence than the latter can hope to override the center.

Of the greatest interest, however, is Mr. King's allusion to his willingness to deal with Progressive premiers, or in other words with leaders of provincial parties not affiliated with either of the two main parties at Ottawa. His statement invites the suggestion that there may well be a positive benefit at the first layer of the Canadian party system that derives from the existence at the second level of provincial parties both nominally and actually autonomous. It was remarked above that the leadership of both of the major parties in contention at Ottawa probably deplores the existence of autonomous parties in the provinces. No doubt a Liberal Prime Minister of the Dominion would, for partisan reasons, much prefer to have provincial Liberal parties in power in every province, just as a Conservative Prime Minister at Ottawa would welcome the unanimous support of provincial Conservatives prevailing everywhere. But how would politics in the Canadian national parliament be served if only the same two parties in contention at Ottawa were available to provincial voters?

The pressures of Canadian federalism, as we have seen, dictate that in time

---

[13]For Mackenzie King's reaction to Hepburn's challenge and his judgment on the Liberal defeat in Ontario in 1943, see J. W. Pickersgill, *The Mackenzie King Record, Volume I*, University of Toronto Press, Toronto, 1960, pp. 62-65, 568-571.

[14]Canadian House of Commons, *Debates*, 3 April 1930, pp. 1227-1228.

the conflict between provincial forces and a government confirmed in power at Ottawa is bound to intensify. The classic cycle of the two layers would therefore indicate that, for example, a Liberal government that had come into power with the support of provincial Liberal parties dominant in most or all of the provinces would soon find itself confronted with hostile Conservative provincial parties coming to power in most or all of the provinces. It would be rather rapidly succeeded by a Conservative government at Ottawa, which would in turn then undergo the equivalent experience.

At least two very grave disadvantages would inevitably seem to follow. First, the precarious national consensus of Canada would suffer. Governments at Ottawa would alternate more rapidly than is now the case, which is not necessarily desirable in itself.[15] It would also seem certain that they would succeed or fall increasingly on the divisive issue of provincial rights. Secondly, each alternation at the Dominion level would presumably be accompanied by the characteristic rewards granted to provincial supporters. The process of pressure for better terms would be opportunistically accelerated, and the present basis of Canadian federalism would be rapidly eroded.

Such dire results might be avoided only if the two Dominion parliamentary parties could discipline and manage their provincial affiliates. This, however, is unlikely to happen so long as provincial governments and political processes serve divergent social and economic forces which are indelibly part of the very essence of Canadian nationhood. With these considerations in mind, the prevalence of parties in office in several provinces that are not affiliated with either of the two contenders for Dominion power may be seen as a vital safety valve in the Canadian political process.

By voting Social Credit into provincial power, for example, the voters of British Columbia can effectively express sectional interest, albeit in the guise of provincial identity, without necessarily damaging thereby the delicate balance of national unity. The autonomous provincial parties in power appear uniquely free to negotiate with both parties at Ottawa. It may well be that this fact offers a vital flexibility, not only to the voters of the provinces, but to the entire national party system. In this sense, then, these autonomous parties in power in the provinces are not merely splinter groups also represented in the Dominion parliament. They constitute part of a second layer of the national Canadian party system, and it is in large measure to their existence that the stable parliamentary life of Ottawa owes its viability.

Professor Brady has written that "Federalism is the most distinctive achievement of Canadian democracy."[16] It is also true that the success of a national system of democratic politics in Canada is *per se* a magnificent achievement in the face of great odds. A century ago John Stuart Mill asserted: "Free institutions are next to impossible in a country made up of different nationalities. Among a people without fellow feeling especially if they read and speak different

---

[15]For the argument that Canadian circumstances make the relatively extended rule of one party in the Dominion parliament advantageous, see my "Massive Alternation in Canadian Politics", *Foreign Affairs*, Vol. XXXVI, No. 4, July 1958, pp. 633-644.

[16]Brady, *op. cit.*, p. 65.

languages, the united public opinion necessary to the working of representative government cannot exist."[17] For Canada at least, Mill's dictum does not hold, though the experience of other nations well justifies his warning. Essentially it is Canadian federalism that has made the difference. More attention is justified to the ingenious and complex political process which animates the successful federal democracy of the Canadian nations. Within this process a two layer national party system appears to have developed.

---

[17]John Stuart Mill, *Representative Government*, Oxford University Press, Oxford, 1948, p. 292.

Part Three

The Constitution and
Canadian Federalism

10 Reflections on the Canadian Constitution After the First Century*

Bora Laskin

Continuing controversy is a hallmark of federalism; and certainly our history is dotted with debates that have been intermittently responsive to constitutional issues. What makes the current debate different from the many that preceded it, is not so much the questioning of the distributive basis of our constitutional system — that has been a recurring feature of constitutional argumentation — but rather the questioning of its political basis. In the result, voices have been raised in support of a new Constitution, without (so far as I have been able to judge) any bill of particulars to demonstrate the fatal shortcomings of our existing one.

Perhaps I mistake the implications of the words "new Constitution," as they are used by the proponents of what on the face of it is a suggestion for revolutionary change. We have been witnesses in recent months to word usages that appear to have lost meaning in translation; we should not be surprised by confusion of thought in communication in the same language. Perhaps all that is sought is revision of the Constitution in some particulars and its consequent repromulgation. If so, this should be underlined, because there are serious problems, legal as well as political, involved in the jettisoning of one Constitution and its replacement by another.

Clamour for a new Constitution has been fed by an increasing politicization of our federalism. It is as if a stalemate has been reached in the legal relations of Canada and the Provinces, but with no legal, no judicial means of resolving current conflicts. In fact, there are such means. But what has been evident for many years is that the mood of our political leaders is less and less for acquiescence in a judicial order of constitutional change through reinterpretation of the division of legislative powers. The courts themselves cannot, of course, force such a mood; their jurisdiction must be activated by the initiative of private litigants or by governments; and above all, the exercise of jurisdiction must be founded on actual or proposed legislation as the subject of challenge.

It is my opinion that this question of mood for orderly constitutional change through judicial action is related to a failure to see the law as a strong strand in the cultural evolution of our country. Law has suffered arrested development as an indigenous, independent force in our lives, because long after we were political masters of our domestic affairs, and even a generation after we were political masters of our external involvements, we still remained judicially subservient to an overseas tribunal. It takes time to develop judicial standards for constitutional evolution; it takes an understanding of shifting social and eco-

---

*Paper delivered at the ceremonies for the opening of the new building of the College of Law, University of Saskatchewan on September 22nd, 1967. It is published with the permission of the College of Law. From the *Canadian Bar Review*, Vol. XLV, No. 3, September 1967, pp. 395-401. Reprinted by permission of the author and the *Canadian Bar Review*.

nomic forces to provide a basis for those standards. The Privy Council had worked towards a particular equilibrium in Dominion-provincial relations; and when
appeals to that court were abolished there was no legacy of working norms to
guide constitutional change through judicial statesmanship. Hypotheses, abstract
standards, could be found in abundance in Privy Council judgments; but the
Supreme Court of Canada, inheriting the Privy Council's role as umpire of our
federal system, was left on its own to give them concreteness; and its function
as such umpire has come under criticism because of anticipated fear that it may
be more activist in constitutional interpretation than was the Judicial Committee.

Moreover, from the late thirties on, the political disposition appeared to be
to rely on constitutional amendment for effective change; and, failing that, to
seek to reconcile the difficulties of divided jurisdiction through administrative
co-operation which would permit unified action while leaving existing judicially-
declared limits of constitutional authority undisturbed. Clearly enough, political
federalism has been, for many years, much more dominant than legal federalism in this country. I do not, indeed it would be foolish to, deprecate ongoing
political adjustments to facilitate harmonious relations between centre and units
in a federal state. The question that I raise, however, is whether freezing the
legal balance at a particular point in time will not ultimately weaken the political foundation upon which any written constitution must rest. Is this not particularly hazardous for Canada when even amendment is more a matter of
convention than of law?

Amendment, as we all know, has also become enmeshed in the politics of
federalism, rather than having a domestic legal base, because the British North
America Act contains no formula for its amendment. No one could sensibly
quarrel with the wish to "patriate" the Constitution; but the recent and ultimately abortive (although nearly successful) attempts to introduce a domestic
amending procedure told us more about the frozen character of Dominion and
provincial legislative jurisdiction than they did about the utility of an amending procedure in a federal constitution. Indeed, it is fair comment, in my view,
to say that both the Fulton and Fulton-Favreau formulas for amendment
reflected a veto theory of Canadian federalism; a new compact theory, if you
will, under which unanimity would be required to accomplish amendments
respecting legislative power. To secure agreement on an amending formula on
the principle that no one need agree is akin to organized chaos. I believe that
a workable federalism requires a disciplined attachment of the units, the Provinces, to the constitutional order; and such a discipline will not be reflected
in an amending procedure which allows the disagreement of any one Province
to scuttle proposals for change.

The existing balance in federal-provincial law-making power is sharply in
favour of the central government in two major fields, taxation and monetary
control. (Another field where the central government has a dominating voice
is transport and communication). Even singly, they are powerful levers; together,
they represent a formidable capacity for regulating social and economic policy.
The taxing power, more than other legislative powers (whether belonging to
the Dominion or to the Provinces) specified in the Constitution, is less an

end in itself than a means of realizing other ends. One of the persistent issues in our constitutional system, an issue more of political policy than of law, is whether the central government should use its taxing power to underwrite, and thus influence if not control, social and economic programmes for which it cannot directly legislate. Involved in this issue are so-called co-operative federalism, with its opting in and opting out features; programmes of subventions and subsidies; price support programmes and the like.

The issue arises because the balance in federal-provincial law-making power is sharply in favour of the Provinces in the field of social welfare and economic regulatory authority. If this is not clearly so in the constitutional text, it is undoubtedly so under the governing judicial interpretation of that text. What is also important is that extensive programmes have been implemented in the respective Provinces on the faith of the immutability of this favourable balance, and I have the impression that the federal authorities and, indeed, federal party leaderships, are not inclined to challenge it.

Many of the provincial programmes, such as those in the fields of health insurance and education, require heavy financing. This cannot be secured without the Provinces coming to an arrangement with the Dominion on the sharing of tax revenue. The Dominion is told, on the one hand, that it must not intrude upon the constitutional responsibilities of the Provinces through resort to its overriding taxing and spending authority; and, on the other hand, that it must yield enough of its taxing power or resulting tax receipts or leave enough play for the exercise of provincial taxing power, to enable the Provinces to meet those responsibilities in whatever manner the Provinces see fit to discharge them.

I do not question the political logic of this position, given the assumption that the constitutional division of powers must remain untouched, either by the molar process of amendment or by the molecular process of judicial review. The assumption is, however, unacceptable to an evolving society, whatever be the political postures of the moment. A federal state is a legal expression of a politically-agreed balance of centralizing and decentralizing features, and of a politically-agreed means of adjusting that balance from time to time without destroying the state in the course of any such adjustment. The responsibility of the courts, and especially of the Supreme Court of Canada, as an agency of adjustment is, of course, a heavy one; but we strike at the legal roots of the country if we deprecate the exercise of this constitutional function or seek to paralyze it when it has achieved a power balance that is particularly congenial to either provincial or federal proponents, as the case may be.

Not all constitutional difficulties in this or any other federal state stem from alleged maldistribution of legislative power or alleged misconstruction of that power by the courts. There are questions that may aptly be termed constitutional that can be answered by an affirmative exercise of legislative power, by the enactment of a statute or by amendment of existing statutes. Among such questions in Canada are distribution of constituencies, size of the legislative assembly, duration of the legislature and so on. I suggest to you that the question of the use of French in the Provinces of Canada other than Quebec, and elsewhere in Canada, is one that can be met by the enactment of legislation by the various provincial legislatures and by the Parliament of Canada. I do not say that this is a matter that should not be made the subject of constitutional protection, but do point out that the federal government is not to be charged with dereliction in a matter that is within provincial constitutional authority in each Province.

Of course, no Province, under present conditions, has extra-territorial rights in another or constitutionally declared claims upon another; and Quebec cannot force the other Provinces to act affirmatively to give their French-speaking inhabitants the linguistic and cultural advantages that they would enjoy in Quebec. It is, hence, not likely that Quebec will be satisfied on this score by anything else than a constitutional amendment. I shall not speculate on the reach of any such amendment, but merely ask the question whether it can reasonably be expected to go beyond linguistic and educational guarantees.

I confront the question whether linguistic and educational guarantees respecting the French language exhaust the scope of the "deux nations," the "two peoples" principle about which so much has been heard. The issue is whether that conception invites a realignment of law-making power between the Dominion and the Provinces, or in favour of the Provinces or any one of them. Let me make myself clear about the "deux nations" conception, at least to indicate my understanding of what it is not. It does not connote two states, two rival political entities exercising similar legislative powers, without any paramountcy of one against the other in the case of inconsistent or incompatible laws. I regard the principle of paramountcy as an operative principle of federalism whether clearly expressed (as in the Australian Constitution and in that of the United States) or not so clearly, as in Canada where it is presently a feature of our Constitution. (I should add that the Supreme Court has in recent years given the principle a narrow scope so as to favour provincial legislation).

On this view of the "deux nations," the "two founding peoples" conception, the view that we are not envisaging two autonomous states, I see no necessary relationship between it and the distribution of law-making power between the Dominion and the Provinces. Acceptance of the "deux nations" conception at the federal level as well as at all provincial levels must surely involve its realization in the exercise of such legislative power as is committed to the one or to the other level of government.

The conclusion from this must be that no special treatment in the way of expanded law-making authority at the expense of the central government should be accorded to Quebec because of its French-speaking majority or to British Columbia or any other Province because of its English-speaking majority. The federal Parliament and government, in exercising legislative and executive power would be expected to reflect application, where appropriate, of the conception of "deux nations," as would the various Provinces in their exercises of authority. One can conceive, for example, of the federal authorities imposing a limitation on the jurisdiction of the Supreme Court of Canada to entertain appeals in matters arising purely under the Quebec Civil Code; and similarly limiting its jurisdiction in respect of appeals from other Provinces in matters arising under peculiarly local legislation.

In short, apart from the guarantees, statutory or constitutional, for underpinning the "deux nations" conception, differences about the appropriate ranges of legislative power must be assessed on the merits of our federal system without intrusion of that conception. I find it difficult to believe that our federal system can endure unless Ottawa is accepted as a source of national power and authority exercisable in respect of and for all citizens of Canada, wherever resident. The manner of exercise may, of course, have to be attuned to regional as well as provincial requirements. This is, however, a familiar situation, common to all federalisms. What I underline is that federal-provincial contentions about the reach of law-making power should not be embarrassed by interposing ethnic-linguistic-cultural qualifications which would make the central government less one for the people of a particular Province than it is for the people of other Provinces.

I take one final point which I shall not attempt to embellish. It is this. Apart from the tax question, to which I have already alluded, is there any such unbalance in constitutional text and constitutional interpretation in favour of the central government and against the Provinces as would, in terms of the experience of other democratic federal systems, suggest the need for remedial action in favour of the Provinces? Or, is there a case to be made for more consonance between federal tax authority and federal responsibility in the fields of social welfare and economic regulatory legislation? On these two related questions I would observe that I know of no federal system in which the constituent units have as extensive a regulatory authority as have the Provinces of Canada and in which the federal commerce power is as truncated as is that of the central government. One need only look at the position in insurance regulation, in securities regulation, in the marketing of natural products, in manufacturing, in the retail, distribution and service trades, in labour relations. I borrow a phrase from my friend Professor Frank Scott, "provincial autonomy [means] national inactivity"; and I would add that the more we have of the one, the more we have of the other. Of course, the issue is that of striking a proper balance. The question that I leave with you is not whether the existing unbalance should be carried further, but whether it should be guaranteed in its present dimensions both against constitutional amendment and constitutional re-interpretation.

I have spoken in the context of a surviving federalism. My words will mean nothing for those who preach separation, whether forthrightly or through verbal obfuscation; and they will probably mean very little to exponents of a limping federalism under which the central government will be one with dependent status, whether in respect of one Province or all the Provinces. I, for my part, reject both.

11 Judicial Review and the Division of Powers in Canada*

Martha Fletcher

One of the most obvious consequences of judicial review is that political questions often come to the courts clothed as legal, constitutional questions. The most notable political questions in federal systems are usually those involving the constitutional division of powers between the two levels of government. The constitutional framework within which the Canadian federation operates and from which judicial adjustment within it proceeds is the British North America Act, 1867 (B.N.A. Act). There the powers of government are divided between the Dominion[1] and the provinces, with section 91 of the Act containing the scope of central government power, and section 92 containing that of the provinces. Yet, because even the most carefully drawn language is subject to multiple interpretations, and because the context in which the arrangements operate changes over time, the division of powers presents to those who govern a continuing problem of adjustment. It is in these areas of adjustment that the choices made by the courts are of political importance, since they may determine which governments may carry out which activities and whether, indeed, some activities may be carried out at all. Thus, judicial review has considerable significance for the way in which the political process responds to the demands placed upon it.

As the court of final appeal for Canada until 1949, it was the responsibility of the Judicial Committee of the Privy Council, sitting in London, to adjudicate conflicts over the division of powers in the Act. Composed of some of the most eminent jurists of the United Kingdom and, later, of the Empire and Commonwealth, the Judicial Committee is technically not a court but rather an advisory body to the Crown, though its "advice" is invariably taken. During much of the time it ruled on Canadian cases it was criticized for its remoteness from the political system and the facts of Canadian life. It was felt by many that an indigenous court would have made different, more "realistic" decisions. The demand for a final court of appeals within Canada ultimately led to the abolition of appeals to the Judicial Committee in 1949 with the Supreme Court of Canada assuming the role of final constitutional arbiter.

Two problems arose in the interpretation of the Dominion and provincial powers conferred by the Constitution under sections 91 and 92. One was the changing definition of what matters are of national concern. The second was the sharp difference of opinion between the courts (particularly the Judicial Committee of the Privy Council) and Canadian political leaders and legal

---

*Published by permission of the author.

[1]Though in recent years the term "federal government" has been the proper designation for the government in Ottawa, the term "Dominion" has been used in this study. Since it is less ambiguous than "federal" and was the term used by the courts in referring to the central authority in nearly all of the cases discussed here, it was felt that greater clarity would result from its use.

scholars concerning both what had been meant in 1867 by the specified functions contained in these sections and how they should be applied to current problems. Further, because the B.N.A. Act has the legal status of merely another statute of the British Parliament, the judges took the view that they were not to go outside the contents of the Act in determining its meaning.

Within sections 91 and 92, four of the constitutional powers which have often been the legal clothing for political disputes concerning the division of powers between Dominion and province are the powers of the Dominion parliament to legislate for the peace, order, and good government of Canada and to regulate trade and commerce; and the powers of the provinces to control property and civil rights in the provinces and to legislate on all matters of merely a local or private nature in the province. Though the litigation involving these powers does not by any means comprise the totality of decisions concerning the federal division of powers, it can serve as an example of the impact of judicial review on the framework of the federal system, for the interpretation of the boundaries of these powers has been perhaps one of the conspicuous areas in which the courts have played the role of arbiter in the federal system.[2]

The Location of the Residuary Power

The residuary power — the general grant of legislative authority to the Dominion on all matters not assigned specifically — is a useful example for the study of the impact of judical review on the working of the federal system. This is true both because the residuary power can be used to legitimate expansion of governmental authority if the court is sympathetic to that expansion and because its expansion or contraction is a sign of the courts' view towards the "proper" division of powers in the federation. Thus it is important both as a source for legitimization of a changing balance of power in the federation and as a sign of the judicial attitude towards such an alteration.

The residuary power in the British North America Act is normally considered to reside in the Dominion authority granted in the opening paragraph of section 91:

> It shall be lawful [for Parliament] to make laws for the peace, order, and good government of Canada, in relation to all matters not coming within the Classes of Subjects by this Act assigned exclusively to the Legislatures of the Provinces; and for greater certainty, but not so as to restrict the Generality of the foregoing Terms of this Section, it is hereby declared that (notwithstanding anything in this Act) the exclusive Legislative Authority of the Parliament of Canada extends to all Matters coming within the Classes of Subjects hereinafter enumerated . . .

The meaning of this grant has been, however, a subject of considerable litigation for nearly a century, and its interpretation in relation to the totality of legislative powers granted in sections 91 and 92 of the B.N.A. Act has varied

---

[2]For a discussion of the ways in which constitutional cases come before the courts see J. A. C. Grant, "Judicial Review in Canada: Procedural Aspects", *Canadian Bar Review*, Vol. XLII, 1964, pp. 195-224.

over time, with the result that other sections at times have taken precedence over it.

From the standpoint of legal interpretation, the meaning of the peace, order, and good government clause can be understood only in the context of the two sections which comprise the division of legislative powers between the Dominion and provincial legislatures, and one must begin with an analysis of the grammar of the two sections. In the *Parsons* case, the Board identified the following grammatical construction as the correct one, and this opinion has been shared by many later writers on the Canadian constitution.[3]

The opening clause of sections 91 — "It shall be lawful [for Parliament] to make laws for the peace, order, and good government of Canada, in relation to all matters not coming within the Classes of Subjects of this Act assigned exclusively to the Legislatures of the Provinces;" — states that the Dominion is to have authority over *all matters* not specifically enumerated in section 92. The next clause — "and for greater certainty, but not so as to restrict the Generality of the foregoing Terms of this Section," — emphasizes that this general grant of power is not restricted by the enumerated heads that follow. The words in parentheses — "notwithstanding anything in this Act" — serve to make explicit that the power of the Dominion to make laws for peace, order, and good government takes precedence over the enumeration in section 92. The final words of the sentence — "the exclusive Legislative Authority of the Parliament of Canada *extends* [emphasis supplied] to all Matters coming within the Classes of Subjects . . . enumerated" — implies that the general grant is the sole authority given to the Dominion and that the authority exercisable under the enumerations comes from the one general grant of power rather than from a separate source to which the general power is merely supplementary (as subsequent decisions were to maintain).

The final paragraph of section 91, coming after the enumerations, says that "any matter coming within any of the Classes of Subjects in this Section shall not be deemed to come within the *class of matters* [emphasis supplied] of a local or private nature comprised in the enumeration of the Classes of Subjects by this Act assigned exclusively to the Legislatures of the Provinces." The significant point in the understanding of this paragraph's place in the Act is to note that the word "class" in the phrase "class of matters" is singular. When read in conjunction with section 92, grammatically, the phrase can only refer to section 92, head 16 — "generally all matters of a merely local or private nature in the province."

In summary, it is argued here that the peace, order, and good government clause was intended to give to the Dominion all subjects of legislation not covered in the provincial list of powers in section 92. The enumerations in section

---

[3]*Citizens Insurance Co.* v. *Parsons* (1881), 7 A.C. 96 at 107-108. For others who agree with this grammatical interpretation see Bora Laskin, *Canadian Constitutional Law*, 2nd ed., Carswell, Toronto, 1960, pp. 65-66; W. R. Kennedy, "The Interpretation of the B.N.A. Act", *Cambridge Law Journal*, Vol. VIII, 1943, pp. 146-159; Frederick P. Varcoe, *The Distribution of Legislative Power in Canada*, Carswell, Toronto, 1954, pp. 18-22.

91 neither add to nor subtract from the Dominion's residuary power over all subjects other than those in the section 92 list, since they are examples of the sorts of powers contemplated in the general grant rather than powers in their own right. The closing paragraph of section 91 was intended to make clear that the mere fact that a matter was of a local or private nature did not remove it from Dominion jurisdiction when it also came within the enumerations of that section. Thus, none of the enumerated heads in sections 91 could, by definition, be considered a provincial matter under any circumstances.

The interpretation of the application of the power to legislate for peace, order, and good government by the Dominion in specific situations has, however, been considerably different from the grammatical reading presented above. In an early landmark case, *Russell* v. *The Queen* (discussed below), the Committee based its decision on a similarly broad interpretation of the Dominion's residuary power. But this view was soon considerably altered by the decisions which followed.

The decisive point in the interpretation of the powers of the Dominion conferred by section 91 came with the *Local Prohibition*[4] case in 1896, in which Lord Watson presented what was to become the prevailing Judicial Committee interpretation of section 91. Watson's decision set out that the power of the Dominion to legislate for the peace, order, and good government of Canada was merely supplementary to the primary power of the Dominion given in the enumerations in section 91. Moreover, the power granted in the section 91 enumerations was not absolute. The closing words of section 91 did not contemplate that the authority of the Dominion under all matters enumerated in section 91 was absolute in its application to local and private matters coming within those subjects, but was merely an authority to legislate on local and private matters when such legislation was necessarily incidental to the exercise of the power over the Dominion as a whole. "It appears to their Lordships that [the closing words of section 91 were] not meant to derogate from the legislative authority given to the provincial legislatures . . . save to the extent of enabling the Parliament of Canada to deal with matters local or private in those cases where such legislation is necessarily incidental to the exercise of the powers conferred upon it by the enumerated heads of clause 91."[5] And, the Board declared, Sir Montague Smith was in error in the *Parsons* case when he declared that the closing words of section 91 applied only to head 16 of section 92. "It appears . . . that the language of the exception in section 91 was meant to include and correctly describe all the matters enumerated in the sixteen heads of section 92."[6] Thus was ruled that the Dominion could not consider its powers listed in the enumerations as paramount over any of the powers given the provinces in section 92. The opening words of section 91 that "(notwithstanding anything in this Act) the exclusive Legislative Authority of the Parliament of Canada extends to all Matters coming within the Classes of Subjects hereinafter enumerated . . ." were ignored rather than explained. The power of the Dominion to

---

[4]*Attorney-General for Ontario* v. *Attorney-General for Canada*, [1896] A.C. 348.
[5]*Ibid.*, p. 359.
[6]*Ibid.*, p. 359.

legislate for the peace, order, and good government of Canada was ruled to be a supplementary power which gave the Dominion authority to legislate "on such matters as are unquestionably of Canadian interest and importance" but it could not in so legislating "trench upon provincial legislation with respect to any of the classes of subjects enumerated in section 92".[7]

What this view of the peace, order, and good government power would mean became clear in the *Insurance Reference,* where Lord Haldane made more explicit what Lord Watson had begun. "It must be taken to be now settled," Haldane said, "that the general authority to make laws for the peace, order, and good government of Canada . . . does not, unless the subject matter of the legislation falls within some one of the enumerated heads which follow, enable the Dominion Parliament to trench on the subject matter entrusted to the provincial legislatures by the enumerations in section 92."[8] Thus only if the matter is not mentioned in section 92 can the Dominion legislate outside the enumeration of section 91 concerning a province. As Frank Scott put it, "the examples swallowed up the rule".[9] The idea of a general power to legislate for peace, order, and good government which would take precedence over provincial claims in section 92 when matters falling under that section became of national importance was rejected. The general power of legislation disappeared into the enumerated heads of section 91 and reappeared as a provincial power in head 16 of section 92.

As the Dominion power to legislate for peace, order, and good government lost its original significance the Judicial Committee developed a new role for the phrase, while attempting to demonstrate that this interpretation was consistent with previous decisions. The most notable of the cases which the Board had either to refute or re-interpret if the new use of peace, order, and good government was to stand was *Russell* v. *The Queen,*[10] decided in 1882. Here the court had ruled that the pith and substance — what the act was actually intended to do — determined whether it was to be viewed from the Dominion or Provincial aspect and the section into which it would fall.

The act in question, the Canadian Temperance Act of 1878, provided, according to its preamble, uniform legislation on the subject of temperance throughout the Dominion: "the objects and scope of the law are general — to promote temperance by means of a uniform law throughout the Dominion". On this ground the Dominion felt the measure properly fell under "peace, order, and good government" and not under the class of subjects "property and civil rights". The fact that the act was applied individually to each particular place could not alter its character as general legislation.[11] The Board agreed with this view of the Act, saying that "their Lordships cannot think that the Temperance Act in question properly belongs to the class of subjects property and civil rights". Instead, they said that it was very similar to laws placing restrictions on

---

[7]*Ibid.*, p. 360.

[8]*Attorney-General for Canada* v. *Attorney-General for Alberta,* [1916] A.C. 588 at 595.

[9]F. R. Scott, "The Development of Canadian Federalism", *Papers and Proceedings, Canadian Political Science Association,* Vol. III, May 1931, p. 247.

[10](1882), 7 A.C. 829.

[11]*Ibid.*, p. 829.

the sale of poisons and drugs, emphasizing that while such items are property, their character is such that their sale and custody can be regulated by the Dominion on the grounds that their use is dangerous to public safety. This sort of regulation, they insisted, does not deal with those items as they are viewed under section 92, head 13. "What Parliament is dealing with is not a matter in relation to property and its right, but one relating to public order and safety," their Lordships maintained. It is this aspect of public order and safety with which the Dominion is concerned, and its overriding interest is not negated by the fact that property is incidentally interfered with. The purpose of the Act is not to interfere with property but to protect public safety, and the section of the B.N.A. Act under which it falls depends on what the Act in question is basically intended to do.[12] As for the local option section of the law, the Board again insisted that the basic intent of the Act was decisive, and this intent was that there should be uniform legislation in all provinces respecting the traffic in intoxicating liquors. "Parliament does not treat the promotion of temperance as desirable in one province more than another. . . . The objects and scope are still general. . . ."[13]

With the redefinition of the Dominion's general power, however, the decision of the Board in the *Russell* case and the meaning of the opening words of section 91 took on new connotations. In the *Board of Commerce* case in 1922[14] Lord Haldane suggested that the decision in the *Russell* case was made to deal with an abnormal, *i.e.*, emergency, situation. Otherwise, the general Dominion powers could not have been called into play. It was in *Fort Francis Pulp and Paper Co.* v. *Manitoba Free Press*[15] two years later that this emergency doctrine was clearly and systematically stated. Here measures taken under the War Powers Act of 1914 were held *intra vires* Dominion authority not under the general powers of peace, order, and good government conferred in section 91, but under an emergency power "discovered" by the Committee. In the event of an emergency, national survival may depend upon the use of exceptional means. It would be suicidal to say that the Dominion could not provide for its own survival, said the Board. Therefore, the interests of the individual might have to be subordinated to those of the community and the Dominion permitted to act under power to legislate for the peace, order, and good government of Canada.

Their application of this heretofore unknown doctrine, however, resulted in some rather unusual legal reasoning. In 1925, basing its opinion on the two earlier Haldane decisions (see above), the Board declared the Industrial Dispute Investigation Act of 1907 *ultra vires* the Dominion on the ground that its subject matter was not among the enumerated subjects of section 91, and its powers trenched upon section 92, head 13, concerning property and civil rights in the provinces.[16] In specifically rejecting the decision in *Russell* v. *The Queen*

---

[12]*Ibid.*, pp. 837-839.
[13]*Ibid.*, p. 841.
[14]*In Re The Board of Commerce Act, 1919*, [1922] A.C. 191.
[15][1923] A.C. 695.
[16]*Toronto Electric Commissioners* v. *Snider*, [1925] A.C. 396.

that an act could be held *intra vires* simply on the grounds that it was to the general advantage of Canada, the court hypothesized in the following terms as to the true grounds upon which the *Russell* case had been decided:

> Their Lordships think that the decision in *Russell* v. *The Queen* can only be supported today, not on the footing of having laid down an interpretation such as has sometimes been invoked of the general words at the beginning of section 91, but on the assumption of the Board, apparently made at the time of deciding the case of *Russell* v. *The Queen,* that the evil of intemperance at that time amounted in Canada to one so great and general that at least for the period it was a menace to the national life of Canada so serious and pressing that the National Parliament was called upon to intervene to protect the nation from disaster. An epidemic of pestilence might conceivably have been regarded as analogous.[17]

To this rather incredible statement by their Lordships came the following Canadian reply:

> I [said Mr. Justice Anglin of the Supreme Court of Canada] cannot find anything in the judgment delivered by Sir Montague E. Smith in the *Russell* case suggestive of such a view having been entertained by the Judicial Committee. On the contrary, the whole tenor of the judgment seems to me inconsistent with its having proceeded on that basis. I should indeed be surprised if a body so well informed as their Lordships had countenanced such an aspersion on the fair fame of Canada even though some hard-driven advocate had ventured to insinuate it in argument.[18]

The peace, order, and good government power, then, was to apply in only two very limited cases.[19] First, in normal times, it was limited to only those items which did not fall into either the enumerations of section 91 or 92 (and these instances were rare indeed).[20] Secondly, it would override the provincial powers in section 91 in times of extreme emergency, with the question of whether the situation was a sufficient emergency to justify the use of the power in this fashion to be determined by the courts.

In 1929, however, a less restricted view of the B.N.A. Act was taken by Lord Sankey, when, in ruling on whether women could be called to the Senate, he said: "The British North America Act planted in Canada a living tree capable of growth and expansion within its natural limits. . . . Their Lordships do not conceive it to be the duty of this board . . . to cut down the provisions of the Act by a narrow and technical construction, but rather to give it a large and liberal interpretation. . . ."[21]

The Sankey "living tree" concept also seemed to carry over in the *Radio* case, decided in 1932, which interpreted the power of the Dominion to implement the International Radiotelegraphy Convention of 1927. Taking notice of the fact that those involved in radiotelegraphy "must so to speak be kept in

---

17*Ibid.,* p. 412.
18*The King* v. *Eastern Elevator Company,* [1925] S.C.R. 434 at 438.
19Laskin, p. 267.
20One of the few examples is the incorporation of companies with Dominion objects. *Great West Saddlery Co.* v. *The King,* [1921] 2 A.C. 91.
21*Edwards* v. *Attorney-General of Canada,* [1930] A.C. 136.

order by legislation and the only legislation that can deal with them all at once is Dominion legislation", the Board stated that control of the field was *intra vires* the Dominion under the general power of Parliament to legislate for the peace, order, and good government of Canada, rather than being divided between Dominion and province, provision by provision, according to the heading in sections 91 and 92 under which each fell.[22]

In 1937, however, court decisions on the scope of the Dominion general power reverted to the extreme of the *Snider* opinion (1925) with the decisions of the Judicial Committee concerning the Bennett "New Deal" legislation. These enactments were perhaps some of the most crucial ones, both economically and politically, to come before the Board during the years in which it ruled on the B.N.A. Act. This legislation was introduced in an attempt to cope with the problems of the great Depression and dealt with a wide variety of subjects.[23] Three of these acts — the Weekly Rest and Industrial Undertakings Act, the Minimum Wages Act, and the Limitation of Hours of Work Act — were defended before the courts both as coming under the Dominion power to implement treaties (since they were enacted in compliance with agreements of the International Labour Organization) and also under the general power of the Dominion to legislate for the peace, order, and good government of Canada.[24] The Board, however, ruled that neither of these grounds was sufficient to bring the legislation under the power of the central government.

To the argument that treaty legislation as a category was a Dominion affair both under section 132 and under the peace, order, and good government clause, their Lordships said: "While the ship of state now sails on larger ventures and into foreign water she still retains the water-tight compartments which are an essential part of her original structure".[25] Rejecting the use of the general power as it had been applied in the *Radio* case, they stated that the true ground of the *Radio* decision was that the legislation fell under the general clause only because it could not be fitted under any of the enumerations in sections 91 and 92.[26]

Finally, to the plea that an emergency situation existed and therefore the acts were valid under power to legislate for the peace, order, and good government of Canada, their Lordships replied that in their view no such overriding emergency existed and ruled the Dominion acts *ultra vires*. In their view,

---

[22]*In Re the Regulation and Control of Radio Communication in Canada*, [1932] A.C. 304 at 312.

[23]For a general discussion on the new deal see J. R. H. Wilbur, ed., *The Bennett New Deal: Fraud or Portent?* Copp Clark, Toronto, 1968.

[24]*Attorney-General for Canada* v. *Attorney-General for Ontario* (Labour Conventions Case), [1937] A.C. 327.

[25]*Ibid.*, p. 354.

[26]*Ibid.*, p. 351. That this interpretation is a patent misreading of the *Radio* decision is shown by quoting from the decision itself: "As their Lordships' views are based on what may be called the pre-eminent claims of section 91, it is unnecessary to discuss the question which was raised . . . whether, if there had been no pre-eminent claims as such, broadcasting could have been held to fall either within 'property and civil rights,' or within 'matters of a merely local or private nature' ". *Radio Reference*, [1932] A.C. 302 at 312.

It is only necessary to call attention to the phrases in the various cases, "abnormal circumstances," "exceptional conditions," "standard of necessity" (*Board of Commerce* case [1922] 1 A.C. 191), "some extraordinary peril to the national life of Canada," "highly exceptional," "epidemic of pestilence," (*Snider* case [1925] A.C. 396), to show how far the present case is from the conditions which may override the normal distribution of powers in sections 91 and 92.[27]

The Employment and Social Insurance Act was also ruled *ultra vires* the Dominion on the ground that the general powers of the Dominion did not apply here any more than in the previous case and that the Act trenched on section 92, head 13, property and civil rights.[28] With these cases, the height of the emergency doctrine was reached, as bitter Canadians noted that the only emergencies which the Privy Council had recognized were World War I and the "public drunkenness" sufficient to be a national emergency read into the *Russell* case.

In 1946, however, the Privy Council showed signs of retreat from the position taken in the "New Deal" cases. In another test of the temperance legislation which had been in question in *Russell* v. *The Queen*, the Board was asked specifically to rule on the meaning of that case. There Viscount Simon expressly repudiated the reasoning of *Toronto Electric Commissioners* v. *Snider* which had postulated the emergency doctrine in its fullest form. To quote him,

> . . . the British North America Act nowhere gives power to the Dominion Parliament to legislate in matters which are properly to be regarded as exclusively within the competence of the provincial legislatures merely because of the existence of an emergency. Secondly, they can find nothing in the judgment of the Board in 1882 which suggests that it proceeded on the ground of emergency; there was certainly no evidence before the Board that one existed. The act of 1878 was a permanent, not a temporary Act and no objection was raised to it on that account . . . . [T]he true test must be found in the real subject matter of the legislation: if it is such that it goes beyond local or provincial concern or interests and must from its inherent nature be the concern of the Dominion as a whole . . . then it will fall within the competence of the Dominion Parliament as a matter affecting the peace, order, and good government of Canada, though it may in another aspect touch on matters specially reserved to the provincial legislatures . . . . It is the nature of the legislation itself, and not the existence of emergency, that must determine whether it is valid or not.[29]

While liquor legislation was considered to be a matter of such general interest to the Dominion as a whole as to fall under the peace, order, and good government clause, the regulation of hours of work of employees of hotels run by the Canadian Pacific Railway was considered, as late as 1950, to be "substantially" a

---

[27]*Ibid.*, p. 353.

[28]*Attorney-General for Canada* v. *Attorney-General for Ontario* (Employment and Social Insurance Act Reference), [1937] A.C. 355.

[29]*Attorney-General for Ontario* v. *Canadian Temperance Federation*, [1946] A.C. 196 at 205-206.

matter of property and civil rights in the provinces rather than of general interest to Canada.[30]

In 1951 the Judicial Committee again utilized the reasoning of the *Labour Conventions* cases, ruling that legislation controlling the manufacture and importation of margarine in the interest of protecting and encouraging the dairy industry throughout Canada could not be justified by appealing to the sufficient interest rule so recently stated in the *Canadian Temperance Federation* case. Without countering the reasoning in that case, Lord Morton quoted the contrary view found in the *Labour Conventions* opinion as controlling in this instance and made no further comment.[31] Thus the final decisions of the Judicial Committee left the matter of the scope of the peace, order, and good government clause in considerable doubt, and the Supreme Court of Canada (which became the court of final appeal in 1949) was presented with a considerable variety of precedents to follow in interpreting the clause.

The Supreme Court was presented with an opportunity to decide on the scope of the general power soon after the Court became Canada's final constitutional authority. The case was a reference on the validity of the Wartime Leasehold Regulations which were adopted during World War II and carried over into the post-war era.[32] The precedent which the Court used in unanimously upholding the validity of Dominion rent controls came directly from the "emergency" doctrine of *Fort Francis Pulp and Paper Co.* v. *Manitoba Free Press*.[33] In deciding that the Act was valid, the Justices emphasized both the "abnormal" and "emergency" situation arising out of the war and its aftermath and the explicitly temporary nature of the legislation. Noting that in normal times the subject of rent control lay exclusively with the provinces through their power over property and civil rights, the Court emphasized that "the rights of the provinces are not . . . permanently suppressed, and their jurisdiction, temporarily suspended . . . flows afresh when the field is finally abandoned".[34] In a spirit unlike that which animated the Judicial Committee in the "New Deal" cases, however, the existence of the emergency in this instance was attested to both by "common sense" (an expression of Mr. Justice Taschereau) and by the view expressed by Kerwin and others that its existence as asserted by the Dominion could only be disregarded in the light of "very clear evidence" or "clear and unmistakable evidence that the Government [was] in error".[35] Nowhere in the decision was the reasoning of the more recent *Canadian Temperance Federation* case considered worthy of more than passing mention, with Taschereau explicitly denying its applicability.

The second case in which the Supreme Court ruled on the scope of this power

---

[30]*Canadian Pacific Railway* v. *Attorney-General for British Columbia*, [1950] A.C. 123 at 142.

[31]*Canadian Federation of Agriculture* v. *Attorney-General for Quebec*, [1951] A.C. 179 at 198.

[32]*Reference Re the Validity of the Wartime Leasehold Regulations*, [1950] S.C.R. 124.

[33][1923] A.C. 695.

[34]*Wartime Leasehold Reference*, [1950] S.C.R. 124 at 140.

[35]*Ibid.*, p. 135.

in the post-Privy Council era was *Johannesson* v. *West St. Paul*,[36] which harks back strongly to the reasoning and tone of the *Aeronautics* and *Radio* references of the early 1930's. Quoting the *Aeronautics Reference*, Mr. Justice Rinfret echoed the view of a unanimous court in declaring aerial navigation to be a "class of subject which has attained such dimension as to affect the body politic of the Dominion".[37] Thus municipal legislation controlling the erection of airports was invalid as encroaching on the power of the Dominion to legislate for peace, order, and good government. Once the determination is made that the subject falls under the Dominion general clause, the Court said, the powers of the provinces over property and civil rights and matters of merely a local or private nature in the province have no standing, even if the Dominion has not exercised its jurisdiction over the matter. In his opinion Mr. Justice Locke quoted approvingly the words of Lord Sankey in the *Aeronautics Reference*:

> While the courts should be jealous in upholding the charter of the Provinces as enacted in section 92, it must be borne in mind that the real object of the Act was to give the central government those high functions and almost sovereign powers by which uniformity of legislation might be secured on all questions which were of common concern to all the provinces as members of a constituent whole.[38]

It took nearly fifteen years for two more cases on the general residuary power to arise before the Supreme Court, and these, like the other two cases from the post-Judicial Committee period, upheld the power of the federal government to act for the "peace, order, and good government of Canada". In the first of these two — a case involving the power of the federal government to expropriate land in Ontario near Ottawa to create a green belt surrounding the national capital — Mr. Justice Cartwright, speaking for a unanimous court, rested the decision firmly on the more generous construction of the *Radio Reference, Johannesson* v. *West St. Paul*, and the *Canadian Temperance Federation* case. Noting that the subject matter of the National Capital Act (the creation of a national capital with the appropriate setting) was not mentioned in either section 91 or 92, and citing both *Johannesson* and the *Radio Reference* as precedents, he concluded that ". . . such legislation [*i.e.*, legislation not mentioned in ss. 91 and 92] falls within the general words at the opening of section 91. . . .[39]

The second ground for the decision, however, followed the slightly different tack of the *Temperance Federation* case. There the reasoning was in the tradition of *Russell's* case, holding that the relevant test was whether the subject matter of the legislation did or did not go beyond local or provincial concern. Again the Court's answer was unequivocal: "I find it difficult to suggest a subject matter of legislation which more clearly goes beyond local or provincial interests and is the concern of Canada as a whole than the development, conservation and improvement of the National Capital Region. . . ."[40] And, to the objection

---

[36][1952] 1 S.C.R. 292.
[37]*Ibid.*, p. 303, quoting the *Aeronautics Reference*, [1932] A.C. 54 at 77.
[38]*Ibid.*, pp. 327-328, quoting the *Aeronautics Reference*, p. 70.
[39]*Munro* v. *National Capital Commission*, [1966] S.C.R. 663 at 670.
[40]*Ibid.*, p. 671.

that the Act trenched on civil rights in the provinces, the Court answered in the same vein: "once it has been determined that the matter in relation to which the Act is passed is one which falls within the power of Parliament, it is no objection to its validity that its operation will affect civil rights in the provinces".[41] There is hardly a more unequivocal statement in support of the Dominion's general power in the entire history of Canadian constitutional interpretation.

The most recent case dealing with the residuary power also supports the Dominion. In the *Off-Shore Mineral Rights Reference*, decided in late 1967, a unanimous court held that the control and exploitation of minerals in the lands under Canada's territorial seas was the sole responsibility of the Federal government, not the provincial government (in this case British Columbia). Basing the judgment squarely on a wide view of Dominion authority, the Court, having found that the lands in question did not fall within the historical boundaries of the provinces and therefore were federal territory concluded that control of mineral rights must be "regarded as a matter affecting Canada generally and covered by the expression 'the peace, order, and good government of Canada' ".[42] Since the lands did not fall within the boundaries of the province they could not, logically, fall within the subjects of section 92. Moreover, the Court ruled, "The mineral resources of the lands underlying the territorial sea are of concern to Canada as a whole and go beyond local or provincial concern or interests".[43] Thus even if the lands had been within the boundaries of the province, their resources would have been of sufficient concern to the nation as a whole to take them out of the ambit of "matters of a merely local or private nature in the province".

With these decisions, the pattern of interpretation of the peace, order, and good government clause would seem to have come full circle to the position taken in *Russell* v. *The Queen*.

Although there have been only four cases from the era of Supreme Court autonomy dealing with the residuary power, the consistency with which the justices have upheld the wider interpretation and the variety of tests they have used in doing so suggest that the Dominion may now be able to rely with some measure of confidence on "peace, order, and good government" as a standard against which to measure proposed legislation.

The Scope of "Trade and Commerce", Section 91(2)

The fates of the peace, order, and good government clause and of the enumerated heads of section 91, were, certainly, closely interrelated. With the interpretation of the closing words of section 91 to mean that the Dominion enumerations could extend only to necessarily incidental control of matters of a local or private nature (this phrase being defined as including the totality of section 92) and the eclipse of the *non obstante* clause, the authority of the Dominion

---

[41] *Ibid.*
[42] *Reference Re Ownership of Off-Shore Mineral Rights*, 65 D.L.R. (2d) 353 at 376.
[43] *Ibid.*

under those enumerations was clearly circumscribed in comparison with what it had previously been.

The trade and commerce power of section 91, head 2, which on its face would seem to have the widest scope of any Dominion enumeration, however, received a still more restrictive interpretation than the other enumerated powers in section 91. Thus it was doubly restricted: first by the generally restrictive interpretation of the relation of section 91 to section 92, and also by a narrow reading of the meaning of the words "the regulation of trade and commerce" themselves. The potential usefulness of this heading to centralists as a device for moving the control of the nation's economy from the provinces to the Dominion as Canada entered her industrial phase can hardly be exaggerated. (This is especially notable when the application of the commerce clause in the United States is compared to the role of its somewhat more forcefully stated counterpart in Canada.) As one observer has noted, there is considerable irony in the fact that the United States has done so much with so little while Canada has done so little with so much.[44] The expansion or contraction of this power has, of course, fundamentally influenced the way in which the federation has approached the crucial issues growing out of the development of a national economy.

The narrowing of the potential scope of the trade and commerce power began the first time the clause was considered by the Judicial Committee in *Citizens Insurance Company* v. *Parsons* in 1881.[45] There the Board rejected the contention of the appellants that the words "trade and commerce" were meant to be "the most generous words which can be used, and include every kind of business which can possibly be carried on". Their Lordships asserted that the Act could not have contemplated such a wide meaning, or several other classes of subjects enumerated in section 91, such as banking, bills of exchange and promissory notes, and weights and measures would not also have been mentioned.[46] Instead, their Lordships speculated that the true intent of the words of head 2 corresponded to those used in the Act of Union between England and Scotland which allowed differing controls and rules of trade in those two kingdoms.[47] "Trade and commerce" in the meaning of the B.N.A. Act, their Lordships said, "would include political arrangements in regard to trade requiring the sanction of Parliament, regulation of trade in matters of interprovincial concern, and it may be that they would include general regulation of trade affecting the whole Dominion." The Board ruled, however, that the phrase did *not* support legislation regulating contracts of a *particular* business or trade carried on in a single province.

When the Supreme Court of Canada had considered the matter, Mr. Justice Taschereau had also maintained that the power of the Dominion parliament to incorporate companies was derived from the trade and commerce power,

---

[44]Alexander Smith, *The Commerce Power in Canada and the United States*, Butterworth, Toronto, 1963, p. 4.

[45](1881), 7 A.C. 96.

[46]*Ibid.*, p. 100.

[47]*Ibid.*, p. 112.

but Sir Montague Smith suggested that this power was more correctly derived from the general power of the Dominion to legislate on all matters not expressly given to the provinces.[48] The *Parsons* case, then, set several precedents. First, the words trade and commerce were not to be taken in their common meaning, for such an interpretation "would all but destroy the autonomy of the provinces". Secondly, the Dominion could not regulate the contracts of particular businesses in a single province. Finally, the tentative definition of the power was that it encompassed political arrangements for trade, interprovincial trade, and perhaps general trade affecting the whole Dominion.

Some of the ramifications of the *Parsons* case became evident in the *Local Prohibition* case. Citing *Parsons* as precedent, the Board confirmed that the Dominion power over trade and commerce did not extend to intraprovincial trade itself. Here the Judicial Committee, however, went beyond that holding and also limited the power of the Dominion to regulate local trade and commerce even as a part of a general regulation of those activities.[49]

While their Lordships noted that "the provisions of the Act of 1878 [involved in the *Russell* case] were in all material respects the same with those which are now embodied in the Canada Temperance Act of 1886 [being tested in this case]",[50] they ruled that it could not also be sustained under the trade and commerce power but only under peace, order, and good government. The reason for this holding, Lord Watson explained, was the distinction between regulation and prohibition:

> A power to regulate, naturally, if not necessarily, assumes, unless it is enlarged by the context, the conservation of the thing which is to be made the subject of regulation. In that view, their Lordships are unable to regard the prohibitive enactments of the Canadian statute of 1886 as regulations of trade and commerce.[51]

Thus the general power to regulate trade and commerce could not include prohibition as a means of regulation.

Again, in the *Insurance Reference*, the Judicial Committee restricted the scope of the commerce powers, declaring that not only were contracts of particular businesses operating in a single province beyond the scope of the power (as held in *Parsons*) and regulation by prohibition invalid, but the regulation of particular *trades* whether local or interprovincial by a licensing system was also beyond the competence of the Dominion.[52] This limiting trend reached its logical conclusion in 1922, when in the *Board of Commerce* case Lord Hal-

---

[48]*Ibid.*, p. 116.

[49]In *Russell* v. *The Queen* the Board had emphasized that, while the prohibitory liquor legislation there in question was primarily to be upheld under the peace, order, and good government power, this "must not be understood as intimating any dissent from the opinion . . . that the Act, as a general regulation of the traffic in intoxicating liquors throughout the Dominion, fell within the class of subject 'the regulation of trade and commerce' . . . and was, on that ground a valid exercise of the legislative power of the Parliament of Canada".

[50][1896] A.C. 348 at 362.

[51][1896] A.C. 348 at 363.

[52]*Attorney-General for Canada* v. *Attorney-General for Alberta*, [1916] A.C. 588.

dane concluded that interference with particular trades and businesses (such as insurance) in any way, was not consistent with a power limited to general regulation of trade (that is, general commercial intercourse), not *trades*.[53]

A more sweeping, if not more serious, limitation on the ambit of section 91(2) came in a series of cases which culminated in *Toronto Electric Commissioners* v. *Snider*. As early as 1912 the Judicial Committee implied that the limitations placed on the peace, order, and good government clause which restricted its application to only those situations where it supplemented a power enumerated in section 91 were also to apply to the trade and commerce clause.[54] It was not until ten years later in the *Board of Commerce* case, however, that this view was expressed explicitly. There Lord Haldane suggested that the trade and commerce power could *only* apply when used in conjunction with another Dominion power, particularly the general power over peace, order, and good government.[55] Thus the trade and commerce clause was not even to have the status of an ordinary enumerated head, but, because of the generality of its terms, the Board ruled that it had to be buttressed by a more explicit, additional authority as well.

In *Toronto Electric Commissioners* v. *Snider*, Lord Haldane stated the point succinctly, saying:

> It is, in their Lordships' opinion, now clear that, excepting so far as the power can be invoked in aid of capacity conferred independently under other words in s. 91, the power to regulate trade and commerce cannot be relied on as enabling the Dominion Parliament to regulate civil rights in the Provinces [in this case the settlement of industrial disputes].[56]

Far from being the most far-reaching of the enumerated Dominion powers, trade and commerce was seen as nothing more than a weak relation.

It was not long, however, until the Judicial Committee beat a retreat from the extravagance of this opinion. In a 1931 opinion Lord Atkin spoke for the Board, saying:

> Their Lordships merely propose to disassociate themselves from the construction suggested . . . in the judgment in the *Board of Commerce* case under which it was contended that the power to regulate trade and commerce could be invoked only in furtherance of a general power which Parliament possessed independently of it. . . . The words of the statute must receive their proper construction where they stand as giving an independent authority to Parliament over the particular subject-matter. . . .[57]

And again, in the *Aeronautics Reference*, heard the following year, the Board intimated that the trade and commerce power might have been a ground for upholding Dominion regulation of aeronautics, had not the treaty power given

---

[53]*In Re The Board of Commerce Act, 1919*, [1922] A.C. 191.

[54]*Montreal* v. *Montreal Street Railway*, [1912] A.C. 333 at 344. See also *John Deere Plow Co.* v. *Wharton*, [1915] A.C. 330.

[55][1922] A.C. 191 at 197-198.

[56][1925] A.C. 396 at 410.

[57]*Proprietary Articles Trade Association* v. *Attorney-General for Canada*, [1931] A.C. 310 at 326.

in section 132 been sufficient ground in itself.[58] The argument that the authority of the trade and commerce clause was supplementary became a dead issue with the *Trade Mark* case (1937), in which Ontario questioned the Dominion's power to establish a national trade mark. In answering the question affirmatively, the Board made it clear that this was an appropriate exercise of the trade and commerce power unaided by any other power of the Dominion. In its view, "there could hardly be a more appropriate form of the exercise of this power than the creation and regulation of a uniform law of trade marks".[59]

But though the extravagance of the "supplementary" view of the trade and commerce power had been discarded, the restrictions of narrow reading of the words and the understanding that none of the enumerations of section 91 could reach farther than a necessarily incidental interference with the provincial matters in section 92 remained. A crucial test of the extent to which these views still applied came with the reference of the Dominion's Natural Products Marketing Act to the courts (also in 1937)[60] The Act was part of the Bennett Government's "New Deal" legislation through which the Dominion sought to cope with the marketing problems of the Depression by claiming sweeping federal authority to regulate time and place of selling and, when necessary, prohibit marketing of any product. This the Board declared wholly *ultra vires* the Dominion on the ground that aspects of the scheme which controlled interprovincial and international trade were so intermixed with control of purely local transactions that the whole scheme was invalid as an infringement of section 92(13). Said the Board, ". . . the regulation of trade and commerce does not permit the regulation of individual forms of trade or commerce confined to the Province".[61]

It was nearly fifteen years before the Judicial Committee was again called upon to comment on the meaning of the trade and commerce power. In 1951 Section 5A of the Dairy Industry Act was referred to the courts for an opinion as to whether it was valid for the Dominion, in an effort to support and develop the dairy industry, to prohibit the manufacture and sale of margarine throughout Canada. Again, noting that the Act prohibited these activities even when carried on solely within the boundaries of a single province, the Board (appealing to the considerable precedent for the view) ruled that such a measure was an invalid encroachment on property and civil rights in the province. In their final word on the subject before appeals were ended, the Board summed up the Judicial Committee view:

> . . . [T]he present case is typical of the many cases in which the Board had
> felt bound to put some limit on the scope of the wide words used in head 2
> of section 91 in order to preserve from serious curtailment, if not from
> virtual extinction, the degree of autonomy which, as appears from the scheme
> of the Act as a whole, the provinces were intended to possess.[62]

[58][1932] A.C. 54 at 73.
[59]*Attorney-General for Ontario* v. *Attorney-General for Canada,* [1937] A.C. 405 at 417.
[60]*Attorney-General for British Columbia* v. *Attorney-General for Canada,* [1937] A.C. 377.
[61]*Ibid.,* p. 387.
[62]*Canadian Federation of Agriculture* v. *Attorney-General for Quebec,* [1951] A.C. 179 at 194.

The end of appeals to the Judicial Committee of the Privy Council left the Supreme Court with a considerable bulk of precedent for a narrow construction of the meaning of section 91, head 2. In 1957, with its first opportunity to rule as the final court in a case involving the commerce power, however, it took a more venturesome tack. The matter in question was the validity of the Ontario Farm Products Act, which was designed to regulate the sale of farm products throughout Ontario.[63] Seven of the eight justices sitting in the case pronounced it *intra vires* the province, but the case was seized as an opportunity to comment on the meaning of trade and commerce as stated in section 91 and the problem of setting the limits of geographical areas of jurisdiction in an integrated economic system. Questioning the validity of considering trade and commerce a part of the power of the provinces over property and civil rights, as it had so often been in the past, Mr. Justice Rand commented: "The production of goods as an economic activity does not take place by virtue of positive law or civil right, it is assumed as part of the residual free activity of men upon or around which law is imposed. It has an identity of its own recognized by section 91(2)."[64] Trade, the Court said, was not static but "dynamic, the creation and flow of goods from production to consumption . . . as an individualized action". Thus, the boundaries of the province and the bounds of provincial authority over trade were not to be considered coextensive. In matters of trade and commerce within the province but with effects beyond the province, the Dominion power under section 91(2) was held paramount. But, though the use of the provincial boundary as the mark of the division of jurisdictions has now been at least temporarily discredited, it is not clear what formula or test of jurisdiction will take its place.

Murphy v. *Canadian Pacific Railway*, decided in the next year, however, offered a more clear-cut test of the Court's view of the commerce power. There Mr. Justice Locke, writing for himself and for Justices Taschereau, Fauteux and Abbott, specifically upheld the Canadian Wheat Board Act. He ruled that the Act was a valid regulation of trade and commerce and added: "the fact that . . . it [necessarily] interferes with property and civil rights in the province . . . is immaterial".[65] To the argument that the Dominion did not have the power to regulate the activities of a particular trade (as held in the *Insurance Reference*), the Justices replied that the Act did not regulate just one trade but several, and, since their activities were directed to the export of grain from the province, the provincial governments were powerless to control them. Though no general trend can be safely inferred from the two rulings of the Supreme Court on trade and commerce since the abolition of appeals to the Judicial Committee, the difference of approach between the Privy Council and the Court is evdent. How far the potential of the pragmatic approach to the matter of whether trade is in fact merely local or interprovincial in import will be developed, awaits the arrival of similar cases before the court.

---

[63]*Re The (Ontario) Farm Products Marketing Act*, [1957] S.C.R. 198.
[64]*Ibid.*, p. 211.
[65][1958] S.C.R. 626 at 632.

Summary and Conclusion

The impact of judicial review on the legal framework within which Dominion and provinces operate, then, has been substantial. The peace, order, and good government clause was transformed from a general residuary power to legislate on all matters not specifically excepted by section 92 to a supplementary power operating (1) only on those matters not covered by either of the enumerated lists, (2) as a supplement to powers possessed independently in section 91, and (3) in time of emergency, when it could temporarily override the normal jurisdiction to save the nation from catastrophe. From the early 1930's until 1949, decisions by the Judicial Committee wavered back and forth between this restrictive interpretation and the broader scope given the clause prior to 1896. Thus, at least until recently, the courts failed to produce even the clarity and certainty as to the meaning of the law which is one of the prime functions of the judiciary.

The interpretation of the trade and commerce power followed a similar pattern. The scope of the power was limited first by a narrow reading of the meaning of the words, then by an interpretation of its relation to section 92 which settled that it could not extend into the realm of the powers given the provinces in section 92 and, finally, by an interpretation which declared it to be operable *only* as a supplement to another federal power. Again, as in the case of the residuary power, the courts retreated from the extremities of their position in the early 1930's only to return to them in the later years of that decade.

After the Supreme Court became the final arbiter of the federal balance in 1949, it began to throw its weight behind broader interpretations of the scope of these two powers. Twice in the past two decades, the Court has shown itself willing to repudiate sharply the more restrictive and abstract elements in the earlier interpretation of the trade and commerce clause. Similarly, in the case of the residuary power, the Court has found it possible to uphold Dominion legislation enacted under the government's authority to provide for the "peace, order, and good government" of Canada, at first tentatively and then with broader sweep. One must proceed cautiously, however, in advancing these trends as settled interpretations, both because of the small number of cases involved and because of the wide fluctuations in interpretation common in the past.

The result of the judicial interpretation of the boundaries of legal authority between Dominion and province with regard to the crucial powers in question here, however, has been primarily to enlarge the provincial area of power and to restrict that of the Dominion. Thus the legal framework has operated as a centrifugal force in the federation, dividing jurisdiction and thwarting attempts to centralize control in important areas of economic and social concern. There can be little doubt that for much of its history, the Judicial Committee brought a "states' rights" bias to its interpretive task. The decisions based on this normative position could not fail to have significant repercussions on the policy-making process in Canada, and thus important consequences for political life. Perhaps the Committee's invalidation of the "New Deal" legislation is the outstanding example of their Lordships' determination to give the provinces their rights —

whether they wanted them or not. In this, as in several other areas, judicial decisions made it more difficult for Canada's governments to cope with their problems than it might otherwise have been.

One of the most important functions of a court which adjudicates constitutional questions in a federal system is to provide flexibility in the allocation of responsibilities between governments, so that the system may adjust, over time, to changing economic, social and political realities. The absence of a settled amendment procedure has made this function particularly important in Canada. The initial rigidity of constitutional interpretation and the unpredictable fluctuations in interpretation which followed have no doubt played their part in discrediting the judicial review process. Among the consequences of this loss of faith are an increase in the use of informal mechanisms of adjustment and, perhaps, a decline in the legitimacy of the courts as arbiters of the federal balance.[66] Bora Laskin sums up the situation as follows:

> It is as if a stalemate has been reached in the legal relations of Canada and the Provinces, but with no legal, no judicial means of resolving current conflicts. In fact, there are such means. But what has been evident for many years is that the mood of our political leaders is less and less for acquiescence in a judicial order of constitutional change through reinterpretation of the division of legislative powers. The courts themselves cannot, of course, force such a mood; their jurisdiction must be activated by the initiative of private litigants or by governments; and above all, the exercise of jurisdiction must be founded on actual or proposed legislation as the subject of challenge.[67]

If, as Professors Corry and Laskin suggest, the courts are no longer a major mechanism for constitutional adjustment, certainly at least part of the explanation of this apparent lack of faith of governments and other potential litigants in the results of judicial decision-making lies in the record of past performance.[68]

---

[66]See J. A. Corry, "Constitutional Trends and Federalism", in A. R. M. Lower, F. R. Scott, *et al.*, *Evolving Canadian Federalism*, Duke University Press, Durham, 1958, pp. 117-118.

[67]Bora Laskin, "Reflections on the Canadian Constitution After the First Century", *Canadian Bar Review*, Vol. XLV, No. 3 September, 1967, pp. 395-396.

[68]Other factors than the trends in interpretation have obviously also played a part in the decline in the role of the Court as arbiter of the federal balance. As Richard Jones points out, one such factor is the doubt that Supreme Court justices, selected solely by the central government, can act as unbiased arbiters in conflicts between the two levels of government. See Richard Jones, *Community in Crisis: French-Canadian Nationalism in Perspective*, McClelland and Stewart, Toronto, 1967, p. 103.

12   The Meaning of Provincial Autonomy*

Louis-Philippe Pigeon

A proper study of the problem of provincial autonomy requires consideration of some fundamental principles. Laws are the framework of society. Without them, relations between men would be governed by individual brute force. Any order of things means laws in one form or in another. Laws in turn imply an authority empowered to make and to enforce them. Under any form of government the power of this authority over individuals is of necessity very great, and very great also is its influence on their living conditions.

For any given group of humans the constitution of the civil authority by which they are governed is therefore of prime importance. Obviously this will cause any human group possessing special characteristics to desire an authority of its own. A group forming what is sociologically termed a "nation" normally aspires to independence. Small states are apt however to encounter very serious difficulties owing to their inherent military and economic weakness. Instead of precarious military alliances or trade agreements, a federation offers stability and permanency. The federal state is an attempt to reconcile the need of military, political and economic strength, which large units only can offer, with the desire for self-government that is inherent in any human group having distinct collective feelings.

Of course federation necessarily implies that some powers become vested in a central authority. The real problem is the definition of these powers or, its corollary, of the powers remaining in the federated states or provinces.

In the eyes of some men, a federal state is an instrument of unification, in other words, a means of bringing about the gradual disappearance of the segmental differences opposed to complete political unity. In the eyes of others, federation of itself implies this complete political unity, the component states or provinces being looked upon as mere administrative entities whose functions should be restricted to the application of general policies defined by the central authority. In the eyes of autonomists, federation implies a division of political authority so that the component states or provinces are free to define their general policy in their own sphere of activity, without being obliged to conform with any pattern set down by the central authority.

In the construction of the British North America Act the courts, and especially the Judicial Committee of the Privy Council, have fairly consistently adopted the autonomist conception of federation:

> They [the Federal Government] maintained that the effect of the statute has been to sever all connections between the Crown and the Provinces; to make the government of the Dominion the only government of Her Majesty in North America; and to reduce the provinces to the rank of independent municipal institutions. For these propositions, which contain the sum and substance of the arguments addressed to them in support of this appeal,

*From *Canadian Bar Review*, Vol. XXIX, 1951, pp. 1126-1135. Reprinted by permission of the author and publisher.

their Lordships have been unable to find either principle or authority . . . .
and a Lieutenant-Governor, when appointed, is as much the representative
of Her Majesty for all purposes of provincial government as the Governor-
General himself is for all purposes of Dominion government.[1]

The scheme of the Act passed in 1867 was thus, not to weld the Provinces into
one, nor to subordinate Provincial Governments to a central authority, but
to establish a central government in which these Provinces should be
represented, entrusted with exclusive authority only in affairs in which they
had a common interest. Subject to this each Province was to retain its
independence and autonomy and to be directly under the Crown as its
head.[2]

Their Lordships do not conceive it to be the duty of this Board — it is
certainly not their desire — to cut down the provisions of the Act by a
narrow and technical construction, but rather to give it a large and liberal
interpretation so that the Dominion to a great extent, but within certain
fixed limits, may be mistress in her own house, as the Provinces to a great
extent, but within certain fixed limits, are mistresses in theirs.[3]

All the arguments advanced against these decisions by numerous writers are
based either on the "Peace, Order and good Government" clause or on the so-
called "historical construction" of the Act.

In support of the first argument it is contended that the courts have failed to
give full effect to the opening words of section 91[4] and that the authority thus
conferred on the federal Parliament should be broadly construed.[5] But it is
significant that seldom do those who advance this contention quote the complete
sentence. They speak of the importance of the grant of legislative authority for
the "Peace, Order and good Government of Canada". They point out that such
expressions were traditionally used to grant general legislative authority; but they

---

[1]*Liquidators of the Maritime Bank of Canada* v. *Receiver-General of N.B.*, [1892] A.C.
437, at pp. 441-443.

[2]*In re The Initiative and Referendum Act*, [1919] A.C. 935, at p. 942.

[3]*"Persons"* case, [1930] A.C. 124, at p. 136.

[4]"It shall be lawful for the Queen, by and with the Advice and Consent of the Senate
and House of Commons to make Laws for the Peace, Order, and good Government of
Canada, in relation to all Matters not coming within the Classes of Subjects by this Act
assigned exclusively to the Legislatures of the Provinces . . .".

[5]See, for example, Bora Laskin, "Peace, Order and good government Re-examined",
Canadian Bar Review, Vol. XXV, 1947, p. 1085. "Some sixty years ago the Judicial
Committee said in *Riel* v. *The Queen* that the words 'peace, order and good government'
were words 'apt to authorize the utmost discretion of enactment for the attainment of
the objects pointed to'. The remark was not made in relation to sections 91 and 92 of the
British North America Act and in the context of the Act it is undoubtedly too wide. But
in its reference to legislative objects it indicates the type of problem which a court
must face in interpreting sections 91 and 92. It is beside the point that the words of the
introductory clause are too large and loose for comfortable adjudication. The Judicial
Committee has not been reticent about its ability to give content to the large and loose
provincial legislative power in relation to property and civil rights in the province,
although it may be noted that it has done so largely in terms of thwarting exercises of
federal legislative power, whether for the peace, order and good government of Canada or
in relation to the regulation of trade and commerce."

pay slight attention to the fact that these pregnant words are immediately followed by the all-important restriction: "in relation to all Matters not coming within the Classes of Subjects by this Act assigned exclusively to the Legislatures of the Provinces". If due attention is paid to these words, it becomes impossible to construe the grant of residuary power otherwise than as saving provincial authority instead of over-riding it.

The "historical construction" is a pretended inquiry into the intentions of the framers of the Canadian constitution, otherwise than by a consideration of the meaning of the words used in the final document. The fallacy of this method lies not only in the fact that it runs counter to a fundamental rule of legal interpretation[6] but also in the fact that it is most unreliable. The B.N.A. Act is not the expression of the intention of one man, whose ideas might perhaps be gathered from extrinsic evidence with a reasonable degree of certainty; it is the expression of a compromise between many men holding different and opposed viewpoints. When agreement was reached on a text, are we justified in assuming that agreement was also reached on intentions?

We know that the Fathers of Confederation were far from unanimous in their conception of the proposed federation. Some, like Sir Charles Tupper, held complete unification as their ideal, while others, like E. B. Chandler,[7] favoured a large measure of provincial autonomy. A compromise formula was finally devised to which both groups assented. Does this mean that their conflicting points of view had been reconciled?[8]

Experience in the practice of law shows that it is extremely difficult to visualize all the implications of a complex statute. Taxation statutes, for example, are prepared by specialists and scrutinized by experienced parliamentary counsel. Even then amendments introduced for the express purpose of avoiding unintended and undesired results are far from uncommon. Obviously, the long-term consequences of constitutional enactments are much more difficult of exact appreciation than the immediate consequences of taxation statutes.

Another important and often overlooked factor contributing to the difficulty of interpreting the B.N.A. Act is the fact that words actually lose much precision of meaning when used to define broad and fundamental political conceptions. The meaning of words is conventional. In final analysis it rests on generally

---

[6]"The question is, not what may be supposed to have been intended, but what has been said": *Brophy* v. *A.G. of Manitoba*, [1895] A.C. 202, at p. 216. See also *Ladore* v. *Bennett*, [1939] A.C. 468. This is not a rule of interpretation of statutes but a general rule applicable to all legal documents, such as wills: *Augur* v. *Beaudry*, [1920], A.C. 1010, at p. 1014.

[7]See Sir Joseph Pope (ed.), *Confederation: Being a Series of Hitherto Unpublished Documents Bearing on the British North America Act*, Carswell, Toronto, 1895, p. 84.

[8]There are definite indications that Sir John A. Macdonald had yielded to the desire of the delegates of Lower Canada, who insisted on a definite measure of autonomy. He is reported to have said at the Quebec Conference (Pope's *Confederation Documents*, p. 86): "New Zealand constitution was a Legislative Union, ours Federal. Emigrants went out under different guarantees. Local charters jarred. In order to guard these, they gave the powers stated to Local Legislatures, but the General Government had power to sweep these away. That is just what we do not want. Lower Canada and the Lower Provinces would not have such a thing."

accepted usage. It is really precise only to the extent that the category of acts or things described by any given word is susceptible of exact and objective definition.

This is the kind of precision which is almost totally lacking in the definitions of legal categories and concepts. They are precise only when applied to a given existing system of laws. Within this existing framework, such words as civil, criminal, municipal, have a clear and unmistakable meaning. But when the same words are used to define fields of legislative activity, any great degree of precision disappears. This is because, to a certain extent, the distinction between classes of laws is not based on an objective classification of the activities which are their subject-matter, but on the technique used in regulating them.[9] In fact, the same activities are the subject-matter of different classes of laws from different aspects. As an illustration of the many judicial pronouncements in which this is recognized, I should like to quote these words of the late Chief Justice Duff:

> The fallacy lies in failing to distinguish between legislation affecting civil rights and legislation 'in relation to' civil rights. Most legislation of a repressive character does incidentally or consequentially affect civil rights. But if in its true character it is not legislation 'in relation to' the subject matter of 'property and civil rights' within the provinces, within the meaning of section 92 of the British North America Act, then that is no objection although it be passed in exercise of the residuary authority conferred by the introductory clause.[10]

On what basis is the "true character" to be ascertained, once it is decided, as it should be, that "civil law" and "criminal law" are not to be confined to the content they had in 1867?[11]

When the question is critically examined it becomes apparent that human activities as a whole are the subject matter of legislation and that these activities are, in our modern society, so inter-related that, if every possible degree of connexity is explored, there is no limit to the permissible extension of any given field of legislation. For instance, in Australia, federal power over "national defence" has, in wartime, been construed as extending to any measure deemed necessary. In Canada, unlimited federal authority for emergency legislation was held to be *implied* in the Constitution:

> It is proprietary and civil rights in new relations, which they do not present in normal times, that have to be dealt with. . . . In a *sufficiently great* emergency such as that arising out of war, there is implied the power to deal adequately with that emergency for the safety of the Dominion as a whole.[12]

It is thus seen that a most important distinction rests on the appreciation of a "degree" of necessity. If any degree were held sufficient, federal authority would be practically unlimited. As illustrations of this principle let me consider briefly the jurisprudence of the Supreme Court of the United States on the

---

[9] If a repressive technique is resorted to, the law is classified as "criminal" or "penal"; if a remedy by private lawsuit is created, the law is classified as "civil".

[10] *Gold Seal Ltd.* v. *A.G. Alberta* (1921), 62 S.C.R. 424, at p. 460.

[11] *Proprietary Articles Trade Ass.* v. *A.G. for Canada*, [1931] A.C. 310.

[12] *Fort Frances Pulp & Power Co.* v. *Manitoba Free Press*, [1923] A.C. 695, at pp. 704-705 (italics added).

"Commerce clause" as contrasted with the decisions of the Privy Council and of the Supreme Court of Canada on the federal power to regulate "Trade and Commerce".

In the United States, pre-New-Deal decisions had established the principle that local activities could be regulated by Congress under the commerce clause only if they were "directly" related to "interstate commerce". More recent decisions of the Supreme Court of the United States have brushed aside this distinction,[13] however, with the result that the commerce clause has acquired practically unlimited meaning: "The federal commerce power is as broad as the economic needs of the nation".[14]

In Canada, on the other hand, federal authority over trade and commerce, although unlimited in its terms, was held to be strictly limited to the regulation of interprovincial operations, because to hold otherwise would have deprived provincial legislatures of powers they were clearly intended to possess:

> The scope which might be ascribed to head 2, s. 91 (if the natural meaning of the words, divorced from their context, were alone to be considered), has necessarily been limited, in order to preserve from serious curtailment, if not from virtual extinction, the *degree* of autonomy which, as appears from the scheme of the Act as a whole, the provinces were intended to possess.[15]

I have italicized the word "degree" in this last quotation because I wish to stress the point that here again, as in the definition of the federal emergency power, it is a question of "degree", not a specific distinction. In my view it is wrong to read the generally accepted definition of legislative autonomy ("that the Dominion to a great extent, but within certain fixed limits, may be mistress in her own house, as the Provinces to a great extent, but within certain fixed limits, are mistresses in theirs"[16]) as implying limits defined with mathematical accuracy. To do so is to conceive political science as an exact science ascertainable in the same manner as the natural sciences.

The government of men is essentially a moral problem. Moral problems are not solved by mathematical formulas but by the exercise of prudent judgment based on fundamental principles of morality. These principles rest on belief in God, and in this sense "Christianity is part and parcel of the law". Moral principles, by their very nature, imply concepts which, in their application to contingencies, cannot be divorced from a certain degree of subjective appreciation, a fact illustrated by the "prudent man" referred to in negligence cases. The proper standard of conduct is not to be ascertained by statistical methods but by a consideration of the "proper" duty to be discharged. What is "proper"

---

[13]"But even if . . . [an] activity be local and though it may not be regarded as commerce, it may still, whatever its nature, be reached by Congress if it exerts a substantial economic effect on interstate commerce, and this irrespective of whether such effect is what might at some earlier time have been defined as direct or indirect." *Per* Mr. Justice Jackson in *Wickard* v. *Filburn* (1942), 317 U.S., 111, at p. 125.

[14]*Per* Mr. Justice Murphy in *American Power and Light Co.* v. *SEC* (1946), 67 S. Ct. 133.

[15]*Per* Duff J. (as he then was) in *Lawson* v. *Interior Tree Fruit Committee*, [1931] S.C.R. 357, at p. 366 (italics added).

[16]"*Persons*" case, *op. cit.*

is a question to be decided according to conscience, not otherwise.

If anyone doubts the correctness of the statement that words used to describe "degrees" in moral (including legal) questions are of necessity imprecise and open to subjective appreciation, let him consider, on the one hand, the meaning ascribed to the word "gross" in the construction of statutes restricting the right of action to "gross negligence" in gratuitous passenger or sidewalk accident cases and, on the other, the meaning ascribed to the same adjective in the application of the wartime wages orders restricting wage adjustments to cases of "gross injustice". In the former, anything short of murder or wilful maiming is held excluded; in the latter the slightest inequality is held included.[17]

As a further illustration of the difficulty of precisely defining fundamental legal terms, let us consider the meaning of the word "free". It was discussed by the Privy Council in the construction of the "free trade" provision of the constitution of Australia and the following observations were then made:

> "Free" in itself is vague and indeterminate. It must take its colour from the context. Compare, for instance, its use in free speech, free love, free dinner and free trade. Free speech does not mean free speech; it means speech hedged in by all the laws against defamation, blasphemy, sedition and so forth; it means freedom governed by law, as was pointed out in *McArthur's* case. Free love, on the contrary, means licence or libertinage, though, even so, there are limitations based on public decency and so forth. Free dinner generally means free of expense, and sometimes a meal open to any one who comes, subject, however, to his condition or behaviour not being objectionable. Free trade means, in ordinary parlance, freedom from tariffs.[18]

The fundamental idea, the basic truth, expressed in those observations is that freedom is not something absolute. This is strikingly revealed by the practical consequence of the political regime that promises absolute freedom: communism. It yields freedom, but for one man: the dictator. It cannot be otherwise: total emancipation of any one man means total domination over all others. True freedom means freedom under the law. Autonomy is nothing else than freedom under the constitution.

The true concept of autonomy is thus like the true concept of freedom. It implies limitations, but it also implies free movement within the area bounded by the limitations: one no longer enjoys freedom when free to move in one direction only. It should therefore be realized that autonomy means the right of being different, of acting differently. This is what freedom means for the individual; it is also what it must mean for provincial legislatures and governments. There is no longer any real autonomy for them to the extent that they are actually compelled, economically or otherwise, to act according to a specified pattern. Just as freedom means for the individual the right of choosing his own objective so long as it is not illegal, autonomy means for a province the privilege of defining its own policies.

It must be conceded that autonomy thus understood allows the provinces on occasion to work at cross purposes. But it would be a grave mistake to assume

---

[17]This observation is not meant as a criticism of the decisions; on the contrary it cannot be doubted that they carry out the intent of the enactments.

[18]*James* v. *Commonwealth of Australia*, [1936] A.C. 578, at p. 627.

that this is wrong in itself, or that it is necessarily against the national interest. Unfortunately this assumption is all too frequently made and it is also all too frequently the only argument invoked against autonomy (if it can be termed an argument). Here is a typical specimen:

> The most serious specific threat to any orderly kind of future for Canada lies in the nature of our Constitution. The "property and civil rights" clause of section 92 of the British North America Act will make short work of our war-time measures and will very quickly reduce us to the bedlam of provincialism again. Can any sane person believe that the competing authorities, mostly parochial, will give us anything but anarchy leading perhaps to revolution?[19]

It will be noted that autonomy is deprecated here as a mark of insanity, but no other argument is advanced. Obviously the underlying assumption is that diversity in legislation concerning property and civil rights is against national interest. Implicit in this assumption is the belief that uniform legislation enacted by the federal Parliament would be better. Of course uniformity has its advantages, but it also has its disadvantages.

The framing of legislation, as already pointed out, is a political task.[20] Hence it is not an exact science but a matter of prudent judgment, on which even popularly elected men may sometimes go wrong. Why should competition be assumed to be undesirable in this sphere of action, when it proves to be such a valuable force in the economic field? It should not be assumed that, in such matters, there is necessarily one right solution, all others being wrong. Human affairs are more complex than that and, very often, several possible courses of action are open among which one may choose. Such is the situation in individual life and such it is in collective action.

This is especially so when the characteristics of individuals or of collectivities are different. Educators have long ago recognized that human beings are not robots and that varying methods and different institutions are necessary to suit varying types of intelligence and differences in character. The same difficulty is met in devising legislation. It is wrong to assume that the same laws are suitable for all peoples. On the contrary, laws have a cultural aspect; hence due consideration should be given in framing them to the character, condition and beliefs of those for whom they are made. Autonomy is designed for the very purpose of meeting this requirement. The French-speaking population of the province of Quebec is obviously the group of Canadian citizens specially interested in it. For them autonomy is linked up with the preservation of their way of life.

Of course, it cannot be denied that the general welfare of a country requires that collective action be made uniform in some important fields, such as defence, tariff, currency. More than that, it must be conceded that the area of uniformity cannot be defined without allowing for extension in emergencies. But the increased need for uniformity in emergencies cannot be relied on as an argument

---

[19]From the introduction by A. R. M. Lower to "War and Reconstruction", a pamphlet published in 1943 by the Canadian Institute on Public Affairs.

[20]In the aristotelian sense, not necessarily in the familiar sense of partisan politics.

against autonomy in normal times. It is already provided for.

All this means that tests of constitutional validity cannot be rigidly devised. Almost invariably they involve judgment on questions of "degree". The courts have therefore been compelled to rest their decisions touching constitutional issues on broad principles and on a general conception of what the B.N.A. Act intended to secure to the provinces and to the federal authority, respectively, rather than on an impossible technical construction:

> Inasmuch as the Act embodies a compromise under which the original Provinces agreed to federate, it is important to keep in mind that the preservation of the rights of minorities was a condition on which such minorities entered into the federation, and the foundation upon which the whole structure was subsequently erected. The process of interpretation as the years go on ought not to be allowed to dim or to whittle down the provisions of the original contract upon which the federation was founded, nor is it legitimate that any judicial construction of the provisions of ss. 91 and 92 should impose a new and different contract upon the federating bodies.[21]

On this basis the courts have consistently refused to allow any particular clause of the B.N.A. Act to be construed in a way that would enable the federal Parliament to invade the provincial sphere of action outside of emergencies. "Such a result would appear to undermine the constitutional safeguards of Provincial constitutional autonomy"[22] was the main reason given by Lord Atkin for his refusal to construe section 132 as enabling the federal Parliament to encroach on provincial matters in order to implement labour conventions adhered to by Canada.

The same principle was applied in dealing with provincial legislation. For instance, the Supreme Court of Canada has invalidated an Alberta law interfering with the freedom of the press, because it would have jeopardized the working of federal parliamentary institutions:

> Some degree of regulation of newspapers everybody would concede to the provinces. Indeed, there is a very wide field in which the provinces undoubtedly are invested with legislative authority over newspapers; but the limit, in our opinion, is reached when the legislation effects such a curtailment of the exercise of the right of public discussion as substantially to interfere with the working of the parliamentary institutions of Canada as contemplated by the provisions of *The British North America Act* and the statutes of the Dominion of Canada.[23]

Let it be noted that, here again, it is a question of "degree". Undoubtedly, the task of construing our constitution would be made lighter for our courts if provincial autonomy could be defined in more specific words, but that hardly appears possible. The great value of the numerous decisions rendered since 1867

---

[21]*In re The Regulation and Control of Aeronautics*, [1932] A.C. 54, at p. 70.
[22]*A.G. for Canada* v. *A.G. for Ontario (Labour Conventions)*, [1937] A.C. 326, at p. 352.
[23]*Reference re Alberta Statutes*, [1938] S.C.R. 100, at p. 134.

lies in the illustrations they afford of the "degree" of autonomy secured to the provinces.

A great volume of criticism has been heaped upon the Privy Council and the Supreme Court on the ground that their decisions rest on a narrow and technical construction of the B.N.A. Act. This contention is ill-founded. The decisions on the whole proceed from a much higher view. As appears from passages I have quoted, they recognize the implicit fluidity of any constitution by allowing for emergencies and by resting distinctions on questions of degree. At the same time they firmly uphold the fundamental principle of provincial autonomy: they staunchly refuse to let our federal constitution be changed gradually, by one device or another, to a legislative union. In doing so they are preserving the essential condition of the Canadian confederation.

13   Le Québec et L'Arbitrage Constitutionnel: De Charybde en Scylla*

Jacques-Yvan Morin

L'intervention d'un tiers indépendant et impartial dans les litiges qui opposent les individus est essentielle, en droit interne, à l'existence de règles de droit effectives. Il n'en va pas autrement des différends et conflits qui surgissent entre les collectivités politiques, Etats ou nations. Certes, l'intervention du juge ou de l'arbitre international est entourée de maints obstacles et restrictions, en raison des intérêts considérables qui sont en jeu, mais les Etats admettent de plus en plus la nécessité de soumettre leurs contestations à des organismes internationaux.

Il ne saurait exister non plus d'union politique ou même économique sans l'existence de tribunaux aptes à concilier les intérêts des Etats-membres et à interpréter leurs accords. C'est ainsi que l'Europe a donné naissance depuis une vingtaine d'années aux tribunaux des communautés économiques et à la Cour européenne des droits de l'homme.

Pareillement, on ne conçoit guère de fédération ou de confédération qui ne comporte un tribunal habilité par la constitution à trancher les débats entre les Etats-membres et le Pouvoir central en ce qui concerne l'interprétation de la loi fondamentale et la validité de leurs lois respectives. A vrai dire, il ne saurait exister de structure politique stable sans la présence du pouvoir judiciaire; plus la structure est homogène sur le plan ethnique et cohérente sur le plan socio-économique, plus les juges auront la tâche facile.

*From *Canadian Bar Review*, Vol. XLV, 1967, pp. 608-626. Reprinted by permission of the author and publisher.

Il existe cependant, encore aujourd'hui, des cas où des collectivités ethniques minoritaires doivent s'en remettre, pour le règlement de leurs différends avec la majorité, à des tribunaux organisés et nommés par cette majorité. Tous les rapports de dépendance politique et notamment les structures coloniales, ont engendré des situations de ce genre; on pourrait donner maints exemples dans lesquels le peuple conquis, plus nombreux même que la population de la métropole, voyait néanmoins l'ensemble de son droit et de ses institutions être soumis au contrôle de tribunaux étrangers et à leurs méthodes d'interprétation.

Le Canada a été soumis à ce système jusqu'en 1949 et le Québec le subit toujours, à cette différence près que des juges québecois font partie de la Cour suprême du Canada, encore qu'ils y soient en minorité, tandis que le Comité judiciaire du Conseil privé n'était composé que de Britanniques. Par ailleurs, le Comité judiciaire relevait du gouvernement de Londres et les membres n'en étaient point choisis par Ottawa, tandis que tous les juges de la Cour suprême, devenue en 1949 le tribunal de dernière instance pour les affaires canadiennes, sont nommés par le gouvernement fédéral.

En outre, le Comité judiciaire avait acquis, en tant qu' arbitre d'un vaste empire, une certaine tradition d'impartialité et de détachement devant les problèmes que soulevait la coexistence d'un grand nombre de peuples; de tous les tribunaux métropolitains créés au siècle dernier par les Etats européens, ce ne fut certes pas le plus oppressif et on lui prête même avec raison un certain libéralisme.

Aussi ne fait-il point s'étonner de voir le Québec, qui n'a échappé aux institutions impériales que pour tomber dans un nouveau péril, regretter l'arbitrage de l'ancien tribunal, malgré tous les inconvénients qu'il comportait pour le Canada français, et réclamer avec insistance l'établissement d'un forum constitutionnel qui ne le laisserait pas à la merci du pouvoir fédéral. Tout en acceptant le maintien d'un certain nombre de liens politiques avec le Canada anglophone et le principe de l'arbitrage constitutionnel, le Québec est à la recherche d'un système juridictionnel qui correspondrait à l'autonomie plus complète à laquelle il aspire comme "foyer national" et "milieu politique fondamental" du Canada français;[1] il réclame la création d'un tribunal constitutionnel qui soit constitué en fonction de l'existence des deux nations canadiennes.

Est-il possible de concevoir et de réaliser une telle institution? Après avoir étudié la nature et la structure du forum constitutionnel existant ainsi que l'attitude du Québec depuis que la Cour suprême a pris la relève du Comité judiciaire, nous tenterons de définir quelles pourraient être la juridiction, le statut et la composition d'un forum constitutionnel adapté aux réalités canadiennes.

Les deux nations devant la Cour supreme

L'évolution générale des arrêts du Comité judiciaire du Conseil privé eut pour résultat de modifier le grand dessein de certains "Pères de la Confédération", en mettant fin à la subordination des provinces canadiennes par rapport au pouvoir

---

[1]Ce sont les expressions employées dans le *Rapport de la Commission royale d'enquête sur les problèmes constitutionnels*, Québec, 1956, Vol. II, p. 85.

fédéral. Bien que la tendance décentralisatrice du Comité judiciaire ait connu quelques fluctuations et retours, l'arrêt *Hodge* v. *The Queen* (1883), suivi de l'affaire de la *Maritime Bank* (1892),[2] donnèrent le ton à l'ensemble de sa jurisprudence. C'est ainsi que, dans les limites de leurs compétences, les législatures provinciales se virent reconnaître un "pouvoir souverain".

Une telle interprétation du *British North America Act* ne pouvait que soulever l'opposition, voire l'irritation, des partisans d'un pouvoir central fort, surtout à l'époque de la crise économique, alors que commençaient à se répandre au Canada des thèses favorables à l'intervention de l'Etat dans le domaine socio-économique. Lorsque le Comité judiciaire rendit ses célèbres décisions de l'année 1937, particulièrement dans l'affaire des Conventions internationales du travail[3] et dans le litige concernant la Loi sur l'emploi et l'assurance sociale,[4] ce fut un véritable tollé chez les juristes anglo-canadiens. Le Doyen V. C. MacDonald se fit le porte-parole d'un grande nombre de ses collègues lorsqu'il déclara que les arrêts révélaient "la nécessité d'étudier sérieusement l'opportunité de mettre fin aux appels en matière constitutionnelle".[5]

Dans un rapport soumis au Sénat en 1939, le conseiller juridique de la Chambre soutint que le tribunal s'était écarté du texte de la constitution "de la façon la plus grave et la plus constante"[6] et le Doyen W. P. M. Kennedy, pour sa part, en conclut que l'abolition du recours au Comité judiciaire était la seule façon "de se défaire de toutes ses décisions passées".[7] Dix ans plus tard une simple loi fédérale écarta définitivement les appels au Conseil privé et la Cour suprême du Canada devint le tribunal de dernière instance en matière constitutionnelle.[8]

La Cour suprême avait été créée en 1875 par le Parlement canadien, en vertu de l'article 101 du *British North America Act*, qui l'autorisait à instituer une cour générale d'appel pour le Canada. Le gouvernement fédéral de l'époque eût souhaité en faire un véritable tribunal constitutionnel habilité à trancher les litiges entre les deux niveaux de gouvernement et entre les provinces, ainsi que toutes les questions relatives à la validité des lois fédérales ou provinciales, mais, comme le constata à regret le ministre de la Justice, la Constitution n'autorisait pas le Parlement à créer un tel tribunal.[9] Cependant, le gouvernement avait imaginé "un expédient selon lequel, avec le consentement des gouvernements

---

[2]*Hodge* v. *The Queen* (1883), 9 A.C. 117; *Maritime Bank* v. *Receiver General of New Brunswick*, [1892] A.C. 437. Voir également *A.G. for Ontario* v. *A.G. for Canada*, [1896] A.C. 348.

[3][1937] A.C. 326.

[4][1937] A.C. 355. Noter que le Comité judiciaire, dans cet arrêt, ne faisait que confirmer l'arrêt antérieur de la Cour Suprême.

[5]"The Canadian Constitution Seventy Years After", *Canadian Bar Review*, Vol. XV, 1937, p. 401.

[6]Sénat du Canada, *Rapport à l'hon. Président par le conseiller parlementaire au sujet de la mise en vigueur de l'A.A.N.B. de 1867*, Imprimeur du Roi, Ottawa, 1939, annexe 4, p. 171.

[7]"The British North America Act: Past and Future," *Canadian Bar Review*, Vol. XV, 1937, p. 393.

[8]S.C., 1949 (2e sess.), chap. 37, art. 3; Loi sur la Cour suprême, S.R.C., 1952, chap. 259, art. 54. Les appels relevant du droit pénal avaient été abolis en 1932-33.

[9]*Debates of the House of Commons* (1875), p. 286.

provinciaux intéressés, on donnerait plein effet aux décisions rendues par la Cour suprême".[10] En outre, le tribunal se verrait reconnaître une "juridiction spéciale", en vertu de laquelle le gouverneur général en conseil pourrait lui soumettre directement les questions relatives à l'interprétation du *British North America Act* ou à la constitutionnalité des lois fédérales ou provinciales, sans toutefois que l'opinion exprimée par la Cour puisse alors être considérée comme un jugement péremptoire.

Le gouvernement de l'époque eût également désiré abolir les appels au Conseil privé, mais hésitait à poser ce geste, qui eût peut-être inquiété l'opinion québecoise, fort sensible sur le chapitre du droit civil;[11] une résolution du député Irving visant à mettre fin aux appels fut d'ailleurs écartée au vote.[12] C'est pourquoi la Loi sur la Cour suprême, telle qu'adoptée en 1875, ne créait de tribunal constitutionnel que dans la mesure où les gouvernements provinciaux y consentiraient;[13] or ceux-ci n'ont pas accédé à la demande du pouvoir central et les dispositions relatives à la juridiction constitutionnelle de la Cour ont dû être abandonnées. Cependant, le haut tribunal fédéral acquit, avec les années, une compétence de fait en matière constitutionnelle. En tant que cour d'appel, en effet, il fut appelé à se prononcer plus de 180 fois sur la validité de lois fédérales ou provinciales; en outre, sa juridiction "spéciale" lui a permis de donner à plusieurs reprises (environ 70 fois) des avis consultatifs.

Avec l'abolition définitive des appels, en 1949, la Cour suprême devint *ipso facto* le tribunal de dernière instance en matière constitutionnelle,[14] sans pourtant jamais avoir obtenu le statut d'une cour constitutionnelle. C'est ainsi que cette Cour qui est appelée constamment à se prononcer sur la validité des lois fédérales et provinciales, dépend du seul gouvernement fédéral, qui en nomme tous les membres.[15] Ce dénouement n'est pas sans rappeler la situation qui prévaut aux Etats-Unis, où la Cour suprême fédérale s'est reconnue elle-même, dans l'arrêt *Marbury* v. *Madison* (1803), le pouvoir de se prononcer sur la validité des lois, alors que la constitution américaine ne confère expressément le *power of judicial review* à aucun tribunal. Or, on connaît le rôle joué par cette Cour suprême, entièrement nommée par l'Exécutif fédéral, en particulier depuis l'époque du *New Deal*.

Le gouvernement du Québec ne fut pas long à réagir à cette nouvelle situation politico-juridique, établie unilatéralement par le Parlement d'Ottawa. Dès la Conférence fédérale-provinciale de septembre 1950, le mémoire soumis par la délégation québecoise fait état de la question en ces termes:[16]

> Nous estimons que la Cour suprême du Canada, en matières constitution-nelles et de relations intergouvernementales canadiennes, doit réunir toutes les conditions exigées d'un tiers arbitre.

[10]*Ibid.*, p. 354.
[11]*Ibid.*, pp. 286, 921, 924, 941.
[12]*Ibid.*, p. 947. Une seconde résolution, destinée à écarter les appels aux tribunaux britanniques autres que le Conseil privé, fut adoptée: *ibid.*, p. 976.
[13]38 *Vict.*, chap. 11, arts 54 à 56.
[14]*Supra*, note 8.
[15]Loi sur la Cour suprême, *ibid.*, art. 4.
[16]Compte-rendu des délibérations de la Conférence fédérale-provinciale, 1950, p. 101.

On se rendait compte à Québec, peut-être un peu tard, des dangers que comportait un tribunal nommé exclusivement par le pouvoir central. Plusieurs arrêts vinrent d'ailleurs confirmer très tôt ces craintes. Dans l'affaire *Johanneson*, jugée en 1952,[17] la théorie des "dimensions nationales", pourtant écartée par le Comité judiciaire en 1937,[18] fut rétablie, et en 1956, dans l'arrêt *Francis* v. *The Queen*, le juge en chef laissa entendre qu'il faudrait peut-être réviser la décision du Conseil privé relative à l'incompétence du Parlement fédéral à l'égard de la mise en œuvre des traités dont l'objet relevait des provinces.[19] Les juristes québecois pouvaient également lire dans les revues savantes des articles qui les laissaient songeurs.[20]

L'enquête de la Commission Tremblay fut l'occasion d'approfondir la question. De nombreuses associations et institutions vinrent en effet devant les commissaires manifester leur inquiétude au sujet de la Cour suprême[21] et ceux-ci firent un exposé des critiques entendues. Tout d'abord, la Cour "est la créature du gouvernement central" et aucune disposition de la constitution ne prévoit l'existence d'un tribunal constitutionnel. En second lieu, le Parlement n'a cessé d'étendre d'année en année la juridiction de la Cour et tous les juges en sont nommés par le gouvernement d'Ottawa, en sorte que le tribunal n'est pas sans ressembler, sur ce point, au Sénat.

> Il suffirait, par exemple, que la coutume s'établisse d'y nommer d'anciens députés ou ministres fédéraux. Passe encore s'il ne s'agissait que de juger les questions civiles et criminelles ordinaires, mais dans les conflits constitutionnels il n'est ni normal ni satisfaisant qu'une seule partie choisisse, nomme et paie tous les arbitres.[22]

Les réformes suggérées par la Commission tendent à donner à la Cour suprême un caractère "d'arbitre impartial et indépendant". Ce haut tribunal devrait posséder un véritable statut constitutionnel, "comme dans les autres constitutions fédératives"[23] et ce statut ne pourrait être modifié unilatéralement ni par le Parlement ni par les Législatures. En second lieu, il conviendrait, pensent les commissaires, de restreindre la juridiction de la Cour. Ils écrivent en effet:

> La province de Québec qui possède un droit civil propre aurait de fort bonnes raisons d'exiger et d'obtenir que les causes en matière civile provinciale soient

---

[17]*Johanneson* v. *Municipality of West St. Paul*, [1952] 1 R.C.S. 303.

[18]Arrêts cités, *supra*, notes 3 et 4.

[19][1956] R.C.S. 618, à la p. 621.

[20]Voir, par exemple, B. Laskin, "The Supreme Court of Canada: A Final Court of and for Canadians", *Canadian Bar Review*, Vol. XXIX, 1951, p. 1038: "The Supreme Court, by the very fact of being entitled to hear an appeal from provincial courts, may establish the law to be followed in those courts. It is thus in a stronger position to develop a unified common law than is the Supreme Court of the United States. . . . This will also be true in connection with Quebec cases, although the fact that the civil law obtains only in that province may well warrant a greater deference by the Supreme Court to local views".

[21]Rapport *supra*, note 1, vol. III, tome 1er, p. 294.

[22]*Ibid.*, p. 297.

[23]*Ibid.*, p. 298.

jugées en dernier ressort par un tribunal suprême québecois. Ce ne serait que juste et raisonnable, en même temps qu'une garantie que ce tribunal jugerait selon la lettre et l'esprit de notre Code civil, et non selon le droit coutumier britannique.[24]

A défaut de pouvoir soustraire à la Cour fédérale les causes relevant du droit civil, le Québec devrait exiger, recommande la Commission, que de telles causes soient jugées par un tribunal composé de cinq juges de la Cour suprême comprenant obligatoirement les trois juges de formation juridique québecoise, ces derniers devant rendre une décision unanime chaque fois qu'il s'agirait de renverser un jugement de la plus haute cour québecoise.

Enfin, les commissaires, se fondant sur quelques constitutions étrangères, recommandent que le mode de nomination des juges soit fixé dans la Constitution. Il conviendrait même de constituer un tribunal constitutionnel spécial et d'associer les provinces à la nomination des membres de ce haut tribunal. Cette participation pourrait être assurée de diverses manières, soit que la Cour constitutionnelle soit formée des neufs juges de la Cour suprême et des juges en chef des dix provinces, soit qu'elle comprenne cinq juges de la Cour suprême et quatre autres choisis par les quatre grandes régions dont se compose le pays, soit encore que la Constitution s'inspire sur ce point de divers tribunaux internationaux.[25]

A la Conférence fédérale-provinciale de 1960, M. Jean Lesage reprit brièvement la thèse de la Commission Tremblay, qui était également celle du gouvernement précédent. Parlant du "rapatriement" de la Constitution devant les premiers ministres réunis à Ottawa, il déclara :

> Il ne faudrait pas oublier de prévoir en même temps l'organisation d'un tribunal constitutionnel conforme aux principes essentiels du régime fédératif. En effet, le principe fondamental de ce régime exige que ni l'un ni l'autre des deux ordres de gouvernement ne puisse toucher au partage des pouvoirs établi par la constitution. Il s'ensuit que l'arbitre des conflits ne doit pas relever exclusivement de l'un d'eux.[26]

Si le Canada anglophone peut se féliciter d'avoir aboli les appels au Comité judiciaire et de s'être donné un tribunal constitutionnel vraiment "national", il n'en va pas de même du Québec. Pour la majorité anglo-canadienne, la Cour suprême, telle qu'établie, est digne de la plus haute confiance et remplace avec avantage un tribunal britannique coupable d'avoir donné au *British North America Act* une tournure trop favorable aux provinces. Pour le Québec français, au contraire, la Cour évoque les dangers séculaires et toujours actuels de la centralisation et de l'impérialisme. Depuis 1960, les Québecois ont eu l'occasion d'étudier l'ensemble de leur situation politique et constitutionnelle et leur volonté de changement ne laisse plus de doute. Quelle serait le rôle et la composition d'un tribunal constitutionnel qui pourrait s'insérer dans le contexte dualiste d'un Canada binational?

---

[24]*Ibid.*, p. 300.
[25]*Ibid.*, p. 301.
[26]*Compte-rendu de la Conférence fédérale-provinciale*, Imprimeur de la Reine, Ottawa, 1960, p. 33.

Statut et Juridiction du Tribunal Constitutionnel

La première réforme qui devrait être apportée au forum constitutionnel canadien consiste à déterminer d'une manière précise la juridiction du tribunal de dernière instance et à en insérer le statut dans la Constitution. Le tribunal devrait posséder une juridiction *originale et exclusive* sur tous les différends qui opposent le pouvoir fédéral au Québec ou à une province, ou encore une province à une autre. Il devrait en outre être investi du pouvoir d'interpréter la Constitution fédérale et de contrôler la validité de toutes les lois du Canada, du Québec et des provinces anglophones.

Ces fonctions devraient-elles êtres confiées à l'actuelle Cour suprême? Dans la majorité des Etats fédéraux, y compris les Etats-Unis, l'Australie, l'Inde et les fédérations latino-américaines, c'est effectivement la Cour suprême fédérale qui joue le rôle d'arbitre constitutionnel, mais, outre le contrôle que le pouvoir central peut de la sorte exercer sur le comportement du tribunal par le jeu des nominations, on peut se demander s'il convient que les questions constitution-nelles soient traitées sur le même pied que les difficultés relatives à l'interpréta-tion ou à l'application des lois ordinaires. C'est l'une des raisons pour lesquelles trois fédérations européennes et l'Italie, Etat unitaire qui possède plusieurs régions autonomes, ont opté pour le système du tribunal spécialisé en droit constitutionnel. A notre avis, le Canada aurait tout avantage à s'inspirer de cette formule, plus conforme à l'esprit du fédéralisme et aux circonstances qui prévalent ici.

La Constitution autrichienne de 1919 voulut assurer l'égalité du *Bund* et des *Länder* devant la constitution. Aussi établit-elle une "Cour constitutionnelle" distincte des cours fédérales.[27] De même, la Loi fondamentale de la République Fédérale Allemande (1949) crée deux tribunaux distincts: La Cour suprême, qui reçoit les appels en matière civile et pénale, et la Cour constitutionnelle (*Bundesverfassungsgericht*), à laquelle sont dévolus l'interprétation de la Loi fondamentale, les questions relatives à la compatibilité des lois fédérales et locales avec les normes constitutionnelles ou à l'exécution des lois fédérales par les *Länder*, ainsi que les litiges d'ordre public entre la Fédération et ses membres.[28] Enfin, la Constitution yougoslave établit également une Cour suprême et une Cour constitutionnelle, laquelle contrôle la validité des lois et juge les conflits entre la République fédérale et les Républiques fédérées ou entre celles-ci.[29]

Une telle solution n'est sans doute pas conforme à la tradition qui prévaut dans le monde anglo-américain, selon laquelle les cours de dernière instance doivent être des tribunaux d'appel de juridiction générale. L'esprit et les tech-niques de la *common law* s'accommodent mieux, en effet, d'un système qui n'établit point des distinctions trop étanches entre le droit constitutionnel, le

---

[27]Constitution de la République autrichienne, arts 137 et 138.

[28]Loi fondamentale, art. 93, par. ler. La Cour possède également d'autres fonctions reliées à la Constitution, v.g., cas de déchéance des droits fondamentaux, de non-constitutionnalité des partis, *etc.* Voir Loi relative à la Cour constitutionnelle fédérale (1951), art. 13.

[29]Constitution de la Yougoslavie, arts 132, 145 à 151, 160, 241, 244 à 246, 249.

droit privé et le droit "statutaire"; toute la tradition britannique, avec le rôle prépondérant qu'elle accorde au juge et l'accent qu'elle place sur le droit coutumier, va à l'encontre de la spécialisation des tribunaux. Le Doyen Le Dain écrivait même récemment qu'un tribunal qui ne possède pas une juridiction d'appel générale n'est pas en mesure de se prononcer en toute connaissance de cause sur les questions constitutionnelles; selon lui, la spécialisation tend à favoriser les opinions abstraites, où les questions de principe l'emportent sur les problèmes concrets.[30]

Si l'on accepte de se placer dans une perspective anglo-américaine, on ne peut nier la force de ces arguments, mais, outre qu'ils ne font aucune place à la tradition européenne, ils forcent les Canadiens français, depuis deux siècles, à se pénétrer d'un système qui est, dans une large mesure, étranger à l'esprit de leurs institutions juridiques. D'ailleurs, comme le fait observer le Professeur E. McWhinney, la tradition des tribunaux d'appel de juridiction générale est quelque peu fétichiste;[31] dans maints pays, aujourd'hui, et même chez ceux qui ont subi l'influence britannique, la tendance est à la spécialisation dans les principaux domaines du droit, particulièrement en matière administrative. Et si les arguments que l'on peut faire valoir en faveur d'une telle spécialisation sont valables dans ces divers domaines, ne sont-ils pas encore plus convaincants lorsqu'il s'agit du droit constitutionnel d'un pays binational? Il y aurait avantage, dans les circonstances particulières du Canada, à s'inspirer sur ce point de la tradition du continent européen.

La Cour constitutionnelle canadienne devrait être dotée par la constitution d'un statut indépendant par rapport à la Cour suprême, mais elle pourrait également constituer une chambre distincte au sein de cette Cour. La première solution est à préférer, cependant, puisqu'elle permettrait de placer la Cour constitutionnelle au-dessus de la Cour suprême et des gouvernements intéressés.

La Cour pourrait être saisie par le moyen d'un renvoi de toute question portant sur la validité d'une loi fédérale ou provinciale au regard de la Constitution. En Allemagne, tout tribunal fédéral ou provincial qui estime qu'une disposition législative est inconstitutionnelle doit surseoir à statuer et s'adresser à la Cour afin d'obtenir un arrêt sur ce point; par ailleurs, si le tribunal inférieur est d'avis que la loi est valide, il n'a pas à s'en remettre à la Cour, mais la partie qui invoque l'invalidité peut y porter la question après avoir épuisé les recours ordinaires.[32] On pourrait également s'inspirer du système nigérien, selon lequel le tribunal régional inférieur doit, à la demande de l'une des parties, renvoyer toute question intéressant la validité des lois ou l'interprétation de la Constitution à la Haute Cour régionale, laquelle doit trancher le point en litige, à moins qu'elle ne soit à son tour obligée de renvoyer le point de droit à la Cour suprême fédérale, si la partie intéressée le requiert; les tribunaux peuvent

---

[30]G. E. LeDain, "Concerning the Proposed Constitutional and Civil Law Specialization at the Supreme Court Level", *Thesis*, Vol. II, 1967, pp. 119, 122.

[31]*Constitutionalism in Germany and the Federal Constitutional Court*, A. W. Sythoff, Leyden, 1962, p. 20.

[32]*Supra*, note 28.

également affectuer le renvoi *proprio motu*.[33] Les deux systèmes, allemand et nigérien, sont fondés sur le même principe, mais le premier nous paraît plus expéditif et moins susceptible d'abus de la part des parties au litige. Enfin, dans les deux cas, le tribunal supérieur saisi du point contesté doit le trancher et retourner le dossier au tribunal primitif, qui rend jugement à la lumière de la réponse reçue. Notons que la Loi sur la Cour suprême du Canada contient déjà des dispositions autorisant les tribunaux à déférer toute question constitutionnelle qui surgit dans une affaire civile à la Cour suprême, à condition que la Législature provinciale ait voté une loi autorisant les juges à utiliser cette procédure.[34] On pourrait également observer qu'il existe une similitude frappante entre le renvoi par les tribunaux inférieurs et la procédure des avis consultatifs, qui n'est autre qu'un renvoi à la Cour suprême par l'Exécutif fédéral.[35]

Il devrait être prévu que la Cour constitutionnelle canadienne ne serait point compétente pour se prononcer sur les questions relatives à la compatibilité des lois québecoises avec la Constitution du Québec; ces questions devraient être tranchées en dernier ressort par le tribunal québecois le plus élevé. Telle est la règle applicable dans la Fédération allemande et elle est conforme au principe de l'autonomie des Etats-membres.[36] D'une manière générale, il conviendrait de mieux distinguer les deux ordres juridiques en attribuant aux tribunaux provinciaux (ceux du Québec tout au moins) la juridiction exclusive en ce qui concerne l'application et l'interprétation des lois provinciales, sauf les questions qui ont trait à la constitutionnalité;[37] il ne devrait y avoir appel à la Cour suprême (distincte de la Cour constitutionnelle) qu'à l'égard des lois fédérales.

Toutes ces propositions soulèvent, il est vrai, quelques difficultés quant à la "qualification" des litiges puisqu'aussi bien le même affaire peut comporter divers aspects qui relèvent tantôt du droit civil, tantôt des lois fédérales ou du droit constitutionnel. Cependant, une fois acceptée l'idée de la spécialisation

---

[33]Constitution de la Nigéria, arts 107 à 114.

[34]Loi sur la Cour suprême, *supra*, note 8, art. 62.

[35]Les lois appropriées ont été votées en Colombie Britannique, à l'Ile-du-Prince-Edouard, au Manitoba, en Ontario, au Nouveau-Brunswick et à Terre-Neuve. A titre d'exemple, voir Dominion Courts Act, R.S.O., 1960, chap. 112. Cependant, cette procédure de renvoi n'a pas été utilisée.

[36]Loi fondamentale, art. 99.

[37]Pour les arguments qui militent en faveur de cette solution dans le cas du droit civil, voir L. Baudouin, *Conflits nés de la coexistence juridique au Canada, La dualité canadienne (1960)*, pp. 106, 109; P. Azard, "La Cour suprême au Canada et l'application du droit civil de la Province de Québec", *Canadian Bar Review*, Vol. XLIV, 1965, p. 555 (le doyen Azard en vient à une conclusion différente de la notre, cependant; il propose en effet la création d'une section civile au sein de la Cour suprême). Les juges des cours supérieures québecoises devraient, à notre avis, être nommés par le gouvernement du Québec. Cf. L'opinion de K. C. Wheare, *Federal Government*, 3e éd., Oxford University Press, London, 1953, p. 71: "The case of Canada, where the appointment of all judges is in the hands of the general government, is an example of a system which contradicts the federal principle. It is a further illustration of the modified or quasi-federal system which the Canadian Constitution established."

et celle d'une plus grande autonomie juridictionnelle pour le Québec, il existe diverses techniques, notamment la création d'un tribunal des Conflits,[38] qui permettent de résoudre ces problèmes. A ceux qui verraient là des complications insurmontables, il faut rappeler que la réalité politique canadienne est également fort complexe et que le système de la *common law* ne recèle pas nécessairement toutes les solutions possibles et raisonnables.

Composition du Tribunal Constitutionnel

Dans plusieurs Etats fédéraux, avons-nous constaté, le rôle d'arbitre constitutionnel est attribué par la Constitution à la Cour suprême fédérale. Ce système entraîne invariablement la nomination des juges constitutionnels par les organes fédéraux.[39] C'est ainsi qu'au Canada, les membres de la Cour suprême sont tous nommés par l'Exécutif fédéral.[40] Une seule disposition, ajoutée au cours du débat de 1875 sur le *bill* de la Cour suprême, restreint quelque peu la liberté de choix du gouvernement: au moins trois juges sur les neuf qui font partie de la Cour doivent être choisis parmi les juges de la Cour d'appel ou de la Cour supérieure ou parmi les avocats du Québec.[41]

On s'est demandé, chez les auteurs, si l'arbitrage des litiges fédéraux-provinciaux et le contrôle des compétences pouvaient être exercés de façon impartiale dans les diverses fédérations qui ont adopté un tel mode de nomination. Plusieurs en tirent même un argument en faveur de la suprématie, voire de la souveraineté du pouvoir central. La jurisprudence dans les Etats fédéraux, écrivait le regretté Professeur M. Mouskhély, montre que l'organe judiciare fédéral "tâche de renforcer le pouvoir central et d'augmenter sa compétence".[42] Certes, ce serait une erreur de croire que les tribunaux constitutionnels sont les seuls responsables des tendances centralisatrices que l'on retrouve dans la plupart des fédérations; on doit également tenir compte de l'action des facteurs sociologiques et économiques, ainsi que de la volonté populaire qui, dans les Etats homogènes sur le plan ethnique, constitue un puissant élément d'uniformisation et d'intégration. En outre, on pourrait citer plus d'un cas où le tribunal suprême de certaines fédérations a favorisé les Etats-membres.

Néanmoins, il demeure vrai que, d'une manière générale, les tribunaux con-

---

[38]En France, le Tribunal des Conflits, constitué sur une base paritaire, est chargé du règlement des conflits d'attribution entre tribunaux judiciaires et tribunaux administratifs. Si les deux juridictions saisies d'un même litige se déclarent toutes les deux incompétentes, il appartient au demander de saisir le Tribunal des Conflits par voie de requête pour faire déterminer le forum compétent. De même, lorsqu'un tribunal judiciaire est saisi d'un litige que l'administration estime être de nature administrative, celle-ci peut lui adresser un déclinatoire de compétence et, à défaut par le tribunal de se dessaisir du litige, peut porter la question devant le Tribunal des Conflits.

[39]Constitution de l'Inde, arts 124, 125, 216, 217; Constitution de l'Australie, art. 72; Constitution du Brésil, arts 60, 98; Constitution de Mexique, arts 56, 86.

[40]Loi sur la Cour suprême, *supra*, note 8, art 4.

[41]*Ibid.*, art 6. Voir les Débats, 1875, p. 972 (à ce moment, deux juges sur six devaient venir du Québec).

[42]*Théorie juridique de l'Etat fédéral* (1931), p. 137; voir également G. Burdeau, *Traité de science politique*, A. Pedone, Paris, 1949, tome II, p. 424.

stitutionnels nommés par les gouvernements centraux ont contribué à la centralisation. Et lorsqu'ils ont refusé de le faire, particulièrement en pèriode critique, les autres organes fédéraux ont été tentés d'intervenir pour briser leur résistance. C'est ainsi qu'en 1870, le Congres américain a augmenté le nombre des juges de manière à transformer rapidement la composition et l'orientation de la jurisprudence de la Cour. En outre, le Président a parfois nommé à ce haut tribunal des partisans de sa politique ou des personnages issus des milieux politiques fédéraux, dans l'espoir de modifier l'orientation de la Cour. Roosevelt lui-même n'a pas hésité à utiliser ce moyen entre 1937 et 1941, alors qu'il tentait de faire triompher son *New Deal*.

Au Canada, l'attitude du Conseil privé provoqua la réaction que l'on sait, laquelle entraîna éventuellement l'abolition des appels au Comité judiciaire par un acte unilatéral du Parlement. De tels procédés sont peut-être justifiables, sur le plan politique, lorsqu'ils sont appuyés par la majorité des citoyens d'une fédération culturellement homogène, mais dans un Etat binational ou plurinational, on ne saurait en user qu'en risquant de perdre la confiance d'une partie importante de la population.

Depuis l'abolition des appels, le pourcentage des arrêts favorables au Pouvoir fédéral en matière constitutionnelle est passé de 51.3% à 56.9%, sur un total de 51 decisions rendues entre 1949 et 1965.[43] Certes, il est difficile de rendre compte en termes quantitatifs d'un phénomène aussi "qualitatif" que celui-là, mais ces pourcentages révèlent néanmoins une tendance, que vient d'ailleurs confirmer la lecture de plusieurs arrêts capitaux comme *Re Validity and Applicability of the Industrial Relations Disputes Investigation Act*, dans lequel il a été décidé que la législation fédérale sur les différends du travail s'appliquait au débardeurs du port de Toronto en raison de la compétence du Parlement central en matière de navigation,[44] ou, tout récemment, *Commission du salaire minimum v. The Bell Telephone Co. of Canada*, en vertu duquel les employés de cette société échappent à la loi québecoise sur le salaire minimum parce que l'entreprise a été classée par le Parlement central parmi celles qui "profitent au Canada en général".[45] Ainsi, par un élargissement subtilisé et graduel des compétences fédérales en arrive-t-on à faire passer sous la coupe du Parlement central une partie croissante du pouvoir législatif des provinces et même de leur territoire. Il n'est que de lire, outre les arraires déjà mentionnées, les arrêts *Winner* et *Munro*[46] pour s'en convaincre.

Il est intéressant de noter aussi que le pourcentage des opinions favorables au pouvoir central s'élève à près de 60% chez les juges qui furent auparavant ministres ou sous-ministres fédéraux (neuf depuis la fondation de la Cour). Comme

[43]Nous devons les chiffres et pourcentages qui suivent à la bienveillance de notre collègue, Me Yves Ouellette, de l'Institut de recherche en droit public de l'Université de Montréal. De l'étude très fouillée qu'il a entreprise sur le comportement de la Cour suprême en matière constitutionnelle, nous n'avons retenu ici que quelques aspects.

[44][1955] R.C.S. 529.

[45][1967] R.C.S. 767. Ce "pouvoir déclaratoire" du Parlement est prévu à l'alinéa 10(c) de l'art. 92 du *British North America Act*.

[46]*Winner v. S.M.T. (Eastern) Ltd. and A.G. for Canada*, [1951] R.C.S. 887; *Munro v. National Capital Commission*, [1966] R.C.S. 663.

le faisait remarquer A. V. Dicey, avec un réalisme tout britannique, si le tribunal de dernière instance relève des organes fédéraux, il y aura toujours danger qu'il ne torde le sens de la constitution en faveur du pouvoir central, tout comme une cour créée par une province serait tentée de la fausser en faveur de l'autonomie.[47]

Quelle pourrait être la composition d'un tribunal constitutionnel qui échapperait à ces dangers et comment seraient nommés ses membres? Dans une première hypothèse, le tribunal constituerait l'une des chambres d'une Cour suprême rénovée ou formerait, comme l'a suggéré le Doyen P. Azard, l'assemblée plénière d'une Cour composée d'une Chambre civile et d'une Chambre de common law.[48] Si cette solution était retenue, il conviendrait d'augmenter le nombre des juges de la Chambre de droit civil à cinq, afin qu'elle soit suffisamment nombreuse, et celui des juges de la Chambre de common law dans une proportion semblable, soit à dix.

Dans les litiges entre l'Etat fédéral et une province autre que le Québec ou lorsqu'une question de droit constitutionnel concernant l'une de ces provinces serait portée devant la Cour, l'assemblée plénière de quinze juges (ou un banc de neuf juges comprenant trois civilistes) trancherait la question à la majorité. Cependant, la composition du tribunal ou du banc devrait être différente dans les litiges entre le pouvoir fédéral et le Québec ou lorsque la question de droit soumise à la Cour porterait sur les compétences particulières du Parlement québecois ou à l'application de la législation fédérale au Québec. C'est dans un tel cas qu'il faut éviter tout particulièrement de remettre le sort de la nation canadienne-française entre les mains d'une majorité anglo-canadienne. La Chambre constitutionnelle pourrait alors être composée de dix juges pris également dans les deux autres Chambres et les décisions seraient prises à la majorité, à condition que cette majorité comprenne trois juges de la Chambre civile. Ce système ne serait pas sans inconvénient puisqu'il se pourrait qu' aucune majorité ne puisse être acquise dans un sens ou dans l'autre à l'égard de l'interprétation qu'il convient de donner de la Constitution. Il serait également possible que deux jurisprudences au systèmes d'interprétation distincts se développent, dont l'un serait applicable aux provinces anglophones et l'autre uniquement au Québec. Néanmoins, à compter du moment où l'on considère, d'une part, la nécessité de maintenir un forum constitutionnel commun et, d'autre part, l'obstacle que constitue pour le Québec un tribunal composé d'une majorité de juges anglo-canadiens, on doit admettre qu'une solution de ce genre s'impose. Quant aux affaires pour lesquelles la majorité requise ne pourrait être atteinte, il n'est pas douteux qu'il ne s'agisse de questions touchant des intérêts fort importants, que la constitution devrait dès lors déférer à la négociation directe entre les gouvernements d'Ottawa et de Québec. Bien que de telles questions ne se présenteraient sans doute que rarement, leur existence ne peut être niée, comme en fait foi le refus du Québec d'accepter l'arbitrage de la Cour suprême dans le litige relatif aux gisements miniers du plateau continental.

---

[47]*The Law of the Constitution*, 10e éd., Macmillan, London, 1960, p. 159.
[48]*Supra*, note 37.

Dans une seconde hypothèse, déjà mentionnée, le tribunal constitutionnel pourrait être distinct de la Cour suprême. En Autriche, où prévaut cette solution, la Haute Cour se compose d'un président, d'un vice-président, de douze autres membres et de six membres suppléants. La Cour ne siège pas de manière permanente, mais selon les besoins et sur convocation.[49] En République Fédérale Allemande, les constituants ont hésité entre le rattachement du tribunal constitutionnel à la Cour suprême et l'établissement d'une cour indépendante. Le rapport de la Commission de Herrenchiemsee (1948), chargée de préparer le projet le Loi fondementale, insistait cependant sur la nécessité de l'indépendance de la juridiction constitutionnelle par rapport au pouvoir politique, de façon qu'elle puisse protéger efficacement les droit des *Länder*.[50] C'est le Parlement qui a dû trancher ces questions, lors de l'adoption de la loi fédérale qui règle la composition du tribunal.[51] On y opte pour une cour indépendante des tribunaux de droit commun et composée de seize membres divisés en deux collèges ou sénats qui se partagent la juridiction constitutionnelle, mais doivent se réunir en *plenum* lorsqu'il y a divergence d'opinion entre les deux collèges au sujet d'un arrêt rendu par l'un d'eux ou lorsqu'il y a lieu de départager leurs compétences respectives.[52] Le tribunal, bien qu'il n'ait guère manqué de travail depuis son établissement, ne siège point d'une manière permanente; plusieurs de ses membres sont des spécialistes du droit public et enseignent dans les universités allemandes.

On devrait, dans une certaine mesure, s'inspirer de ces modèles au Canada. L'expérience de la Haute Cour spéciale créée en 1946 pour arbitrer les différends constitutionnels entre le pouvoir central italien et la Région sicilienne, dont les membres sont nommés en nombre égal par les Assemblées de l'Etat et de la Région, pourrait également servir d'exemple.[53] Le fonctionnement en a été satisfaisant jusqu'à ce que Rome s'engage dans une politique de centralisation et tente de restreindre fortement l'autonomie des Régions italiennes.[54] En ce qui concerne le Québec, une juridiction spéciale, indépendante des tribunaux de droit commun, paraît désormais nécessaire; les incidences politiques des arrêts constitutionnels, particulièrement importantes dans un pays binational, exigent une solution de ce type. Le tribunal pourrait être composé de quinze membres, dont cinq de formation civiliste, et fonctionner selon le système que nous avons décrit ci-dessus. La Cour suprême pourrait, de son côté, faire l'objet d'une réforme distincte ou demeurer ce qu'elle est actuellement, si la Cour d'appel du Québec connaissait en dernier ressort des causes relevant uniquement du droit civil.

---

[49] Constitution autrichienne, art. 147.

[50] C. Lassalle, *Le fédéralisme dans la Loi fondamentale de la République Fédérale Allemande*, Presses Universitaires de France, 1954, p. 121.

[51] Loi du 12 mars 1951 réglant la constitution et les compétences du Tribunal constitutionnel fédéral, art. ler.

[52] Sur le fonctionnement de la Cour, voir E. McWhinney, *Comparative Federalism*, University of Toronto Press, Toronto, 1962, pp. 24, 30.

[53] Statut de la Région sicilienne, décret-loi no. 455 du 15 mai 1946, converti en loi constitutionnelle no. 2, du 26 fevrier 1948, arts 24 à 29.

[54] Voir C. Palazzoli, *Les Régions italiennes*, 1966, p. 475.

Il reste à traiter du mode de nomination des membres du tribunal constitutionnel. En Autriche, les membres de la Haute Cour sont nommés par le président de la Fédération, sur proposition du gouvernement fédéral dans le cas du président, du vice-président, de six membres et de trois substituts, et sur proposition des chambres fédérales pour les autres. La Chambre haute (*Bundesrat*), composée de représentants élus par les législatures locales, élit trois membres et un substitut.[55] Ce sont donc toujours les organes fédéraux qui élisent les juges, mais on a cherché à diversifier le corps électoral et à assurer une certaine participation des *Länder*. Le mode de nomination adopté en Allemagne donne un rôle plus considérable aux Etats-membres. Les membres du Tribunal constitutionnel y sont élus en nombre égal par la Diète (ou Chambre basse) fédérale et par le Conseil fédéral, lequel est composé de délégués des *Länder*.[56] Les candidats ne peuvent appartenir ni aux organes législatif et exécutif fédéraux, ni à ceux d'une *Land*; ils ne peuvent exercer aucune autre activité, si ce n'est celle de professeur de droit. Six doivent être choisis parmi les juges des tribunaux fédéraux supérieurs et sont nommés à vie; les autres sont élus pour huit ans et sont rééligibles.[57] Comme on peut le constater, ce ne sont par les solutions qui font défaut; chaque fédération a inventé la sienne en fonction de ses besoins et de l'équilibre qui y régne entre les facteurs de centralisation et les forces décentralisatrices.

Quel serait le mode de nomination le plus approprié aux circonstances canadiennes? Pour les raisons que nous avons énoncées, il paraît essentiel d'assurer la participation du Québec et des provinces à cette étape critique de l'établissement du tribunal constitutionnel, car il ne suffira pas de créer des Chambres de droit civil et de *common law* pour rétablir la confiance nécessaire entre le pouvoir central et les Etats-membres, si tous les juges continuent d'être nommés par le gouverneur général en conseil. Il n'est pas sûr, par exemple, que les juges canadiens-français nommés par Ottawa depuis 1875 se soient, dans l'ensemble, beaucoup écartés des tendances de leurs collègues anglophones.[58] Certes, il ne s'agit nullement de mettre en cause les qualités intellectuelles des dix juristes canadiens-français qui ont siégé à la Cour suprême depuis cette époque et qui ont été pour la plupart d'excellents techniciens du droit, mais on doit constater qu'ils étaient prisonniers du système. On comprend mieux leur situation dès que l'on sait que les juges francophones rédigent leur opinion en anglais dans la plupart des arrêts portant sur des questions constitutionnelles. Le juge H.-E. Taschereau, pourtant farouche adversaire de la Confédération au cours des débats de 1865, rédigea en anglais 33 de ses opinions, sur 35; le juge P.-B. Mignault, 17 fois sur 19; le juge D. Girouard, toutes ses opinions; le juge L. Brodeur, 17 fois sur 20; le juge T. Rinfret, 28 fois sur 35.[59]

---

[55] Art. 147, par. 2.

[56] Loi fondamentale de la République Fédérale Allemande, art. 94.

[57] Loi, *supra*, note 51, arts 2 à 10.

[58] Alors que les juges anglophones se sont prononcés en faveur du pouvoir fédéral dans 53.3% des cas, les juges canadiens-français ont fait de même dans 48% des cas où ils ont participé a la décision.

[59] Ces renseignements sont extraits des travaux de Me Y. Ouellette, *supra*, note 43.

Il existe de multiples formules qui permettraient d'assurer la participation du Québec et des provinces à la nomination des juges constitutionnels. Nous ne retiendrons ici que le mode qui nous paraît le plus approprié au type de tribunal proposé ci-dessus. Si le tribunal constitutionnel était composé de quinze membres, en effet, le pouvoir fédéral et les provinces anglophones pourraient se partager les nominations des dix membres de *common law*, soit également, soit en accordant la majorité des nominations à l'un ou à l'autre des niveaux de gouvernement, les provinces étant groupées par régions pour cette fin. Le Québec, pour sa part, nommerait trois membres du groupe civiliste et la nomination des deux autres reviendrait au Pouvoir central. De la sorte, tous les intérêts en cause seraient représentés.

Pour assurer la plus grande objectivité possible dans le choix des membres du tribunal constitutionnel, il conviendrait que les nominations soient soumises au suffrage du Parlement fédéral dans le cas des juges choisis par l'Exécutif central, et à l'approbation des législatures dans les cas des membres nommés par les provinces ou régions. La majorité des deux tiers devrait être exigée pour ces ratifications.[60]

Tombé de Charybde en Scylla avec l'abolition des appels au Comité judiciaire du Conseil privé et l'avénement de la Cour suprême du Canada en tant que tribunal constitutionnel de dernière instance, le Québec réclame la création d'un forum constitutionnel qui tienne compte de la place qu'il doit occuper dans la Fédération en tant que milieu politique fondamental du Canada français. Après avoir exprimé très tôt sa crainte de voir la Cour suprême modifier au profit du pouvoir fédéral l'équilibre constitutionnel établi par le Comité judiciaire, le Québec a pu constater que cette prévision s'avérait exacte; la Cour suprême laissa bientôt entendre, en effet, qu'il conviendrait de reviser plusieurs arrêts fondamentaux de la jurisprudence du Comité et elle obliqua effectivement vers des positions plus favorables au pouvoir central.

Tant que le Québec choisira de faire partie de l'Union canadienne, quelle que soit la formule constitutionnelle ou conventionnelle adoptée, il faut reconnaître la nécessité d'un forum où puissent être tranchées la plupart des questions d'interprétation de la loi fondamentale et les différends qui surgissent entre Etats-membres ou entre ceux-ci et le Pouvoir central. La plupart des questions touchant l'interprétation ou la validité des lois surgissent dans les litiges entre particuliers et il importe d'être en mesure, dans le cours normal des affaires, de les régler rapidement.

Cependant, tout système d'arbitrage constitutionnel qui aurait pour effet de soumettre systématiquement le Québec aux arrêts d'un tribunal dont les membres seraient en majorité anglo-canadiens ou nommés en majorité par le gouvernement central, ne saurait rallier la confiance et l'appui des Québecois, comme le montrent les déclarations que nous avons mentionnées. On ne saurait nous objecter que tous les Etats, même souverains, acceptent désormais de soumettre

---

[60]C'est la majorité requise à la Chambre haute allemande pour l'élection des juges de la Cour constitutionnelle; le Sénat américain approuve les nominations faites par le Président à la même majorité.

leurs différends aux tribunaux car, dans ce cas, les juges on arbitres appartiennent presque tous à des Etats tiers, tandis que dans le système canadien actuel, le pouvoir central est à la fois juge et partie. On ne saurait non plus prétendre que cette question est de peu d'importance, comme le soutiennent parfois les partisans du *statu quo*; il suffit en effet d'imaginer quelle serait l'attitude des milieux fédéraux si les provinces nommaient tous les juges de la Cour suprême. . . .

L'arbitrage constitutionnel canadien, tel qu'il est constitué à l'heure actuelle, traîne toutes sortes de résidus de l'époque victorienne et du colonialisme britannique; il place le Québec dans la dépendance du pouvoir central, lequel s'est substitué graduellement au pouvoir impérial. Tout système juridictionnel qui prétendrait perpétuer un tel état de choses constituerait une source constante de tension, voire de division, entre le Québec et la Fédération canadienne.

14   Federalism For the Future*

Lester B. Pearson

The Government of Canada rejects both centralization and fragmentation as alternatives to federalism. Centralization, a trend toward a unitary state, would be inconsistent with Canada's character — with its cultural diversity, with a geography which calls for the extensive decentralization of government, and with the freedom which is characteristic of states where the powers of government are not concentrated in the hands of a few.

The opposite course — a loose association of political units in which the effectiveness of the national government is dependent upon the will of provincial governments — is equally incompatible with Canada's goals. It would jeopardize the ability of the federal government to contribute to rising living standards for the people of Canada; it would weaken the willingness of individual Canadians to contribute toward the well-being and progress of their fellow citizens in other provinces; and it would threaten the very existence of our country in a world where size as well as excellence count in the struggle for economic, technological and cultural achievement.

Canadian federalism must be a balance between these extremes, and we should expect to find this sense of balance expressed in our constitutional arrangements. We should expect to find this sense of balance in the constitutional guarantees of the rights of Canadian citizens including their linguistic rights — balanced as

*From *Federalism for the Future*, a White Paper published by The Right Honourable Lester B. Pearson, Prime Minister of Canada, Ottawa, February 1968. Reprinted by permission of the Queen's Printer. The document was published for the Constitutional Conference held in Ottawa, February 5, 6 and 7, 1968.

to the rights of individuals and their obligations to one another and to society, and balanced as to their rights as members of one of Canada's linguistic communities and their concern for those who are members of the other. We should expect to find central institutions of Canadian federalism capable of ensuring a balanced representation in the governing of the nation — representation on the basis of population where the general power to legislate is concerned and representation related to Canada's regions and linguistic groups where the power to legislate is particularly concerned with identity and the rights of these regions and groups. We should expect to find a balanced division of the power to govern between the federal and provincial governments — balanced in the powers it assigns to each and balanced in its concern for the needs of the present and those of the future.

Having formulated these goals and these guiding principles, the Government of Canada believes it is appropriate for it to present to the people, the Parliament and the Provinces of Canada its general views on Canada's Constitution.

The Rights of Citizens and Canada's Linguistic Duality

The first goal of the Canadian federation, in the opinion of the Government of Canada, is the protection of the rights of the individual. This means to begin with, the guarantee of individual human rights for all Canadians. This is a fundamental condition of nationhood; take these rights away and few Canadians would think their country was worth preserving. In a country such as ours, with its two founding linguistic groups, the preservation of individual rights also must mean the guarantee of the linguistic rights of both groups. For language is at once the extension of the individual personality and an indispensable tool of social organization: fail to recognize the linguistic rights of either French or English speaking Canadians and their will to preserve Canada will be seriously weakened, if not destroyed.

The rights of the individual — human and linguistic — are so fundamental to the will of the nation to survive, that the Government of Canada suggests as the first step in reviewing Canada's Constitution the guarantee of these rights in the fundamental law. For this purpose we propose the incorporation into Canada's Constitution of a Charter of Human Rights as quickly as the federal and provincial governments and legislative bodies can agree. For the same purpose we propose that the recommendations in Book I of the Royal Commission on Bilingualism and Biculturalism be considered by this Conference, and that each government here represented agree now to the declarations of principle and of objectives set forth in the recommendations, and set in motion the machinery for realizing these goals as soon as possible.

A Canadian Charter of Human Rights

An important forward step was taken when the Parliament of Canada enacted in 1960 a Bill of Rights which guaranteed the rights of Canadians, to the extent that Parliament could do so by statute. The same can be said about the provincial enactments which guaranteed some of the rights of the citizens in certain of the provinces of Canada, again to the extent that such guarantees can be given by statute. But we do not yet have in this country a comprehensive Charter of Human Rights which assures to Canadians all of the rights they believe to be fundamental, nor do we have a Charter which would prevent these rights from being infringed by the legislative bodies of Canada. This can be achieved only by placing a Charter of Human Rights in the Constitution of our country. Such a Charter, unlike most proposed constitutional amendments, would not involve a transfer of legislative power from one government to another. It would not, for instance, affect provincial jurisdiction over property and civil rights any more than federal jurisdiction over criminal law and procedure in criminal matters. Instead, it would involve a common agreement to restrict the power of all governments.

Central Institutions of Canadian Federalism

The guarantee of the rights of individual Canadians, including linguistic rights, would be the first step in adapting Canada's constitutional and governmental arrangements so as better to achieve the goals of our federation. The second step, in our view, would be the adaptation of our national institutions of government so as to ensure that they too were making their most effective contribution toward the realization of these goals.

The Government of Canada believes that the central institutions of government must be designed to ensure that the essential character of the country is preserved. Federalism is not just a matter of dividing up the powers of government between the federal and provincial governments in the hope of achieving an appropriate balance between the forces of unity and diversity in the nation. The division of powers is, of course, a central element of federalism, and it must be fully considered at the Conferences which are to follow. But it should not be finally decided until the central institutions of federalism provided for in the Constitution have been re-examined.

The Parliament of Canada

The first such institution is the Parliament of Canada. The Constitution provides for two kinds of representation in Parliament; representation on the basis of population in the House of Commons, and representation on a regional basis in the Senate. But because Canadians gradually have come to believe that the Senate should not be able to overrule the will of a popularly elected body, the House of Commons, the Upper House has almost ceased to use its right of veto. This has imposed an effective limitation on its exercise of legislative power.

There are of course other important if informal methods by which Canada's diversity is represented in the national organs of government. We refer to the representation in federal cabinets of the several provinces of Canada, or both of the country's basic linguistic groups, and of much of the diversity in religion and culture in the nation. Similarly the major political parties in the House of Commons have organized so as to ensure in their caucuses and otherwise that these interests are adequately represented.

We believe, however, that the role and the powers of the Senate should be reviewed. It might well be reconstituted so as to enable it to play a new role in representing the federal character of our country. It might, for example, be called upon to make a special contribution in securing the rights of Canadians and in protecting the bilingual character of Canada. It might also be expected to reflect better than it does now the regional interests of our country.

If the role and the powers of the Senate were to be changed, it would also be appropriate, in the judgment of the Government of Canada, to consider changes in the method of appointment. For the method of selecting Senators clearly should be related to the particular role and functions of an Upper House in a federal form of government.

The Supreme Court

Another essential element of federalism is the system under which disputes as to the meaning or application of the Constitution are adjudicated. There have been serious discussions in Canada concerning the composition, jurisdiction and procedures of our final constitutional court, the Supreme Court of Canada; these properly should be considered in any review of the Constitution. For example, the Supreme Court both as a general court of appeal and the final court in constitutional matters now operates under an ordinary statute of the Parliament of Canada. It has been urged that its Constitution and role should be set forth in the fundamental law.

The Government of Canada will be prepared to discuss questions such as these at the constitutional meetings to follow. At this time, however, we would set forth the fundamental principles which in our view should guide us in such discussions. First, there is a functional need, in a federal system such as ours, for a body to settle the jurisdictional conflicts and uncertainties to which all federal Constitutions inevitably give rise. Secondly, if such a body is to enjoy the respect and authority which it needs in order properly to discharge its functions, it must retain a judicial character and be able to perform its functions impartially. Thirdly, the independence of the judiciary is a fundamental principle of the Constitution which must be protected accordingly.

These principles, we acknowledge, are self-evident; they are essential if Canada is to continue to be governed by the rule of law. Unquestionably they would guide both federal and provincial governments in their review of the Supreme Court of Canada.

The Public Service of Canada

The public service of Canada should also be looked upon as one of the institutions of federalism. This means, as the Royal Commission on Bilingualism and Biculturalism has said, that English and French must be the language of work in the federal public service, particularly in Ottawa and other areas where both languages are spoken. It also means that in its composition the public service should in a general way reflect the character of the nation.

The fact that the Government recognizes the public service as an institution of federalism was evident in its announcement almost two years ago of its intention to make the public service progressively bilingual, and its determination to increase the numbers of French-Canadians in the service. A great deal of progress has been made in this direction, and more can be expected as our capacity for language instruction improves, and as our ability to attract to the public service French-Canadians, and Canadians from all regions and walks of life in the country, increases. The problems we face are not constitutional; they are very practical. Canada's public servants are the products of Canada's educational systems, and if the educational systems have not produced bilingual graduates public servants cannot be expected to be bilingual. There are therefore very difficult problems of adjustment, for the Government and for the public servants. We intend protecting as a matter of justice civil servants who have rights to security and expectations for advancement under past language practices. But we are resolved, while according such protection, to make the required changes. To this end we are providing extensive language training facilities for civil servants who are not bilingual. For the future, it is the provincial governments which can contribute most of this change by making available to all students the opportunity of learning to speak French as well as English.

The National Capital

If the organs of government in Ottawa should reflect the federal character of the country, the nation's Capital should be a symbol of Canada. Ottawa and the Capital region should be a model of what we think Canada should be — in particular, as our capital, it should be a model of bilingualism and biculturalism. The Government of Canada has begun discussions with the Provinces of Ontario and Quebec under whose jurisdiction the Ottawa/Hull area falls, on arrangements which could be made to achieve this goal. These discussions will have to take into account both the jurisdictional and the municipal interests which are the proper concern of the Provinces of Ontario and Quebec. We are pleased that the Prime Ministers of these Provinces have been so ready to discuss this question with the Government of Canada.

Canada in the World

Before turning to the third element of Canada's Constitution which we would expect to discuss in the series of constitutional conferences we have proposed, the Government of Canada feels special mention should be made of Canada's international presence.

Canada can have only one international personality. We think that Canadians generally want and expect their country to be seen abroad as a single united country — as Canada. This requires, in our view, that the Government of Canada continue to have full responsibility for Canada's foreign policy and for the representation abroad of Canada's interests.

This is not to deny the interest that provincial governments have in international matters which touch upon their own jurisdiction. This interest can be recognized and protected by ensuring that the Government of Canada exercises its international responsibilities in the proper manner, and by co-operative arrangements between the federal and provincial governments in international matters of mutual concern. There is no evident need to provide the Provinces with special powers in this field. Indeed no federal state has found it necessary or desirable to confer independent treaty-making powers on its provinces or states, or, with the single exception of two of the republics of the USSR for very special reasons in 1945, to allow for a separate presence in international bodies or independent diplomatic representations. The reason is obvious. Such powers or representation would divide or fragment a federal union into separate international entities. In Canada's case, it would destroy our influence and our presence abroad, and undermine our unity at home.

This would not only be tragic; it would be unnecessary. The Government of Canada has been seeking progressively to ensure — in its foreign policy and in all its actions abroad — that it reflects the bilingual character of the country and that it takes into account the proper and developing interests of the Canadian provinces in various international activities. For example, delegations to international conferences where provincial interests are affected increasingly contain a provincial component; provincial desires to benefit from co-operation and interchanges with foreign states are fully recognized and assisted; the provincial governments can, where it is necessary, make agreements with other jurisdictions, with Federal Government agreement; and provincial interests in other forms of international co-operation are also facilitated. Indeed any provincial requirement that calls for some international action can be met by the federal government, save of course for actions which would undermine the ability of the Government of Canada to represent the country abroad. The Government intends, in full co-operation with the provinces, to continue to pursue and develop this policy.

Canadians will understand that talk of separate international personalities or a divided presence abroad is not just academic talk of interest to constitutional lawyers. It strikes at the roots of our existence as a country. Indeed the achievement of independent status for Canada rested a great deal on gaining for our country a separate international voice. To extend this right and power to the provincial governments could mean the same result for them: separate foreign policies, separate relations with other states, separate representation in the U.N. and other agencies, and separate ambassadors and embassies. But it would mean more than that. Separatism abroad would lead to separatism at home. We should make no mistake about it.

The Division of Powers

The third important aspect of Canada's Constitution which should be reviewed is the division of the powers of government between the federal and provincial governments. It is the part of the Constitution over which most differences between governments arise; inevitably it will occupy a major part of our attention in the course of the constitutional conferences we have suggested.

This is understandable and desirable. It is understandable because of the enormous growth in the role of government, federal, provincial and municipal. As the scale of government has increased, the tendency of governments to propose policies or undertake measures which affect the policies or measures of other governments also has increased. Concern as to whether governments' taxing powers match their spending responsibilities has increased correspondingly. And as the range of government activities and programme planning has widened, there has been a growing tendency on the part of governments to extend their planning to cover the activities of other governments operating in the same area.

It is important that the federal and provincial governments review seriously the consequences of proposed constitutional adjustments in this field, in view of the differences which currently divide them. We should be frank about these differences. The governments of the provinces believe that their powers of taxation are too limited; the federal government believes that provincial taxing powers are virtually as great as its own. The governments of some provinces do not believe the Parliament of Canada should use the spending power in the way it has; but in fact, the use of this power has been responsible for much of Canada's social and economic progress. There have been demands for wholesale transfers of taxing and spending powers from the Parliament of Canada; the federal government has replied that transfers to the provinces of powers of such magnitudes would make it impossible for it to discharge its responsibilities for the whole country.

All of these differences are serious. And all of them stem from genuine differences of opinion over how the powers of government are or ought to be divided between the Parliament of Canada and the legislative assemblies of the provinces. The Government of Canada has concluded that the point has been reached where the federal and provincial governments should meet to discuss, formally and fully, the whole question as to how the powers of government should be divided in Canada. We should examine the claims that are made for the transfer or the clarification of powers, and the consequences of these claims. These meetings would, of course, involve difficult discussions of complex and sensitive questions, including the division of powers, the spending power, the residual power, and the power of delegation. But meetings on these questions would be preferable, in our opinion, to dealing with forever recurring disputes over particular powers, in a partial or a piecemeal fashion.

Discussions on the division of powers should take place, in the opinion of the Government of Canada, after the constitutional conferences have considered the other principal elements of the Constitution — the rights of individual Canadians, including linguistic rights, and the central institutions of federalism. We say this because provincial interests and the interests of Canada's two linguistic groups are not and cannot be represented simply through the device of transferring powers from the federal government to provincial governments. These interests are and must be reflected as well in constitutional guarantees and in the central institutions of federalism. It follows that a balanced judgement as to the powers required by the provincial governments for the primary purpose of protecting linguistic or provincial interests can only be made in the perspective of the constitutional guarantees and the representation of such interests in the central organs of government. To jeopardize the capacity of the federal government to act for Canada, in the name of protecting linguistic and provincial rights, when what is essential could be accomplished through constitutional guarantees and the institutions of federalism, would be to serve Canadians badly. Furthermore, the division of powers between orders of government should be guided by principles of functionalism, and not by ethnic considerations. Such principles can best be applied after issues concerning the protection of linguistic rights have been settled.

The Government of Canada would propose, therefore, that discussions on the division of powers take place at subsequent conferences. However, in anticipation of these discussions, and as a guide to the direction of the Government's thinking we believe we should place before the Conference some of the principles by which we feel we would have to be guided.

First, we are committed to the view that Canada requires both a strong federal government and strong provincial governments. The field of government now is so wide, and the problems of government are so many, that it is not a contradiction to speak in these terms. Governments themselves confirm this view when they argue that their spending responsibilities exceed their ability to raise revenues. There is another reason for achieving a balance between the powers of the federal and provincial governments: the freedom of the individual is more likely to be safeguarded if neither order of government is able to acquire a preponderant power over the citizen.

Secondly, the Government of Canada believes that there are certain areas of responsibility which must remain with the federal government if our country is to prosper in the modern world. The Parliament of Canada must have responsibility for the major and inextricably inter-related instruments of economic policy if it is to stimulate employment and control inflation. It must have control over monetary and credit policy, the balance-wheel role in fiscal policy, tariff policy, and balance of payments policy. It must be responsible for inter-provincial and international trade. It must be able to undertake measures for stimulating the growth of the economy, some of which inevitably and some of which intentionally will affect regional economic growth. Without such powers Canada's federal government would be unable to contribute to many of the central objectives of federalism, including the reduction of regional disparity.

We believe that the Government of Canada must have the power to redistribute income, between persons and between provinces, if it is to equalize opportunity across the country. This would involve, as it does now, the rights to make payments to individuals, for the purpose of supporting their income levels — old age security pensions, unemployment insurance, family allowances — and the right to make payments to provinces, for the purpose of equalizing the level of provincial government services. It must involve, too, the powers of taxation which would enable the federal government to tax those best able to contribute to these equalization measures. Only in this way can the national government contribute to the equalization of opportunity in Canada, and thus supplement and support provincial measures to this end.

The Government of Canada believes it must be able to speak for Canada, internationally, and that it must be able to act for Canada in strengthening the bonds of nationhood. We have said what we think this implies in international matters. Internally it seems to us to imply an active federal role in the cultural and technological developments which so characterize the 20th century. We acknowledge, of course, that the nourishment of Canada's cultural diversity requires imaginative provincial programmes, as well as federal ones. But there is a role for the Government of Canada, too; indeed cultural and technological developments across the country are as essential to nationhood today as tariffs and railways were one hundred years ago.

These are central areas of responsibility essential to the apparatus of the modern sovereign state — economic policy, the equalization of opportunity, technological and cultural development, and international affairs. There are among these, of course, areas of responsibility which are shared with the provinces — including cultural matters, regional economic policy, and social security measures. However to catalogue these now, or federal powers generally, would be to depart from a statement of guiding principles and to anticipate the discussions of future conferences.

The third principle which would guide the Government of Canada in discussions concerning the division of powers is that most services involving the most immediate contact between the citizen and the government, and those which contribute most directly to the traditions and heritages which are uniquely provincial, should generally be provided by Canada's provincial governments. Strong provincial governments, able to adapt public services to the particular needs of their people, are as essential to meet the facts of diversity in Canada as a strong federal government is to the preservation of Canadian unity.

The governments of the provinces have responsibility for education, and their own power to support technological and cultural development — so often associated with educational institutions. These powers play an important part in the flourishing of Canada's linguistic groups, and of the diverse traditions to be found in our country. We acknowledge, of course, that many of the institutions involved serve the nation as well as the province but this fact should not be allowed to diminish the capacity of the provinces to perform their role.

The Government of Canada believes that the provinces must have the power to provide health and welfare services. For instance, the provincial governments rather than the federal government should operate hospitals or public health clinics and determine the needs of persons requiring social assistance. Provincial administration of services such as these makes possible the variation of levels of service to accord with local priorities. The role of the federal government should be to provide for those transfers of income between people and between provinces which generally support the incomes of people and the services of governments in the different provinces.

The Government of Canada recognizes too that the provinces should continue to have the constitutional powers required to enable them to embark upon regional economic development programmes. Provincial programmes inevitably will affect national policies for economic growth, and vice versa, and the programmes of the several provinces may well be competitive with one another. But the aims and the expectations of people in the several provinces should find expression in provincial as well as federal economic measures. The provinces must continue, too, to have responsibility for the many intra-provincial matters which call for local rather than national action.

The Government of Canada holds the view that in the exercise of these responsibilities — which under the present division of powers are at least as wide ranging as those of the federal government — each province should be able to develop its own unique approach. The range of powers we would expect the provinces to have would extend, as they do now, into the areas which are vital to the preservation of Canada's several cultural and regional identities.

We believe, finally, that the provincial governments like the federal government must have taxing powers sufficient to enable them to finance their responsibilities. However, we suspect that in assigning to governments the power of taxation — the capacity for financing public services in Canada — the principle of access to tax powers will supersede the principle of an exact division of tax fields. We would do well to remember that it is as difficult to predict what technological or social or international changes will have increased the role of the provincial or federal governments in 30 years as it would have been to predict the changes between 1938 and 1968.

The fourth generalization we would advance concerning the division of powers has to do with the effect each government's activities inevitably will have upon the activities of the others. This applies both to individual programmes and to the totality of government activity. For example, federal income redistribution measures inevitably have an effect upon provincial social welfare programmes and provincial resource development policies inevitably affect the rate of growth of the nation's economy. Similarly the aggregate use by the provinces of their spending and borrowing powers inevitably affects federal fiscal, and monetary and balance of payments policies, and the use of the federal spending power affects provincial policies in different ways. Obviously the total volume of spending by each order of government affects the priorities of the other.

We question whether it is any longer realistic to expect that some neat compartmentalization of powers can be found to avoid this. Instead we suspect that the answer is to be found in the processes by which governments consult one another and by which they seek to influence each other before decisions are finally taken. This remedy has been prescribed so often as to appear commonplace. But there is much to be done even in coming to understand the processes of intergovernmental influence, to say nothing of perfecting the machinery by which intergovernmental consultation takes place. Nor will we find the "participation" of provincial governments in federal government decisions, and vice versa, to be an easy answer to the problems of consultation. The federal government must remain responsible to Parliament, and the provincial governments to their legislatures: federal-provincial conferences must, it seems to us, occupy themselves with the art of influence rather than the power of decision-making.

Both federal and provincial governments will recognize, too, the unresolved question as to whether there should be a federal government role when there is a "national interest" in provincial programmes (or the lack of them), or whether there should be a provincial government role when there is a "provincial interest" in national programmes (or the lack of them). Examples abound: What the provinces do or do not do about urban development unquestionably affects the national interest, and what the federal government does or does not do about tariff policy affects the provincial interest. We have to consider seriously whether there should be a way for the federal government to seek to influence the provinces in cases where a national interest is involved, and a way for provincial governments to seek to influence the federal government when a provincial interest is involved.

There are, we think, no easy solutions. What is required is a comprehensive review of the federal-provincial conferences and committees which now exist, how they function, and how their work is co-ordinated. We must be prepared, it seems to the Government of Canada, to give more systematic recognition to these new forms of federalism.

We must be prepared to consider new methods for bringing provincial influence to bear on developing federal policies, and federal influence on developing provincial policies, before decisions have finally been taken. We must be prepared for innovations in the machinery of government which will enable us to preserve the essence of Canada's two great governmental traditions — federalism and parliamentary government.

Part Four

Federal-Provincial Financial Relations

15   Federal Provincial Fiscal Relations*

James H. Lynn

I Problems of Fiscal Arrangements in a Federal State

A federal state is one in which sovereign rights are enjoyed both by a federal or central or general government and by regional or state or provincial governments.[1] Of course, there is considerable scope for variation in the size of the spheres assigned to the two types of government; indeed, all federal states may be classified on a spectrum ranging from "highly centralized" to "highly regionalized", depending on the division of powers. The exact nature of the division of powers as set out in the Constitution and developed by judicial interpretations depends on the traditions, fears, and desires of the citizens of the particular federation in question. This allocation of powers with respect to both revenues and expenditures gives rise to certain problems which are common to all federal states, but are not found, at least in such explicit form, in unitary states. Although the Government of Canada still legally has the right to reserve or disallow provincial legislation, these practices have fallen into disuse, and for practical purposes Canada has all the attributes of a true federal state, and, needless to say, is therefore confronted with all the unique problems of a federal state. It should be noted that the federal form of organization is chosen for specific reasons and with an awareness of the problems it will create; presumably it is felt by the founders that the advantages of the federal form are such that they outweigh the problems entailed.

Basically, three major problems arise as a consequence of the federal form of governmental organization. Other problems ancillary to these major ones also arise and, in addition, general problems of government found in the unitary form as well, may be aggravated by the federal form of organization.

The three major problems arise in:

1. Allocating expenditure responsibilities and revenue sources between the two levels of government, so that the financial resources and requirements of each level are maintained in balance over time;[2]
2. Adjusting for differences in the ability of regional governments to meet their responsibilities so that each regional government is able to provide a nationally acceptable level of services wtihout having to

---

*From *Federal-Provincial Fiscal Relations*, Studies of the Royal Commission on Taxation, Number 23, Queen's Printer, Ottawa, 1967. Reprinted by permission of the author and publisher.

[1]K. C. Wheare, after an exhaustive study of several countries, concludes that federal states may be distinguished by their adoption of the "federal principle", by which he means ". . . the method of dividing powers so that the general and regional governments are each, within a sphere, co-ordinate and independent". K. C. Wheare, *Federal Government*, 4th ed., Oxford University Press, London, 1963, p. 10.

[2]The word "level" may imply that the central government is superior to the regional governments in a legal or constitutional sense, but this is not intended and the word "level" is used simply because there does not appear to be a more suitable word available.

resort to tax levels far in excess of those levied by other regional governments; and,

3. Maintaining the effectiveness of the fiscal and monetary policy tools necessary to combat economic fluctuations and to promote the most desirable rate and geographic distribution of economic growth.

Allocating Expenditure Responsibilities and Revenue Sources

In a unitary state, the central government alone is responsible for determining the tax structure and the expenditure pattern. Local governments, of course, usually exist, but they are created by the central government, just as municipalities are created by the provincial governments in Canada, and they, therefore, have no independent powers. There are no impediments to the central government's altering the expenditure pattern as its assessment of the scale of priorities desired by the public changes, nor to its altering the tax structure in order to achieve the most desirable mix of various taxes. Furthermore, it is free to vary the level of total revenues and expenditures in order to achieve whatever size of surplus or deficit it desires.

In a federation the total government sector is, in effect, divided into two independent sectors and expenditure responsibilities and revenue sources must be allocated between these two sectors. This division, which is written into the Constitution, reflects the bias toward more or less centralization of the founding fathers and, to some extent, their assessment of which level of government is best suited to administer particular services. An effort to preserve regional differences in culture, religion, and language, which is perhaps the main reason for instituting the federal form of governmental organization, also has a significant influence on the division of powers. Once the allocation of expenditure responsibilities is agreed upon, available revenue sources must then be allocated so that each level of government can meet its obligations. This may be accomplished by providing each level of government with access to all revenue sources, or by dividing the sources and arranging for a system of transfers from one level to the other to ensure that sufficient funds are available to both. Obviously, very neat and precise arrangements can be made for any one year, but what of later years?

If the public suddenly increases demand for a particular type of service in a unitary state, the government can raise whatever tax is most socially acceptable or economically desirable to finance the expanded service. But, in a federal state, the level of government responsible for satisfying this new demand may find it has reached the limit of its ability to exploit the revenue sources allocated to it by the Constitution, or that further exploitation of these sources will disort the tax mix in an undesirable manner. At the same time, the other level, facing a constant or perhaps even a declining demand for its services, may find its revenues actually increasing because of a high elasticity with respect to the growth of the economy. Unless the latter level of government is responsive to the problems of the former and a mechanism for shifting resources exists, serious problems may arise. Such situations actually occur in all federal states because changing times and circumstances radically alter the balance between the revenues and expenditures of each level which was established when the Constitution was created. Obviously this problem does not arise in unitary states, but it is a fundamental problem encountered in all federal states, and it is vital that arrangements be made to ensure that the balance between revenues and expenditures at each level is maintained over time.

Adjusting for Differences in the Ability of Regional Governments to Provide a Nationally Acceptable Level of Services

Within the boundaries of any unit of government — a central government, a provincial or state government, or even a municipality or school board — those living in certain areas will have higher real incomes than those living in adjacent areas because of differences in such factors as natural resources endowment, population concentration, and ability to attract entrepreneurial ability and capital. Differences in real income levels between areas are found everywhere regardless of the form or unit of government. When incomes are lower in certain areas, tax bases are lower, and per capita yields from the same tax structure are therefore lower. If real incomes are lower because of higher costs, per capita tax yields might be equal, but the higher costs will account for differences in the level of services.

Most public services for which any single government is responsible, however, are generally provided indiscriminately to all residents, regardless of the area in which they reside, and, consequently, irrespective of how much they contribute through the tax system to the cost of providing these services or of how much the services cost in their area. The fact that some areas contribute more on a per capita basis, therefore, is not a serious problem within the jurisdiction of any one governmental unit. In effect, an "implicit equalization" of service levels takes place; that is, each resident contributes according to the same tax structure and is provided with the opportunity to enjoy the same level of services regardless of the absolute amount of his contribution. The transfers which effect this "equalization" are hidden by the government's budgetary processes.[3]

---

[3] A distinction must be made between equalizing the consumption of public goods and equalizing the consumption of private goods. A progressive tax structure and personal transfer payments, such as old age pensions, welfare payments and family allowances, are intended to equalize the consumption of private goods at least to some extent. The distinguishing feature of public goods is that their consumption generally is not or cannot be confined to certain individuals within the boundaries of the governmental unit (often consumption cannot even be confined within the borders). The benefits of defence services, for example, are enjoyed or consumed equally by all citizens regardless of their contribution. Some services, such as parks, have to be rationed and some individuals may, therefore, not be able to consume as much as others, but this is a function of their location rather than of their contribution to the costs of providing the services. But, while all residents enjoy equal consumption of public goods, their absolute contributions vary with their income, expenditures, or wealth, depending on the tax structure. If their consumption of public goods was dependent upon their contribution, some people would have a right to more than others, but instead, consumption of public goods (or at least the right to consume public goods) is equalized by the budgetary process.

In a federal state, it inevitably happens that some of the higher and lower real income areas roughly coincide with the jurisdictions of the regional governments. When it is realized that all regional governments are obliged for political or other reasons to provide the same services, and must rely primarily on revenues from taxes levied within their own borders, it becomes apparent that some regions will be able to enjoy a higher level of services given uniform rates of taxation, or lower rates of taxation given uniform levels of services in all regions. Some differences in service levels between regions of a federal state are acceptable as a logical consequence of the autonomy enjoyed by the regional governments, but if the differences become intolerable to those in the lower income regions, the federation may dissolve. The second major problem confronting federal states, therefore, is to implement suitable policies to enable all regional governments to provide a nationally acceptable level of services without having to levy relatively high tax rates. Although many reasons have been advanced over the years to justify such policies, the fundamental justification of all policies designed to ensure a more uniform level of public services in the various regions of a federal state is the national sentiment which opposes extreme variations in service levels within the nation and which endorses the sacrifice that may be necessary to raise service levels in low income areas. This sentiment inevitably arises and expresses itself through the national political process, and it overrides the conflicting sentiment which, at certain times, may arise and assert itself in some of the more fortunate regions.

Although this national sentiment is based to some extent on the welfare consideration that all Canadians, wherever they reside, should enjoy the same level of public services simply because they are Canadians, there are other telling factors supporting this national sentiment. Since the consumption of public goods and services cannot be confined, particularly when there are no border impediments, the spill-over effects between regions of a federal state may be quite large. This factor is particularly significant in the fields of education and health, as well-educated and healthy members of the labour force may move to higher income areas after they have been raised and educated and are then most productive. In addition, national policies, such as minimum wage laws and tariffs, may have detrimental effects on certain regions. Minimum wage laws may raise the marginal cost of a unit of labour over its marginal productivity and, therefore, discourage industry from establishing in certain regions. Tariffs may prevent certain areas from purchasing materials from foreign producers at lower costs, while reciprocal tariffs prevent their selling in those foreign markets. Finally, the region in which income is received is not necessarily the region in which it is earned. Corporate income in particular is rarely earned solely in the region in which corporate taxes are paid or dividends received. Even personal income is often ultimately due to sales in other regions. These three factors, although they may not be quantified, are nevertheless real and significant, and they provide strong support for the national sentiment in favour of a more uniform level of those public services for which regional governments are responsible.[4]

---

[4]References to these factors are continually made by the Canadian provincial govern-

K. C. Wheare defends adjustments of this nature on yet another ground. He believes the federal form of governmental organization is valuable because it enables the people of the various regions to govern themselves in many respects, and this alone justifies policies intended to raise the level of services in certain regions. As he states:

> This exercise in self-government is sufficiently valuable to be worth the cost it entails. If a region cannot support itself, then it is entitled to be guaranteed in a federal constitution access to sufficient resources under its own control to help it to perform its functions.[5]

Policies designed to raise the level of public services in low income areas are, therefore, abundantly justified, not on the basis of analogy with a unitary state or single unit of government, but on the basis of the factors mentioned above which combine to produce a national sentiment. Often these policies must take the form of transfer payments of various sorts between governments, and here a great difference between unitary and federal states becomes apparent. In a unitary state, the transfers which enable all residents, regardless of their contribution, to enjoy the same level of public services, are hidden or implicit, but in a federal state, these transfers must be made explicit. The fact that they are explicit can give rise to much misunderstanding and turmoil within federations.

An integral part of the problem of compensating for differences in ability to provide services is the reconciliation of these policies with policies designed to achieve other goals. The classic conflict which has received extensive treatment

---

ments in their negotiations with the federal government. For example, a perusal of the proceedings of recent Federal-Provincial Conferences reveals the following statements:

"Again, it should be emphasized that Nova Scotia has traditionally educated, and is today educating young men and women who move to other provinces. Other provinces of Canada are benefiting thereby, because of the movement of our trained people to those other provinces." *Dominion-Provincial Conference 1960*, Queen's Printer, Ottawa, 1960, p. 38.

"The present national tariff policy primarily protects the domestic-based manufacturing industries in the central Provinces of Ontario and Quebec. Consequently, individuals and industry in British Columbia pay much higher prices for consumer and production goods . . . . The national tariff policy adds to the already high costs of our provincial services and makes it difficult for British Columbia industry, which is primarily dependent on foreign markets, to compete at world prices." *Federal-Provincial Conference 1963* Queen's Printer, Ottawa, 1964, p. 70.

"In order to collect taxes, administrative assumptions are made about where a tax was earned, but allocation on this basis bears no necessary relation to the contribution each area makes to the national economy." *Ibid.*, pp. 92-93.

These statements were made by the Provinces of Nova Scotia, British Columbia, and Saskatchewan respectively.

[5] K. C. Wheare, *op. cit.*, p. 244.

in the literature on federalism is that between "equity" and "growth" policies.[6] Some argue that policies designed to raise service levels (or incomes) in low income regions necessitate an interference with the most efficient allocation of resources primarily by reducing the mobility of labour and, therefore, lowering the national rate of growth which could otherwise be achieved. While under certain circumstances this is no doubt true, the significant point is that both policies are justified and desirable, but, unfortunately, to some extent incompatible. This commonly cited example of conflict illustrates an important aspect of the political economy of federalism — the continual necessity for balancing conflicting policies. What must be achieved in such cases is a compromise, and successful federal statesmen must possess the rare ability to perceive the point at which an acceptable balance between conflicting policies is being attained. Unfortunately, problems of this nature usually cannot be quantified and technical advisers, therefore, cannot ease the burden placed on federal statesmen; they alone have to make the decisions regarding the proper blend of conflicting policies.

Maintaining the Effectiveness of Economic Policy Tools

Government responsibility for promoting stable economic growth is now an accepted objective in our way of life. When there is more than one government capable of pursuing policies of this nature, it is obvious that conflicts may arise. Although the regional governments in a federation rarely have control over monetary policy, they do have control over some part of the normal fiscal tools, namely, revenues and expenditures. How large a part they will control, of course, depends upon the degree of centralization of the federation. Also, they are generally free to develop their resources and encourage industrial development, and, consequently, to influence economic growth within their boundaries. It is therefore possible for one level of government to be carrying out expansionary policies while the other is carrying out restrictive policies; the net effect of the total government sector's policies could possibly be neutral. Again, with regard to growth policies, regional governments could be carrying on intensive campaigns by tax incentives, grants, or other means to encourage industries to establish in their areas without considering the total effect of all such campaigns and their consequences for individual regions. Once again the federal system gives rise to potentially serious conflicts, both between levels of government and among the individual regional governments. The interrela-

---

[6]This conflict was thoroughly debated in the early 1950's by A. D. Scott and J. M. Buchanan in the following articles: A. D. Scott, "A Note on Grants in Federal Countries", *Economica*, New Series, Vol. XVII, No. 68, November 1950, p. 416; J. M. Buchanan, "Federal Grants and Resource Allocation", *The Journal of Political Economy*, Vol. LX, No. 3, June 1952, p. 208; A. D. Scott, "Federal Grants and Resource Allocation", *The Journal of Political Economy*, Vol. LX, No. 6, December 1952, p. 534; J. M. Buchanan, "A Reply", *The Journal of Political Economy*, Vol. LX, No. 6, December 1952, p. 536.

Incidentally, as discussed above, there are several factors besides equity considerations which justify transfers in a federal state, and it is somewhat unfortunate that this name alone has been applied to such transfers.

tionship between conflicts of this nature and those discussed earlier are clear, as is the need for compromise and reconciliation.

Other Problems

In addition to the major problems discussed above, other problems common to all types of government are aggravated by the federal form of organization. In fact, these additional problems are closely related and could possibly be considered as aspects of the three major problems. First, if particular tax sources and responsibilities are shared by the two levels of government, efficiency in administration may be impaired and costly duplication of effort may occur. The multiplicity of decision-making units aggravates the common government problem of maintaining administrative efficiency.

Secondly, it becomes more difficult for the public to make clear the degree of priority it wishes to assign to each government function. The fact that the public must express its wishes to two levels of government, each of which is naturally more attentive to pressures to increase those services for which it is responsible, no doubt retards the reaction of the total government sector to a shift in priorities. Once again it is obvious that the two levels of government cannot operate independently of each other, but must co-operate in solving these problems.

A third problem which is commonly discussed in the literature on federalism may arise as a consequence of the policies taken to solve the second major problem discussed above. As we shall see, the central government or certain regional governments may choose to raise the levels of services in other regions by transferring some of their funds to other governments. Consequently, the latter governments may gradually lose their sense of financial responsibility as the transfers grow and the degree of responsibility to their electorates correspondingly diminishes. Again, they may lose some of their autonomy if the contributing government attaches qualifications to the transfers.

Transfer payments between levels of government may also have a detrimental effect on the public's awareness of government financial operations. As residents of a level enjoying transfers from the other, the public may delude themselves into believing that these are gifts and forget that there is ultimately only one taxpayer in a federal state despite the two distinct levels of government. All transfers from one level to the other must be financed by taxes and those taxes will be borne ultimately by the same people.

It is readily apparent that the problems of federal finance all involve conflicts. It therefore becomes imperative that there be active participation by all governments in developing effective and continuing machinery to facilitate the co-ordination and the co-operation which are vital to the success of a federation. All governments must be willing to give as well as take and, when necessary, to put considerations for the whole country above considerations for their own particular spheres of activity. The final and perhaps most comprehensive problem therefore is that of achieving a high degree of mutual trust and respect among all the governments and the machinery or facilities for reconciling the many conflicts which continually arise.

II Alternative Solutions to Problems of Fiscal Arrangements in a Federal State

[Part] I presented a formidable array of problems which must be solved if a federation is to thrive harmoniously. Many different types of arrangements have been devised to meet these problems at different times and they have met with varying degrees of success depending upon the nature of the particular federation in question and the economic, social and political circumstances of the various periods. It is worth while, therefore, to gather together and classify the different types of arrangements and to examine their relative advantages and disadvantages.

Allocating Revenue Sources

The first basic problem discussed in the previous section involved the division of expenditure responsibilities and revenue sources between the two levels of government. This division, or the first variation of it at least, is written into the federation's Constitution. It is possible to vary the division of both expenditure responsibilities and revenue sources; however, since the division of expenditure responsibilities is generally more rigid than the division of revenue sources (particularly in Canada), throughout this study, attention will be confined to the division of revenue sources.

There are two fundamental methods by which each level of government may obtain funds (excluding borrowing); first, by levying its own taxes and, secondly, by obtaining transfer payments from the other level of government. Since most types of transfers will be considered when examining solutions to the second major problem, they will be discussed in more detail later; however, there is one type of transfer which is relevant to the problem under discussion here and it will be discussed in turn.

The following classification summarizes the various arrangements which can be employed to facilitate the basic division of revenues given the allocation of expenditure responsibilities:

> Rigid separation of revenue sources
> Joint access to all (or major) revenue sources
> > Tax jungle
> > Tax rental system (derivation transfers)
> > Tax-sharing system
> Supplementary arrangements
> > Tax credits
> > Tax deductions
> > Revenue guarantees
> > Reciprocal taxation policies

Rigid Separation of Revenue Sources

The first and most primitive method of dividing revenue sources between the two levels of government is to rigidly separate the major tax sources when creating the Constitution. For example, income taxes might be assigned to the central government and commodity taxes to the regional governments. While such an arrangement avoids administrative duplication and may be suitable at the time of federation, it lacks the flexibility necessary to adapt to changing circumstances. The expenditures of the regional governments may increase at high rates because of the demand for the services they provide and, unless they can tap the tax sources assigned to the central government, they may be forced to seriously distort the tax mix. They may even find it impossible to meet their responsibilities because of public opposition to an increase in rates on the types of taxes they must impose. While this arrangement does meet some problems it is obvious that the lack of flexibility seriously impairs its usefulness.

Joint Access to All (or Major) Revenue Sources

The second basic method of dividing revenues is to grant each level of government complete legal freedom to levy whatever types of taxes it chooses at whatever rates it chooses. Depending on the maturity of the federation and its leaders, this type of arrangement can either create the worst possible situation or be the keystone of the best possible situation.

At one extreme, complete lack of co-operation or co-ordination can result in what is commonly known as a "tax jungle". Here, both levels may be levying the same types of taxes with a consequent duplication of administrative effort and with the possibility of the total tax rate being extremely high or even exceeding 100%. Fiscal policies implemented by one level employing a particular type of tax may be nullified by the other level's action in the opposite direction with the same tax. Smaller regional governments may find it difficult or impossible to maintain the collection machinery required in some tax fields while larger regional governments may easily be able to bear such costs. Businesses carrying on activity in two or more regions may run into major accounting problems and extremely high total effective tax rates if all regions are taxing business income without co-ordinating their provisions for allocating a firm's total income among regions. A high degree of utilization of a particular tax field by one level may effectively prevent the other level from utilizing that field.

The situation under this general type of arrangement, on the other hand, can be improved considerably if the governments are willing to work together. First of all, they may agree to divide the tax sources between them so as to avoid administrative duplication and to improve their efficiency as fiscal policy tools. Minor tax sources which can be efficiently administered by either level of government may be allocated to either level and even transferred over time, if shifts in relative expenditure requirements occur. Major taxes such as income taxes may be allocated to the central government so that everyone in the country is treated equally; this is particularly advantageous to business firms. Also, the central government may then carry out fiscal policies without fear of their being nullified.

If necessary, the central government might transfer a certain amount of the collections to the regional governments under what is, in effect, a "rental" system whereby each regional government agrees not to levy that particular tax and, in return, receives a certain portion of the collections made within its region from the central government. Tax rental transfers are actually "derivation transfers", that is, the amount of the transfer or grant is determined by the amount of revenue derived from within the jurisdiction of the receiving government. This is the only major type of transfer payment the function of which is to meet the problem of allocating revenues between the two levels of government. Derivation transfers could also be made under a rigid separation of revenue sources system; one level of government could simply make grants to the other based on tax returns from the latter's jurisdiction.

While it has the advantages outlined above, a tax rental system suffers from certain disadvantages. The difficulty of allocating corporate income taxes or any type of commodity tax other than a retail tax is encountered if such taxes are rented. The renting governments give up a certain degree of their autonomy since they can no longer vary the tax base or rate. Changes in the rental rate can only be made after protracted negotiation and the system, therefore, is somewhat inflexible and similar to the system of rigid separation of sources. Also, the public's awareness of which government is really receiving the tax revenue is obscured unless it is made clear on the tax returns.

Another alternative is to attain agreement on a technique for sharing the major taxes between the two levels of government. Both levels might agree on the tax base, but remain free to vary their rates as they choose. The governments might agree to have only one level collect the tax or to have each government collect its own. If one level only collects the total tax, the arrangement is similar to a rental arrangement, but it has the advantages of permitting all governments to vary their rates of tax as they choose and of enabling the public to realize the rates being levied by each government. If each collects its own tax, there is, of course, a duplication of administration. A tax-sharing arrangement does not erode the autonomy and responsibility of any government, but it may possibly lead to conflicting fiscal policies. One level of government might increase its tax rates at the same time as the other level reduces its rates. Of course, if they revert to independently altering their tax bases as well, they may possibly find themselves back in the tax jungle; it is, therefore, imperative that the tax bases be kept identical, particularly if the taxes are to be administered by only one level. The ability of all governments to vary their rates under a tax-sharing arrangement ensures the maintenance of their autonomy and financial responsibility and provides a greater degree of flexibility.

When each level has no restrictions on its taxing powers, it is clear that the success or failure of the governments in developing the most appropriate arrangements depends on their ability to agree on a system and to co-operate with each other in making it effective.

Supplementary Arrangements

The basic division of revenues can also be supplemented by various techniques. First, one level of government can create more tax room for the other level by permitting a tax credit for taxes paid to the latter. Total taxes or a certain fixed or maximum amount paid to one level might be permitted as a credit or reduction from tax payable to the other level. This technique is obviously similar to a tax-sharing arrangement and, indeed, the two might be identical under certain circumstances. Generally, though, the difference between the two lies in the fact that the government permitting the credit is in a dominant position; it determines the amount of the credit and may, therefore, effectively dictate the tax rate to be levied by the other level.

Another method of leaving some tax room to one level is to permit the deduction of expensing of taxes (or a portion of them) paid to that level under the income tax. This enables the latter to raise tax rates and obtain more revenue. It should be noted that with tax deductions, the full amount of any tax increase is not offset by the government permitting the deduction; the value of the deduction will depend on the permitting government's tax rates.

Under tax rental or tax-sharing arrangements, where the two levels of government have agreed upon the method of exploiting a tax field, the level of government best able to withstand decreases in revenue due to economic fluctuations (generally the central government) might provide guarantees to the other level to maintain its revenues at such times. Although these payments would in effect be transfers, they would constitute part of the basic allocation of revenues just as derivation transfers do under rental arrangements. Regional government revenues might be guaranteed at the absolute level effective as of a certain date (with or without a growth factor), or the effective sharing or rental rate might be guaranteed at the rate existing as of a certain date; that is, if the central government reduced its effective rate by increasing exemptions, (thus reducing the tax base) it might automatically increase the rental or sharing rate to compensate for this effective decrease in the regional government tax rate. If regional government rates are a percentage of central government tax collections, rather than a percentage of the tax base, the same type of provisions could be applied to the nominal tax rate.

Finally, governments may have a marginal effect on the basic allocation by their policies in taxing other governments. Although governments may be constitutionally exempt from taxation by another government, they may choose to make grants in lieu of taxes which would otherwise be payable. A government may even agree to voluntarily pay taxes to other governments.

Adjusting For Difference in the Ability of Regional Governments to Provide A Nationally Acceptable Level of Services

Arrangements for dividing total government tax revenues between the two levels of government are concerned only with the first problem introduced in [Part] I, and, by themselves, contribute nothing toward solving the second major problem of federal finance — that of compensating in some manner for differences in the ability of regional governments to provide a nationally acceptable level of services. There are two basic methods of attacking this problem.

The first method involves a long-range comprehensive attack on the fundamental factors causing variations in tax yields and standards of living as between regions, while the second method involves what should be short-run temporary expedients designed to compensate for the more serious deficiencies, but which often become permanent arrangements. During the discussion of this problem in [Part] I, it became apparent that there is sufficient justification for national policies of this nature.

Long-Run Regional Development Programmes

Because variations in tax yields as between regions are due to variations in returns to the factors of production, particularly labour, the logical procedure to solve this problem is to introduce long-run policies to adjust regional growth rates in order to bring the returns to the same factors in different regions into line. While it is traditionally argued that the free market mechanism will bring the rates of returns to the same factors into line provided the factors are mobile and there is no interference with the market mechanism, it is apparent in all federations that this just does not occur.[7] Whether it is due to an inherent inefficiency in the market mechanism, immobility of the factors of production, or various types of government interference which have developed for various reasons is irrelevant because, the efficiency of the market in this respect cannot be empirically measured, the factors of production are clearly becoming less responsive to negative pressures to migrate, the degree of government interference which has been demanded by the people through the political process and is therefore justifiable is clearly not going to diminish.

The solution, therefore, is to introduce positive policies to equalize the returns to the same factors of production in different regions to the extent that this is compatible with other goals. This will involve all the means available to governments to raise rates of growth in low-growth regions. Such policies will inevitably conflict with other policies such as those designed to increase the total national rate of growth and, as stated in [Part] I, a balance must be struck. If the regional development policies are watered down in this process of compromise, it may strengthen arguments for putting some of the temporary expedients on a permanent basis. Regional development has only recently attracted the concentrated attention of governments and economists and it is therefore difficult to generalize about the required procedures and policies.[8]

[7]Several observers of comparative regional growth rates have been struck by the persistence of differences over time and conclude that this may be inevitable for various reasons despite the free market mechanism. See for example, Albert O. Hirschman, *The Strategy of Economic Development*, Yale University Press, New Haven, 1962, Ch. 10, "Interregional and International Transmission of Economic Growth"; Richard E. Caves and Richard H. Holton, *The Canadian Economy: Prospect and Retrospect*, Harvard University Press, Cambridge, 1959, pp. 164-169, "The Economics of Retarded Regional Growth"; T. N. Brewis, "Regional Development: The Need for a Federal Policy", *The Business Quarterly*, Vol. XXVII, No. 3, Fall 1962, pp. 41-45.

[8]For a summary of techniques employed in the rapidly developing field of regional economic analysis and an extensive bibliography, see John Meyer, "Regional Economics: A Survey", *American Economic Review*, Vol. LIII, No. 1, March 1963, pp. 19-54.

Indeed, the most appropriate policies will vary from country to country and each individual country must devise the imaginative policies required to meet its particular problems. The important point is that the problems of regional development are fundamental to the problems of federalism.

Intergovernmental Transfer Payments

While the fundamental solution to the problems created by differences in tax yields as between provinces require an effective programme of regional development, temporary transfer payments will be necessary during the transitional period. Although elements of these policies will survive indefinitely because it is unlikely that rates of returns to the same factors of production in different regions will ever become exactly equal, the transfer payments should be considered as temporary and supplemental to the main attack. This is important because once these transfers come to be accepted as permanent more fundamental solutions may be neglected. Transfer payments may take the form of payments either from the central government to lower income regional governments or from higher income regional governments to lower income regional governments. Subsidies and other types of aid to industry are also part of the long-run development programmes, but unfortunately, they too, often come to be considered as permanent arrangements. Intergovernmental transfer payments are designed to reduce disparities in the levels of public services available for consumption.

Two Concepts of Intergovernmental Transfer Payments

As noted above, intergovernmental transfer payments may take two forms. First, they may take the form of transfers explicitly from one regional government to another. Secondly, they may take the form of transfers from the central government to regional governments. In principle these two types are quite different, but confusion between the two can arise if transfers of the second type (central government to regional government) are considered as being in reality transfers of the first type (regional government to regional government), with the federal government merely acting as a clearing house or agent. This gives rise to two conceptions of central government transfers to regional governments.

The distinction between these two concepts or interpretations of central government transfer payments is both very subtle and very important. Indeed, the distinction is analogous to the distinction between foreign aid transfers from one country to another which are clear and explicit, and government expenditures within different areas of its own jurisdiction which form part of its normal policies. In the latter case the fact that there are differences in the amounts spent in different regions is irrelevant because all expenditures are part of national policies, and the national government is responsible to the entire electorate of the country and not to individual regional governments. The central government obtains its revenues from a nationally uniform tax structure and spends it in a manner designed to achieve the ends of the national policies. If these ends include national unity and, therefore, nationally accept-able levels of public services in all parts of the country, as it has been argued they should, then differential expenditures in geographic areas may be required. If so, the source of these funds by areas or regions is irrelevant; they are raised through the national tax structure for national purposes.

Transfers between nations, or between regions within a nation, are some-what like gifts or a form of charity. Transfers of this nature may take place through the clearing house mechanism of the central government (or an inter-national agency), in which case the amounts donated by various regions to provide the funds to be transferred to other regions may become obscured. But if the transfers are recognized as interregional transfers and not as an element of a national policy, the sources should be made explicit.

Within a federation, regional development programmes and intergovern-mental transfers carried out by the federal government are national policies. Indeed, the factors discussed in [Part] I which justify the national sentiment in favour of nationally acceptable levels of public services indicate that such policies must be considered as national policies. Funds spent on these pro-grammes by the federal government, in whatever form they take, must be considered as federal funds being expended for national purposes, and not as transfers between regional governments carried out by the federal govern-ment on behalf of the regional governments.

Four Types of Intergovernmental Transfer Payments

The foregoing has been a rather lengthy introduction to an examination of intergovernmental transfer payments, but a proper understanding of the con-cepts involved is essential if fruitful discussion is to be stimulated and effective, acceptable policies developed. Federal transfers to regional governments may take four forms, each having a different primary function.

The first type of transfer is not relevant to the second problem under dis-cussion here, but was referred to during the discussion of the basic sharing of revenues. This is the derivation transfer or grant; its purpose is to transfer funds from the federal to the regional governments according to the amount derived from within each regional government's jurisdiction. Such grants, obviously, are not designed to compensate for differences in the ability of regional govern-ments to provide a nationally acceptable level of services.

The second type of federal transfer is that designed to compensate for differ-ences in the per capita fiscal capacity of the regional governments. Fiscal ca-pacity is simply an indicator of the relative ability of regional governments to raise revenues as measured by the income or tax bases of the regional govern-ments. This ability varies due to differences in the economic base of the regions and, therefore, the tax yields of the regional governments. Transfers of this nature may be designed to raise the per capita tax yields in each region up to any specified level. The term "equalization grant" has often been applied to this type of transfer payment and this is unfortunate because the term implies that there is some objective, proper level to which the transfers should raise a regional government's per capita tax yields. This is not so because transfers must continually be balanced with other policies and there is, therefore, no inherent justification for per capita tax yields being raised to any particular level. The significant point about fiscal capacity adjustment transfers is that the criteria governing the degree of difference in the size of the transfers to the various regional governments is the variation in their fiscal capacity or ability to raise revenue, and not the amount raised by the federal government in the various jurisdictions or the different amounts the regional governments require to supply a given level of services.

This leads to a third type of federal transfer — the fiscal need transfer. While fiscal capacity transfers are concerned with variations in revenue yields only, fiscal need transfers are concerned with both revenue yields and expenditure requirements. Differences in fiscal need transfers are based on the differences in per unit service costs between regions caused by geographic terrain, population composition, price levels, degree of urbanization and other factors, as well as with variations in per capita revenue yields.

If and when both fiscal capacity and fiscal need can be measured in a manner acceptable to all governments concerned, perhaps the ideal transfer would simply be one which fills the gap between a regional government's capacity to raise revenues and its financial requirements.[9] This is probably the most popular theoretical transfer found in the literature on federalism. Unfortunately, the problems encountered in attempting to measure the two relevant concepts are so great that this type of transfer system has never been fully implemented in any federal state.

The fourth type of transfer has yet another function. Under certain circumstances, the central government in a federation may be in a better position to perceive the need for a programme on a national scale in a field which falls within the constitutional jurisdiction of the regional governments. Again, the effectiveness from a national point of view of a particular programme being carried out by the regional governments may depend upon common standards being adhered to by all regional governments. In these cases the federal government may make transfers to the regional governments to stimulate and assist them to undertake such a programme or to introduce common standards.[10] Of course, a transfer of this type will often have effects similar to those

---

[9]Perhaps the most rigorous analysis of various types of intergovernmental transfers is contained in a recent article by Professor Musgrave. In this article, he examines seven different methods of calculating the size of federal grants to regional governments and concludes that one filling the gap between capacity and need is his favourite. Professor Musgrave is relatively optimistic about the possibility of instituting such a system although he is aware of the immense problems involved. See Richard A. Musgrave, "Approaches to a Fiscal Theory of Political Federalism", *Public Finance: Needs, Sources and Utilization*, A conference of the Universities — National Bureau Committee for Economic Research, Princeton University Press, Princeton — 1961, pp. 97-122.

[10]Donald V. Smiley, in a recent study of this type of grant in Canada, concludes: "Grants in aid are appropriate under these circumstances: (1) when the implementation of a vital federal policy can be conclusively demonstrated to be dependent upon certain provincial action which would not be undertaken without some form of federal financial inducement; and (2) when provincial and local residence requirements frustrate the free access of citizens to health and welfare services provided by these jurisdictions." Donald V. Smiley, *Conditional Grants and Canadian Federalism*, Canadian Tax Papers No. 32, Canadian Tax Foundation, Toronto, 1963, p. 61.

achieved by the three types of transfers previously discussed, but such effects are secondary to the primary purpose of stimulating and assisting the regional governments. If the primary purpose of these transfers could be achieved by other means, the secondary effects might be achieved more effectively by explicit derivation, fiscal capacity, or fiscal need transfers.

The central government can also provide a general stimulus to regional governments to increase their expenditures by varying any or all of the first three types of transfers according to regional government expenditures from their own sources or the degree to which they exploit their fiscal capacity.[11] Such a policy does not seem advisable as it constitutes a serious infringement upon regional government autonomy. The regional governments, for the reasons discussed in [Part] I, should be provided with the ability to provide nationally acceptable levels of services in the areas for which they are responsible, but whether or not they do so is their own concern, and they should not be penalized if they choose not to do so.

Measures of Fiscal Capacity [12]

Grants designed to raise the tax yields in regions with relatively low yields must be based on some measure of the differences in the potential tax bases or tax capacity of the regional governments as measured on a comparable basis. The now commonly used expression "fiscal capacity" simply refers to the ability of a government to raise revenue relative to other governments, assuming, of course, they are making the same "tax effort" or, in other words, are exploiting their potential revenue sources to the same degree. Naturally, it is meaningless to compare the fiscal capacity of two or more provinces by comparing actual revenue yields if the governments are employing different tax bases or different tax rates on the same bases; some basic comparable measure of capacity must be developed. Given present national statistical collection procedures, there are two basic methods of measuring and comparing fiscal capacity.

First, one of the concepts of the national accounts system of measuring national aggregates could be employed. Preferably a measure of gross or net domestic regional product or, as an alternative, regional personal income might be employed. Since all types of taxes are eventually paid out of income received or product produced, such a measure is the most comprehensive single measure generally available. Unfortunately, certain types of income may be created in a particular region, but may not be accessible for taxation by that regional government, whereas that same income might be accessible for taxation in another region where the income is received but not created. For example, if regional governments levy only a personal income tax, dividends which are due to income created in region A may be subject to taxation in region B. Also,

---

11See Musgrave's seventh grant plan. Musgrave, *op. cit.*, p. 111.

12For an excellent discussion of the techniques and problems of measuring fiscal capacity and tax effort, see, United States, Advisory Commission on Intergovernmental Relations, *Measures of State and Local Fiscal Capacity and Tax Effort*, A Staff Report, G.P.O., Washington, October 1962.

measures of flows such as income or product do not measure stocks, such as property, which are a common base for taxation, nor variations in consumption of commodities liable for commodity taxation. Again, if measures of regional product are unavailable, and reliance must be placed upon personal income, certain types of activity affecting the product of a region, but not appearing as personal income in that region, such as natural resource production will not be encompassed in a measure of regional income, and capacity will therefore be underestimated. Certain types of income (or product) may be amenable to higher rates of taxation and, although they will receive the same weight in the comprehensive measure of capacity, they may give rise to considerable variation in actual capacity if there is variation in the income mix among regions. Although commonly accepted as the best general measure of fiscal capacity, personal income is obviously subject to serious deficiencies.[13]

A second method of measuring fiscal capacity is to measure the yields from a common or average tax structure applied to all regions at the same rates. This method has considerable merit if the regional tax structures are quite similar. All types of taxes regardless of their bases may be included. All that is necessary is to determine the size of the base in each region on a comparable basis and apply an average or standard rate to this base. Taxes, the base of which do not appear in income statistics, such as property or natural resource taxes, may also be included. Consideration may also be taken of variations in the consumption of alcohol or gasoline or other goods which may be taxed at relatively high rates.

Once a comparable measure of fiscal capacity is agreed upon, the actual per capita revenues of the low yield provinces may be raised to whatever level is compatible with other national objectives and obligations. In determining the per capita level to which the yields are to be raised or the size of the transfers, consideration must be taken of other factors such as the effect of the size of the transfers on the responsibility and autonomy of the receiving governments and the morale of those governments not receiving grants, and their effect on the most efficient utilization of the nation's resources.

Measures of Fiscal Requirements

The second type of transfer payment is that designed to compensate for significant differences in the cost of providing services among the regions, or any peculiar circumstances, including temporary ones, which give rise to an exceptional need in a region, as well as variations in tax yields. The most apparent need for such transfers occurs when natural disasters such as floods or droughts hit certain regions. Sudden shifts in demand for certain goods due to changing international trade arrangements or new discoveries may also justify special need grants. If such fiscal occurrences affect tax yields or fiscal capacity, what were

---

[13]An alternate measure of fiscal capacity which may be useful, depending on the tax powers of the regions, is some measure of average consumer unit income. Such measures are commonly made during the national census. If the regional tax structures are limited to personal income taxes and sales taxes, such a measure may have validity, but if the regions are able to tax corporate income or natural resources production, it will not provide an acceptable measure.

originally special fiscal need transfers may become part of the first type of transfer discussed.

Fiscal need transfers may also be required on a continuing basis. If certain regions are called upon to provide expensive services which are not required in other regions, but contribute to the national welfare, this should be considered. Again, if there are great differences in the cost of providing a unit of service, this may justify special transfers. Of course, rather than supplying special transfers, adjustments might be made in the calculation and application of the basic fiscal capacity adjustment transfer for cost or need factors.

One of the great problems in determining fiscal need transfers is the problem of measuring differences in need on a comparable basis. It is particularly difficult to incorporate measures of fiscal need into simple and acceptable formulae as may be done with fiscal capacity measures; considerable scope for personal judgment is generally required. These factors, of course, make it difficult to gain agreement from several governments on the procedures and personnel required to implement fiscal need measures into the fiscal arrangements.

One method of measuring fiscal need is to start with the actual per capita expenditures on major government programmes in certain regions, or on the national average, and to make adjustments to these according to an agreed upon formula taking into account the various determinants of provincial-municipal expenditures.[14] This approach is based on the assumption that the required levels of services in all regions are those attained in certain regions or on the average. Although actual need may be higher (or lower), this approach is reasonable since, due to the necessary rationing of resources, it is not possible to achieve the highest level of services in all regions. The real problems arise in determining what factors to use in adjusting the average per capita or per unit data and the weights to assign each factor.[15]

A second method of measuring fiscal need is to determine what levels of services are desired and what it would cost each regional government to provide

---

[14]In the United Kingdom, basic per capita grants to local governments are supplemented in various ways for such factors as:
  (i) number of children under 5 and old persons over 65,
  (ii) proportion of school children in population,
  (iii) high population density,
  (iv) low population density,
  (v) declining population,
  (vi) metropolitanism.

[15]Several studies in the United States have isolated the major determinants of state-local expenditures. Unfortunately the most important determinant is invariably some measure of income or fiscal capacity, including transfers from other governments. If income is the major determinant of regional government expenditures, actual expenditures may be a very poor basic indicator of fiscal need.

See: 1. Glen W. Fisher, "Interstate Variation in State and Local Government Expenditure", *National Tax Journal*, Vol. XVII, No. 1, March 1964, pp. 57-74; 2. *The State and Local Government . . . . The Role of State Aid*, New York State Department of Audit and Control, Comptroller's Studies in Local Finance No. 3, 1963; 3. Solomon Fabricant, *The Trend of Government Activity in the United States since 1900*, National Bureau of Economic Research, New York, 1952, Chapter 6, "Interstate Differences in Government Activity".

these levels. This method requires objective assessments of required service levels and differences in per unit costs of services. For this reason an independent body may be necessary to determine how much each regional government requires.[16]

Shared Cost or Conditional Transfer Payments

The third type of transfer payments is that designed to stimulate the development of certain services or to ensure national standards where they are necessary for the success of a programme. Although these ends may sometimes be gained by other means, such as voluntary co-operation and agreement, use of the "power of the purse" is a proven and effective way of achieving these ends. Therefore, "conditional grants" or "shared cost transfers", as they are commonly called, have been introduced by the central governments of many federal states.[17] By making the transfer payments or contributions "conditional" upon the performance of certain prescriptions by the receiving regional governments, a central government is generally able to achieve its ends.

A wide variety of arrangements are possible, as the central government share might be a lump sum, matching or fixed proportion of total expenditures, or a per capita or per unit of service grant. It might also contain provision for consideration of variations in fiscal capacity.[18] If an adjustment for tax yield or fiscal capacity is included in the conditional formula, these transfers may be employed to partially achieve the basic aim of fiscal adjustment transfers.

The primary purpose of each of the four types of central government transfer is clear. It is also clear that any one actual transfer may be modified or adjusted to achieve more than one of these purposes.

Maintaining the Effectiveness of Economic Policy Tools

The third major problem confronting a federation is that of ensuring the effectiveness of the policy tools which modern governments employ to combat economic fluctuations and to encourage economic growth. This problem arises due to two factors. First, the existence of two levels of government, each with control over a part of the tools, means that two independent lines of action may be taken on each problem. Secondly, the policies introduced to meet the first two major problems of federal financial arrangements may conflict with other national economic policies and thereby reduce their effectiveness. Since

---

[16]The Australian Commonwealth Grants Commission is probably the most commonly cited example of an independent body appointed to recommend grants after studying the capacity and need of certain states.

[17]Actually, "conditional grants" may be in respect of programmes which are not shared and "shared-cost transfers" may be made without conditions attached. Generally, though, the two elements are combined.

[18]This technique is employed in several United States conditional grant programmes. Generally, such grants are adjusted by the inverse of each state's personal income. For a comprehensive report on this subject, see United States Advisory Commission on Intergovernmental Relations, *The Role of Equalization in Federal Grants*, A Commission Report, G.P.O., Washington, January 1964.

monetary policy is generally controlled by the central government, it is primarily in the field of fiscal policy that these problems arise.

There appear to be two basic methods of maintaining the effectiveness of fiscal policy tools. First, when it is possible for both levels of government to independently undertake policies regardless of the actions of the other level, effective fiscal policies can only be assured by common agreement on the problems faced and the proper solutions. Of course, one level may be in a better position to realize the problems and develop policies sooner. This level should then take the initiative in inducing the other level to co-operate in making their combined policies as effective as possible. Secondly, if one level finds itself for various reasons unable to take the proper action or even forced by circumstances to take perverse action, the other level should provide positive aid to minimize the degree of perversity or maximize the degree of accentuation.

Stabilization Policies

Basically, modern stabilization policies require the maintenance or expansion of government expenditures and reduction of tax rates during recessions and the reverse during inflationary periods. Agreement on forecasts of economic conditions during the next year is fundamental to agreement on appropriate fiscal policies. This may be achieved, at least to some extent, by close contact between ministers and officials in developing major fiscal policies during the preparation of annual government budgets.

If one level finds it is unable to carry the deficit expected during a recession, almost any of the policies discussed in the first two sections of this [Part] could be introduced or expanded. Ideally, provision for special transfers or guarantees should be planned ahead so that they may come into effect automatically. It may be more difficult for one level to induce the other to undertake proper restrictive policies during an inflationary period, and in such cases voluntary agreement on proper anti-flationary policies must be achieved by co-operation.

Economic Growth Policies

Total economic growth policy in a federal state must combine policies to maximize the national rate of growth, and policies to raise the relative growth rate in low income or slow growth areas.[19] The latter are of particular interest to regional governments and for this reason it is important that the federal government develop national regional development policies to ensure that regional policies are not conflicting and self-defeating.

---

[19]An interesting comment on the relationship between these two ends is contained in the July 1964 *A.P.E.C. Newsletter*, Vol. 8, No. 7, Atlantic Provinces Economic Council (Halifax). After noting that the gap between the rate of growth of personal income in the Atlantic Provinces and the national rate of growth had declined in 1963 over 1962, the Newsletter comments: "This suggests that as the current business expansion in Canada became deeper and spread to more sectors, the Atlantic Provinces felt the effects more strongly. If so, the implication is that a healthy national growth rate is almost a prerequisite for regional expansion." (p. 1).

The long-run national growth rate can be increased by government action in the fields of education, resource development, installation of transportation and communication facilities, and aid to research in all industrial sectors. Financial resources must be made available to the level of government responsible for these fields of government activity; this is essentially an aspect of the basic division of revenues. Again, it is important that development plans be nationally co-ordinated to ensure that a gross misallocation of resources is avoided.

Another growth factor which governments can influence is the direct-indirect tax mix. While there is considerable debate on the influence of this factor on growth, it is essential that governments have the conscious ability to vary it as they see fit. This means that there must be flexibility in the employment of both major direct and indirect taxes.

Although it is beyond the scope of this study, the problems of regional governments in borrowing funds through the capital markets to finance long-run development policies should not be ignored in a thorough examination of federal fiscal arrangements.

16 Quebec Speaks*

Jean Lesage

The State of Quebec has fiscal powers and it exercises them. From the time of Confederation, there has been a certain development in this field, and I do not wish to describe its causes and its tendencies today. I will content myself with facing the facts as they are and the situation which I find arouses in me, as in many other people in Quebec, reflections that I should wish to relate to this assembly, Mr. Speaker.

Anyone who is responsible for public administration knows that the absence or insufficiency of fiscal powers seriously limits his scope. In other words, the fiscal system can in itself constitute an instrument of economic growth. Planning as practiced in certain European countries is an eloquent proof of this.

Now, the fiscal system is the one instrument of economic growth over which the Quebec Government still has the least control. The share of income tax collected by our Province is greater now than it has been for several generations, but it still remains clearly insufficient.

*From *Budget Speech*, delivered in the Quebec Legislative assembly by the Honourable Jean Lesage, Prime Minister and Minister of Finance, Queen's Printer, Quebec, 1963, pp. 55-64. Reprinted by permission. Italics are in original.

The Prior Needs of Quebec

At federal-provincial conferences, I have time and time again insisted on Quebec's legitimate demands, basing my claim, with reason I believe, on what I have called and still call the "prior needs of Quebec". Last year, in my Budget Speech, I dealt with this question at great length. As a result of the particular situation in which we find ourselves this year, I believe that it is useful and pertinent to repeat, word for word, the thesis on prior rights as it appeared in the budget speech of 1962:

> In fiscal matters it is always indispensable to apply a good dose of realism. Because available resources are always limited in one way or another, it must happen that altogether justifiable social and economic objectives cannot be realized or that their realization may have to be postponed. This could have been the case with the objectives that we have set for ourselves in Quebec in response to the needs for our population. If we were living for example in wartime, our duty would be to consecrate all our energy and all our resources to victory while retarding the development of important projects. That is exactly what happened here in Canada from 1939 to 1945 when every Canadian was concerned with the "war effort". Domestic consumption was reduced, production of military goods came before the production of civilian goods and that was normal for that period.
>
> After the war and for about ten years the Canadian economy had to readapt itself to new conditions. A serious economic recession of the type that followed the First World War had to be avoided. Also our economy had to be so fashioned as to ensure stability and control the danger of inflation while taking into account our country's role in the post-war world and its dependence on international markets.
>
> To attain these ends it was necessary for the constitutional framework of our country to lean on the central government whose needs at this time took precedence over those of the provinces. The central government thus developed its principal instruments of economic policy, fiscal policy, exchange controls and control of the volume of credit, etc. . . . To guide the fluctuations of the economy and to curtail the effects of economic cycles it had to possess extended fiscal powers. During this time, provincially, the sources of revenue were less, but this situation could be justified by the importance of the role the Federal government had to play in matters of economic stability and international exchanges. The Federal government had to give the post-war economy the means of securing for Canadians the high standard of living to which they had the right to aspire, especially after the period of wartime restrictions. In certain ways the very future of the country itself was at stake.
>
> The fiscal arrangements necessary to meet this situation were to be only temporary. At the beginning it was believed that the spirit of federalism would be reasserted as soon as hostilities were over but the economic consequences of the war lasted several years longer, years during which the former arrangements were maintained.
>
> But now we are living in 1962. There is no longer a state of war and the economic problems that confronted Canada after 1950 are not those of today. It is the needs of the provinces which, after all these years have to take precedence over those of the Federal government. Let me explain myself.

When I say that our needs have to take precedence, I am not expressing an entirely subjective point of view. I am basing myself on facts that everyone can verify for himself. In other words, our needs have not become prior because we wish them to be so but rather because their nature renders them so.

We know that Quebec's needs are essential needs. I have insisted on this point already. We have to improve our level of education since the goal of national affirmation for which we are now striving would otherwise be short-lived. We have to raise the level of public health and social welfare here so that our citizens can play a more efficient role as producers and so that they may become happier human beings. It is finally necessary that the province henceforth be in a position to acquit itself of its responsibilities in the economic field.

Another of the reasons for which these essential needs have to take priority is that there is in practice no longer any reason for the Federal government to keep for itself sources of revenue for which it has not the same needs as in the past. Its anti-inflationary function does not necessarily require tremendous revenues; the Federal government can fulfil this function thanks to the controls it possesses over money, the banks and the rates of exchange. As to its stabilizing function, as fundamental as it was during and after the war, it is now less significant. For we must not overlook that for several years now private enterprises of every kind have been planning their development for the long run. They are not so easily subject, as formerly, to all sorts of influences the nature of which they could not fully fathom; today, with the progress of economic research and thanks to market studies, their operations fluctuate much less than in the past from year to year. In the public sector the social security system that exists in Canada and thanks to which Canadian citizens receive each year more than two billion dollars in the form of transfer payments, permits the maintenance of effective demand at such a level that we can no longer expect an economic depression like the one that started in 1929. I will not go so far as to say that the problem of economic instability has become non-existent but I believe that it is less acute for the reasons that I have just outlined.

Thus the arguments that were valid to justify the prior needs of the Federal administration during the war and post-war periods have lost, since then, a great part of their pertinence. But we continue to live in a framework conceived for an outdated situation.

The fact that the Federal government has closed its recent fiscal year with record deficits does not weaken the preceding argument; it arises from another phenomenon which I would not be justified to develop at the moment.

At the same time as the reasons for which the Federal government could have considered its needs prior to those of the provinces were losing their validity, another factor was manifesting itself, a factor of which all the developed countries of the world were conscious and whose presence reversed completely the situation prevalent from 1939 to about 1956. This factor is the new orientation that modern economic policy must take.

For many years, as I have pointed out, the problem of economic instability and the problem of inflation justly preoccupied those who were responsible for the economic development of the country and incited them to adopt the measures that were required. From the very fact of their action and of the cooperation of the private sector, these problems without entirely disappearing, have nevertheless been considerably attenuated. The problem remaining today, and in an acute fashion, is that of economic development, and this problem is far from being resolved; on the contrary, it may very well be the cause for a large proportion of the unemployment that is prevalent in the Canadian and Quebec economy.

With respect to this problem, if not a new one, at least more timely than ever before, I have only one question to put, which jurisdiction, the Federal government, or the Provincial government, can best favour its solution? And my answer is: the two levels of government can participate in its solution, — but it is undeniable that the provinces have in this matter, a great role to play.

The reason is very simple. By the Canadian constitution the important elements of economic growth and of the development of the riches of the soil, which are but one aspect of the question, fall within the jurisdiction of the provinces. The provinces actually control the greater number of the factors through which a true policy of development can materialize and can have a chance of success. The provinces are also in a position to influence the rate of their own industrial progress by their action in the location of secondary industries, by laying out roads to facilitate access to the basic resources and by their absolute jurisdiction over municipal structures. They can furthermore participate directly in investments, for the development of resources and industry where economic conditions make it desirable. In other words, the provinces are better situated than the Federal government to instigate a policy of economic development because they are nearer to the essential problems, their people and the regions that compose their territory. They can better undertake rational planning in the matter of regional development. In all the developed countries of the world, the United States, France and elsewhere, the accent has been placed on this type of policy. It is hard to see then why, in a country that is so widespread and diverse as ours, we should not adopt the necessary measures. Besides the Federal government itself recognizes the necessity of regional action and we realize that such action can only be effective if the provinces themselves assume the greater share of the responsibility. I do not wish to exclude forever the Federal government from the initiation of a policy of economic development; my one aim is to recall the basic role that the provinces have to play in this matter, since there is obviously a tendency to overlook this consideration in our country's capital.

Moreover, if any policy of growth must involve the development of physical capital, it must equally be concerned with the development of human capital by appropriate education, health, and welfare measures. We are dealing here with fields, within the provincial jurisdiction and whose importance I have noted a short while ago, especially for us in Quebec.

The provinces thus have an obvious responsibility in the economic development of their territory. The constitution implicitly foresees this in the allocation between provincial and federal powers; facts demand that the provinces acquit themselves of the responsibility but the heart of the problem is that at present they are incapable of doing so, because they lack the necessary means. They are incapable of doing so because the Federal government keeps for itself sums of money over which the province should have a first call to accomplish a very essential task. What is more serious is that our people — and the people of Quebec in particular — put up with a lower standard of living than that they could obtain if the Federal government handed over to the provinces which are entitled to it, the means of collecting the revenues that the provinces, conscious of their responsibilities, could devote to the institution of a rational and balanced policy of development, established on the basis of concrete situations existing at the regional level.

Well this was our theme last year. It has been the theme that has guided our attitude since 1960. It remains the same today and *I do not foresee anything that could modify it*. We have undertaken a project of national renovation in Quebec and *we will not tolerate — no matter which Party takes office next Monday — a refusal, whatever the excuses given, to turn over to us the means of action that we still lack.*

I would even add that by the limited amount of attention that the federal government has paid up till now to Quebec's demands, it has acted as though it wished to slow down the economic and social progress of our Province. Its attitude in the application of certain joint programmes has only strengthened the grounds for the lack of confidence in which it is held by a growing number of people in Quebec. Unless there is, during the next few months, a marked reorientation in federal policy regarding fiscal matters and the redistribution of fiscal powers, we will not quickly regain our faith in the federal government's understanding of a federal regime.

This year again . . . the departments of the provincial administration will be deprived once more of an amount of $161,323,800 which they sorely need. As Minister of Finance I have to recognize that their demands for credits have been altogether reasonable. They had been compiled with care and contained no exaggerations. Obviously, as I had asked of them, the authorities of the various Departments have taken into account, in their budgetary demands the fact that Quebec's financial resources are limited. However that may be, once again because the distribution of the sources of revenue between the different governments in Canada continues to be unacceptable, the people of Quebec will be unable to undertake immediately the enterprises that they consider important.

Quebec's Requirements

In three days, federal elections will take place. We do not yet know to which political group the Canadian people will entrust the administration of their country. *Whatever the result of the election, it will be absolutely necessary that the new government should give satisfaction to Quebec.* For the benefit of the federal administration to be elected on April 8th, I reiterate briefly that Quebec requires, *at the moment*, as minimum fiscal powers: 25% of personal income tax, 25% of corporation income tax and 100% of succession duties. Furthermore we want equalization payments to be calculated on the basis of the yield of personal and corporation income tax in the province where it is the highest. These are, *for the moment*, our minimum requirements. It will be necessary later on the basis of the work of the Royal Commission on Taxation that has just been set up, to reconsider the whole question of the division of the fiscal powers between the central government and that of the State of Quebec.

I have asked the federal government to amend the Criminal Code to allow the institution of lotteries for provincial purposes. I reiterate the firm desire of the Quebec Government to have recourse to this method of financing.

As to joint plans, I wish to repeat what I said on this subject at the Federal-Provincial conference of July 1960. The federal government should stop participating in them; it should withdraw from them. The joint plans were instituted at a time when they could be of service to the Canadian economy, *but they are no longer justified*. The flagrant injustice to which Quebec has just been treated with regard to professional and technical training shows that the federal government has not only deprived us of our needs and our rights but that it has also used joint plans to favour certain provinces at the expense of ours. I recall the facts:

Since the years 1960 and 1961, besides having set up a study committee on technical and professional education that has just submitted its report, the government has had a continuing desire to insure the normal development of its network of specialized training schools. It was for this purpose that it decided, in September 1961, to participate in the joint federal-provincial plan on professional and technical training and to recover from the federal government all the sums to which it might possibly be entitled.

Up till 1961, the agreement foresaw a 50-50 division of capital expenditures between the federal and provincial governments. Such a division, was then based on a total sum determined annually and assigned to the provinces on a pro rata basis (proportional to the 15-19 year old population).

The new 1961-67 agreement embodies a new idea; the sum to be distributed to the provinces is no longer determined in advance. Each province receives an amount in proportion to the amount that it has spent within a period prescribed by the agreement. No more pro rata basis.

The 1961-67 agreement also contains a second peculiarity. During the first two years, the contribution of the federal government is fixed at 75% of capital cost. After this period, that is to say, from April 1st, 1963, the federal contribution drops to 50%.

At the time of signing the agreement in 1961 Quebec found itself in a disadvantageous position as compared to the other provinces from various points of view:

The agreement based on the federal act exactly met the needs of the other provinces but did not take into account the special features of Quebec's educational programs.

Having ceased, in 1956, to participate in joint plans on technical training — as a result of the blind policy of the administration that preceded us — Quebec did not, in 1961, have any body set up for the implementation of the agreement from the time of its signing.

Quebec had no program whatsoever for the expansion of specialized training.

In every Quebec milieu, and especially industrialists, businessmen and trade unionists openly questioned the possible efficiency of our technical training as it was then organized.

It was necessary to make a general survey of the situation in technical training and to prepare a complete plan — something that the other provinces had already done through their royal commissions on education and that the present Government initiated in January 1961 by the setting up of a study committee on technical and professional training.

Despite the short period of two years in which the federal government would contribute 75%, Quebec could not launch investments of hundreds of millions of dollars without preparation, without a plan, without exact knowledge of our aims and our needs, without evaluating the benefits of the investments to be made. We had the duty, as a responsible government, to obtain the best yield on the taxpayers' money.

Thus, for Quebec, the years 1961-63 have been years of planning a program and creating a framework for carrying it out. Construction started during this period will enable us to recover, from the federal government, a sum of about $28,000,000, while in the same period our neighbouring province of Ontario received about $200,000,000.

The Quebec Government claims its just share of the money that the Federal Parliament is making available to the provinces for capital expenditures, on technical instruction. *The fair share of Quebec, its total share, should be proportional to its school age population and not to the speed with which it can initiate the construction of buildings.* At least $200,000,000 should be recovered by the Province of Quebec for capital expenditures under the present federal-provincial agreement.

Since the joint plan is designed to assist in the training of young people with regard to the needs of industry, the result of the federal government's action is to favour provinces that were already better prepared in this respect and to penalize those that were less so — despite the fact that Quebec's administration cannot be held responsible for the ostrich policy of the preceding administration. We are thus faced with a situation that is contrary to the fundamental objectives of Confederation.

How can we speak seriously of the reorientation of Confederation when we are not even treated with the most elementary justice?

At the very moment when a large number of our people are questioning the advantages offered to Quebec by Confederation, the attitude of the present federal government is far from dissipating the accumulated bitterness and newer anxieties.

The only acceptable solution, within Confederation, is the replacement of joint plans by the restoration to the provinces of the fiscal powers to which they are rightly entitled.

Joint plans on matters within exclusive provincial jurisdiction, such as education, should be rejected. In participating in them, the provinces are only allowing infringement on their autonomy. Actually, they involve the channelling of public funds through the federal treasury meant for specifically provincial ends. Furthermore, the federal government, having established certain objectives and certain priorities, now determines the conditions under which it invites the province to participate in the realization of these objectives. It imposes a precise framework for the carrying-out of the provincial activity. *Such a situation is absolutely unacceptable to Quebec.*

The renewal of the fiscal arrangements between the federal and provincial governments should normally take place with 1967 in view. However, the Quebec Government cannot wait so long. If some people could have trusted in the past that the joint plans were functioning well, proof to the contrary is now available. The regime of joint plans is not only lame; it is injust. It should be abandoned, particularly in the field of education, without delay; it has to give way to the restoration of fiscal rights to the Province, so that the latter can utilize its own resources to satisfy the specific needs of its own population.

I am submitting these ideas to the three serious parties taking part in the present federal electoral campaign: the Liberal Party of Canada, the Progressive-Conservative Party and the New Democratic Party. The parties in question have made statements on this subject which we, in Quebec, consider of greatest importance. In closing, I should like to consider briefly what the newspapers have indicated as their positions.

The programme of the Liberal Party of Canada proposes the surrender to the provinces of succession duties, a widening of their power of direct taxation and an increase and adjustment in equalization payments. Thus, it recognizes the principle of fiscal decentralization and allows the provinces, by compensating them, to retire from joint plans. There are, in this program, several interesting elements that correspond roughly to the requirements of the Government which I lead, at least to its present requirements. Nevertheless as to the percentage of personal income tax and corporation income tax that should be reserved for the provinces, I find a lack of precision. And regarding the clause concerning compensation for the provinces that would withdraw from joint plans, it would have to be improved for the provinces to achieve full justice.

The leader of the Progressive-Conservative Party has told us that Quebec has received from the Government of Canada, in 1962-63, a sum of $517,000,000. He suggests that this should satisfy us. However, at no time has his party taken a stand on the principles in question. It has revealed nothing original or precise on joint plans, on equalization payments, on the fiscal powers that should revert to the provinces.

Mr. Diefenbaker is content with the presentation of a figure which he draws from I do not know where, and offers us nothing new. What is he including in this sum of $517,000,000? Equalization payments? No doubt. The amount is $73,000,000. Joint plans? Probably. This would be $203,000,000. If one adds to these two amounts a sum of $3,900,000 for the subsidy paid under the constitution and another $4,500,000 paid out of the tax on public utilities, we arrive at a total of $286,000,000.

How does he make up the difference of $231,000,000? Does he include family allowances? Possibly. Old age pensions to persons 70 years and over? Possibly too. In no way does the head of the Progressive-Conservative Party give a clear accounting.

Or again, does he count as federal payments the proportion of personal income tax and corporation profit tax that the provinces themselves collect? I hope not. That would indicate a most curious understanding on the part of the leader of the Conservative Party of provincial rights in general and Quebec's rights in particular.

The New Democratic Party, through its leader, has just announced that it is offering the provinces 40% of personal and corporation income tax, a proportion that would increase to 50% within ten years. This shows a remarkable improvement in this party's program but this proposition is far from satisfying us. In the first place no mention is made of succession duties. Moreover, the total of 40% for the first year, and even that of 50% for the tenth year, cannot meet our needs. What we are asking for with regard to the re-distribution of fiscal powers, with regard to succession duties, with regard to abolition of joint plans, with regard to the compensation that should replace them, and with regard to equalization payments, represents much more, as a total, than the share of income tax that this party would consent to return to the provinces. The New Democratic Party is very vague on these different subjects and today, three days before the election, we still do not know what to expect from it on these important issues.

As to the fourth of the federal parties, I should declare that its opinion means nothing to me. The useless and erroneous comments that its deputy leader has recently ventured to issue on the financial policy of the Government that the people of Quebec have elected for themselves, renders unacceptable any semblance of opinion that he might have on questions that concern French Canada.

In closing, I solemnly declare that I have no intention to continue to speak indefinitely of the needs of Quebec, nor will I be satisfied to continue to present these demands to the central government in the hope that it will condescend to meet them. As I have just said, the matter is of primary importance and I do not intend, as Prime Minister and as Minister of Finance, to repeat myself year after year without tangible results. So this is the last time that I will revert in those terms to this matter in a Budget Speech.

Twelve months will go by before the next Budget Speech. Either the central government, *whichever party is elected on April 8th* and I repeat *whichever party is elected on April 8th*, will have taken advantage of the twelve months to meet Quebec's requirements, or else, we, in Quebec, will, during the same twelve months, see to it that the necessary action is taken in fiscal matters. And this action will be that dictated to us by the objective of economic, social, and cultural affirmation that we have set for ourselves, impelled as we were by the clearly indicated wishes of the people of Quebec.

17   Nova Scotia Speaks*

Robert Stanfield

Although this federal-provincial conference is called primarily to discuss fiscal matters, it would appear that discussion of fiscal matters may relate very closely to the fundamental nature of Confederation. It is clear that certain problems have developed within the framework of Confederation which must be given the most careful consideration.

This is not the first time in our history of almost 100 years when stresses and strains developed within the framework of our federal system of government. Indeed it may be said that stresses and strains within the colonies of British North America contributed in no small measure to the creation of this nation. Certainly, these stresses and strains became very evident in the Province of Nova Scotia immediately following Confederation, resulting in at least two attempts by well-meaning, public spirited citizens to take the Province of Nova Scotia out of Confederation. However, moderation prevailed, and the strength of the framework of Confederation was preserved . . . .

Nova Scotia, in 1867, made sacrifices in order to play its full part in creating a new nation. It held grievances for many years and some of them are still with us, but we are citizens of Canada as well as Nova Scotians and we intend to do everything within our power to preserve this nation and to solve our difficulties and differences in a moderate reasonable manner around the conference table.

Nova Scotia, in 1867, supported a federal system of government as opposed to a unitary state and in 1963 we still hold the same belief. However, a federal constitution must be so framed as to serve all the citizens of the nation and not just those who happen to live in certain geographical parts of the nation. Each of us has a responsibility to his own province but surely each of us has a greater responsibility to the nation as a whole.

Nova Scotia believes in a federal system of government but we do not believe in a form of federalism which creates a central government with no responsibility for the social and economic well-being of the various parts of the union, or a central government charged with the responsibility but without the means to discharge that responsibility. Some government in Canada must be charged with the responsibility of assuring to Canadian citizens a national standard of essential services and that responsibility can only be discharged effectively by the federal government.

In fact, that responsibility has been accepted by successive Governments of Canada. The proposals presented to the federal-provincial conference in 1945 by the Government of Canada contained the following statements:

> These proposals assume a broad federal responsibility in co-operation with provincial governments for establishing the general conditions and framework

---

*From *Federal-Provincial Conference 1963*, Queen's Printer, Ottawa, 1964, pp. 51-54. Reprinted by permission.

for high employment and income policies and for support of national minimum standards of social services. . . . The third requirement of post-war financial arrangements is that they should make possible at least an adequate minimum standard of services in all provinces while not denying to any province the advantages which its resources give to it nor the freedom to establish its own standards. The fourth requirement is that the dominion-provincial financial arrangements must be such as to strengthen, not weaken, the federal system established in our constitution.

The Prime Minister of Canada, addressing the federal-provincial conference on October 3, 1955, stated:

> Our present problem is twofold — to achieve some method of sharing of the revenue available from the direct tax field and some reasonable degree of equity and stability in the revenue of the various provinces. The latter involves some recognition of the fiscal need of those provinces whose tax potential is less than others — payment of subsidies in one form or another. There is nothing repugnant to the spirit or the letter of our constitution in this; the original British North America Act provided what was then substantial subsidies and recognized fiscal need. Throughout our history the forces of economics and geography have been tempered by some measure of national consciousness and solidarity. But this process requires judgement and discretion and due regard to the interest of the nation as a whole.

The Prime Minister discussed very briefly the history of the tax rental agreements and went on to say:

> The present government had no intention of abandoning the objective of the tax rental agreements which is to make it financially possible for all the provinces, whatever their tax base, to perform their constitutional functions themselves and to provide a reasonable Canadian level of provincial services without an abnormal burden of taxation. That is the foundation of the policy of Federal government. This is the principle of paying an element of fiscal need subsidies to provinces with lesser tax potential than others.

The Prime Minister of Canada at the federal-provincial conference, July 25, 1960, in somewhat different terms, reaffirmed the objective of the Government of Canada when he stated:

> Again I wish to emphasize that the federal government remains firmly committed to the principle of equalization and of financial assistance to those provinces in which incomes and taxable capacity are below those of the richer provinces. . . . The Government believes that the principle of fiscal aid and equalization to assist the less wealthy provinces stands on its own feet and is accepted on that basis, and is quite separate from the question of tax rental or tax sharing.

The Government of the Province of Nova Scotia assumes that the Government of Canada is still committed to those objectives.

The need for subsidization of one government by another government is not to be desired and every effort should be made to eliminate the conditions which create the need. Nova Scotia is making a determined effort to improve the economic life of the province and it is having a measure of success. It has joined with the Provinces of New Brunswick, Prince Edward Island, and Newfoundland to form a conference of Atlantic Premiers to deal with matters of mutual concern. As a committee of that conference, the Atlantic Provinces Research Board was constituted to study and analyze the factors which have contributed to our economic disabilities and to consider ways and means whereby those disabilities can be overcome.

Atlantic House in London has been established to represent the trade interests of the four provinces. Nova Scotia has established Industrial Estates Limited as an agency through which industry can be attracted to our province. Nova Scotia has embarked on a program of Voluntary Economic Planning designed to achieve the maximum rate of economic growth and thereby create a higher rate of employment, higher incomes, better social and public services. Nova Scotia wants to mobilize the knowledge, skill, energy and creativity of all its people and to increase its rate of economic growth without regimentation or compulsion.

The Government of the Province of Nova Scotia believes that our efforts will be productive but it all takes time and in the meantime, we must look to the Government of Canada for assistance so as to achieve and maintain a national standard of service for the citizens of Canada domiciled in the Province of Nova Scotia.

Someone may suggest that an attempt to establish a national standard of services is impractical and that each province should provide only a standard of services which its own economy can support. The Government of the Province of Nova Scotia suggests that there are some services which as a nation we can ignore or maintain at a sub-standard level in some provinces, only at the peril of all Canada, namely, education, social welfare and public health. We repeat, at the peril of all Canada, because in these days of mobility of population, the problems created by sub-standard services in one province will inevitably spill over into the other provinces of Canada. As a nation, we must assure to our youth equality of educational opportunity and for the ill and needy a degree of assistance which recognizes the dignity of each Canadian citizen . . . .

We recognize that great demands are being made upon the financial resources of all governments in Canada but we respectfully suggest that the establishing and maintaining of national standards in the fields of education, public welfare and public health are matters of national concern.

The Government of the Province of Nova Scotia suggests that the present fiscal arrangements cannot achieve the objective of enabling each province to provide a national standard of essential services. The present fiscal arrangements and our share of the Atlantic Provinces Adjustment Grants have benefited greatly the Province of Nova Scotia. However, the Government of the Province of Nova Scotia asserts that fiscal arrangements incorporating an equalization factor based only on the returns from income tax, corporation tax, succession duties and natural resource revenue completely disregard the fact that the tax return from these tax sources or the tax return from these sources plus the equalization amount furnish but a portion of the required revenue of each province. The Province of Nova Scotia must raise the major portion of its requirements from other tax sources.

Any plan which recognizes tax deficiencies in limited tax fields and which disregards tax deficiencies in all other tax fields will not enable some of the provinces to furnish a national standard of essential services without imposing an excessive burden of taxation.

We wish to point out that based on 1963-64 estimates, the portion of our revenue coming from individual income tax, corporation tax, succession duties and natural resources is approximately $18,960,000. This is about 21 per cent of the total amount we raise from our own sources of revenue. In short, under the present fiscal arrangements, about 21 per cent of our revenue is equalized to the national average and 79 per cent is not. Under this arrangement, national standards of services cannot be maintained in all fields without imposing an abnormal burden of taxation. Some services will have to suffer; in fact, without the Atlantic Provinces Adjustment Grant, we would not be able to maintain even our present standard of services. Nova Scotia is making a determined effort to encourage and stimulate our economic growth, but an excessive burden of taxation could nullify all our efforts.

The Government of the Province of Nova Scotia wishes to state again the principles on which it believes federal-provincial fiscal arrangements must be based if all Canadians in all provinces are to have a reasonable standard of essential services.

First: that the constitutional responsibilities of each government in Canada must be coupled with financial ability to discharge those responsibilities.

Second: that in the light of the disparity in natural resources and economic development in the various provinces, the federal government must retain a sufficient portion of the tax fields in Canada to enable it to discharge its direct constitutional responsibilities and to assist provinces with low tax potential so as to enable them to furnish a national standard of services to the Canadian citizens residing within their boundaries.

We recognize that through conditional and shared cost programs, the Government of Canada has participated in the development of programs which are under provincial jurisdiction but we do not oppose that participation although we would welcome consultation before the Government of Canada initiates programs involving participation by the provinces.

For the federal government to simply withdraw from certain tax fields or to turn over a lump sum of money to each province without regard to the tax potential of each province, or without regard to the future costs of existing shared cost programs, would be virtual abandonment of federal objectives which have been stated clearly since 1945.

Whatever plan is proposed, it must recognize the necessity of providing for standards of services not only for the present but also the future. It must recognize the financial inability of some provinces to provide a reasonable standard of essential services without imposing an excessive burden of taxation.

The Province of Nova Scotia helped to create this Confederation of Provinces and we want to preserve it. We know that few countries in the world present greater problems of government than does Canada with its great variance in natural resources and regional rates of economic development.

The Government of the Province of Nova Scotia is not seeking through equalization grants a standard of services comparable to the richest provinces in Canada. It is seeking to obtain the necessary financial resources to maintain a good average standard of services without imposing an abnormal burden of taxation.

18   Ontario Speaks*

John P. Robarts

Tax Sharing

As already suggested, the Ontario Government strongly believes that the basic requirement in the area of federal-provincial tax sharing is to secure a division of tax resources which closely matches the distribution of expenditure responsibilities between the two levels of government. In this regard, the existing set of arrangements is manifestly defective. The nature of the problem is well known. On the one hand, the federal government occupies and dominates what are commonly called "growth-tax" fields, consisting primarily of the personal and corporate income taxes. On the other hand, the provincial governments and municipal authorities who, in turn, receive substantial financial assistance from the provinces are largely responsible for the growth fields of public expenditure such as education, health, highways, and water and sewage facilities. This resulting imbalance of revenue sources compared with expenditure responsibilities has placed a disproportionately high burden on the provinces and municipalities in securing funds through tax increases and debt financing. . . .

During the past 12 years, the average annual rate of growth in provincial-municipal expenditure responsibilities was about 12 per cent, compared to about 4 per cent for the federal government. While this tremendous disparity in growth rates was accompanied by a gradual return to the provinces of part of the personal income tax field, provincial revenues lagged far behind provincial expenditure responsibilities. This problem was partly resolved by increased assistance by the federal government through cost sharing and by provincial-municipal borrowing on a large and growing scale. Provincial-municipal debt charges rose from almost $100 million in 1952-53 to almost $400 million in 1964-65, or at an average annual rate of over 12 per cent. In spite of stepped-up federal assistance, the debt burden of the provinces and municipalities has

*From *Federal-Provincial Tax Structure Committee*, Queen's Printer, Ottawa, 1966, pp. 37-46. Reprinted by permission.

accelerated, reaching an average annual rate of growth in debt charges of 16.7 per cent during the past six years. This compares with only 7.3 per cent for the federal government.

The historical record . . . clearly points up the imbalance which has developed in the financial position of the two levels of government. In spite of an annual amount which is now more than one billion dollars in federal assistance through cost sharing in provincial areas of jurisdiction, provincial and municipal expenditure requirements have grown so rapidly that a disproportionate amount of debt financing has been necessary in most provinces. Starting from this seriously imbalanced provincial position, the provincial and municipal governments are faced with a period of continued rapid expansion in their expenditures.

The forecasts made for the Tax Structure Committee reveal that provincial and municipal expenditures can be expected to continue to increase faster than those of the federal government. Moreover, the anticipated growth of provincial and municipal expenditures may prove to be conservative in the light of price increases and upward revisions of expenditure demands. In particular, the provincial and municipal authorities can expect to be faced with an increasing need to undertake expensive types of expenditures, such as urban renewal, commuter transportation, regional development, and school, university and hospital construction. This clearly demonstrates the need to secure a significant reallocation of tax resources between the federal and provincial governments.

This brings us to the question of how tax resources should properly be redistributed. In our view, the present negotiations must result in new tax-sharing arrangements which provide the provinces with a greater share of the personal income tax. Since the personal income tax is the most significant growth tax and since it has been amply demonstrated that the provinces have the largest and most rapidly growing expenditures, it is only reasonable that they should have greater occupancy of this tax field if subsequent readjustments are to be kept to a minimum. Therefore, the Ontario Government believes that an immediate additional abatement of the personal income tax is the rational approach to the problem of tax sharing. . . .

Furthermore, we do not believe that any arbitrary limit such as 50 per cent need be imposed on the provincial share to ensure that the federal government remains in a position to finance its own expenditures, undertake effective anti-cyclical fiscal action and control the form and structure of the income tax. We believe that these responsibilities can be effectively discharged with less than 50 per cent of the personal income tax. The federal government has other tax sources, of course, in addition to personal income tax from which to finance its own expenditure requirements. In our opinion, the federal government would still be in a position to make any required budgetary adjustments and changes in personal income tax rates for normal anti-cyclical and fiscal policy purposes. Moreover, we believe that the way to ensure effective contra-cyclical policies in Canada is through the development of mechanisms for joint federal-provincial fiscal action. Finally, if the provinces do not receive a sufficient increase in their share of the personal income tax, they may be forced to develop their tax fields with little regard to the overall form and structure of Canadian taxation, thereby diminishing federal influence. . . .

In short, Ontario maintains that a significant reallocation of the personal income tax field must take place regardless of the future form of federal-provincial financing arrangements. In this process, the need to contain total governmental expenditures within the limits of a tolerable burden of taxation on private economic activity dictates a natural decline in the federal government's share of total governmental revenues.

Cost Sharing

Ontario recognizes the significant and constructive role that shared-cost programmes have played in assisting the provinces to provide more and better services and in establishing uniform minimum standards across the country. There are, however, deficiencies in present shared-cost arrangements and these should be corrected. As well, the shared-cost form of intergovernmental financing has mushroomed into an unwieldly proliferation of specific programmes. It is our contention that a major review and rationalization of the whole area of cost sharing is in order.

In our view, cost-sharing arrangements require revision along the following lines:

(1) The implicit equalization hidden in some shared-cost programmes should be evaluated and removed. The equalization component in such programmes as hospital insurance arises because the present sharing formula does not adequately account for interprovincial differences in costs. That is, each province receives part or all of its federal assistance on the basis of national average costs, while actual costs in different provinces vary from well above to well below the national average. The result of this procedure is a federal overpayment to provinces in which costs are relatively low and a penalty to provinces in which costs are high. These differences are not compensated for in the federal transfers. In addition, cost-sharing formulae based on national average costs can actually operate as a deterrent to the improvement of standards in some provinces. To the extent that low costs in such provinces reflect inadequate or at least lower standards, these provinces would have to pay an increasing proportion of higher costs in order to upgrade services. Surely these inadequacies in existing shared-cost arrangements should be corrected, or at least compensated for in the final equalization arrangements. Moreover, we strongly urge that such implicit equalization be avoided in any future cost-sharing programmes such as medicare.

(2) Shared-cost programmes should be re-examined periodically to see that they continue to serve the needs and purposes for which they were set up. Programmes that have become obsolete or that can be handled more efficiently in other ways should be discontinued rather than carried on indefinitely.

(3) Programmes should be continued where federal participation is neces-

sary to maintain national standards or to ensure common eligibility and portability.

(4) New programmes should be introduced only after extensive prior federal-provincial consultation and agreement and in situations of temporary
national emergency, such as university capital financing.

Ontario has never adopted a doctrinaire position on cost-sharing, believing
that the circumstances of each case must be treated in specific practical terms.
Nor have we chosen to contract out of programmes simply for the sake of
assuming control over programmes to which we were committed. Clearly any
proposal to hand back to the provinces total responsibility for mature programmes, in exchange for additional tax capacity in order to continue these
essential programmes, offers no real gain to the provinces. Rather, our concern
is to be assured of adequate financial resources to undertake our responsibilities,
singly or jointly. Before accepting any transfer of well established shared-cost
programmes, Ontario wants to explore further the matters of tax sharing and
equalization so that we can properly evaluate the whole package of financial
arrangements available to us. . . .

Equalization

The Ontario Government supports the principle of equalization as a basis for
developing the Canadian nation. Through equalization payments, Canadians
in every province have been able to enjoy at least a minimum level of welfare
and public services. As a large, resources-rich province, Ontario has for many
years been the paymaster for much of these federal transfers to the poorer
provinces. We accept this situation but would caution against carrying equalization so far that the growth and development of the wealthier provinces is
retarded. Excessive inter-regional transfers will inevitably have detrimental
effects on Canada's competitive position in the world economy.

We agree that the current federal equalization proposal is a major improvement in principle over the present formula because all provincial revenue
sources are included and equalization is to the national average. In addition,
the proposed formula has the merit of incorporating the Atlantic Provinces
Adjustment Grants. These changes remove some of the weaknesses and arbitrary features of the old formula. However, we feel that the new formula still
is deficient in that it does not reflect interprovincial differentials in the cost of
providing services. To equalize the fiscal capacities of provinces to the national
average may over-subsidize provinces which have lower costs than the national
average. The equalization proposal is also incomplete in that there is implied
equalization in some shared-cost formulae. As we have suggested, we feel that
this implicit equalization should be eliminated from cost-sharing arrangements.
Failing that, the formal equalization payment should be adjusted to take into
account the equalization hidden in shared-cost formulae. We are convinced
that there should be a single lump sum payment which includes all forms of
equalization. As a paying province we want to know explicitly what the equalization bill amounts to.

We also believe that the proposed formula can be further strengthened by a simple modification in the weighting of natural resource revenues. Rather than weighting all natural resource revenues at 100 per cent, as in the proposed formulae, we suggest a weight of 50 per cent for revenues accruing from non-renewable natural resources such as metallic and non-metallic minerals, oil and gas reserves, and the products of quarries. In a real sense, these resources are once for all revenue resources; once extracted or used, they yield no further revenues to a province. Royalties, bonus bids and other such once for all revenues have a good deal more in common with a receipt from the sale of a capital asset than with a current revenue from the permanent tax base. On the other hand, some provinces now enjoy large revenues from such non-renewable resource fields and are inclined to regard such revenues as part of their total revenue picture. Accordingly, we suggest a 50-50 weighting for such revenue, thus taking into account their importance as a source of revenue, while recognizing at the same time their terminating nature.

Finally, it must be emphasized again that Ontario regards the renegotiation of tax sharing to be of basic importance to a viable reconstruction of federal-provincial relations. Because of this, it would be unwilling to consent to any fiscal settlement on interprovincial equalization until our position in tax sharing has been satisfactorily determined.

Conclusion

Since government is divided in a federal state, there must be provision for properly coordinated policy formulation along with properly distributed financial capacity. There is ample evidence to support the contention that the provinces are now major sources of economic power. Between them, the provinces and municipalities now constitute nearly 55 per cent of overall government expenditure in Canada and over 80 per cent of capital investment expenditures by all levels of government. Much of the apparent criticism of this situation would appear to be based on a wish that Canada were a unitary state rather than a recognition of the fact that we are a federation. We do have eleven governments and we have jurisdiction in the provinces which, at this time, compels us to undertake heavy responsibilities requiring a large share of the public purse.

In this situation, we must work out some system whereby our national interest will be met. Since we have a federal system, this means that the national interest includes, perforce, proper provision for provincial needs. We have only one set of problems, but several levels of government. Our governments should be regarded not as competitive but as complementary, not as opponents at the bargaining table but as partners in progress. Therefore, we should not be engaged in a process of competition between governments for tax sources; rather, we should be seeking a tax system which best suits the present requirements of our federation. In devising a reallocation of financial resources to correspond to national requirements as presently constituted within the federal system, our objective must be to equip governments with the financial capacity to carry out their constitutional responsibilities.

19 The Federal View *

Mitchell Sharp

The Objectives of Canadian Federalism

It is evident to us that the federalism of the future must recognize even more than the federalism of the past that intergovernmental arrangements must serve the two purposes which concerned the Fathers of Confederation. One was to establish a federal system which would define the roles of the federal and the provincial governments in the management of the public affairs of Canada. The other purpose was to provide the means for promoting the social and cultural development of our two societies, a goal which has come to include the cultivation of the enriching heritages that have come to us from other lands. In this twofold purpose lies the uniqueness both of the spirit of Canadian federalism and of the intergovernmental arrangements which our system calls for.

It will be equally self-evident, I think, that the economic and social developments of our first century have changed substantially the roles both of the federal and the provincial governments, and the inter-relationship between these roles. The Depression, the war and then the years of reconstruction taught governments everywhere that they must assume the new and difficult task of managing their economies, in the interest both of full employment and balanced economic growth, and the Federal Government assumed the primary responsibility for this role in Canada. These years taught us, too, that Canadians everywhere want and expect certain basic government services wherever they live, and that they expect their federal and provincial governments to find the methods by which this can be achieved.

It was during these years too that the role of the provinces was similarly enlarged, by the expectations imposed upon them by the people of the provinces, by the technological changes and urban developments which created new needs, and by the renewed realization of provincial potential by provincial politicians. So the responsibilities of provincial governments grew both in scale and in scope, involving programmes in the fields of health and welfare, education, urban development, transportation, and resource and economic development.

Out of these developments emerged still another and a different role for the Federal Government, and new interpretations of the role of the provinces. The Federal Government assumed the responsibility for ensuring that the poorer provinces should, through a system of equalization payments, be put in a position to finance their new and heavier responsibilities. The provincial governments in turn, exercised both their taxing and spending powers in such a way and on such a scale as to increase, in practical terms, both their fiscal powers and their influence over the nation's economy. In the process of these

*From *Federal-Provincial Tax Structure Committee*, Queen's Printer, Ottawa, 1966, pp. 12-27. Reprinted by permission. This statement was presented to the Tax Structure Committee, September 14, 1966.

changes, many of the programmes of the federal and the provincial governments, each of them acting within its own constitutional domain, have come to overlap, with the consequent need for harmonization of government plans and programmes.

These are the forces the federalism of the future must accommodate. We must somehow fashion machinery which will permit a strong Federal Government to accomplish the economic and social responsibilities which properly belong to it, but without impairing the fiscal freedom and responsibility of the provinces. We must on the other hand fashion machinery which will strengthen the ability of the provinces to provide the greatly expanded and improved public services which are expected of them, but without at the same time hobbling the Federal Government or forcing it to have different laws for different parts of Canada — differences which might have the effect of obscuring or weakening its proper role as a government which governs all Canadians and protects equally the interests of all of them.

We in Canada, in other words, cannot solve the problems of twentieth century federalism by subordinating one level of government to another. Nor can we do so by adopting a kind of compartmental federalism, under which the federal and provincial governments would attempt to function in isolation. We must find another way.

Any general appreciation of the objectives of federalism in Canada, such as this, must lead to a statement of the guiding principles which flow from it, if it is to be useful in discussions such as those we are about to begin. The following, then, are the principles by which we believe we should be guided in trying to develop a system of federal-provincial fiscal arrangements which will be consistent with the federalism of the future.

(1) The fiscal arrangements should give both the federal and provincial governments access to fiscal resources sufficient to discharge their responsibilities under the constitution.

(2) They should provide that each government should be accountable to its own electors for its taxing and spending decisions and should make these decisions with due regard for their effect on other governments.

(3) The fiscal arrangements should, through a system of equalization grants, enable each province to provide an adequate level of public services without resort to rates of taxation substantially higher than those of other provinces.

(4) They should give to the Federal Government sufficient fiscal power to discharge its economic and monetary responsibilities, as well as to pay its bills. In particular they should retain for the Federal Government a sufficient part of the income tax field in all provinces — both personal and corporate — to enable it to use variations in the weight and form of that tax for economic purposes and to achieve a reasonable degree of equity in the incidence of taxation across Canada.

(5) They should lead to uniform intergovernmental arrangements and the uniform application of federal laws in all provinces.

(6) The fiscal arrangements should seek to provide machinery for harmoniz-

ing the policies and the priorities of the federal and provincial governments.

These then are the principles or the objectives which have guided us in formulating our approach to the new fiscal arrangements. I would like now to say something about the fiscal environment in which these principles would operate during the next five years, before discussing their application to the four main elements of fiscal relations — equalization arrangements, the use of shared-cost programmes, tax-sharing, and intergovernmental liaison on fiscal and economic matters.

The Fiscal Outlook for the Next Five Years

Since the early 1950's provincial and municipal expenditures have increased from an amount equal to less than one-half of federal expenditures to an amount greater than the total amount the Federal Government now spends. The provincial use of major tax fields has grown correspondingly. All provinces now receive twenty-five per cent of the personal income taxes paid and Quebec receives an additional 23 per cent in return for assuming equivalent additional expenditures under the contracting-out arrangements. The ten provinces taken together receive almost twenty-five per cent of corporation income taxes paid in Canada. They collect about forty per cent of all commodity taxes, including about the same percentage of general sales taxes, some fifty per cent of liquor taxes (or mark-ups), and virtually one hundred per cent of gasoline taxes. And the provincial/municipal governments collect virtually all of the property taxes and natural resources levies paid in Canada.

Federal revenues and expenditures are growing too, but at a slower rate. Indeed the Federal Government was able in the past, because its revenues had been growing more rapidly than its expenditures, to facilitate the rise in provincial revenues through the progressive reduction or abatement of certain federal taxes.

The outlook for the future according to studies made for the Tax Structure Committee indicates a number of trends. First, provincial/municipal expenditures will continue to rise more rapidly than those of the Federal Government. Secondly, provincial and municipal expenditures will also rise more rapidly than will their revenues from existing taxes. Thirdly, federal government revenues from existing taxes, on the other hand, are expected to grow at a rate more nearly equal to the pace at which its expenditures will increase.

These are the fiscal prospects which we have had to take into account in the application of our guiding principles.

Equalization arrangements are one of the four central features of federal-provincial fiscal relations. They represent one of the dividends of Canadian unity, designed as they are to enable all Canadians to enjoy an adequate level of provincial public services. Where circumstances — whether natural or man-made — have channelled a larger than average share of the nation's wealth into certain sections of the country, there should be a redistribution of that wealth so that all provinces are able to provide to their citizens a reasonably comparable level of basic services, without resorting to unduly burdensome levels of taxation.

To accomplish this goal and in the spirit of the principles I spoke of earlier, we have concluded that we must undertake a fundamental reform in our equalization arrangements. We should seek in the future to measure the whole revenue or fiscal capacity of the provinces — to develop a comprehensive "prosperity index" if you will — in place of the partial measure now in use. Instead of selecting certain taxes and equalizing them to the level of the top two provinces, we should take into account all of a province's revenues and equalize them to the national average. This would be a good deal more expensive to the federal treasury but far more equitable. Secondly, the arrangements should be sensitive to the revenue requirements of the provinces, taken together — that is, they should grow as provincial responsibilities increase — and they should be equally responsive to changes in the tax capacity of individual provinces. Finally, to develop a formula that meets these requirements, we must take into account objective factors only, recognizing at the same time the need to deal with any special problems which may arise in the transition from the present to the new arrangement.

The proposed formula is estimated to cost the federal treasury about $490 million, about $140 million more than the present one. These estimates are based upon the hypothetical application of the proposed formula to 1966-67 revenues. They also take into account transitional arrangements which it was recognized from the beginning would be required if there were substantial reductions in the payments to any province under the new formula, as compared with the old. The results, for individual provinces, are [found in Table 1].

The Joint Use of Tax Fields

The major element of federal-provincial fiscal relations, by far the most important one in the post-war period, is the division and use of tax fields by the federal and provincial governments. What this has come to mean to most of us is periodic federal-provincial disputes over what share of personal income tax should be federal and what share provincial. We have come to the conclusion that it is time to try to recast this whole question of tax sharing in broader and more comprehensive terms. I say this both because negotiations over tax shares have increasingly tended to be divisive rather than unifying forces in Canadian federalism, and because this conventional approach to the use of tax fields is misleading.

The real problem confronting us, if we are to take seriously the projections of government revenues and expenditures our officials have presented to us, is how the federal, provincial and municipal governments — and particularly the provincial and municipal governments — are going to finance their continually rising expenditures. This in turn leads to the difficult question as to whether the provinces have access to sufficient revenue sources to finance these increasing expenditures, for unless they do we would be forced to the conclusion that

Table 1

ESTIMATED EQUALIZATION PAYMENTS TO PROVINCES
UNDER FEDERAL PROPOSALS OF SEPTEMBER, 1966
AND UNDER PRESENT ARRANGEMENTS

(Using 1966-67 figures for illustrative purposes)
(All figures estimated)

Province	Total Payment			Per Capita Payment			Payment as Percentage of Provincial Revenues from Own Sources[2]		
	Present Arrangements[1]	Proposed Arrangements	Change	Present Arrangements[1]	Proposed Arrangements	Change	Present Arrangements[2]	Proposed Arrangements	Change
	$000'000	$000'000	$000'000	$	$	$	%	%	%
Newfoundland	37.2	59.8	+22.6	73.96	118.89	+44.93	49.9	80.3	+30.4
Prince Edward Island	10.6	10.8	+ 0.2	98.15	100.00	+ 1.85	73.1	74.5	+ 1.4
Nova Scotia	50.2	69.0	+18.8	66.14	90.91	+24.77	46.7	64.1	+17.4
New Brunswick	44.6	60.3	+15.7	71.25	96.33	+25.08	46.6	62.9	+16.3
Quebec	149.5	235.3	+85.8	26.08	41.04	+14.96	10.7	16.9	+ 6.2
Ontario	—	—	—	—	—	—	—	—	—
Manitoba	27.5	29.1	+ 1.6	28.68	30.34	+ 1.66	14.5	15.4	+ 0.9
Saskatchewan[3]	33.2	27.2	− 6.0	34.84	28.54	− 6.30	13.2	10.9	− 2.3
Alberta	—	—	—	—	—	—	—	—	—
British Columbia	—	—	—	—	—	—	—	—	—
Total	352.3	491.5	+138.7						

Notes: 1 The amounts shown for present arrangements include the Atlantic Provinces Adjustment Grants.
2 "Provincial revenues from own sources" consists of provincial net general revenues less all transfers from the federal government (based on D.B.S. statistics), i.e., it includes all provincial revenues from taxes, licences, fees, fines, etc.
3 The payment to Saskatchewan under the proposed arrangements is a transitional payment which would be paid in 1967-68, and would decline during 1967-68 to 1971-72.

they do not possess that measure of fiscal strength which is an essential element of twentieth century Canadian federalism.

An examination of the tax sources now being used by the provinces reveals that these governments do in fact have access to revenue fields capable of yielding the required revenues. The real question is not whether they have access to such sources but rather whether there are practical considerations making it difficult for them to use their taxing powers. Under the constitution the provinces have access to the income tax fields, both personal and corporate, just as the Federal Government has. Indeed their use of these fields has risen substantially since the war: from five per cent of personal income tax fifteen years ago to twenty-five per cent now, and from $\frac{1}{10}$ of the corporation income tax to about one quarter today. They are now levying taxes on commodities at the consumers level, while the Federal Government levies such taxes at the manufacturers level. As I have indicated earlier the provinces now collect some forty per cent of all commodity taxes imposed in Canada, including nearly forty per cent of the general sales taxes, some fifty per cent of liquor taxes, and virtually a hundred per cent of gasoline tax. The provinces have full access as well to the asset tax field; they and their municipalities now receive close to a hundred per cent of all the property taxes collected, and seventy-five per cent of estate taxes or succession duties. The provinces also have access to resource revenues, as does the Federal Government; indeed provincial resource revenues now represent close to one hundred per cent of the revenues from this source. Only the customs duties can be said to be exclusively collected by the Federal Government.

The conclusion seems clear: the problem is not lack of access to revenue sources, but rather the difficulties the provinces face — in company with the Federal Government — in raising tax levels that are already high.

The conventional approach to this problem, during the post-war period has been to argue that the Federal Government should reduce its taxes so as to give the provinces more "tax room". This is an understandable argument if federal tax yields are rising more rapidly than required. But when federal revenues are required to meet federal expenditures, or to reduce a deficit or create a surplus for economic reasons, then this approach is unhelpful and even misleading. For the Federal Government would not be justified in these circumstances in reducing one of its taxes simply to make it easier for the provinces to increase the same tax. What would be involved would be a reduction in one federal tax to enable the corresponding provincial tax to be raised and then an increase in some other federal tax to restore the necessary budgetary position. The end result of this process would be a net increase in this other tax, with the Federal Government having imposed the increase. The provinces would get the extra money. Surely a more appropriate course would be for the provinces to finance their expenditure increases by increasing the taxes they think should be increased, just as the Federal Government is expected to do in financing its expenditure increases.

The proposition that the Federal Government should reduce its taxes to ease increases in provincial levies must, in circumstances such as those I have described, be based on the assumption that Parliament is appropriating money for purposes less important than those being served by provincial expenditures. That governments should reduce expenditures is a proper subject for argument —taxpayers make it regularly, and apply it equally to federal, provincial and municipal governments. But we cannot accept as a general principle that federal expenditures are less important than provincial ones. The principle that *does* call for recognition is a different one: namely that both Parliament and provincial legislatures must accept their financial responsibilities and that each should look to its own electors for direction as to what money should be raised and how it should be spent.

This is not to say that the Federal Government rejects the notion of federal-provincial consultation concerning public policy priorities. We must have such consultations and increasingly so, in order to ensure a proper concern for the taxpayers' interests. Consultations involving discussions about the size and direction of revenues and expenditures, must be a two-way street.

What I am suggesting then, is that we must get away from what is tending to become a conventional notion that the Federal Government can and should be expected to give greater tax room to the provinces, when they find their expenditures rising more rapidly than their revenues. This has been possible, and has been done, in the past decade, but it cannot be accepted as a general duty. Our basic duty is the ancient one — to tax no more than we need, and to reduce taxes when we can and should.

The second convention of federal-provincial fiscal relations that must be questioned is that there is some particular share of income tax and estate taxes and succession duties, the so-called "shared taxes", which is rightly federal or rightly provincial. The fact is that both have constitutional rights in these fields.

What we must share now is the responsibility for the total taxes imposed on Canadians, taking into account what each other is doing. We must find ways of harmonizing federal and provincial tax actions, to ensure that the interests of the taxpayers of Canada are protected, both in the way and the extent to which the several tax fields are used. This must include the determination of what taxes tend to have national as opposed to provincial characteristics. The corporation tax is one of these, because corporation profits may be earned elsewhere than in the province where the head office is located and profits recorded. I submit too that the Federal Government must have a predominant share of this tax field by reason of the importance and the peculiar value of this tax as an instrument of national economic policy — as we saw in this year's federal Budget.

There are also compelling reasons for the federal government to maintain a substantial position in the personal income tax field. This is the principal tax by which equity is achieved between the rich and the poor across the nation. This implies that a substantial share of this tax should continue to flow to the national government. This tax, too, is one of the central instruments for regulating total demand in the economy, and Canadian governments must not allow total federal income taxes to be abated so much that they can no longer be used for this purpose. This means that the Federal Government must maintain a strong position in this field, despite the pressures it will continue to face for reducing its share in favour of the provinces. We have already made arrangements with Quebec which have enabled that Province to bring its tax to levels equalling those of the federal tax. We have made proposals here which would enable the other provinces gradually to reach the Quebec position. The position that will have been attained under those proposals is, we think, a reasonable one for the provinces, and leaves the Federal Government with a personal income tax adequate to serve the purposes of equity and economic policy.

For these reasons we have concluded that we must look elsewhere than to the further and continuous abatement of federal income taxes for the solution to provincial fiscal problems. We must look instead, I think, to provincial access to all tax fields in provincial jurisdiction. For access can be limited by practical as well as legal obstacles.

Provincial use of the personal income tax field has been impeded and provincial responsibility for the use of this tax has been diluted by the designation under federal-provincial tax arrangements of a certain provincial income tax rate as being the "standard rate". This standard rate, now 24 per cent, has been used in determining equalization payments, and in determining the extent to which the federal personal income tax would be abated. The provinces have been free to impose any rate they chose, but they have had to recognize that any rate above the standard rate would expose them to the charge of "double taxation". In fact, where provincial rates do exceed the standard rate, the excess has been called a "surtax".

It is a nice question as to whether the Federal Government should by inference or otherwise suggest the rate of provincial tax it considers to be appropriate. We have concluded that it should not. In saying this we recognize, as I have said, that each of us should take into account in our fiscal decisions the levels of the other's taxes. But this need not and should not extend to the point that either of us states or implies the level of taxes appropriate for the other. We therefore propose to recommend to Parliament the elimination of reference to "standard rates" (of personal income tax) in the Income Tax Act. This would be done at the time of any major revisions to this Act pursuant to the recommendations of the several Royal Commissions on Taxation. I should note that the equalization formula proposed will similarly make no reference to "standard rates", but will use instead actual average provincial rates.

I should emphasize that this action would in no way weaken the incentives which exist in present fiscal arrangements for uniform tax laws, and should not therefore lead to different definitions of income or other differences in our tax laws. Canadians are justly proud of their accomplishments in achieving uniform income tax laws across the country, and the Federal Government will continue to bend every effort to maintain this uniformity. For this purpose, tax collection agreements will be offered again to the provinces in the period 1967-72, without any charge being made for the collection of provincial taxes under them. The one condition will be that the form of the provincial tax laws must accord with the model Act, a requirement of present tax collection agreements.

In all of this I have scarcely mentioned the details of our tax structure, or the impending Royal Commission reports which may, with the Quebec Royal Commission report, propose extensive changes in it. This is not because I attach little importance to the form and the burden of taxes in Canada, but because I felt the first question to occupy our attention should be a new approach to tax sharing. This, indeed, has always been the aspect of taxation most considered at federal-provincial meetings, and is one upon which the Commissions were not asked to make recommendations.

I regret, as I know some provincial representatives do, that we were unable to have before us at this meeting the report of the Royal Commission on Taxation, for it would enable us to view our problems in the wider perspective which a broad study of this kind makes possible. I hope that this committee will be meeting next year to discuss changes in our tax laws arising out of the revisions that will be undertaken in the light of the commission's report.

I would hope, in the meantime, that the Tax Structure Committee will give serious consideration to the new approach to the joint use of tax fields which I have outlined. I believe it is the approach best suited to the long-term requirements of the provinces and their proper desire for fiscal freedom and responsibility. It equally will serve to preserve the ability of the Federal Government to act effectively on matters of national importance.

20   The Agreements*

Canadian Tax Foundation

Important grants of a general character are made to the provinces, to the territories and to municipalities. . . . The principal grants to the provinces consist of those made under the *Federal-Provincial Fiscal Arrangements Act*, the so-called statutory subsidies and the provincial share of income tax on power utilities. Payments to the territories cover the deficiency on ordinary account, capital needs and amortization of debt. The general payments to municipalities take the form of grants in lieu of taxes on federal property.

The federal government also makes conditional payments or grants-in-aid to the other levels of government for specific purposes such as hospital insurance, assistance to the aged, the blind and the disabled, the Trans-Canada highway, vocational school training, airport development and various resource projects. These conditional grants are not described in this chapter . . . [but] in order to

*From *The National Finances, 1967-68*, Canadian Tax Foundation, Toronto, 1967, pp. 127-138. Reprinted by permission.

provide a comprehensive view of federal assistance to other levels of government, a summary table showing both unconditional and conditional payments is included.

Grants to Provinces

Total actual and estimated general payments to the provinces for fiscal years 1958, 1962 and 1966 to 1968 are set out in Table 2. . . . The table shows that unconditional grants in 1967-68 are expected to total $636 million, about 62% more than a decade ago in 1957-58. However, in the intervening ten years there have been major changes in the fiscal arrangements. The grants reached a peak of $541 million in 1961-62, the last year of the 1957 tax rental agreements, dropped to a low of $254 million in 1963-64 due to the substitution of tax abatements for tax rental payments, and have since been rising steadily as equalization payments grew and a larger share of the estate tax was transferred to the provinces. The equalization payments have increased because of changes in the formula and growth in the yield of the taxes on which the formula is based.

The federal government has partially withdrawn from the income and estate tax fields, all provinces now levy their own income taxes and three have provincial succession duties. The extent of the federal government's withdrawal is indicated by the figures for the estimated value of the federal abatements for personal and corporate income tax and estate tax which are shown at the bottom of Table 2, together with the figures in the top part of the table showing the share of the estate tax and the power utilities income tax paid to the provinces. In 1965-66 the abatements totalled $1,137 million and in 1967-68 they are expected to reach $1,873 million including the new abatements to all provinces for post-secondary education but not the extra abatements to which Quebec is entitled as a result of "opting out" of certain conditional grant programs and operating its own scheme of Youth Allowances. Quebec's extra abatements for these purposes are estimated to be worth about $292.0 million but they are offset by reductions in federal outlays for the programs concerned.

For the 1957 to 1961 tax years both Ontario and Quebec levied corporation income taxes, the former at an 11% rate and the latter at 9% from 1957 to 1959, at 10% for 1960 and at 12% for 1961. A federal abatement of 9% was allowed for both provinces until 1960 when the abatement for Quebec was raised to 10% to compensate for Quebec not receiving federal university grants. During these five years Quebec also continued to impose its own personal income tax and tax-payers received an abatement of federal tax equivalent to 10% in 1957 and 13% from 1958 to 1961. Both Quebec and Ontario continued to impose succession duties in the five-year period and their taxpayers received a 50% abatement of federal estate tax.

Federal-Provincial Tax-Sharing Arrangements (1957-1962) [1]

All provinces and territories except Quebec and Ontario signed agreements relating to the three tax fields covered by the federal-provincial tax-sharing

[1]For a description of the history of federal-provincial financial arrangements since 1941, see *The National Finances, 1966-67*.

arrangements in effect for the fiscal years 1958 to 1962 and covering tax years 1957 to 1961. Ontario chose to rent only the personal income tax field to the federal government and Quebec stayed out entirely, accepting only the unconditional equalization payment. The *Tax-Sharing Arrangements Act* provided for payments by the federal government to the provinces as follows: (1) A rental payment covering the personal income tax, corporation income tax and inheritance fields, and calculated on the basis of the yield of specified "standard taxes" in these fields. (2) An equalization payment, to bring a province's per capita yield from the three standard taxes up to the weighted average per capita yield of such taxes in the two provinces with the highest per capita yields. (3) A stabilization payment to bring a province's yield from the equalization payment and standard taxes up to a minimum which was the greater of (a) the previous financial arrangements extended into current years; (b) the last payment under the previous arrangements adjusted for population changes; or (c) 95% of the average payments for the previous two years under the 1957-62 arrangements.

Standard taxes at January 1, 1957 were (a) a personal income tax equivalent to 10% of federal personal income tax collections in the province, less Old Age Security tax; (b) a corporation profits tax of 9%; and (c) a succession duty equivalent to 50% of federal duties in the province, based on a three-year average of assessments. In 1958 the rate of the standard tax on personal income was increased to 13%. For the provinces which retained their right to impose taxes in these fields, an abatement of the federal tax was granted to alleviate double taxation. As of January 1, 1957, these abatements were the smaller of the amount of the provincial personal income tax paid or 10% of the federal personal income tax, 9% of the federal corporation income tax base, and 50% of the federal tax on estates. In 1958 the abatement of personal income tax was increased to 13%.

In 1960 the legislation was amended to provide that the corporation tax abatement could be increased from 9% to 10%, commencing with the 1960 tax year, in the case of a province not wishing to accept federal per capita grants for universities. Quebec was the only province to take advantage of this abatement and increased its own corporation tax by 1%. Where the value of the additional abatement was less than the $1.50 per capita university grant that would otherwise have been paid, an additional payment was to be made to the province. Conversely, if the value of the 1% abatement was more than the per capita grant, the difference was to be refunded to the federal government.

Special Atlantic Provinces Adjustment Grants were incorporated in the 1958 amendments to the *Federal-Provincial Tax-Sharing Arrangements Act* under which annual payments totalling $25 million were made to the Atlantic provinces as follows: Prince Edward Island, $2.5 million; Nova Scotia, New Brunswick and Newfoundland, $7.5 million each. The payments began in the 1958-59 fiscal year.

Under the *Newfoundland Additional Grants Act, 1959*, an annual payment for the five years ending in 1961-62 of $8 million, less the transitional payment, was granted to Newfoundland. The transitional payments were a series of special grants given to Newfoundland on union with Canada in 1949 in order to facilitate the adjustment of Newfoundland to the status of a province of Canada. These grants totalled $42.8 million and were paid on a declining scale over a period of 12 years commencing in 1949.

Federal-Provincial Fiscal Arrangements (1962-1967)

In 1961 Parliament passed the *Federal-Provincial Fiscal Arrangements Act* which applied to the tax years 1962 to 1966 inclusive. Under this legislation the federal government undertook to withdraw from the corporation income tax field by 9 percentage points of corporate income and from the personal income tax field by 16% in 1962 and by an additional 1% in subsequent years up to 20% in 1966. Following the federal-provincial conference in the spring of 1964 an additional withdrawal of 2% was offered for the 1965 tax year and a further 2% for the 1966 tax year so that the total withdrawal amounted to 24% for the 1966 tax year. The withdrawal or abatement was calculated on the tax payable under the federal *Income Tax Act* before abatement and excluding the Old Age Security tax. The withdrawal applied only to income arising in the provinces, not to income arising in the territories or outside Canada.

The *Fiscal Arrangements Act* also provided for the payment of 50% of the federal estate tax collections in a province to those provinces which did not impose their own succession duties. The 50% abatement of the federal estate tax was continued for provinces with succession duties — currently British Columbia, Ontario and Quebec. At the federal-provincial conference in November 1963 the payment or abatement was increased to 75% of the federal estate tax, effective from April 1, 1964.

The base on which the equalization payment was previously calculated was modified by the addition to the standard taxes of 50% of a three-year moving average of natural resources revenues. The difference between the national average per capita yield of this base and the per capita yield in the province was multiplied by the population of the province to derive the equalization payment. Formerly equalization had been to the weighted average of the top two provinces rather than to the national average and resource revenues had not been counted. The standard taxes in 1962 were 16% of the personal income tax, 9% of corporation income, and 50% of the estate tax. (The definition of the "standard estate tax" was not altered by the increase in the estate tax payment and abatement mentioned above.)

The federal-provincial conference of November 1963 produced a further revision of the equalization formula, effective April 1, 1964. The base of the equalization payment was again confined to the per capita yield of the standard taxes, with each province equalized up to the average in the top two provinces instead of the national average, but there was a deduction for provinces in which natural resource revenues were above average. This deduction was 50% of the amount by which the three-year average of natural resources revenue per capita in the province exceeded the national average, multiplied by the population of the province.

A stabilization payment was guaranteed to any province in which the yield of the standard taxes plus equalization fell below 95% of the average receipts from tax rental, or tax sharing, equalization and stabilization for the two preceding years.

Atlantic provinces additional grants were paid for the term of the 1962-67 agreements in an amount of $35 million each year — $3.5 million to Prince Edward Island, and $10.5 million each to Newfoundland, New Brunswick and Nova Scotia. In addition Newfoundland received a special grant of $8 million annually. An Act was passed in 1966 authorizing payment of this grant in perpetuity.

There were also several other arrangements in effect which were not covered by the *Fiscal Arrangements Act*. These included the sharing of the income tax on power utilities, the statutory subsidies, and the credit against income taxes for provincial logging taxes. These provisions are explained in greater detail in the description of the federal-provincial fiscal arrangements for 1967-72.

In addition Quebec received an extra 1% abatement of the corporation income tax in lieu of federal university grants.

Further 1964 Changes in Fiscal Arrangements

In addition to the specific changes in the 1962-67 fiscal arrangements already mentioned (the increase in the personal income tax abatements for 1965 and 1966, the alteration in the equalization formula and the transfer of the extra 25% of the estate tax), a number of further modifications were made in the fiscal relationships of the federal and provincial governments following the federal-provincial conference in the spring of 1964 and subsequent negotiations. The most important are the following.

Youth Allowances

A federal scheme of providing allowances for 16 and 17 year olds who remain at school or are incapacitated was introduced in 1964. Since Quebec was already in the field of schooling allowances and wished to continue its own program, the federal government agreed to provide an additional abatement of 3% of personal income tax to a province which was in the field at the time the federal program commenced. If the abatement yields more than the federal program would have cost in the province, the excess will be collected back by the federal government, and conversely, if it falls short, the province will receive the difference from the federal government. Quebec is the only province which qualifies for this abatement. The yield of the abatement exceeded the cost of the program by $12 million in 1966-67.

Student Loans

In 1964 the federal government passed the *Canada Student Loans Act* authorizing a program of guaranteeing bank loans for university students and paying the interest on them while the student is at college. In the legislation it offered to provide equivalent fiscal compensation to any province which wished to operate its own loan scheme. The Act specifies that the compensation will be the same proportion of the federal expenditures for the plan in the participating provinces as the 18 to 24 age group in the contracting-out province bears to the same age group in the participating provinces. Only Quebec accepted the option to operate its own plan.

Crown Corporation Immunity from Provincial Taxes

In 1964 the federal government passed a law removing part of the immunity from provincial taxes enjoyed by most federal Crown corporations. The legislation makes 27 Crown corporations and agencies liable for provincial retail sales taxes, gasoline and motor fuel taxes and motor vehicle fees after April 1, 1964. While the amount of revenue involved in this concession is not very significant, the change eases the administrative problems of provincial tax collectors. Because the legislation authorizing this change had been proposed in 1962, the federal government undertook to make a retroactive payment to the provinces to cover the revenue which they would have obtained if the legislation had been effective from April 1, 1962. This payment was made in 1964-65 and amounted to $3.8 million.

1965 Changes in Fiscal Arrangements

Further legislation was passed in 1965 affecting the relationship between the federal and provincial governments. The most significant items were the *Canada Pension Plan Act* and the Act authorizing the "opting-out" arrangements. In addition, the federal government made several proposals at the July 1965 federal-provincial conference relating to medicare, joint programs in various fields and sharing of the income tax on power utilities. At an earlier conference with provincial welfare officials the federal government proposed an integration and expansion of existing federal-provincial welfare plans.

Canada Pension Plan

The first version of the Canada Pension Plan was introduced in Parliament in 1964. Following extensive discussions with the provinces, a considerably modified plan was finally enacted in 1965 to become effective January 1, 1966. The most significant feature of the plan from the point of view of federal-provincial relations is the provision that all funds generated by the plan available for investment will be allocated to the provinces in proportion to the pension contributions coming from each province. The provinces must guarantee the fund a specified rate of return but beyond that they will be free to invest the funds as they see fit.

The *Canada Pension Plan Act* also permits a province to opt out providing it operates a similar comprehensive pension plan and ensures portability of pensions between provinces. Quebec is operating its own pension plan under this arrangement.

"Opting-Out" Arrangements

The conditional grant programs were examined in detail at the federal-provincial conference in the spring of 1964 in an attempt to meet the desire of some provinces to "opt out" of such programs without losing the financial benefits associated with them. After further discussions following the conference, the Prime Minister sent a letter to all provincial premiers in August 1964 detailing a federal proposal for opting-out arrangements for programs of a permanent nature which involved a fairly large annual expenditure. The main features of this proposal were embodied in the *Established Programs (Interim Arrangements) Act* which was assented to in April 1965.

Under the Act the programs which provinces may opt out of are set forth and divided into two categories. For the first category abatements of the personal income tax are offered in lieu of federal payments. For the second group cash compensation is available for provinces carrying on similar programs. Provinces taking advantage of "opting-out" must undertake to continue the program along the same lines as the joint program for a specified interim period ranging from two to five years and must submit "information and accounts in the form and manner described in the authorizing instrument" as well as permit such federal inspections and audits as are necessary for the purposes of the opting-out agreement.

The tax abatements offered were equalized abatements — i.e. an equalization payment was made to bring the per capita yield from the abatement points specified for each program up to the average per capita yield of the same number of points in the top two provinces. If the equalized abatement provided more than the federal contribution to the program would have been had the province not opted out, a recovery was made; conversely, if the equalized abatement fell short, an additional payment from the federal government was forthcoming.

Provinces had until October 31, 1965 to accept or reject "opting-out". Quebec alone entered into supplemental agreements with respect to the various programs. It contracted out of all of the category I programs and the forestry program of category II. Consequently, it was entitled to 20 additional equalized points of personal income tax for the 1965 and 1966 tax years.

The legislation authorized opting-out for the following programs.

Category I	*Equalized Abatement*	*Interim Period*
Hospital Insurance	14 points	January 1, 1965 to December 31, 1970
Old age assistance, blind and disabled allowances	2 points	April 1, 1965 to March 31, 1970
Welfare portion of unemployment assistance	2 points	April 1, 1965 to March 31, 1970
Specified technical education programs—operating costs	1 point	April 1, 1965 to March 31, 1967
Health grants	1 point	April 1, 1965 to March 31, 1967

Category II — Provinces were allowed to opt out of the following additional programs and receive cash compensation equivalent to the federal contribution to which the province would be entitled under the program:

> Agricultural lime assistance
>
> Forestry programs
>
> Hospital construction program
>
> Campgrounds and picnic areas program
>
> Roads to resources program.

Other

In 1965 the federal government proposed that the joint programs covering old age assistance, allowance for the blind and disabled and unemployment assistance be consolidated and expanded into the Canada Assistance Plan. This was inaugurated April 1, 1966.

1966 Changes in Fiscal Arrangements

In 1966 legislation was passed to implement the Canada Assistance Plan, and to increase to 95% the provincial share of the income tax on power utilities. In addition legislation was passed authorizing the payment of part of the costs of provincial medicare programs after July 1, 1967. (The effective date was subsequently changed to July 1, 1968.) As already mentioned, the $8 million annual grant to Newfoundland was written into the statutes in perpetuity. Federal university grants were increased from $2 per capita to $5 per capita but were later superseded by new arrangements in the *Federal-Provincial Fiscal Arrangements Act, 1967*. Two important federal-provincial conferences were held in 1966, leading to the new federal-provincial fiscal arrangements.

Canada Assistance Plan

In July 1966 the Canada Assistance Plan was enacted. It provides a basis for co-ordinating the various public welfare programs in each province and permits, at the option of the province, the existing categorical shared-cost assistance programs (Old Age Assistance, Blind and Disabled Persons Allowances and Unemployment Assistance) to be replaced by one general co-ordinated program. Under the Canada Assistance Plan legislation was introduced to change the rate of the income tax abatement. The original agreement allotted (a) a total of 2 points to the old age assistance, blind and disabled allowances and (b) 2 points to the welfare portion of unemployment assistance. Under the new arrangements, both are included under the heading of special welfare and allotted a total of 4 points. In addition to the welfare portion, all other forms of unemployment assistance are now included.

The Canada Assistance Plan is a comprehensive public assistance plan based on need rather than categories and income limits and includes medical services for welfare recipients. It is also extended to needy mothers and children. Its costs are shared jointly by the federal and provincial governments but the opting-out arrangements apply if a province chooses to operate its own plan.

University Grants

In February 1966 the Prime Minister announced that the federal university grants would be increased from $2 to $5 per head commencing with the 1966-67 academic year which began September 1. No change was proposed in the rate of corporation tax abatement which Quebec received in lieu of the $2 per capita grant to cover the increase. Instead provision was made in the 1966-67 Estimates for payment of the additional $3 per head in the form of a cash payment to both Quebec and the Association of Universities and Colleges of Canada which distributes the grants in the other provinces. The payment to Quebec for the extra $3 has been estimated at $11 million for 1966-67.

Federal-Provincial Conferences

A number of important proposals were put forward at two conferences during the Fall of 1966. At the first of these conferences, in September, the federal government outlined the equalization and stabilization formula to be used for the period 1967-72, and proposed that the provinces take over certain shared-cost health and welfare programs with the federal government withdrawing further from the personal income tax field as compensation. Under the federal proposals the provinces would take over hospital insurance, the health grants programs and the programs grouped under the Canada Assistance Plan. In return the federal government would cede an additional 17% of the personal income tax to the province, and the associated equalization payment plus a final adjusting payment or refund would make the total transfer equivalent to what the federal share of these programs would have been. It was intended that eventually this transfer would not be tied to provincial program costs but would instead be an unconditional grant of equalized abatement points and federal supervision would be eliminated. None of the provinces has accepted this proposal to date.

At the October meetings the federal government stated that it was prepared to increase the transfer to the provinces for higher education, to extend the provisions for capital grants for technical and vocational schools due to expire March 31, 1967, and to assume full responsibility for adult retraining programs. These provisions and the new equalization and stabilization formulae are discussed in greater detail in the section on the fiscal arrangements for 1967-72.

Federal-Provincial Fiscal Arrangements (1967-72)

The *Federal-Provincial Fiscal Arrangements Act, 1967*, passed in March 1967 provides for a number of significant changes in the structure of federal payments to the provinces. The federal government increased its abatement of the personal income tax — excluding the abatements under the *Established*

Programs (Interim Arrangements) Act — from 24% to 28% of the federal tax payable in the provinces. The abatement of the corporate income tax, which stood at 9% of taxable income in provinces other than Quebec and 10% of taxable income in Quebec, was raised to 10% in all provinces effective for the 1967 taxation year. The same arrangements hold for estate taxes and succession duties as held during the last year of the previous agreements. For provinces which levy their own succession duties at the same rate as in 1964 (i.e. Ontario and Quebec), the federal government will abate its estate tax by 50% of the federal estate tax payable, and will make a payment equal to 25% of the estate tax payable in the province. For provinces which have increased their succession duty since 1964 (i.e. British Columbia) the federal government will abate its estate tax by 75% of the federal tax payable. For provinces which do not levy a succession duty the direct payment will be 75% of the federal estate tax due in the province.

Whereas earlier abatements of the personal and corporate income taxes by the federal government to provide taxing room to the provinces had usually been unconditional (the exception was the *Established Programs (Interim Arrangements) Act*, which in effect applied only to Quebec), the extra 4 points of personal income tax and 1% of corporate income granted to the provinces in 1967 was linked to expenditures for post-secondary education and was a substitute for the per capita grants for university costs.

Both the equalization formula and the stabilization formula have been expanded by changing their form — relating them to all provincial revenue sources instead of the "standard" taxes and natural resource revenues.

Financing Post-Secondary Education

The federal government in the *Federal-Provincial Fiscal Arrangements Act* has agreed to increase its transfer to the provinces for post-secondary education from $5 per capita to either $15 per capita or 50% of the operating costs of post-secondary education, whichever is greater. In addition to changing the formula for calculating this transfer, the federal government has changed the method by which payment is to be made. In future the provinces will receive the revenue from the additional abatement of the personal and corporate income taxes already mentioned and the equalization payment associated with this additional abatement; a final adjusting payment or refund will make the total transfer equal to the amount due the province under the new formula.

Certain expenses are not considered to be operating expenditures. Capital costs, depreciation, and specified rents for land, buildings, physical plant, facilities or equipment are all excluded as are interest payments and repayment of capital debt. Student financial aid and prescribed ancillary enterprises are also listed as excluded items. For purposes of this Act some revenue items must be deducted from expenditures as well. Thus, amounts received for sponsored, assisted, or contract research, amounts received by the post-secondary institutions from the federal government or the Canada Council, and any amount received by the provinces and designated as paid for "post-secondary education" reduce "operating expenditures".

Variations in the structure of education in the various provinces tend to make the definition of "post-secondary education" difficult to frame. In the Act it is defined as any course of more than 24 weeks which requires the attainment of junior matriculation for admission and which has been certified as such a course by the Lieutenant-Governor in Council or by someone he designates for that purpose.

Conditional grants to the provinces under the *Technical and Vocational Training Assistance Act* were originally scheduled to expire on March 31, 1967 but transitional arrangements have been made whereby capital grants are available, without limit as to time, until they reach for each province, $800 per capita of its population aged 15 to 19 as of 1961. The federal government has taken over the full cost of training allowances to adults taking occupational training and the full cost of the training programs

Equalization[2]

In contrast to the equalization formula for 1962-67 which included only the three "standard" taxes and natural resource revenue, the new formula is based on the 16 provincial revenue sources listed below.

> Personal income tax
> Corporation income tax
> Succession duties and shares of estate tax
> General sales tax
> Motor fuel tax
> Motor vehicle revenues
> Alcoholic beverage revenues
> Forestry revenues
> Oil royalties
> Natural gas royalties
> Sales of Crown leases and reservations on oil and natural gas lands
> Other oil and gas revenues
> Metallic and non-metallic mineral revenues
> Water power rentals
> Other taxes
> Other revenues

For each revenue source a base is chosen which is as close as possible to the actual base of the revenue source in all provinces. Then for each revenue source a "national average provincial revenue rate" is calculated by dividing the total revenue for all provinces by the total base for all provinces. This national average rate is multiplied by the base in each province and divided by the population of the province to give the per capita yield of a "tax" levied at the national

[2]See "Equalized Unhappiness", *Canadian Tax Journal*, Vol. XIV, No. 6, November-December 1966, p. 530 for an examination of the new equalization formula.

average rate. To obtain the equalization payment for the particular revenue source in the province the population of the province is multiplied by the difference between the per capita yield in all provinces and the derived per capita yield in the province at the national average rate. . . . The total equalization payment for the province is the sum of its payments, positive and negative, for each revenue source.

There is a simpler method of calculating this payment. The percentage of the total base attributed to a particular province is calculated as well as the percentage of the total population in the province. The difference between the percentage of the base and the percentage of the population multiplied by the total revenue in all provinces from a source gives the equalization payment for the revenue source in the province. Again the total payment is the sum of the payments for each source of revenue.

Saskatchewan which has been receiving an equalization payment under the old arrangements would lose its payment as a result of the new formula but provision was made for its equalization payment to phase out gradually over five years. The Atlantic Provinces Additional Grants were abolished under the new arrangements but the provinces of Nova Scotia, New Brunswick and Newfoundland are guaranteed an additional equalization payment of $10.5 while Prince Edward Island is guaranteed an additional $3.5 million. These are the same amounts as were previously paid in the form of Additional Grants.

Stabilization

The change in the stabilization formula is closely related to the change in the equalization formula. All provincial revenue sources, including equalization and stabilization payments, are to be used in determining the size of this payment, and not just the standard taxes, equalization, and stabilization. In two cases actual revenues are to be replaced by average revenues: a three-year average of estate tax and succession duty revenue and a five-year average of sales of Crown leases and reservations on oil and natural gas lands will be used instead of actual revenue. The stabilization payment is then the amount needed to bring the current year's revenue at the previous year's tax rates up to 95% of the previous year's revenue.

"Opting-out"

The "opting-out" arrangements are to be very similar to the arrangements described under 1965 changes in fiscal arrangements. Two changes result from the *Federal-Provincial Fiscal Arrangements Act, 1967*. An agreement entered into for health grants under the *Established Programs (Interim Arrangements) Act* was to be in force only up to March 31, 1967. This terminal date has been moved to March 31, 1970, the terminal date for other programs under this Act. The one point abatement of the personal income tax related to the operating costs of certain technical education programs was allowed to expire on March 31, 1967 as scheduled. This change is connected with the federal government's takeover of adult retraining expenses. As a result the total additional abatement received by Quebec for opting-out was reduced from 20 to 19 points.

Current Situation

Table 1 shows how the payments to the provinces under the current fiscal arrangements are calculated and summarizes the estimates of the amounts each province will receive in the form of unconditional payments for the 1967-68 year. The table also contains an estimate of the value of the federal tax abatements in each province, including the value of the extra abatements for post-secondary education. It should be noted that this estimate does not include the extra abatements which Quebec will receive as a result of opting-out of certain conditional grant programs and operating its own youth allowances program.

The table shows that all provinces except Ontario, Alberta and British Columbia will qualify for an equalization payment in 1967-68. Equalization payments are estimated at $544.8 million and other payments at $91.7 million. The federal government will collect an estimated $1,090.5 million of income taxes on behalf of the provinces with which it has collection agreements, including an estimated $226.6 million toward the cost of post-secondary education in the provinces.

Quebec is the only province to take advantage of the opting-out alternative under the *Established Programs (Interim Arrangements) Act*. The value of the extra abatements of income tax to Quebec during 1967-68 for the various programs it has opted out of has been estimated as follows.

Program	Tax Abatement	Equali-zation	Operating Cost Adjustment	Estimated Total Value
	(dollar figures in thousands)			
Health insurance	14% $153,356	$70,154	—$28,179	$195,331*
Special welfare programs (old age assistance, blind and disabled persons allowances)	2% 21,908	10,022	— 12,655	19,275
Unemployment assistance	2% 21,908	10,022	—	31,930
Health grants	1% 10,954	5,011	— 6,742	9,223

The value for 1967-68 of the 3% abatement to Quebec in lieu of youth allowances has been estimated at $32.9 million.

*Estimate for calendar year 1967.

Table 1

ESTIMATED PAYMENTS TO THE PROVINCES UNDER THE FEDERAL-PROVINCIAL FISCAL ARRANGEMENTS 1967
For Fiscal Year 1967-68

(All dollar figures except per capitas in thousands)

	Nfld.	P.E.I.	N.S.	N.B.	Que.	Ont.	Man.	Sask.	Alta.	B.C.	Total
Estimated population April 1, 1967	499	109	756	619	5,854	7,115	961	955	1,483	1,938	20,289
Provincial revenues											
Individual income tax 28%b	11,439	2,328	25,782	17,953	306,701a	549,816	55,353b	49,926b	77,965	137,248	1,234,511
Corporation income tax 10%c	7,740	942	8,967	7,659	158,298a	279,364a	23,202	15,336	34,378	64,464	600,350
Estate tax (75% of 3-year average)	1,010	231	5,069	1,928	39,437a	59,422a	3,749	2,850	5,890	10,237a	129,823
Estimated revenue from all sources	86,802	16,597	123,451	157,698	1,617,122	2,154,014	236,689	279,221	478,473	646,497	5,796,564
Equalization (for all revenue sources)											
Yields at national average rates	74,923	18,576	138,768	110,556	1,422,971	2,227,629	231,036	261,437	624,348	686,320	5,796,564
Per capita yield at national average rates	150.00	170.78	183.63	178.58	243.07	313.07	240.47	273.83	421.08	354.06	285.70
Deficiency from national average ($285.70)	135.70	114.92	102.07	107.12	42.63	—	45.23	11.87	—	—	—
Equalization amount from above	67,781	12,500	77,133	66,317	249,560	—	43,456	11,333	—	—	528,080
Guaranteed equalization	48,159	14,071	60,672	55,228	—	—	—	26,438	—	—	204,568
Payments to provinces											
Equalization paymentd	67,781	14,071	77,133	66,317	237,560e	—	43,456	26,438	—	—	532,756
Individual income tax collected	11,439	2,328	25,782	17,953	—	549,816	55,353	49,926	77,965	137,248	927,810
Corporation income tax collected	7,740	942	8,967	7,659	—	—	23,202	15,336	34,378	64,464	162,688
Share of estate tax collected	1,010	231	5,069	1,928	13,146	19,807	3,749	2,850	5,890	—	53,680
Share of income tax on power utilities (50%f)	329	67	650	34	628	1,111	94	13	3,094	233	6,253
Statutory subsidies	9,656	657	2,132	1,745	4,023	4,624	2,127	2,155	2,955	1,673	31,747
Total payments	97,955	18,296	119,733	95,636	255,357eg	575,358	127,981	96,718	124,282	203,618	1,714,934e
Value of income tax abatements for post-secondary education included in above											
4% of individual income tax	1,634	333	3,683	2,565	43,814	78,545	6,709	6,052	11,138	19,607	174,080
1% of corporation income tax base	704	94	897	766	13,192	23,280	2,109	1,394	3,438	6,596	52,470

aQuebec collects its own personal and corporation income taxes and Ontario its own corporation income tax. Quebec and Ontario collect 50% of their shares of income taxes through their succession duties and B.C. collects its 75% share through its succession duties. Amounts entered are value of federal abatements for income taxes and full 75% abatement of estate taxes. bIndividual income tax rate in Manitoba and Saskatchewan is 33%. cThe provincial corporation income tax rate is 12% in Ontario and Quebec which collect their own corporation income tax, 11% in Manitoba, Saskatchewan and Newfoundland and 10% in the other five provinces. Amounts entered for Ontario and Quebec are value of federal abatement. dSee text for bases of equalization payment. eEqualization payment to Quebec of $249,560,000 is reduced by $12.0 million because of excess value of abatements in lieu of youth allowances. fFigures relate to 1965 tax year. gDoes not include value of extra abatements to Quebec for opting out of certain joint programs.

Source: Department of Finance.

Table 2

SUMMARY OF FEDERAL CONTRIBUTIONS TO THE PROVINCES, MUNICIPALITIES AND TERRITORIES

1958, 1962 and 1966 to 1968
($ million)

	1958	1962	1966a	1967ab	1968ab
A. PAYMENTS TO PROVINCES					
Unconditional grants					
Tax rentals	217.1	312.6c	1.0d	—	—
Equalization and stabilization	140.1	165.7e	349.3f	319.2	532.8g
Share of federal estate tax	—h	—h	42.7	44.7	53.7
Atlantic provinces grants	8.0	33.0	43.0	43.0	—
Power utilities income tax	7.4	6.4	6.4	7.3	6.3
Statutory subsidies	20.6	23.5	23.6	23.7	31.7
Total unconditional grants i	393.2	541.1	466.0	437.9	636.4
Conditional grants					
Recreation and culture	—	1.7	.8	.6	—j
Hospital insurance	—	283.2	318.5	549.5	600.0
Other health	34.6	49.0	45.3	55.3	—
Welfare	48.1	143.6	148.5	194.9	321.0
Education	4.8	35.9	152.6	246.7	521.5
Transportation	50.9	52.6	98.6	91.2	—j
Agriculture	1.0	5.4	20.2	25.1	—j
Other natural resources	4.3	7.4	20.9	38.7	—j
Civil defence	1.0	3.1	5.1	5.4	5.2
Municipal winter works	—	21.2	41.0	51.8	40.0
National centennial	—	—	4.5	—	—
Other	.1	.4	—	—	194.8j
Total conditional grants i	144.8	606.5	856.0	1,261.1	1,682.5
Total payments to provinces i	548.0	1,147.6	1,322.0	1,700.6	2,318.9
B. PAYMENTS TO MUNICIPALITIES					
Grants in lieu of property taxes	17.5	24.9	39.6	39.2	41.7
Other grants	4.2	11.0	58.6	44.0	12.5
Total payments to municipalities i	21.8	36.0	98.2	82.1	53.7
C. PAYMENTS TO TERRITORIES					
Statutory subsidies and tax rentals	1.0	1.1	5.5	6.3	9.8
Other grants	.4	1.4	2.3	2.4	2.5
Total payments to territories i	1.4	2.5	7.8	8.7	12.3
TOTAL FEDERAL PAYMENTS i	570.2	1,186.1	1,428.0	1,791.4	2,384.9
Federal grants to universities					
Per capita grants	16.6	27.3	39.1	78.1	—
Estimated value of federal "standard" tax abatements (income and estate taxes)	—	327.2	1,136.7	1,432.8	1,873.1

a Estimates only. b Conditional grants include value of tax abatements to Quebec plus equalization and operating cost adjustments for those programs from which Quebec has opted out. c Before deduction of $1 million for overpayments under 1952 agrements. d Completion of payments under 1957 agreements. e After adjustments to Quebec on account of corporation income tax and adjustments in previous years' payments. f Includes value of extra abatements to Quebec for opting out of certain programs. g After adjustment to Quebec because of excess value of abatements in lieu of youth allowances. h Included in rental payments. i May not add because of rounding. j Included in "other" total of $194.8 million. — Nil or not available.

Sources: D.B.S. *Financial Statistics of the Government of Canada, 1957, 1961*; Department of Finance; Dominion Bureau of Statistics; *Public Accounts*; *Budget Papers*; *Estimates*.

21 Conditional Grants and Canadian Federalism: The Issues*

Donald V. Smiley

The First Issue:
Does the Importance Justify Federal Assistance?

A common general argument for conditional grants is that such subventions are useful devices for the promotion of the "national interest" in respect to particular functions which are, perhaps unfortunately, outside the jurisdiction of Parliament. An official of the Department of National Health and Welfare has put it this way: "There are certain aims national in scope within the provinces' field of jurisdiction which the provinces might not be willing to carry out; conditional grants are a device to remedy this situation."[1] The growth of nationalistic sentiments in Canada and elsewhere has made the argument appealing that there is a national interest in nearly any matter considered to be of importance, and that the federal authorities have a moral if not a constitutional responsibility to promote this interest. This doctrine was asserted in its most explicit form by the Royal Commission on the Arts, Letters and Sciences: "If the Federal Government is to renounce its right to associate itself with other social groups, public and private, in the education of Canadian citizens, it denies its moral and intellectual purpose, the complete conception of the common good is lost and Canada, as such, becomes a materialistic society."[2]

A classification of provincial functions into those for which direct federal assistance is available and those for which it is not demonstrates that decisions in these matters have been guided by influences other than a systematic notion of the national interest. Grants are available for the training of health personnel and vocational education instructors but not for social workers or elementary school teachers; for roads to relatively undeveloped resources but not for roads (apart from the Trans-Canada Highway) where development has already taken place; for general but not tubercular or mental hospitals, and so on. In 1937 Professor V. O. Key, Jr., said of federal grants-in-aid to the American States what is essentially true of the current Canadian situation:

> There is no mystic standard by which it may be determined that one activity is affected with a national interest and another is purely a local matter. Federal-aid acts are generated in precisely the same fashion as other legislation. Pressure groups interested in particular activities attempt to persuade Congress to make appropriations for that service. Action is urged primarily on the basis of the importance of the particular activity, but arguments are

*From *Conditional Grants and Canadian Federalism*, Canadian Tax Paper No. 32, Canadian Tax Foundation, Toronto, 1963. Reprinted by permission of the author and publisher.

[1]*Proceedings of the Fifth Annual Conference of the Institute of Public Administration of Canada*, Toronto, 1953, p. 370.

[2]*Report*, King's Printer, Ottawa, 1951, p. 8.

usually added to show that peculiar circumstances make that function one of national concern. . . . The selection of the state activities to be aided is . . . a question which may be determined by the free play of political forces and in no other way.[3]

There are two implicit assumptions behind the argument that the importance of a matter *as such* justifies federal involvement in that matter: (1) that the federal government is the repository of national values; and (2) that the judgment of the federal authorities on important public functions is superior to that of the provinces. I find neither of these propositions convincing.

A comprehensive examination of the first assumption would lead more deeply into political theory than I am equipped to go. I feel little of the mystique attached to the federal government voiced by the Massey Commission in the statement already quoted, and prefer to regard that and other jurisdictions in Burke's terms as "contrivances of human wisdom to provide for human wants". From this instrumental point of view the federal government is seen as nothing more than a vehicle for realizing certain specific purposes whose claims, in an analytical rather than a legal or historical sense, to participation in particular functions rests on purely expedient and pragmatic considerations. These considerations should take into account two broad sets of factors. The first is the effectiveness of the federal government's activities in relation to the function at hand relative to the effectiveness of these activities being performed by other levels of government or by private groups. The second involves broad social and political values related in the Canadian federal system, more particularly the desirability of preserving regionally based particularisms and the effective accountability of governments to their respective electorates.

The argument from the national interest is sometimes stated in terms of the interdependence of modern society. No reasonable person would deny that under existing circumstances all Canadians are affected by the kind of education available in the elementary schools of Newfoundland, the way in which Ontario develops its forest resources and the standards of welfare administration in British Columbia. Thus, it is argued, Ottawa has at least a residual responsibility in this kind of matter. Some appeal is usually made to a view which sees matters of only local concern dealt with by the local authorities, functions of provincial concern assigned to the provinces and affairs relating to "Canada as a whole" made the responsibility of the federal authorities.

The implications of the national interest argument are far-reaching. In our interdependent society, if a matter is of importance only to the citizens of Manitoba or of Quebec or of Prince Edward Island it is of only marginal concern to them. Dr. Donald Rowat has put the matter succinctly ". . . Because of the interdependence of modern society there is a national interest in almost everything the provincial government does. If you agree that the Federal Government should regulate every provincial service in which there is a national

---

[3]*The Administration of Federal Grants-in-aid*, Social Science Research Council, New York, 1937, p. 376.

interest, then it would be laying down the terms of operation for almost every-thing that the provinces do."[4] Professor Rowat's pragmatic approach to the circumstances in which grants-in-aid are appropriate is in general harmony with my own views: "I was not arguing that grants be made for every provin-cial service that is of national interest. I say that conditional grants should be made only where there is a clear-cut need of developing a service on a uni-form, nation-wide basis. This is something quite different."[5]

Those who argue for federal participation in a particular provincial or local function on the basis of the importance of those functions almost never spell out the implications of their proposals for the broader governmental process. Do these proposals attenuate the accountability of provincial and local jurisdic-tions? Are they compatible with the preservation of regionally-based particular-isms? What is their impact on the administrative process? These and other questions which put particular proposals for the extension of federal involve-ment in provincial functions in the broader framework of the Canadian federal system must logically be answered.

When a person says that there is a national interest in a particular matter under the jurisdiction of the provinces he is doing nothing more than to assert that the problem is of considerable significance and that the provinces cannot adequately meet it. As Professor David B. Truman remarked about the claims of an "inclusive public interest", the argument from the national interest is "a tremendously useful promotional device" but does not "describe any actual or possible situation within a complex modern nation".[6] The argument from the national interest is incantation rather than analysis.

In much of the justification for conditional grants is the assumption that at least in the particular circumstances under review the judgment of the federal authorities is superior to that of the provinces. In its more extreme form this doctrine asserts that the decisions reached by the federal government are in-herently better than those coming out of the provincial capitals — that there is somehow an irresistible attraction to Ottawa for Canadians of superior wisdom or, alternatively, that their presence on the federal pay-roll somehow purges elected and appointed officials of the assumed parochialisms associated with the provincial administrations. Suspicion of the provinces can be based on either or both of two considerations. The first is that they give particular functions an unduly low priority in their expenditure patterns. The second judgment asserts that the provincial governments lack the expertise or the integrity, or both, to carry out particular responsibilities adequately. Thus it is appropriate for Ottawa to "buy control" over particular provincial functions. The following points can be made about this line of argument:

First, the assertion that the expenditure patterns determined by the provincial administrations are "wrong" implies that the federal authorities are in posses-sion of some objective standards for evaluating the provincial priorities. The

---

[4]*Proceedings of the Fifth Annual Conference, ibid.,* p. 385.

[5]*Ibid.* I am less hopeful than Dr. Rowat about the possibility of attaining uniform standards of service through the grant-in-aid technique.

[6]*The Governmental Process,* Alfred Knopf, New York, 1951, pp. 370-371.

source and nature of these criteria have never been analyzed. I would agree with Professor Herman Finer when he asserted in arguing for the subserviency of appointed to elected officials that ". . . the people can be unwise but cannot be wrong".[7] According to this line of argument, democracy is a *procedure* by which public decisions are made and thus if one has a commitment, as I do, to democracy as a primary value he cannot logically submit decisions made by this procedure to *substantive* standards.[8] The priority-determining function has rightly been called the "supreme act of government"; it thus seems appropriate, in the absence of very decisive considerations to the contrary . . . to let popularly-elected provincial administrations make and take responsibility for the decisions allocating the scarce resources available to them among competing public needs. Barbara Wooton's vision of a mature political system in which "rival political programs . . . reach a stage of precision where they are expressed *throughout* in quantitative terms"[9] is to me a worthy one. The comments of the Rowell-Sirois Commission in rejecting proposals made to it recommending federal aid for education are relevant here:

> . . . the representations appear to us to go too far in denying the right of each province to decide the relative importance of expenditure on education and expenditure on other competing services . . . . Our financial proposals aim at placing every province in a position to discharge its responsibilities for education (on a scale that is within the means of the people of Canada) if it chooses to do so. Once this position is established it seems best to us that education, like every other form of welfare service in a democratic community should have to fight for its life, and that a generous provision for the education of the children of the nation should depend, not on any arbitrary constitutional provision, but on the persistent conviction of the mass of the people that they must be ready to deny themselves some of the good things of life in order to deal fairly by their children. . . .[10]

Many supporters of particular conditional grant programs openly regard these arrangements as devices by which the priority-determining functions of provincial administrations can be inhibited; I would regard this purpose as wholly unacceptable except in the extenuating circumstances to be described later in this chapter. In general, then, it seems inappropriate for the federal authorities to intervene between the provincial administrations and their respective electorates.

Second, in most of the constitutional grant programs, with the possible exception of some of the more highly specialized health services, all but the smaller

---

[7]In Donald C. Rowat (ed.), *Basic Issues in Public Administration*, Macmillan, New York, 1961, p. 470.

[8]For a discussion of "democracy as method" see Henry B. Mayo, *An Introduction to Democratic Theory*, Oxford University Press, New York, 1960, pp. 30-34. See also Glendon A. Shubert, *The Public Interest*, Atherton Press, New York, 1961. In Shubert's terminology the viewpoint taken here is that of "party rationalism".

[9]*Freedom under Planning*, University of North Carolina Press, Chapel Hill, 1945, p. 171.

[10]*Report of the Royal Commission on Dominion-Provincial Relations*, reprinted, 1954, Queen's Printer, Ottawa, 1964, *Book II*, p. 51.

provinces have in their bureaucracies a larger and more specialized supply of expertise than has the federal government. Thus to the extent that access to expertise is necessary to the making of adequate judgments about such functions as highways, welfare services and the conservation of natural resources, the supply of specialized knowledge and skills in the provincial departments carrying out these functions is usually better than that of the federal agencies supervising provincial activities in shared-cost programs.

Third, it is superficial to assert that the frames of reference of federal officials involved in conditional grant arrangements are broader or more meaningful than those of their provincial counterparts simply because the former's concerns extend over a more extensive geographical area. The professionalization of the provincial public services has brought into these bureaucracies a very large number of persons whose horizons are wider than purely provincial, and Professor Richard Leach's study of the very great number of inter-provincial contracts — most of them of an informal and continuing nature — has demonstrated that provincial agencies are by no means unaware of what is going on outside the geographical limits of their jurisdictions.[11] At the more senior levels in the provinces, the official's context is often an integrated pattern of health or highway or educational services. The federal employees engaged in shared-cost arrangements are more apt to be exclusively interested in the particular program in which Ottawa participates. Little in general can be said here except that the breadth of vision of appointed officials is a function of other factors than the area or population of the area in which they work, and there is no reason to suppose that these factors always work in favour of the federal government.

The Second Issue:
Exclusive or Joint Responsibilities?

If one denies that there are exclusively national and exclusively provincial interests involved in particular public functions it is plausible to argue that the responsibilities for these functions should be shared between the two levels of government. Maurice Lamontagne in Chapter XII of his *Le Fédéralisme canadien*, published in 1954, comes to this conclusion in asserting that because "*la politique économique et sociale est devenue quasi indivisible*" that "*la participation de tous les gouvernements aux principales fonctions de l'Etat . . . doit devenir la règle générale*". Unfortunately Lamontagne does not spell out the administrative implications of his general argument. By defining the principal public functions in very broad terms — those related to unemployment, commerce, culture, labour relations, etc. — his proposition is compatible with two very different models of federalism: one in which the major *functions* are divided but in which the exclusive responsibilities for particular *programs* are assigned to one level of government; and one in which the norm is collaboration between the federal and provincial authorities through shared-cost arrange-

---

[11]"Interprovincial Co-operation", *Canadian Public Administration*, Vol. II, No. 2, June 1959, pp. 83-99.

ments or other devices. In spite of this conclusion, however, the general tenor of Lamontagne's thought is sympathetic to conditional grants.

In a brilliant essay "Practice and Theory of Federalism" P. E. Trudeau has recently made a strong plea for the "exclusive jurisdiction" situation. He says ". . . the federal spending power or so-called 'power of the purse' is presently being construed as a federal right to decide (at the taxpayers' expense!) whether provincial governments are properly exercising any and every right they hold under the constitution".[12] Thus:

> . . . it almost seems as though whenever an important segment of the population needs something badly enough, it is eventually given to them by one level of government or the other, regardless of the constitution. The main drawback to such an approach is that it tends to develop paternalistic instincts in more enterprising governments at the expense of democratic maturation in others. In areas where there exists a clear division of responsibilities between the federal and provincial levels, there is no doubt that the only proper censor of a government which incompetently discharges its obligations is the electorate of *that* government and not some other government responsible to some other (level of) electorate. And if, for example, federal politicians are convinced that by their very nature the totality of the provincial governments *cannot* discharge their duties in some area, surely the proper procedure is for those politicians to seek the overt transfer of such areas into federal jurisdiction, either by way of constitutional amendment . . . or by invoking federal powers under section 92, paragraph 10(c).[13]

There are two general difficulties inherent in arrangements which divide the responsibilities for a particular activity between two or more levels of government. The first relates to the hesitations, delays and procedural burdens which are concomitants of shared-cost programs. The second and, in my set of preferences, much more significant problems, involve the dilution of accountability which is inherent in such procedures.

The Rowell-Sirois Commission was keenly aware of the administrative problems of conditional grants. Hesitations and delays in implementing public policies are inevitable when decisions either of a broad or of a routine nature can be made only with the agreement of two levels of government. No adequate technique for resolving conflicts between the two levels of government are available, and disputes which can be expeditiously resolved at relatively junior levels if the matter were the exclusive concern of one government may complicate the work of officials of senior appointed or Cabinet ranks. The procedural burdens, particularly those imposed on auditing officials, are considerable. Although these difficulties are undeniably present there are . . . more possibilities for mitigating them than the Rowell-Sirois Commission, on the basis of Canadian experience up to that time, believed.

---

[12]In Michael Oliver (ed.), *Social Purpose for Canada*, University of Toronto Press, Toronto, 1961, p. 382.

[13]*Ibid.* p. 383. Section 92 10(c) confers upon Parliament the authority to bring "Local Works and Undertakings" under federal jurisdiction by declaring them to be "for the general Advantage of Canada or for the Advantage of Two or more of the Provinces".

The more basic problem which arises when particular activities are shared between levels of government relates to the attenuation of accountability inherent in such sharing. The peculiar virtue of the British parliamentary system is that it places the responsibility for the way in which the authority conferred on a particular jurisdiction is wielded squarely in the hands of a particular group of people — cabinet solidarity and party cohesion of course reinforce the effectiveness of this accountability to the governed through periodic elections. However, there is an increasing number of important public functions for which the federal authorities assert the provinces have the primary responsibilities but on behalf of which federal financial assistance is available. In these circumstances it is almost impossible to enforce accountability, and no satisfactory answer can be given to the broad question of whether the provinces have in fact been delinquent in not providing adequate support for particular services or, alternatively, whether some or all of them could not reasonably be expected to do better in the light of the existing distribution of tax resources and revenues and functional responsibilities. Further, if we were to assume that the federal government has *some* direct responsibilities in relation to particular provincial programs, it is almost impossible to gauge whether their level of support for these activities has been satisfactory. On a day-to-day basis, also, it is sometimes open to the provinces to avoid responsibility for their actions in conditional grant programs by attributing alleged deficiencies to federal policies.

Many of those who have been involved in conditional grant programs assert that collaboration between officials of the two levels of government has a salutary influence in raising the levels at which particular services are provided.[14] This consideration is of course most important in fields like public health and hospitalization, where the federal agencies provide a relatively wide range of specialized competence; provincial public health officials have told me that it is a valuable exercise for them to be required to justify to federal specialists in the fields concerned, particular projects for which health grants are requested.

No reasonable person would wish to inhibit this kind of constructive collaboration, but it seems appropriate to suggest that perhaps somewhat the same results might be obtained outside the framework of conditional grant arrangements. The allocation of exclusive responsibilities to the provinces for a wide range of public functions does not mean that it is inappropriate for the federal authorities to involve themselves directly in efforts to improve provincial performance of many of these functions. The following general kinds of activities, apart from shared-cost programs, can still be undertaken by the federal government: (a) specialized consultative services to be used by the provinces at the latter's discretion; (b) statistical research and reporting; (c) the dissemination of knowledge and experience through publication, periodic or annual conferences, etc.; and (d) the devising, in collaboration with the provinces and interested individuals and groups, of suggested standards of performance in respect of particular functions. I would hope that in the future much of this sort

---

[14]See the remarks of a British Columbia Health official in this respect in *Proceedings of the Fifth Annual Conference of the Institute of Public Administration of Canada, ibid.*, pp. 385-386.

of activity would be undertaken under interprovincial rather than federal auspices, but in the absence of this the federal government can play a valuable role in helping to raise the standards of provincial performance without the complications and the restrictions on provincial freedom of action inherent in conditional grant programs. The provinces with smaller populations suffer not only from their limited fiscal capacities in their attempts to provide adequate standards of some of the more important services but also from the absence of the kinds of specialized competence that it is practical for the larger jurisdictions to employ; thus the provision by the federal authorities of supplementary services to the provincial departments and agencies can in the long run be an important device in inter-provincial equalization.

The Third Issue:
Can Grants-in-Aid Be Justified on Egalitarian Grounds?

The dependence of the provinces on federal subventions dates from Confederation, although the extent of this dependence has varied from period to period. In the face of the existing inequalities in provincial fiscal capacities and needs, and the increasingly influential sentiments of nationalism and egalitarianism, it is doubtful whether the Canadian federal system would last a decade if federal transfer payments were withdrawn, whatever redistribution of tax sources was implemented as a concomitant measure. The alternatives then are conditional as against unconditional grants as the primary device by which these inequalities are mitigated.

Unconditional subsidies enable the provinces to discharge their responsibilities more effectively by increasing the financial resources at their disposal. The federal government takes no responsibility for ensuring that the proceeds from these subventions are expended prudently or that they are used to provide services commonly regarded as being within the social minimum. The Rowell-Sirois Report states that rationale for this kind of financial help in respect of the proposed National Adjustment Grants to the provinces:

> It should be made clear that while the adjustment grant proposed is designed to enable a province to provide adequate services (at the average Canadian standard) without excessive taxation (on the average Canadian basis) the freedom of action of a province is in no way impaired. If a province chooses to provide inferior services and provide lower taxation it is free to do so, or it may provide better services than the average if its people are willing to be taxed accordingly, or it may, for example, starve its roads and improve its education, or starve its education and improve its roads. . . . But no provincial government will be free from the pressure of the opinion of its own people and if when it applies for an increased adjustment grant on the basis of need, it has to produce figures which indicate that although it might, without specially heavy taxation, have provided better education but did not do so, it has, of course, to justify this to its own electors.[15]

The purposes of grants-in-aid are quite different. When such grants are

---

[15]*Book II*, p. 84.

made the federal government defines precisely what provincial activities are to be assisted and enforces some minimum conditions to which the provinces must adhere if they are to receive such assistance. From the federal viewpoint at least the primary purpose of their participation is the enhancement of the quantity and quality of the aided function and not a sharing of financial burdens. The then Minister of National Health and Welfare stated this kind of assumption in defending the government's refusal to include mental hospitals and tuberculosis sanitoria in the provisions of the hospitalization legislation enacted in 1957, on the grounds that such facilities were already being provided by the provinces from their general revenues. "I am sure that the honourable member is not arguing that we should use the hospital insurance plan to subsidize provincial governments. A hospital insurance plan is intended to subsidize individuals in connection with their hospital costs."[16] It cannot of course be taken for granted that in each case federal assistance will "trigger" an extra expenditure on the aided function exactly equal to the amount of that assistance. It may prove expedient for Ottawa to offer inducements to the provinces to participate which do not increase the amount of spending on the program assisted, like the federal payments on behalf of integral parts of the Trans-Canada Highway built between 1928 and the date that the Trans-Canada program began; and in other circumstances, such as those relating to hospitalization, federal contributions may be made to some provinces on behalf of services provided at comparable levels prior to the inauguration of the shared-cost arrangements. On the other hand, it is reasonable to suppose that in many instances federal participation encourages a higher expenditure on the aided service from provincial sources than the provinces would otherwise choose to make.

A plausible case can be made that conditional grants are inherently superior to unconditional subventions as an equalizing device. A thorough-going egalitarian would argue perhaps that the important inequalities relate to the inaccessibility of adequate health, welfare, educational and other basic public services to very large numbers of Canadians. The federal government cannot, according to this argument, discharge its responsibilities by disbursing unconditional subventions from which each province can as it chooses "starve its roads and improve its education or starve its education and improve its roads". Thus if the ethical claim of all residents of Canada to the social minimum is to be met, the federal government must select the provincial and local functions where otherwise there would be deficiencies and induce these jurisdictions to carry out these functions at certain defined standards.

There are several broadly egalitarian features in the existing conditional grant arrangements, although it is not always possible to determine whether the inequalities which are being mitigated are between provinces or between individuals.

First, the bulk of the federal moneys made available are for health and welfare functions. The bias of the complex of conditional grant programs is thus in the direction of basic amenities made directly to individuals, either as social assistance payments or as public health and hospital services.

---

[16]*House of Commons Debates,* March 25, 1957, p. 2657.

Second, federal participation in shared-cost activities has done much to overcome the inequities which arise when Canadian residents are denied hospitalization and social assistance because they fail to meet the legal residence requirements of particular provincial and local jurisdictions.

Third, the bases of cost-sharing in the Trans-Canada Highway and hospitalization programs and in some of the vocational training and health grants take into account the needs of the respective provinces in relation to these activities.

Fourth, the consultative and advisory services provided by the federal government in connection with some of the shared-cost programs, particularly those in the fields of hospitalization and public health, put at the disposal of the provinces with both low *per capita* income and small populations, skills they would not otherwise have. The Maritime provinces in particular are at a disadvantage not only because they are poor but because even under the most favourable financial circumstances their respective populations would be too small to justify the employment of the specialized expertise which is necessary to the effective provision of an increasing number of public services; unconditional subventions have obvious limitations in remedying this second kind of deficiency.

In spite of these influences, there are other features of the existing conditional grant arrangements which modify this egalitarian impact.

First, in many of the programs the federal government pays the same proportion of shareable costs to all provinces, and even in the other programs it can reasonably be argued that the sharing formulae do not adequately take into account either the relative fiscal capacities or needs of the provinces, or their peculiar problems in respect to particular aided functions.

Second, it seems likely that in the poorer provinces the expansion in services for which federal grants are given has taken place at the expense of those provincial and local functions for which no moneys from Ottawa are available, and if this is true the total impact of shared-cost arrangements has been to increase the disparities among the provinces in their abilities to carry out these latter responsibilities, particularly in the field of elementary and secondary education.

Third, the present arrangements allow the federal authorities little discretion in allocating the funds made available by Parliament to the provincial and local jurisdictions where the deficiencies in aided services are greatest. Conditional grants are thus an effective device in inducing a greater volume of an existing service than would otherwise be provided; but the distribution of federal funds is somewhat indiscriminating and the more prosperous provinces, and those who have chosen to support a particular function generously prior to the establishment of a grant-in-aid program, often receive help to maintain a level of service which other provinces will not attain in the foreseeable future. Nowhere has this circumstance been demonstrated more clearly than in regard to the arrangements which came into effect in 1961 relating to vocational training. The Minister of Labour, in introducing legislation under which the new federal-provincial agreements had been concluded, was extremely vague in answer to Opposition questions about the capacity of the existing training facilities or the need for new facilities.

"In this respect I am advised that all we can do is to take the word of the provinces. They are the ones who advise us in respect to these matters and it is the provinces who say that they feel that a 50% increase in present capacity is necessary over the coming years."[17] Under further questioning as to his justification for requesting Parliament to appropriate funds for a problem whose precise dimensions he was unable to describe, the Minister went on to say:

> . . . the jurisdiction for education lies with the provinces. The federal government does not direct the amount of education that is to be undertaken. . . .
> The federal government is in this position. We feel that our surveys reveal that there are people unemployed who are not trained to fill the vacancies that exist. In an effort to rectify the situation we say to the provinces, we will pay more for the construction of more schools to train people with these skills. . . . We say we will pay more so you will undertake to build these schools, and we will pay more toward the training of these people. I think no more is needed as an incentive to the provinces to go ahead and bring about some results.[18]

These statements are indicative of the somewhat indiscriminating process by which federal moneys are distributed among the provinces in the shared-cost programs; one might have expected that because of the federal government's exclusive responsibilities for job-placement services and unemployment insurance, the government would have had more precise and definite policies in respect of this particular function. However, in designing conditional grant arrangements the federal government endeavours to provide inducements for all the provinces to participate and thus it may prove impossible to make provision, except in a few isolated instances, to channel federal support to those provinces where it can be demonstrated that the deficiencies in the aided function are greatest.

Fourth, the very great degree of provincial autonomy which exists in the major shared-cost programs militates against a uniform nation-wide standard of service. The concept of a conditional grant arrangement as a device by which a national policy is provincially administered is wholly inaccurate if by this it is implied that the major decisions relating to the program, except perhaps the initial one of whether it is to be undertaken or not, are made by the federal authorities. The provinces, for motives rather more substantial than mere perversity, are jealous to preserve their discretionary authority on those matters which the federal government continuously asserts are their responsibility. Under the existing circumstances it is impractical to attempt to establish a hierarchical relation between federal and provincial agencies, and any constructive pattern of inter-governmental relations must proceed on a collaborative basis in which a large measure of provincial autonomy prevails. Thus although the standards of services available under federal legislation to veterans and immigrants are fairly uniform across Canada, significant differences remain in old-age assistance, hospitalization and other shared-cost functions, and these differences cannot be explained entirely by the differing fiscal capacities of the

---

[17]*House of Commons Debates* (unrevised), December 9, 1961, p. 677.
[18]*Ibid.*, p. 678.

respective provinces. Thus, if one believes that the demands for uniform standards of a particular service are compelling, the realistic alternative is the direct provision of that service by the federal government, after a constitutional amendment if necessary, rather than a conditional grant arrangement.

The possibilities of unconditional fiscal-need subsidies in equalizing access to certain basic services should not be overlooked. It is possible to imagine a situation in which the priorities that the various provinces gave to particular functions would be infinitely varied — in which one province provided lavish school facilities but had only rudimentary welfare programs, and another where health facilities were generously supported but virtually no moneys were made available for resource development. However, in practice there are strong influences at work to prevent such extremes from developing. The level at which a particular function will be supported in a jurisdiction appears to be determined by a complex interaction between: (1) the expectations of the public, "the consumers", about an adequate level of service; (2) the influence of groups, both inside and outside government, who have a particular interest in promoting the function; and (3) the financial resources at the disposal of the government. We may assume that as there is greater integration of our national society tendencies toward a more homogenous pattern of expectations about an adequate range and quality of public services will develop. The influence of the various specialized elites (health, highway construction, welfare, etc.) is increasing and these groups almost always share common beliefs about standards applicable to the functions with which they are concerned. Thus if all the provinces are provided with the funds to make it feasible to provide particular services at levels in harmony with popular expectations on these services, there are effective influences present to induce broad adherence to national minimum levels of performance.

Conditional grants have thus no *inherent* superiority over unconditional subventions as an equalizing device, whether equalization is conceived primarily in terms of the abilities of the provinces to provide minimum standards of service or the availability of services to individuals living in different provinces. Inter-provincial equalization through the existing conditional grants has occurred largely because the bulk of the federal moneys available have been for health and welfare services. If, as seems not unlikely, more emphasis comes to be placed on federal assistance in the development of natural resources, the equalizing impact will be less important. More significantly perhaps, the principle of inter-provincial equalization has won widespread acceptance in regard to the various schemes of unconditional subsidies.

The same is not true of conditional grants. At the Federal-Provincial Conference of July 1960 the Prime Minister stated in announcing his government's financial proposals for the period beginning on April 1, 1962: ". . . I wish to emphasize that the federal Government remains firmly committed to the principle of equalization and of financial assistance to those provinces in which incomes and taxable capacity are below those of the richer provinces"[19] and

---

[19]*Report*, p. 10.

even the Premier of Ontario paid at least lip-service to ". . . fiscal need or adjustment payments . . . for the provinces which need them to enable them to maintain adequate standards of public service, and to promote the even development of our country."[20] However, there is no similar consensus on conditional grants. An official of the federal Department of Finance, speaking in his personal capacity, put forward in 1953 a view which has widespread acceptance:

> The purpose of a conditional grant is not to share burdens — the tax rental agreement is designed to do that job. A conditional grant should have attached to it meaningful conditions. It should not be merely financial assistance to a province. If the province needs financial assistance, why should Federal financial assistance be directed to a particular service rather than to all provincial services? The case for a conditional grant must rest pretty heavily upon the existence of a national interest as indicated by widespread public support right across the country, coupled with provincial unwillingness to finance the service themselves.[21]

Any attempt at thoroughgoing inter-provincial equalization, through either conditional or unconditional subventions or a combination of the two, is inevitably frustrated by the necessity of designing arrangements in which the wealthier provinces will choose to participate. However, a very considerable degree of progress has been made since 1945 in the direction of equalization through various forms of unconditional grants, and it is reasonable to expect that this principle will become even more influential in the future pattern of federal-provincial financial relations. There is no corresponding expectation, it seems to me, that conditional grants will move in this direction.

---

[20]*Ibid.*, p. 25.
[21]*Proceedings of the Fifth Annual Conference of the Institute of Public Administration of Canada, ibid.*, p. 357.

Part Five

Cooperative Federalism

22 Public Administration and Canadian Federalism*

Donald V. Smiley

An increasing number of students of the American and Canadian federal systems are coming to concern themselves with the intergovernmental administrative relationships which now appear as essential mechanisms in the functioning of the modern federal state. The Reports of the President's Committee on Intergovernmental Relations and the specialized studies undertaken under its direction in the 1950's are a rich mine of description and analysis. Professor Morton Grodzins of the University of Chicago has developed important insights into the interrelationships between political parties and bureaucratic structures in sustaining the American federal system;[1] Grodzin's student, Daniel J. Elazar, has written a stimulating history of federal-state relationships from 1789 onward[2] around the hypothesis that "virtually all the activities of government in the nineteenth century United States were cooperative endeavors, shared by federal and state agencies in much the same manner as government programs are shared in the twentieth century."[3] F. J. C. Vile's recent book on American federalism gives more attention to intergovernmental administrative cooperation than is usual in such discussions.[4] The Canadian literature on cooperative federalism is much less adequate. Some of the most interesting analysis in this field has been done by the natural resource specialists in papers prepared for the federal-provincial Resources for Tomorrow Conference held in Montreal in 1960.[5] R. M. Burns[6] and Allen Kear[7] have written on the mechanisms of

*From *Canadian Public Administration*, Vol. VII, No. 3, September 1964, pp. 371-300. Reprinted by permission of the author and the Canadian Institute of Public Administration.

[1] See especially "American Political Parties and the American Federal System", Bobbs-Merrill Reprint Series, Political Science 111; "The Federal System" in *Goals for Americans*, The American Assembly, Columbia University, New York, 1960, pp. 265-284 and "Local Strength in the American Federal System" in M. Irish (ed.), *Continuing Crisis in American Politics*, 1963, pp. 132-152.

[2] *The American Partnership*, University of Chicago Press, Chicago, 1962.

[3] *Ibid.*, p. 1.

[4] *The Structure of American Federalism*, Oxford University Press, New York, 1961, particularly Chapter IX.

[5] *Reports*, Queen's Printer, Ottawa, 1961. See especially D. W. Carr, "Resource Adjustment in Agriculture, Effects of the Legislative and Administrative Framework", pp. 123-139; T. M. Patterson, "Administrative Framework for Water Management", pp. 227-279; and David A. Munro, "Legislative and Administrative Limitation on Wildlife Management", pp. 867-879. See also the brilliant article by one of the major participants in the Conference: Morris Miller, "The Developmental Framework for Resource Policy and its Jurisdictional-Administrative Implication", *Canadian Public Administration*, Vol. V, No. 2, 1962, pp. 133-155.

[6] "Cooperation in Government", *The Canadian Tax Journal*, Vol. VII, No. 1, January-February 1959, pp. 5-15.

[7] "Cooperative Federalism: A Study of the Federal-Provincial Continuing Committee on Fiscal and Economic Matters", *Canadian Public Administration*, Vol. VI, No. 1, 1963, pp. 43-56.

federal-provincial fiscal relations. Donald V. Smiley's monograph[8] on federal grants-in-aid to the provinces published in 1963 analyzed the interrelationships between program specialists and financial officers from both levels of government in shared-cost programs. Professor Richard Leach has made a study of inter-provincial relationships, mostly of an informal and continuing nature,[9] and Professor J. H. Aitchison has examined the possibilities of formal institutions of inter-provincial cooperation in the light of American experiences with the Council of State Governors.[10] Finally, the federal Royal Commission Report on Governmental Organization discussed briefly "Federal-Provincial Cooperation in Joint and Allied Services",[11] although it seems to me that its analysis was a superficial one. In general then, students of federalism have come to be less preoccupied than in the past with such matters of formal constitutional structure as constitutional amendment, judicial review, residual and concurrent powers and so on and have come increasingly to concern themselves with the kind of administrative arrangements which make for coordination and integration of public policies in political systems where the powers to enact legislation in relation to various classes of subjects are divided between two levels of government.

It is plausible to suggest that the increasing range of public activities and the growing interdependence of modern life bring about almost inevitably a growth in intergovernmental relations in a modern federation.[12] However, what might appear to the observer as the need for articulation between the two levels does not ensure that this need will be met. Indeed it is possible to postulate a federal system in which the powers, privileges and responsibilities of government are so distributed, that there is relatively little need for interjurisdictional collaboration, another in which most public activities are shared by the two levels. Among the critical factors which encourage the extension of joint federal-provincial action in Canada are the following:

1. The relative inflexibility of the system in effecting periodic redistributions of the powers and responsibilities of government between the two levels by constitutional amendment, judicial review or the delegation of legislative powers by one level on the other.

It can be taken for granted that as new circumstances arise within a federation the distribution of legislative powers made by the original constitutional document will, if unchanged, result in the frustration of important public objectives. There are two alternatives. The first is a re-allocation of powers through

[8]*Conditional Grants and Canadian Federalism*, Paper No. 32, Canadian Tax Foundation, Toronto, 1963, particularly Chapter III.

[9]"Interprovincial Cooperation", *Canadian Public Administration*, Vol. II, No. 2, 1959, pp. 83-99.

[10]"Interprovincial Cooperation" in J. H. Aitchison (ed.), *The Political Process in Canada*, University of Toronto Press, Toronto, 1963, pp. 153-170.

[11]Vol. III, pp. 124-131.

[12]Maurice Lamontagne asserts that because "la politique économique et sociale est devenue quasi indivisible," that "la participation de tous les gouvernements aux principales fonctions de l'Etat . . . doit devener la règle générale." *Le Fédéralisme canadien*, Les Presses de l'Université Laval, Québec, 1954, pp. 245-248.

constitutional amendment, changing patterns of judicial review or inter-governmental agreement. The second alternative is to attempt to overcome the difficulties by piecemeal collaborative arrangements between the two levels of government. In Canada, the major vehicle of constitutional adjustment has been the latter kind of procedure.

2. The increasingly powerful pressures for federal action to equalize the range and quality of public services available to citizens throughout Canada.

If we assume a relatively stable distribution of legislative powers between the two levels, the need for inter-governmental collaboration increases as the expectations as to what constitutes acceptable standards of public services become more homogeneous. The interplay between nationalism and regional inequalities in per capita fiscal capacity has propelled the federal government into an equalizing role and has created the circumstances for a very large number of federal-provincial joint arrangements.

3. The will and the ability of the executives of the two levels of government to devise and implement collaboration arrangements.

Again, the need for collaboration does not ensure that it will take place. Effective federal-provincial relations involve interactions where the participants are not organized within a common pattern of hierarchical authority as in situations involving a single jurisdiction. This kind of collaborative arrangement can be successful only if the participants share a bureaucratic ethic which provides for the resolution of difficulties by other means than the exercise of hierarchical authority.[13] Later in the essay I shall argue that the professionalization of the federal and provincial public services has been the strategic factor in this process.

The term "cooperative federalism" has had a wide although somewhat uncritical acceptance in Canada[14] and the United States as being the distinctive characteristic of the contemporary federal systems of these countries. Within the framework of executive collaboration there are two patterns of interaction which I shall call "joint federalism" and "consultative federalism" respectively.

"Joint federalism" is distinguished by the sharing of decision-making powers and financial responsibilities for particular programs or projects between the two levels of government. Its typical device is the grant-in-aid made by the federal authorities to one or more of the state or provincial jurisdictions.

In "consultative federalism" the exclusive financial and administrative responsibility for particular matters rests with one level or the other with formal and informal devices to communicate the values and objectives of each level to the other where the interests of both are involved. Federal-state or federal-provincial relations thus proceed by mechanisms akin to those of effective international diplomacy.

To anticipate the analysis of this essay, between 1945 and about 1960 the

---

[13]For a stimulating analysis of bureaucracy in terms of the clash between hierarchical authority and functional competence see Victor A. Thompson, "Hierarchy, Specialization and Organizational Conflict", *Administrative Science Quarterly*, Vol. V, 1961, p. 485.

[14]The term appears in the national programs of both the Liberal Party and the New Democratic Party adopted in 1961.

Canadian system developed along a direction in which joint federalism was dominant. However, toward the end of this period these arrangements began to show signs of strain which could be effectively lessened only by more effective devices of consultative federalism. We have as yet made little progress in moving toward these.

A Critique of "Joint Federalism"

There is almost no literature available on federal-provincial administrative relationships prior to the 1930's. Vernon Fowke's brief account of these relations in the concurrent fields of agriculture and immigration points up the fact that relations were not constructive ones in the period after Confederation.[15] The Depression crisis of the 1930's resulted in three analyses of particular aspects of the Canadian experience of intergovernmental sharing of administrative functions. The studies of both J. A. Maxwell[16] and Luella Gettys[17] came to the conclusion that the major defect of the existing shared-cost arrangements was that the federal authorities had failed to impose standards of performance on the provinces with sufficient vigor. The Royal Commission on Dominion-Provincial Relations which reported to the Government of Canada in 1940[18] made a straightforward attack on what I have called "joint federalism" and recommended a master-solution of redistributing functional responsibilities and revenue sources between the Dominion and the provinces so that each province could provide as it chose an average level of services without subjecting its citizens to taxation above the national average.[19] Its general conclusion about collaborative arrangements was this: "The experience with conditional grants leads us to doubt whether the joint administration of activities by the Dominion and a province is ever a practical way of surmounting constitutional difficulties. Where legislative power over a particular subject is divided, it is ordinarily desirable that these powers should be pooled under the control of a single government in order to secure unified effort in administration."[20] To this end the Commission recommended that there be established, by constitutional amendment if necessary, a procedure whereby the Dominion or the provinces might delegate particular legislative powers to the other either permanently or for a limited period.

The Rowell-Sirois Commission appears to have been very much influenced in its appraisal of "joint federalism" by a study undertaken at its direction by Professor J. A. Corry of Queen's University and entitled "Difficulties of Divided Jurisdiction." Corry studied four areas of regulatory activity where formal federal-provincial arrangements had been established — related to the market-

---

[15]*Canadian Agricultural Policy*, University of Toronto Press, Toronto, 1946.

[16]*Federal Subsidies to the Provincial Governments in Canada*, Harvard University Press, Cambridge, Mass., 1937.

[17]*The Administration of Canadian Conditional Grants*, Public Administration Service, Chicago, 1938.

[18]*Report*, King's Printer, Ottawa, 1940.

[19]*Ibid.*, Book II, "Abstract of the Leading Recommendations", pp. 269-276.

[20]*Ibid.*, Book I, p. 259.

ing of agricultural products, insurance, fisheries and industrial disputes — and also the federal conditional grant programs to the provinces. His conclusion was: "... Canadian experience so far seems to indicate that administrative performance in these joint activities . . . falls short of the standards of reasonably good administration."[21] Corry admitted that there were other criteria than "administrative efficiency" by which "a final assessment of the distribution of powers in a federal state" might reasonably be measured.[22] However, by the efficiency standard alone, not only had the existing collaborative arrangements fallen short but it was almost inevitable that they should do so; "there are some good reasons for thinking that two bureaucracies so placed tend to be 'rival centres of power' rather than eager cooperators for the fulfilment of a grand national purpose."[23] Corry advanced a somewhat deterministic account of bureaucratic behaviour to explain why this should be so:

1. Officials of different bureaucracies find both their desire to express themselves through their work and their career prospects inhibited by entering into constructive intergovernmental relations.[24] The capable and ambitious official will try to "master the uncertainties which interfere with his control of the situation." One of these "uncertainties" will be the actions of the other jurisdiction and he will thus try to extend his influence to all aspects of the shared activity. Further, if the provincial official shows himself to be relatively passive in the face of his federal collaborators, he is demonstrating to his superiors that he has lost his originality. Conflicts thus cannot be attributed to the "perversity of civil servants" but rather to factors inherent in the situation and are more likely than otherwise to occur when able and zealous people are involved.

2. It is almost inevitable that federal and provincial officials will disagree on the objectives of particular public policies and the most appropriate means by which they may be attained. In speaking of conditional grants Corry asserts: "Hope for harmonious and efficient cooperation depends largely on the discovery of clear-cut objective criteria for measuring the activity — criteria which command agreement by their clarity. Such criteria are almost impossible to find."[25]

3. When administrative conflict between two independent bureaucracies occurs there is no hierarchical superior by which the dispute may be expeditiously resolved. "The real advantage of unified administration is that it provides a single authority which can break a deadlock and whose very existence is a deterrent to prolonged bickering."[26]

"Joint Federalism" from 1945 Onward

The recommendations of the Rowell-Sirois Commission were accepted by the

[21]*Ibid.*, p. 8.
[22]*Ibid.*
[23]*Ibid.*, p. 9.
[24]*Ibid.*
[25]*Ibid.*, p. 30.
[26]*Ibid.*, p. 10.

federal Government as a basis for discussion at the Dominion-Provincial Conference called in 1941.[27] No agreement with the provinces was possible along these lines. During the last months of the European War the energies of a very large number of officials in Ottawa were marshalled to devise a comprehensive series of interrelated measures looking forward to fundamental changes in Canadian federalism in the post-war period. These emerged as the so-called "Green Book" proposals presented by the federal Cabinet at the Dominion-Provincial Conference which opened in Ottawa in May 1945.[28]

The Green Book proposals showed none of the hostility to federal-provincial joint arrangements which characterized the approach of the Rowell-Sirois Commission. Although the 1945 recommendations suggested, as had the Commision, that the federal government have exclusive occupancy of the individual and corporate income tax and succession duty fields, there was no provision for inter-provincial equalization through federal unconditional subventions; the final offer of Ottawa was that the provinces in return for refraining from entering the three direct taxation fields would receive annual subsidies of $15 per capita based on either their 1941 or 1942 populations with provisions for future per capita increases proportionate to the growth of the Gross National Product. Whatever inter-provincial equalization was contemplated was in provisions for exclusive federal responsibility for pensions to those over 70, extensions of federal activities to ensure full employment and to assist the unemployed and in a very large number of collaborative activities to be carried out by the two levels of government. Among the most important of the latter were:

1. The establishment by stages of a comprehensive system of health insurance.

2. The construction of a Trans-Canada Highway and access roads to undeveloped mining and forest resources.

3. The establishment of a system of non-contributory pensions to persons in the 65-69 year group who met requirements of Canadian residence and a means-test.

4. A program for the occupational rehabilitation of the physically-handicapped.

5. Expansion of federal-provincial cooperation in vocational training.

6. The establishment of new collaborative arrangements in natural resource development.

7. Payments to provinces and municipalities to encourage them to undertake particular capital developments when the federal government decided that this was appropriate for anti-cyclical considerations.

The Green Book proposals were presented as a "package deal" and as no agreement between Ottawa and the provinces could be reached in regard to them the last plenary session of the Dominion-Provincial Conference on Recon-

---

[27]*Proceedings*, King's Printer, Ottawa, 1941.

[28]*Dominion-Provincial Conference (1945), Dominion and Provincial Submissions and Plenary Conference Discussions*, King's Printer, Ottawa, 1946, pp. 55-118.

struction adjourned *sine die* on May 3, 1946. However, almost from the day the Conference was finished federal officials began to seek limited and piecemeal agreements with the provinces on particular matters. The five-year tax-sharing arrangements which came into effect in 1947, 1952, and 1957 not only provided for more inter-provincial equalization than was contemplated by the Green Book proposals but also contained options to meet the circumstances of particular provinces. By 1960, too, a very large number of federal-provincial conditional grant programs had been established relating to the fields of hospitalization, general and categorical public assistance, public health, the development of agricultural and forestry resources and the Trans-Canada Highway. The federal government had also participated in shared-cost ventures with particular provinces through the Maritime Marshland Redevelopment Administration, the St. Mary Irrigation project (Alberta) and the South Saskatchewan development. In general then, federal-provincial relations were "factored" in the sense that agreement proved possible on a very large number of particular enterprises in the absence of agreement on a comprehensive redistribution of privileges and responsibilities between the two levels as recommended by the Rowell-Sirois Report and the Green Book proposals.

In the fifteen years or so after the end of World War Two relations between federal and provincial officials involved in shared cost arrangements were very much more cordial and constructive than the somewhat deterministic theories about bureaucratic behaviour presented by Professor Corry believed they could be. The strategic factor in this developing pattern of cooperation was, I believe, the increasing influence of program specialists at both the federal and provincial levels. The Rowell-Sirois Commission saw the characteristic relation between officials in implementing joint programs as involving provincial personnel responsible for substantive activities confronted by federal financial officers whose major objective was to protect the national Treasury and on this basis it was reasonable to believe that these relations would be characterized by conflict.[29] Although the activities of provincial civil servants engaged in shared-cost programs were of course subject to certain financial controls by federal officers in the period after 1945, a new and different kind of interaction became influential as the bureaucracies at both levels became more specialized and professionalized. The late Dr. Harry Cassidy of the University of Toronto School of Social Work made the point well in 1949 when contrasting the federal-provincial relations concerned with agriculture and forestry with those which involved old age pensions and unemployment relief he said of the former:

> There you have a situation in administration where the professionally equipped and disposed person talks with his professional friend in Ottawa. They talk the same kind of language, they work from common premises, and they can reach certain common understandings about procedures fairly easily and they can settle many issues without the Ministers in the Provinces or in Ottawa intervening. Such negotiation is a quiet kind of thing, pro-

---

[29]*Report of the Royal Commission on Dominion-Provincial Relations,* King's Printer, Ottawa, 1940, Book I, pp. 257-258.

posals seem sensible so they are accepted without fuss or fury. Hence the issue never comes up to the political level, with pressures from Alberta or from Nova Scotia or from Ontario coming up to influence the Federal Minister. It seems to me that this is a point of fundamental importance regarding programmes staffed with professional personnel which distinguishes them sharply from other programmes, such as unemployment relief and old age pensions.[30]

In general, federal-provincial relations in shared-cost arrangements have been harmonious and constructive to the extent that they have been dominated by program specialists from both levels of government. The following influences are at work to encourage this kind of collaboration and to inhibit conflict between officials of the two levels of government:

1. The attitudes, procedures and values common to particular groups of program specialists — foresters, social workers, civil engineers, experts in occupational therapy and so on — provide common standards to which officials from federal and provincial levels defer. Membership in such a group almost always involves not only the sharing of a body of knowledge and techniques but also adherence to a common set of standards and objectives related to the public policies with which the group is professionally concerned. What Seymour Lipset has said of bureaucracies generally applies to these federal-provincial complexes of specialists: "Inherent in bureaucratic structures is a tendency to reduce conflicts to administrative decisions by experts, and thus over time bureaucratization facilitates the removing of objects from the political arena. Constant emphasis on the need for objective criteria as a basis for the settlement of conflicts enables bureaucracies to play major mediating roles."[31]

2. Program officials know that if they do not resolve intergovernmental disputes "within the guild" these conflicts will be settled by outsiders who are motivated by different considerations than those which prevail within the specialized group — by senior departmental officials with more generalist perspectives, by treasury officers, by politicians, perhaps in some cases by the courts of law. In the broadest of terms, shared-cost programs are subject to less effective political and treasury control than are those activities for which one jurisdiction assumes full responsibility and it is in the interest of the program specialists to maintain this relative independence.

3. Powerful factors of self-interest are at work to encourage federal and provincial officials involved in grant-in-aid functions to regard their respective roles as complementary rather than competitive. If Ottawa withdrew from some or all of the present arrangements, groups of federal officials would have to be assigned to new tasks, with possible losses in their power and status. Provincial program officials, along with their federal counterparts, usually believe that more financial resources are expended on their functions when shared-

---

[30]*Proceedings, First Annual Conference of the Institute of Public Administration of Canada 1949*, Toronto, 1950, pp. 164-165.

[31]R. K. Merton, L. Brown and L. S. Cottrell (eds.), *Sociology Today*, Basic Books, New York, 1959, p. 102.

cost arrangements prevail than would be the case if the provinces had equivalent funds at their disposal with no strings attached.[32]

4. Professionalization leads to increased formal and informal contacts among those involved in the same kinds of work and strengthens "in-group" attitudes. Specialized journals are published, advisory committees are set up, *ad hoc* and regular conferences are held and so on. It is part of the contemporary ethic that much is to be gained by sharing experiences with those engaged in the same kind of work and modern developments in transportation and communication facilitate this kind of interaction.[33] It may also well be true, contrary to the Corry analysis, that officials in these specialized intergovernmental groupings do not look single-mindedly to their hierarchical superiors for rewards. Once such a community of interest and purpose is established officials may come to that community for influence and status. If and when this is so, the conduct that will result in the desired rewards being conferred will be based on the ability to establish and sustain cooperative relations with officials of other jurisdictions.

In general, federal-provincial administrative relations in the post-1945 period developed in quite a different direction than the Rowell-Sirois Commission with its somewhat deterministic views of bureaucratic behaviour believed possible. Adjustments to changing circumstances were made for the most part as highly particularistic responses to the demands of groups inside and outside governments for individual projects and programs. The formal constitution proved remarkably resistant to change through amendment or evolving patterns of judicial review. Further, the development of effective devices for intergovernmental articulation at the political-executive and treasury levels was retarded. Adjustments thus were made largely by officials involved in specific functions.

The dominance of highly particularistic considerations under joint federalism in the 1945-60 period cannot be over-emphasized. As we have seen, shared-cost functions attained a relatively high degree of independence of political and executive control. Elazar in his history of federal-state relations asserts that the functional relations between Washington and the Southern States went on very much as usual almost to the eve of the Civil War and that recent program relations have been very little disturbed by conflicts over the race issue.[34] Similarly, it is my observation that the joint programs involving British Columbia were not much affected by the vendetta between the Diefenbaker and Bennett governments relating to hydro-electric development. Also, the whole matter of the financial relations between Ottawa and the provinces hammered out in the tax-sharing agreements was done in almost complete isolation from the devising and implementing of shared-cost arrangements.

"Joint Federalism" under Stress

From about 1960 onward there was a combination of circumstances signifying

---

[32]Smiley, *op. cit.*, p. 39.

[33]". . . there may be and probably usually is more group consultation in modern bureaucratic organizations than the objective facts of interdependence warrant." Thompson, *op. cit.*, p. 501.

[34]Elazar, *op. cit.*, p. 330-331.

that the particularistic and program-dominated patterns of intergovernmental relations were failing to meet the interests of either level. The following seem to be the crucial factors giving rise to these new stresses:

First, several of the provincial administrations came to be administratively mature enough to commit themselves to comprehensive objectives and to allocate the resources at their disposal according to long-term plans. From the late 1950's onward, Alberta began to plan its capital expenditures on a five-year basis. The Quebec Government in office since 1960 is committed to economic planning. Ontario has drastically reformed its budgetary procedures in the direction of a more rational process of decision-making. The Manitoba Government has assumed a general commitment to the proposals of the Committee on Manitoba's Economic Future which reported early in 1963. The provinces have been increasingly successful in attracting able and aggressive officials in both their treasury and program departments and have increasingly guided their conduct in terms of long-term projections of the needs for roads, schools, hospitals, and other public amenities. Provincial commitment to budgetary and program planning gave rise to dissatisfaction with the inherent paternalism of the grant-in-aid device, particularly when Ottawa took action to sponsor new shared-cost programs or change the terms of existing ones without adequate prior consultation with the provinces. The complex of highly specific shared-cost arrangements was compatible with harmonious relations between the two levels so long as provincial administration was somewhat haphazard and the "fifty-cent dollars" available from Ottawa looked attractive because the provinces were not committed to rational procedures of priority-allocation.

Second, there was a discernible increase in federal-provincial relations of the influence of officials who were not involved in particular programs. In 1954 the St. Laurent Government established a small Federal-Provincial Relations Division in the federal Department of Finance and provincial administrations have shown an increasing disposition to devolve the immediate responsibility for financial relations with Ottawa on particular officials or sections; a Federal-Provincial Relations Department was established in Quebec in 1961. As a result of the 1955 Dominion-Provincial Conference, the Continuing Committee on Fiscal and Economic Matters composed of senior appointed treasury officials was constituted and meets twice yearly.[35] The Institute of Public Administration of Canada which reflects the concerns and values of general administrators more than those of program specialists became more influential.[36] Legislation introduced into Parliament by the Pearson Government in the summer of 1963 provided for the establishment of the Economic Council of Canada to formulate national economic goals and to coordinate through persuasion the activities of

---

[35]Kear, *op. cit.*

[36]The incumbent President and three immediate past Presidents of the Institute have been financial officials. The annual convention of the Institute held each September is scheduled just before the semi-annual meeting of the Federal-Provincial Continuing Committee on Fiscal and Economic Matters so that the same officials can conveniently attend both meetings in the same city.

public and private bodies toward these goals.[37] At the political level there have been annual meetings of the provincial Premiers since 1960[38] and the federal Government has established a Cabinet Committee to deal with federal-provincial relations. There are thus new kinds of interactions between Ottawa and the provinces in the making, interactions not directly related to particular programs and projects.

Third, the Lesage administration, with the support of some of the other provinces on particular issues, is making a more effective challenge to the extension of federal influence than did the Union Nationale leadership. In retrospect, it is surprising how little Mr. Duplessis's efforts on behalf of provincial autonomy influenced the course of federal-provincial relations between 1944 and his death in 1959 and it is difficult to cite any major concession made by Ottawa to Quebec during that period apart from the increases in federal tax abatements after that province began to levy personal income taxes in 1954. The crucial new factor is that the Lesage administration, unlike its predecessor, is committed to the aggressive pursuit of social and economic goals through provincial action. There are thus more areas in which specific policy objectives of the federal and Quebec administrations clash. Further, the present Quebec Government is committed to costly programs and its demands for increased fiscal autonomy are less symbolic in nature than were those of the Union Nationale. The influences of a revitalized Quebec have contributed to other pressures on the centralized variant of Canadian federalism that developed in the period immediately after World War Two.

Fourth, relatively high levels of unemployment and unsatisfactory rates of economic growth since 1957 have given rise to the increased necessity of the articulation of federal and provincial activities, particularly fiscal policies. An essential part of the Green Book "package deal" of 1945 was a proposal that the provinces and municipalities would receive grants to plan shelves of public works and that Ottawa would pay twenty per cent of the costs of projects executed in a period designated by the federal authorities. However, the high levels of income and employment in the decade after World War Two did not encourage this kind of federal-provincial collaboration in capital investment and, at the 1955 Federal-Provincial Conference, Prime Minister St. Laurent formally announced that his Government would not act on the anti-cyclical proposal made ten years before and had decided that ". . . it would be better and more practical to make whatever cooperative arrangements are justified in specific fields. We think that the Federal Government should not suggest that it get involved in having to make judgments in regard to thousands of public projects of the normal type carried out by the Provinces and the municipalities."[39] The relatively high rates of unemployment combined with unsatisfactory economic growth which have prevailed since 1957 have led to renewed demands for the articulation of federal and provincial economic policies. There

---

[37]For a lucid account of the rationale of the Council see the speech by Dr. Pauline Jewett, M.P., *House of Commons Debates* (unrevised), July 15, 1963, pp. 2206-2209.

[38]Aitchison, *ibid.*

[39]*Proceedings*, Queen's Printer, Ottawa, 1956, p. 9.

has also come the conviction that in part at least these circumstances have been due to structural defects in the economy rather than deficiencies in gross demand and that appropriate remedies can thus come only through federal-provincial collaboration. Further, the steadily increasing proportion of public expenditures made by provinces and local authorities combined have made more necessary than in the preceding period the coordination of the fiscal policies of all levels of government.

The strains on the complex of highly specific adjustments effected through shared-cost agreements were shown in the attacks on the grant-in-aid device made by several of the provincial Premiers at the Federal-Provincial Conference held in July, 1960.[40] The arguments of Lesage of Quebec and Manning of Alberta were phrased in terms of a concern for provincial autonomy on somewhat dogmatic grounds. Robichaud of New Brunswick, Roblin of Manitoba and Shaw of Prince Edward Island made the criticism that the existing programs did not meet the needs of the less prosperous provinces. Douglas of Saskatchewan, the leader of a government more committed than most to long-term budgetary and program planning, was concerned with the "distortions" in provincial budgets induced by conditional grants and both Shaw and Roblin expressed similar concerns about the impact of these arrangements on provincial procedures. For the first time since the 1930's, the grant-in-aid device had been strongly challenged by influential Canadian politicians other than those from Quebec.

The 1961 statement on conditional grants adopted by the federal Liberal Party constituted a further challenge to "joint federalism".[41] This statement asserted that the federal government should withdraw from continuing shared-cost functions once these were well established throughout the country. If new programs were begun requiring "permanent and fairly regular expenditures" they should be terminated after a period of not more than five years. Arrangements should also be made by which a province might opt out of particular shared-cost plans without suffering "financial discrimination" thereby; this was a new idea — it had been taken for granted previously in Canada as in other federations that a jurisdiction which decided not to accept a specific conditional grant would be subjected to the full financial penalties of its decision. In general terms, the Liberals showed a marked preference for dealing with the financial needs of the provinces through increased equalization payments made unconditionally and an increased provincial share of the income tax and succession duty fields rather than conditional grants.[42]

In spite of the circumstances I have described, the complex of functional relationships built up around the grant-in-aid device will no doubt continue as an important aspect of the Canadian federal structure in the foreseeable future. There are a very large number of interests both inside and outside government

---

[40]*Proceedings*, Queen's Printer, Ottawa, 1960. See also Smiley, *op. cit.*, pp. 12-15.

[41]See also the Hon. Lester Pearson's speech made in Quebec City on November 6, 1961, National Liberal Federation (mimeo.).

[42]Opening Statement by the Prime Minister of Canada at the Federal-Provincial Conference, November 26, 1963 (mimeo.), pp. 10-11.

who will use their influence to perpetuate the existing system of grants-in-aid and to influence federal financial support for new provincial functions. The Pearson Government since coming to power has increased its contributions to vocational training and has agreed to new forms of cooperation with the provinces in the field of welfare. The Prime Minister has also made clear that his Government would terminate existing shared-cost arrangements only after consultations with the provinces[43] and it is by no means certain whether forms of compensation, in the forms either of subsidies or of increased "tax room" can be agreed upon, particularly in respect to functions where there is an expectation that costs will increase. There are also possibilities of making the grant-in-aid procedure more palatable to the provinces. The Continuing Committee on Fiscal and Economic Matters has had some success in rationalizing the procedures by which the provinces are reimbursed by Ottawa.[44] It seems likely that the federal authorities will be less prone than in the past to announce their willingness to support new provincial and local functions or to alter existing arrangements without prior consultations with the provinces. There may be a tendency for Ottawa to support broader functions than in the past; the forestry agreements which came into effect in 1962 are a step in this direction, there has been some discussion of consolidating the categorical and general public assistance programs within one framework and the suggestion has from time to time been made that Ottawa support broadly-defined provincial activities like health, welfare and vocational training in place of its present assistance for specific programs and projects. The contracting out device may also encourage the federal government to undertake new shared-cost activities in the absence of agreement from one or more of the provinces to a greater extent than in the past. Joint federalism as I have defined the term will thus remain a central feature of federal-provincial relations.

The Federal-Provincial Conference of November 1963 and Consultative Federalism

The Federal-Provincial Conference held in November 1963 seems to have presaged a development toward consultative federalism. The events of the months immediately preceding made more obvious than before the necessity of more continuous consultation between the two levels of government. The newly-elected Liberal Government had in the summer of 1963 introduced legislation into Parliament providing for a municipal loan fund and a Canada Pension Plan. These measures had been introduced as a fulfilment of promises made by the Liberals prior to the general election of 1963. The provinces had not been consulted and the provincial reaction was so hostile that a Federal-Provincial Conference was hurriedly called in July at which the federal Government made very considerable changes in both proposals as a result of provincial pressure. The Government had also encountered some opposition from individual provinces on designating particular areas where the percentage of federal assistance

43*Ibid.*

44*Dominion-Provincial Conference, 1960,* Queen's Printer, Ottawa, 1960, p. 13.

paid for winter works would be higher than elsewhere and others where certain tax concessions would be made in respect to capital investment. The federal Cabinet had thus been made aware in a somewhat dramatic way of the results of unilateral action in respect to matters in which the provinces felt an interest.

The Pearson Government gave every indication prior to and during the November Conference of wanting to work toward more effective high-level consultation with the provinces. The meeting was regarded by the Government as the first of a series of such gatherings which were to be held more regularly than in the past. The agenda included as an item for discussion "federal-provincial liaison arrangements". The Prime Minister in his opening address to the Conference suggested new matters for federal-provincial consultation toward (1) defining the criteria for designating areas of slow economic growth, (2) making more effective the work of the newly-established Economic Council of Canada and Department of Industry, (3) terminating certain well-established joint programs.[45] Mr. Pearson, in a somewhat oblique way so as not to imply any federal interference in the affairs of the provinces, suggested more effective internal machinery for consultation.[46] The stage had thus been set for major new developments in federal-provincial relations.

Within the existing division of powers and responsibilities between the federal and provincial governments there are too many ways in which the activities of one level can vitally affect the interests and objectives of the other to make tolerable a situation in which policies are decided upon and implemented unilaterally. The strains on the federal system occasioned by the lack of effective procedures of intergovernmental articulation can be expected to become more severe as both levels commit themselves more explicitly to comprehensive and long-term goals than in the past; a case can be made that Canadian federalism has up until now been sustained through one or the other level being relatively immobilist in economic matters, a circumstance which now appears to be changing. The aim must be to work toward a set of political and administrative conventions by which neither Ottawa nor any province embarks on a major policy without taking the other into its confidence and being willing to consider the latter's assessment of the implications of this policy for its interests. To be more concrete, it would mean that no province would go ahead with a major program of hydro-electric development or of changing the terms under which municipalities might borrow in the domestic or international capital markets without prior consultations with the appropriate federal agencies. Further, there is no *a priori* reason why consultations should not include matters within the jurisdiction of the federal government — Premier Lesage at the November Conference suggested that the provinces "should have their voice in determining tariff structures, transportation and even the monetary policies of Canada";[47] something can be said for the argument made by Jean-Marc Leger that what is now commonly understood as "cooperative federalism" relates

---

[45]*Ibid.*

[46]*Ibid.*, pp. 17-18.

[47]"*Address*", Nov. 25, 1963 (mimeo.), p. 38. I am not suggesting that I believe that these are the kinds of matters about which consultations would be appropriate.

almost exclusively to matters within the jurisdiction of the provinces and is therefore "the new face of centralization."[48]

Consultative relationships between sovereign governments are extraordinarily subtle and it is impossible to predict with any precision the kinds of devices by which they might be facilitated in Canada. What seems certain is that the establishment of new institutional machinery, however ingenious, will not of itself bring effective consultation about. The following general points can be made:

1. The new procedures for federal-provincial articulation should not be allowed to frustrate close and harmonious relations between functional agencies of the two levels. The relative success of joint federalism can be attributed in part to the highly specific nature of the interactions which developed; i.e., program agencies could work closely together because their collaboration did not depend on federal-provincial agreement on more comprehensive objectives. One can postulate a quasi-diplomatic pattern of relations in which Ottawa and each of the provinces designed a coherent policy toward the other and implemented this policy through an agency specifically charged with this responsibility. Such a development might well lead to situations in which federal-provincial cooperation on particular issues was inhibited by the lack of agreement about more fundamental concerns. Although this kind of circumstance is to be avoided there is room for Ottawa and the provinces to have the "presence" of officials whose concern is with broad public policies in the dealings between functional agencies.[49]

2. If considerations more comprehensive than those related to particular programs and projects are to be more influential than before in federal-provincial relations, experience with conditional grants suggests the usefulness of establishing centres of bureaucratic power at both levels devoted to these considerations and of creating circumstances in which interactions between these centres can be continuous rather than sporadic. A first step in this direction would be for each jurisdiction to confer the responsibility for relations between the two levels on particular departments or agencies whether these are Departments of Federal-Provincial Affairs, branches of the Treasury or groups within the Prime Minister's or Privy Council office.[50] However, the preconditions of success of consultations between such groups have not been met in some of the jurisdictions: (a) the consultative agency must be able to speak authoritatively for its government; (b) functional agencies must be under the effective control of agencies with more comprehensive goals. Even if these circumstances did exist

---

[48]"Cooperative Federalism or the New Face of Centralization", *The Canadian Forum*, October 1963, pp. 155-156.

[49]In the conditional grant programs there has sometimes been the complaint that financial officials were not informed at an early enough stage of the negotiations between program officials from each level. See Smiley, pp. 37-42, for a discussion on the conflicts between treasury and program officers in shared-cost programs.

[50]I am indebted to a letter from Dr. A. W. Johnson for a perceptive discussion of the significance of the administrative relations of these intergovernmental agencies in relation to their own Cabinets and Finance Departments.

it would be unrealistic to contemplate these federal-provincial organizations developing the kind of allegiance to common procedures and values which so much facilitates intergovernmental relations among program specialists as the concerns of the former relate to fundamental political choices about which consensus is more difficult to establish than in respect to more technical matters. However, it is tempting to speculate about the results of having these posts filled by a Canadian "administrative man" devoted to what has been called "the political economy tradition" and the rapidly developing profession of general administration. Perhaps the Institute of Public Administration of Canada will come to provide a focus for the concerns and values of this group or perhaps it might come to be recruited from among the graduates of a federal-provincial administrative staff college yet to be established.

It is prudent to realize the limits of consultative procedures. Consultations among governments having different responsibilities allow men to discover common ground where it exists; they do not provide any means of reconciling interests which are incompatible. If one believes that there are single values, such as full employment or economic growth or provincial autonomy or the equalization of public services throughout the nation which in any and all circumstances should over-ride conflicting considerations, he cannot reasonably defend federalism; war-time experience in Canada and elsewhere demonstrates that when a single national objective is to be pursued federalism must of necessity be in abeyance. There are several kinds of public policy situations in which there are likely to be differences of emphasis if not in ultimate aims between Ottawa and the provinces and it is in regard to these that more effective consultative procedures are desirable:

1. The federal authorities can be expected to be more concerned with the income and employment impact of provincial and local capital expenditures than are the provinces, which are likely to regard these expenditures in part at least in the light of service needs for roads, schools, hospitals, and so on.

2. The objectives of some of the provinces are likely to lie in the direction of more differentiated and autonomous provincial economies than are compatible with national economic objectives.

3. In some cases provincial policies may inhibit the federal government's interest in maintaining the mobility of labour and capital within the national boundaries.

4. In respect to the capital expenditure policies of local authorities the provinces may be expected to emphasize local financial stability, Ottawa the impact of projected expenditures on employment and income.

5. In some circumstances individual provinces will press for a closer integration with contiguous areas in the United States than is compatible with national economic policies.

6. Ottawa may choose in some circumstances to achieve its purposes through grants-in-aid with some or all of the provinces preferring federal financial assistance through unconditional subventions or increased access to tax sources to cooperation in attaining federal objectives.

7. There can be expected to be permanent conflicts in the sharing of tax sources and the distribution of public revenues between the two levels.

When the Right Honourable Lester B. Pearson was Minister of External Affairs, he wrote about consultative procedures among the nations of the Western Alliance in terms which are almost directly applicable to the needs of federal-provincial relations in the mid-1960's:

> . . . Consultation means the opportunity to participate in the give and take of ideas, the weighing of pros and cons; and the formulation of policy based on the highest common denominator of agreement. It is a method of harmonizing divergent interests, a process which makes it possible so to adjust and adapt measures which any one government may have in mind that are least likely to disturb, and most likely to consolidate, the unity of the greater . . . society to which we all belong.
>
> This broader responsibility does not in any sense remove or weaken the direct constitutional responsibility of each democratic government to its own nation. It is something additional. It is less a matter of formal agreement between governments than an attitude which must be developed by men, a quality of outlook that must be achieved by politicians, editors, teachers, and businessmen, by all those whose views and actions make up public opinion.[51]

23   The Machinery of Federal-Provincial Relations: I *

Edgar Gallant

Let me say at the outset — before it becomes obvious — that I have come to the field of federal-provincial relations only recently. I came to it from work in other fields including that of international trade relations where I have had the opportunity to observe intergovernmental consultation in international organizations.

We are all aware of the growing importance of consultation between the federal and provincial governments in Canada, in this age of "cooperative federalism," and I should like to begin with an indication of this growth. Some of you no doubt remember an address given by Dr. K. W. Taylor at the Ninth Annual Conference of this Institute in 1957 on the subject of "Coordination in

[51]*Democracy in World Politics*, Princeton University Press, Princeton, 1955, pp. 50-51.

*From *Canadian Public Administration*, Vol. VIII, No. 4, December 1965, pp. 515-526. Reprinted by permission of the author and the Institute of Public Administration of Canada.

Administration."[1] The list of federal-provincial committees which he appended to his paper contained 64 items. At the Federal-Provincial Conference of Prime Ministers and Premiers last July, a calendar of federal-provincial conferences and meetings for 1965 was distributed. There are 125 items in this list. To judge by these comparisons, the number of conferences and committees doubled over a period of eight years!

This rapid growth, it could be observed, is not out of line with the striking development of international machinery for intergovernmental consultation. Since the Second World War we have witnessed the birth of several new international organizations, and new ones seem to appear every now and then. If independent countries have found it in their interest, in this age of growing interdependence, to set up such elaborate machinery for intergovernmental liaison, should it not be expected that different levels of government within a federal country would provide machinery for even closer consultation?

Before I attempt to analyse the federal-provincial machinery we now have, it might be useful to reflect briefly on the need for consultation as it has developed in the past and as it is now evolving.

The Need for Consultation

In theory there would appear to be two types of federal state: one in which all fields of responsibility are precisely defined and properly allocated, requiring little machinery for intergovernmental consultation; and one in which many fields of responsibility are shared by two levels of government, requiring much more elaborate machinery for coordination. The Canadian constitution did provide for a fair amount of abutting or overlapping jurisdictions — for example, in the fields of agriculture and immigration. Nevertheless, I would suggest that the Fathers of Confederation intended to establish the first type of federal state. Over the years, however, as Canada evolved into a modern and increasingly complex industrial economy, and as the role of government underwent drastic changes, our federal system evolved into the second type.

In the early days of confederation there was not much need for federal-provincial consultations. At the beginning, relations between the federal government and the provinces were of a formal legal character, with the Secretary of State and the Lieutenant-Governors being the channels of communication. Subsequently there were periods when federal-provincial relations played an important role at the political level, and other periods when they subsided. Since then, increased use of financial power has expanded fields of influence and concern of the federal and the provincial governments. Through the use of such devices as shared-cost programs, and grants and loans to institutions under provincial jurisdiction, the federal government has considerably expanded its field of influence, though not its field of jurisdiction. Parallel to this growing role of both levels of government, and as a consequence of it, there has been an increasing crowding of the tax fields. Obviously, given such a large scale of

---

[1]*Proceedings of the Sixth Annual Conference of the Institute of Public Administration of Canada,* Toronto, 1954, p. 253.

government activity, together with this high degree of interaction between levels of government, effective intergovernmental consultation has become a basic requirement.

It is in matters relating to the over-all management of the economic affairs of the country that this requirement is becoming, in my opinion, particularly pronounced. Like other modern industrial countries, Canada seems to be paying increasing attention to the use of government economic policies for the achievement of basic social and economic objectives. While, broadly speaking, the citizens of a country will tend to look to their national governments for leadership in reaching such goals, we have to recognize that in Canada all levels of government are active in matters having definite implications for the economy as a whole. Let me try to illustrate this with a few obvious examples.

Consider first the objective of economic growth. It goes without saying that the behaviour of the public sector as a whole has a definite impact on the growth of the national economy. This applies not just to the sheer magnitude of government activity — and total government expenditure amounted to 31 per cent of the G.N.P. in 1964 — but also to the priorities given to the different functions of government, the timing of public expenditure, and the means by which the funds are raised. In all of these decisions, governments may stimulate or retard growth.

When one considers that the provincial-municipal governments spent $8.1 billion in 1964, compared to $6.5 billion spent at the federal level (excluding intergovernmental transfers), and that provincial-municipal expenditures have grown by over 200 per cent in the last ten years compared to 56 per cent for federal expenditures, it becomes more than obvious that the management of government financial transactions to maximize economic growth is a matter of concern for all levels of government in Canada. We can also illustrate this point by passing from the aggregate activity to individual government measures, particularly those specific programs relating to economic growth, in which both levels of government are active. Think, for instance, of the many programs relating to the provision of trained manpower — the technical and vocational training programs, the financing of institutes of technical training and higher learning, the rehabilitation of disabled persons, and so on. Think, also, of the programs for development of primary resources — the dual roles in agriculture and fisheries, ARDA, PFRA, roads to resources, etc. One could mention also many undertakings involving both levels of jurisdiction in such important fields as energy, transportation, communication, and industrial development.

Now let us consider some further illustrations by referring to economic stabilization. Generally speaking, governments can alleviate the effects of short-term fluctuations in the economy by building automatic stabilizers into the fiscal system or by making discretionary fiscal changes. An important automatic stabilizer is, of course, the personal income tax with its basic exemptions and progressive rates. We are all aware of the recent developments in the sharing of this revenue source, and the growing importance of the provincial shares. On the expenditure side of the budget, we have an example of automatic stabilizers in unemployment insurance and other programs of assistance to the unemployed

— the one involving the federal government, and the others involving the provincial and federal governments.

Turning to the ability of federal and provincial governments to implement discretionary stabilization policies, as opposed to automatic ones, an examination of the 1964 National Accounts shows that provincial and municipal governments spent over $5.6 billion on goods and services in that year while the federal government spent about $3.0 billion. One could also note that expenditures of a capital nature, which are generally more susceptible to changes in timing, are estimated to be about five times as great at the provincial-municipal level as at the federal level. Clearly, there is more potential for implementing discretionary stabilization policies through the timing of purchases in the provincial-municipal sphere than in the federal.

I have mentioned a few examples to establish the point that the two levels of government are both intimately involved in many matters which bear heavily on economic policy. This is just one, although a very important one, of several areas of joint federal-provincial concern, but it serves to illustrate, I think, the increasing need for consultation which our machinery will have to meet.

The Machinery for Federal-Provincial Relations

I now move back to the machinery. I mentioned previously that there are now some 125 committees and conferences. These do not, of course, encompass all federal-provincial consultations. There are many informal or *ad hoc* meetings to deal with particular problems. Also, and this is perhaps even more significant, individual contacts between officials and between ministers, by letter, telephone, or visits, appear to be increasing. Therefore, when one speaks of the machinery for federal-provincial relations, one has in mind much more than just the formally constituted bodies with a more or less continuing role in facilitating federal-provincial consultations and coordination. In this paper, however, I intend to analyse mainly this ensemble of federal-provincial committees.

The first point that strikes me about this machinery is a notable difference between it and that which exists for intergovernmental liaison at the international level. At the international level, we have, as I said earlier, a vast structure of international organizations and specialized agencies, conferences and committees, covering a very broad range, if not all areas of governmental activity. In addition, we have a large network of diplomatic missions which, it should be noted, was established well before the rapid growth of specialized agencies and specialized missions.

In our federal-provincial relations, our machinery has evolved in a reverse order. We have first developed numerous committees and conferences at a specialist level. We have not had a comparable network of intelligence concerned with the total picture of intergovernmental relations. While Canada has over 400 professionals engaged in international relations, we still have very few engaged full-time in a professional way in federal-provincial relations, and our machinery makes relatively little provision to ensure continuous liaison with respect to the over-view of matters which concern both the federal and provincial governments.

The central body of our federal-provincial machinery is the Plenary Conference of Premiers and Prime Ministers. It seems to me to have been concerned more with specific policy issues than with the continuous over-view of federal-provincial matters. It began meeting sporadically in the early years of Confederation, but only in recent years has it taken on the role of a more continuing body for federal-provincial consultations. It now meets at least annually.

The rest of the machinery reflects the concentration on special program areas that I mentioned. As would be expected, this machinery tended to develop first where the constitution provides specifically for concurrent roles, notably in the agricultural sector. Then, as the country matured and the activities of government increased, we witnessed a growing interdependence between the programs of the federal and provincial spheres. Associated with this was the growth of shared-cost programs and the appearance of new consultative machinery to facilitate coordination in the areas where federal and provincial activities were coming together. This machinery sometimes developed at the ministerial level, and sometimes it involved deputy ministers or other officials. Several different committees, at different levels, have evolved within particular fields to meet specific needs.

This process has taken us to the point where in 1965 there are some 125 committees and conferences meeting on federal-provincial matters. They have taken so many different forms that a simple, concise description of the machinery becomes difficult. However, I think it will contribute to our understanding of the subject if I attempt a brief description. Before I do, I should make the point that federal-provincial machinery by no means included every body which exists to facilitate coordination of government activity in Canada. There is also a substantial body of interprovincial machinery committees and conferences which bring provincial representatives together to deal with matters of purely provincial concern. And there are the intragovernmental machinery devices which operate within one government for the purpose of dealing with federal-provincial matters. They include cabinet committees, interdepartmental committees of officials, and specialist federal-provincial relations divisions. The latter exist in the federal government, and in some if not all of the provinces. They aid in developing the positions which are taken at conferences, and in facilitating communication between conferences.

Taking all of these together, we have a large package of committees; and there are those who still disparage the committee as a device. They belong to the school of thought which defines a committee as "a collection of people who individually believe that something must be done and who collectively decide that nothing can be done," or which says of a committee's labours, "Never have so many spent so much time to accomplish so little."

The Federal-Provincial Conferences and Committees

When one is faced with the task of describing a collection of many entities, one seeks first a convenient system for classifying them. I see several different possible classifications for these committees and conferences: the broad structure, the participants, the subject matter, and the broad purpose or type of consultation. I think it could be illuminating to give a little attention to each of these possibilities.

1. The Broad Structure

Under the heading of what I call, for lack of a better word, the broad structure, I would identify seven groupings.

a. Federal-Provincial committees as such. These, I think, are what we would normally think of first when considering the subject of federal-provincial machinery. I consider them to be federal-provincial bodies in the truest sense of the word. They are composed of ministers or officials from the federal and provincial governments, who come together as official representatives of their governments to work on matters of mutual concern. Note first that they are definitely committees of government. Note next that they are made up by the participation of individual governments, each in its own right. The federal government by virtue of its central position usually provides the chairman and secretarial services. I would place most of the committees — approximately 100, including sub-committees — in this category, and I would offer, as examples, the Plenary Conference of Prime Ministers and Premiers, the Conference of the Ministers of Welfare, the Continuing Committee on Economic and Fiscal Matters, and the meeting of Federal and Provincial Directors of Vocational Education.

I should note, also, that committees may be national in scope, involving all provinces, such as the examples I have given, or they may be regional in nature, with representation from only a few provinces plus the federal government. Of the 100 noted above, about 30 could be considered to be regional in nature. The Atlantic Fisheries Committee is one example.

These federal-provincial committees are established with varying degrees of formality. Some annual meetings are called as a matter of tradition, some are handled more casually, being called together as circumstances dictate.

b. Federal advisory councils. A compilation of federal-provincial committees and conferences has to include certain councils which are appointed under federal statute or order-in-council to act as advisory bodies to federal ministers. As such, they would not appear to belong in a classification of federal-provincial bodies. However, their composition, with representation from all provincial governments, is such, that they do, in effect, function as federal-provincial committees to a large extent. The process is roughly as follows. The council deliberates on a matter with the benefit of the provincial points of view. When it decides to recommend something to its minister, this means that its provincial members are in agreement or go along with the decision and will be ready to advocate acceptance in their provinces. If the minister accepts the advice of his council and gains the approval of the federal goverment, he can then make a proposal to the provinces with reasonable prospects for ready acceptance. In effect, then, this body has been instrumental in facilitating the development of federal-provincial policy.

Examples of these advisory councils include the Dominion Council of Health, the National Advisory Council on Rehabilitation of Disabled Persons, the Technical and Vocational Training Council, and the National Council of Welfare.

These councils all have members not only from the governments, but from outside organizations, as well. The wide representation means they tend to become quite large, and they look as if they could be somewhat cumbersome to handle. It is interesting to speculate on the reasons for their formation. Are they needed primarily as a source of ideas, or as a public relations device to satisfy all interest groups by giving them a voice? Or are they meant to serve primarily as a device for federal-provincial consultation, but with these other elements thrown in for good measure? Whatever the answer, it seems clear that their federal-provincial role has been substantial.

c. Quasi-independent associations. There are certain bodies which are made up wholly, or almost wholly, of ministers or civil servants, and which are supported by government, but which are not federal-provincial committees in the usual sense of the term. They are constituted as associations and function to some extent as professional organizations or special interest groups. Their stimulus comes more from within themselves than from the governments, and the participants function more as association members than as representatives from governments. And yet, because they do bring together people in a particular field from all governments, they serve to some extent as a vehicle for federal-provincial consultation and coordination.

Examples of bodies I would place in this category include the Canadian Council of Resource Ministers, which has its own letters patent and its own staff, the Canadian Association of Administrators of Labour Legislation, and the Association of Canadian Fire Marshals.

d. Interprovincial conferences. A relatively new but in my view very significant development in intergovernmental liaison in Canada is the growth of the interprovincial machinery for consultation. One compilation, which may be incomplete, indicates that there are now about 60 formally constituted inter provincial bodies, some of which could be defined as quasi-independent or independent associations. They convene for the purpose of discussing matters of interest primarily to the provinces, or perhaps for agreeing on a joint approach to the federal government, and the provinces usually take turns acting as host to them. These conferences and committees at ministerial and official levels have a definite impact on federal-provincial relations. Indeed, they can be regarded as essential for the effective functioning of the country. I mention them here in this classification of federal-provincial devices because some do in fact assume a considerable federal-provincial role.

The Provincial Ministers of Mines Conference is an interesting example. One of the things the provincial ministers do at these conferences is to agree on the substance of a brief to be submitted to the federal government. However, the federal minister or his representatives are present as observers so that, when the provincial ministers make their formal presentation a few months later, the federal minister has had time to consider their conclusions and is in a position to discuss them.

Other examples in this category include the Conference of Provincial Premiers, which was held in Winnipeg this year, the Trade and Industry Council, and the Conference of Provincial Deputy Ministers of Public Works. (I think I should like to be invited as an "observer" to the Motion Picture Censor's Association Conference — at least I should if they compare cuttings.)

e. Subcommittees. Perhaps I can complicate the picture somewhat now by noting that there are also subcommittees. Committees seem to have two tendencies which are sometimes thought to be unfortunate: they tend to live forever, and they tend to produce offspring. The former possibly suggests something angelic about their nature; the latter, however, might be taken to invite a description of their activities which is really too uncharitable to be used here.

There are about 30 committees in my list which I would call subcommittees because they seem to have a direct reporting relationship to some other committee. They are usually at a technical level, with terms of reference requiring them to give attention to a specific problem area. The Dominion Council of Health has several such committees reporting to it, for example. Sometimes a description of the organization becomes difficult. For example, I would describe the Committee on Technical and Vocational Training as a federal-provincial committee since it works to achieve coordination of technical and vocational training programs at an administrative level. However, it is considered to be subordinate to the Technical and Vocational Training Council, a federal advisory body.

f. Provincial advisory committees. At the risk of extending this list excessively, I should note that in individual provinces there are some provincial committees with federal representation created to advise on matters relating to federal-provincial programs. They may be formed and chaired by provincial authorities but can be initiated on the basis of a federal proposal. Examples are the Coordinating Committees on Indian Affairs and the ARDA Joint Advisory Committees.

g. Non-government associations. There are some organizations which are quite independent of government, unlike the quasi-independent associations noted earlier, but which play an important role in federal-provincial relations nevertheless. Such associations have a substantial number of members representing governments across the country and are interested in subjects relating directly to some area of government activity. When the membership comes together to discuss its area of interest, it is inevitable that ideas will be born, thinking influenced, and policy eventually affected. The Canadian Good Roads Association is a notable example of this type of organization. Perhaps I might be so bold as to suggest that the Institute of Public Administration is another.

I have attempted so far to describe the federal-provincial machinery under a classification I have called "the broad structure." This became complicated enough, but I am now going to compound the problem by introducing a number of other possible classifications. I shall deal with them more briefly, however.

2. The Participants

The first of these I call "the participants." One could classify the federal-provincial meetings by the people who attend them. When I group them by hierarchial levels, I come up with the following count (excluding non-government associations):

Level	No. of 1965 Conferences & Committees
Prime Ministers and Premiers	2
Ministers	13
Deputy Ministers	14
Directors	27
Professional and Technical	65

I should explain that this was a rough classification involving some arbitrary judgments about the level of meetings, and that the picture is frequently not clearly defined. Deputy Ministers may attend meetings which are primarily technical in nature, and so on.

I might also note that when Dr. K. W. Taylor did this exercise in 1957 he counted 5 conferences at the Ministers level, 13 at the Deputy Ministers level, 18 at the Directors level, and 28 professional or technical meetings. He, also, was modest about the absolute validity of his figures.[2]

This classification does not match up in any way with the broad structural classes previously defined. To take the ministerial conferences only, some of them could be defined as federal-provincial committees as such, while some are inter-provincial, and at least one, the Resource Ministers Council, I have described as a quasi-independent association. Ministers may also meet at non-government organizations such as the Canadian Good Roads Association. Technically, it would be possible for provincial ministers to appear on some of the federal advisory councils, since the composition of some councils includes representation from some organizations to which provincial ministers belong.

3. The Subject Matter

Another obvious classification which may be used is based on the subject matter discussed by the committee. In the lists of conferences and meetings I have referred to, the committees are grouped under headings of Agriculture, Finance, Health and Welfare, and so on. As one would expect, the largest number of committees occur in those fields where the activities of both levels of government overlap the most. For example, in the 1965 calendar of meetings the two areas with the most committees listed are Health and Welfare with 21 and Agriculture with 16.

It is of interest to note that there is a wide variety in the character of the committees which have developed for each class of subject matter. Some sectors have ministerial conferences, others do not. Some have advisory councils, others

---

[2]*Proceedings of the Sixth Annual Conference of the Institute of Public Administration of Canada*, Toronto, 1954, p. 255.

do not. Some have an extensive network of technical sub-committees, while others do not.

4. The Broad Purpose or Type of Consultations

One might also attempt to group the committees according to broad categories of purpose. Some, such as the Plenary Federal Provincial Conference, have very broad terms of reference. Others obviously have a restricted field of activity, as, for example, the National Potato Breeding Committee. Some have elaborately spelled-out terms of reference, perhaps as a part of a formal constitution, requiring them to work toward uniformity of legislation across Canada in their field, or toward objectives of comparable significance. Others have no terms of reference other than to provide an opportunity for an exchange of views on matters of mutual interest. Some are created to advise a minister, others to advise other committees, and so on.

One might define a range of the different kind of purposes which have to be served by intergovernmental consultation in Canada. I should like to suggest the following spectrum of purposes:

a. Public relations. I use the term "public relations" here, even though the public is not involved, to designate the process of getting to know one's counterparts in other governments, to the extent that a sense of *rapport* and conviviality is established. This presumably helps to oil the channels for smoother intergovernmental consultations in future.

b. Professionalization. There are some areas of specialized activity which lie almost entirely within the governments, and the specialists involved tend to want to express themselves as a professional group. A federal-provincial meeting sometimes serves as the vehicle for such expression. This type of gathering does much to advance an area of specialization through the exchange of ideas, and it also permits the development of a brotherly feeling of togetherness.

c. Advancement of knowledge. The exchange of information is a frequent purpose behind the function of a committee. Also, some federal-provincial technical committees are created specifically to inquire into a problem area to learn more about it or to encourage research for this purpose. I believe these committees have convincingly demonstrated the truth in the old adage that eleven heads are better than one.

d. Harmonization. I use this word to describe the process by which purposes are explained, suspicions are assuaged, and conflicts are removed.

e. Coordination. This is a step farther than harmonization. It implies a conscious effect to work together toward some mutually acceptable goal. In our more sceptical moments, we might describe it as the process by which activities which would otherwise be completely unintelligible become merely muddled.

f. Persuasion. This type of consultation is getting closer to the policy level. Governments may use a committee to attempt to influence the actions of others in directions deemed to be desirable.

g. Negotiation and decision-making. At this end of the spectrum is the consultation which results in a decision being reached either through agreement or through compromise. This may sound impressive. Sometimes, however, the decision may be to refer the matter to another committee.

The wide diversity in the committees' terms of reference and the problem in some cases of determining what the terms of reference are, if there are any, would make it a difficult exercise to attempt to assign present committees to these categories. For that matter, many of the committees probably work at some or even most of these objectives at some time or another. However, one might speculate that a more consistent committee structure could be established if it were formed on the basis of an accepted definition of purposes.

Concluding Observations

I hope that the approach I have taken of outlining a number of possible classifications of the federal-provincial committees will have left a reasonable over-all impression of the formally established machinery which exists. By way of conclusion I would like to make a few observations on the relationship between the *need* for consultation between the provinces and the federal government — about which I spoke earlier — and the *machinery that exists* for this consultation. Is the present machinery adequate to meet present and future needs, and how might it be improved?

I think one could say, first of all, that machinery exists in most of the individual program areas where both levels of governments are active. I will go even further and say that in most if not in each of these individual program areas consultation seems to have been reasonably effective. Certainly, if these consultations have had anything to do with the rapid growth in shared-cost programs, I am impressed with their success.

I would say secondly, however, that we have to take a close look at our provision for coordination of this machinery. When a complexity of devices exists to permit consultation on a multitude of intergovernmental activities, we run the risk, unless there is adequate provision for coordination, of having a situation in which the right hand does not know what the left hand is doing. More than once I have seen this happen in international organizations. It is not inconceivable to me that it could happen in federal-provincial relations and that the position taken by the representative of one government at one federal-provincial meeting may not be wholly consistent with the position taken by another representative of the same government on a related question at another meeting.

Another and related observation that could be made on the relationship between the need and the machinery for consultation has to do with the basic economic objectives I have referred to earlier in this paper. The various federal, provincial, and joint programs may be proceeding satisfactorily, taken individually, but how do we assess their combined effect on the economy, or determine which area should receive emphasis relative to another at a particular time? Similarly, what machinery exists to facilitate consultation and coordination with regard to other areas of fiscal and economic management? I note that the federal and provincial ministers of finance and provincial treasurers held a pre-budget meeting for the first time last December. If this new ministerial committee holds annual meetings, as I hope it will, it could well develop into a body which meets this need, at least in part.

Finally, I would like to raise a question concerning the direction in which the process of federal-provincial relations is evolving. At the start we relied largely on the connections built up within the political parties representing Canadians in the House of Commons and in the provincial legislative assemblies. This machinery proved to be not entirely adequate: it was not always reliable, it was often not available when needed, and governments could not hold it responsible. Over the years we developed a considerable number of committees and other devices for consultation. The majority of these provide for contacts among specialists in a wide range of specific areas of government activity. We appear to see now the need for more frequent contacts among those who see the over-all picture of federal-provincial relations. The establishment of units responsible for federal-provincial relations in a broad way in some provinces and within the federal government indicates that our governments are responding to this need. The question which I would like to raise is this: where does this evolutionary process lead us? How far are we going to go in providing machinery for improving intelligence and coordination in Canadian federal-provincial relations?

24   The Machinery of Federal-Provincial Relations: II *

R. M. Burns

The subject we have before us is one of the most easily talked about and most difficult to deal with that we encounter in this presently confused political organism which we call the Canadian Federation. However, in the present mood of self-determination which we share with so many newly emerging nations, it seems likely that we must resolve it or the country will degenerate into a loose "balkan-like" confederacy rather than the national entity so many of us have come to think we know.

It is not my intention to retrace the ground of Mr. Gallant's paper which clearly indicates the scope of the problem and some of the measures currently being taken to meet it. We should by now be reasonably familiar with the various bodies and mechanisms that exist to make the necessary cooperation

*From R. M. Burns, "The Machinery of Federal-Provincial Relations: II", *Canadian Public Administration*, Vol. VIII, No. 4, December 1965, pp. 527-534. Reprinted by permission of the author and the Institute of Public Administration of Canada.

possible. What I hope to be able to do is to treat — in a somewhat subjective manner, perhaps — some of the more important aspects of the question. Some of these are: the continuing intergovernmental contacts at departmental levels, including "ad hoc" committees on particular problems; continuing committees in certain categorical areas; the rather broader interests of the Federal-Provincial Continuing Committee on Fiscal and Economic Matters; the various ministerial gatherings; and the federal-provincial conference themselves.

From what we have been told already and from what we know of our own experience, cooperation between governments is not a new concept in Canada, born of this recent mood of provincial self-determination to which I have referred. But it has of necessity spread more broadly in recent years as our problems have become more interwoven and complex and as our responsibilities have grown.

In some important areas of joint interests, steps taken over the years have been relatively successful and have met the challenge of the changing problems with considerable success. I think here of agriculture, statistics, health, mining, roads, and some areas of education and welfare. In most cases success has been achieved by direct intergovernmental contacts at the official level or through the ad hoc committees to which I have referred, although ministerial interest has not been lacking.

In the resource field, we have a somewhat different approach, with the fairly recent creation of the Council of Resource Ministers. While it is too early to make any final judgment on this somewhat corporate approach to the question of intergovernmental cooperation, there can be no doubt that it has interesting possibilities, especially where there is a predominant provincial interest. Personally I have some reservations with regard to what appear to me to be policy-oriented approaches, but it may be I am seeing shadows where none exist.

It has been in the more general field of finance and economic matters that the successful resolution of our problems by cooperative efforts, while often productive, has proved more difficult. I know that this is not for lack of will but is perhaps due rather to the inevitable connections with basic aspects of government policy — in the natural reluctance of quasi-sovereign governments to accept any limitations on their traditional powers. There is this rather noticeable reluctance in some quarters, both federal and provincial, to accept the fact that intergovernmental cooperation, if it is to be effective, involves some surrender of individual initiative even if it does not involve any surrender of constitutional rights.

Having acknowledged that the ad hoc groups and the departmental relationships appear to work with reasonable success in their limited or specialized areas, and having noted some shortcomings in the broader financial and economic fields, I am brought to more detailed consideration of the functions of the Federal-Provincial Continuing Committee, the meetings of the Ministers of Finance and Provincial Treasurers, the Plenary Conferences and, if I may be permitted, the meetings of Provincial Premiers which have now been in existence long enough to give us some idea of their own direction and purpose.

First to the Continuing Committee on Fiscal and Economic Matters. As Kear indicates in the journal of March, 1963,[1] its greatest successes have been where it has been specifically concerned with particular aspects of proposed or existing fiscal arrangements. This to some extent flows from its original development as the Preparatory Committee of the 1956 conferences, where it had a most auspicious start, but probably it is also due to the fact that its membership is primarily interested in the fiscal approach and finds this a good deal more practicable to deal with than the more nebulous area of economic analysis and planning. Its problems are largely in the short term where decisions and judgments are generally closely aligned with policy.

As it has completed its responsibilities as a preparatory working group in fiscal negotiations, the Committee has tended to transfer its interests to broader areas. Many of these, such as revenue trends, capital markets, and similar financial problems, have been matters of administrative concern to the treasuries in particular. A good deal of interest has been taken in the short- and middle-term economic forecasts.

There has also been consideration of other areas of government involvement, as in health, welfare, technical education, etc., and in such cases it has been the custom for the officers of the departments directly interested to be brought into the discussions.

There has been a great deal of value in such procedures. While the direct results have not always been obvious, the consideration of mutual problems and the advancement of understanding has been most useful indeed. But we must admit that the value is limited in many cases by the fact — as is quite proper — that the committee is an official body and determination of policy is quite beyond its own initiative.

As it is manifestly somewhat frustrating to try to discuss official matters in a policy vacuum, the committee has not always been effective where it has lacked the direction of the responsible ministers. This judgment can be supported by a look at past experience. It was most successful in its earlier years when it had specific and delineated objectives within a frame of policy reference but, when this period was over, it tended to lose its drive and sense of identity.

There were no doubt a number of reasons for this, not the least of which was the loss of some of the more positive personalities from its meetings. The hiatus between fiscal agreements and a consequent lessening of the demand on its energies probably contributed. But most important of all was, I think, a realization of a reduced status, which can largely be attributed to the fact that after the conclusion of the 1957 agreements (in 1956) its services were not used to the same extent, and in the 1959 and 1960 negotiations it played little more than a mechanical role.

If the short history of the committee illustrates anything, it is that a committee of officials can only be a fully effective body if it enjoys the full confidence and appreciation of all governments and in particular of the Ministers

---

[1]A. R. Kear, "Cooperative Federalism: A Study of the Federal-Provincial Committee on Fiscal and Economic Matters", *Canadian Public Administration*, Vol. VI. No. 1, 1963, pp. 43-56.

directly responsible. This shows probably better than anything else that its potential strength lies not so much in its own status as in its role in support of a ministerial group charged in the same area of responsibility, for it is with governments themselves that the power of policy determination and executive authority must remain. I think the relationship of the Continuing Committee to the Tax Structure Committee illustrates an effective use of the resources of this body.

Now, having put all my friends and former colleagues in their places, I turn to their lords and masters, the Ministers. As I have indicated, one of the least effective measures designed to advance the cause of intergovernmental effectiveness and felicity has been the Committee of Ministers of Finance and Provincial Treasurers. This group — and I doubt that its history can justify the use of the term committee — was first convened in early 1959, as a preparatory step to a plenary conference. It has met on two occasions since: in the fall of 1959, and last year. I cannot see where its activities have been crowned with any great success. Part of the difficulty may be in the fact that a number of the Ministers are also the Premiers and are divided in their objectives. Part may be that its interests circulate closely around the area of budgetary policy, a field where "togetherness" is not easily achieved. But it seems to me both necessary and desirable that some greater continuing effort be made to have this important group make a more useful contribution toward cooperative federalism.

It is all too easy to be critical of these limited results to date, and in fairness we must recognize that in trying to bring into regular consultation a group of ministers of divergent political views, all with their own responsibilities in an area where policy determinations are most difficult to reconcile, we are asking a good deal, perhaps more than we can ever hope to achieve. It would be — and I suggest that we must recognize this — quite inconsistent with the present concept of parliamentary responsibility for the Minister of Finance or a Provincial Treasurer to discuss in any but the most general terms the future budgetary policies of his government.

This is not to say, however, that there is no future for the Ministers of Finance and Treasurers operating as a group for mutual benefit. There are many areas of like interests which do not touch directly on the sensitive area of budgetary policy — questions of broad economic and fiscal trends, financial administration, capital markets, and many others. In this way the Ministers could provide an effective background of policy interest in which their officials of the Continuing Committee could work more effectively than they have sometimes been able to do in the past.

The future of the Federal-Provincial Continuing Committee on Fiscal and Economic Matters would, therefore, seem to be in its function as the principal technical and coordinating committee for such a permanent ministerial group charged with the responsibility of the various governments of Canada in the broad fiscal field. In the process it could serve in many useful and effective ways, given the support and direction that flows from positive ministerial policy. However, I do not suggest its relegation to the role of an administrative group. It has a greater part to play in a dynamic and constructive approach to the many and varied problems that will face it. This will bring it close to policy considerations from time to time and it will not be an easy task to draw the line. But with the experience of the past and the willingness to take a few chances that is part of the role of the responsible official, it should be possible — providing the governments wish it to be.

This now brings us to the summit of our structure for intergovernmental cooperation — the Federal-Provincial Plenary Conference. These conferences have a long history, but it is only in very recent times that they seem to have assumed the continuing status that is the product of our current confused relationships.

The conference was originally a consultative body for the exchange of views and information which could then be the subject of report and appropriate action by the respective legislative bodies concerned. Mr. King, at the Conference of 1935, noted this role in the following terms: "A Dominion-Provincial Conference is neither a cabinet not a Parliament. It is an institution which enables the Government of Canada and the governments of the Provinces of Canada to confer together and exchange information which can be presented to the governments concerned and to the Parliament of Canada and the Legislatures of the Provinces."

It is of course unavoidable and even necessary that some statements of government intentions should be made at these conferences and, if these statements are kept in the form of intentions, there can surely be no objections. However, there is a developing tendency for governmental representatives to seek agreements and make firm commitments in matters of policy which have not had the sanction of either Parliament or the provincial legislatures.

I would not want to take the position that government representatives should not express a clear indication of proposed policy. Not to do so would effectively paralyse the conference. But a statement of intention should always clearly be indicated only as a proposal subject to legislative will, which of course it is and must be.

I do not go so far as some who have tried to create in the minds of the public the bogey of the Federal-Provincial Conference as a sort of super-parliament. But this growing tendency toward "summitry" will likely create more problems in the long run than it will solve in the short, for in some cases I suspect the real will of the country could be easily overlooked or misinterpreted and a point of no return reached which would not be generally acceptable.

This seems as good a time as any to make a brief reference to the Conference of Provincial Premiers which started at Premier Lesage's urgings back in 1960. These conferences are not the first in Canada's history, for there have been others in the past, with perhaps less altruistic motives than those of today. There has always been some scepticism as to the value of such meetings. Provinces have not been noted for their ability to form common fronts — probably a very good thing for the nation. But the concern lest these conferences become the vehicle of such a common front or pressure group has been very real in the minds of some. It is, however, to the great credit of the premiers that despite the many temptations so to do, they have all firmly rejected such an approach and held to the principle that matters which involved Canada should not be dealt with at these meetings.

As no official documents other than the usual official communiqués issue from these meetings, it is not possible to form any worthwhile opinion as to their real value. However, what evidence we have would seem to show no great influence directly on the course of events even though they may well have served a useful purpose as a base for greater understanding — and indeed they are reputed to be very pleasant affairs. Perhaps this serves to point up a moral: that without the effective cohesive force of strong central government, unity and direction of purpose are difficult to achieve.

The development of effective means of communication will not come easily, and various alternative mechanisms and approaches will have to be studied and tested before any final answer is likely to be found. Such communication is not enough at the official level alone, it must extend into the policy level as well. There must be consultation before the fact of decision, and such consultation must be reasonably continuous. But how is this all to be achieved?

First of all, I believe very strongly that before we go to the trouble of developing methods, the principals must be willing to accept that cooperative federalism means the surrender of some degree of individual initiative and freedom of action in the common cause. Cooperation is a two-way street. It has its obligations as well as its benefits. Sometimes it has appeared that our various representatives have failed to consider it in these terms.

What I have tried to emphasize throughout these remarks is that the key is in a more effective means of cooperation at the ministerial or policy level. This points to a need to revise our present system of meetings at three levels of responsibility.

First, the Prime Minister of Canada should meet at reasonably regular intervals, perhaps yearly would be sufficient, with provincial premiers. Few advisors and a limited agenda dealing with broad matters of policy which overlap jurisdictional bounds would seem called for. This could in most respects take the place of the present Provincial Premiers' Conferences, which have not so far indicated that they are particularly productive. It would be hoped that in this way some degree of national consensus and mutual understanding could be developed.

Second, the existing Federal-Provincial Plenary Conference could continue for the more specific consideration of the larger problems of policy and, where necessary, matters could be "hived off" to sub-conferences of ministers specifically concerned with the particular affair.

Third, there should continue to be regular meetings of federal and provincial ministers in their appropriate fields of particular interest, as often as required to provide the necessary policy guidance in such fields as agriculture, welfare, health, resource development, and finance. These would, of course, be supplemented as necessary by individual departmental communication. It is under this heading that I would place the rather moribund meetings of Ministers of Finance and Provincial Treasurers in the hope that their mutual interests might develop to the common advantage.

Fourth, underpinning this whole apparatus would have to be the necessary departmental or official technical exchange and collaboration which could go forward along the lines indicated by the ministerial groups. Presumably a coordinating body would be required, and the Federal-Provincial Continuing Committee on Fiscal and Economic Matters would seem the logical centre for this purpose. It would have to continue to be supported as necessary by those additional representatives whose knowledge and experience would be germane to the particular subjects referred to the committee.

In this connection, I hope that when the Tax Structure Committee has made its report every consideration will be given to its possible use as a major coordinating body in the field of taxation. It could perhaps be absorbed by the Committee of Ministers of Finance and Provincial Treasurers, should this latter committee develop the necessary vitality.

It would be idle to undertake such a complex program without adequate commitments of staff, time, and organizational effort by all concerned. Cooperative federalism is not going to be anything more than a subject for pious discussion in the absence of communication on a flexible and consistent basis. The effective work of ministers will depend on this. Ultimately the success of cooperative decision-making must live or die with the success of the liaison mechanism.

For success in any workable measure, governments concerned must be prepared to accept the full and continuing responsibility to work as a federal partnership within the agreed constitutional framework, accepting obligations as well as advantages. I think this applies with special emphasis in the case of many of the provinces, just as I believe that in some cases more than *ex post facto* lip service to consultation with the provinces is necessary on the federal side. It will not be enough to agree in private and disagree for the political benefit of public consumption.

While I have urged the need of a sound organizational background, I have emphasized that it must exist in the partnership and not as a superimposed façade. On analysis, I do not find any strong arguments for a permanent secretariat for Dominion-Provincial Conferences. The position would create or support the concept of a third tier of government, something that I do not think would be generally acceptable.

To the extent that administrative arrangements are required, the Department of Finance and Privy Council Office are fully capable of meeting any demands. The provinces themselves should be able to provide for their own needs within their own organizations.

In concluding these remarks, may I emphasize my belief that the important thing to be remembered is that the machinery of intergovernmental relations is a means to an end and not an end in itself. Certainly, consultation is no substitute for action. I suspect that the people of Canada, with some voluble exceptions, are less concerned about constitutional rights than their political representatives, and are more concerned in obtaining honest and effective government.

25   Cooperative Federalism: A Study of the Federal-Provincial Continuing Committee on Fiscal and Economic Matters*

A. R. Kear

"The sphinx would be a good emblem for Canada itself, put together in defiance of all natural law, yet amazingly solid and permanent, with dominion-provincial relations forming its unsolved riddle and its inscrutable smile."[1] The purpose of this paper is to examine an institution created to solve some of the problems of federalism.

In a country as diverse as ours with a population having a variety of traditions and cultures, that lives in distinguishable economic regions with unique local conditions, and being a highly industrialized community pursuing a variety of occupations with all the complexities inherent in an interdependent society in a welfare state with a mixed economy, good intergovernmental relations are a necessity if Canadians are to move toward broad political, fiscal and economic goals. Dominion-provincial relations are exceedingly complicated and if intergovernmental cooperation, even some degree of coordination, is to be achieved some flexible and creative machinery is necessary to give flesh to the spirit.

The Deputy Provincial Treasurer of Saskatchewan expressed some of his feelings thus:

> There is a surprisingly substantial area of agreement among the provinces, and between them and the federal government. The reason is that they accept common — if broadly defined — goals. The disagreements, which are also substantial, arise because of the difference in emphasis given to these objectives. Furthermore, the grounds upon which disagreements are based constantly shift, since the provinces themselves change their emphasis on their objectives.
>
> Here is the basis for optimism about Dominion-provincial relations. If there were disagreement over the objectives themselves, then the differences would be profound indeed. In fact, they would likely be irreconcilable. But as long as we differ in degree only, and as long as governments change and the differences themselves shift, then it is reasonable to expect continuing improvements in Dominion-provincial fiscal arrangements.[2]

The Continuing Committee on Fiscal and Economic Matters had its birth

*From *Canadian Public Administration*, Vol. VI, No. 1, March 1963, pp. 43-56. Reprinted by permission of the author and the Institute of Public Administration of Canada.

This paper is based on my experience while a member of the Federal Provincial Relations Division of the Department of Finance, and attendance at Committee meetings between 1959 and 1961. Any opinions expressed are personal and do not reflect a statement of official views.

[1]H. Northrop Frye, *By Things Liberal*, Clarke, Irwin, Toronto, 1959, p. 5.

[2]A. W. Johnson, *Federal-Provincial Fiscal Relations — An Optimistic View*; An Address to the Senior Officers Course in Government Administration, Arnprior, Ontario, August 30, 1960, p. 17.

at the meetings of the federal and provincial officials gathered to prepare and assemble information in anticipation of the 1955 Dominion-Provincial Conference. It was formally established at that Dominion-Provincial Conference. Since the Committee has operated for several years, now appears to be an opportune time to examine it and its workings.

This study will describe its history, nature, composition and function, and the relationships between the Continuing Committee and other cooperative devices in our federal system.

The Constitutional Background

What kind of federal system do Canadians want? The Tremblay Report expressed its opinion thus:

> Is the Canadian state in future to be unitary, frankly federal, or will it continue to practice the halting and unaware federalism which carries with it all the inconveniences and none of the advantages of true federalism, and in which current constitutional practices threaten to engulf it?[3]

There would appear to be four general methods of dealing with the problems of modern federalism; and they cannot be sharply delineated one from the other:

first, by a greater centralization of power in the national government;

second, by re-writing sections 91 and 92 of the British North America Act in the light of almost a century of experience;

third, by decentralizing responsibilities following the principles of countervailing power;[4] and

fourth, by a mutual sharing of responsibilities and by making necessary adjustments within the present constitutional arrangements of fiscal and economic powers so that the latter will conform more closely to changing national and social goals.

The Continuing Committee exists to help apply the third and fourth methods. Since formal constitutional changes in the B.N.A. Act are rare, it is not surprising that most attention has been paid until recently to the fourth approach. With a gradual return to peacetime conditions, the "revolt", so to speak, of the provinces by the establishment of the annual Inter-Provincial Premiers' Conference, and the growing strength of provincial political, economic and administrative resources, the third method may assume more prominence in the immediate future.

With respect to the basic principles and techniques upon which fiscal agreements are to be based, the Tremblay Report argued for a financial equalization organism to help the less well endowed provinces. "However, the distinction

---

[3]*Royal Commission of Inquiry on Constitutional Problems*, Quebec, 1956, Summary, p. 25. This report is better known as the Tremblay Report.

[4]The first, second and fourth methods are from R. M. Burns, "Cooperation in Government", *The Canadian Tax Journal*, Vol. VII, No. 1, January-February 1959, pp. 5-15.

must be made between *fiscal equalization*, whose object is to restore to each province the revenues to which it is entitled, and *social equalization*, whose object is to assure the really handicapped provinces of social services in conformity with the minimum standards of the country as a whole."[5]

Some explanation must be advanced as to why this Committee has been established only fairly recently. The reasons lie partly in the fact that relations in a federal state are between governments constitutionally authorized to operate independently and partly because there was not a demonstrable need for some permanent institution for formal cooperation other than correspondence, Dominion-Provincial Conferences, and intermittent meetings. Cooperation and coordination between sovereign governments, it may be argued, may imply some willingness to surrender or dilute their sovereignty and in addition some loss of initiative though not necessarily or inevitably any surrender of constitutional rights. Cooperation is essential where two governments share in governing the same people in the same area. Federal-provincial relations can be viewed as cooperation between *de jure* equals and not as between principal and agents. In addition, coordination takes place when policies are shifted in the light of policies implemented by another government. Coordination includes the situation where a government seeks advice in the implementation of a program. Cooperation and coordination in a federal system evolve from many currents of policy, personalities, and fiscal and economic conditions. Cooperative federalism must be viewed in its context, arising from the acceptance by Canadians of certain national goals, including social welfare measures, low levels of unemployment, modification of industrial strife, defence policies arising from the global situation, and other national fiscal and economic policies.

History of the Continuing Committee

The first attempt at cooperation occurred after Confederation when for several years there was a Secretary of State for the Provinces. Lack of any concrete purpose and function led to the abolition of this office in 1873. Besides, the Fathers assumed that intergovernmental relations would be conducted through the office of the Lieutenant-Governor. Coordination developed by correspondence and visits by Ministers and officials, which was sometimes consummated by formal agreements, and, beginning shortly before World War I, by the establishment and later the extension of the conditional grant and its shared-cost techniques of administration.

Dominion-Provincial and Inter-Provincial Conferences have been held over the years to settle and discuss specific issues. At the Dominion-Provincial Conference in 1935 several sub-committees were set up to study the problems on the agenda. It was decided to establish a permanent committee of the Minister of Finance and all the Provincial Treasurers. Nothing came of this proposal, although Mr. King was in favour of continuity and permanence because cooperation was so important.

The Rowell-Sirois Commission came to the same conclusions and stressed

[5]Tremblay Report, Summary, *op. cit.*, p. 25.

that means should be found to promote cooperation, so essential to efficiency and economy in administration. The Commission was impressed with the problems arising from divided jurisdiction and was hopeful of promoting cooperation to advance the public welfare.

> Two separate governments, neither one of which has any authority over the other, must agree on objectives, on the means of reaching them, and on the daily application of these means to new situations.[6]

The Commissioners adopted a Nova Scotia suggestion and recommended a permanent secretariat to serve annual Dominion-Provincial Conferences to facilitate cooperation.[7]

Less precise references were made at the 1945 Reconstruction Conference to some kind of permanent board at the ministerial level with a secretariat. Two continuing committees were proposed by Ontario: The Dominion-Provincial Coordinating Committee of Ministers with executive powers for timing public investment and distributing fiscal-need payments to the provinces; and the Dominion and Provincial Economic Board composed of officials to examine and advise on financial problems of mutual concern. These proposals received broad support but were not adopted. Mr. Duplessis supported in general terms the ideas put forward for cooperation, especially the creation of an officials' committee. And later, Mr. King

> . . . suggested that one of the sub-committees of the Conference which had been set up, the Economic Committee, might continue to operate with a permanent secretariat. He suggested that this committee might meet twice yearly to exchange information at the technical level and put its members in a position to advise their respective governments on ways and means of furthering the objectives of the agreement and on the other subjects of mutual and national interest. This proposal actually had much in common with that which finally came to fruition with the setting up of the Continuing Committee ten years later.[8]

At the time of signing the 1952 agreement Mr. Frost, like Mr. Drew in 1945, urged the constitution of a Continuing Committee of Ministers. The objectives for this committee were to study the Canadian tax structure, including the distribution of taxes and revenues and the allocation of governmental functions, and to report on the fiscal measures best suited for all governments. Mr. Frost also urged a permanent secretariat but did not go into details.

Over the years there was a growing recognition of the need for some better form of fiscal cooperation and coordination. While the Department of Finance at Ottawa handled the periodic problems of intergovernmental fiscal relations, it was not until 1954 when a senior official with many years of provincial experience was recruited from a provincial government to study and deal with all matters of federal-provincial finance that the need for continuing considera-

---

[6]*Report of the Royal Commission on Dominion-Provincial Relations,* reprinted, Queen's Printer, Ottawa, 1954, Book I, p. 255.

[7]*Ibid.,* Book II, p. 275.

[8]R. M. Burns, *op. cit.,* p. 10.

tion and attention was acknowledged. He was named Director of the Federal-Provincial Relations Division, a new branch of the department. The Director became responsible for some continuing if rather extraneous duties, such as the administration in 1954 of the Municipal Grants Act R.S.C. 1952, C. 182, as amended, and the Municipal Winter Works Incentive program in 1958, as far as this program concerned the Department of Finance working in cooperation with the Department of Labour. The Director is the senior adviser in the Department of Finance to the minister and the deputy minister on federal-provincial relations. He is responsible for the administration of the fiscal agreements for 1952-57 and 1957-62. The Director had tried to visit each province at least once a year. Sometimes these visits, as in 1959 and 1960, were undertaken to draw up agendas in advance of meetings of the Minister's Committee and the Dominion-Provincial Conference. Besides these more systematic visits the Director has travelled to provincial capitals to discuss particular problems as they arose. When the Prime Minister was invited to attend the Inter-Provincial Premiers' Conference in December, 1960, the Director went as an observer for the federal government (a task that has become customary).

This Director was useful in helping to prepare the Dominion's approach to the April 1955 preliminary or agenda Conference. At this Conference there were some vague misgivings and doubts as to the need and value of a continuing organization. Some support came from Premier Frost in his official submission when he suggested the creation of a Federal-Provincial Technical and Advisory Committee on a permanent basis as a fact-finding body with no executive powers. Premier Hicks of Nova Scotia, Bennett of British Columbia and Douglas of Saskatchewan made similar proposals.

As a result, the Preparatory Committee for the Federal-Provincial Conference was created following the April Federal Provincial Conference under the chairmanship of the Deputy Minister of Finance of Canada and his counterparts in the provincial treasury departments. The Director was appointed Secretary to this Preparatory Committee. Five meetings were held between April and September to provide the technical and statistical information needed for the main conference in October. The Dominion Bureau of Statistics assisted by preparing a publication of comparative statistics of public finance (publications now appear regularly).

Premier Douglas of Saskatchewan specifically recognized the value of the Committee's work at the main conference in 1955. Nova Scotia, New Brunswick and British Columbia supported the idea, also, with no province raising a dissenting vote. The press communiqué issued at the close of the Conference on October 3 stated:

> By general agreement the Conference established a committee of federal and provincial officials to meet from time to time to exchange information and examine technical problems in the field of federal-provincial fiscal and economic relations. Representation on this committee will be designated by the Prime Minister or Premier of each government respectively and the chairman will be designated by the Prime Minister of Canada. The Com-

mittee will not take collective action but each of its members will report to his own government on the subjects discussed.[9]

All meetings and the work of the Committee were to be confidential and, like any intradepartmental work and most discussions at Dominion-Provincial Conferences, meetings would not be open to the press. Part of the understanding implied that the Committee would not make corporate recommendations unless especially requested to do so. The latter rule of operation avoids completely even a hint that the Committee as a body could exercise any executive power or be directly responsible for policy, or that the two levels of government must agree. The Committee first met on February 2, 1956, in Ottawa.

In 1956 the Quebec Royal Commission of Inquiry on Constitutional Problems recommended the creation of a permanent secretariat for Federal-Provincial Conferences.

Status of the Committee

The Continuing Committee, a creature of the Federal-Provincial Conference, is its Secretariat. The Committee lacks original jurisdiction and is answerable ultimately to the Conference. Its subordinate status[10] is pointed up further by the fact that Committee members are also responsible to the principals composing the Conference. This is the constitutional position of the Committee, but to what body or to whom is the Committee answerable when it is not working under the general direction of the Conference? (This question will be discussed later.)

Nature and Composition of the Committee

Representation on the Committee follows the statement in the 1955 press communiqué. The chairman, who has a kind of authority associated with his office in the federal government, is the Deputy Minister of Finance and, in his absence, is either the Clerk of the Privy Council or a senior officer of the Department of Finance. In most cases provincial members are treasury deputies although, in some provinces, the spokesman is an official with similar interests and responsibilities. Territorial and municipal governments are not represented on the Committee, but new provinces would join the Committee. While the Committee consists of eleven people, and there has been a small turnover in its personnel, attendance at meetings averages between twenty-five and thirty. Both levels of government normally include other officials as may be appropriate to the occasion. The latter officials, including the Federal-Provincial Relations Division, constitute the Secretariat of the Committee.

The Secretary of the Committee is the Director of the Federal-Provincial Relations Division of the federal Department of Finance.[11] His responsibilities

---

[9]*Proceedings of the Federal-Provincial Conference 1955*, Queen's Printer, Ottawa, 1955, p. 127.

[10]K. C. Wheare, *Government by Committee*, The Clarendon Press, Oxford, 1955, p. 5.

[11]*Cf.* K. C. Wheare, *op. cit.*, p. 36. The secretary is usually an official of the central government in British Committees to inquire, to advise and to negotiate.

are those usually associated with a secretary including the supervision of the preparation of notes of Committee discussions by a rapporteur from the Division. The Secretary provides the Committee with information both when it is assembled and when its members are dispersed across the country. When the Committee undertakes research, he is the central coordinator and with his staff he helps to prepare the required material. In his other role as Director, he must be informed about the federal-provincial fiscal relations of all federal departments and agencies. The second secretary, unlike the first, was chosen in September, 1959, from the federal civil service as most of the staff of the Division have been. Without in any way implying any criticism of the past or the present Secretary, who has also had some provincial experience, it is an open question whether the Secretary should come from the federal government or from the provinces. If the latter is to be the case, internal promotion within the federal Department of Finance would be stifled. There are three officers in the Division, including the Director. I believe quite strongly that the personnel of the Division should be drawn from all parts of the country. While no doubt the department has tried very hard to meet this ideal, failure to meet it in the future may pose serious problems when a Federal-Provincial Relations Department may be established. As a start toward achieving this ideal, I suggest that the next addition to the staff be a French-speaking Canadian from Quebec, then the next a person from the Atlantic Provinces.

What Does the Committee Do?

Because of the nature of the Committee's role its terms of reference are broad and are in conformity with the 1955 declaration: "Discussion and exchange of information on fiscal and economic matters, and to examine questions that may be referred to it by the federal-provincial Premier's Conference."[12] The terms of reference are clearly understood by all members. With the creation of the Committee of Ministers of Finance and Provincial Treasurers in 1959, which met twice (July 6-7 and October 15-16), the terms of reference were extended informally to embrace the study of problems under the direction of the Ministerial Committee. The Continuing Committee's role is neutral concerning policy as the Committee membership is concerned primarily with examining all facets of problems and presenting the facts to the Federal-Provincial Conference, the Ministerial Committee, and to their own individual ministers.

Much of the Committee's work is concentrated in the areas of concurrent or overlapping jurisdiction and administration. Since the members are at the deputy minister level they are concerned with "top level administration, which is sometimes almost indistinguishable from policy questions . . ."[13] The committee members agree on facts, clarify problems, discuss memoranda submitted by members, but make no independent decisions, take no votes, exercise no executive powers

[12]K. W. Taylor, "Co-ordination in Administration", *Proceedings*, The Institute of Public Administration of Canada, Toronto, 1957, p. 261. The premier's Conference is different from the Inter-Provincial Conference of Provincial Premiers and is a Dominion Provincial Conference.

[13]*Ibid.*, p. 255.

as a committee, do not lobby as a body and do not bind their principals in any way. They do however pursue a consensus of views, and a collective judgment, indulge in cooperative studies, and participate in the fiscal discussions that constitute the bulk of their daily responsibilities. Firm agreements between governments are made more possible when the Committee has reached a consensus.

It is not possible to describe the inner operations of the Committee and what approach it takes to questions under consideration because its meetings are held in camera. Part of the difficulty arises because members may touch on and influence policy without having the power to direct or ultimately determine policy. The Committee has been invaluable in settling purely administrative problems arising during the negotiations at the ministerial level for the 1957-62 and 1962-67 fiscal agreements. Its work concerning these five-year fiscal agreements passes through these stages before the cycle is repeated: preparation, finalization, agreement, operation and revision. The Committee has no set approach to problems. The only exception arose when it worked out procedures, at the request of the Ministers' Committee in 1959, that were accepted by all governments in 1960 for the payment and accounting of monies under conditional grant and shared-cost programs. Its most important work lies in the five-year taxation arrangements.

At least two meetings are held each year, one in the spring in Ottawa and the other in the fall. Sittings last up to four or five days. The fall meeting usually follows the annual Conference of the Institute of Public Administration of Canada. Normally the Committee also meets following a formal Federal-Provincial Conference or a meeting of the Finance Minister's Committee. All meetings are held in camera, no press communiqués are issued, and agreed minutes are not adopted as they would be more binding than the extensive unofficial notes.

The Committee is interested in both general and specific subjects, those of continuing and long-range significance, and those that arise periodically, rarely or only once. Some questions of intergovernmental relations are unchanging in nature although personalities, time, fiscal and economic conditions influence the importance and relevance of specific topics or aspects of them. Questions of fiscal administrative cooperation arise repeatedly and, in the case of the procedures for payment and accounting under conditional grant and shared-cost programs, discussions led to new arrangements based completely on agreement having been reached by the Committee, after the Committee of Ministers of Finance and Provincial Treasurers had asked the Committee for a report.[14] While the Continuing Committee is useful to all governments for airing irritations and new suggestions concerning responsibilities not coming directly under treasury control, it does not act as a review body for decisions reached by other federal-provincial committees of officials.

A knowledge of fiscal information, particularly the latest estimate of payments under the current federal-provincial fiscal arrangements, is eagerly sought after by the provincial members. All this information is given on a confidential and

---

[14]*Dominion-Provincial Conference, 1960*, Queen's Printer, Ottawa, 1960, p. 13.

unofficial basis and is not binding in any way upon the federal authorities.

As the name of the Committee may suggest, discussions of economic conditions are of less importance than fiscal matters. The custom has developed that at the fall meeting the members report on the economic situations in their own jurisdictions as a means of exchanging mutually useful information that is of assistance in their daily responsibilities. No special meetings are called to discuss the economic situation and these discussions take place after the main business is completed. The Committee may be becoming another important forum for the discussion of national economic affairs. It would be premature to comment upon the effect of these discussions. Perhaps the Committee of Ministers of Finance and Provincial Treasurers should discuss economic conditions also, especially because the ministers could talk about policy.

How does the Continuing Committee Fit into the Fabric of Intergovernmental Relations?

The Continuing Committee on Fiscal and Economic Matters is the most important of many committees furnishing cooperation and a degree of coordination in fiscal and program administration between Ottawa and the provincial capitals. A good many of the committees discussed in an article by Mr. K. W. Taylor[15] are concerned primarily with the implementation of programs and services to the public. However, only the Continuing Committee is charged with the role of cooperation in the general field of fiscal and economic matters, the real bedrock of governmental operations and the second most important function of government. The Committee is an important keystone to the whole federal system and has relations, both as a body and through its members acting in their normal capacities, with other cooperative machinery. Committee members attend all Dominion-Provincial Conferences in their role as advisers to their own governments and then meet in the Committee. The same procedure takes place in respect to the Committee of Ministers of Finance and Provincial Treasurers. Less direct relations, and with increasing remoteness, are maintained when the Director, as a federal observer, attended the Inter-Provincial Premiers' Conference in December, 1960; with the Secretary as Director attending meetings of federal government committees concerned with the Territories; and once in April, 1959, when a member of the Federal-Provincial Relations Division attended a meeting at which the Canadian Federation of Mayors and Municipalities presented a brief to the Cabinet.

Conclusions

While this paper has described the Continuing Committee on Fiscal and Economic Matters and the environment in which it functions, six questions need answering.

What should be the proper structure for federal-provincial fiscal relations in Canada? There is no permanent answer to this question but the Continuing

---

[15]K. W. Taylor, *op. cit.*, p. 251.

Committee is a most vital forum for working out a moving answer as circum-stances change. One criticism of the Committee's structure was expressed at the July, 1960, Dominion-Provincial Conference. Premier Lesage of Quebec felt that the Continuing Committee concept was inadequate from several points of view:

> We propose that a permanent Secretariat for Federal-Provincial Conferences be established and that it be financed and administered jointly by the Federal and Provincial Governments. We believe that with such a permanent secre-tariat, the Federal-Provincial meetings at the ministerial or the official level would be better prepared and more fruitful. Moreover, such a secretariat would establish intergovernmental relations on a permanent and continuous basis.[16]

At the present time the Federal-Provincial Relations Division by itself is the Secretariat neither to Conferences nor to the Committee. Establishment of a Secretariat to the Inter-Provincial Premiers' Conference should meet, in part, provincial needs.

How does the Continuing Committee square with the theory and realities of a federal union as we know it? It is possible only to allude to the intricate theories of a federal state rather than enter into a lengthy discussion. Provinces have some of the attributes of nation states. Dominion-Provincial relations ex-hibit some of the characteristics of international relations, especially when it is realized that both levels of government encompass concentrations of political and economic power that for the most part operate independently of each other. There is no overriding authority for cooperation or coordination other than the public. But one cannot pursue this line of reasoning too far for Canadian federal-ism exhibits a growing degree of interdependence as the public requires govern-ments at all three levels to expand their functions and cooperate in an increasing range of activities. Hence, a body such as the Continuing Committee is valuable to promote cooperation and its existence is proof of growing federal-provincial cooperation in the post-World War II years.

A third question is: What, more precisely, is the nature of the Continuing Committee? Through usage it has been woven into the fabric of cooperative fed-eralism and it represents a marked step beyond the classical definition of federal-ism. It is now a constitutional organism based on mutual consent as to its continuing existence and purposes, operating in the fiscal world that joins policy and administration. The Committee can be compared to diplomacy at the official or ambassadorial rather than the ministerial level where ministers may commit their governments. The Committee cannot and does not exercise any executive power as a body even though individual members do exercise power within their own jurisdictions. Members of the Committee influence and are influenced by delegates from the other levels of government. In their delegate role, members can bind their principals only to the extent the principals permit and members usually report back to them for instructions. Even in their Com-mittee role, members never abdicate their prime function as advisers to their own governments. Members are delegates of their governments and are not repre-

---

[16]*Dominion-Provincial Conference, 1960, op. cit.,* p. 126.

sentatives to a supragovernmental body. Members are not expected to give up their provincial or federal sentiments but members do usually observe a restraint and tact arising from their membership. The committee helps to ensure technical continuity between Dominion-Provincial and Ministerial Conferences, brings together documentation, establishes contact between the fiscal experts of the two senior levels of government and prepares and facilitates the exchange of views. Whereas Australia has developed the Commonwealth Grants Commission, a quasi-independent body that determines fiscal need subsidies and centralizes debt adjustment, Canada has not adopted the recommendation of the Rowell-Sirois Commission for a Finance Commission. Instead the quinquennial fiscal arrangements are hammered out by federal-provincial conferences of heads of governments, assisted since 1956 by the Continuing Committee. This system is more practical, flexible and fluid than the Australian and is more suited to our plural cultural society. This system provides that politicians make policy decisions ultimately rather than experts, no matter how highly regarded the latter may be.

The fourth question is: is the Committee just an advisory body or does it also negotiate solutions? While the Committee, representative of all the interests that need to be accommodated, does negotiate on some problems, this is a secondary aspect of its work. Members do not negotiate to the extent of making speeches as this is the role of their political superiors. Members do negotiate and compromise on solutions but only to the extent permitted by their principals. Pursuing a consensus approaches negotiation to the extent that the solution is acceptable to the member governments if it is also remembered that members are not delegates from equally powerful governments. The quinquennial tax agreements are based in part on the consensus of fiscal agreements reached by the Committee. A clear example of administrative cooperation arose between July 1959 and July 1960 when after complaints from provincial governments ". . . that the claims, accounting and audit procedures in connection with many of the shared-cost programs were unnecessarily complicated . . ."[17] the problems were referred to the Continuing Committee for study and report. The Prime Minister said, "The Government of Canada has approved the recommendations *agreed upon* by the committee of officials and is prepared to give effect to them as rapidly as possible."[18]

Fifth: Has the Committee adequate research resources to deal properly with the questions it faces? Each government has done the research necessary to prepare its delegates for meetings, except during the period when the Ministers of Finance Committee met and then cooperative research studies were undertaken. Are the present governmental research activities adequate? I do not believe that the Committee would then exercise corporate power directly. Acting as a body, even under supervision, might mean the beginning of another "force" in federal-provincial relations and the Committee should not play this role. Cooperative research studies are a better solution. Other solutions should be sought to the problems arising from the increasing complexity of intergovernmental relations.

[17]*Dominion-Provincial Conference 1960*, p. 13. The Prime Minister is speaking.
[18]*Ibid.*, p. 13, my italics.

Finally, does the Committee operate under the best conditions to enable it to do its work? It meets under political direction provided by Federal-Provincial Conferences and the Finance Ministers' Committee (when this body was meeting). It also meets without political direction, except that provided by members' individual ministers, during the technical administration of the tax agreements between the quinquennial negotiations. Should the Committee meet under continuous political direction, remembering that unlike intragovernmental committees it has no continuous political head, or should its present ambivalent position be continued? Professor W. J. M. MacKenzie writing about the British government says:

> Even when a committee is formally appointed with limited terms of reference and a direction to report back for authority to act, its job is still to reach decisions. It will only advance business if it goes back to the main body saying 'These points are clear; accept these, give us direction on the others' .... [19]

Business is still advanced now, but I feel that the Committee operates best under political direction because the sense of purpose is stronger, because the locus of responsibility is clearer, and because as civil servants they feel more secure of goals than when forced by circumstances to carve out a role for themselves. It is a fine tribute to Canadian civil servants that governments permit the Committee to meet without continuous political direction. Perhaps the situation would be improved if the Finance Ministers' Committee met regularly. Also, economic policy could be discussed by the Finance Ministers, in addition to the exchange of fiscal information by the Continuing Committee. The lack of regular meetings of the Finance Ministers' Committee suggests that Canadian governments are not willing to take this further step toward greater cooperation and coordination in fiscal economic policy. Since 1960 the Commonwealth Economic Consultative Council, composed at the highest level of the Finance and Economic Ministers of the Commonwealth, has met on several occasions for consultation on economic matters.

What of the Future?

> At any rate, we are likely to have to live for a long time with the equivocal structure called cooperative federalism. It has arisen because several separate governments share a divided responsibility for regulating a single economic and social structure. It is most unlikely that any constitution could be devised which would enable each to perform its specific functions adequately without impinging seriously on the others. So their activities are inevitably mingled, and cooperative arrangements must be worked out.[20]

As a device for improving the standards of communication, cooperation and

---

[19]W. J. M. MacKenzie, "Committees in Administration", *Public Administration*, Vol. XXXI, Autumn 1953, p. 238.

[20]J. A. Corry, "Constitutional Trends and Federalism", in R. M. Clark (ed.), *Canadian Issues: Essays in Honour of Henry F. Angus*, University of Toronto Press, Toronto, 1961, p. 20.

coordination, the Continuing Committee is in a vital position to advance harmonious intergovernmental relations and to achieve that sane balance between the tendencies of centralization and decentralization, nationalism and provincialism, which is the basis of a federal system and on which true Canadian unity must rest. As a forum for the discussion of national fiscal and economic conditions, the Continuing Committee may grow in value. Finally, if the Finance Ministers' Committee were to operate on a continuing basis with the additional task of planning Canada's economic growth, the Continuing Committee would be an excellent advisory intelligence agency.

Postscript

This article was written before all the reports of the Royal Commission on Government Organization became available. The Royal Commission recommended that the Federal-Provincial Relations Division be given enlarged terms of reference and increased staff to serve these needs of the federal government:

> To review federal-provincial consultative and cooperative arrangements generally.
> To stimulate federal initiatives in areas where existing arrangements appear inadequate.
> To formulate general principles for the removal of existing anomalies and to guide further federal initiatives.
> To advise departments and the Treasury Board on the possible use of provincial administrative machinery to meet federal needs.[21]

If these recommendations were adopted the Continuing Committee would be a useful instrument to advance federal-provincial cooperation from the federal viewpoint. As for the provinces, the Committee would be useful to ensure that federal initiatives did not harm provincial interests by using the principles and practices of countervailing power described previously as the third method of cooperative federalism.

26   Le "fédéralisme coopératif" ou le nouveau visage de la centralisation *

J. M. Leger

C'est sous le signe du "fédéralisme coopératif" que va s'ouvrir la semaine pro-

---

[21]The Royal Commission on Government Organization, *Supporting Services for Government* (continued), Vol. 3, Queen's Printer, Ottawa, 1962, pp. 124-131, contains an initial brief description of Federal-Provincial Cooperation in Joint and Allied Services.
*From *Le Devoir*, Montréal, Mardi, 3 Septembre, 1963. Reprinted by permission of the author and *Le Devoir*. For a translation see the *Canadian Forum*, October 1963, pp. 155-156.

chaine la grande saison des conférences fédérales-provinciales: le 9 septembre,
réunion consacrée au projet de régime pan-canadien de retraite universelle;
quelque temps plus tard, conférence sur les grands axes routiers; en novembre,
la première d'une série de réunions sur le partage des ressources fiscales. Et il
est fort possible que d'autres rencontres s'ajoutent à ce calendrier déjà chargé.

L'expression de "fédéralisme coopératif" lancée à Ottawa voici quelques mois
a fait fortune dans certains milieux et a notamment été reprise par une large
partie de la presse de langue anglaise. Notons tout de suite le pléonasme: qui
dit fédéralisme, en effet, dit forcément coopération; le fédéralisme est impossible
là où il n'y a ni volonté ni moyens de coopération, là où il n'y a pas intention
ferme de respect mutuel des juridictions. Le fait d'insister lourdement aujourd-
'hui sur le caractère "coopératif" du fédéralisme canadien ne peut être que
l'aveu implicite d'un échec, l'expression d'un repentir ou celle d'un voeu pieux.

Qu'est-ce donc que le "fédéralisme coopératif"? Quelles conceptions, quels
soucis inédits véhicule cette formule dont on pourrait croire, à entendre certains
hommes politiques, qu'elle a valeur de panacée? On nous présente ce prétendu
néo-fédéralisme comme l'expression d'un tournant historique dans les relations
entre Ottawa et les Etats provinciaux, comme l'aube d'une ère nouvelle et la
reconnaissance implicite par le gouvernement central de ce qu'il a trop longtemps
agi comme si les provinces n'existaient pas. La formule aurait politiquement du
sens et serait acceptable (malgré son caractère pléonastique) si elle marquait la
soudaine et ferme résolution du gouvernement central de renoncer à intervenir
dans les domaines réservés aux Etats provinciaux et d'évacuer sans retard les
champs qui ne relèvent pas de sa juridiction.

Nouvelle formule, même réalité

Or à quoi assistons-nous? Exactement au phénomène contraire. L'expression de
"fédéralisme coopératif" s'accompagne d'un nouvel et vigoureux assaut contre
certaines prérogatives des Etats provinciaux et d'une nouvelle manifestation de
la philosophie centralisatrice qui est, en vérité, sous-jacente à la constitution de
1867 et que les gouvernements d'Ottawa sont fatalement portés à incarner de
plus en plus dans les faits.

Ainsi, a-t-on salué comme une expression de "fédéralisme coopératif" la
conférence de fin juillet et l'accord qui l'a suivie: pourtant, malgré les modifications et les aménagements divers, malgré l'alternative offerte au Québec en
particulier, personne ne peut nier qu'il s'est agi là d'un nouveau progrès de la
centralisation et d'une violation de l'esprit et de la lettre de la constitution; par
le biais de la lutte au chômage et des "travaux d'hiver", le gouvernement central
est entré dans le domaine des affaires municipales. C'est encore au nom de ce
fédéralisme coopératif qu'est convoquée une conférence sur le projet fédéral de
caisse générale de retraite, par quoi Ottawa continue d'accaparer l'important
secteur de la sécurité sociale; ce sera sous le même signe que, d'ici un an, Ottawa
invitera les gouvernements provinciaux à étudier un projet de système fédéral de
bourses pour les étudiants des universités et "collèges", etc.

En somme, Ottawa veut "aider les provinces à remplir leurs obligations" en même temps qu'il cherche au nom de "l'unité nationale", du "bien commun canadien", de l'efficacité et de l'uniformisation, à partager avec les provinces le domaine de leur souveraineté.

Faire coopérer les provinces . . . à la centralisation

L'entreprise ne manque pas d'habileté: il s'agit de faire consacrer par les Etats provinciaux eux-mêmes leur démission progressive, de les amener, sous le couvert de la coopération et par le moyen de la consultation approfondie, généralisée, à s'associer à l'insidieux et patient effort de centralisation. Bien sûr, deux fois sur trois, Ottawa devra réviser son projet initial, consentir des aménagements, des formules d'option, des régimes particuliers pour telle ou telle province: peu lui importera, l'essentiel aura été acquis, le principe de son intervention aura été admis, fût-ce de mauvaise grâce, le mécanisme de contrôle aura été mis en place. Le reste sera affaire de temps, de sens politique, de pressions exercées au bon moment, de moyens financiers.

Dans la fédération canadienne, Ottawa assume déjà toute la souveraineté externe et une large partie de la souveraineté interne; il entend évidemment (il l'a suffisamment démontré depuis 1945) conquérir par étapes la partie de souveraineté interne qui lui échappe. Il tente d'abord de pratiquer la "co-souveraineté", de partager avec les Etats provinciaux la juridiction de ceux-ci, ensuite il l'assume totalement.

C'est uniquement dans le cas de mesures intéressant les domaines de juridiction provinciale (municipalité, sécurité sociale, enseignement, travail, santé, planification, aménagement du territoire, etc.) qu'Ottawa découvre les vertus du fédéralisme coopératif, c'est-à-dire d'une formule qui lui permette d'intervenir là où, jusqu'à présent, il n'avait pas à le faire. Nous assistons au début de la plus redoutable offensive centralisatrice encore déclenchée par Ottawa, d'une offensive d'autant plus dangereuse qu'elle porte le masque de la coopération: nous n'imposons rien, nous vous offrons de vous aider à faire face à vos obligations, de partager avec vous un terrible fardeau et des tâches difficiles, de vous fournir des moyens financiers, techniques et même, si vous l'acceptez, un cadre juridique . . . ce qui importe ce n'est pas de discuter "mesquinement" le partage des ressources et des compétences mais bien d'assurer ensemble le progrès commun de tous les Canadiens . . . et comment ne pas admettre que le gouvernement central est le mieux équipé, à tous égards, pour remplir cette mission dans tous les domaines, avec, bien sûr, la "coopération" des provinces!

Seul est dupe qui le veut bien

Le "fédéralisme coopératif" est évidemment le nouveau visage de la centralisation, la formule et le slogan de la centralisation habile et perfide. Avec une naïveté déconcertante, de braves gens veulent voir dans le souci nouveau d'Ottawa de multiplier les conférences avec les provinces l'indice d'une ère nouvelle: vous voyez bien que la centralisation est révolue, Ottawa consulte désormais les gouvernements provinciaux! Mais sur quoi les consulte-t-il et que leur propose-t-il, sinon de nouvelles incursions du gouvernement central dans les domaines de juridiction provinciale ou l'extension de l'ingérence déjà accomplie dans tel ou tel secteur? Imaginerait-on un seul instant la convocation par Ottawa d'une conférence fédérale-provinciale pour étudier les modalités du retrait par le gouvernement central de tout le champ de la sécurité sociale, l'évacuation par lui du domaine des impôts directs ou, encore, pour faire un examen critique de la politique étrangère du Canada? Poser la question, c'est y répondre. Le "fédéralisme coopératif" a une seule signification et joue à sens unique: ce sera sans doute l'une des plus monumentales duperies du siècle.

L'enterprise est d'ailleurs favorisée par la fausse conception qu'entretiennent trop de gens, même dans le Québec, du système fédéral, de l'image qu'ils s'en font: celle d'une pyramide, couronnée par Ottawa. Dans cette vision grossière, et qu'entretiennent naturellement les centralisateurs, il y a, à la base, les munici-palités, ensuite les gouvernements provinciaux ou "régionaux", enfin, le "grand gouvernement", celui qui est comptable du "bien commun de tout le Canada", c'est-à-dire Ottawa. Il est clair que cette conception est pratiquement admise par l'immense majorité des anglophones, pour qui Ottawa est "le gouvernement national" et a naturellement primauté sur les provinces et priorité dans presque tous les ordres.

La centralisation est dans la constitution, elle est dans la mentalité du Canada anglais, elle est dans la volonté des gouvernements d'Ottawa comme dans l'esprit de la fonction publique fédérale. A moins qu'il ne capitule dans une cascade de "pis-aller" (ce qui hélas n'est pas exclu), le gouvernement du Québec va se rendre compte qu'il est engagé dans une bataille décisive, permanente, de plus en plus dure et sur tous les plans, bataille qui ne prendra fin que par l'éclatement de la fédération ou l'adoption d'une constitution entièrement nouvelle, de type réellement confédéral.

27   Co-operative Federalism *

Jean-Luc Pepin

To my mind, co-operative federalism is the best answer to the two main political problems which Canada must solve to guarantee her political future: the prob-lem of relations between the central government and the regional governments, that of Quebec in particular; the problem of relations between French-speaking

*From a translation in *The Canadian Forum*, Vol. 44, No. 527, December 1964, pp. 206-210. A speech to the Conference de l'Institut canadien des Affaires publiques, September 12, 1964, by the author who was then the member of Parliament for Drummond-Arthabaska and Parliamentary Secretary to the Minister of Trade and Commerce. Reprinted by permission of the author and the publisher. Italics are the author's.

and English-speaking Canadians. These two problems are intimately related.

Any political system involves 1) a philosophy, that is, a concept of man, society and political action . . . ; 2) a technique of government. Technique is useless without philosophy . . . and vice versa.

Co-operative federalism does not escape this rule.

The philosophy of co-operative federalism

. . . First of all, after several others, I would like to warn my fellow French Canadians against the *cult* (I mean the excessive concern) for the particularities of race, language, culture, nation and state. . . . All these particularities which some people delight in over-stressing, in dramatizing (to such an extent that we are given the impression that, for example, between the French culture and the English culture there is a gap which cannot be bridged, that English institutions are totally incompatible with the French mentality), . . . have their importance, but only a relative one: they are useful only inasmuch as they serve man. And then, not exclusively, as every language, every culture and every nation is largely made up of borrowings. Voltaire, who before Montesquieu and de Tocqueville and others since them, had studied the Anglo-saxons carefully, write: "The English have taken good advantage of the works in our language; we should in turn borrow from them, having loaned so much to them. The English and our-selves came only after the Italians who in everything were our masters, and whom we have surpassed in a few things. I do not know to which of the three nations we should give preference, *but fortunate is he who can gauge their various merits.*" Therefore, there should be no question of opposing cultures, languages, and nations within Canada. We should rather seek to link them, achieving a syn-thesis mindful of the rights and obligations of each of them.

Let us therefore guard ourselves against exaggeration. We French Canadians, should not switch from a stupid inferiority complex to a stupid superiority com-plex; we should not let our lazy shyness of yesterday be converted into pre-tentious arrogance. *The assertion of oneself does not compel us to deny the rights of others.* The value of our quiet revolution stems from the fact that it is revolt against ourselves, against our past deficiencies, and especially a will to become competent, to achieve progress for the future. Let us therefore assume with vigour, assurance and enthusiasm our rightful place in Canadian and world society.

It seems to me that with particularities respected, protected and constantly enriched, the building of a cooperative federal state can allow Canadians of French, English and other origins to give the world a fine example of political wisdom and human brotherhood.

Otherwise, what the devil are we doing in Cyprus and Rwanda?

May I also raise my voice against "Quebec sovereignism," a concept which stems from the old principle of nationalities of the 19th century according to which every nation, every association which is sociologically homogeneous is entitled to political independence.

Mr. Pierre E. Trudeau magnificently deflated the balloon of "Quebec National Sovereignism" in the April, 1962, issue of the *Cité libre*, showing that a large number of contemporary States are bi- and multi-national and do not fare worse than the uni-national States, and that an appeal to the principle "one-nation-one-state" would immediately unleash a hundred wars throughout the world. . . .

We can defend Quebec's autonomy, the "politique de grandeur" and the principle of "maîtres chez nous" without advocating the national sovereign Quebec State. Several times last evening, we heard that sovereignty was a totally outmoded concept as the interdependence of peoples and governments has now become evident. We fool people by intimating that once independence is won, everything will be peace, happiness and prosperity in the State of Quebec. The philosopher Locke shows us that the people, who in his time struggled over religious matters, would easily find other reasons for fighting against neighbouring peoples and even among themselves unless they first acquired a spirit of tolerance. The internal division of the RIN are a good example of this truth.

Thus, co-operative federalism aims at and allows us to achieve political bi-nationalism in Canada.

One last excerpt from my creed. It has almost become fashionable in our province to denounce in the name of purity, compromises, pragmatism, package deals, "constitutional laxity" and "political horsetrading," to quote Jean-Marc Leger, as if all this were immoral and disgusting.

You know as well as I do, ladies and gentlemen, that politics, in a federal State as in a unitary State, in a State with a mainly written constitution as in a State with a mainly customary constitution, in a latin society as in an anglo-saxon society, yesterday in Athens and Rome and today in Istanbul and in the Vatican, politics, I say, is the art of achieving the greatest possible common good for the whole community by applying wisdom, caution, and also charity, to the solution of conflicts which are *unavoidable*, since we are all stained by the original sin, in the relations between individuals and groups.

Under these conditions, the political man, the politician since we must call a spade a spade, improvises, must improvise and cannot help improvising in conformity with the image which the society he governs and himself are making of harmony, justice and happiness. He is constantly looking for equilibrium, the immediate solutions which do not contradict long term objectives, the happy medium (where Aristotle places virtue) between equally inaccessible extremes. Negotiation, haggling, compromise, package deals . . . are his stock in trade. As every good craftsman, he is proud of his tools. "Compromise," said the honourable Guy Favreau, "is the meeting-point between the thought of two intelligent beings."

May the Lord allow great men of compromise to be born into Canada in order to assure the success of Co-operative Federalism!

Let us recapitulate: Co-operative Federalism, as any other federalism, "calls on the virtues which have given birth to civilization, the sense of human brotherhood, Christian charity, the spirit of tolerance, the art of compromise, the desire to build collectively great works, the hope of making a better world where peace and justice shall prevail." If my lyricism amazes you may I specify that my past paragraph was taken from the brief of the Saint Jean-Baptiste Society of Montreal to the parliamentary committee for the constitution at the Quebec Legislative Assembly, page 22.

The Technique of Co-operative Federalism

Co-operative federalism is also a set of rules, techniques, and government institutions.

We should take time to situate this co-operative federalism in our constitutional history, to compare it to previous forms of Canadian federalism, to trace its origins; we should above all describe the present social, economic and political situation which has made it possible and even necessary. But it would no doubt be more useful to seek this evening to define it with a few key statements. Here again, I should like to be able to draw generously from the text of recent laws and the recent speeches of Federal and Quebec leaders in order to demonstrate that there is among them a broad consensus of opinion concerning the nature and the implications of co-operative federalism.

What are these propositions?

1. Economic decentralization and bi-nationalism

Co-operative federalism can be defined on the basis of a few forceful ideas. Some of them are *philosophical*; I singled out a few of them a while ago (for example the relative value of particularism, the necessity of compromise . . .). Others are related to *economy*. For example, there is no doubt that the recent popularity of economic decentralization helps to justify co-operative federalism, which advocates a much greater dose of political decentralization. In the *cultural* field the vitality of French culture in general (I am thinking especially of technology) and the progress of science, arts and letters in French Canada contribute in supporting the political arguments of Quebec.

In the *socio-political* field, *the theory of two nations*, whether true or false in the eyes of history, is now recognized by the best Canadian constitutionalists and political leaders, leaders in both nations; Mr. Pearson first, Mr. Diefenbaker, somewhat behind. Canadian society is bi-national; the Canadian state is the result of at least a moral agreement between the two founding nations.

Here is a fact which, if not new, has at least been recently accepted. Henceforth, the question runs as follows: *How shall we transpose to the Government level this socio-political reality of bi-nationalism?* In other words, how will the presence of a French-Canadian nation affect the rules, the techniques and the political institutions of Canada?

Some people do not want such a transposition: the *separatists*, English and French speaking; some deny it partially: the bi-statists and the *confederalists*; some believe that this transposition is possible within the framework of a revised Canadian federal State: these are the *co-operative federalists*. We note that there are among the defenders of this idea varying views as to the methods and amount of economic and political decentralization which are possible and the methods and desirable amount of recognition of the French reality and the Quebec reality.

2. "To each level of Government according to its aptitudes"

As "Canada is a vast continental domain — too big, too spread out, too cut up to be governed exclusively, or even dominantly, from one centre" (Mr. Pearson, May 26, 1964), co-operative federalism proclaims, against separatists and centralizers alike, *the necessity of two orders of government in Canada*. But how shall be divided the responsibilities between them?

The traditional *criterion*, the 1867 criterion, of the division of function — that is, matters of general interest will be attended to by the central government and matters of local interest, by the provincial governments, is not worth much. Everything can in some way be of general interest: agriculture, highways, education ... temperance!

We must therefore replace the former criterion with two others drawn from common sense and from the Act of '67: 1) *the criterion of aptitude*: We must allot to each order of Government what it is particularly able to do well in principle and in the present situation (Mr. Hirsch said last night that each decision should be taken at the level where it can best be made); 2) *the criterion of agreement between the two nations*: we must not assign to the central government matters over which there is clear-cut dissension between the two nations. The report of the Tremblay Commission also stated this principle, extrapolating it from the Act of 1867.

I admit that these two criteria do not provide an easy solution to all problems. The concepts of "aptitude" and "agreement" are themselves relative. A socialist does not think of "aptitude" like a conservative in the matter of social legislation. A French Canadian does not have the same philosophy of education as an English speaking Canadian. Nor is it always easy to know whether French Canadians agree among themselves: tonight's meeting is sufficient proof of this!

Thus, encounters and conflicts cannot be prevented. We will always need discussion and compromise.

I do not have enough time to state in which fields of government activity Ottawa is more competent *in principle*, and in which fields *in principle*, the provinces are more competent. I underline "in principle" because, in practice, we have already seen provinces, including Quebec, refuse, due to a lack of personnel or merely a lack of will-power, to take over fields of jurisdiction which were, in principle, rightfully theirs.

3. Unavoidable overlapping: inevitable interdependence

Without denying the usefulness of dividing as accurately as possible the duties between Ottawa and the provinces, we must observe the unavoidable overlapping of central and regional authorities in most segments of Government activity, especially in a period of interventionism as the present one and the next one. I hear Messrs. Lesage, Kierans and others assert that the provinces should participate in the determination of Canada's tariff policies, in her transportation policy and even her monetary policy, her trade policy, her tax policy, etc. I agree wholeheartedly. Co-operative federalism leaves room for consultation, co-operation and co-ordination even in these traditionally federal fields. I could read you, only as an example, a speech made by Mr. Sharp and speak to you of the Federal-Provincial conferences on international trade promotion, where the participation of the provinces is not only accepted but solicited. However, the provinces, especially Quebec, cannot claim a kind of right to be consulted in sectors of jurisdiction which are considered as "exclusively" *federal* (i.e. monetary policy) while refusing a similar right to Ottawa in sectors of jurisdiction which are considered to be "exclusively" *provincial* (i.e. highways).

The inevitable overlapping, the overall interdependence is thus a reality which has to be acknowledged.

Hence, it is not possible anymore, in my view, to divide clearly and once and for all the fields of activity. *The sharing of power* between Ottawa and the provinces is no longer the sole major problem of Canadian federalism. The true key problems are: 1) the establishment of *priorities of action*: the decisions as to what must be done first and how, it being understood that everything cannot be done at the same time; 2) *pre-consultation and continuous co-operation* in the establishment of priorities of action as well as the implementation of measures which have been adopted jointly.

4. Provincial priorities

Another key proposition of co-operative federalism: the claim by the provinces, especially Quebec, and the acknowledgement by Ottawa of the priority, not in principle, but "actual" (Mr. Lesage, himself, used this word), i.e. in the social, economic and political situation in which we Canadians are now living *of certain provincial requirements*: education, social security, highways and economic development. Once again I repeat, these priorities are essentially relative; the situation could change (unfortunately, a world war is not impossible), the order of priority also. But we can say that co-operative federalism *is essentially a decentralizing force*, that it brings about a certain decrease in Ottawa's role, at least the gradual withdrawal by the central government from essentially provincial sectors. Ottawa's offer to hand over to the provinces a large number of joint plans, announced today, is but one of several proofs.

5. The division of income: "to each according to its needs"

The distribution of government income and especially the powers of taxation between Ottawa and the provinces has been going on since 1957 and especially since 1961, not by virtue of the powers of taxation or methods of taxation described in the British North America Act, but, on the basis of the above-mentioned propositions, by virtue of the responsibilities accepted by each level of government at a given period. "To each order of government according to its needs." There is agreement between Ottawa and the provinces in this respect.

The provinces have submitted their financial needs to the central government, especially in their acknowledged fields of priority as of now. The central government has acknowledged the merits of these claims and for some years, has been making major tax concessions to the provinces. Mr. Diefenbaker boasted the other day in the House of Commons that he had paid to the provinces from 1957 to 1961, $439 million more in unconditional subsidies and $698 million more in conditional subsidies than the previous government. The agreements concluded following the Federal-Provincial Conferences of November 1963 and April 1964 resulted in an additional displacement during the years 1963-64 to 1966-67 of $523 million in favour of the provinces including $323 million in favour of Quebec. *Tax decentralization is already a reality.* The provinces have recently obtained a larger share of the individual income tax and of the estate tax. The equalization formula has been improved. Other federal laws: assistance for technical and vocational training, assistance to municipalities, youth allowances, the submission of federal crown corporations to provincial taxes, student loans, especially the transfer to the consenting provinces of certain joint plans with a corresponding share of the powers of taxation and what is more important, the capitalization now contemplated for the pension fund, which will apparently make no less than $4 billion (and probably more) available to the provinces within the next ten years, . . . all this is contributing not only toward making funds but also additional powers available to the provinces. Mr. Laporte said "we must reverse steam": it is obvious that steam has already been reversed.

6. The repatriation of joint programs

Few commentators deny the theoretical unconstitutionality and the practical difficulties of several joint plans although most of them recognize the past and future usefulness of the device "in certain circumstances" (Mr. Lesage). We have just said so: co-operative federalism recommends "that the provinces which so desire be entrusted with the full responsibilities of certain well-established programs which at any rate are presently administered by the provinces" (Mr. Gordon) and "which entail relatively stable, annual expenditures", with, of course, the equivalent financial resources or better still the equivalent powers of taxation.

This very day, it was announced that twelve joint plans will be offered to the provinces.

Co-operative federalism also recommends that Ottawa should not introduce any more joint plans unless it has the provinces' consent.

7. Co-operation and co-ordination

As a result of all that we have said, co-operative federalism proclaims the necessity of consultation, co-operation and co-ordination on a permanent basis between the two levels of Government. You will tell me that this principle was violated in some cases. That is true, and by both sides. However, the overall progress is no less evident. Mr. Lesage has acknowledged that there has never been so much co-operation between Ottawa and the provincial capitals as now. Agreed, but we must do better still . . . .

In the event of irreparable conflicts of ideology or interests, co-operative federalism acknowledges that the provinces have 1) a right of *option*: i.e., to a different method more respectful of provincial autonomy, of putting into practice a law which stems mainly from the Federal Government; 2) the right of *contracting out*; i.e., the right to waive all participation in a federal-provincial plan: (i.e., assistance to universities), without being penalized.

Instruments of co-ordination are already in place and others will be created to make common action more efficient: a federal-provincial secretariat, a joint economic committee, etc.

8. The particular status of Quebec

Co-operative federalism acknowledges the right of the French Canadians, a "minority not like the others," the right of Quebec "a province not like the others," to a particular status.

All we have just set forth makes possible a particular status for *Quebec* within Canadian federalism if, for example, it wants to take advantage of options, "contracting out," and withdrawal from joint plans.

Other questions will arise. I agree for my part that the lieutenant-governor could be appointed by the Provincial Governments; I am sure that the right of the provinces, especially Quebec, to diplomatic or quasi-diplomatic action within the purview of its traditional jurisdiction will soon be acknowledged.

The rights of *French Canadians* are partially acknowledged by the text of 1867; the only thing to do is to make the facts comply with this act . . . and to draw from its texts certain implications. It is the purpose of the Laurendeau-Dunton Commission to have the French language acknowledged everywhere in Canada where this is possible; it is the objective of the Pearson Government to have bilingualism recognized within the federal civil service. If they succeed, as I think they will, major constitutional amendments will have been achieved since Section 133 of the Act of 1867 does not go so far.

9. Constitutional Pragmatism

How did the recent changes come about and how will future changes be carried out? Will we have to rewrite the Canadian Constitutional text? Here we have conflicts of mentality, a rift between the formalists, who are not all French Canadians, and the pragmatists who are not all English Canadians. . . .

A study of Canadian federalism shows that *circumstances* explain its original formulation as well as the subsequent changes, and that judicial interpretation, conventions of the constitution, ordinary legislation and in rare cases, formal amendment, have been used in the past *to legalize changes*.

From now on, we cannot rely too much on formal amendments and judicial interpretation: major changes, present and future, are and will be legalized by constitutional practice and by ordinary acts adopted by the federal and by the provincial governments following consultation and federal-provincial agreements. For example, it should be observed that the recent tax arrangement between Ottawa and the provinces constitutes a de facto revision of sections 102 to 120 of the British North America Act.

At this time, a complete redrafting of the Act of 1867 seems to me, considering the present discussions and the nebulousness of the situation, not only impossible but dangerous even if co-operative federalism does not discard it for the future.

You will tell me that I am anglicized, that co-operative federalism is an Anglo-Saxon philosophy and technique. I will reply that even some great jurists of France do not think otherwise about the usefulness of written constitutional documents. We could benefit from reading the article written by George Burdeau in *Les Etudes en l'honneur de Achille Mestre*, an article entitled: "A Survival: the idea of a Constitution." For Burdeau real powers exist which are infra, supra and para-constitutional, but which are not liable of perfect integration in a constitutional text. He writes:

> Considering the forces of this type, it would seem that *the idea of the constitution is outmoded*. Politics is similar to an instinctive or internal function in that it admits only the law of possibility and requirements. The truth is that constitutions do not encompass the manifestations of political life. The latter evolves *independently of their provisions* and that is what explains the favour now being enjoyed by studies in political science.

Unfortunately, to my mind, too many French-Canadian politicians are suffering from *legalitis* especially with regard to our constitution. They seem to want to settle problems by fabricating legislation. Fortunately, in practice, the pragmatism of the majority overrides them.

Conclusions

Thus, here are the key propositions which I might use to define Canadian co-operative federalism:

1) profitability, even from the economic standpoint, of economic and political decentralization;
2) the existence of two nations and the necessity of transposing this fact at the political level;
3) the division of taxation between the central and regional governments according to the principle "to each according to its ability" to find a better solution for such and such a problem;
4) the unavoidable overlapping of activity between the two levels of government;
5) the present "actual" priority of provincial authority in certain fields;
6) the distribution of tax income and taxation powers between Ottawa and the provincial capitals according to the principle "to each level of government according to its requirements";
7) the necessity of constant co-operation and co-ordination between the central and the regional governments;
8) the particular status of the French Canadians and of Quebec;
9) pragmatism, empiricism, in the legal formulation of the new system.

Someone underscored last evening the need for world federalism. Very well.

But before offering the formula to the world, let us try to prove that federalism can work in Canada.

28   Federalism and International Conferences on Education: The Indivisibility of Foreign Policy*

Mitchell Sharp

The issues raised by the question of provincial attendance at intergovernmental conferences are not related merely to form or protocol, as has sometimes been suggested. In fact, they raise two fundamental policy questions, which go to the heart of our Canadian federal system:

First — can Canadian foreign policy and foreign relations be divided?

Second — if foreign policy is indivisible, and Canada must speak with one voice, is the Federal Government willing to promote the interests of all Canadians, of both major linguistic groups?

The answer to the first question is "no".

The answer to the second is "yes".

The central problem at issue concerns the very nature of foreign policy in the modern world. What precisely are external relations and foreign policy? Can some relations with states be considered to be part of the foreign policy of a country while others can be considered to be outside this sphere?

The question involved is one of principle: who is responsible for Canadian representation abroad, whether in matters of education or any other matters within provincial jurisdiction?

It has sometimes been suggested that the provinces have this right in matters over which they have domestic legislative competence, and that this has been shown by court decisions, for example in the celebrated *Labour Conventions Case* of 1937. This interpretation is not well-founded. The question at issue in that case was whether the Parliament of Canada could, in order to implement a treaty entered into by the Canadian Government, legislate in fields of domestic provincial jurisdiction under the British North America Act. The case decided that the Parliament of Canada could not legislate in areas of provincial jurisdiction simply as a result of the Canadian Government's entering into international agreements. However, the judges of the Supreme Court of Canada explicitly recognized that the Canadian Government could enter into treaties

*From *Federalism and International Conferences on Education*, a White Paper published by the Hon. Mitchell Sharp, Secretary of State for External Affairs, Queen's Printer, Ottawa, 1968. By permission of the Queen's Printer.

on all subjects, and the Judicial Committee of the Privy Council, which was the final court in that case, did not challenge this opinion. Thus, in no respect did the judges question the external affairs power of the Canadian Government as such or support the view that provincial competence extended abroad.

In light of this decision, both federal and provincial governments have worked on a co-operative basis toward the implementation of international agreements. The principles underlying this co-operation are described in *Federalism and International Relations*, where proposals are also made for strengthening procedures for federal-provincial collaboration.

There would be obvious problems involved in accepting the view that, in a federal state, a member or part can be responsible for international relations in respect of subjects concerning which it has, or shares, competence domestically. If this were the case, a province would be free to pursue an independent foreign policy in certain fields to the exclusion of the Federal Government. It would have to be accepted, in particular, that a province would be free to pursue its own foreign policy or external relations, not only in respect of education but in fields such as labour, health and welfare, and agriculture, and other areas where the provinces share jurisdiction with the Federal Government. Because so large a part of contemporary international relations concerns matters of this nature, the members or parts of a federal state would then be responsible for a major proportion of the country's foreign policy.

Acceptance of the above proposition would have further serious international consequences. In the case of Canada, ten or eleven voices could speak for the country on various questions. Some might not agree with others, which would exacerbate conflicts of interest within the country, and could in turn be exploited by foreign countries. Moreover, although a province might reflect adequately its own separate interest, it would not be likely to take full account of the larger Canadian interest. Neither the Government of Canada, nor that of any other country, could accept such a state of affairs. And, in fact, none has.

Furthermore, if a province were free to conduct its own foreign policy in areas under its domestic jurisdiction, it would thereby be at liberty to conduct relations with all countries without regard to national policy considerations. Thus, for example, a province could attempt to establish or maintain relations with a country with which Canada did not have diplomatic relations. Common sense indicates that, at the very least, this would place very serious strains on national unity.

The additional argument that intergovernmental conferences of a "technical" nature do not raise problems having foreign policy implications fails to take account of the realities of international relations in the modern world.

Educational matters, when they involve participants from other governments at an international conference, cease to be purely technical and domestic questions and take on a new dimension, involving foreign policy. And foreign policy deals with the outside world in matters which involve the whole country and all its parts.

The very nature of international affairs is such that it is not possible to divide external relations into one category that relates to "technical" or "provincial" matters and another which deals with "foreign policy". The work of various UN agencies, such as UNESCO, the ILO, WHO and FAO, all of which deal in part with matters of provincial interest and concern, affords ample proof of the political character of international co-operation in technical fields.

Foreign policy is the external expression of a country's sovereignty and it must harmonize various domestic policies which have external ramifications. That a country should have several separate votes at an intergovernmental conference can mean that it would have more than one foreign policy. Foreign policy cannot be fragmented. If it is, internal divisions are immediately exported and compounded.

Moreover, if countries deal with a government other than the national one, without prior agreement, questions will arise whether such acts constitute recognition of another entity at the international level. In these conditions, if a dialogue is sustained by one country with a state or province of another country, rather than with the national government, harmonious relations become very difficult to maintain. As a result, countries have accepted as law among themselves that in their relations with each other they will use only one channel with regard to matters of official business or policy. Over the years, cases have arisen which have required the Government to draw to the attention of various provinces and foreign governments concerned that the conduct of external relations is the concern of the Government of Canada. No state, no matter how powerful internally its component parts may be, has ever been in a position to divide external sovereignty.

In the internal world, there may be large and small units. There are and can be no half units. . . .

The Constitutional Conference and Proposals for the Future

At the Federal-Provincial Conference held in Ottawa from February 5 to 7, 1968, it was decided to establish a Continuing Constitutional Conference composed of the prime ministers and premiers, or their delegates, to supervise a process of constitutional review. It was also decided to set up a Continuing Committee of Officials to assist the Constitutional Conference in its task It was agreed that among the questions to be examined by the Constitutional Conference and the Continuing Committee of Officials would be the distribution of powers.

The Canadian Government considers that, in connection with a discussion of the distribution of powers between the federal and provincial governments, the Constitutional Conference should give attention, at an early date and together with other constitutional problems of an important character, to questions in the field of foreign affairs.

In the expectation that the foreign affairs question would receive attention in the process of constitutional review, the Government made available to the Constitutional Conference in February the document *Federalism and International Relations*. As noted above, this paper outlines both the general principles relating to Canada's participation in international affairs, which the Canadian

Government believes to be of fundamental importance in maintaining the unity of the country, and proposals and procedures designed to facilitate federal-provincial co-operation in the foreign affairs field. The present document — *Federalism and International Conferences on Education* — is intended as a companion volume to the earlier paper. As such, it is designed to elaborate upon procedures and arrangements for federal-provincial co-operation in devising representative Canadian delegations to international conferences in fields of provincial interest, particularly education.

The Government considers that the proposals which it has put forward to the Province of Quebec in connection with representation at international meetings of French-speaking states concerning education, together with procedures established in the past for participation in meetings of the Commonwealth, UNESCO and the IBE in this field, represent a sound foundation on which a basis for arrangements acceptable to the federal and provincial governments might be found.

In summary, the Federal Government's proposals for attendance at international conferences which deal with matters of interest and concern to the provinces, particularly those in the educational field, are based on the following principles:

(1) Delegations to be sent to such conferences should be Canadian delegations. They should speak, act and vote on behalf of Canada.

(2) There should be a substantial provincial component in all such delegations.

(3) In international conferences on education, a subject concerning which provinces have domestic jurisdiction, Canadian delegations should normally be headed by provincial ministers or, as appropriate, by other persons acceptable to all concerned, for example, leading university figures, and should include ministers of education or officials of interested provinces.

(4) Where the meeting is one of ministers from French-speaking countries with responsibilities in the educational field, the head of the delegation should normally be a Quebec minister or, where appropriate, a minister of another province with a large French-speaking population. The delegation should, in any case, include, in the capacity of delegate or adviser, persons from provinces with substantial *francophone* populations.

(5) In meetings on educational matters, the Council of Ministers of Education should be consulted in order to obtain agreement on a satisfactory delegation; in the case of UNESCO meetings, liaison should also be continued with the Canadian National Commission for UNESCO.

(6) The role of the Council of Ministers of Education in the process of selecting delegations should be strengthened.

(7) Federal officials should normally be attached to Canadian delegations to international meetings on education to advise on foreign

policy and other issues of concern to the Federal Government.

(8) The general guidance provided by the Government to Canadian delegations attending international meetings on education should not deal with education matters as such but be limited to questions with foreign policy implications, Canadian budgetary contributions and any other matters of federal concern which may be under consideration. The position to be followed on educational matters as such should be for decisions by provincial governments, or, as appropriate, by the Council of Ministers of Education.

(9) Canadian delegations to international meetings on education should take into account in an appropriate manner the bilingual character of Canada. At the same time the interests of Canadians whose mother tongue is neither English nor French should also be given appropriate recognition.

(10) Canadian delegations to international meetings on technical matters concerning which both the federal and provincial governments share domestic jurisdiction should follow, in taking account of both federal and provincial interests, the general principles outlined in *Federalism and International Relations*.

In the field of external co-operation and aid, the Canadian Government made known in *Federalism and International Relations* the proposals which it has made to the provinces for establishing improved methods of co-operation in respect of external aid. These proposals can be summarized as follows:

(1) The Federal Government will consult with the provincial authorities on the development of programmes which could have a substantial impact on the personnel requirements of the provinces.

(2) Recruitment of teaching personnel in particular will be carried out in consultation and collaboration with interested provinces.

(3) Appropriate arrangements will be made with respect to the payment of provincial personnel and the retention of their seniority, pension and related rights.

(4) Where possible, a decision as to termination of employment will be made in consultation with the provinces.

(5) The provincial authorities will be kept informed as to federal administrative arrangements, and provision will be made for inspection visits which should include provincial officials in the Canadian team.

(6) Arrangements will be made for effective communications through Canadian diplomatic missions.

(7) In order to ensure coherent policies and programmes, procedures should be established to provide for federal-provincial consultation with regard to aid projects financed or supported by the provinces.

(8) In connection with aid projects financed or supported by the provinces, it should be understood that formal liaison with foreign states and any formal agreements which might be required with them

should be undertaken by, or with the agreement of, the federal authorities.

(9) Clear recognition should be given to the provincial role.

In putting forward the above suggestions with respect to participation in international conferences and programmes of external aid and co-operation, the Government wishes to emphasize that they are intended as a basis for discussion.

The Government hopes that they will be given careful consideration by all concerned.

It will welcome additional comments and suggestions which may be put forward, and it will adopt a flexible attitude toward all aspects of the problem.

It is not committed to any particular solution and is ready to consider all proposals which recognize Canada as one country and provide opportunities for Canadians from all provinces to share, as part of a united Canada, in the benefits of international co-operation.

Part Six

Quebec and Canadian Federalism

29   Quebec and Canadian Federalism*

Alexander Brady

Canada's federation is distinct from the other two major federations in the English-speaking world in resting upon an alliance of two peoples and two cultures. Other differences exist, but this is fundamental. Since 1867 the dualism of culture has been slowly woven into the political fabric of the nation, although outside Quebec its implications are still not always appreciated or wholly accepted. With the appearance in 1956 of the *Report of the Royal Commission of Inquiry on Constitutional Problems*,[1] English-speaking Canadians have little excuse for misunderstanding the position of their French-speaking compatriots. The Commission was appointed by provincial statute in January, 1953, under the chairmanship of Judge Thomas Tremblay. Its bulky report is never likely to be widely read. It is prolix and sometimes repetitious to the point of tedium; its analysis would have been more telling had it been tidier and more compressed. Yet, despite such flaws, it is a landmark in the literature of federalism: it describes and explains more fully than any other public document the position and anxieties of Quebec in the federal state, and defends the concept of a strict federalism as the essential basis for the success of Canada's national experiment. For the Tremblay Commissioners the issue of Quebec in the federation and the issue of the French in the nation are one and the same. In harmony with their theme they submit numerous recommendations. We cannot, however, assess these or do justice to their premises, without first reviewing briefly the historical position of Quebec in Canadian federalism.

At Confederation the political thinking of leaders in British North America swung between two positions, both empirical. Some of the Fathers had originally feared that the federal principle, especially as exemplified in the neighbouring republic, implied a dispersal of power that would drain the strength, increase the cost, and jeopardize the survival of a new state in North America. Sir John A. Macdonald's first preference, like that of Sir Charles Tupper, was a legislative rather than a federal union. Yet he and his associates quickly yielded to the logic of the fact that the existing colonies enjoyed local autonomy and were unwilling to surrender it.[2] The two Canadas, moreover, possessed a single legislature, but had been compelled by the differences in their cultures to conduct their affairs almost as in a federation. This was the main circumstance which changed Macdonald's mind on the nature of the new state: the French as a minority feared that in legislative union "their institutions and their laws might be assailed, and their ancestral associations, on which they prided themselves, attacked and prejudiced."[3] The French were emphatic in

*From *The Canadian Journal of Economics and Political Science*, Vol. XXV, No. 3, August 1959, pp. 259-270. Reprinted by permission of the author and the Canadian Political Science Association.

[1]Four vols., Quebec, 1956. Hereafter called the *Tremblay Report*.
[2]See, e.g., *Parliamentary Debates on the Subject of the Confederation of the British North American Provinces*, Quebec, 1865, reprinted Ottawa, 1951, p. 29.
[3]*Ibid.*

contending for genuine federalism, and those among them who opposed the projected confederation did so because it appeared to offer a provincial autonomy that was shadowy and insufficient. The presence of dual cultures and diverse social values among the people of the St. Lawrence Valley was thus basic in shaping the decision of the Fathers for a federal state.

Since 1867 Quebec has remained consistently attached to a strict federalism as a protector of its own culture and the cultural dualism of Canada. It has been the chief citadel of resistance to centralizing conceptions and homogenizing tendencies. Its position has sometimes been backed by Ontario, which usually however acts independently for reasons of its own. In the first three decades after Confederation Ontario might seem to have been even more emphatic in assailing the centralizing pretensions of Ottawa. Under Oliver Mowat (1872-96) it checkmated the manoeuvres of Sir John A. Macdonald, who never wholly subdued his original bias for a legislative union and persistently endeavoured to restrict the role of the provincial legislatures and to exalt that of the national Parliament. But, in Mowat's successive legal contests and triumphs before the Privy Council, Quebec was Ontario's vigilant and reliable ally. Its jurists and politicians were equally keen to elaborate the powers of the provinces under section 92. In Judge T. J. J. Loranger among others it had a constitutional expert who in the eighties presented with distinguished clarity the provincial case. "If the federal pretensions prevail," wrote Loranger in 1883, "and if the principle of the provinces' inferiority and dependence of their legislatures with regard to the federal authority is recognized, in less than half a century their absorption will be accomplished and the federal system will give way to the legislative union so rightly feared in our province."[4]

In politics, two Quebec figures in the first half-century of federation especially advanced the provincial cause: Honoré Mercier and Wilfrid Laurier. Both reflected the inflamed feelings of French Canadian nationalism in the eighties provoked by the sorry events of the Riel Rebellion and its aftermath. Both, and especially Laurier, also responded to the more stable emotions about provincial rights which in greater or lesser degree have inspired all French leaders since 1867. Mercier's principal achievement was his convening an interprovincial conference in 1887 to examine the relations of the provinces with the federal government. Under the chairmanship of Oliver Mowat five provincial premiers there adopted resolutions that challenged and rejected the centralist policies of Macdonald. Although their requests, including a surrender by the federal government of its power to disallow provincial acts, were not acceptable to Ottawa, the case for provincial autonomy received an important impetus from its formal affirmation.

Laurier's leadership of the national Liberals (1887-1919) secured, by quiet persuasion at the highest levels in Ottawa, a sympathy for Quebec's position and for provincial autonomy in general. "The only means of maintaining Confederation," he declared in 1889, "is to recognize that, within its sphere assigned to it by the constitution, each province is as independent of control by the

---

[4]Quoted in *Tremblay Report*, Vol. I, p. 67.

federal Parliament as the latter is from control by the provincial legislatures."
This dictum is important, not for its novelty, but for the fact that it influenced
Laurier's tactics and policies throughout his career. It was evident in his
stand on the Manitoba school question before his electoral triumph in 1896,
and in office he never lost a French Canadian's anxiety for the autonomy of the
provinces. Admittedly he was aided by the stream of events. In successive
decisions from that of *Hodge* v. *The Queen* in 1883, the Privy Council consolidated and fortified the power of the provincial legislatures, while the growth
in population and industry of Quebec and Ontario enhanced the prestige of
their governments and goaded them to seek in the courts that larger legislative
competence essential for developing their natural resources. In employing the
power of disallowance Laurier and his colleagues sought to pursue a fresh
course. They did not consider the power obsolete (although privately Laurier
told Blake that it was alien to the federal idea), but generally avoided its use
as a corrective of the alleged errors and injustices committed by provincial
legislatures, and confined it to cases where the legislation affected federal or
imperial interests. No other view, they were convinced, could secure provincial
autonomy and local democracy. Laurier's governments between 1896-1911 admittedly disallowed thirty provincial statutes, but of these twenty issued solely
from the legislature of British Columbia and affected both Canadian and
imperial interests by dealing adversely with the employment and status of
Asiatics. Since 1896 only one Quebec act has been disallowed compared with
five in the preceding twenty-nine years and only two Ontario acts compared
with eight in the earlier period.[5]

Soon after the passing of the Laurier régime, there appeared fresh threats to
provincial autonomy, which were mainly related, as they still are, to the issues
of finance. On a small scale before the First World War and on a larger scale
after it, national governments began to make grants to the provinces on conditions which implied a federal control over their use. This new procedure
came from a quickened and wider sense of national interest in the policy-
makers at Ottawa, coupled with a desire to circumvent the restrictions imposed
on them by the constitution. They were persuaded that, without loss of provincial autonomy, the provinces and the national government might create an
ad hoc partnership for certain desirable ends with funds jointly contributed.
Grants, such as those provided in 1919 to encourage technical education,
trespassed on the legislative field of the provinces, but the provincial governments could not resist the temptation to accept virtual supplements to provincial revenue.

From the outset leaders in Quebec viewed this form of federal largesse with
disquiet or positive disfavour. Ernest Lapointe, a prominent French Canadian
spokesman in the Liberal Opposition at the close of the First World War,
attacked conditional grants. In his view they intruded on provincial jurisdiction and were unfair to non-concurring provinces, whose citizens were taxed to

---

[5]See G. V. La Forest, *Disallowance and Reservation of Provincial Legislation*, Queen's
Printer, Ottawa, 1955, Appendix A.

benefit those in other provinces.[6] Indirectly but forcibly, a federal government thus exerted coercion in fields where its action was either constitutionally ambiguous or invalid. It practised generosity at the price of provincial autonomy, and employed its own relative affluence to entice and bribe impecunious provinces, whittle away their independence, and generally impair their freedom to manoeuvre. In Quebec this argument has ever since rendered doughty service in the polemic of federal-provincial relations.

The inter-war ministries of Mackenzie King, wherein Ernest Lapointe sat as an influential member, were on the whole unsympathetic to conditional grants, although the social and political compulsions of the time involved them in this policy in some degree. In July, 1924, a special committee of the Commons advocated that the federal and provincial governments should share the costs of old age pensions for needy persons over seventy. The Liberals were reluctant to reject a proposal that might win popularity. King himself was deeply interested in policies of social welfare and alert to their importance in political strategy. Hence in 1927 his Government sponsored a scheme whereby it would pay half the cost to every province which agreed to provide old age pensions. The provinces, beginning with British Columbia, made such agreements, and finally in 1936 New Brunswick and Quebec participated, although the Quebec government still viewed old age pensions as an undesirable federal intrusion into the provincial field. It could not, however, continue to ignore the unpalatable facts that if it remained outside the scheme its people would be helping to pay for pensions they were not free to enjoy.

Despite the precedent of old age pensions, the inter-war administrations of Mackenzie King, influenced by their French Canadian supporters, never displayed enthusiasm for conditional grants. Quebec resented them as the vehicle of a vigorous federal policy. Its leaders had no wish to see the national government in a position to exert pressure on the provinces. Such grants placed it in this position because they implied centralized authority in making decisions by lawmakers and officials in Ottawa, the majority of whom were English Canadians.[7]

Since 1939 profound changes in Canadian society and ways of thought have involved a heavier subsidization of the provinces. National enactments have multiplied conditional grants until today there are half a hundred different kinds. Some, such as those relating to the reclamation of land and to fisheries, mainly concern specific provinces and regions. Others, such as those in public health and old age assistance, appeal to all the provinces, and enlist the active support of all, including Quebec. This accentuated trend in federal action is traceable to social forces linked with industrialism and nationalism, accelerated by war and the preparation for war. The appetite of a growing industrial people for public services within provincial jurisdiction has sharpened, especially for highways, welfare and health services, and education. Federal governments, of course, might have left the provinces alone to cope with these services

---

[6]*House of Commons Debates*, 1919, p. 3794.

[7]For Mackenzie King's concern for the position of the provinces in this matter see *ibid.*, 1931, pp. 1959 ff.

as best they could, but they have been persistently pressed by public opinion to feed them with federal funds. In some cases the pressure has been strongest from people in the relatively poor and less favoured areas, but it commonly comes from certain organized interests in all the provinces and especially from the more industrialized regions. The more rapid the pace of urbanization, the more varied and insistent are the demands on the national treasury. On their part federal politicians are loath to miss an opportunity of winning votes by spending money, and now find it easy to justify expenditure on the grounds of a compelling national interest. Since their primary concern is to placate the electors, they must listen to the numerous pressure groups, which often are indifferent to the political and legal facts of federalism and rationalize their own interests in terms of a national interest. Thus the Liberal party, ascendant in Ottawa for the first dozen years after the Second World War, became fired by a stronger nationalism, and rapidly retreated from its former scruples about encroaching on provincial jurisdiction. In successive enactments after 1940 it sponsored abundant grants, conditional and unconditional.

The Tremblay Commission, in surveying this panorama of post-war change, admit with evident sorrow that "a vast network has been spread which binds the provinces to the central government and which, to a certain extent, provides them with the financial means of discharging their legislative functions, but always at the discretion and on the terms of the wealthy and powerful donor."[8] In all this the French Canadians as the chief defenders of traditional federalism face a difficult dilemma. Either they must patiently resign themselves to a course of events that threatens to erode the older federalism or pursue more resolutely than hitherto the policy of survival by withdrawal. Some fear that they have no choice, and that the decision is made for them by the speed and inexorable strides of an industrialism which transforms their society, exposes them to a stream of influences from outside, and assimilates them in character to English-speaking Canadians. Since 1939 Quebec, with rich mineral resources, abundant water power, and a high birth rate, has shared substantially in the country's material expansion. Its industrial production has multiplied five-fold, and light industries such as textiles have yielded ground to heavy industries such as mining and metallurgy. Industrialism in the province was born long before, but the Second World War accelerated its growth. The drift from farm to factory was quickened. The old rural framework of life, in which for generations the relatively isolated culture of the French Canadians was sustained, is crumbling now that only a fifth of the people live in strictly rural areas. As urban dwellers and industrial workers they undergo much the same experience as labour elsewhere in Canada, respond to the prevalent appetite for social security, and are likely to be no less eager for the services that the federal treasury can ensure. With the progress of industrialism a variety of interests in French Canadian society, notably organized labour, establish a rapport with like interests in Ontario and other provinces, and become less diffident in dealing with a government in Ottawa. Quebec may still resemble a cultural

---

[8]*Tremblay Report*, Vol. II, p. 214.

island within the nation, but an island now with numerous bridges that diminish its isolation.

The Union Nationale party led by Maurice Duplessis has held office in Quebec since 1944, and in the face of these forces has vehemently defended the province's autonomy. It has freely exploited the sentiments of French Canadian nationalism aroused by the depression of the thirties and the subsequent tensions of the Second World War. Yet it is difficult to determine precisely how much the longevity of M. Duplessis' régime is due to his display of autonomist convictions. Other obvious factors contribute: his smoothly working political machine, his rare art in winning support by dexterous use of patronage, and his gains from an electoral distribution of seats that bears little relation to the rapid urbanizing of the population. Despite his strong position, he has found it expedient to accept many conditional grants from Ottawa; others he has brusquely rejected. His criterion for acceptance or rejection is the extent of the threat to the traditional autonomy of the province. Thus he entered into agreements to obtain substantial grants from the federal treasury for health services, including hospital construction, general public health, and the control of tuberculosis and cancer. Although he also accepted the conditions prescribed in 1952 for joint provincial and federal old age assistance for the needy, he rejected the federal subsidies to aid in building the Trans-Canada Highway through Quebec. Even more emphatically he rejected the subsidizing of Quebec universities from federal funds because it touched, not merely traditional provincial jurisdiction, but the sensitive nerves of culture. For him this was an appropriate battle ground. "What counted in Judas' betrayal of Christ," he declared, "was not the sum of thirty pieces of silver but the fact that Judas had betrayed his Master." Acquiescence in such federal action would merely stimulate Ottawa to indulge further in an interference all the more unwarranted in being needless, since the provincial government itself could adequately sustain the colleges of the province, especially if the federal authority left it appropriate fields for direct taxation. This point raises the controversial and basic question of the taxing power, which has occasioned the most prolonged and wordy debates between Ottawa and Quebec.

The modern issue of taxation originated as a by-product of the First World War, when the national government in 1916 resorted to direct taxes on war profits and in the next year on general income. After the war the income tax survived as an important instrument in federal policy, and provoked in Quebec strong protests. "Ottawa," asserted Premier Taschereau in 1920, "has unceremoniously arrogated to itself our own sources of revenue." But the federal income tax was there to stay, and the facts of the depression in the thirties helped to secure its permanence. The depression, however, had contrasting and conflicting effects within the federation. In English-speaking Canada, especially in the west, the current of opinion now ran more strongly than before towards a heavy reliance on Ottawa. The taxing power of the federal government was accepted as an inevitable adjunct to its responsibility. In Quebec, by contrast, the current of opinion ran turbulently in the opposite direction. The harsh tensions of the depression merely exacerbated French Canadian nationalism, raised more urgently the persistent theme of cultural survival, and made the régime of M. Duplessis after 1936 more uncompromising than any previous government in clinging to every element of provincial autonomy. In the economic and social facts of the time Quebec sensed a new and greater menace to the position that it was obligated by long tradition to defend. The Sirois Commission (appointed in August, 1937) was naturally viewed by M. Duplessis as objectionable because it was appointed without prior consultation with the provinces and unilaterally investigated matters that were crucially important to them. His government made explicit to the Commission its opposition to any abridgement of provincial rights, or any significant change in the federal pact unless accepted by all the provinces.

At that time, however, Quebec's position was not isolated. Four other provincial governments also argued before the Sirois Commission against any drastic change, fiscal or otherwise, in the existing distribution of federal power. Only the four then most needy provinces, Manitoba, Saskatchewan, Nova Scotia, and Prince Edward Island, were ready to barter their right to tax for provincial aid. All four proclaimed fidelity to federalism, but, in their precarious financial plight, a secure revenue had more appeal than fiscal liberty. The conference of January, 1941, convened by Ottawa to get agreement for implementing the principal recommendations of the *Sirois Report*, adjourned in failure on the second day because Ontario, British Columbia, and Alberta rejected a revision of the federal system on the terms recommended, and the national Government could consider no others. From September, 1939, to August, 1944, Quebec was ruled by the Liberals under Adélard Godbout, who cautiously did not commit himself. "We are here," he remarked, "to study; we will listen and we are ready to co-operate."

After the Second World War the issue of federal taxation appeared to Quebec in a more ominous light. To meet the urgent necessities of war the federal Government had secured (in 1942) the agreement of all the provinces to vacate in its favour the right to levy personal income and corporation taxes and to accept compensation in annual grants. Here was a means that with provincial consent and without a constitutional amendment might at any time augment the fiscal initiative of Ottawa, and for many reasons Ottawa was anxious that it should endure into the peace. Public sentiments at the time incessantly pressed the federal Government to do and prepare for countless things. Fears of a post-war depression and haunting memories of unemployment in the thirties were in the air. Conceptions of an economy managed through fiscal controls seeped into the thinking of federal ministers and public servants. The ideas of Maynard Keynes took root in the Department of Finance, and to lend them scope it seemed essential to have federal control over the major and most remunerative taxes. Hence at the Dominion-Provincial Conference on Reconstruction (1945-6) Ottawa submitted to the provinces far-ranging proposals, buttressed by a series of supplementary studies, which among other things would have left to it an exclusive access to personal income and corporation taxes and succession duties, while in return Ottawa provided per capita provincial grants.

Quebec, like some other provinces, viewed these plans of Ottawa as a serious menace to federalism. If they were fully implemented, the major initiative in social policy would irretrievably shift to the national capital, and provincial independence in finance and manoeuvrability in policy would drastically diminish. In the words of the Quebec brief the proposals would "exclude the provinces from the most important fields of direct taxation and to that extent deprive them of the exercise of the powers assigned to them by the constitution." Ontario's plea was similar. It denied, moreover, that centralization could provide protection against depression, although it would certainly violate federal principles. Yet neither Quebec nor Ontario outdid in vigorous and eloquent protest the Premier of Nova Scotia, who declared that if the proposals were accepted, "provincial autonomy will be gone. Provincial independence will vanish. Provincial dignity will disappear. The provincial governments will become mere annuitants of Ottawa."

The Conference of 1945-6 dissolved in acrimony and without accomplishment. The wartime agreements, however, ran their course to 1947. In the interval certain fundamental facts in the situation worked inexorably in favour of Ottawa, especially the inequality of the provinces in economic and financial strength and hence their divergence in interpreting the nature of the federal bond. The financially weak or less favoured naturally saw advantages in retaining payments from Ottawa. On principle they were not really averse to rental agreements provided that they got good terms, although for purposes of bargaining they might appear appropriately coy. Their outlook on the federation fundamentally differed from that of Quebec, because they were not preoccupied with the feeling of having to defend through federalism a distinct culture. Consequently they were disposed to take a short-run view of federal matters. The necessities of the day dominated, for under pressure from their electorates they thought primarily of services to which they were committed and must become committed, and of how to secure the revenue necessary to finance them. Even the strong and affluent among the English-speaking provinces do not act very differently, but their strength commonly permits them to take longer views.

This circumstance in the situation makes plain why Ottawa, after failing to obtain agreement for a general scheme, could successfully resort to the tactic of individual agreements on the basis of new formulae. By the beginning of 1948 seven provinces and in 1949 Newfoundland had signed such agreements. Quebec and Ontario then alone remained outside, but in 1952 Ottawa, armed with different formulae, was able to win Ontario and isolate Quebec. The history of these years illustrates how expediency dominates in Canadian federalism. With the rapidly changing society an elaborate process of individual and constant bargaining between the federal and provincial governments is the accepted norm, and the provinces rarely present a united front. On such a basis the federation will continue to operate, for it serves best the shortrun interests of Ottawa and all the provinces except Quebec.

The Tremblay Commission, aided by the numerous briefs of organized interests in the province, assess Quebec's place in the federation in the light of history and philosophy. Much of their detailed report, with its wealth of facts, surveys the past and analyses the present in order to underline the special identity of the French community in Canada's evolution, its relation to the federal structure after 1867, and the threats to its survival and the survival of federalism that result from the forces of the twentieth century, especially industrialism, depression, and war.

The historical section of the report is invaluable, and, despite a bias on some matters, is likely to be acceptable to scholars outside Quebec. Agreement on facts, however, does not imply agreement on their interpretation. The historical struggle of the French Canadian for cultural survival gives him a special point of view, which the Tremblay Commission express in terms of an appropriate philosophy. This philosophy is a form of Catholic pluralism, emphasizing the necessary freedom for cultural groups to operate and survive, combined with the assumptions of a liberal nationalism. Federal policy, it is argued, should be determined, less by the material conditions and appetites of the society, than by the wholesome impulses towards the freedom of cultural groups and the freedom of the individual to develop his personality in a group. The goals of the Canadian nation should be association not assimilation, diversity not uniformity, the vitality of all the distinct groups in the state and not their standardization. These concepts of liberal Catholic philosophers, such as Jacques Maritain, are readily translated into the traditional French Canadian attachment to a strict federalism, stressing the full autonomy of the province with its aggregate of usages and traditions. This pluralist philosophy might have found an uncongenial environment in the Quebec of the nineteenth century under its dominant ultra-montanism. But in the 1950's it seems to fit comfortably into the French Canadian heritage.

What kind of offspring in practical recommendations does this marriage of history and philosophy produce? The Tremblay Commission are explicit about what it should produce. They formulate many recommendations, some of which differ greatly in content and purpose from those of the Sirois Commission twenty years ago. They primarily seek to stop the erosion of federalism, threatened by the centralizing pressures of Ottawa especially in finance. They launch what they hope are destructive assaults against the "new federalism" and its apologists, English and French, and single out for criticism the views of a French Canadian advocate, Maurice Lamontagne, author of Le Fédéralisme canadien.[9] "To believe and to try to have it believed," they wrote, "that there is respect, in Canada, for the autonomy of the provinces, because they are allowed to exist as mere administrative units to which the central authority will distribute living allowances, is mere self-deception and an attempt to deceive others. It confronts true federalism with mere administrative decentralization which is to be found in any state but which does not truly allow autonomy of the regional and local communities."[10]

The Tremblay Commission think of a genuine federal state as one wherein financial and political powers are so apportioned between the federal and unit

---

[9]Les Presses de l'Université Laval, Quebec, 1954.
[10]*Tremblay Report*, Vol. II, p. 276.

governments that their self-operating and self-governing functions are un-
fettered by interferences from one another. "There can be no federalism," they
write, "without autonomy of the state's constituent parts, and no sovereignty of
the various governments without fiscal and financial autonomy."[11] Such a
federal structure must ensure the identity of the whole and the identity of the
parts. It implies, not isolation, but close co-operation among the several governments. This general concept of federalism is one to which many modern political
theorists would readily subscribe. The inevitable question, however, is, what
division of power has most logic in a given situation? Even among genuine
liberal pluralists it is far from easy to secure agreement on this thorny issue in
view of the speed of economic and social change. The modern industrial
economy never stands still, and every major innovation affects profoundly the
federal jurisdiction.

The Tremblay Commission naturally enough use a criterion calculated to
ensure for a province an authority sufficiently broad to protect its culture. They
are confident that the constitution drafted by the Fathers provided this authority,
and that in the past the Judicial Committee and the Supreme Court of Canada
jealously upheld it. The real threat to the federation in the present generation
comes from the centralizing actions of an Ottawa forgetful that federalism implies two orders of government and not one. The national authority has employed various expedients, such as conditional grants, to encroach on provincial
jurisdiction. It has freely invoked ancillary powers in the B.N.A. Act, and has
used the financial incapacity of the provinces as an excuse for doing countless
things, while its own inroads in the field of direct taxation accentuate their
incapacity. The Commission are particularly critical of the national government
for exercising powers, as in some forms of education, allegedly ancillary to those
in section 91. Ottawa may properly legislate for the Indians, the penitentiaries,
the armed forces, agriculture, immigration, and radio, but assumes that each
of these subjects has an educational aspect that justifies its intervention in the
field of education associated with the subject. Judge Tremblay and his colleagues
comment caustically on the manner in which the Massey Commission, by what
they deem a series of specious arguments, establish a right of the federal government to intervene in certain fields of education and then transfer this right
into a duty in the name of the public welfare and spiritual values. They think
that the extravagant use of ancillary powers seriously threaten the survival of
the federation, and quote with approval Justice Duff's view that the "division
of legislative authority is the principle of the British North America Act, and
if the doctrine of necessarily incidental powers is to be extended to all cases in
which inconvenience arises from such a division, that is the end of the federal
character of the Union."[12]

On this premise the Tremblay Commission consider that for the future federal
power should be employed, not to displace the provinces, but to establish the
conditions, including a sufficient and independent revenue, that would allow

[11]*Ibid.*, Vol. III, p. 294.
[12]*Ibid.*, Vol. II, p. 236.

them to play the special role assigned to them under the constitution. The provinces need fiscal powers commensurate with their legislative powers, and can secure them only by a logical division of the field of direct taxation between them and the national government. Yet, even with a careful division of the taxing power, some provinces would likely remain unable to obtain revenue sufficient to finance services comparable with those of their wealthier or more industrialized neighbours, and for this situation the Commissioners think that the appropriate remedy is a "financial equalization organism."[13] Instead of leaving solely to Ottawa the major task of combatting economic depressions, the provinces should for this purpose be brought into a close co-operative relation with Ottawa and be organized to participate in the anti-cyclic policy according to their capacity and the requirements of their constitutional role.[14] In a period of depression they, like the federal government, should be able to sell bonds to the Bank of Canada. The Commission emphasize the value of a permanent committee of the federal-provincial conferences to secure continuity of co-operation in the interval between conferences, and in addition a permanent council of the provinces, confined exclusively to them, somewhat on the lines of the Council of State Governments in the United States. One body that they have in mind now already exists in the Federal-Provincial Continuing Committee on Fiscal and Economic Matters.

Such briefly is the main case of the Tremblay Commission for a revitalized federalism. It is both radical and controversial. Its chief argument and proposals are derived from briefs submitted to the Commission, and unquestionably represent important bodies of opinion in the province of Quebec, although not all that province's opinion is necessarily well represented. A convinced federalist elsewhere in Canada could accept the main thesis of the Tremblay Commission that decentralization is desirable to invigorate local autonomy in all the provinces. But the patent fact is that in English-speaking Canada, in the postwar years especially, the current of nationalism has run powerfully in the opposite direction and has been stimulated by the evident insecurities of the national state in the contemporary world. The dangers to Canada's survival as a political entity have among English-speaking Canadians weakened the federal spirit. Moreover there is a growing sense that many problems of social life can best be settled nationally and that social progress demands national standards. Hence the pressure of special interests for action from Ottawa has increased rather than diminished. With its larger and more flexible source of income Ottawa can most effectively achieve what these special interests want. Federal politicians, moreover, with the indispensable help of the national treasury, never cease to angle for votes by promising many things and doing many things. The very nature of democracy is contributory to this end. Here are nationalizing forces, which at present are not easy to control in order to guarantee the complete integrity of the federal system.

Yet federalism in Canada has not suffered a final eclipse. It is not on the road

---

[13]*Ibid.*, Vol. III, p. 297.
[14]*Ibid.*, Vol. III, p. 299.

to dissolution. Many of the provinces constitute immense territories with abundant resources, and already have grown into populous and prosperous communities which are destined to become more populous and more self-confident. They will increasingly require all the legislative and administrative powers that they now possess to achieve effective regional planning and development. Consequently their political leaders will be anxious to erect defences against the continued seepage of power and initiative to Ottawa. Much of the distinctiveness in Canada's nationality in the future must derive from the recognition of its cultural dualism, and the more this fact is appreciated the more sensitive will be the concern for federalism. In the meantime Quebec's devotion to the federal idea has served a national purpose; it has helped to lessen the danger of excessive centralization in Ottawa and the equal danger of a rigid framework advantageous to Ottawa. Rigid arrangements acceptable today may be intolerable tomorrow. Flexibility is a prime condition for a healthy federalism, and paradoxically Quebec by its unbending position has been its guarantor.

30   Concepts of Federalism:
Some Canadian Aspects *

Eugene Forsey

The problems of Canadian federalism, in my opinion, are not, for the most part, problems of federalism at all, but of Canadian dualism. If the whole country were solidly English-speaking, or solidly French-speaking, we should probably be able to settle questions of distribution of power between the Dominion and the provinces as we settle questions of public and private ownership, by asking simply, "Which can do the better job in this particular field at this particular time?" But with most of the provinces overwhelmingly English-speaking, and one overwhelmingly French-speaking, there is, for the French-speaking, an added question: "Which will better protect 'us' against 'them'?" So, if the English-speaking majority arrives at the conclusion that a particular function is best entrusted to the Dominion, it must try to convince the French-speaking that this need not mean simply entrusted to the English-speaking. If the existing Constitution already gives the function to the Dominion, then the English-speaking have to try to persuade the French-speaking that it is safe to leave it there; if the existing Constitution gives it to the provinces, then the English-speaking have to try to persuade the French-speaking that it is safe to transfer it.

    The Fathers of Confederation thought they had found an easy way around

*From Gordon Hawkins (ed.), *Concepts of Federalism*, 34th Couchiching Conference, Canadian Institute on Public Affairs, Toronto, 1965, pp. 22-28. Reprinted by permission of the author and the Canadian Institute on Public Affairs.

this difficulty. In effect, they guaranteed to Quebec, which was then virtually synonymous with French Canada, the specific rights which French Canada then felt to be indispensable to its survival and development: first, the use of its language in the legislature and courts of Quebec, and in the Dominion Parliament and any courts created by that Parliament; second, its own Civil Law, including the legal right of the Roman Catholic Church to collect the tithe from its own members; third, complete control of its educational system, subject to certain guarantees for the Protestant minority.

All this was written into the British North America Act; the right to use the French language in the legislature and the courts of Manitoba was written into the Manitoba Act. No special rights for the French language or French schools, let alone French Civil Law, were written into the Constitution for Ontario, the Atlantic provinces or British Columbia. No such rights appear to have been even asked for, for the simple and sufficient reason that the French-speaking population outside Canada East was then so small, and seemed likely to remain so small, except in Manitoba, that no one even thought of it. Nor does there seem to be any evidence that the Fathers of Confederation ever thought of giving the French language or French schools or French Civil Law any special position in the Northwest Territories; official bilingualism made its appearance in their constitution only in 1877, and then only as the result of a Senate amendment moved by a private member of that body at the tail end of the session.

Of course Quebec was also guaranteed a fixed number of posts in the House of Commons, and twenty-four in the Senate, though the provisions for entry of other provinces made it plain that its original proportion of one-third of the total Senators could not be preserved.

Apart from the limited guarantees written into the strict law of the Constitution, there appears to have been one unwritten understanding which hardened into convention: Quebec was to have approximately one-third of the members of the Dominion Cabinet, and the French-Canadians were to have three quarters of the Quebec Ministers, that is, about one quarter of the total.

All the provinces, including Quebec, were given exclusive power over a relatively short list of specific matters, subject to the Dominion's power to disallow any provincial Act within one year. Any legislative power not explicitly given to the provincial legislatures belonged automatically to the Dominion Parliament.

Several things have happened to upset this neat and simple equilibrium.

First, the Judicial Committee of the British Privy Council so interpreted the British North America Act as to give the provinces far wider powers than the Fathers had ever intended.

Second, this process for many decades provoked little opposition in Canada; on the contrary, it was ardently welcomed and fostered, first by Ontario, later by Quebec.

Third, changing concepts of the function of government made both the original provincial powers, such as education, and the new powers, such as jurisdiction over many social questions, far more expensive than the Fathers could ever have dreamt, and increasingly so.

Fourth, Privy Council decisions did not provide adequate extra revenues to meet these extra expenditures. The Dominion had untrammelled power to tax; the provinces' taxing powers remained limited.

Fifth, French Canada has spread out beyond the bounds of Quebec. True, the French-speaking people of Manitoba were early swamped by English-speaking immigrants; but substantial and growing French-speaking communities have made their appearance in northern and eastern Ontario, and the Acadians, and French-speaking immigrants from Quebec, have grown to be well over a third of the population of New Brunswick.

Sixth, Quebec has become more and more predominantly French-speaking. In 1861, Montreal had been more than half English-speaking, Quebec City nearly half, eight counties overwhelmingly English-speaking, and several others had had large English-speaking minorities. Now there is not a single county with an English-speaking majority, and very few with even a large minority; and all the cities are overwhelmingly French-speaking.

Seventh, Quebec has become industrialized, and its people want what they feel is their due share of the benefits. The new technical and administrative middle class wants big jobs in industry and public administration. The ordinary people want a twentieth century North American standard of living. And they want it all in French, so to speak. They are keener than ever on doing things in their own distinctive French-Canadian way. But they want to do a great many more things in that way than they used to, and they want at the same time to be just as well off materially as other North Americans doing things quite differently.

Eighth, there has been a new flowering of French-Canadian culture: literature, art, philosophy, theology, political thought; and this has coincided with the emergence of a whole host of new French-language states and General de Gaulle's restoration of France to the position of a major factor in European and world affairs. There is a new surge of pride not only in the achievements of French Canada itself but in being part of a great, new French-speaking international community.

Very naturally, all this has led to a questioning of all established institutions. Politically, it has led, on the one hand, to demands that Quebec should have wider powers; on the other, that French-Canadians should have more rights all over Canada, and a much bigger share in running the whole of Canada. Indeed, most Quebec French-Canadians probably want both.

The demand for wider powers for Quebec takes a variety of forms: sometimes only minor changes in the distribution of legislative powers, leaving the main structure of Confederation intact; oftener, outright independence; oftener still, the division of Canada into two loosely associated states. There is also at least one proposal for a sort of in-and-out associate state, an associate with knobs on, very large knobs. Under this scheme, the central Parliament would have jurisdiction over Quebec only in relation to defence, currency, interprovincial trade and transport, central banking and monetary policy, customs tariffs, broadcasting (because the maintenance of coast-to-coast French networks would be too expensive for Quebec to handle), equalization grants to the provinces and such external relations as had to do with these subjects. Even for these subjects, policy would be drafted by Advisory Boards half French-Canadian, half English-Canadian; and the Senate would be elected half by French-Canadians, half by the rest of us, and would be given the power to reject treaties (even those dealing with the rest of the country, not Quebec), to veto the appointment of judges and ambassadors, and possibly still further powers. Over the rest of the country, the central Parliament would exercise the far wider jurisdiction which it has at present, or even more; Quebec Ministers would presumably continue to make up about a third of the central Cabinet, and to preside over departments which dealt only with the other provinces; and the full number of Quebec members of the House of Commons would remain, speaking and voting, and very possibly wielding the balance of power, on measures which dealt only with the other provinces. There is also a very recent suggestion, from a very high quarter, that the association of Quebec with the rest of Canada already is, essentially, and should become more and more, an "alliance". As a description of what is, this is unmitigated nonsense: historically, legally, constitutionally, politically. As a statement of what should be, it is hair-raising. NATO would no doubt provide a model; and it is not hard to guess who would play the part of le grand Charles.

Most numerous and influential of all, as far as I can judge, are the Quebec voices which reject separatism, reject the associate state, have at least not pronounced in favor of the in-and-out associate state, but demand a complete revision of the Constitution, or a completely new Constitution, giving Quebec jurisdiction over at least such things as banking, a very large chunk of external affairs, most of all of social security, broadcasting, employment services, and a variety of other things summed up under the usefully vague phrase, "and the list is far from being exhausted." With all this would go also a pretty complete bilingualization of the Dominion public service, and guarantees for French education for French-speaking children in the other nine provinces.

These last two points, of course, are essential demands of those French-Canadians, in Quebec and still more outside it, who want a much bigger share in running the whole country.

Now I am going to be brutally frank in stating my own opinion on these various proposals and some other things.

First, if Quebec really wants independence, we have neither the right nor the means to stop her. All we can do is sit down and do some very hard bargaining on the terms, along the lines sketched out in a recent article by Professor McNaught. I think separation would be bad for Quebec and bad for the rest of us; indeed, probably fatal to both succession states. For many Canadians, of both languages, it would be a heartbreak. For the world, it would be the end of what long looked to be at least a hopeful experiment in co-existence.

Second, if Quebec really wants to divide the country into two associate states, or nine provinces plus an in-and-out associate state, or an "alliance", then I think the answer of English Canada will be, in Cromwell's words, "In the name of God, go!" Schemes of this sort simply will not work, and are not worth the effort. Better outright separation.

Some French-Canadians seem to believe that the rest of us are so enamoured of them, or so convinced we cannot get on without them, that we will pay almost any price to preserve even the most tenuous connection with them. This is a dangerous delusion.

Third, some Quebec French-Canadians who call themselves "moderates", and who, I think, genuinely believe that they want to preserve a single Canadian economic and political community, are nevertheless asking for Quebec powers which are totally impossible within any such community. These people are, to adapt a delightful phrase of the late M. Duplessis, "separatists without knowing it." They do not want separation, but they do want things which can be got only by separation. They are asking for dry water, boiling ice, sour sugar, stationary motion.

Those are pretty hard words for some French-Canadians. Now I have a few for some English-Canadians who seem to me, in different but equally disastrous ways, just as foolish and unrealistic.

First, the Dominion of Canada is not, never was, and never will be, a country of one language and one culture. The French language and French-type Civil Law always have had and always will have a special position. French-Canadians are not just one among many ethnic groups, or even just the largest among many minorities.

Second, Quebec is not just "one province like the others." It always has had, and always will have, a special position, a special status. It is the citadel of French Canada. That is written into the BNA Act plainly, unequivocally.

Third, we cannot simply maintain the Confederation settlement unchanged. The industrialization of Quebec, its cultural renaissance, the continuous extension of French Canada beyond Quebec, all call for adjustments, though not for the return to 1860 which some people are in effect proposing.

Fourth, if we really want to keep one country, we must be willing to pay a price for it. If we are not willing to pay the price, then we do not really want one Canada, we only un-really want it.

Fifth, in my opinion, the minimum price of holding the country together includes: first, the quickest and most complete bilingualism of the central administration possible; second, official bilingualism in New Brunswick, just as far and as fast as possible; third, the same, in municipal government and the courts wherever there is a substantial French-speaking minority that wants it; fourth, French education for French-speaking children wherever the parents want it and there are enough such children to make it possible. I know all this will not be easy. But if we really want Canada to survive, then I think we must give French-Canadians much more of a feeling that the whole country is their show as well as ours than many of them seem to have now, and must give them outward and visible signs of it.

Sixth, I think we English-speaking Canadians must be willing to sit down with our French-speaking fellow-citizens and discuss *any specific* changes. I do not myself see how we can maintain recognizable or visible Canadian economic or political community with any substantial reduction in the present powers of the Dominion Parliament. But I would be willing to look at any grievance whatever, and discuss it, and try to find means of meeting it.

Of course this ought to work both ways. We have *our* grievances too, our rights, our traditions, our history, our feelings, our way of looking at things, our culture, though this is sometimes forgotten. We also are part of the "bi" in "biculturalism".

And note that I say "discuss". That means examine, on the basis of facts, and by the light of reason, and decide accordingly; it means give and take, within the limits of what is tolerable and practicable. It does *not* mean saying "Yes", automatically, to anything and everything Quebec or French Canada asks. I think one thing English Canada more and more resents is the tendency of French-Canadian spokesmen to present a list of demands with a peremptory, "Sign here, and sign quick, and no noise from the English-Canadian cheap seats!", the tendency to tell us that we must simply "adjust" ourselves to French-Canadian wishes, must be mere clay in the hands of the French-Canadian potter. Nor does it help to be told that the changes we must accept only embody "the legitimate aspirations" of French Canada. No one would refuse to satisfy "legitimate aspirations"; but the question is, what is "legitimate"? Calling a demand that does not make it so. If English-Canadians announced that their "legitimate aspirations" required the transfer of jurisdiction over health from the provinces to the Dominion, and no questions asked, French-Canadians would want to know why; and they would be right. What's sauce for the English-Canadian goose should be sauce for the French-Canadian gander.

Either automatic acceptance or automatic rejection of proposals for constitutional change, whether from French Canada or English, is a flight from reason, and can only end by making civilized life in this country impossible. The best of us, at the best of times, are unreasonable enough; but surely few of us would deliberately embrace unreason as *the* method of conducting public affairs, deliberately give anyone or any group a blank cheque.

I will add, finally, just four footnotes.

First, I suggest English-Canadians should try to imagine how we would feel, think and act if the United States and all the provinces except Ontario spoke French.

My second footnote is that simply saying, "Yes", to anything any French-Canadian says he wants is paying French-Canadians a very poor compliment. Indeed it is treating them with contempt. It implies that they are not rational, not grown up, not equal fellow citizens, with whom we can really engage in "dialogue" (to use the great camp word of the moment), but irrational, spoiled children, neurotics, inferiors, who can only be humoured and appeased, not argued with. This is an insult to French-Canadians of which I refuse to be guilty. I would a thousand times rather appear grossly discourteous, as perhaps I have now.

Third, I would not be scared of any specific change in the Constitution by the cry that it would give Quebec a special status, a right, a power, a privilege that no other province would have. Quebec already has a special status, has had from the beginning. So have several other provinces, in various ways. There may be perfectly good reasons for giving any one province something further the others have not got and do not even want. There are, of course, things no province can have as long as it remains part of Canada. If it insists on having them it will have to get out. But any specific proposals short of that should be examined on their merits, not just damned on the ground that no province has a right to anything unless every other province gets it too.

Finally, I hope that in any constitutional discussions we shall stick to specifics and forswear those abstract principles which, in a pluralistic society like ours, are almost certain to set everybody by the ears to no purpose. That is why I dread any attempt to write a whole new Constitution instead of simply dealing with the specific, practical issues, "claw by claw," as one of our old Newfoundland trade unionists used to say when he began collective bargaining. That very distinguished French-Canadian, my friend and former colleague Guy Hudon, used to say: "The Judicial Committee of the Privy Council never laid down a general principle but once, when it laid down the general principle that it would not lay down general principles. The Cour de Cassation, in France, starting from totally different premises, arrived at the same conclusion." I think that in this at least those two great embodiments of our two great Canadian legal traditions set us a salutary example.

31   What Does Quebec Want?*

Government of Quebec

Introduction

Our delegation is delighted to have this opportunity to set forth, before the representatives of the various governments gathered here, Québec's objectives regarding the constitution she desires for the Canada of tomorrow.

Nor can she fail to acknowledge the great merit redounding to her sister province for having undertaken, at a most appropriate moment, to convene this conference whose historic import we fully appreciate, and which historians will record as a decisive step in our country's development.

We have prepared this document especially for our English-speaking fellow-countrymen and we should like them to study it with the same equanimity as we sought to attain in preparing it. For we are here to open a dialogue and we take it for granted that this conference is only the first of many. For us, it represents the initial stage in an exchange of views, an exchange for which the pressing need is now apparent and whose scope will be unprecedented.

The many difficulties along our road cannot serve as an excuse for refusing the

---

*Government of Quebec, *Preliminary Statement*, Presented to the "Confederation of Tomorrow" Conference, Toronto, November 1967. Reprinted by permission.

challenge confronting us. And, at the present juncture, we do not believe we are really in any position to do anything but accept it.

Statement of the Issue

If we are to determine as fittingly as possible what the "Confederation of Tomorrow" should be, we must first examine Canada as it is today.

An Imperilled Confederation

We are now living in a divided country searching for identity and racked by inner tensions.

Why is this so? Why, when a few short years ago most people did not have the slightest premonition of such a crisis, why are some of us now suddenly obliged to accept as a working hypothesis the hitherto unthinkable possibility of Canada's dissolution? What has taken place which can account for the astonishment in some circles, the dismay in others at such a development?

What has happened is that Québec, mainstay of French Canada, questioning the validity of the country's political structure, seeks a reallocation of powers between the two orders of government and concrete recognition for French Canada of rights equal to those always enjoyed by English-speaking Canada. Such aspirations, expressed more forcefully and consistently than ever before, first surprised English-speaking Canada and then produced opposition to what seemed a threat to the established order. In fact, we have reached the point where quite a few French-speaking Canadians believe that persistent misunderstanding makes any statement of their aspirations to English-speaking citizens a waste of time. A considerable number among the latter, we realize, are satisfied with the present political system and hold that no concession should be made to the vague demands of what they believe to be a vociferous and extremist minority. Thus the two groups which a century ago established Canadian Confederation are becoming more firmly entrenched in their "two solitudes". More seriously still, these two solitudes are increasingly out of touch with each other's reality; in the end, lack of co-operation between them can destroy Canada.

Québec's representatives at this conference are in an excellent position to assess the present state of mind among French-speaking Canadians living in Québec and to foresee where it may lead if our country's two main cultural groups do not soon reach an understanding to rebuild Canada on new foundations.

A Century-old Experience

French Canadians assume that the 1867 confederative act was designed to let them develop in accordance with their own culture.

One hundred years ago, the Fathers of Confederation entrusted to the provinces both those spheres of activity which, at the time, seemed properly to depend on local initiative and those which seemed essential to protect language, religion and culture.

Today, after a century's experience, French Canadians have become aware of three things. First of all, whenever members of their community living in provinces other than Québec have sought to obtain rights equal to those enjoyed by English-speaking Canadians, the 1867 constitution has proved impotent. Of course neither English Canada's nor the French-Canadian nation's rights are expressly acknowledged in the constitution. Yet we might have expected French Canadians living outside Québec to have been treated with more understanding and greater broad-mindedness. Unfortunately this did not happen and numerical superiority was often used to withhold from French-language minorities basic community rights essential to their survival and development. They were even stripped of rights they already had. Eventually, French Canadians were, to all intents and purposes, reduced to feeling truly at home only within Québec's borders, even though, despite everything, some French-speaking groups continue to survive in all provinces, especially in certain areas of Ontario, the Atlantic Provinces and Manitoba.

The second thing French Canadians have noticed is that there has always been a clear tendency for the federal government to take over, partly or wholly, responsibilities assigned to the provinces in the 1867 constitution. In Quebecers' eyes, the constitutional or political justifications with which the central government has sought to explain its encroachments have often smacked of sophistry. Certainly no one would say that during the last twenty-five or thirty years the federal government has acted against its will. All it needed as an excuse for action was inaction by some provinces. Provincial governments wanting to act on their own behalf then had to follow suit or lose major financial advantages. The story of joint programmes is a good case in point.

And thirdly, French-speaking Canadians realize that the 1867 division of responsibilities between governments no longer permits the French-Canadian nation to develop as effectively as it desires. During these last hundred years, the economic, social and administrative roles assigned to the public sector have grown enormously. State activities have become vastly more complex, and are sure to become more so as time goes on. Citizens are now directly affected by government action on a host of matters for which local and private initiative were formerly responsible. French-speaking Canadians feel that several such new realms of government intervention are, like education in 1867, vital instruments for their collective self-expression. They now want to keep control over these fields because, in the long run, not merely their full development as a people but their very survival will depend on it.

An Inevitable Crisis

Quebecers have always known that if their enterprises are to attain success in Canada, they must exert themselves more than other Canadians, who have the dual advantage of numerical superiority and favouring Canadian economic and political institutions. But in addition, they now find their road to full self-achievement encumbered with fresh obstacles, including some which, under present conditions, seem more difficult to overcome than those they have met in the past. In general, during the last decade, not a minority but a majority of

Quebecers have become aware that their situation is likely to grow worse if they do not act promptly to remedy it.

In sociological terms, Quebecers have witnessed the disintegration of the way of life which traditionally protected them. They had survived in good part because they lived in isolation, locked in upon themselves, clinging to the past in a typically rural environment where the state's presence was marginal. Almost overnight, they found themselves in an industrial society requiring massive intervention by the state, open to the whole of North America and exposed to the influence of foreign, especially American, culture, backed by such powerful means of communication as speedy transport, highways, cinema, radio and television.

In demographic terms, they have become aware that, even though they form some thirty per cent of Canada's population, they constitute a tiny group in comparison with the North American English-speaking community.

On the economic level, they have come to understand that the industrial society in which they were henceforth to live had not been created by them, but by others not sharing their cultural values. And also that, in a world where economic might confers enough *de facto* advantages to make *de jure* claims unnecessary, they were — not always through their own fault — seriously lacking in means for effective action.

In political matters, as we have already said, they have realized that Canada's structure itself worked to their disadvantage and that the 1867 constitution was far from giving them the protection they had traditionally anticipated.

Taking all this into account, it is incontrovertibly evident that our nation no longer has a choice. If it passively accepts the present situation, it will inevitably take the road to slow but sure assimilation into the great North-American mass.

Hence, it has become vital that it do everything in its power to correct the present situation.

As French-speaking Canadians, we have the unshakeable conviction that we form a viable community sharing one of the greatest cultures in the western world, speaking an international language and endowed with vast human potentialities. That is why, despite all difficulties, we are resolved to preserve our identity. But there is more than this. The very act of asserting ourselves as a nation will certainly help greatly in giving Canada the identity she needs to distinguish herself from her powerful neighbour to the south. Moreover, we are convinced that, in future, nations like ours will have a role to play out of all proportion to their demographic strength. In short, we are willing to gamble on our possibilities as a people and want to act accordingly. Several obstacles we now face as a nation can be overcome by our own efforts and by Québec Government action. But there are other aspects of this problem for which we alone cannot find a solution. We know that it can be solved if English Canada makes a serious effort. Up to a point, this community will have to alter its traditional approach to relations between our two linguistic groups. It will also have to abstain from opposition to substantial change in the country's political structure and in the present division of powers between the Canadian and Québec governments.

What we in Québec have become accustomed to call the Canadian constitutional problem is thus not wholly juridical in nature. We are dealing with a basically political and social problem, one of whose causes stems from the present constitution.

An Impotent Constitution

A country's constitution is its fundamental law. To some extent, it lays down the rules of the game. In doubtful cases, appeal should be had to it, and it should be interpreted by appropriate tribunals. Governments under its sway must conform to it. Therefore, it is essential that a constitution properly reflect sociological reality in the country to which it applies and truly derive from the aims and aspirations of the human communities making up that country.

Does the 1867 British North America Act, even as interpreted and amended since its passage, meet these requirements, which are certainly not unreasonable for so obviously important a document as a constitution? To ask the question is already to suggest the answer, which is a forthright negative. The 1867 constitution no longer in any sense conforms to present Canadian reality. We shall not undertake here any juridical analysis or study in semantics. We shall merely point out specific characteristics of today's Canada and her problems, then try to see how closely the present constitution does reflect these characteristics and whether it can contribute to solving new problems as they arise. The conclusions will be self-evident.

1) In Canada there exists a French-Canadian nation of which the mainstay is Québec. It can likewise be said that there exists an English-speaking nation, although its cohesion and self-awareness may, for understandable reasons, be less apparent than they are among French Canadians. Each of these two nations must have its fundamental right to full development recognized by the other, in law and in fact, if we want Canada to be able to operate as a political entity and advance as an economic entity. The most serious Canadian problem today is precisely that of the relation which should obtain between these two communities. Here the present constitution offers no guidance, since it wholly ignores this essential aspect of Canadian reality. Our constitution does not recognize the existence in our country of sociological groups called "nations", "nationalities" or "societies". Even though it refers to some individual religious rights and regulates the use of the English and French languages in a few federal and Québec public bodies it provides no specific rights for the communities which speak those languages.

2) Canada now comprises ten provinces, no one like any other in people, size, climate, problems or resources. Logically, it would not seem desirable to formulate policies conceived as though all the country's provinces had been cast in the same mold. Yet except for a few provisions of secondary importance — accidental or transitory — our constitution in principle now keeps all provinces on the same footing. It provides no opportunity for special federal-provincial arrangements adapted to conditions in a given province. In practice, these special arrangements can be effected but, whatever the intention may be, they cannot help appearing exceptional or temporary. In short, our consti-

tution makes some allowance for special situations existing when a given province entered confederation; but, divorced from day-to-day reality, it does not allow for continuance and even intensification of differences between provinces once they became members of confederation.

3) Because of changes in the technical and social order, Canada today is faced with a whole series of problems which the Fathers of Confederation, however vivid their imagination, could not conceivably have foreseen. Consider, for instance, town-planning policy, regional development, economic stability, telecommunications, atomic energy, the space age, manpower policies, educational television and many other contemporary developments. Our constitution is silent on these matters. Therefore, when a new problem arises in Canada, we are more and more likely to base each government's responsibilities for it, not on constitutional principles, but on considerations of the moment which, in turn, derive from a variety of factors such as relative capacity to act, financial resources or merely the political power wielded by a given area of government. Hence, even though there is a written document called the British North America Act from which we may expect some light to be cast on such traditional fields as education and municipal institutions, the allocation of new tasks among governments has not been guided by this document but by decisions mainly based on exigencies of the day. In some instances, the old constitution has been amended to furnish grounds for action that was predetermined in any case. In others, the method used was to imagine the opinions Fathers of Confederation would have held. Whether or not the provinces have participated in reaching such decisions, it is still true that our present constitution, perhaps admirable during the age of steam trains, no longer suits Canada's needs in this era of interplanetary rockets.

4) In addition, the modern world has stimulated more frequent and continuing relations between nations, groups and regions. This is as true at the Canadian as at the international level. Within Canada, developments in recent years have led governments to have increasing recourse to federal-provincial or interprovincial conferences to settle problems as they arose. Such meetings have become a necessity. It is hard to imagine how Canada could function efficiently today were not the representatives of the various governments to gather at more or less regular intervals to discuss among themselves policies to be followed. For the moment we do not intend to say how we believe these conferences should be prepared and managed; the fact remains that so essential a means for co-ordination and consultation is not even mentioned in the country's present constitution. Hence, intergovernmental meetings in Canada result far more from political, financial or administrative accidents than from rational and formal machinery for reciprocal consultation. In theory, nothing prevents their being eliminated at any time, even if such a turn of events is at present unlikely. It is also significant that a good many of these conferences are now made necessary by the ill-defined division of powers between the country's governments. So we are faced with a constitution which, over the years, has become vacuous whenever there is need to allocate public responsibilities whose very existence could not be foreseen in 1867, a constitution, moreover,

including no clear provision or procedure for implementing the intergovernmental coordination often made necessary by its own omissions.

5) In international affairs, the situation created by the present constitution is equally confused. Practice established during the past half century, and not any constitutional text, gives the federal government responsibility for what we call foreign policy. Yet nowhere is this defined. Nor does the constitution say anything about the bonds of every kind which, more tightly and in increasing number, link modern nations in fields almost all of which it reserves to the provinces. As a result, efforts to resolve any differences which may arise today between governmental sectors over relations they may or may not have with foreign countries or organizations are based on more or less acrobatic interpretations of the constitution or of constitutional practice.

6) Nothing in our constitution clearly provides for settling such disagreements, whether they relate to international relations, culture, manpower or the administration of justice. In several essential matters, there is not even provision in the constitution for amending it. Until now, every attempt to reach an acceptable amending formula has been based on an inaccurate interpretation of Canadian society.

To our minds, these few examples constitute sufficiently obvious evidence of the rift between our constitution and the reality to which it supposedly applies. If to this be added the fact that no clear-cut rule, still valid today, governs the sharing of tax resources among Canadian governments, the only straightforward conclusion to be drawn, in our view, is that our country's fundamental law not only has a superannuated look, but is in fact a compilation of various unrelated customs, conventions and juridical documents and no longer fits the needs of modern government for the aspirations of the French-Canadian nation.

Alarming Empiricism

Some people have claimed that the present constitution has been flexible enough to adjust to the changing conditions which marked the last few generations and that it did not prevent us from finding workable solutions to several federal-provincial problems in recent years. We feel that such arguments are invalid on two counts.

First, the constitution has never been instrumental in settling federal-provincial disagreements. When we did work out temporary or permanent compromises, especially for Québec, they came as a result of intergovernmental discussions which at times had every aspect of open warfare. Indeed, it was lack of an explicit constitution, complicated by basic political factors, that led to these clashes, costing both sides much wasted energy and creating misunderstandings which have yet to be cleared. Surely, in a country such as ours, there must be a better way of reaching an effective and lasting solution to difficulties attending allocation of responsibilities and distribution of the resources needed to carry them out. At any rate, we in Québec are probably most directly concerned and we do not see why negotiations between governments in Canada should always take place in such an atmosphere of conflict.

Second, the French-Canadian nation considers the present constitution no longer capable of providing the guarantees that should properly be expected from it. It is no secret that, even if our constitution is always subject to interpretation whenever new problems spring up, both the interpretation and resulting practical arrangements usually favour the government sector whose political position is stronger; at times, this may be the federal government, at others, the provincial governments. Nothing in Canada today indicates which way the scale will tip in future. In a country with a single society, such a situation would at worst create administrative complications or regional uneasiness; in ours, it spells a lasting threat to the French-Canadian community and, with time, creates unbearable conditions. French Canada is quite prepared to take up the awesome cultural challenge it faces on the North-American continent, but cannot be reconciled to the prospect of fruitless struggles in its own country caused by its permanently unsettled situation.

Levelling criticism at a constitution because it is inexplicit or behind the times does not necessarily mean that the critic wants an inflexible replacement. We would readily agree that, however well drafted, a constitution cannot possibly contain answers to all problems

True, constitutional problems seldom seem to take priority; but when they do, particularly in a federal system, political rather than legal implications become the issue. It seems to us that we are indeed going through one of those rare phases when, owing to their direct repercussion on the citizen's daily life, questions related to our country's constitution — therefore our political institutions — take precedence. We must tackle them at the earliest opportunity, lest conditions grow worse, and so that we may concentrate our efforts on the solution of other urgent problems.

The Canadian Duality

The two languages widely spoken in our land, English and French, are both international languages. Those who speak French live mostly in one part of Canada, Québec, where they constitute the great majority of the population.

Being the first Europeans to settle in this country, they are convinced that they form a nation in the sociological sense of the word. They have their own government, public and private economic, financial and administrative and cultural institutions. In short, they have a civilization of their own.

Because she also happens to be the home of an English-speaking society with a culture of its own, Canada is thus a binational country. Indeed, it is one or other of these two nations or cultural communities which have been joined by those of various origins whose arrival has enriched Canada since the beginning of the century.

In its relationship with the rest of the country, Québec, as the mainstay and homeland of French Canada, is confronted by two kinds of problems which are not easily differentiated because in practice they often overlap.

When we consider for instance highway construction, some financial arrangements between governments, sales tax collection, measures designed to reduce water pollution, there are a host of questions where all provinces, Québec included, meet on common ground.

But when we come to socio-cultural problems, Québec's position is altogether different from that of the other provinces. We have in mind not only education, culture and language, but also social security, health, municipal institutions, certain credit establishments, regional development, adult training, manpower policies, cultural exchanges with other countries or, to put it briefly, everything that may be used as instrument for French-Canada's assertion and promotion of her economic, social and political institutions.

A New Covenant

What then must be done to pave the way for the Canada of tomorrow is to lay the foundation of a covenant without which we shall continue to live in confusion, victims of contradictions arising daily between our anachronistic constitution and Canadian reality.

The last half of this statement contains certain proposals in this respect for purposes of discussion.

The Canada of Tomorrow

If Canada of Tomorrow is to endure, it must rest on a new constitution that, as now, must group within the country a certain number of territories, which may be called provinces or states. More important however, it must also permit association by two societies co-operating within common institutions as well as respect for the basic collective rights and legitimate aspirations of each.

In the following paragraphs, rather than submit the draft of a new constitution in legal form, we shall elaborate briefly on issues which we feel should be the object of constitutional provisions. In each instance, we shall formulate opinions on which we would heartily welcome open discussion; we would like to know what English-speaking Canadians think of them, for what really matters — and such is the immediate purpose of our meeting — is that we get our heads together in order to examine the broad elements of the problem, without embarking on discussion of details. Besides, the Government of Québec will have to weigh the implications of positions taken by the Estates General of French Canada and study the report prepared by our Parliamentary Committee on the Constitution. Naturally, we are also awaiting the report of the Royal Commission on Bilingualism and Biculturalism.

We feel that the new constitution should be aimed at four goals:

(1) defining clearly the principles that are to guide Canadian political life;
(2) working out a new distribution of powers and resources to promote development of the French-Canadian nation and free evolution of English-speaking Canada;

(3) institutionalizing or establishing certain machinery for intergovernmental consultation, co-ordination and action;

(4) modifying the operation of some Canadian organization and institutions, modernizing others and creating new ones so that, as a whole, they may reflect Canada's binational identity.

Fundamental Principles

A constitution is much more than a legal document; it is a guide and a source of inspiration. Objectives shared by all citizens must be embodied in the fundamental principles on which it rests as well as the ties which bind together nations, communities, groups and individuals of different language, history and culture.

With these considerations in mind, we believe that the constitution should begin by proclaiming Canada's absolute sovereignty.

The constitution should also acknowledge the existence in Canada of two nations, bound together by history, each enjoying equal collective rights. The new constitution must clearly spell out the principle that English and French are the country's two official languages.

The constitution must include a charter of human rights applying to the central government's constitutional jurisdictions. As for us, the Québec Government intends to insert in Québec's constitution a charter of human rights covering matters under provincial control.

Finally, a provision must sanction the principle of economic interdependence, mutual support and co-operation between states or provinces, with every regard for the country's binational character.

As for Québec's internal constitution, it must naturally fall under its own exclusive jurisdiction.

Distribution of Powers

The division of powers between central government and member-states remains the keystone of any federal constitution. To make headway, we submit certain proposals.

We believe that, as is the case in most other federations, provinces or member-states of Canada must retain all powers not expressly granted to the central government. In this way, we should have a better idea where the latter's jurisdiction begins or ends, and friction caused by encroachment from the centre would be greatly reduced.

Needless to say, we want to have reserve and disallowance powers eliminated from federal prerogatives and the Parliament of Canada divested of its declaratory power. Perhaps these provisions had some justification in earlier days, but we think that today, in matters within their jurisdiction, the provinces must be given complete internal sovereignty.

Other Québec positions have already been made known. Thus, in the brief submitted in September 1966 to the fourth meeting of the federal-provincial Tax Structure Committee, we stated: "As the mainstay of a nation, it wants free rein to make its own decisions affecting the growth of its citizens as human beings (i.e., education, social security and health in all respects), their economic development (i.e., the forging of any economic and financial tool deemed necessary), their cultural fulfilment (which takes in not only arts and literature, but the French language as well), and the presence abroad of the Québec community (i.e., relations with certain countries and international organizations)."

Further in the brief, we stated that, while awaiting a new constitution, we would first have to proceed with a re-arrangement of functions, which might even be initiated within the framework of our present constitution: "By this process, the Québec Government would gradually become solely responsible within its territory for all public expenditures on every form of education, old age security, family allowances, health, employment and training of the labour force, regional development and, in particular, municipal aid programmes, research, fine arts, culture, as well as any other social or cultural service within our jurisdiction under the present constitution. Existing federal programmes in these fields would be taken over by Québec, which would maintain their portability where applicable."

It is not our place to tell the other provinces how powers in the Confederation of Tomorrow should be divided between them and the federal government. We merely wish to make a few comments which may be pertinent.

We have just outlined the Québec Government's general objective. To reach it, Québec will necessarily have to obtain a new constitutional distribution of tasks giving her broader powers than she now exercises. We feel these broader powers are vital to Québec, but this does not mean that we in any way object to the other provinces seeking exactly the same powers if they so desire.

If in fact they are willing to assume the same tasks as Québec, it is quite conceivable to envisage a new constitution which would confirm much greater decentralization of powers to all provinces than now exists.

Naturally, we realize that other provinces may be prepared to entrust the central government with some powers which Québec believes she must herself exercise. In our view, such an arrangement is not incompatible with federalism and solutions of this kind should be used without hesitation whenever sociological conditions in the country make them necessary. In this case, all provinces would at the outset, be granted identical constitutional powers, provided that constitutional provision would make possible administrative or legislative delegation to the federal government. This way, the provinces themselves would decide the actual extent of their responsibilities under the new system.

Not wanting to prejudge their attitude on this matter, we thought it might be helpful to open the dialogue by stating some of our own positions, for later comparison with theirs.

Intergovernmental Co-operation

If it is important to establish clearly the responsibilities of each area of government, it is equally essential to indicate here the methods of co-operation which should exist between each. The modern world no longer tolerates impassable barriers between governments, any more than it permits attributing any particular problem to a single cause. Quebec is fully aware of this fact; she feels she must increase her jurisdictional range in the Canada of tomorrow, not in order to isolate herself, but rather to be in a better position to bring her own contribution to collective wealth through interdependence. Each government must be concerned with the impact of its actions on other governments.

Thus, even though the federal government has jurisdiction over currency, it must always reckon with the fact that monetary policy has concrete repercussions on other governments' action. Similarly, nobody will deny the provinces' exclusive responsibility for municipal affairs, but does this mean that their activities in this field have no effect on decisions required of the federal government in others? Not at all. And certainly the influence which provinces exert on one another is often apparent, even if each merely acts within the limits of its own jurisdiction.

As far as we are concerned, we prefer to establish a clear division between governmental responsibilities, then provide machinery for intergovernmental co-operation.

Above all, it is our feeling that we should institutionalize federal-provincial and interprovincial conferences. Of course, the constitution could not fix the frequency or agendas of such meetings. That would be unrealistic. It would probably be sufficient to stipulate the right of any government to take the initiative for convening such conferences.

Similarly, we should provide for the existence of well defined machinery for intergovernmental consultation and co-operation on economic policy. Here again, it would not be necessary to enter into details, but merely to express juridically the practical consequences of our incontestable economic interdependence. Economic policies in Canada cannot and must not depend exclusively on one government, in this instance federal. The provinces have and will continue to have a major interest in this field. There can be no question of excluding them from formulating and implementing various economic policies, particularly fiscal policies, if only because of the size of their own budgets and their influence on the economy. In any case, Quebec cannot agree to stay out of the economic policy field, for that would be tantamount to allowing another government to decide the course of her whole economy.

Fiscal matters, and more specifically fiscal arrangements are not on the agenda of this conference, in accordance with the wishes of the Ontario Government which convened it. It is obvious that in the context of a new constitution to exclusive jurisdictions must correspond exclusive or paramount fiscal powers.

Further, in order to ensure the right of each citizen to comparable services, wherever he may live in Canada, the mechanisms of fiscal arrangements should be improved and, if necessary, institutionalized.

It is also our impression that we would have everything to gain by setting up a permanent interprovincial secretariat which, among other functions, would help keep provincial governments better informed on one another's legislation, administrative reforms, problems as well as the solutions adopted, policies and other matters. In addition, such a secretariat would permit more thorough preparation for interprovincial meetings of cabinet ministers and civil servants.

Canadian Institutions

Whatever their immediate functions, it seems essential to us that federal institutions in the Canada of tomorrow take clear count, in their structure and aims, of the country's binational character. We want to express a few thoughts on the subject, in spite of the fact that this meeting is not a federal-provincial conference.

Steps should first be taken, by required means, to ensure genuine, effective and proportionate participation in the federal public service by French-speaking Canadians. There have been recent improvements in this respect, but this movement should be stepped up; above all, definite mechanisms should be provided to translate it rapidly into fact. In addition, it is vital that French become a current working language within all administrative services directly or indirectly dependent on the federal government, both in Ottawa and in areas with a French-language population. The same should be done in the Armed Forces.

We also think the federal capital should reflect the linguistic duality of the population. Equality of the two official languages should be confirmed in all capital area government services, be they federal, provincial or municipal. To this end, the purely federal "National Capital Commission" should become a tripartite "Federal Capital Commission" in which the three governments most directly concerned, those of Canada, Ontario and Québec, would have equal prerogatives, each delegating to it the powers needed to administer an appropriate territorial area and assuming a proportionate share of its operating costs.

We further think it advisable to create a genuine constitutional tribunal whose composition would reflect the federal character of our institutions and the Canadian cultural duality.

We believe, also, that it would be advantageous to investigate the possibility of transforming the current Senate into a true federal House having a bicultural character.

Finally, we believe that establishment of a permanent federal-provincial commission on linguistic rights would do a good deal to ensure the recognition, in practice, by all governments concerned, of the equal rights of our two communities in this respect. Citizens and corporate bodies who felt their linguistic rights had been prejudiced would be entitled to lodge grievances or complaints with the commission. This advisory institution should in no way limit the competence of the constitutional tribunal with respect to language rights.

Of course, there are many things we might add concerning changes we think necessary in other Canadian institutions, such as the Canadian Broadcasting Corporation, the National Film Board, etc.

The Language Question and French-Canadian Minorities

In concluding, it is important to draw very special attention to one of the major Canadian problems of the day: the status of French in Canada. We have already touched several times on this question, which we consider basic.

The Québec Government is committed to making French a true national language in Québec, while respecting the linguistic rights of the minority. We are currently studying various means of promoting generalized use of French throughout our territory, so that French-Canadian Quebecers in their home province may live and work in their mother tongue, just as English-speaking Canadians live and work in their own language in the other provinces.

But this will not solve the whole problem. Essentially, what French Canadians want is to be themselves and develop normally like any other people; in Québec and in other parts of Canada. More particularly, they want to create in Québec an environment conducive to their own growth. They also want it to be possible for members of their community settled in other provinces to develop as English-speaking Canadians can do in Québec.

In a country like ours, we must begin by ensuring public education at all levels in Canada's two official languages wherever the English or French-speaking group is sufficiently large. Obviously, this does not rule out the necessity of providing the French or English-speaking groups with means of acquiring good command of the majority language in their environment. As for other government services such as departments, courts, administrative bodies, we believe the best way to avoid problems and render justice to the greatest number of people concerned is to deal with the question on a regional basis, without regard to provincial boundaries.

We expect to continue the dialogue initiated here at subsequent meetings.

32   Report by the Constitution Committee of the Quebec Liberal Federation Policy Commission*

Introduction

Quebec, A Distinctive Society

1. Ever since 1760, French Canadians have had to grapple with critical problems in order to ensure the survival of their community.

2. Different from all other North-American communities, concentrated within a well-defined territory, not given their own government until 1867, French Canadians have maintained the distinct identity which they succeeded in retaining under every political system they had previously known.

---

*This Report was presented to the Annual Convention of the Quebec Liberal Federation in October 1967. The document is a first draft translation and is subject to change. By permission.

3. Today, French Canadians constitute the large majority in Quebec where they have developed a society whose language and culture are predominantly French. Their determination to ensure this society's progress in accordance with its own characteristics is stronger now than it has ever been.

4. Until recently, the survival and growth of French Canadians in Canada and Quebec was largely attributable to a high birth rate and to their withdrawal into a rural society sealed off from outside influences.

5. In the past few years, however, they have become aware that the past no longer holds out any guarantee for the future. They have come to realize that only their own state and government can undertake the tremendous effort towards self-assertion and progress which would enable them to meet modern world requirements. Because of the forces moving them closer every day to the rest of North America, to which they are bound by countless ties, they know they must identify more fully with Quebec, the only state which can organize and sustain their growth.

6. Witnessing a world-wide move towards emancipation by peoples less well equipped and organized than themselves, fully alive to the extraordinary challenges which the technological revolution and the staggering economic power of the United States present to any society, they have grown more demanding and more determined to carve out a future in which they and their children may take pride. They are now convinced that their being and fulfilment are linked with the existence of a Quebec state endowed with all the essential powers needed to this end.

7. In recent years — particularly since 1960 — French-Canadian society has begun this effort towards self-assertion and progress, primarily by dynamic state action in three key areas: modernization of Quebec's educational system; establishment of her own social security program tailored to her special conditions and aims; planning and guidance of economic growth (by taking over a number of controls, creating certain financial or fiscal conditions, organizing services or making other promotional efforts).

8. It was while carrying out this program that Quebec discovered the deep resistance which the Constitution sets up against its implementation: duplication of effort between the federal and provincial governments, directly conflicting jurisdictions and policies, or lack of provincial powers.

9. This is the crux of the constitutional problem, raised today more than ever before. If Quebec intends to remain a distinct society, she can no longer accept the 1867 constitutional framework, but must seek and obtain institutions commensurate with her new situation.

Quebec's Powers

a) Present Powers

10. As constituted by the 1867 British statute, Quebec shares with the central Canadian state the many legislative and administrative powers generally associated with statehood — each, in theory, exercising its own powers fully and exclusively.

11. Quebec can thus govern with complete sovereignty in a great many areas, encompassing such spheres of activity as natural resources (water, soil and sub-soil), education, civil law, hospitals and public health, municipal organization and others.

12. Under the B.N.A. act of 1867, the Quebec state also obtained powers in many other fields which it has neglected to exercise; these include activities in which leadership or direct action by the state might have been and still is expected. We must not overlook the vast powers and accompanying control levers which Quebec holds under the 1867 constitution and which she is free to use without constitutional amendment. The constitutional problem should certainly not serve as a handy excuse to cover up the incompetence and inaction of those who have at their command full sovereignty in a wide range of fields demanding bold and energetic action by public authorities in the people's interest.

13. This does not alter the fact that the 1867 constitution puts a great many obstacles in the path of legislation by Quebec in areas which are vital to her existence and growth as a distinct personality. The Act expressly reserves sole exercise of certain powers to the federal parliament. However, the central authority has made further inroads into fields where Quebec should have jurisdiction, as a result of interpretations of the Act by the Privy Council of England and the Supreme Court of Canada.

14. It is important to mention various loopholes in the Constitution through which the central government has moved obliquely into fields otherwise allocated exclusively to the provinces. At the risk of entering into technicalities, attention should be drawn to the significance of provisions concerning "Peace, Order and good Government", "residual" power, "accessory" or "incidental" power, "declaratory" power and, above all, the authority to spend for any purpose monies raised under an unlimited taxation power. This screen of legal jargon conceals not only direct obstacles but also the most artfully contrived impediments to implementation of Quebec policies.

15. Areas which the federal government has thus penetrated cover radio and television, university grants, social assistance and vocational training, control of the insurance field and highway construction. And what are we to think of the over-subtle distinction made between education and culture?

16. Surely this is sufficient to justify the conclusion that, in its present form, the constitution is a constant source of frustration and wasted energy, duplication of effort and conflict. This situation must be completely changed to provide for effective government of the modern state needed by Quebecers. This necessarily implies a new division of powers.

b) New Powers Required

17. That being the case, the next step is to consider what new legislative and administrative powers Quebec requires in order to organize her citizens' community life in terms of their own needs and aspirations.

18. It might be said that, in a way, a state's every act, and thus its every

power, has a direct or indirect influence on the growth of its people's collective personality. However, now that interdependence of nations is such a daily fact of life that all states are led to seek formulas for rapprochement and co-ordination, we must attempt to define the minimum powers which cannot be left to an outside authority without endangering our collective personality.

19. Mention of our collective culture immediately brings to mind every factor having a direct influence on language and culture: personal culture through educational institutions and the arts; mass culture through cinema, radio and television. These are areas in which Quebec must assume primary responsibility and must have the constitutional jurisdiction required to do so.

20. Equally important to cultivation of our collective personality is a state immigration policy, drafted by Quebec in terms of her own cultural and economic aims. Therefore, Quebec must obtain more complete jurisdiction than she now has in this field, particularly as regards selection criteria and actual choice of immigrants.

21. Social security and assistance, including health, are too directly linked with a society's structure and values to be left in outside hands. In addition, political and administrative efficiency requires these matters to be the responsibility of a single government, Quebec's.

22. Manpower, a field already bound with two of Quebec's major jurisdictions — education and labour — and creating special problems in Quebec because of the language and culture of our work force, certainly cannot escape our state's control, any more than can adult education or vocational training.

23. Quebec's current and future responsibilities dictate that she be given broader powers to direct her economic development. It is unthinkable that the state have no voice in such matters as currency, credit or tariff policy when economic expansion is so influential in determining government activity and collective fulfilment, and is in turn so conditioned by education, manpower, labour, social security, fiscal policy and public investment. This does not imply that Quebec should introduce her own currency or customs duties, but she must play a direct part in deciding monetary and tariff policies, instruments much too important in community-growth planning to be kept out of Quebec's hands.

24. Jurisdiction over marriage and divorce, so closely tied in with civil law, must be vested in the Quebec state. The same is true of insurance, business and financial corporations, all of utmost importance to our economic development.

25. If Quebec intends effectively using her powers to ensure maximum attainment in today's world by her citizens, both individually and as a community, she must possess complete sovereignty in her fields of sole jurisdiction; consequently, she must obtain recognition as an international personality empowered to negotiate agreements and serve in international bodies whose activities extend to areas over which she is sovereign.

26. Finally, it is obvious that Quebec's sovereignty would lose much significance if our state did not have unrestricted power to amend its own constitution. This competence must therefore be clearly established.

27. We have listed these matters — using as source material various studies prepared in recent years as part of the work done by the Parliamentary Committee on the Constitution or in university and political circles — in order to illustrate the powers we want for Quebec in addition to those she now has. This list is neither complete nor definitive; far from it. Among others, we might add off-shore rights, maritime fisheries and certain categories of transport. A number of studies to be carried out during the next few months will enable us to complete it, either by including new powers or by clearing up certain cloudy areas. The Quebec state must exercise this set of powers with full sovereignty, free from such existing impediments as we have brought out.

28. Above all, it must be clearly understood that Quebec could not possibly exercise these powers without substantially increased financial resources. Assuming a division of legislative jurisdictions between our state and a central Canadian state, provision would thus have to be made for a different tax sharing system to reflect the redistribution of responsibilities resulting simultaneously from a new constitution and from the change in nature and relative importance of present-day government obligations.

29. Sovereignty in this range of basic fields constitutes the measure of self-determination which seems necessary from now on to ensure the growth and maturity of Quebec's collective personality.

A New Canadian Constitution

a) Special Status for Quebec

30. To point out that a people needs sovereignty to safeguard its collective personality is to reveal only one facet of an infinitely complex reality. While there was a time when communities might lay claim to absolute sovereignty in practice to the extent that they were content to live in isolation, sovereignty today is counterbalanced by interdependence brought about by ever farther-reaching, speedier and more sophisticated communications and exchanges.

31. For Quebec as for the other communities in Canada's population, mutual interdependence is now a fact of life, quite apart from the constitutional structures which unite us. In fact, these groups have been steadily weaving intor relationships for close to a hundred and fifty years. Their labours have resulted in a tightly-knit fabric; thus, the question for Quebec is not to decide whether our mutual dependence can be ignored or combatted, but rather what advantage we can draw from it and in what political framework we want it contained in relation to the freedom to which we aspire.

32. Although a good many forms of association are open to Quebecers as a frame for their interdependent relations with the rest of Canada, in the final analysis they can be boiled down to two basic options.

33. The first — that of full juridical sovereignty — would give Quebec complete freedom, independence or constitutional sovereignty. Some feel this option should include co-operation or "union" with English-speaking Canada for the pooling arrangements best suited to our common economic interests; monetary, tariff and postal union, debt management, co-ordination of fiscal policies and

the like. Others have suggested extending this list to take in the minority question, defence and foreign policies. However, if there were pooling arrangements, they would be subject to continuing negotiation between two equal partners who might, if necessary, set up co-management bodies. The salient characteristic of this option — and of its "confederal" variant — is that it rules out existence of a central parliament elected by popular vote and provides for top-level administration by a council or other agencies composed of an equal number of delegates from two sovereign states (Quebec and English-speaking Canada), but probably without powers of decision.

34. Unlike the first, the second option — a new federal system — provides for a government and a popularly elected central parliament, existing independently from the provinces or member-states and exercising powers determined by a constitution. Under this original new federal system designed especially for Canada, one member-state would have its individual, different system; this would give Quebec full legislative and administrative powers in a great many fields which the other provinces or states might leave to the jurisdiction of the federal authority.

35. From the standpoint of theory, it is not easy at this time to say exactly and with certainty what advantages and disadvantages each option would entail for Quebec and the rest of Canada or for French Canadians and English-speaking Canadians. However, a number of practical considerations and facts press for immediate attention.

36. Thus, at the core of the economic system in which Quebec is now integrated, we find a monetary system based on a single Canadian currency which is stable and inspires confidence. As things now stand, it seems likely that the absolute sovereignty option would affect currency to the point of upsetting Quebec's economy, at least during a transition period lasting ten, fifteen or twenty years.

37. First, it is inconceivable that a Canadian currency could be maintained under the ultimate authority of a political body made up of equal delegations from political powers (governments and parliaments) free to dissociate themselves from it at any time, or even at stated periods.

38. Second, any separate Quebec currency created in the foreseeable future would encounter very serious obstacles, among them pressures on reserves, devaluation, possible deterioration of the financial climate which could lead to flight of capital, declining investments, added borrowing difficulties for public bodies, repercussions on retirement plans and, above all, lower real income for workers and a manpower exodus.

39. The absolute sovereignty option also raises serious questions regarding fields which, though diversified, are interconnected: for instance, the central bank, interprovincial and international trade, tariff policy, defence, foreign policy. So far, these questions have not been answered. At best, we might conclude common policy agreements, but that would require unanimity which might remain nothing more than a pious hope; at worst, there is no telling what the situation would be. In any event, Quebec would be committed to never-ending negotiations whose success is anything but a foregone conclusion, and in which she will always be the weaker partner.

40. Many people will prefer a different approach to the choice between these two options. Instead of assuming a people without any political structure of its own being forced to elect one of several options, wisdom and political prudence will prompt them to determine, in the light of past experience, whether our present institutions whose components we know in detail cannot serve as a basis for a new start which will enable Quebec to attain her aims without serious risk to her economy or other values which loom large in her life as a community.

41. It was while weighing these two possibilities — first, the serious if not disastrous economic implications of absolute sovereignty; second, the working base afforded by our existing institutions — that we first outlined the option of a new federalism. Now that it has been developed in detail, it appears to us as the best choice for Quebec.

42. We are alive to all the bonds, complementary activities and countless close economic relationships to which citizens throughout Canada have grown accustomed as backing for the Canadian venture. As a number of people have properly pointed out, nothing compels us to wreck this structure we have built up in common; on the contrary, we all have every good reason to maintain its framework. Interdependent as we are, if we destroy it we shall sooner or later be forced to rebuild it as best we can.

43. Advocates of absolute sovereignty would like to base this framework simply on continued harmony of purpose, without any permanent juridical structure. However, we believe a juridical structure is necessary to ensure more effective operation, provided of course it does not prevent the Quebec community from developing in accordance with its basic characteristics and aspirations. In our view, such a structure, with powers set forth in a constitution and exercised with sufficient participation by the federated communities, would encourage mutual co-operation, promote reconciliation of certain conflicting interests and facilitate the pursuit of common aims.

44. Federalism appears to us all the more desirable as a basis for a new Canadian association in that it lends itself to endlessly diversified combinations and procedures. As Professor Georges Burdeau so aptly expressed it:

> Federalism extends far beyond the framework of the federal state; its justi-
> fication and value lie in the variety of juridical combinations which it makes
> possible; consequently, there would be no point in confusing it with institutions
> and procedures. Its strength and future stem from the consent it assumes
> between parties whom it brings together, from the harmony of purposes
> joined without loss to any. Thus the form of institutions which express this
> harmony is unimportant. Whenever such solidarity takes juridicial shape, you
> have federalism.[1]

45. This spirit, we believe, would make it possible to associate in a form of federalism with the rest of Canada a Quebec endowed with all powers necessary for her development. Such a political system might enable us to attain our dual aim of guaranteeing Quebec full sovereignty in fields essential

---

[1]*Traité de science politique*, t. 11: L'Etat (Paris Librairie générale de droit et de jurisprudence, 1949), p. 502.

to her growth as a collective personality, while allowing her to draw all the benefits which interdependence has to offer.

46. Canada's other communities do not have the same reasons for claiming the degree of sovereignty to which Quebec aspires; it can never be taken for granted that they wish to retain a much stronger central government than Quebec is prepared to accept.

47. Hence it is with a view to meeting the most cherished aims of both Quebec and the rest of Canada that we propose our own type of federation, devised by Canadians to fit their particular situation. This Canadian-made federation would give Quebec sovereign authority in areas which she considers essential to the fulfilment of her collective personality, while concentrating in federal government hands a large proportion of that sovereignty with respect to the other provinces.

48. Many observers may feel that this form of federation will be hard to achieve; but despite the undeniable problems it raises, it seems to us the most desirable formula for Quebec to adopt so as to reconcile the objective of sovereignty with the requirements of interdependence in a context such as ours. For the entire country, and particularly for English Canada, it also appears to be the formula most likely to ease the internal tensions which divide Canada more sharply every day, and to maintain a Canada which still has meaning on the international scene as well as for all Canadians.

49. Will this form of association be acceptable to the rest of Canada? We certainly have no right to expect a refusal. On the contrary, we should assume that English Canada and Quebec will tackle, with the same open-mindedness and determination to succeed, the problem of continuing Canada's existence as the large country it is today, while satisfying the deep-seated aspirations of both groups.

b) Transformation of Federal Institutions

50. Although it goes to the root of the present constitutional problem, definition of a new Canadian federalism affects only part of Canada's political institutions. We still have to decide whether central government agencies are designed to meet the aspirations and needs of our day.

51. On this score, there should be no hesitation in saying that the Senate needs complete reform as to composition, the method of appointing members and the functions assigned to it; the constitutional tribunal responsible for settling differences in interpreting the constitution between federal authorities and member-states should depend for its own constitution and appointment of its members on all parties concerned, rather than on the central authority alone; the rest of Canada would be well advised to consider whether our monarchical system should not be replaced by an institution originated solely by the Canadian people, which would lead to creation of a Canadian federal republic. Obviously, transformations of this magnitude would entail other changes in the machinery of federal political institutions.

c) Bill of Community Rights

52. A new federal constitution would afford an ideal opportunity to adopt a bill setting forth the community rights of Canada's majorities and minorities. One advantage of maintaining a federal link would be to make it easier to safeguard and increase basic guarantees regarding French as the language of instruction in schools and of communication in public services throughout Canada. This question is certain to remain a cornerstone of the new Canada which Quebecers want to build, together with Canadians in the other provinces.

Quebec's Internal Constitution

a) Present Constitution

53. Any study of the Canadian constitutional problem implies a study of Quebec's internal constitution. Although the Quebec community had existed for a long time by 1867, it was the British North America Act which created a Quebec state and gave it the essentials for survival as a state: a well defined territory, its own legislative and executive branches as well as a judicial system, although it should be noted that the latter is not altogether dissociated from the federal power. While it is true that Quebec's sovereignty is limited to certain categories in legislative and administrative fields, her sovereignty in those fields of provincial jurisdiction has been recognized by the highest juridical authorities.

54. However, the political institutions thus determined for Quebec in 1867 have failed to keep pace with evolving political customs and no longer answer the needs of a modern state. Still less do they reflect the current aspirations of the Quebec community.

55. Where do we look for the statutes and parliamentary papers which decide our political institutions? Just as many can be found in Ottawa and London as in Quebec. What justification can there be for constitutional documents which give Ottawa power to disavow legislation adopted by Quebec's parliament? What is the relevance in Quebec today of a head of state known as the Lieutenant-Governor, appointed by and primarily responsible to the federal government (right to reserve bills)? What have we to do with parliamentary protocol handed down through the centuries and now completely out-dated? Where is the symbol in all this to express the pride, spirit of solidarity and collective aspirations of Quebec's people?

56. From a purely functional standpoint, Quebec's political institutions are simply not geared to modern conditions: countless popularly elected local governments, scattered and powerless to cope with absolutely centralized provincial administrative authority; a Legislative Assembly which foils members' efforts to give their best or to perform their dual role in checking and stimulating the executive branch of government; a Legislative Council too frequently used to reward faithful party hacks and thwart the democratically expressed will of the people.

57. There are also grounds to question the part which the British North America Act assigns to the central government in Quebec's judicial system; we refer particularly to appointment of higher court judges and to the constitution of the final court of appeal for all cases, including those governed exclusively by Quebec civil law.

b) New Constitution

58. It would be difficult to argue against the need to consolidate in a strictly Quebec-made document the basic rules intended to govern the organization and administration of our state. We must have an orderly, clear document, stripped of non-essentials, to set forth these basic rules, leaving the practical methods of application to various other legislative texts; it must be couched in elegant but current language and infused with the breath of life so necessary in a document meant to uplift a people and serve as an inspiration to its youth.

59. Quebec's new constitution must contain a bill of rights, guaranteeing individuals their political and civil rights, their public and personal freedoms, their collective economic and social rights.

60. Quebec's new constitution must replace our archaic monarchial institutions with new home-grown ones emanating from the will of our people. The office of lieutenant-governor will have to be changed accordingly.

61. Our new state constitution must provide for a legislative body in which the population of all Quebec will be equitably represented. Without destroying the party system, this parliament must be designed to enable members to play an active part and make a personal contribution, particularly by introducing a system of parliamentary committees or commissions and giving them sufficient independence from cabinet control.

62. Should the new constitution make provision for an economic and social advisory council? Some form of constitutional council? A council of state to act as an administrative tribunal? These questions will have to be explored and answered so that the new state structures will keep the executive and legislative branches of government in constant touch with every sector of society and give citizens practical and reasonably speedy machinery for protecting their rights in dealings with the state.

63. The new constitution must obviously provide for a complete judicial system under Quebec's sole jurisdiction. This means that final decision on legal disputes in Quebec will be handed down by courts and judges wholly dependent on our state's constitution and authority.

64. And surely Quebec's constitution is the logical document in which to lay the foundations for the municipal, administrative, economic and cultural regionalization needed to focus our economy on growth points which are genuine centres of dynamism and regional community life? It is impossible to overstress the fact that development of a Quebec whose culture is basically French depends, to a great extent, on our collective ability to ensure that such growth points exist and thrive throughout Quebec, outside the metropolitan Montreal area.

65. Montreal itself is destined to remain a great cosmopolitan North American city. This does not mean it will not be an active centre for French cultural expansion, but its character will always be more universal, if not more all-embracing than that which we should strive for in the rest of Quebec. Moreover, neither the wording of a constitution nor a regionalization policy will guarantee authentic French culture its proper place in Montreal. While state action in this area will necessarily differ from that needed elsewhere in Quebec, this is a challenge which public authorities are duty-bound to accept with equal courage and wisdom if, instead of an instrument for cultural Americanization of all Quebec, Montreal is to be a source of cultural as well as economic enrichment for the rest of our territory.

Conclusion
Two New Constitutions, Two Deadlines

66. From the foregoing, it clearly follows that Quebec requires both a new Canadian and a new internal constitution. There was a time when judicious patching, even a few specific amendments, might have answered our needs. However, present requirements, from the standpoints of national symbolism and effective government, call for entirely new documents, conceived, drafted and adopted at home with the assent of the sovereign people.

67. The urgent need for a new Canadian constitution can no longer be denied. For several years now, this question has been as widely discussed in public as in university and government circles. It is even fair to say that, as things now stand, debate on the constitution is a source of unrest and insecurity. Unless immediate action is taken, this unstable mixture may deteriorate quickly and reach the explosion point.

68. This question certainly concerns every part of Canada; thus the central government and those of all ten provinces are equally responsible for analysing the situation, drafting proposals and gathering around the conference table to hammer out a solution.

69. Four years ago, Quebec took the initiative by setting up a parliamentary committee with specific instructions to begin and continue working in this area. Though it had made considerable headway, it has been completely inactive since the government changed hands in June 1966. This committee should be reconvened without delay to draft a plan for submission by Quebec to the rest of Canada during 1968 at the latest. In fact, it is Quebec's prerogative to determine herself the powers she deems essential to fulfilment of her aspirations.

70. Furthermore, the task of drawing up her new internal constitution is one for Quebec alone. Even if it should require amendments to the 1867 British North America Act, immediate responsibility for its formulation and adoption can only rest with the parliament and people of Quebec.

71. The Parliamentary Committee on the Constitution has so far not tackled the problem of Quebec's own constitution. It must do so without delay, meanwhile continuing preparatory work on a new Canadian constitution. Since a

decision in our own case depends merely on what we want, it seems reasonable to assume that this aim can be attained more quickly. We can expect that early adoption of a new Quebec constitution would convince not only Quebec citizens but all Canadians that we do not intend to equivocate on adoption of a new Canadian constitution.

72. Quebec can and must show real leadership in this double task. In recent years, she has shown herself capable of certain great achievements expected of modern, dynamic states. She must now take concrete steps to overhaul the major institutions which are to govern the collective progress of a people aware of its destiny.

33   Quebec and Foreign Relations*

Government of Quebec

Public opinion in our province is becoming increasingly alive to the necessity for Quebec to look beyond her boundaries and take an active interest in the work of certain international organizations. It would therefore seem that, unless their constitutional jurisdictions respecting foreign relations are clearly defined, the Governments of Canada and Quebec are bound to have disagreements and misunderstandings of growing seriousness.

In today's world, there is an inevitable tendency for closer links to be established between governments, not only in the areas of traditional diplomacy but also in those of education, research, cultural affairs, labour, health and technology in general. Unless Canada means to live in isolation, she will necessarily be led to seek more and closer bonds with other countries in these very sectors.

Now most of these sectors are a provincial responsibility, and Quebec obviously cannot allow them to be dealt with internationally by the federal government alone. The content of agreements in these fields has such a close bearing on the implementation of day-to-day policies that, if the federal government were to have a monopoly on international affairs, it would gradually take over *de facto* — if not *de jure* — internal jurisdiction over matters which, constitutionally, do not fall within its competence. This result would be hard enough to justify in a federal state with only one language and culture. In our federation where, because of her geographic and demographic position, Quebec remains the mainstay of French Canada, it would also be tantamount to ignoring Canada's cultural duality.

*From Quebec, *Brief on the Constitution*, Quebec, 1968, pp. 13-15. A document submitted to the Canadian Intergovernmental Conference, Ottawa, 1968. Reprinted by permission.

We wish to reiterate for the record that Quebec has never questioned the federal government's jurisdiction in matters of foreign policy. The areas in which we are interested are, in the field of co-operation and technical or cultural exchanges.

In our view, therefore, Quebec should have, within the limits of Canadian foreign policy, a recognized capacity to negotiate and sign her own agreements with foreign governments on matters subject to her internal jurisdiction. The Quebec Government should also be regularly invited to participate in the Canadian delegation at international conferences and at meetings of international organizations of which Canada is a member, and which touch on fields of provincial competence. Similarly, she should be empowered to attend international conferences of provincial interest in which Canada is not a participant. Finally, the Quebec Government should be in a position to play a more substantial role in external aid. If these requests were given thoughtful examination, we are confident that solutions could easily be found which would satisfy both Quebec's legitimate desire for self-assertion and the requirements of federalism.

Besides, we believe that Canada as a whole stands to gain by allowing the provinces to take more than an academic interest in the international dimension of fields which, under domestic law, fall within their jurisdiction. As we just pointed out, these matters are taking on growing significance in relations between countries. And in every instance, it is the provinces which have the human and institutional resources needed to make Canada's contribution worthwhile. Thus, it is not only important but useful that the provinces be called upon, one way or another, to participate more fully in our country's international endeavours. Juridical concepts formulated in bygone days when international activity centred mainly on questions of war and peace will have to be adapted accordingly.

34   Quebec in World Affairs *

Marcel Cadieux

. . . Quebec's presence on the world scene is, I believe, not merely a fact; it is an obvious fact. That Quebec must be more active on that scene also appears obvious to me. The real problem is how Quebec is to play its role in the world: alone, by and for itself, or as one element in Canada's representation. In other

*From Department of External Affairs, *Statements and Speeches*, No. 10, 1968. Speech by Mr. Marcel Cadieux, Under Secretary of State for External Affairs, to the Annual Meeting of the Club des Relations internationales, University of Montreal, March 2, 1968. By permission.

words, are Quebec's activities abroad to be separate from Canada's or are they to be Canadian?

The problem is basically the same at home and abroad, and amounts to this: is a Quebecker a Canadian as well, or are the two loyalties mutually exclusive? If the answer to the latter question is yes, then, obviously, no compromise is possible. If not, then I think there is every possibility that an accommodation can be worked out.

But let us define our terms: when we say "Quebecker", we mean a person living in the Province of Quebec. We do not mean "French-Canadian". Certainly, 85 per cent of the Quebecers are French-Canadians, but there are almost one million French-Canadians living elsewhere in Canada, mainly in Ontario, New Brunswick and Manitoba. Bearing this in mind, it remains a fact nevertheless, that Quebec is, to employ a familiar phrase, the "homeland of French-Canadians". But this does not mean that the Quebec government is the only one with an obligation to promote and protect the interests of French-Canadians.

By the time the federal-provincial conference last February had ended, it was clear that the warnings and recommendations of the Dunton-Laurendeau Commission had been understood by the majority of the other provinces and by the Federal Government. Doubtless their motives were not entirely magnanimous; they realized that, if the country was to survive as a unit, equal status had to be given to the French and English languages and cultures. While this reasoning is not entirely selfless, it does show clear recognition of their vested interests. How many world crises and problems could be settled by this kind of approach! Let us examine, if you will, this area of clearly-recognized interests and ask ourselves one question: what is the interest of French-Canadians and Quebeckers in the field of foreign relations?

We all know, and the papers constantly remind us, as they echo the statements of politicians in Quebec and Ottawa, that it is essential for the survival of the French language and culture in Canada that Quebec play a part in the world's French-speaking community, that it strengthen its ties with the French-speaking nations of the world, and with France in particular. I am struck by the fact that, not only does everyone agree on this but both the federal Government and the provincial governments are taking positive and effective steps to carry out this purpose. To some commentators it even seems as if the governments are attempting to outdo one another. Even if we accept this interpretation, which I do not, what does it prove? Simply that the Canadian Government considers it as much its duty as Quebec's to maintain the closest possible ties with the French-speaking world. In short, there is no difference in this area between the goals of Quebec and Ottawa, both of which are seeking closer contacts with the French-speaking community in order to assist in the development of French culture at home and to make our version of this culture known abroad. But it makes a difference whether this policy is conducted by Quebec or Ottawa. If conducted by Quebec, it will to some extent serve the interests of Quebeckers, but only *their* interests. If it is undertaken on a broader base by the Canadian Government, it can serve the interests not only of Quebeckers but also of the French-speaking people of Ontario, Manitoba and New Brunswick, not to mention those English Canadians who are willing to accept the "French fact". But there is an even more serious consideration; if that part of Canada's foreign policy which is concerned with our relations with the French-speaking world became the monopoly of the Province of Quebec, the tendency people have to identify Quebec with French-Canada would become that much stronger, at the very time (and this is the supreme paradox) when the "French fact" has finally acquired its rights in the other provinces. In other words, at the very moment when the rest of Canada is discovering that it has a real interest in French culture, and when the French minorities in the other provinces can hope to breathe more easily and, so to speak, in French, Quebec, by insisting that it is the sole genuine representative of French Canada on the International level, risks undoing what is now finally, after 100 years, being accomplished in our country to realize an objective which has always been uppermost for Quebeckers. Instead of working for the diffusion of the French language, Quebec may succeed, perhaps unintentionally, in helping to restrict it. It is, in fact, obvious that, if we accept the idea that French Canada is Quebec, by the same token we must accept the idea that the rest of Canada is English. In short, I see a danger that, if we accept the premise that only Quebec is logically entitled to represent French Canada in the French-speaking community, then we must accept the conclusion that what is not part of Quebec may be excluded from this French-speaking community. By doing this we should isolate Quebec from the rest of the country, deprive French-Canadians outside Quebec of the right to be French, and discourage those English-speaking Canadians who are willing to accept French culture.

If, on the contrary, we accept the fact that in foreign countries it is the voice of Canada that is to be heard, if we accept the idea that it is the Government of Canada which is to make formal commitments on behalf of the whole country, then, if this voice is to be heard in a French-speaking environment, we automatically accept the idea that it will be a French voice. In view of the demographic and political situation in Canada, this voice, if it is to ring true, must have an accent that English-speaking Canadians can recognize without difficulty. There is no reason why a Canadian delegation to a meeting of the French-speaking community could not include, besides Quebeckers, French-Canadians from other provinces, and perhaps even a few English Canadians. Obviously, such a practice would permit Quebec's voice to be heard on the world scene; but it would also give another dimension to Canada's French voice, which could thus reach beyond Quebec's borders and, at the same time, assist in its development both in this country and abroad.

If, as I hope, I have shown that the clear interests and ideals of Quebeckers, French-Canadians and all other Canadians are more accurately reflected in the international French-speaking community by French-oriented federal action than by exclusively provincial and necessarily more restricted action, it goes without saying that, in those fields that do not relate exclusively to the French-speaking community, Quebec's interests must also be served within a Canadian context. In saying this, I may appear to be tilting at windmills, inasmuch as no one, to my knowledge, is contesting the Federal Government's jurisdiction in external policy; the only fields where there is, in fact, any disagreement are those relating to the French-speaking community and those under provincial jurisdiction. But it is essential, in my opinion, to distinguish very clearly between Canada's internal and external relations. Within our borders, there is no hierarchy among the various governments. We have a central government which has jurisdiction in certain fields; and we have provincial governments which have jurisdiction in certain other fields. Our constitution (or what passes for one, the British North America Act) was written 100 years ago and naturally contains a certain number of vague points that must be clarified in the light of modern reality. On this, the Prime Minister and the provincial premiers agreed at the federal-provincial conferences that took place early in February. Whatever changes they may make to the constitution, jurisdiction in internal matters will remain divided between the Federal Government and the provinces. Education, for instance, is clearly within the competence of the provinces, while national defense is a federal responsibility. Thus, each government, whether federal or provincial, is completely sovereign in its own field.

We are so used to this situation that the division of powers between the Federal Government and the provincial governments seems quite normal — as, indeed, it is in domestic matters. At the international level, however, the situation is quite different. As seen from abroad, Canada, like all countries, whether federal or unitary, is a single entity and international law is not concerned with whether this agreement or that convention falls within federal or provincial jurisdiction. In international law, there is only one Canada possessing international personality and it is the Federal Government which represents this Canada. There could no more be any question of a sovereign country or international organization signing a treaty with a province of Canada than of that country or body signing an international agreement with the Canton of Berne in Switzerland, Croatia in Yugoslavia or the State of Massachusetts in the United States. This rule of international sovereignty, which was not invented by Canada, derives from international law, international usage and plain good sense. Under this rule, therefore, each federal state must settle within its borders the problem of how each of its component parts is to obtain the benefits which accrue from contacts and relations with foreign countries and international bodies. In almost all federal states, the central government has maintained exclusive control over international relations. In Canada, we have acted differently; the central government has long had a flexible policy in the field of external relations. You will not see a "Valais House" or find representatives of a German *land* or Mexican state in Montreal, Toronto or Vancouver. There have, however, been delegations from Quebec, Ontario and the Maritimes in London for many years. There are provincial representatives in New York and many other American cities. Quebec also has a delegation-general in Paris, and another in Milan; and this list is by no means exhaustive. Some of these provincial delegations abroad have been in existence for many years, and their existence has never posed any problems or caused the federal government to object. Yet they concern themselves with a host of matters that could be considered rather directly connected with international relations. Anything, in fact, can be considered as coming under the heading of international politics and anything can, moreover, change its nature under certain conditions and become highly political. That is why, for example, commercial or cultural relations with a friendly country are not in themselves political matters. But if the same type of relations are established with other countries, the case may be quite different. Recall, if you will, the uproar caused by the sale of trucks to Cuba by France and Britain a few years ago. Imagine the reaction in certain countries if Canada or one of its provinces decided to negotiate a cultural agreement with Communist China. In any case, these provincial houses or delegations in other countries have concerned themselves for years with tourism, immigration, trade, teacher exchanges, investment, etc. — all matters that may serve the interests of the provinces concerned and come within provincial jurisdiction.

No problems arose, since these provincial delegations did not claim to be embassies or consulates. These provinces were successfully engaged in promoting their own special interests. The Federal Government has encouraged, and continues to encourage, the international activities undertaken by the provinces to promote their own interests in matters within their jurisdiction. This is a reasonable approach; yet very few federal countries allow such freedom of action on the international scene to their provinces. Such an arrangement does not and should not create any conflict between the Federal Government and the provincial governments as long as both respect the basic principle that, on the international plane, there is only one Canada. Basically, what this means in practice is that only representatives of the central government may represent the country in its dealings with other countries or on international organizations and that only the representatives of the central government may sign international agreements. Essentially, this is all a question of procedure, and heaven knows how important procedure is in diplomacy.

In substance, Quebec loses nothing in respecting this procedure; on the contrary, it is in Quebec's interest to play a role both on the world scene and in Canada   to play its part in the French-speaking community of the world, benefiting from the cultural enrichment which it may derive from exchanges, and also to play its part in the national life of Canada. There would, of course, be a conflict between these two aims if the Federal Government opposed the movement toward closer relations with the French-speaking community. But the fact is that Canada is becoming bilingual; it is opening its doors to French culture. Quebec was isolated for many years. This is no longer true. From now on other provinces are going to be bilingual and therefore increasingly interested in the French-speaking world, as has been the case for some time now with the governments at Ottawa and Quebec. What was once a dream can now become a reality. It is this reality which must be developed and reflected abroad. By working in co-operation with the Federal Government, Quebec gains in two ways: first, by ensuring its contacts with the world French-speaking community just as though Quebec itself had dealt with these countries directly;

secondly, by helping to develop the French fact in Canada in association with other provincial governments and with the Federal Government.

You may, perhaps, be familiar with the document entitled *Federalism and International Relations*. From the legal point of view, this paper makes a number of clear-cut statements. Indeed it asserts, and supports the assertion with evidence, that only the federal authorities may represent a federal state in its relations with other states. I repeat that this is true for all federal states and that the Canadian federal system is as flexible in its attitude toward the provinces as any. However, in the manner in which it recommends that this federal control be applied, this document is very broad and flexible. The document, in fact, opens the way to all possible forms of co-operation with the provinces and allows them full scope in this area, on the condition that a certain form of procedure or, better still, a certain attitude, be respected.

I mentioned a moment ago certain provincial delegations abroad which were set up with the approval and co-operation of the Federal Government. It was also the Federal Government that authorized the cultural exchange between France and Quebec. This exchange was negotiated directly between Quebec and France but, following the usual practice, before it was initialled, federal approval was given in a diplomatic note to the French Government. Why should it be otherwise? In substance, this agreement benefits Quebec and, by the same token, Canada. In form, the result would have been the same if Quebec had signed the agreement itself, but with this difference — it would have been contrary to practice and to international law and, above all, the signing would then have had solely provincial, rather than national significance. By initialling the exchange of notes, the Federal Government signified its approval of the policy of closer relations between France and Quebec, which, of course, was and still is in line with the Federal Government's policy of drawing closer to France.

That simple gesture of initialling has a symbolic value. It was a sign of co-operation.

So it is in the other fields of international politics. If Quebec is represented in a national delegation to an international meeting, the Federal Government is thereby aided by Quebec in developing the Canadian "French fact" to the fullest extent on an international level, by ensuring that the interests for which the provincial government is responsible will be directly represented.

Moreover, the interests of French-Canadians are not limited to the French-speaking world. These interests include all areas of external affairs. Conversely, the French-speaking world should not interest only Quebeckers, or even French-Canadians, but all Canadians. When the Commonwealth Conference on Education was held in Ottawa in 1965 (and another will soon take place in Lagos), it was not only English-speaking Canadians who took part. French-Canadians were also there. This is only reasonable. In addition, the Quebec provincial government is invited to appoint representatives on such occasions, and does so. For my part, I should like to see the French-speaking world do the same: allow English-speaking people and provinces with English-speaking majorities to be represented as well. In this way the problem of the French-speaking community would be of concern not only to French-Canadians or to the Quebec Government but to all Canadians. Is this utopian? Perhaps. Yet five years ago, if anyone had said that Ontario would become a bilingual province, he would have been called a dreamer. Why should it be thought advisable for Quebec to participate in the Fourth Commonwealth Conference on Education and inadvisable for New Brunswick, for example, to participate in a similar conference dealing with education in the French-speaking countries?

The basic ideal for French-speaking people, and, in particular, for the people of Quebec, is to develop their culture as far as possible. However, in order to do this, we must go out into the world, not shut ourselves in. Going out into the world does not mean locking ourselves safely inside our own little world but, on the contrary, being seen and felt in as many areas and places as possible. It is important for French Canada, all of French Canada, to be represented in the French-speaking community, but it is also important for it to be represented in Washington or at the United Nations. That is what we are trying to do in the Department of External Affairs. In the field of foreign relations the policy of the Government and its officials is very clear — it is to reflect abroad, to an ever increasing extent, the image of a bilingual Canada.

If this action is to be pursued and developed, the Federal Government and its officials must obviously maintain contact and co-operate with the provincial governments and their officials. And that is precisely the intention, and increasingly the practice, of our Department. When an international conference which may be of interest to the provinces is announced, the provinces are informed and invited to appoint someone to the national delegation. If a group of provincial officials wishes to negotiate some arrangement with a foreign country, we facilitate the matter. What more can you ask in the way of co-operation? All we ask is to be consulted in time, so that we can assure ourselves that the projects do not conflict with Canada's national policy and that the arrangements observe the proper forms and respect Canada's international personality. And I am not speaking here of what we intend or plan to do, but of current and accepted practice.

35 De la vérité et de la liberté en politique: Les Canadiens français et le défi fédéral*

Pierre Elliot Trudeau

Chesterton, le grand journaliste catholique, aimait à répéter le paradoxe suivant: "Il faut un grand courage, il faut presque de l'héroïsme, disait-il, pour monter sur une tribune à affirmer à haute voix que 2 et 2 font quatre."

C'est cette espèce de courage que je voudrais avoir aujourd'hui. Car j'ai l'intention de vous parler en toute franchise et la franchise, commande, exige même à certains moments qu'on ait la force de proclamer des évidences.

J'ai pleinement conscience de me présenter devant un auditoire qui n'a rien de partisan, qui n'attend pas de moi un discours partisan, qui veut seulement savoir, et cette curiosité m'honore, ce que je pense de l'avenir québécois et de l'avenir canadien, comment j'envisage le sort du Canada français et celui du Canada tout court.

De la vérité en politique

C'est cela que j'essaierai de vous dire. Et je vous le dirai sans détour, aussi directement que possible, avec un minimum de précautions oratoires. Du reste, je réussirais fort mal, même si je m'y efforçais, à dissimuler ma pensée. Car je crois le temps venu pour les hommes politiques, et particulièrement dans notre pays, de dire clairement les choix qui s'imposent et de les présenter comme ils les voient.

Je sais que tout le monde n'est pas de mon avis à ce sujet. Je sais que certains préfèrent l'ambiguïté, parce que celle-ci est plus confortable. D'autres la préfèrent parce qu'ils croient que le Canada ne peut vivre que dans l'ambiguïté. D'autres enfin, par je ne sais quelle étrange conception de l'éthique professionnelle, voudraient que les hommes politiques placent l'habileté au-dessus de la vérité, dans leur échelle de valeurs. D'une part, ils reprochent aux politiciens en général de toujours aborder de biais les situations, au lieu d'y faire face. Mais, d'autre part, si un homme politique dit carrément ce qu'il pense (et surtout quand cette pensée ne coïncide pas avec les idées courantes) on dira volontiers qu'il manque de sens diplomatique.

Mais qu'est-ce donc que le sens diplomatique? Il ne faudrait tout de même pas confondre la souplesse de caractère avec le fait de ne pas avoir en tête une seule idée qui vaille la peine d'être exprimée, ou pas une seule à laquelle on tienne suffisamment pour la défendre. Car on aboutirait ainsi à un curieux résultat. L'homme politique idéal, ce serait alors celui qui ne croit à rien, toujours prêt à céder devant la première contradiction et à tourner sa voile dans le sens du vent, d'où qu'il vienne.

---

*Discours prononcé, 2 avril 1968 à Montréal, par le ministre fédéral de la justice, devant les membres des clubs Richelieu de la région métropolitaine. Voici la première tranche du texte intégral de l'important discours prononcé par M. Trudeau pour marquer la clôture de sa campagne dans la course au leadership libéral.

Le vérité, je pense, est ailleurs et vous le pensez aussi. Votre invitation de ce soir en est la preuve. Vous savez que l'existence du dialogue civil, de la discussion ouverte, de la libre confrontation des idées, est l'une des plus hautes traditions démocratiques, l'une des fonctions les plus nécessaires à la vie politique d'un pays. Votre hospitalité, ce soir, permet que cette fonction, s'exerce. Et vous savez que le déroulement de débats publics, dans une communauté humaine, est un signe de santé, une preuve de vitalité. Or, comment ce débat pourrait-il se poursuivre si l'on devait considérer comme inflexible tout homme politique qui exprime sans détour les convictions qui l'animent, qui accepte de dire tout haut ce qu'il pense tout bas?

Pour ma part, je plaide coupable à l'accusation de parler trop franchement. J'accepte d'avance le reproche. Je refuse de me défendre. Et je me prépare à récidiver dans l'instant même.

Ce que je veux vous exposer, aussi brièvement mais aussi clairement que possible, ce sont mes convictions politiques de Québécois canadien.

Foi dans le fédéralisme

Je n'étonnerai sans doute personne, parmi vous, en affirmant d'abord ma foi profonde dans une forme de gouvernement qui se nomme le fédéralisme. Je voudrais préciser d'abord qu'à mes yeux, le fédéralisme n'est ni un expédient, ni un compromis, encore moins un pis-aller comme certains ont tendance à le croire. C'est au contraire une formule politique d'avant-garde, à laquelle je souscrirais pour ma part même en-dehors du contexte canadien.

Pourquoi?

Ce qui prime toute autre considération, quand on fait le choix d'un système politique, c'est la personne humaine. Non pas la personne comme notion abstraite; ce qui importe ce sont les gens bien concrets, vous, moi, les cultivateurs, les ouvriers, les hommes d'affaires, les locataires de la rue Delorimier et les habitants de Lethbridge, les travailleurs de Windsor et les pêcheurs de la Gaspésie ou de Terre-Neuve. La politique, comme on dit chez nous, c'est fait "pour le monde", et non pas "le monde" pour la politique.

Je voudrais vous citer ici une phrase du Frère Untel, une phrase qui va très loin, pour peu qu'on s'arrête à y réfléchir: "Socialisme, capitalisme, doctrine sociale, écrit le Frère Untel, j'ai mon critère pour les juger: les pauvres que je connais. Dès qu'une mesure sociale se traduit, ou aurait pu se traduire, par un peu plus de sécurité ou de dignité pour les pauvres que je connais, elle a mon appui".

Voilà aussi ma conviction. Et ce n'est pas vrai seulement pour les mesures sociales et les pauvres, cela est vrai de toutes les formes de gouvernement, de toutes les lois et de tous les citoyens. Légiférer, mettre en oeuvre une politique, c'est améliorer le sort quotidien de personnes humaines en chair et en os. Et mieux les gouvernements sont adaptés, ajustés aux problèmes qu'ils doivent résoudre, meilleures sont leurs chances de faire des lois pour les hommes.

L'immense avantage du fédéralisme, c'est d'abord de rapprocher l'Etat du citoyen, c'est de permettre qu'on légifère localement pour des besoins locaux, régionalement pour des besoins régionaux, et au niveau fédéral quand il s'agit de faire face aux problèmes d'ensemble.

Ma deuxième raison de préférer le fédéralisme, je pourrais l'exprimer par un dicton si célèbre qu'il en est devenu banal: "Gouverner, c'est prévoir". Je veux dire que toute politique digne de ce nom est par définition tournée vers l'avenir. Or, l'avenir c'est le rapprochement entre les peuples, c'est la mise en commun des richesses du monde, c'est la marche vers l'unité — ou bien alors, c'est la guerre atomique.

Mais rapprochement, mise en commun, unité, cela ne veut pas dire uniformité. Il y a des gens qui rêvent d'une société humaine internationale où tout le monde parlerait la même langue, vivrait de la même manière, mangerait les mêmes plats, et regarderait les mêmes émissions de télévision. Ce monde aurait peut-être ses avantages, mais on risquerait fort d'y crever d'ennui.

Il reste certain cependant que nous évoluons vers une union de plus en plus étroite entre les peuples. S'il est une tendance qui paraît irréversible, aujourd'hui, c'est bien celle-là.

Or le fédéralisme, c'est très précisément le système politique qui permet l'union dans la liberté et l'unité dans la diversité. C'est pourquoi sans doute des centaines de millions d'hommes vivent déjà en régime fédéral, aussi bien en Inde qu'aux Etats-Unis, au Brésil, en Allemagne et en URSS; c'est pourquoi aussi des centaines de millions d'autres s'acheminent vers le fédéralisme, à travers diverses étapes qui s'appellent unions douanières, marchés communs ou communautés économiques.

Voilà, si vous voulez, le fondement de l'attitude que j'ai prise, et tenue depuis vingt ans, dans le débat constitutionnel qui occupe le Québec et le Canada.

Je crois à une politique axée sur la personne, soucieuse en premier lieu d'assurer aux hommes et aux femmes de ce pays la plus grande mesure possible de bien-être et de liberté.

La société canadienne-française et son avenir

Et puisque nous parlons aujourd'hui en famille, c'est-à-dire entre Canadiens français, nous partirons, si vous le voulez, de cette société canadienne-française qui nous préoccupe en premier lieu, qui constitue pour nous tous, dans cette salle, le point de départ aussi bien physique que culturel, de toutes nos réflexions politiques. "Citoyen de ce pays, ai-je écrit récemment (et je m'excuse de me citer) j'aurais été Canadien français d'adoption, si je ne l'avais déjà été de naissance." Je me sens donc bien à l'aise pour réfléchir avec vous en partant du fait français.

Et la première question à nous poser, c'est, je pense, la suivante: "Comment pouvons-nous le mieux assurer aux personnes qui composent notre communauté canadienne-française, ce maximum de bien-être et de liberté?"

Quand je parle de bien-être, je ne pense pas seulement aux avantages matériels, aux salaires, aux logis, aux autos et aux réfrigérateurs. Je pense aussi et surtout à notre épanouissement culturel, au progrès humain dans sa totalité. Il faut bien comprendre que tous ces éléments sont inséparables. Comment pourrait-on promouvoir une collectivité dont les individus, pris un à un, n'auraient pas les moyens d'augmenter leur compétence, leur efficacité, leur qualité humaine? Et comment assurer ce progrès collectif si nous ne pouvons pas mettre au service des personnes qui composent la collectivité les immenses moyens qu'exige un tel avancement?

Le standard de vie, ce n'est pas le "confort des fesses" comme l'exposait récemment, avec une étonnante légèreté, un jeune instituteur. Le standard de vie ce sont avant tout les universités, les bibliothèques, les laboratoires, les réacteurs atomiques et les instituts spécialisés dans les sciences de l'avenir. C'est sur tout cela que le Québec et le Canada français doivent compter, c'est de tout cela qu'ils doivent se pourvoir s'ils veulent s'assurer autre chose qu'une survie misérable, marginale, où notre langue elle-même, isolée des courants majeurs du monde moderne, serait bientôt réduite à la condition de résidu culturel ou de curiosité historique.

Notre premier objectif, en politique, c'est de permettre au Canada français de participer pleinement à tout ce qui compose la substance même du monde moderne. Il faut nous mettre à l'heure de la science contemporaine, du progrès contemporain dans tous les domaines. Il faut, non pas réduire la dimension de nos outils techniques et politiques, mais nous pourvoir au contraire d'instruments plus considérables et plus puissants.

Nous avons franchi déjà d'importantes étapes, dans cette entreprise de modernisation. Mais nous nous causerions à nous-mêmes un tort incalculable si nous refusions de voir et de reconnaître qu'il nous reste encore une très longue route à parcourir.

Quant au maximum de liberté, c'est là encore un objectif inséparable des précédents. Puisque l'épanouissement de la personne humaine est notre priorité absolue, il est bien évident qu'il ne saurait s'accomplir que dans la liberté des personnes, intégrées à leur tour dans une société libre.

Or, quel homme ou quel peuple peuvent se dire libres s'ils sont en proie à la pauvreté? Et que vaudrait une "égalité" de droits qui ne pourrait pas s'appuyer sur une égalité de moyens? Ce serait l'égalité décrite par Anatole France, quand il vantait ironiquement la loi de son temps qui permet également, disait-il, aux pauvres comme aux riches, de dormir sous les ponts en hiver.

Il est clair aussi que le progrès humain exige une large ouverture sur le monde extérieur, et qu'un Québec isolé, replié, coupé même des minorités françaises qui vivent hors de ses frontières, deviendrait vite suffocant.

Comme francophones, nous possédons l'un des héritages les plus riches du monde, en matière de progrès et de liberté. La tradition française a toujours été marquée par un courant très fort de résistance à la tyrannie, d'accueil aux idées nouvelles et d'ouverture sur l'avenir. Etre français, c'est refuser les idées toutes faites, c'est battre la marche, c'est risquer quand l'entourage hésite, c'est foncer vers le lendemain. Comme Canadien français, nous n'avons pas encore donné le quart de notre mesure véritable. Le Canada sait que nous représentons déjà un énorme potentiel pour le pays, dans son ensemble. Mais nous seuls savons de quoi nous sommes vraiment capables et le reste du pays sera saisi d'étonnement et d'admiration quand nous aurons enfin décidé de jouer le jeu à fond. Je suis convaincu, pour ma part, que la culture française, représentée par des hommes qui n'ont pas froid aux yeux et qui ne craignent pas le risque, peut donner au Canada et à toute la vie canadienne, une dimension nouvelle et insoupçonnée jusqu'ici.

Ce que je propose, c'est que nous entreprenions dès aujourd'hui de jouer à fond le jeu du fédéralisme. Je voudrais donc, dans la seconde partie de mon exposé, vous dire comment je conçois les conditions à réaliser pour réussir dans cette entreprise.

Commençons, si vous le voulez bien, par les conditions que nous-mêmes devons remplir.

L'option fondamentale: Le fédéralisme ou la rupture

La première, à mon avis, c'est précisément de mettre à l'épreuve ce fédéralisme canadien. Mais non pas seulement par la critique, les spéculations intellectuelles ou l'échafaudage abstrait de solutions théoriques. Non. Il faut l'éprouver par l'action, directement, c'est-à-dire par une participation active, énergique, agressive même, à tous les aspects de la politique fédérale.

Cela suppose, évidemment, qu'on ait résolu au préalable certaines contradictions à mon avis illusoires, mais qui paralysent tout de même certains esprits. D'aucuns prétendent, vous le savez, que le progrès du Québec est incompatible avec celui du Canada — et vice-versa, qu'ils se détruiraient l'un l'autre en continuant de vivre ensemble.

Je vous propose que nous partions de l'hypothèse exactement contraire, à savoir que le plus sûr gage de progrès pour le Canada tout court, c'est un Canada français fort et dynamique, sûr de lui-même, délivré de toute peur et engagé à fond dans tous les aspects de la vie canadiennne. Corollairement, le plus sûr moyen de construire un pays solide, prospère et libre, sur la frontière des Etats-Unis, c'est pour le Canada anglophone de jouer à fond le jeu de la collaboration honnête avec l'élément français du pays.

Nous sommes donc ici devant un choix clair. La première hypothèse, celle de l'incompatibilité quel que soit le nom qu'on lui donne, tend vers le séparatisme auquel elle nous conduira à plus ou moins brève échéance, si nous l'acceptons. La seconde hypothèse, c'est l'expérience fédéraliste, abordée avec une résolution nouvelle et les moyens nouveaux, les ressources nouvelles du Québec moderne.

Entre les deux, il faut choisir. La plus mauvaise attitude que nous puissions prendre, ce serait d'hésiter, de balancer entre l'une et l'autre, et de laisser les événements décider pour nous. Ce n'est pas un hasard si deux ouvrages sont parus récemment dont l'un s'appelle *Option Québec* et l'autre *Option Canada*. Mais si j'avais été l'auteur du second, j'aurais choisi un titre plus nuancé, qui n'aurait laissé croire à aucune opposition. Car il est pour moi très clair que, si *l'Option Québec* de M. Lévesque exclut l'option Canada, en ce sens qu'elle détruit le pays, *l'Option Canada* au contraire, *inclut l'Option Québec*. En d'autres termes, la première option préconise une rupture alors que la seconde propose une solidarité.

Je l'ai répété souvent, les Etats ne sont pas des réalités imposées aux hommes par la nature, ni par aucune autre force surnaturelle. Un Etat, c'est l'expression d'une volonté commune à plusieurs hommes, c'est le fruit d'un choix.

Je ne choisis pas le Canada parce que le passé nous l'impose ni parce que le présent nous le commande. Je le choisis, et vous propose de le choisir, parce qu'il représente un défi plus exigeant, plus excitant et plus enrichissant, que la rupture séparatiste, parce qu'il offre à l'homme québécois, à l'homme canadien-français, l'occasion, la chance historique de participer à la création d'une grande réalité politique de l'avenir.

Pour créer cet avenir, il faut non seulement nous y mettre résolument, mais il faut aussi nous donner les moyens, les instruments de sa réalisation. Nous avons commencé déjà; il faut continuer. Le Québec et le Canada français se sont engagés dans la voie du progrès; ils doivent y rester. La seule chose qui pourrait nous empêcher de bâtir le Canada et d'y élargir notre place au soleil, ce serait un retour à l'immobilisme des années 50, ou encore la complaisance dans les débats stériles et théoriques qui ont trop longtemps tenu lieu chez nous d'action sociale, économique et politique.

Permettez-moi de faire, en passant, un bref retour sur cette histoire récente.

Il s'est mené ici, dans les années 50, un combat pour la liberté. J'ai lutté moi-même avec ceux qui voulaient secouer le joug de l'autoritarisme, de la dictature larvée, de la corruption politique. J'ai combattu avec ceux qui dénonçaient l'autonomisme verbal, prétexte commode qu'on utilisait alors pour justifier l'inaction et l'incurie de notre gouvernement provincial. J'ai fait ma part pour dissiper nos illusions les plus soigneusement entretenues, quand on nous racontait, par exemple, que nous possédions le meilleur système d'éducation au monde, alors que nous ne possédions même pas un ministère de l'éducation.

Mais la nécessité d'une autonomie véritable pour les provinces, et singulièrement pour le Québec, je n'ai jamais cessé de l'affirmer, de la défendre, parfois même contre mes amis.

Et la véritable révolution tranquille, en 1960, fut le résultat d'un effort pour faire "fonctionner" l'autonomie plutôt que de se contenter d'en parler, c'est-à-dire pour exercer réellement les pouvoirs que possède le Québec, en vertu de la constitution. Après s'être évertué si longtemps à protéger nos droits, on a décidé enfin de les mettre en oeuvre. Il en est résulté des réalisations authentiques, qui ont grandement contribué à l'avancement de la communauté québécoise. C'est cela qui a éveillé l'intérêt de la population et l'enthousiasme des jeunes. Mais chaque fois que la révolution tranquille a oublié ce point de départ pour bifurquer vers le verbalisme et les belles formules, chaque fois elle a cessé d'avancer.

Appliquer au domaine fédéral l'esprit de la "révolution tranquille"

Aujourd'hui, le défi qui se présente à nous, Canadiens français, c'est d'appliquer l'esprit authentique de la révolution tranquille à la réforme du gouvernement central. Ce que nous avons entrepris au niveau provincial, il faut le continuer au niveau fédéral. Là non plus, il ne faut pas nous contenter de défendre des droits: il faut les exercer pleinement, comme nous avons déjà commencé de le faire. Il nous faut agir et assumer nos responsabilités dans tous les domaines de compétence fédérale, qu'il s'agisse des opérations financières, du commerce, des affaires extérieures ou de la défense. Aucun de ces domaines ne nous est fermé, aucun ne doit nous être étranger, rien ne peut nous empêcher d'y jouer un rôle de premier plan. Et c'est en jouant ce rôle que nous ferons rayonner notre culture propre à travers tout le pays. C'est dans ce sens-là qu'Ottawa peut devenir, pour le français, une caisse de résonance, un instrument de diffusion plus puissant que tous ceux dont nous disposons ici.

Je sais bien que beaucoup de gens, parce qu'ils songent au passé, refusent de reconnaître les possibilités de l'avenir que j'évoque. Et certes, il ne manque pas de problèmes que seuls nos compatriotes anglophones peuvent résoudre, pour que cet avenir devienne possible. C'est là un aspect de la réalité canadienne qui s'impose avec la dernière évidence.

J'écrivais moi-même, voici trois ans déjà, les lignes qui suivent.

"Non seulement je ne suis pas indifférent (aux problèmes suscités au Canada par la présence des deux grandes communautés linguistiques qui y cohabitent depuis deux siècles) mais je crains que si, par entêtement, indifférence ou fanatisme, ces problèmes ne trouvent pas de solution convenable dans un avenir rapproché, la Confédération puisse subir de sérieux contre-coups. "Le Canada doit vraiment devenir un pays bilingue où la majorité linguistique cessera de se comporter comme si elle était investie de droits prioritaires et exclusifs; cette majorité devra de plus accepter le caractère fédératif du pays avec toutes les implications que cela entraîne.

"Que la majorité anglophone ne se soit comportée historiquement comme si les Canadiens français n'étaient qu'une des minorités ethniques du pays, avec quelques privilèges particuliers, cela me paraît bien évident. Le fonctionnarisme fédéral où la langue anglaise est, à toutes fins pratiques, la seule langue de travail, en est le plus bel exemple. Dans le passé, le Ministère des Affaires extérieures du Canada a créé l'image d'un pays unilingue anglais. Je pourrais en dire presque autant des autres ministères et des compagnies de la Couronne. La capitale fédérale est une capitale anglaise. L'armée canadienne est une armée anglaise dans laquelle les Canadiens français ont à surmonter des handicaps sérieux, surtout du point de vue linguistique.

"Sur le plan de la langue et de l'éducation, les Canadiens français des autres provinces ne jouissent pas de droits comparables à ceux des Canadiens anglais du Québec. Et cela, même au Nouveau-Brunswick où les Acadiens forment environ les deux cinquièmes de la population.

"La Radio-télévision d'Etat, malgré les efforts déployés depuis quelques années, n'a pas encore réussi à étendre ses réseaux français d'un bout à l'autre du pays.

"Dans un grand nombre de cas, des compagnies installées au Québec n'ont pas respecté la langue et la culture de leurs employés, non plus que celle de la population. Pour les promotions et l'embauchage, les Canadiens français ont été et sont encore souvent en position d'infériorité."

Il y a dans ces quelques paragraphes tout un programme de réformes à entre-

prendre. Mais la preuve que cette situation peut être corrigée, c'est que les réformes en question ont été amorcées depuis que ces lignes furent écrites.

Les réformes à entreprendre

Ce qu'il faut faire, désormais, c'est d'en mettre en route de nouvelles. Il est
indiscutable, et cela n'a jamais fait dans mon esprit le moindre doute, que plusieurs institutions fédérales (j'en veux pour exemple la Cour suprême et le
Sénat) ne correspondent plus aux nouveaux rapports qui se sont établis au
Canada pendant les dernières décennies. Il est non moins évident que le Parlement et sa procédure, que le fonctionnement même du gouvernement central
ont besoin de sérieuses révisions, pour s'adapter aux transformations majeures
qu'une évolution accélérée impose à toute la société canadienne. Je ferai seulement remarquer que tous nos parlements ressentent ce même besoin et que, par
exemple, les députés qui siègent à Québec réclament à cor et à cri la même
réforme parlementaire, la même redéfinition de leur rôle que les députés fédéraux tentent d'accomplir depuis plusieurs années.

Nous en sommes tous conscients: un programme politique, au Canada, en
1968, ne peut pas se contenter de définir le contenu des lois à faire, il doit porter
aussi sur notre façon de faire les lois, sur nos mécanismes parlementaires et minis-
tériels qui sont devenus désuets. Je ne peux donc concevoir de gouvernements
nouveaux qui ne soient pas profondément, et résolument réformistes. Non
seulement les hommes politiques doivent se laisser pousser par le vent de réforme
qui souffle aujourd'hui; ils doivent orienter cette poussée vers les secteurs
essentiels de la politique.

La réforme constitutionnelle

Cela m'amène à poser une question que vous attendez sans doute et que je
formulerai dans les termes suivants: "A quelle réforme faut-il donner la priorité?" ou encore. "Devons-nous privilégier de façon absolue la question constitutionnelle, comme tant de journalistes, de juristes et de professeurs nous pous-
sent à le faire, au Québec, depuis quelques années?"

A cette question, j'ai toujours répondu selon mes convictions. Or, il s'est trouvé
qu'elles ne coïncident pas, ces convictions, avec celles de tous les journalistes,
avocats et professeurs du Québec et du Canada qui se préoccupent de la question.

J'ai dit et je répète que les réformes constitutionnelles constituent pour moi
une priorité, parmi d'autres. J'ai dit, et j'en suis toujours persuadé, que nous
aurions tort, comme Québécois et comme Canadiens français, d'investir toutes
nos énergies dans ce domaine.

Voilà ce que je pense, et je ne m'en excuse pas.

Mais mon attitude n'en est pas une de refus global, je n'ai jamais été un apôtre
du statu quo constitutionnel et j'ai toujours accepté, voire recherché la discussion avec ceux qui ne pensent pas comme moi.

Depuis que je suis à Ottawa, à cause de mes fonctions mêmes, j'ai dû accorder
plus d'attention peut-être aux questions constitutionnelles qu'à n'importe quelle
autre, d'abord comme secrétaire parlementaire du premier ministre, ensuite

comme ministre de la Justice. J'ai annoncé en septembre, au nom du gouvernement, que la discussion était ouverte sur l'ensemble de la constitution et que nous étions prêts à négocier sur tous et chacun des points que voudraient soulever les provinces en général et le Québec en particulier. Pour assurer que le débat s'engage dès le départ sur un mode positif, j'ai visité tous et chacun des premiers ministres provinciaux et toutes ces rencontres, sans exception, ont été cordiales.

Enfin, vous vous souviendrez qu'au début de février, nous avons mis en marche les négociations au cours d'une conférence fédérale-provinciale, la plus importante, a-t-on dit, depuis le début de la Confédération.

Plaidoyer pour la clarté

Mais, sauf erreur, négocier, c'est discuter, c'est chercher un accord, c'est affronter des points de vue parfois divergents. Ce serait trop simple s'il suffisait que l'une des parties formule une demande pour que l'autre y accède aussitôt. Et ce serait l'anarchie si chacune pouvait décider qu'elle s'attribue tel ou tel pouvoir nouveau sans consulter l'autre.

Enfin, il ne faudrait pas croire que la volonté de négocier, la souplesse d'esprit essentielle à toute négociation, interdit aux négociateurs de faire connaître au préalable les positions qu'ils entendent adopter, ou de réclamer que les autres précisent leurs positions.

Au contraire, dans tout débat public de cette importance, qui met en jeu le sort même de la communauté, les citoyens ont le droit d'exiger des prises de positions claires et les hommes politiques ont le devoir d'expliciter leur pensée; de faire connaître ouvertement les conséquences éventuelles et les implications diverses des solutions qu'ils préconisent.

Mener une telle négociation en cachette, dissimuler sa pensée ou se tenir délibérément dans l'équivoque, ce serait refuser tout rôle aux citoyens et mépriser la démocratie. Les décisions doivent être prises en pleine connaissance de cause, ce qui implique pour tous les hommes politiques intéressés le devoir d'exposer clairement leur attitude, de dire sans ambiguïté à quelle enseigne ils logent.

J'ai conscience, pour ma part, d'avoir fait connaître mon attitude avec toute la clarté et toute la franchise dont je suis capable.

Les prétentions de certaines "élites"

Certains ont prétendu déjà, et sans doute le feront-ils encore, que cette position va à contre-courant de ce que pensent aujourd'hui les élites québécoises.

A ce sujet, je me permets d'entretenir des doutes et de contester d'abord la définition même des élites qui se trouve sous-entendue dans cette proposition. Il est exact que beaucoup d'intellectuels tiennent mordicus à certaines nouveautés constitutionnelles dont ils font presque un absolu. N'est-il pas présomptueux toutefois d'affirmer qu'il s'agit là de "nos élites" et que leur attitude reflète la volonté, les aspirations profondes de la société canadienne-française?

J'ai toujours cru, pour ma part, que l'élite, dans une société, ne se définit pas par les titres universitaires, les postes d'influence ou le compte en banque. Dans la conception que je me fais d'une élite, j'inclus tous ceux qui savent réfléchir et orienter leurs efforts vers le bien commun. Ils peuvent être manoeuvres, militants syndicaux, hommes d'affaires, gérants de coopératives, balayeurs de rues, fonctionnaires ou professeurs d'université. Ils peuvent être banquiers ou journalistes, techniciens ou ferblantiers, voire même politiciens! Mais ce qui fait d'eux une élite, ce ne sont ni leurs fonctions ni leurs titres; c'est, je le répète, l'aptitude à réfléchir et le souci du bien général, le dépassement des égoïsmes et des intérêts particuliers.

Or qui peut prétendre, à l'heure actuelle, que ces élites là, dans leur ensemble ou seulement dans leur majorité, adhèrent à telle ou telle thèse particulière en matière constitutionnelle? Ont-elles eu l'occasion de s'exprimer clairement? Sait-on vraiment ce que pense le peuple québécois?

Je refuse pour ma part de proclamer que je parle en son nom. Je me contente de proposer une pensée, je tente de persuader que je préconise des solutions justes. Mais en vertu du même principe, je me demande qui peut prétendre qu'il parle au nom de tous et se comporter comme si la pensée canadienne-française était unanime et monolithique.

Avant tout, la liberté de l'esprit

Quand on croit à la liberté des personnes et qu'on travaille à l'édification d'une société vraiment libre, on annonce la fin des monolithismes. A cet égard, le Québec et le Canada français ont subi une véritable mutation, depuis vingt ans, mutation dont les conséquences positives sont partout visibles.

Si nos chansonniers, par exemple, ont retrouvé le chemin de la poésie véritable, si nous avons produit de grands peintres, comme Pellan, Borduas et Riopel; si Marie-Claire Blais, Réjean Ducharme ou Anne Hébert ont créé des oeuvres fortes et accédé à la renommée internationale, si l'évolution sociale s'est accélérée chez nous de façon spectaculaire, dans de nombreux secteurs, dont celui de l'éducation, c'est que la liberté des personnes et celle de l'esprit ont franchi des étapes capitales.

Il nous reste à canaliser cette énergie enfin libérée vers des objectifs politiques toujours plus précis et plus valables, vers le risque calculé, vers les défis du progrès lui-même.

Et nous aurions grand tort de profiter de cette liberté pour créer entre les hommes des conflits artificiels.

Ceux que la chose publique intéresse s'engagent, dans une société libre, au niveau d'action qui leur plaît. Certains choisissent la scène municipale, d'autres la politique provinciale, d'autres encore le niveau fédéral. Et chacun, dans son option, poursuit le plus honnêtement, le plus efficacement qu'il peut, les objectifs qu'il croit les plus importants pour l'avancement de la communauté qu'il représente. Il est non seulement vain, il est néfaste et dangereux d'opposer, comme si elles étaient contradictoires, les loyautés diverses que ces engagements commandent.

En nous engageant dans la politique fédérale, mes collègues à Ottawa et moi nous servons notre communauté d'origine, nous le faisons de notre mieux et nous refusons les entreprises de confusion de certains pêcheurs en eau trouble qui voudraient en quelque sorte nous exclure de la communauté.

Je disais tout à l'heure que pour moi, la question constitutionnelle ne constituait qu'une priorité entre plusieurs autres. Mais si vous me demandiez maintenant de dire laquelle des priorités m'apparaît la première, laquelle se rapproche davantage d'un absolu, voici ce que je répondrais.

Faire de ce pays une société politique libre, ouverte et forte qui puisse, en tout premier lieu, effacer de nos villes et de notre milieu rural la honte que constituent la misère au milieu de l'abondance et la pauvreté côtoyant la richesse. On dit, avec raison, que les jeunes, en particulier, ont besoin de s'enthousiasmer; c'est vers cet objectif-là que le voudrais orienter en tout premier lieu leur enthousiasme politique.

Et sur ce fondement solide, nous pourrons édifier une culture française rayonnante, créatrice, délivrée de la plus terrible des oppressions; celle de l'insécurité et de la peur.

Maîtres chez nous? J'en suis.

Mais chez nous, c'est le Canada tout entier, de Terre-Neuve à Victoria, avec ses immenses richesses qui nous appartiennent à nous tous et dont il ne faut pas abandonner une parcelle. Ce pays que nous avons exploré une première fois, que nos pères les tout premiers ont foulé dans un émerveillement extraordinaire, il faut repartir à sa découverte et cette fois pour de bon.

Nos jeunes ingénieurs ne s'arrêteront pas à la Manic: ils s'intéresseront bientôt, ils s'intéressent déjà aux sables pétrolifères de l'Athabaska ou aux gisements de potasse de la Saskatchewan. Nos hommes d'affaires, nos marchands, nos entrepreneurs, nos manufacturiers n'ont pas renoncé aux marchés de l'ensemble canadien. Nos artistes ont déjà conquis de larges auditoires à travers tout le Canada.

C'est cela que nous devons continuer; c'est cette effort que nous devons poursuivre. Il faut ouvrir le compas et non le refermer.

35   Of Truth and Freedom in Politics: French-Canadians and the Federal Challenge*

Pierre Elliot Trudeau

The great Catholic journalist, Chesterton, used to repeat the following paradox: "A great courage is required, heroism almost," he used to say, "to stand on a platform and proclaim that 2 and 2 are 4 . . . ." This is the type of courage that

---

*Translation of a speech delivered April 2, 1968 in Montreal to the members of The Richelieu Club, Metropolitan Area, by the Federal Minister of Justice. This is the full text of the important speech given by M. Trudeau announcing the close of his campaign in the race for the Liberal leadership. By permission.

I would like to have today. My intention is to speak to you in all frankness, and frankness commands, demands sometimes, that we have enough strength to proclaim the obvious.

I am fully aware that I am not addressing myself to a partisan audience, which therefore does not expect to hear a partisan speech, but only wishes to know, and this curiosity honours me, what I think of Quebec's future, and Canada's future, how I see the fate of French Canada, and that of Canada.

Of Truth in Politics

This is what I shall attempt to tell you. I will tell it to you simply, as directly as possible with a minimum of oratorical precautions. Moreover, even if I tried to dissimulate my ideas I would not succeed very well. I believe that the time has come for politicians, especially in our country, to enunciate clearly the available choices, and present them as they see them.

I know that not everybody thinks the way I do on this topic. I know that some people prefer ambiguity because it is more comfortable. Some choose ambiguity because they believe that it is the fate of Canada to live in such ambiguity. There are those, finally, who, motivated by some strange conception of professional ethics, would like to see politicians place cleverness higher than truth in their scale of values. On one side, they blame politicians in general for attacking problems tangentially instead of facing them. But, on the other hand, if a politician honestly says what he thinks (and especially if his ideas do not coincide with current opinion) he will be accused of lacking diplomatic sense.

But what is diplomatic sense? We ought not to confuse flexibility of character with not having a single idea worth expressing, or not having a single idea to which we hold strongly enough to stand up for it. The consequences would be strange. The ideal politician would be the one who does not believe in anything, always ready to give up when coming face to face with contradiction, and promptly turning his sail in the direction of the wind, no matter where it comes from.

Truth, I believe, resides somewhere else, and so do you believe. Your invitation stands as a proof of this. You know that the existence of civil dialogue, of open discussion, of the free confrontation of ideas, is one of the most important democratic traditions, one of the functions most essential to the political life of a country. Your hospitality, tonight, allows the exercise of this function. And you know that the process of public debates, within a human community, is a sign of health, a proof of vitality. Now, could we carry on this debate if we considered as inflexible the politician who expresses his ideas directly and frankly, who dares proclaim in a clear voice what he silently thinks?

For my part, I plead guilty to the charge of speaking too frankly. I accept the blame in advance. I refuse to defend myself against the accusation. And I shall repeat the offence this very minute.

What I want to expose to you, as briefly but as clearly as possible, are my political convictions as a Canadian from Quebec.

Faith in Federalism

You will not be astonished if I affirm my faith in a form of government called federalism. I would like to state precisely that, as far as I am concerned, federalism is not an expedient, nor is it a compromise. Far less is it a makeshift as some people believe it to be. On the contrary, it is an avant-garde political formula, to which I would subscribe even outside the Canadian context.

Why?

The first priority, when we choose a political system, is the human person. Not the person as an abstract notion; what is of prime importance is concrete human beings, you, me, the farmers, the workers, the businessmen, the tenants on Delorimier Street and the residents of Lethbridge, the workers of Windsor and the fishermen of Gaspésie or Newfoundland. Politics, as we say here, is made "for the people", and not "the people" for politics.

I would like to quote Brother Anonymous here; it is a phrase which goes very far if we just stop and think about it for a minute: "Socialism, capitalism, social doctrine," writes Brother Anonymous, "I have a criterion to judge them: the poor people that I know. If a social measure translates, or could have been translated, into a little more security or dignity for the poor people that I know, it has my support."

This is my conviction as well. It does not hold only for social measures and the poor; it is true of all forms of government, of all the laws and all citizens. To legislate, to work out a policy, is to improve the daily lot of flesh and blood human beings. And the better adapted and adjusted governments are to the problems they are called on to solve, the better are their chances to frame legislation for men.

The great advantage of federalism is that it brings the State and the citizen closer, it allows for local legislation for local needs, regional for regional needs, and federal for confronting global problems.

I could express the second reason for my preference for federalism in a phrase so popular that it has become banal: "To govern is to foresee". I mean that any political formula worth the name is by definition oriented toward the future. Now, the future is the rapprochement between peoples; it consists of pooling the wealth of the world; it is the march towards unity — or it is atomic warfare.

But rapprochement, pooling, unity, do not mean uniformity. Some people dream of an international society where everybody would speak the same language, would live in the same way, would eat the same meals, and would watch the same television programs. This type of world would have certain advantages, but chances are that we would die of boredom.

It remains certain that we are evolving toward a closer union among peoples. If there is an irresistible tendency in the modern world, that is the one.

Now, federalism is the very political system which allows for union in freedom and for unity in diversity. It is undoubtedly why hundreds of millions of men live within a federal framework, in India and the United States, in Brazil, in Germany and the U.S.S.R.; this is why hundreds of millions more are moving toward federalism, through stages that are called customs unions, common markets, or economic communities.

This is the basis for the attitude that I adopted, and maintained for twenty years, in the constitutional debate which occupies a central place in Quebec and Canada.

I believe in a political formula centred on the person, a political formula whose prime consideration is to secure for the men and women of this country the greatest measure of welfare and freedom possible.

French-Canadian Society and Its Future

And since we are having a family chat, that is, we are all French-Canadians, we will start, if you so wish, with this French-Canadian society, which is our first preoccupation, which for all of us here constitutes the point of departure, physical as well as cultural, of all our political reflections. Recently I wrote (and I apologize for quoting myself), "Citizens of our country, I would have been French-Canadian by adoption, had I not been French-Canadian by birth." Therefore, I feel quite free to talk with you using as my starting-point the French fact.

And the first question we must ask ourselves is, I think, the following: "How can we best secure for the people who make up our French-Canadian community this maximum welfare and freedom?"

When I speak of welfare, I do not think of material welfare only, of wages, residences, cars, and refrigerators. I think also and especially of our cultural fulfilment, of human progress in its totality. It is important to understand that all of those elements are inseparable. How could we promote a collectivity in which individuals, one by one, would not have the means to improve their competence, their efficiency, their human quality? And how can we secure this collective progress if we cannot make the immense resources required for such progress available to the persons who compose the collectivity?

The standard of living is not "comfort of the buttocks", as a young teacher recently wrote with incredible frivolity. The standard of living is first and foremost the universities, the libraries, the atomic reactors and the institutes specializing in the sciences of the future. This is what Quebec and French Canada must take into account, this is what they must secure for themselves if they wish to have more than just a marginal and miserable survival, where our language itself, isolated from the major currents of the modern world, would very soon be reduced to the status of mere cultural residue or historical curiosity.

Our first objective, in politics, is to allow French Canada to participate fully in everything that makes up the very substance of the modern world. We have to be up-to-date in contemporary science and in contemporary progress in all sectors. This is not the time to reduce the size of our political and technical tools; but, on the contrary, we must acquire bigger and more powerful tools.

We have traversed important stages, in this enterprise of modernization. But we would inflict upon ourselves incalculable harm should we refuse to acknowledge that we still have a long trip ahead of us.

As far as maximum freedom is concerned, this objective is inseparable from the former ones. Since the fulfilment of the human being is our absolute priority, it is clear that it can be reached solely within the freedom of persons, in their turn integrated within a free society.

Now, can we call a man, can we call a people free, if they are in the throes of poverty? And what is the value of "equality" in law if it cannot find its support in equality of means? This would be the equality described by Anatole France, when he ironically spoke of the law of his day which allows the poor and the rich equally to sleep under bridges in winter.

It is clear that human progress requires wide access to the external world, and if Quebec were isolated, withdrawn, even cut off from the French minorities living outside its borders, it would suffocate very quickly.

As francophones we possess one of the most imposing traditions of progress and freedom. The French tradition has distinguished itself by a strong current of resistance to tyranny, of receptivity to new ideas, of openness to the future. To be French is to refuse conservative thinking to open up the march, to risk when those about you hesitate, to move ahead toward the future. As French Canadians we have not yet given the quarter of our true capacities. Canada knows that we have enormous potential for the country as a whole. But we alone know exactly what are our capacities, and the rest of the country will be struck with wonder and admiration, once we decide to play the game thoroughly. I am convinced that French culture, represented by daring men who are ready to gamble, could give Canada and Canadian life a new, unsuspected dimension.

What I propose is that right now we start playing the game of federalism, and playing it thoroughly. In the second part of my exposé I would like to outline the necessary conditions if success is to be achieved in this enterprise.

Let us start, if you wish, with the requirements that we ourselves must fulfil.

The Fundamental Option: Federalism or Rupture

The first requirement, in my opinion, is precisely to put Canadian federalism to the test. But not only by criticism, intellectual speculations, the framing of abstract, theoretical solutions. No, we must test it through action, directly — that is, through active participation, energetic, aggressive even, in all aspects of federal politics.

This, of course, presupposes that we resolve certain contradictions, illusory as far as I am concerned, but which stifle some minds. Some people assert that Quebec's progress in incompatible with Canada's — and vice versa, that they would destroy one another if they went on living together.

I propose that we start with the contrary hypothesis, namely that the safest token of progress for Canada is a strong and dynamic French Canada, sure of itself, freed from fear, and thoroughly involved in all aspects of Canadian life. Equally, the safest way of building up a solid country, prosperous and free, on the border of the United States is for English Canada to play thoroughly the game of honest collaboration with the French element of the country.

We are facing a clear choice. The first hypothesis, that of incompatibility, whatever its name, leads to separation where we will end up sooner or later if we accept it. The second hypothesis is the federalist experience, approached with boldness, and with the new means and resources of modern Quebec.

We have to choose between the two. The worst attitude would be hesitation, to shift from the one to the other, and let the events decide for us. The recent publication of two books called *Option Quebec* and *Option Canada* is not an accident. Had I been the author of the second work, I would have chosen a more subtle title, not giving rise to the opposition implied in the titles. Because it is very clear to me that, if Mr. Lévesque's *Option Quebec* excludes option Canada in the sense that it destroys the country, *Option Canada* on the contrary includes *Option Quebec*. In other words, the first option presupposes a rupture, while the second offers solidarity.

I have often repeated that States are not realities imposed on men by nature or any other supernatural agency. A State is the expression of the common will of various men; it is the product of a choice.

I do not choose Canada as an imposition of past history, nor as a commandment of present times. I choose it, and propose the same to you, because it represents a greater, more exciting, more fufilling challenge than the separatist rupture, because it offers the man from Quebec, French-Canadian man, the occasion, the historical chance of participating in the creation of a great political reality of the future. In order to create this future, we not only have to get definitely involved, but we also have to give ourselves the means, the instruments of its realization. We have started already; we need to go on. Quebec and French Canada have taken the road to progress — they must go on travelling this road. The only thing which would prevent us from building Canada, and from increasing our share of its available resources, would be a return to the inactivity of the 50's, or the complacency of the sterile and theoretical debates, which for too long in Quebec took the place of social, economic and political action.

Allow me to go back briefly over this recent history. In the 50's a struggle for freedom was fought here. I myself fought next to those who attempted to shake off the chains of authoritarianism, of latent dictatorship, of political corruption, I fought with those who denounced verbal autonomy, a useful pretext used to justify the inactivity and carelessness of our provincial government. I did my share to shatter the carefully entertained illusions, when we were told, for instance, that our educational system was the best in the world, while we did not even have a ministry of education.

As far as the necessity for genuine autonomy for the provinces is concerned, and especially for Quebec, I have never ceased to affirm it. I have always stood up for it, sometimes even against my friends.

And the true quiet revolution, in 1960, was the outcome of an effort to make autonomy functional rather than just talk about it; that is, to really exercise the powers that Quebec possesses in virtue of the constitution. After struggling for so long for the protection of our rights, we finally decided to set them to work. The outcome was authentic achievements which have greatly contributed to the progress of the Quebec community. This is what stirred up interest among the public and captivated the enthusiasm of the youth. But each time that the quiet revolution forgot this starting-point to bifurcate into verbalism and niceties, its advance was stifled.

The Spirit of the Quiet Revolution
Applied at the Federal Level

Today the challenge that faces French Canadians is that of applying the genuine spirit of the quiet revolution toward a reform of the central government. The efforts we have expended at the provincial level must be translated to the federal level. Here again we cannot remain content to simply defend our rights: they have to be exercised fully as we have already started doing. We must act and assume our responsibilities in all domains of federal competence whether it be finance, commerce, external affairs, or defence. None of those domains is closed to us, none foreign to us, nothing can prevent us from playing a leading role. It is in playing this part that we will be able to diffuse our own culture through the whole country. It is in this way that Ottawa can become an amplifier, a more powerful instrument of diffusion than all those we possess here.

I know that a lot of people, because they still think about the past, refuse to acknowledge the possibilities of the future that I evoke. And of course, there are many problems that only our English-speaking compatriots could solve, if this future is to be realized. This is an irreducible aspect of Canadian reality.

Three years ago, I wrote the following:

> Not only am I not indifferent (to the problems that arise in Canada from the presence of the two great linguistic communities of which Canada has been made up for two centuries) but I fear that if through stubborness, indifference, or fanaticism, those problems become impossible to solve in the near future, confederation may be under severe strain. Canada must really become a bilingual country where the linguistic majority will stop behaving as though it were invested of priority and exclusive rights; this majority, moreover, will have to accept the federal character of the country with all its implications.

> That the anglophone majority behaved historically as though French Canadians were nothing but one of the ethnic minorities of the country, with a few special privileges, seems to me obvious. The federal civil service, where for all practical purposes the English language is the everyday language, is the most obvious example. In the past, the Minister of External Affairs of Canada projected the image of an English unilingual country. I could almost say the same of the other ministries and crown companies. The federal capital is an English capital. The Canadian army is an English army in which French-Canadians have to overcome serious handicaps, especially from the linguistic point of view.

> As far as language and education are concerned, French Canadians in other provinces do not enjoy comparable rights to those of English Canadians in Quebec, even in New Brunswick where Acadians account for about two-fifths of the population.

> The CBC radio and television network, in spite of its efforts in the last years, has not succeeded in extending its French network from coast to coast.

> In a great number of cases, companies established in Quebec have not respected the language and culture of their employees, nor of the population. As far as promotions and hiring are concerned, French Canadians are still often in an inferior position.

There is contained in those few paragraphs a whole program of reforms to be undertaken. But the proof that this situation can be remedied is that the above reforms have been set in motion since those lines were written.

The Reforms to be Undertaken

What is required, now, is to set new reforms in motion. It is indisputable, and I never had the shadow of a doubt about it, that many federal institutions (for example, the Supreme Court and the Senate) do not correspond any more to the new relations set up in Canada during the last decades. It is no less obvious that Parliament and its procedures, that the very functioning of the central government, require serious reforms in order to be adapted to the major changes that an accelerated evolution has imposed on Canadian life. I will simply bring to your attention that all our parliaments feel the same need and that the deputies in Quebec urgently call for the same parliamentary reform, the same redefinition of their role, that the federal members have attempted to set up for years.

We are all aware of it: a political program in Canada, in 1968, cannot remain content with defining the contents of future legislation, it must include the way we frame legislation, and our ministerial and parliamentary mechanisms which have become obsolete. I cannot therefore conceive new governments that would not be deeply and resolutely reformist. Not only must politicians be influenced by the contemporary movement of reforms; they have also to orient this current towards the essential sectors of politics.

The Constitutional Reform

This leads me to ask a question which you undoubtedly expect; I will formulate it in the following terms: "Which reform should be granted priority?" or again: "Should we give the constitutional question absolute priority, as so many journalists, jurists and professors have urged us to do in Quebec in the last few years?"

I have always answered this question according to my convictions. It happens that my convictions do not coincide with those of all the journalists, lawyers and professors in Quebec who are concerned with the problem.

I said, and I repeat, that constitutional reforms are, as far as I am concerned, a priority among others. I said, and I remain convinced, that we would be wrong as Quebeckers and French-Canadians, to invest all our energy in this sphere.

This is what I think, and I do not have to apologize for it.

But I do not adopt an attitude of global refusal, I never preached the constitutional status quo, and I always accepted and even sought to discuss my views, with those who think differently than I do.

Since I came to Ottawa, because of my duties, I have had to devote more time to constitutional problems than to any others, first as parliamentary secretary to the Prime Minister and then as Minister of Justice. I announced in September, on behalf of the government, that discussion was open on the whole of the constitution, and that we were ready to negotiate on each and every point brought up by the provinces in general and especially by Quebec. To make sure from the start that the debate moves along positive lines, I have visited each and every Provincial Prime Minister, and those meetings, without exception, were cordial.

Finally, you will remember that at the beginning of February we set the negotiations into motion at a Federal-Provincial conference, the most important, it was said, since the beginning of confederation.

A Plea for Clearness

But, unless I am mistaken, to negotiate is to discuss, to seek agreement, to confront diverging points of view. It would be too easy if the only requirement were that one of the parties submit a demand to which the other party would accede immediately. And it would be anarchy if each party could decide as to what new power it is going to acquire without consulting the other.

Finally, it should not be thought that openness for negotiations, the flexibility of mind essential to all negotiation, prevents the negotiators from making their positions known in advance, or from asking that the other party make their positions clear.

On the contrary, in any public debate of this importance, when the fate of the community is at stake, the citizens have the right to ask where each party stands, and politicians are under the obligation to make their ideas explicit, to make everybody aware of the eventual consequences and implications of the solutions they propose.

To negotiate behind the scenes, to dissimulate one's thought or to deliberately remain equivocal, amounts to denying any participation to the citizenry and means contempt for democracy. Decisions must be taken in full awareness, which implies that all politicians have the duty to express their attitude clearly, to say without ambiguity where they stand.

For my part, I am aware that I have made my position clear, with all the clearness and frankness that I am capable of.

The Pretensions of Certain "Elites"

Some people have claimed before, and undoubtedly will go on claiming, that this position goes against what Quebec elites think today.

On this point I have serious doubts, and I wish to contest the implicit definition of elites used in this proposition. It is true that some intellectuals believe very strongly in some constitutional novelties, as in an absolute. Is it not presumptuous to assert that they are "our elites" and that their attitude represents the will, the true aspirations of French-Canadian society?

I have always believed that the elite in a given society cannot be defined by university diplomas, influential posts or the bank account. In my mind an elite includes all those who can think and orient their efforts towards the common good. They may be manual labourers, trade union militants, businessmen, industrial managers, street sweepers, functionaries or university professors. They may be bankers or journalists, technicians, tinmen, even politicians. But what makes them an elite is not their functions nor their titles; it is, I repeat, the aptitude to think and care for the general good, overcoming egoism and private interests.

Who would maintain, at this moment, that those elites as a whole, or as a majority, favour this or that particular thesis on constitutional matters? Did they have a chance to express their ideas clearly? Does anybody know, really, what the people of Quebec thinks?

I refuse to proclaim that I speak in its name. I remain content with formulating an idea. I am attempting to convince you that the solutions I propose are just. But in virtue of the same principle, I ask: who claims to speak in the name of all? Who acts as though French-Canadian thought is unanimous and monolithic?

Before Everything, Freedom of Thought

If one believes in the freedom of the individual, and works towards the edification of a really free society, one proclaims the end of monolithisms. In this matter Quebec and Canada have experienced a real mutation in the last twenty years, the positive consequences of which are everywhere visible.

If our *chansonniers*, for instance, have found again the road which leads to genuine poetry, if we have produced great painters such as Pellan, Borduas and Riopel; if Marie-Claire Blais, Réjean Ducharme or Anne Hébert have come out with real creations, and acquired international fame, if social evolution here has moved at a spectacular pace in numerous sectors, including education, it is because the freedom of the individual and that of the mind have traversed important stages.

We now must orient those liberated forces towards political objectives ever more precise and valuable, towards calculated risk, towards the challenges of progress itself.

And we would be wrong to use this freedom in order to create artificial conflicts between men.

Those who are interested in public life get involved, in a free society, at the level of action they prefer. Some choose the municipal scene, others provincial politics, others the federal level. And everyone, according to his own choice, pursues in the most honest and efficient manner the goals he believes to be the most important for the progress of the community that he represents. Not only is it vain, it is nefarious and dangerous to oppose those different loyalties as though they were contradictory.

Through our involvement in federal politics, my colleagues in Ottawa and myself serve the community of our origin, we do it in the best way we can, and we refuse to get involved in the confusing projects of those who would like somehow to exclude us from the community.

I said a moment ago that, as far as I am concerned, the constitutional question is one priority among many others. But if you asked me now which of the priorities is the first one, which one comes closest to an absolute, here is my answer.

To make out of this country a free political society, open and strong, which could in the first place erase from our cities and rural districts the shame of misery in the midst of abundance and poverty in the midst of wealth. We hear, rightfully, that youth needs enthusiasm; it is towards this objective that in the first place I would like to orient their political enthusiasm.

On this solid foundation we could build a radiating French culture, creative, freed from the most terrible of oppressions: insecurity and fear.

Masters in our own house? I agree.

But our own house is the whole of Canada, from Newfoundland to Victoria, with its immense resources which belong to all of us and of which we should not give up even a patch. This country which we have explored a first time, which our fathers were the first ones to explore with extraordinary amazement, we must now set off again to discover, and this time once and for all.

Our young engineers will not stop with Manic: they will soon be interested, they are already interested, in the Athabaska tar sands or the potash mines of Saskatchewan. Our businessmen, our tradesmen, our entrepreneurs, our manufacturers have not given up on the markets of Canadian society. Our artists have captivated large audiences through the whole of Canada.

That's what we must continue; that's the objective we must pursue. We must open the windows and not close them.

36   Changing Canadian Federalism*

Lester B. Pearson

For the next three days you will be discussing a very important subject, the economics of Canadian unity within the context of nationhood as a whole; including its social and cultural and political aspects as well as the economic.

Your talks will take place, too, in the context of the many forces at work in our country today — vigorous forces, dynamic forces, sometimes deeply disturbing ones; but always as challenging as they are disturbing.

It is reassuring to remember that federalism — the source of so many of these forces — by its very nature is always in a state of flux. For it combines opposing forces — forces of unity and of diversity, of regional power and of central power — and these forces are in a constant state of adjustment in the face of changing economic, technological, and international circumstances.

*Text of the Prime Minister's address to the conference on the Economics of Canadian Unity, Banff, Alberta, October 15, 1967. Reprinted by permission of the author.

It is the continuing responsibility of any national leader in a federal country to try to keep these forces in balance; to recognize when positive action will reinforce the bonds that unite us, and when accommodation is required to reinforce the diversity which enriches us; and which, moreover, is an essential factor in unity. This has been my job — and my principal domestic concern — during my four years in office.

My colleagues and I have tried to give added meaning to nationhood in Canada — by contributing toward common achievements in the arts and in science; by providing universal national services in the fields of health and of social security; by increasing the benefits of economic growth and distributing them more evenly across the country. We have tried to give focus to our common bonds by recognizing the symbols of nationhood — the flag and the national anthem; by giving encouragement to our Centennial celebrations and Expo. We have tried, at the same time, to find some accommodation with the provinces when a centralized approach to social or economic progress in Canada would have conflicted with the interests or the aspirations of one of Canada's societies or regions.

It was for this reason, for example, that the Canada Pension Plan was adapted to co-exist with the Quebec Pension Plan, and that the Atlantic Development Fund was created to meet the special needs of the Atlantic Provinces. These are but two examples.

The forces of change in Canada today, however, have been so accelerated, and the turmoil of adjustment has become so intense, that customary processes of initiative and accommodation are no longer sufficient.

We must engage in a more fundamental sort of questioning — the kind which in times of social stress can turn risk into opportunity, danger into challenge, even crisis into progress. We must identify and clarify the issues and the alternatives which the country faces. They must not only be discussed by political leaders but, more important, by the people themselves. For it is the people who will determine our destiny, our very existence as a sovereign Canadian state.

Today all countries are subjected to stresses and tensions. Technological progress, increasing urbanization, the growing international interdependence of economies and of societies, and the confusion and bewilderment of change: all have caused major social adjustments throughout the world.

Canada, though a "promised land" if there ever was one, could not expect to be immune. One of the most unexpected reactions to these changes has been the increased determination of peoples and of societies to find, or to retain, some cultural or social identity in the face of the rising uncertainty and insecurity associated with change, national and international.

In Canada today, for example, there is a greater emphasis than in earlier years upon regional identity, upon the powers and prerogatives of regional governments, even upon the marks of regional diversity. And in particular, and this is a dominant force which all of us recognize, the French-speaking Canadian society has made known its determination not merely to survive but to flourish; not in poverty and in isolation, but as a participant in, and a beneficiary of, the growth of the western world.

If we are to develop, or even survive, as a Canadian state, we must understand both the nature and the power of this determination; recognize that it is stronger than before. And we must accommodate our federal system to this situation, just as we must accommodate it to the other social, economic and technological developments. The question is how.

One suggestion that is sometimes made is that we should wait for forces to spend themselves; assuming that French-speaking Canadians will recognize sooner or later that participation in North American society requires their adaptation to that society. They should, therefore, either accept — so it goes — the gradual absorption of their culture, of their society in a larger North American one; or revert to the kind of pastoral last-century isolation in which that culture once existed. After all, the Scottish clans still have their Highland Games and the chief gives out prizes in Gaelic! In such a "solution", English-speaking Canadians would feel no need to make those changes and accommodations which would contribute to the preservation of the French-speaking Canadian society in centres outside of Quebec: in the Nation's capital and government, in the Ottawa Valley, in Northern Ontario; in St. Boniface; in the Acadian parts of the Maritime Provinces; wherever there is a sizeable and a flourishing community of French-speaking Canadians.

I need hardly add that there is no future for Canada in this approach. If it were attempted, French-speaking Canadians would be forced to look upon Quebec, not Canada, as their sole cultural home; and Quebec, not Canada, would soon be their sole political home. Separatism would be inevitable and the powers exercised by a government in Ottawa which no longer pretended to represent the interests of French-Canada would be transferred to Quebec City. A French Canadian might put it bluntly this way: if you must live in a cultural ghetto, it is better to run it yourself, rather than try to preserve it in an unreal and unequal federal partnership.

So French Canadians would have been forced to choose between a cultural island within Canada, or an independent cultural one outside Canada. Fourteen million English-speaking Canadians would be saying, in effect, that they valued the contribution of the French-Canadian society and culture so lightly that they were prepared to risk its separation from the country rather than make any significant adjustments themselves which would give that culture an honourable and respected place in all of Canada.

I do not believe that English-speaking Canadians are so insensitive as this, or that they are so little interested in the future of their country. Such an attitude would represent a kind of English-speaking separatism, born out of indifference to anything but absorption or isolation of nearly one-third of our population. We must reject this approach as being totally inconsistent with the essential character of this country, with its history, and with its future.

We hear less about it today, however, than we do of the separatism brought about by a revolutionary political decision on the part of the French-speaking minority; asking not for adjustments but for a break-up. Separation of this kind would not occur in a tranquil or a rational way. It would shatter the hopes and the dreams of millions of Canadians, particularly young Canadians.

It would create an atmosphere of disillusionment and bitterness. In a disruption so great as this, all other historic and traditional bonds would be called into question.

The problem would not be merely one of Quebec versus Canada. It would also become one of wider fragmentation.

A separated Quebec could not expect any easy, automatic economic union with a continuing Canada, to ease the dislocations and losses that would follow. The economic results of separation have lately been widely discussed; the loss of development and investment, of jobs and of income; the effect upon the standard of living of Quebeckers, and upon the taxes they would have to pay, if separation led to the movement out of Quebec of business and commerce, and federal administration.

But the most serious result would be the loss of opportunity for Quebeckers to participate in the development of a confederation covering half a continent and which could become one of the great countries of the world. It would not be the intellectuals, the technocrats, the bureaucrats who would suffer this loss. It would be the workers, the farmers, the merchants, the housewives, the children, the students, who would lose most in the limitation of their opportunity for social development and material progress.

Nor would French-Canadian society as a whole be better preserved or strengthened or enlarged under such circumstances. The one million French-speaking Canadians living outside of Quebec, one-sixth of the whole, would be abandoned. The effort to preserve French-Canadian culture, after separation, would have to be solely within Quebec.

I am confident that when Canadians in Quebec have fully measured the gains and losses from separating themselves from the rest of Canada in the atmosphere of tension and hostility which would prevail, they will not regret having chosen Confederation and Canada. But with this choice, can there not be a particular, a special status for Quebec inside Confederation? Many moderate people and good Canadians ask this question.

The answer, of course, depends on what is meant by particular status. If it means that the special position in Canada of the French-Canadian language and culture and tradition must be officially recognized and protected, that the unique national characteristics of French-Canadian people should be encouraged to develop, then I respond with warmth and with understanding to this direction for Canadian federalism.

To me, indeed, this approach is implicit in the B.N.A. Act that made Canada possible in the first place.

It is not being soft or "giving in" to Quebec to agree that Quebec is not a province like the others, and that Canadians should recognize this fact. This is already being done in many ways. Where federal programmes impinge upon or affect the special characteristics of French-Canadian society, they can be and have been adapted to that society. The CBC, for instance, has a French network. The National Film Board produces films for French-Canadians as well as English-Canadians. The ARDA programme is being planned differently in Quebec than in Nova Scotia. Other examples could be given.

Examples could be given, too, of the adaptation of federal programmes to the needs of other provinces and regions: the Atlantic Development Fund for the Atlantic Provinces; the coal-mining phase-out programme in Nova Scotia; the Prairie Farm Rehabilitation Administration for the Prairies; harbour developments in British Columbia.

There is a considerable scope for further changes of this kind. Federal governments may have been too slow in adapting their programmes and their administration to the different regions in Canada. But progress is being made.

I have no difficulty in accepting this kind of "particular status", which affects Quebec most directly but is not exclusive to Quebec. Indeed, it represents the kind of federalism which is not only essential generally to a country so vast and regionally disparate as Canada; it is also an essential ingredient of the two-societies concept of Confederation.

But to some others, "particular status" is more than this. It is defined to mean a special transfer of federal jurisdiction in certain fields to the provincial government of Quebec. This, in effect, would give more constitutional power to the Government of Quebec than that enjoyed by other provinces, including the largest province in Canada, Ontario.

The corollary is that the influence of Members of the Federal Parliament and ministers in the federal government from Quebec would be reduced in comparison with that of members and ministers from the rest of Canada. This kind of "particular status" could lead to a "separate state", a result that cannot be accepted.

We should be very clear, therefore, about what we mean when we talk about special or particular status. Prime Minister Johnson, for instance, has suggested that the Parliament of Canada should forego its constitutional right to make income maintenance payments to the people of Quebec within provincial jurisdiction as well as its right to operate certain other federal programmes for equalizing opportunity for the individual in that province. He has suggested that these should be transferred by Ottawa to the Government of Quebec. He has also suggested that the Parliament of Canada should stop levying personal and corporate income taxes in that province, leaving the whole income tax field to his government.

This would, of course, mean a substantial increase in the powers of the Government of Quebec, and an important reduction in the jurisdiction of the Parliament of Canada in that province. Such a change would carry implications more serious than the immediate effect of the fiscal transfers involved.

Canadians in Quebec would have to look to the Quebec Government *alone* for all income maintenance measures such as family allowances and old age security. Quebeckers would in the future have to depend solely upon increases in the wealth of Quebec to finance the improvements that would be derived from these programmes. The Parliament of Canada would cease to have jurisdiction over these matters in Quebec. It would legislate in respect of such matters only for the rest of Canada. This, clearly, is a vital change in Canadian federalism which Canadians, whether in Quebec or elsewhere, would wish to consider very carefully.

It raises certain questions which would have to be faced.

Would Canadians outside Quebec be prepared to contribute money through Parliament to a particular provincial *Government*, if they were barred constitutionally from making payments to the *people* of that Province?

Would other Provinces *not* ask for the same increase in powers as that received by the Government of Quebec; particularly for complete control over income taxes and over the payment of family allowances and old age security pensions?

Would other provinces agree to a preferential status for the Government of Quebec; for example, in the competition for industry through tax incentives?

Remember that Quebec would control 100 per cent of the corporation income tax field and the other provinces only some 25 per cent.

Would the other provinces accept the present arrangements for the equalization and stabilization of the revenues of the Quebec Government, given the fact that four of the remaining nine provinces already receive virtually no benefit from these measures?

These are questions which would be asked and would have to be answered, if a particular kind of "particular status" for the Government of Quebec was to be discussed seriously and properly.

While radical constitutional reform might precipitate far less friction than the threat of separation, we must be absolutely clear as to how such radical reforms would affect the country as a whole and how they would serve the interests of the French-Canadian people, as individuals.

The same difficulty arises over the use of the expression "two nations", or *deux nations*.

These words have come to mean so many different things to so many different people that their real meaning has often been lost in sterile semantics.

One thing, however, is clear and unequivocal. There do exist in Canada two distinct cultural and linguistic societies, one English-speaking, one French-speaking, with each including members of other cultural and ethnic groups.

The English-speaking society is less homogeneous, less cohesive, than the French-speaking one, but there is a common strand running through it.

One needs only to travel across Canada to perceive that the Nova Scotian, or the British Columbian, feels relatively at home in the other's province. They know without thinking that they are in the same country wherever they may be.

But few of them feel so much at home in Trois Rivières or Isle de la Madeleine, where French is the language of everyday use. Even more does this apply to the French-speaking Canadian who leaves Trois Rivières. He feels at home in the rest of Quebec, but far less so — or not at all — in those areas where little or no French is spoken, and where the way of life seems different.

This situation reflects the fact that there *are* two societies in Canada. So what are we prepared to do to preserve and develop and enjoy them; and to make it possible for *both* to contribute to a better Canada?

It is not a question, I repeat as to whether there *should* be or *will* be, a French-Canadian society. There is one *now*; and it will exist so long as French

Canadians have a will to survive, with their own language and traditions and culture. If English-speaking Canada tries to isolate this French-Canadian society, whether by design or, more likely, by indifference, it will simply encourage separatism.

So we are left with a clear and simple question: what price are we prepared to pay to preserve our total identity as Canadians; in a country which history has built on a "dual foundation"?

What are we prepared to do not only to preserve our two cultural societies in a federal political unity but also to allow them both to develop fully?

This is the question we must face, and urgently.

It will not be solved until English-speaking Canadians understand the difference between equal treatment for individuals and equal treatment for societies, or peoples.

It is easy to treat a French-Canadian individual at a conference in Banff as a full and equal member of the group; yet deny him, by collective action, the respect for and recognition of his culture, heritage and language that he is entitled to, as a citizen of Canada.

Social action is often more difficult than individual action. Yet it is social action we must take. It will involve, for many English-speaking Canadians, a change in attitude and approach to, and a greater respect for "the French fact" in our country, in our Confederation.

It means that we must make all Canada, and not merely Quebec, a homeland for all French-Canadians and to take the steps necessary for that purpose.

Selected Bibliography

Part One

Birch, A. H. *Federalism, Finance and Social Legislation in Canada, Australia and the United States.* Oxford: Clarendon Press, 1955.

Bowie, R. R., and Friedrich, C. J. (eds.) *Studies in Federalism.* Boston: Little, Brown and Company, 1954.

Center for the Study of Democratic Institutions. *Two Faces of Federalism: An Outline of an Argument about Pluralism, Unity, and Law.* Santa Barbara, California, 1961.

Davis, Rufus. "The Federal Principle Reconsidered", *Australian Journal of Politics and History,* I (November, 1955), 59-86; II (May, 1956), 223-245.

Dicey, A. V. *The Law of the Constitution.* 16th ed., London: Macmillan and Co. Ltd., 1959.

Friedrich, C. J. "New Dimensions of Federalism", *Proceedings of the American Society of International Law* (1962-1963), 238-240.

Livingston, W. S. (ed.) *Federalism in the Commonwealth; A Bibliographical Commentary.* London: Cassel, 1963.

Livingston, W. S. *Federalism and Constitutional Change.* Oxford: Clarendon Press, 1956.

Macmahon, A. W. (ed.) *Federalism, Mature and Emergent.* Garden City, New York: Doubleday, 1955.

McWhinney, E. *Comparative Federalism: States' Rights and National Power.* Toronto: University of Toronto Press, 1962.

Mill, J. S. *Considerations on Representative Government.* Chicago: Henry Regnery Company, 1962. See Chapter XVII.

Morin, J.-Y. *Le Fédéralisme: Théorie et Critique.* Montréal: Université de Montréal, 1963.

Riker, W. *Federalism; Origin, Operation, Significance.* Boston: Little, Brown and Company, 1964.

Rockefeller, N. A. *The Future of Federalism.* New York: Atheneum, 1963.

Sharma, B. M. *Federalism in Theory and Practice.* 2 vols. Chandausi, India: Bhargava and Sons, 1951.

Watts, R. L. *New Federations; Experiments in the Commonwealth.* Oxford: Clarendon Press, 1966.

Wheare, K. C. *Federal Government.* 4th ed., New York: Oxford University Press, 1963.

Part Two

Aitchison, J. H. (ed.) *The Political Process in Canada.* Toronto: University of Toronto Press, 1963.

Angus, H. F. "The Working of Confederation: A Western View", *Canadian Journal of Economics and Political Science*, III (August, 1937), 345-353.

Beck, J. M. "Canadian Federalism in Ferment", in Leach, R. H. (ed.), *Contemporary Canada*. Durham, N. C.: Duke University Press, 1968.

Black, E. R. "Federal Strains Within a Canadian Party". *The Dalhousie Review*, XLV (1965), 307-323.

Brunet, Michel. "M. Maurice Lamontagne et sa conception du fédéralisme canadien", *Revue d'Histoire de l'Amérique Française*, VIII (September, 1954), 262-278.

Burns, R. M. *The Evolving Structure of Canadian Government*. Winnipeg: The University of Manitoba, 1966.

Cairns, Alan C. "The Electoral System and the Party System in Canada", *Canadian Journal of Political Science*, I (March, 1968), 55-80.

Clarkson, Stephen. "A Programme for Binational Development", in Russell, Peter (ed.). *Nationalism in Canada*. Toronto: McGraw-Hill of Canada, 1966.

Cole, Taylor. "Commonwealth Federations Old and New: Canada and Nigeria", in Hamilton, W. B. Robinson, K., and Goodwin, C. D. W. (eds.) *A Decade of the Commonwealth 1955-1964*. Durham, N. C.: Duke University Press, 1966.

Creighton, D. G. "Confederation: The Use and Abuse of History", *Journal of Canadian Studies*, I (May, 1966), 3-11.

Crépeau, P.-A. and MacPherson, C. B. *The Future of Canadian Federalism*. Toronto: University of Toronto Press, 1965.

Dubuc, Alfred. "The Decline of Confederation and the New Nationalism," in Russell, Peter (ed.). *Nationalism in Canada*. Toronto: McGraw-Hill Co., 1966.

Engelmann, F. C. and Schwartz, M. A. *Political Parties and the Canadian Social Structure*. Scarborough, Ontario: Prentice-Hall of Canada Ltd., 1967. *passim*.

Falardeau, J.-C. *Quelques épines du fédéralisme canadien*. Toronto: Canadian Institute of International Affairs, 1945. 15-23.

Forsey, Eugene. "Present Problems of Confederation", *Journal of Canadian Studies*, I (August, 1966), 13-23.

Hawkins, Gordon (ed.). *Concepts of Federalism*, 34th Couchiching Conference. Toronto: Canadian Institute on Public Affairs, 1965.

Hurley, James Ross. "Federalism, Co-ordinate Status and the Canadian Situation", *Queen's Quarterly*, LXXIII (Summer, 1966), 157-166.

Maheux, A. *Problems of Canadian Unity*. Quebec: Editions Bois-Francs, 1944.

Mallory, J. R. *Social Credit and the Federal Power in Canada*. Toronto: University of Toronto Press, 1954. *passim*.

Meisel, John. "The Stalled Omnibus: Canadian Parties in the 1960's", *Social Research*, XXX (Autumn, 1963), 367-390.

Ontario. Advisory Committee on Confederation, *Background Papers and Reports*. 3 vols. Toronto: Queen's Printer, April, 1967.

Paltiel, K. Z. "Federalism and Party Finance: A Preliminary Sounding", in Committee on Election Expenses, *Studies in Canadian Party Finance*. Ottawa: Queen's Printer, 1966, 1-21.

Porter, John. *The Vertical Mosaic*. Toronto: University of Toronto Press, 1965. *passim*.

Rogers, N. "Federal Influences on the Cabinet", *Canadian Bar Review*, II (1933), 103-121.

Rogers, N. "The Political Principles of Federalism", *Canadian Journal of Economics and Political Science*, I (August, 1935), 337-347.

Rowat, D. C. "Recent Developments in Canadian Federalism", *Canadian Journal of Economics and Political Science*, XVIII (February, 1952), 1-16.

Scarrow, H. A. "Federal-Provincial Voting Patterns in Canada", *Canadian Journal of Economics and Political Science*, XXVI (May, 1960), 289-298.

Scott, F. R. "The Development of Canadian Federalism", *Papers and Proceedings of the Canadian Political Science Association*, III (1931), 231-247.

Scott, F. R. "Social Planning and Canadian Federalism", on Oliver, M. (ed.) *Social Purpose for Canada*. Toronto: University of Toronto Press.

Smiley, D. V. *The Canadian Political Nationality*. Toronto: Methuen, 1967.

Smiley, D. V. "Federalism, Nationalism and the Scope of Public Activity in Canada", in Russell, Peter (ed.). *Nationalism in Canada*. Toronto: McGraw-Hill Co., 1966.

Smiley, D. V. "Two Themes of Canadian Federalism", *Canadian Journal of Economics and Political Science*, XXXI (February, 1965), 80-97.

Smith, Denis. "Prairie Revolt, Federalism and the Party System", in Thorburn, Hugh G. (ed.) *Party Politics in Canada*. 2nd ed., Scarborough: Prentice-Hall of Canada Ltd., 1967.

Trudeau, P.-E. "The Practice and Theory of Federalism", in Oliver, Michael (ed.). *Social Purpose for Canada*. Toronto: University of Toronto Press, 1961, and in Trudeau, P.-E, *Federalism and the French Canadians*. Toronto: Macmillan of Canada, 1968.

Part Three

General

Ares, Richard. *La Confédération: Pacte ou Loi?* Montréal: Editions de l'Action Nationale, 1949.

Borden, R. L. *Canadian Constitutional Studies; The Marfleet Lectures*. Toronto: University of Toronto, 1922.

Canada. *Memorandum on Dominion Power of Disallowances of Provincial Legislation*. Ottawa: King's Printer, 1938.

Forsey, Eugene. "Disallowance of Provincial Acts, Reservation of Provincial Bills and Refusal of Assent by Lieutenant-Governors Since 1867", *Canadian Journal of Economics and Political Science*, IV (February, 1938), 47-59.

Forsey, Eugene. "Disallowance of Provincial Acts, Reservation of Provincial Bills, and Refusal of Assent by Lieutenant-Governor, 1937-47", *Canadian Journal of Economics and Political Science*, XIV (February, 1948), 94-97.

Hendry, M. L. *Memorandum on the Office of Lieutenant-Governor of a Province: Its Constitutional Character and Functions.* Ottawa: Queen's Printer, 1955.

Keith, A. B. "The Principles of the Canadian Constitution", *Journal of Comparative Legislation and International Law*, XXII, Series 3 (1940), 216-217.

Kennedy, W. P. M. *The Constitution of Canada, An Introduction to its Development and Law.* 2d. ed., London: Oxford University Press, 1938.

Kennedy, W. P. M. *et al.* "A Symposium on Canadian Constitutional Problems", *Canadian Bar Review*, XV (June, 1937), 393-507.

La Forest, G. V. *Disallowance and Reservation of Provincial Legislation.* Ottawa: Queen's Printer, 1955.

Le Dain, G. E. "Reflections on the Canadian Constitution After the First Century", *Canadian Bar Review*, XLV, No. 3 (September, 1967), 402-408.

Mallory, J. R. "Compact Theory of Confederation", *Dalhousie Review*, XXI (October, 1941), 342-351.

Mallory, J. R. "Disallowance and the National Interest: The Alberta Social Credit Legislation of 1937", *Canadian Journal of Economics and Political Science*, XIV (August, 1948), 342-357.

Mallory, J. R. "The Lieutenant-Governor's Discretionary Powers: The Reservation of Bill 56", *Canadian Journal of Economics and Political Science*, XXVII (November, 1961), 518-522.

O'Hearn, P. J. T. *Peace, Order and Good Government; A New Constitution for Canada.* Toronto: Macmillan, 1964.

Rogers, N. "The Compact Theory of Confederation", *Canadian Bar Review*, IX (June, 1931), 395-417.

Saywell, J. T. *The Office of Lieutenant-Governor: A Study in Canadian Government and Politics.* Toronto: University of Toronto Press, 1957.

Stanley, G. F. G. "Act or Pact? Another Look at Confederation", in Cook, R., Brown C., and Berger, C. (eds.) *Confederation.* Toronto: University of Toronto Press, 1967.

Varcoe, F. P. *The Distribution of Legislative Power in Canada.* Toronto: Carswell, 1954.

Confederation

Canada. *Parliamentary Debates on the Subject of the Confederation of the British North America Provinces.* 8th Provincial Parliament of Canada, 3rd Session. Quebec: Hunter and Rose, 1865.

Creighton, D. G. *British North America at Confederation.* Ottawa: Queen's Printer, 1939.

Creighton, D. G. *The Road to Confederation: The Emergence of Canada: 1863-1867.* Toronto: Macmillan, 1964.

Mayo, H. B. "Newfoundland's Entry into the Dominion", *Canadian Journal of Economics and Political Science,* XV (November, 1949), 505-522.

Morton, W. L. "Geographical Circumstances of Confederation", *Canadian Geographical Journal,* LXX (March, 1965), 74-87.

Pope, Joseph (ed.). *Confederation Documents: A Series of Hitherto Unpublished Documents Bearing on the British North America Act.* Toronto: Carswell, 1895.

Trotter, R. G. "Some American Influences Upon the Canadian Federation Movement", *Canadian Historical Review,* V (September, 1924), 213-228.

Waite, P. B. (ed.) *The Confederation Debates.* Toronto: McClelland and Stewart, 1963.

Waite, P. B. *The Life and Times of Confederation, 1864-1867.* 2nd ed., Toronto: University of Toronto Press, 1962.

Constitutional Amendment

Alexander, E. R. "A Constitutional Straight Jacket for Canada", *Canadian Bar Review,* XLIII (March, 1965), 262-313.

Angers, F.-A. "La formule Fulton-Favreau et la théorie du pacte", *Action Nationale,* LV (septembre, 1965) 31-42.

Angers, F.-A. "Le livre blanc sur l'amendement de la constitution", *Action Nationale,* LIV (avril, 1965), 824-30.

Canada. *Constitutional Conference of Federal and Provincial Governments, Proceedings ... January 10-12, 1950.* Ottawa: King's Printer, 1950. *Second Session, September 25-28, 1950.* Ottawa: King's Printer, 1950.

Canada. *Method of Amending the British North America Act: Report and Minutes of Evidence before the Special Committee of the House of Commons.* Ottawa: King's Printer, 1935.

Favreau, G. (Minister of Justice). *The Amendment of the Constitution of Canada.* Ottawa: Queen's Printer, 1965.

Gérin-Lajoie, Paul. *Constitutional Amendment in Canada.* Toronto: University of Toronto Press, 1950.

Goldenberg, H. C. and Underhill, F. H. "The Problems of Constitutional Amendment in Canada", *Papers and Proceedings of the Canadian Political Science Association,* VI (1934), 238-250.

Laskin, Bora. "Amendment of the Constitution: Applying the Fulton-Favreau Formula", *McGill Law Journal,* XI (1965), 2-18.

Lederman, W. R. *et al.* "Constitutional Amendment in Canada", *McGill Law Journal,* XII (1966-67), 337-612.

The Courts and the Constitution

Browne, G. P. *The Judicial Committee and the British North America Act.* Toronto: University of Toronto Press, 1967.

Freund, Paul A. "A Supreme Court in a Federation: Some Lessons from Legal History", *Columbia Law Review,* LIII (May, 1953), 597-619.

Freund, Paul A. "Umpiring the Federal System", in Macmahon, A. W. (ed.) *Federalism: Mature and Emergent.* Garden City, New York: Doubleday, 1955.

Gibson, Dale. "Constitutional Law . . . Federalizing the Judiciary", *Canadian Bar Review,* XLV (December, 1966), 674-678.

Gray, V. E. "The O'Connor Report on the British North America Act, 1867", *Canadian Bar Review,* XVII (May, 1939), 309-337.

Johnson, C. O. "Did Judah P. Benjamin Plant the 'States Rights' Doctrine in the Interpretation of the B.N.A. Act?" *Canadian Bar Review,* XLV, No. 3 (September, 1967), 454-477.

Laskin, Bora. *Canadian Constitutional Law: Cases, Text and Notes on Distribution of Legislative Power.* 2d ed., Toronto: Carswell, 1960.

Laskin, Bora. "Peace, Order and Good Government Re-examined", *Canadian Bar Review,* XXV (December, 1947), 1054-1087.

Laskin, Bora. "The Supreme Court of Canada; A Final Court of Appeal of and for Canadians", *Canadian Bar Review,* XIX (December, 1951), 1038-1079.

Lederman, W. R. "The Concurrent Operation of Federal and Provincial Laws in Canada", *McGill Law Journal,* IX (1962-1963), 185-199.

Lederman, W. R. (ed.) *The Courts and the Canadian Constitution.* Toronto: McClelland and Stewart, 1964.

MacDonald, V. C. *Legislative Power and the Supreme Court in the Fifties.* Toronto: University of Toronto Press, 1961.

MacDonald, V. C. "Privy Council and the Canadian Constitution", *Canadian Bar Review,*" XIX (December, 1951), 1021-1037.

McWhinney, E. "Federal Supreme Courts and Constitutional Review", *Canadian Bar Review,* XLV (September, 1967), 578-607.

McWhinney, E. *Judicial Review in the English Speaking World.* 3rd ed., Toronto: University of Toronto Press, 1960.

Mallory, J. R. "The Courts and the Sovereignty of the Canadian Parliament", *Canadian Journal of Economics and Political Science,* X (May, 1944), 165-178.

Olmsted, R. A. *Canadian Constitutional Decisions of the Judicial Committee, 1864-1954.* Ottawa: Queen's Printer, 1954.

Palmer, E. E. "Federalism and Uniformity of Laws: The Canadian Experience", *Law and Contemporary Problems,* XXX (Spring, 1965), 250-269.

Rogers, N. "Constitutional Impasse", *Queen's Quarterly,* XLI (November, 1934), 475-486.

Russell, P. H. (ed.) *Leading Constitutional Decisions; Cases on the B.N.A. Act.* Toronto: McClelland and Stewart, 1965.

Russell, P. H. "The Supreme Court's Interpretation of the Constitution Since 1949", in Fox, P. (ed.) *Politics: Canada.* 2nd ed., Toronto: McGraw-Hill of Canada, 1966.

Scott, F. R. "Centralization and Decentralization in Canadian Federalism", *Canadian Bar Review,* XXIX (December, 1951), 1095-1125.

Scott, F. R. "The Consequences of the Privy Council Decisions", *Canadian Bar Review,* XV (June, 1937), 485-494.

Senate of Canada. *Report to the Honourable the Speaker Relating to the Enactment of the British North America Act, 1867.* (O'Conner Report) Ottawa: Queen's Printer, 1939.

Smith, Alexander. *The Commerce Power in Canada and the United States.* Toronto: Butterworth and Co., 1963.

Treaty-Making and Foreign Affairs

Eayrs, J. "Canadian Federalism and the United Nations", *Canadian Journal of Economics and Political Science,* XVI (May, 1950), 172-183.

Fitzgerald, G. F. "Educational and Cultural Agreements and Ententes: France, Canada, and Quebec . . . Birth of a New Treaty-Making Technique for a Federal State?" *American Journal of International Law,* LX (July, 1966), 529-537.

Hendry, J. M. *Treaties and Federal Constitutions.* Washington: Public Affairs Press, 1955.

Lederman, W. R. "Legislative Power to Implement Treaty Obligations in Canada", in Aitcheson, J. H. (ed.) *The Political Process in Canada.* Toronto: University of Toronto Press, 1963.

MacDonald, V. C. "Canada's Power to Perform Treaty Obligations", *Canadian Bar Review,* XI (November, 1933), 581-599. (December, 1933), 664-680.

Martin, Paul (Secretary of State for External Affairs). *Federalism and International Relations.* Ottawa: Queen's Printer, 1968.

Morin, J.-Y. "Treaty-Making Power — The Position of the Government of Quebec", *Canadian Bar Review,* XLV (March, 1967), 160-173.

Morris, G. L. "The Treaty-Making Power: A Canadian Dilemma", *Canadian Bar Review,* XLV (September, 1967), 478-512.

Sabourin, L. "Biculturalism and Canadian Foreign Policy", in Gordon, J. King (ed.). *Canada's Role as a Middle Power.* Toronto: The Canadian Institute of International Affairs, 1966.

Sharp, Mitchell (Secretary of State for External Affairs). *Federalism and International Conferences on Education.* Ottawa: Queen's Printer, 1968.

Soward, F. H. "External Affairs and Canadian Federalism", in Lower, A. R. M., Scott, F. R., *et al. Evolving Canadian Federalism.* Durham, N. C.: Duke University Press, 1958.

Civil Liberties

Canada. *A Survey of the Contemporary Indians of Canada, I.* Hawthorn, H. B. (ed.) Department of Indian Affairs and Northern Development, Ottawa: Queen's Printer, 1967.

Lederman, W. R. "The Nature and Problems of a Bill of Rights", *Canadian Bar Review,* XXXVII (March, 1959), 4-15.

Lysyk. "The Unique Constitutional Position of the Canadian Indian", *The Canadian Bar Review,* XLV, No. 3 (September, 1967), 513-553.

MacGuigan, R. "Civil Liberties in the Canadian Federation", *University of New Brunswick Law Journal,* XVI (May, 1966), 1-15.

Schmeiser, D. A. *Civil Liberties in Canada.* London: Oxford University Press, 1964.

Scott, F. R. *Civil Liberties and Canadian Federalism.* Toronto: University of Toronto Press, 1959.

Scott, F. R. "The Privy Council and Minority Rights", *Queen's Quarterly,* XXXVII (October, 1930), 668-678.

Tarnopolsky, Walter S. *The Canadian Bill of Rights.* Toronto: Carswell, 1966.

Trudeau, P.-E. (Minister of Justice). *A Canadian Charter of Human Rights.* Ottawa: Queen's Printer, 1968.

Part Four

Angers, F. A. "Conséquences des nouveaux arrangements fiscaux proposés par le gouvernement Diefenbaker", *Canadian Public Administration,* V (mars, 1962), 1-8.

Angers, F. A. "La dernière conférence fédérale-provinciale (le mémaue du Québec)", *Action Nationale,* LVI (novembre, 1966), 251-255.

Bladen, V. W. "The Economics of Federalism", *Canadian Journal of Economics and Political Science,* I (August, 1935), 348-351.

Brady, Alexander. "Report of the Royal Commission on Dominion-Provincial Relations", *Canadian Historical Review,* XXL, No. 3 (September, 1940), 245-253.

Breton, A. "Theory of Government Grants", *Canadian Journal of Economics and Political Science,* XXXI (May, 1965), 178-179. Weldon, J. C. "Reply with Rejoinder", *Canadian Journal of Economics and Political Science,* XXXII (May, 1966), 230-242.

Bryden, M. H. *Occupancy of Tax Fields in Canada.* Canadian Tax Paper No. 42. Toronto: Canadian Tax Foundation, 1965.

Burns, R. M. "Choices for Canadian Federalism", *Canadian Tax Journal,* XIII (November-December, 1965), 512-518.

Burns, R. M. *et al.* "Federal-Provincial Implications", *Report of Proceedings at the Nineteenth Tax Conference on the Report of the Royal Commission on Taxation.* Toronto: Canadian Tax Foundation, 1967, pp. 385-407.

Canada. *Dominion Government and Canadian Municipalities Informal Conference.* Ottawa: Queen's Printer, 1958.

Canada. *Dominion-Provincial Conference; 1935, Record of Proceedings, Ottawa, December 9-13, 1935.* Ottawa: King's Printer, 1936.

Canada. *Dominion-Provincial Conference on Reconstruction, 1945; Dominion and Provincial Submissions and Plenary Conference Discussions.* Ottawa: King's Printer, 1946.

Canada. *Dominion-Provincial Conference; January 14-15, 1941.* Ottawa: King's Printer, 1941.

Canada. *Dominion-Provincial Conference, 1957.* Ottawa: Queen's Printer, 1958.

Canada. *Dominion-Provincial Conference, 1960.* Ottawa: Queen's Printer, 1960.

Canada. *Federal-Provincial Conditional Grant and Shared-Cost Programs, 1962.* Ottawa: Queen's Printer, 1962.

Canada. *Federal-Provincial Tax Structure Committee, Ottawa, September 14-15, 1966.* Ottawa: Queen's Printer, 1966.

Canada. *Proceedings of the Conference of Federal and Provincial Governments, December 4-7, 1950.* Ottawa: King's Printer, 1951.

Canada. *Proceedings of the Federal-Provincial Conference, 1955.* Ottawa: Queen's Printer, 1955.

Canada. *Report of Proceedings of the Federal-Provincial Conference, 1963.* Ottawa; Queen's Printer, 1964.

Canada. *Report of the Royal Commission on Dominion-Provincial Relations* (Rowell-Sirois Report). Ottawa: King's Printer, 1940.

Canada. *Report of the Royal Commission on Financial Arrangements Between the Dominion and the Maritime Provinces* (White Commission). Ottawa: King's Printer, 1935.

Canada. *Report of the Royal Commission on Maritime Claims* (Duncan Commission). Ottawa: Queen's Printer, 1957.

Canada. *Report of the Royal Commission on Taxation.* 6 vols. Ottawa: Queen's Printer, 1966. *passim.*

Canada. *Statements, Notes on Proceedings, Communiqué of the Federal-Provincial Conference, October 14-15, 1964.* Ottawa: Privy Council Office, 1964. (mimeographed)

Curtis, C. A. "Municipal Finance and Provincial-Federal Relations", *Canadian Journal of Economics and Political Science,* XVII (August, 1951), 297-306.

Dupré, J. Stefan. "Contracting Out: A Funny Thing Happened on the Way to the Centennial", in *Report of the Proceedings of the Eighteenth Annual Tax Conference, 1964.* Toronto: Canadian Tax Foundation, 1965, pp. 208-218.

Eggleston, Wilfred and Kraft, C. T. *Dominion-Provincial Subsidies and Grants*. Ottawa: King's Printer, 1939. (mimeographed.)

Gettys, Luella. *The Administration of Canadian Conditional Grants*. Chicago: Public Administration Service, 1938.

Goldenberg, H. C. "Social and Economic Problems in Canadian Federalism", *Canadian Bar Review*, XII (September, 1934), 422-430.

Graham, John F., Johnson, A. W. and Andrews, J. M. *Inter-Government Fiscal Relationships*. Canadian Tax Paper No. 40. Toronto: Canadian Tax Foundation, 1964.

Hanson, E. J. *Fiscal Needs of the Canadian Provinces*. Canadian Tax Paper No. 23. Toronto: Canadian Tax Foundation, 1961.

Hood, W. C. "Economic Policy in Our Federal State", *Canadian Tax Journal*, XII (November-December, 1964), 389-397.

La Forest, G. V. *The Allocation of Taxing Power Under the Canadian Constitution*. Canadian Tax Paper No. 46. Toronto: Canadian Tax Foundation.

Lynn, J. M. *Studies of the Royal Commission on Taxation, No. 23, Federal-Provincial Fiscal Relations*. Ottawa: Queen's Printer, 1967.

MacKintosh, W. A. *The Economic Background of Dominion-Provincial Relations*. Ottawa: King's Printer, 1939. Reprinted: Toronto: McClelland and Stewart, 1964, J. H. Dales (ed.).

McLarty, R. A. "Organizing for a Federal-Provincial Fiscal Policy", *Canadian Tax Journal*, XV (July-August, 1967), 413-420.

McQueen, R. "Economic Aspects of Federalism: A Prairie View", *Canadian Journal of Economics and Political Science*, I (August, 1935), 352-367.

Maxwell, J. A. *Federal Subsidies to the Provincial Governments in Canada*. Cambridge: Harvard University Press, 1937.

Moore, A. Milton, Perry, J. Harvey and Beach, Donald I. *The Financing of Canadian Federation, the First Hundred Years*. Canadian Tax Paper No. 43. Toronto: Canadian Tax Foundation, 1966.

Musgrave, R. A. *Theoretical Aspects of Fiscal Federalism, Part II: The Fiscal Theory of Political Federalism*, Conference on Public Finances, April 10-11, 1959. New York: National Bureau of Economic Research, 1959.

Nova Scotia. *Report of the Royal Commission, Provincial Economic Inquiry* (Jones Report). 2 vols. Halifax: King's Printer, 1934.

Perry, J. H. "What Price Provincial Autonomy?" *Canadian Journal of Economics and Political Science*, XXI (November, 1955), 432-446.

Ratchford, B. "Constitutional Basis of Public Expenditure in Canada", *Canadian Tax Journal*, VIII (1960), No. 5, 330-336. No. 6, 423-429.

Richardson, J. H. *Economic and Financial Aspects of Social Security*. Toronto: University of Toronto Press, 1960.

Salyzyn, Vladimir. "Federal-Provincial Tax Sharing Schemes", *Canadian Public Administration*, X (June, 1967), 161-166.

Scott, F. R. "The Constitutional Background of Taxation Agreements", *McGill Law Journal*, II (Autumn, 1955), 1-10.

Smiley, D. V. *Conditional Grants and Canadian Federalism: A Study in Constitutional Adaption*. Canadian Tax Paper No. 32. Toronto: Canadian Tax Foundation, 1963.

Part Five

Aitchison, J. H. "Interprovincial Co-operation in Canada", in Aitchison, J. H. (ed.) *The Political Process in Canada*. Toronto: University of Toronto Press, 1963.

Bowland, James G. "Geographical Decentralization in the Canadian Federal Public Service", *Canadian Public Administration* X (September, 1967), 323-365.

Cole, Taylor. *The Canadian Bureaucracy and Federalism, 1947-1965*. Denver: University of Denver, 1966.

Corry, J. A. *Difficulties of Divided Jurisdiction*. Ottawa: King's Printer, 1939.

Dehem, Roger, *et al.* "Concepts of Regional Planning", *Canadian Public Administration*, IX (June, 1966), 152-200.

Doern, G. Bruce. "The Role of Royal Commissions in the General Policy Process and in Federal-Provincial Relations", *Canadian Public Administration*, X (December, 1967), 417-433.

Gouin, L. M. and Claxton, Brooke. *Legislative Expedients and Devices Adopted by the Dominion and the Provinces*. Ottawa: King's Printer, 1939.

Hodgetts, J. E. "Regional Interests and Policy in a Federal Structure", *Canadian Journal of Economics and Political Science*, XXXII (February, 1966), 3-14.

Innis, H. A. "Decentralization and Democracy", *Canadian Journal of Economics and Political Science*, IX (August, 1943), 317-330.

Kristjanson, B. H. "Some Thoughts on Planning at the Federal Level", *Canadian Public Administration*, VIII (June, 1965), 143-151.

Leach, R. H. "Interprovincial Co-operation: Neglected Aspect of Canadian Federalism", *Canadian Public Administration*, II (June, 1959), 83-99.

Lederman, W. R. "Some Forms and Limitations of Co-operative Federalism", *Canadian Bar Review*, XLV (September, 1967), 409-436.

Lindenfield, R. "Hospital Insurance in Canada: An Example in Federal-Provincial Relations", *Social Service Review*, XXXIII (June, 1959), 148-160.

Plumptre, A. F. W. "Regionalism and the Public Service", *Canadian Public Administration*, VIII (December, 1965), pp. 548-557.

Taylor, K. W. "Co-ordination in Administration", in *Proceedings of the Ninth Annual Conference, 1957*. Toronto: Institute of Public Administration of Canada, 1957, 253-273.

Part Six

Allard, M. *The Last Chance, The Canadian Constitution and French Canadians.* Québec: Editions Ferland, 1964.

Bonenfant, J.-C. and Falardeau, J.-C. "Cultural and Political Implications of French-Canadian Nationalism", *Canadian Historical Association Report*, Ottawa, 1946, 56-73.

Brunet, Michel. *La presence anglaise et les Canadiens; études sur l'histoire et la pensée des deux Canadas.* Montréal: Beauchemin, 1958.

Canada. *Report of the Royal Commission on Bilingualism and Biculturalism*, Vol. I. *The Official Languages.* Ottawa: Queen's Printer, 1967.

Cook, Ramsay. *Canada and the French-Canadian Question.* Toronto: Macmillan of Canada, 1966.

Cook, Ramsay. "The Canadian Dilemma", *International Journal*, XX (Winter, 1964-65), 1-19.

Corbett, E. M. *Quebec Confronts Canada.* Baltimore: Johns Hopkins Press, 1967.

Dawson, R. McG. *The Conscription Crisis of 1944.* Toronto: University of Toronto Press, 1961.

Dufour, André. "Le Statut Particulier," *Canadian Bar Review*, XLV (September, 1967), 437-53.

Faribault, M. and Fowler, R. M. *Ten to One: The Confederation Wager.* Toronto: McClelland and Stewart, 1965.

Forsey, Eugene. "The B.N.A. Act and Biculturalism", *Queen's Quarterly*, LXXI (Summer, 1964), 141-149.

Forsey, Eugene. "Canada: Two Nations or One?" *Canadian Journal of Economics and Political Science*, XVIII (November, 1962), 485-501.

Forsey, Eugene. "Professor Morin's Modest Proposal", *Canadian Forum*, XLIV (September, 1964), 121-125.

Guindon, H. "Social Unrest, Social Class and Quebec's Bureaucratic Revolution", *Queen's Quarterly*, LXXI (Summer, 1964), 150-162.

Jones, R. *Community in Crisis.* Toronto: McClelland and Stewart, 1967.

Keyfitz, N. "Canadians and Canadiens", *Queen's Quarterly*, LXX (Summer, 1963), 163-182.

Kwavnick, D. "The Roots of French-Canadian Discontent", *Canadian Journal of Economics and Political Science*, XXXI (November, 1965), 509-523.

Lamontagne, Maurice. *La fédéralisme canadien: évaluation et problemes.* Québec: Les Presses de l'Université Laval, 1954.

Le Conseil de la Vie Française en Amérique. *Nothing More; Nothing Less.* Toronto: Holt, Rinehart and Winston, 1967.

Lesage, J. *Un Quebec fort dans une nouvelle confederation.* Quebec: Queen's Printer, 1965.

Lower, A. R. M. "Two Ways of Life: The Primary, Antithesis of Canadian History", in Cook, Ramsay, Brown, C. and Berger, C. (eds.) *Approaches to Canadian History*. Toronto: University of Toronto Press, 1967.

Manning, H. T. *The Revolt of French Canada*. Toronto: University of Toronto Press, 1962.

Morin, J.-Y. "The Need for a New Canadian Federation", *Canadian Forum*, XLIV, No. 521 (June, 1964), 64-66.

Oliver, M. "Confederation and Quebec", *Canadian Forum*, XLIII (November, 1963), 179-183.

Oliver, M. "Quebec and Canadian Democracy", *Canadian Journal of Economics and Political Science*, XXIII, No. 4 (November, 1957), 504-515.

Quebec. *Royal Commission of Inquiry on Constitutional Problems* (Trembly Report). Quebec: Queen's Printer, 1956.

Quinn, H. F. *The Union Nationale: A Study in Quebec Nationalism*. Toronto: University of Toronto Press, 1963.

Rioux, Marcel and Martin, Yves (eds.). *French Canadian Society: I*. Toronto: McClelland and Stewart, 1964.

Ryan, Claude. "L'égalité est-elle possible?" *Journal of Canadian Studies*, I (August, 1966), 3-13.

Scott, F. R. and Oliver, M. (eds.) *Quebec States Her Case*. Toronto: Macmillan of Canada, 1964.

Trudeau, P.-E. *Federalism and the French Canadians*. Toronto: Macmillan of Canada, 1968.

Trudeau, P.-E. (ed.) *La grève de l'amiante*. Montréal: Editions Cité Libre, 1956.

Wade, Mason (ed.). *Canadian Dualism: Studies of French-English Relations*. Toronto: University of Toronto Press, 1960.

Wade, Mason. *The French-Canadians, 1760-1967*. rev. ed. 2 vols. Toronto: Macmillan, 1968.

Wilson, Frank. "French-Canadian Separatism", *Western Political Quarterly*, XX (March, 1967), 116-131.

426

Index